# Procedural Due Process

**Recent Titles in**
**Reference Guides to the United States Constitution**
*Jack Stark, Series Editor*

The Right to the Assistance of Counsel
*James J. Tomkovicz*

Prohibited Government Acts
*Jack Stark*

State Sovereign Immunity
*Melvyn R. Durchslag*

Constitutional Remedies
*Michael Wells and Thomas A. Eaton*

Privileges and Immunities
*David Skillen Bogen*

Searches, Seizures, and Warrants
*Robert M. Bloom*

The Supremacy Clause
*Christopher R. Drahozal*

# Procedural Due Process

## *A Reference Guide to the United States Constitution*

Rhonda Wasserman

Foreword by the Honorable
Joseph F. Weis, Jr.,
United States Circuit Judge

REFERENCE GUIDES TO THE
UNITED STATES CONSTITUTION, NUMBER 8
Jack Stark, *Series Editor*

PRAEGER

**Westport, Connecticut**
**London**

**Library of Congress Cataloging-in-Publication Data**

Wasserman, Rhonda, 1958–
Procedural due process : a reference guide to the United States Constitution / Rhonda Wasserman; foreword by Joseph F. Weis.
p. cm.—(Reference guides to the United States Constitution; no. 8)
Includes bibliographical references and index.
ISBN 0-313-31353-9
1. Due process of law—United States. I. Title. II. Series.
KF4765.W37 2004
347.73'5—dc22 2004052302

British Library Cataloguing in Publication Data is available.



Library of Congress Catalog Card Number: 2004052302
ISBN: 0-313-31353-9
ISSN: 1539-8986

First published in 2004

Praeger Publishers, 88 Post Road West, Westport, CT 06881
An imprint of Greenwood Publishing Group, Inc.
www.praeger.com

10 9 8 7 6 5 4 3 2 1

For Howard, who has brought much light,
love and laughter into my life

It is during our most challenging and uncertain moments that our Nation's commitment to due process is most severely tested; and it is in those times that we must preserve our commitment at home to the principles for which we fight abroad.

*Hamdi v. Rumsfeld* (U.S. 2004) (plurality op.)

# Contents

# Series Foreword

Jack Stark

One can conceive of the United States Constitution in many ways. For example, noting the reverence in which it has been held, one can think of it as equivalent to a sacred text. Unfortunately, most of its devotees have had less knowledge and even less understanding of the document than they have had reverence for it. Sometimes it is treated as primarily a political document and on that basis has been subjected to analysis, such as Charles Beard's *An Economic Interpretation of the Constitution of the United States*. One can plausibly argue that the Constitution seems most astounding when seen in light of the intellectual effort that has been associated with it. Three brief but highly intense bursts of intellectual energy produced, and established as organic law, most of the Constitution as it now exists. Two of those efforts, sustained over a long period of time, have enabled us to better understand the document.

The first burst of energy occurred at the Constitutional Convention. Although some of the delegates' business, such as the struggle between populous and non-populous states about their representation in Congress, was political, much of it was about fundamental issues of political theory. A few of the delegates had or later achieved international eminence for their intellects. Among them are Benjamin Franklin, Alexander Hamilton, and James Madison. Others, although less well known, had first-rate minds. That group includes George Mason and George Wythe. Many of the delegates contributed intelligently. Although the Convention's records are less than satisfactory, they indicate clearly enough that the delegates worked mightily to constitute not merely a polity—but a rational polity that would rise to the standards envisioned by the delegates' intellectual ancestors. Their product, though brief, is amazing. William Gladstone called it "the most wonderful work ever struck off."

Despite the delegates' eminence and the Constitution's excellence as seen from our place in history, its ratification was far from certain. That state of affairs necessitated the second burst of intellectual energy associated with that document: the debate over ratification. Soon after the Convention adjourned, articles and speeches (some supporting the Constitution and some attacking it) began to proliferate. A national debate commenced—not only about the document itself but also about the nature of the polity that ought to exist in this country. Both sides included many writers and speakers who were verbally adroit and steeped in the relevant political and philosophical literature. The result was an accumulation of material that is remarkable for both its quantity and its quality. At its apex is the *Federalist Papers*, a production of Alexander Hamilton, James Madison, and John Jay that deserves a place among the great books of Western culture.

Another burst, although not as impressive as the first two but highly respectable, occurred when the Bill of Rights was proposed. Some delegates to the Constitutional Convention had vigorously asserted that such guarantees should be included in the original document. George Mason, the principal drafter of the Virginia Declaration of Rights, so held, and he walked out of the Convention when he failed to achieve his purpose. Even those who had argued that the rights in question were implicit recognized the value of adding protection of them to the Constitution. The debate was thus focused on the rights that were to be explicitly granted, not on whether any rights ought to be explicitly granted. Again many writers and speakers entered the fray, and again the debate was solidly grounded in theory and was conducted on a high intellectual level.

Thus, within a few years a statement of organic law and a vital coda to it had been produced. However, the meaning and effect of many of that document's provisions were far from certain; the debates on ratification of the Constitution and the Bill of Rights had demonstrated that. In addition, the document existed in a vacuum, because statutes and actions had not been assessed by its standards. The attempt to resolve these problems began after Chief Justice John Marshall, in Marbury v. Madison, asserted the right of the U.S. Supreme Court to interpret and apply the Constitution. Judicial interpretation and application of the Constitution, beginning with the first constitutional case and persisting until the most recent, is one of the sustained exertions of intellectual energy associated with the Constitution. The framers would be surprised by some of the results of these activities. References in the document to "due process," which seems to refer only to procedures, have been held also to have a substantive dimension. A right to privacy has been found lurking among the penumbras of various parts of the text. A requirement that states grant the same "privileges and immunities" to citizens of other states that they granted to their own citizens, which seemed to guarantee important rights, was not held to be particularly important. The corpus of judicial interpretations of the Constitution is now as voluminous as that document is terse.

As judicial interpretations multiplied, another layer (interpretations of interpretations) appeared, and also multiplied. This layer, the other sustained intellectual effort associated with the Constitution, consists of articles, most of them published in law reviews, and books on the Constitution. This material varies in quality and significance. Some of these works of scholarship result from meticulous examination and incisive thought. Others repeat earlier work, or apply a fine-tooth comb to matters that are too minute even for such a comb. Somewhere in that welter of tertiary material is the answer to almost every question that one could ask about constitutional law. The problem is finding the answer that one wants. The difficulty of locating useful guidance is exacerbated by the bifurcation of most constitutional scholarship into two kinds. In "Two Styles of Social Science Research," C. Wright Mills delineates macroscopic and molecular research. The former deals with huge issues, the latter with tiny issues. Virtually all of the scholarship on the Constitution is of one of those two types. Little of it is macroscopic, but that category does include some first-rate syntheses such as Jack Rakove's *Original Meanings*. Most constitutional scholarship is molecular and, again, some fine work is included in that category.

In his essay, Mills bemoans the inability of social scientists to combine the two kinds of research that he describes to create a third category that will be more generally useful. This series of books is an attempt to do for constitutional law the intellectual work that Mills proposed for social science. The author of each book has dealt carefully and at reasonable length with a topic that lies in the middle range of generality. Upon completion, this series will consist of thirty-seven books, each on a constitutional law topic. Some of the books, such as the book on freedom of the press, explicate one portion of the Constitution's text. Others, such as the volume on federalism, treat a topic that has several anchors in the Constitution. The books on constitutional history and constitutional interpretation range over the entire document, but each does so from a single perspective. Except for a few of the books, the special circumstances of which dictate minor changes in format, each book includes the same components—a brief history of the topic, a lengthy and sophisticated analysis of the current state of the law on that topic, a bibliographical essay that organizes and evaluates scholarly material in order to facilitate further research, a table of cases, and an index. The books are intellectually rigorous (in fact, authorities have written them) but, due to their clarity and to brief definitions of terms that are unfamiliar to laypersons, each is comprehensible and useful to a wide audience, one that ranges from other experts on the book's subject to intelligent non-lawyers.

In short, this series provides an extremely valuable service to the legal community and to others who are interested in constitutional law, as every citizen should be. Each book is a map of part of the U.S. Constitution. Together they map all of that document's territory that is worth mapping. When this series is complete, each book will be a third kind of scholarly work that combines the macroscopic and the molecular. Together they will explicate all of the important constitutional topics. Anyone who wants assistance in understanding either a topic in constitutional law or the Constitution as a whole can easily find it in these books.

# Foreword

THE HONORABLE JOSEPH F. WEIS, JR., UNITED STATES CIRCUIT JUDGE

Justice Holmes had a knack for expressing important legal doctrine in memorably pithy terms. One of the better examples of this ability is, typically, found in a dissenting opinion. "Whatever disagreement there may be as to the scope of the phrase 'due process of law,' there can be no doubt that it embraces the fundamental conception of a fair trial, with opportunity to be heard." Frank v. Mangum, 237 U.S. 309, 347 (1915).

That statement is deceptively simple and might lull the less inquisitive into feeling that further exposition would be superfluous. But subjecting that quote to the journalistic queries "who, what, when, where and why" reveals a complex, critical and fascinating area of the law.

Professor Rhonda Wasserman has devoted most of her legal career to a searching examination of the many facets of due process. In this easily readable book, she wends her way through the thicket of case law and scholarly commentary to arrive at a well-organized and informative presentation of an often misunderstood subject.

Dispute resolution is a weighty process that cannot function effectively in the absence of a highly organized system. Granting everyone, everywhere and any time the right to be heard on any issue would create a cacophony accomplishing little but confusion and obfuscation.

When all speak at once, no one is heard. When speech rambles interminably over immaterial and irrelevant matters, the fact finder's efficiency plummets to unacceptable levels. Rules to regulate the right to be heard in the litigation milieu become not merely desirable but essential.

Modern society has more than enough experience with unproductive babble in other institutions to recognize its destructive effect in the courtroom setting. Yet, at the same time, the fundamental right to be heard must be safeguarded zealously. Patience and understanding, not unsympathetic or excessively rigid rulings, must be the prevailing practice.

Professor Wasserman not only explains the practical importance of procedural rules but explores their constitutional basis. *Where* litigation is to be conducted invokes fairness in a constitutional dimension. Limitations on *who* may be heard are necessary so that facilities may be available to those who have immediate and pressing needs. *When* a matter is to be heard may vary from the expedited emergency proceeding to one in which years of preparation and gathering of evidence are essential.

My service as chairman of the Standing Committee on Rules of Practice and Procedure of the Judicial Conference of the United States, and of the Advisory Committee on Civil Rules has given me an intense exposure to matters affecting, and affected by, due process. That experience, in addition to years on the bench when due process is a day-to-day consideration, underlies my admiration for this excellent book that Professor Wasserman has written. It is a valuable addition to the legal literature of our time.

# Acknowledgments

Jules Lobel, Bill Luneburg, Jack Stark and the Honorable Joseph F. Weis, Jr. graciously agreed to read and critique portions of this book in draft form. Their insightful comments and suggestions helped me to improve the quality of the final product; any errors that remain are mine.

Tracey Balliet, Erica Burgess, Nat Croumer, John Haller, Nancy Harris, Ryan Keenehan, Michelle McCreery, Portia McGonigal, Rodney Miller, Sara Beth Reyburn, Michael Rhodes, Jeff Robinson, Jo Rosenberger, Joshua Siebert, John Vitale, Jordan Webster, Peter Weeks and Tara Willke provided dedicated and invaluable research assistance. My secretary, Amy Heggemeyer, and the staff of the Document Technology Center of the University of Pittsburgh School of Law, LuAnn Driscoll, Karen Knochel, Darleen Mocello, Valerie Pompe and Barb Salopek, were an enormous help in preparing the manuscript for publication. Dean David Herring of the University of Pittsburgh School of Law provided financial support for this project.

I never would have been able to complete this book without the remarkable support and patience of my husband, Howard A. Stern, and the understanding of my sons, Eric, Scott and Benjamin Wasserman Stern. I am grateful to them beyond words.

Rhonda Wasserman
Pittsburgh, Pennsylvania
February 2004

# 1

# The History of Due Process

***"The history of American freedom is, in no small measure, the history of procedure."***[1]

The Fifth and Fourteenth Amendments to the United States Constitution bar the government from depriving any person of life, liberty or property without due process of law.[2] These Due Process Clauses afford both substantive and procedural protections. As substantive limits on governmental action, the Due Process Clauses bar the government from interfering with certain interests that are so basic, personal or fundamental that they may not be regulated by government absent a compelling interest, regardless of the procedural protections afforded (Reno v. Flores, 1993).[3] Among the interests protected are reproductive freedom (Planned Parenthood v. Casey, 1992; Roe v. Wade, 1973) and the right to raise one's children autonomously (Troxel v. Granville, 2000; Pierce v. Society of Sisters, 1925).

Our concern in this volume, of course, is with the *procedural* protections afforded by the Due Process Clauses. The terseness of the phrase "due process of law" belies an enormously powerful check on governmental power: before the government can deprive a person of a protected interest, it must provide her with notice and an opportunity to be heard, among other procedural protections. Our primary objective is to explore the content, scope and significance of these protections as well as their limits. But before we begin, let us first understand the historical context in which these clauses of the Constitution were adopted and the early understanding of the phrase "due process of law."

## THE ORIGINS OF DUE PROCESS: MAGNA CARTA AND EARLY ENGLISH LAW

Although the words "due process of law" are not found in the Magna Carta, that charter is commonly viewed as the historical antecedent of the Due Process Clauses. Adopted as a personal treaty between King John and his rebellious barons in 1215, the Magna Carta protected not only the nobility but also the freemen, stating generally that "No freeman shall be taken and imprisoned or disseized or exiled or in any way destroyed, nor will we go upon him nor send upon him, except by the lawful judgment of his peers and by the law of the land."[4]

The key phrase "by the law of the land" is derived from the Latin, "per legem terrae." By assuring the barons and freemen a trial by their peers according to the customary laws of the kingdom, the charter barred execution before judgment and other arbitrary action by the King, at least with regard to criminal procedure.[5] According to Hermine Herta Meyer, the phrase "law of the land" required a particular proof procedure, including the compurgation oath and the ordeal.[6] Others have advocated a broader meaning, not confined to the methods of procedure, but referring instead to "the entire tone and substance of the law."[7]

As successive kings ascended to the throne, each reissued and reaffirmed the charter, sometimes with modifications.[8] The phrase "due process of law" was first introduced in a 1354 statutory reissue of the charter: "That no man of what estate or condition that he be, shall be put out of Land or Tenement, nor taken, nor imprisoned, nor disinherited, nor put to Death, without being brought to Answer by due Process of the Law" (28 Edw. III ch. 3 (1354)). Like the original Magna Carta, the 1354 statute meant that a person could be deprived of life, liberty or property only pursuant to regular court proceedings that afforded him a right to defend himself and included a proof procedure.[9] According to Meyer, the King changed the language from "law of the land" to "due process" to sanction the use of new forms of procedure in the King's Council. As revised, the charter no longer guaranteed a particular procedure, but rather "the procedure due to [a given] case pursuant to law."[10] Thus, "due process of law" meant a regular procedure for summoning people to trial and adjudicating their liability.[11]

As initially crafted, the Magna Carta constrained the King and the 1354 statute constrained the courts, but neither expressly regulated the Parliament, which, in 1215, had not yet been created.[12] By the seventeenth century, however, the great English commentator Sir Edward Coke took the position that Acts of Parliament, too, were subject to the "law of the land." For instance, in Dr. Bonham's case, Coke, then Chief Justice of the Court of Common Pleas, declared, "that in many cases, the common law will controul Acts of Parliament, and sometimes adjudge them to be utterly void" (Bonham's Case, C.P. 1610).[13] As we will see, this reading of the "law of the land" was later invoked by the American colonists to challenge the legality of legislation enacted by Parliament. Coke also read the phrases "law of the land" and "due process of law" synonymously,[14] a reading that was initially disputed but came to be widely accepted, especially in America (Murray's Lessee v. Hoboken Land & Improvement Co., 1856).[15]

## THE COLONIAL CHARTERS AND EARLY STATE CONSTITUTIONS

The colonists who moved to America claimed for themselves the same legal protections they had enjoyed in England. Thus, the colonial charters and early laws preserved in some form or other the protections originally provided by the Magna Carta and the 1354 statute. For example, the General Laws of New-Plimouth (1671) barred deprivations of "Life, Limb, Liberty, Good name or Estate, under colour of Law," unless the person was "brought to Answer by due process thereof."[16]

In the minds of the colonists, due process meant not only procedural protections in judicial proceedings and a regular indictment and jury trial in criminal proceedings, but also a more general check against arbitrary government. As Rodney Mott put it, "It is but a small step from the view that the procedure in a civil case must be according to the law, to the conception of the law of the land as a limitation upon the impairment of vested rights or the tyrannical exercise of the police power."[17]

The colonists invoked due process and the "law of the land" language from the Magna Carta in their struggles with England leading up to the Revolutionary War. Thus, when British officials sought to enforce the Navigation Acts in Boston by means of general search warrants, a Massachusetts attorney, James Otis, argued that the court should invalidate Acts of Parliament that were contrary to the constitution of England and the "law of the land" provision of the Magna Carta. Otis relied on Lord Coke's view that the "law of the land" limited the powers of Parliament, as well as the King and his courts.[18] Likewise, in challenging the Stamp Act, the colonists argued that it violated the Magna Carta by authorizing trials of offenders in the admiralty courts without the protection of trial by jury.[19] Thus, the colonists believed that the "law of the land" constrained the legislature as well as the other branches of government.[20]

The Declaration of Independence, drafted before the war, was an "indictment of England's misdeeds," but it was not a bill of rights and contained no legal assurances of personal freedom or due process.[21] Nor did the Articles of Confederation address personal freedom, as it was accepted at the time that each state retained sovereignty, including the responsibility to protect the rights of its own citizens.[22] Thus, it was the states themselves that first adopted permanent constitutions, including bills of rights to protect the individual liberties of their citizens.[23] Several of these constitutions paraphrased or copied the Magna Carta, barring deprivations of life, liberty or property except "by the judgment of his peers or by the law of the land" (Maryland Declaration of Rights, 1776; Massachusetts Constitution, 1780; New Hampshire Constitution, 1783). By Rodney Mott's count, eight of the thirteen states had constitutions containing the equivalent of a due process clause before the Fifth Amendment was adopted, although none of them used the words "due process of law," and none were interpreted until after the federal government was established in 1787.[24]

The Continental Congress did not presume to enact a bill of rights to protect citizens of the states, but it was obliged to protect the rights of those living in the territories, including the territory northwest of the Ohio River.[25] In 1787, it adopted the Northwest Ordinance, which included a full bill of rights for the inhabitants of the Northwest Territory and, borrowing language from the Magna Carta, assured that "No man shall be deprived of his liberty or property but by the Judgment of his peers or the law of the land."[26] Unfortunately, the records of the Continental Congress do not reveal the meaning that was attached to the phrase, the "law of the land."[27] The ordinance nevertheless is highly significant, for as Robert Rutland notes, "For the first time, civil rights became a factor in national legislation."[28]

## THE FEDERAL CONSTITUTION AND THE FIFTH AMENDMENT

In time, the Articles of Confederation came under attack and a Constitutional Convention was called to draft a constitution that would strengthen the national government and protect private property rights against legislative attack.[29] The early debates did not focus on personal liberties, as the protection of civil rights had been a matter of state, not national, concern under the Articles and there was widespread satisfaction among the public with the protections thus afforded.[30] As the debates continued, however, and it became clear that the national government would have enormous powers under the new Constitution, a group of delegates grew concerned about potential federal interference with the rights of individual citizens. During the last week of the Convention, these delegates moved to appoint a committee to prepare a bill of rights, but the motion was defeated. Even last-ditch efforts to add specific protections in piecemeal fashion—to preserve the liberty of the press, for example—were unsuccessful.[31] No specific reference was made to a due process clause during the entire four months that the Constitutional Convention sat, which is noteworthy given the significant role that "due process" and the "law of the land" had played in England and colonial America.[32]

During the months following the close of the Convention, the Antifederalists, who opposed ratification of the Constitution, cited the lack of a bill of rights as a primary flaw. Thomas Jefferson, who was then serving as American Minister to France, added his voice to those advocating a bill of rights, while George Washington was far more skeptical.[33]

Ratification debates in the states were sometimes fierce, with vigorous arguments raised in letters, newspapers and pamphlets. Much of the debate centered on the need for a bill of rights, with the Federalists arguing that a bill of rights was unnecessary because nothing in the Constitution divested the people of the rights already secured to them by the state constitutions, and the Antifederalists countering that, in the absence of a bill of rights, freedom of religion and other personal liberties would depend "on the will and pleasure" of their rulers.[34] Although the precise contours of the Antifederalist vision of a bill of rights were vague and none of the pamphlets referred specifically to the need for a due process clause, it is clear that proponents believed that Congressional power had to be limited "by principles of liberty . . . based upon the fundamentals of the common law and Magna Carta."[35]

A compromise was reached in Massachusetts to ratify the Constitution but also to submit a set of proposed amendments to the new Congress for its consideration.[36] Other states followed suit, with New York circulating a letter to the other states suggesting another federal convention.[37] Of the seven states that submitted proposed amendments to Congress, four included the "law of the land" text from the Magna Carta.[38] Ultimately, all states but North Carolina and Rhode Island ratified the Constitution, with the widespread expectation that a bill of rights would be added.[39]

When the new Congress met in New York in April of 1789, James Madison offered a set of amendments gleaned from both the Virginia Declaration of Rights and the amendments submitted by the states, including only those proposals that he thought were likely to gain approval by Congress and the states.[40] One of his proposed amendments stated that "No person shall . . . be deprived of life, liberty, or property, without due process of law. . . ."[41] Since the Constitution already provided that "the Trial of all Crimes, except in Cases of Impeachment, shall be by Jury,"[42] it would have been "in part superfluous and inappropriate" to use the language of the Magna Carta and declare that no person shall be deprived of life, liberty or property except by the judgment of his peers or the law of the land (Murray's Lessee v. Hoboken Land & Improvement Co., 1856). Instead, Madison used the words "due process of law," which Coke had declared to be synonymous with the "law of the land."

Madison may also have chosen the phrase "due process of law" to avoid confusion. After all, the phrase "law of the land" was used in the Supremacy Clause of the Constitution.[43] Since "law" in the Supremacy Clause referred to positive enactments (i.e., the Constitution, federal statutes and treaties), while "law" in the Magna Carta's "law of the land" meant common law, it might have been confusing to employ the phrase "law of the land" in the Fifth Amendment.[44]

In all events, Madison's proposals were vetted by a committee, thoroughly reviewed by the House sitting as a committee of the whole, and ultimately forwarded (in revised form) to the Senate.[45] After some initial wrangling about whether to postpone consideration of the amendments until the next session of Congress, the Senate agreed to consider the seventeen amendments forwarded by the House. The Senate rejected several of them and consolidated the rest (including the Due Process Clause) into twelve revised amendments, which it then sent back to the House for its concurrence. After some further revisions by a conference committee, both houses approved the twelve amendments, which ultimately were transmitted to the states.[46] With this check on federal power now in the hands of the states, North Carolina finally ratified the Constitution.[47]

As the states debated whether to ratify the amendments, two of the proposals—one regarding the apportionment of seats in the House and the other on Congressional salaries—were defeated. There was no opposition, however, to the Due Process Clause of the Fifth Amendment.[48] On December 15, 1791, more than two years after the amendments had been approved by Congress, Virginia ratified the Bill of Rights and became the last of the eleven states needed to make the amendments effective.[49]

As adopted, the Fifth Amendment to the United States Constitution followed the general organization of the eighth article of the Virginia Declaration of Rights. Both dealt largely with criminal procedure, and both promised due process in a clause that immediately followed one that barred forced self-incrimination. While the Virginia Declaration employed the time-honored "law of the land" language of the Magna Carta and the Fifth Amendment employed the phrase "due process of law," it is well-accepted that the framers, like Coke before them, read the words synonymously.[50]

Notwithstanding the Fifth Amendment's focus on criminal procedure, Rodney Mott concludes that "There is no doubt that the Fifth Amendment was expected to limit arbitrary abuses of the powers of government from whatever source abuse might come, and it is a perfectly tenable hypothesis that the due process provision was intended to serve as a general limitation to check tyranny in any kind of case in which it should arise."[51] To bolster this conclusion, Mott notes that one of the primary arguments in favor of a bill of rights had been the need to curb Congressional power. In his view, of the five amendments that possibly could be read to limit Congress, only the Due Process Clause of the Fifth Amendment was broad enough to serve as a "catch-all phrase for popular liberty."[52] While agreeing that the Due Process Clause was intended to provide general procedural protection as well as the specific "process" guarantees contained elsewhere in the Bill of Rights, William Crosskey nevertheless maintains that the Due Process Clause was not intended to authorize courts to review the substantive fairness of Congressional legislation.[53]

## DUE PROCESS BEFORE THE CIVIL WAR

The elasticity and potential breadth of the words "due process of law" have provided the Supreme Court with countless opportunities for interpretation. But in the early years of our nation's history, the Due Process Clause of the Fifth Amendment was "largely irrelevant" and, in the words of Judge Easterbrook, "fell into desuetude."[54] In fact, sixty-five years passed before the United States Supreme Court first examined the Due Process Clause in Murray's Lessee v.

Hoboken Land & Improvement Co. (1856). There, an auditor for the federal treasury found that a collector of the customs for the port of New York owed over a million dollars to the government. The solicitor of the treasury issued a distress warrant as authorized by federal statute, which placed a lien on the collector's property. The collector was provided no opportunity to be heard. When the property was sold to satisfy the obligation, the collector challenged the constitutionality of the warrant and the sale thereunder, arguing that he was deprived of liberty and property without due process of law.

In addressing this challenge, the Court first noted the Fifth Amendment's opacity: "The constitution contains no description of those processes which it was intended to allow or forbid. It does not even declare what principles are to be applied to ascertain whether it be due process." Notwithstanding the text's terseness, the Court had no trouble inferring that the Fifth Amendment Due Process Clause restrained Congress as well as the executive and judicial branches of government; Congress was not "free to make any process 'due process of law,' by its mere will" (Murray's Lessee v. Hoboken Land & Improvement Co., 1856).[55]

In assessing whether a process enacted by Congress constituted "due process," the Court applied a two-part analysis. First, it looked to those "settled usages and modes of proceeding" under English law that were adaptable to American civic life, and second, the Court "examine[d] the constitution itself, to see whether this process be in conflict with any of its provisions" (Murray's Lessee v. Hoboken Land & Improvement Co., 1856). Thus due process was defined in terms of historically accepted practice (except as modified by the Constitution itself).[56]

Applying this historical analysis, the Court noted that while due process of law generally implied "regular allegations, opportunity to answer, and a trial according to some settled course of judicial proceedings," among other protections, England had long treated those owing debts to the Crown more summarily than ordinary debtors. In fact, "'the law of the land' authorized the employment of auditors, and an inquisition without notice" to ascertain the existence and amount of debts to the Crown. In light of this history and the states' nearly universal use of distress warrants to collect taxes before adoption of the federal Constitution, the Court concluded that the proceedings comported with due process (Murray's Lessee v. Hoboken Land & Improvement Co., 1856).

*Murray's Lessee* is noteworthy not only for its historical analysis, but also for its recognition that due process applies beyond the criminal procedure context to protect private property rights. In Charles Miller's words, "it is this side of due process/law-of-the-land, the side of property rights and, to a considerable degree, natural rights, which is the genuine American 'contribution' to the due process tradition."[57] Put differently, *Murray's Lessee* foreshadowed the "due process revolution" of the 1960s, which recognized that government benefits, employment and other forms of largess are protected by due process.[58]

During the mid-nineteenth century, social reform movements, including the temperance and abolitionist movements, attempted to infuse due process with greater substantive content.[59] Although these efforts are beyond the scope of this volume, one pre-Civil War substantive due process case, Wynehamer v. People (N.Y. 1856), foreshadows another important development in procedural due process. In *Wynehamer*, a man was convicted of selling intoxicating liquors in violation of a state temperance law. On appeal, the New York Court of Appeals concluded that intoxicating liquors were property and held that the law violated the state Due Process Clause. In striking down the law, the court made clear that it is a judicial function, not a legislative function, to determine what process is due:

> To say . . . that "the law of the land," or "due process of law," may mean the very act of legislation which deprives citizens of his rights, privileges or property, leads to a simple absurdity. The constitution would then mean, that no person shall be deprived of his property or rights, unless the legislature shall pass a law to effectuate the wrong, and this would be throwing the restraint entirely away (Wynehamer v. People, N.Y. 1856).

Thus, *Wynehamer* not only reinforces the conclusion that due process restrains the legislature, but it also foreshadows the Supreme Court's later conclusion that the scope of procedural protections required by due process is a federal constitutional matter, which state legislatures cannot limit by enacting summary procedures to govern the deprivation of state-created rights (Cleveland Bd. of Educ. v. Loudermill, 1985; Vitek v. Jones, 1980).[60]

## ADOPTION OF THE FOURTEENTH AMENDMENT

The earliest drafts of the Fourteenth Amendment were introduced in Congress in December 1865, eight months after the end of Civil War and just days before the Thirteenth Amendment was ratified. The Fourteenth Amendment was intended to insulate from constitutional challenge the far-reaching legislative program of the Thirty-ninth Congress, embodied in the Civil Rights and Freedmen's Bureau Acts, and to enshrine their protections in the Constitution itself so that a later Congress could not eliminate them.[61] While earlier drafts of the Fourteenth Amendment would have granted Congress *affirmative* power to enact legislation to ensure equal enjoyment of civil rights (e.g., "Congress shall have power . . . ."),[62] in its final form, the Fourteenth Amendment used *negative* language:

> No State shall make or enforce any law which shall abridge the privileges or immunities of citizens of the United States; nor shall any State deprive any person of life, liberty, or property, without due process of law; nor deny to any person within its jurisdiction the equal protection of the laws (U.S. Const. amend. XIV, § 1).

While the drafters may have changed the affirmative language to the negative to appease those concerned about states' rights,[63] they also may have changed it to ensure that protection of civil rights would not depend upon which party held a majority of the seats in Congress, but rather would be built into the Constitution itself.[64]

The Due Process Clause of the Fourteenth Amendment was the least discussed provision in the amendment.[65] Understandably, the primary focus of the framers was on equality under the law. In fact, while all drafts of the amendment included an Equal Protection Clause of some kind, no Due Process Clause was proposed until April 1866, a full four months after the original proposal for a Fourteenth Amendment was offered.[66] Even in explaining the relevance of the Due Process Clause to the Senate, Jacob Howard of Michigan emphasized its role in "protect[ing] the black man in his fundamental rights as a citizen with the same shield which it throws over the white man."[67] Likewise, in explaining the amendment to the House of Representatives, Thaddeus Stevens emphasized the goal of equality, but in doing so, mentioned the judicial protections to be afforded to blacks:

> Whatever means of redress is afforded to one shall be afforded to all. Whatever law allows the white man to testify in court shall allow the man of color to do the same. These are great advantages over their present codes. . . . Now color disqualifies a man from testifying in courts, or being tried in the same way as white men.[68]

This language suggests that the framers of the Fourteenth Amendment intended to ensure that blacks would have the same access as whites to state judicial proceedings under the same rules.[69]

By failing to specify particular procedural safeguards in the Fourteenth Amendment itself—such as the Fifth Amendment presentment or indictment requirement—the framers may have intended to leave the states "free to make their own procedural rules with the sole obligation that they had to be the same for every person."[70] As the Supreme Court of Wisconsin put it in 1872,

> the object of [the Fourteenth] [A]mendment was to protect [blacks] especially from any arbitrary exercise of the powers of the state governments, and to secure for [them] equal and impartial justice in the administration of the law, civil and criminal. But its design was not to confine the states to a particular mode of procedure in judicial proceedings . . . (Rowan v. State, Wis. 1872).

This conclusion was reaffirmed by the United States Supreme Court, which noted that due process in the Fourteenth Amendment refers to the "law of the land in each State" and that "[e]ach State prescribes its own modes of judicial proceeding" (Hurtado v. California, 1884; Missouri v. Lewis, 1879; see also Walker v. Sauvinet, 1875).

## PROCEDURAL DUE PROCESS IN THE POST-CIVIL WAR PERIOD

Although there had been few challenges to federal governmental action brought under the Due Process Clause of the Fifth Amendment before the Fourteenth Amendment was ratified, many suits were filed to challenge state action under the Due Process Clause of the Fourteenth Amendment. The Supreme Court soon recognized that if it could define all those state actions that would violate due process and distinguish all those that would not, "no more useful construction could be furnished by this or any other court to any part of the fundamental law" (Davidson v. New Orleans, 1877). But the Court declined to attempt to craft such a definition: "there is wisdom, we think, in the ascertaining of the intent and application of such an important phrase in the Federal Constitution, by the gradual process of judicial inclusion and exclusion, as the cases presented for decision shall require, with the reasoning on which such decisions may be founded" (Davidson v. New Orleans, 1877).

The Supreme Court's first opportunity to interpret the Fourteenth Amendment came in the Slaughter-House Cases (1873). There, a group of butchers challenged the constitutionality of a Louisiana statute that granted a monopoly to a newly-chartered slaughterhouse and ordered the closing of all other slaughterhouses in New Orleans. The case is best known for its distinction between state and federal citizenship and its much-criticized holding that the Privileges and Immunities Clause of the Fourteenth Amendment does not protect the fundamental rights of all citizens in a free society, but only those rights that "owe their existence to the Federal government, its national character, its Constitution, or its laws" (Slaughter-House Cases, 1873). But Justice Bradley's dissenting opinion invoked the Due Process Clause of the Fourteenth Amendment, both harking back to the Magna Carta and foreshadowing the later expansion of protected liberty and property rights. "In my view," Bradley wrote,

> a law which prohibits a large class of citizens from adopting a lawful employment, or from following a lawful employment previously adopted, does deprive them of liberty as well as property, without due process of law. Their right of choice is a portion of their liberty; their occupation is their property (Slaughter-House Cases, 1873, Bradley, J., dissenting).[71]

If a majority of the Court paid short shrift to the Due Process Clause in the Slaughter-House Cases (1873), it gave it greater attention a decade later in its first significant procedural due process decision following enactment of the Fourteenth Amendment, Hurtado v. California (1884). There, the state of California charged Joseph Hurtado with murder. Rather than convene a grand jury to indict him, the district attorney filed an information against him pursuant to state law. An information is a formal criminal charge made without a grand jury indictment.[72] Upon conviction and imposition of a death sentence, Hurtado argued that due process required an indictment or presentment by a grand jury and that the procedure employed violated the Fourteenth Amendment.

The Supreme Court began with the proposition that "when the same phrase ['due process'] was employed in the Fourteenth Amendment to restrain the action of the states, it was used in the same sense and with no greater extent" than in the Fifth Amendment (Hurtado v. California, 1884). Since the Fifth Amendment contained a separate provision regarding the grand jury, the Court concluded that the Due Process Clause did not itself require grand juries. Likewise, "if in the adoption of [the Fourteenth] [A]mendment it had been part of its purpose to perpetuate the institution of the grand jury in all the states, it would have embodied, as did the fifth amendment, express declarations to that effect" (Hurtado v. California, 1884). Thus, the Court concluded that the Fourteenth Amendment Due Process Clause did not require grand juries in state criminal proceedings. Harlan in dissent and Crosskey in commentary sharply criticize *Hurtado*'s paradoxical principle: that "every element of 'process' that was prescribed in the Constitution was to be excluded as an element of 'due'—that is to say, 'appropriate'—'process of law' thereunder."[73]

In addition to resolving the precise issue before it, the *Hurtado* Court offered further insight into the general meaning of due process. First, notwithstanding its earlier emphasis on tradition, the Court clarified that new procedures that were not part of the inherited common law might nevertheless qualify as due process. In parsing its prior interpretation of "due process" in *Murray's Lessee*, the Court gleaned "that a process of law, which is not otherwise forbidden, must be taken to be due process of law, if it can show the sanction of settled usage both in England and in this country; but it by no means follows, that nothing else can be due process of law" (Hurtado v. California, 1884). If only pedigree qualified law as due process, the law would be "incapable of progress or improvement." Citing the common law's "flexibility and capacity for growth and adaptation" as its "peculiar boast and excellence," the Court declined to conclude that the phrase "due process of law" had a "fixed, definite and technical meaning" (Hurtado v. California, 1884). Thus, in the words of J. Roland Pennock, under *Hurtado*, "historical precedent was no longer a necessary condition of due process."[74] In its place, the Court considered the fundamental fairness of a challenged procedure.

Second, the *Hurtado* Court clarified that not every legislative act qualified as "law" or "due process of law." Rather, due process referred to "the general law," not "a special rule for a particular person or a particular case . . ." and "exclud[ed], as not due process of law, acts of attainder, bills of pains and penalties, acts of confiscation, acts reversing judgments, and acts directly transferring one man's estate to another, legislative judgments and decrees, and other similar special, partial, and arbitrary exertions of power under the forms of legislation" (Hurtado v. California, 1884).

Third, the Court reiterated that each state had authority to prescribe "its own modes of judicial proceeding." Due process in the Fourteenth Amendment did not require the states to adopt particular modes of procedure, but instead "refers to that law of the land *in each state*, which derives its authority from the inherent and reserved powers of the State, exerted within the limits of those fundamental principles of liberty and justice which lie at the base of all our civil and political institutions. . . ." (Hurtado v. California, 1884 (emphasis added); see also Rogers v. Peck, 1905). This language is reminiscent of the framers' statements that the Fourteenth Amendment Due Process Clause was intended to ensure equal access to state judicial proceedings, rather than to require the states to afford particular procedural protections.

There is a tension, however, between *Hurtado*'s conclusion that the Due Process Clause left the states free to prescribe their own procedures, and the earlier understanding that due process and the "law of the land" limited the legislature as well as the judiciary and the executive. Ralph Whitten argues that "the pre-fourteenth amendment context . . . possesses a much higher degree of reliability in establishing the meaning of due process of law" and rejects the proposition that the Due Process Clause was "designed *only* as a direction to the states to give everyone access to judicial processes under the same rules."[75] Instead, he posits that while the framers and ratifiers of the Fourteenth Amendment intended the Due Process Clause to assure all persons equal access to judicial proceedings and to bar state courts from departing from legally prescribed procedures in specific cases, these were not the *only* meanings of due process.[76]

The Supreme Court's decision in Pennoyer v. Neff (1877) is consistent with Whitten's reading and demonstrates that the post-Civil War Court did not repudiate the earlier understanding that due process restricted the legislature. In fact, *Pennoyer* concluded that the Due Process Clause of the Fourteenth Amendment *did* limit the freedom of the states to craft their own procedures, at least with regard to state court jurisdiction (or the authority of a court to compel a defendant to appear and defend in its courts).

To understand *Pennoyer*, we must first understand the flexibility regarding jurisdiction that state courts enjoyed before *Pennoyer*. The Fifth Amendment restrained only the federal government, not the states (Barron v. Baltimore, 1833; Withers v. Buckley, 1858; Twining v. New Jersey, 1908), so it did not inhibit state courts from rendering judgments against defendants who had not been personally served with process or otherwise brought within a court's jurisdiction.[77] And since the states retained sovereignty, they were treated as independent governments at liberty to prescribe their own methods of judicial process (Thompson v. Whitman, 1873). Thus, in the years before the Fourteenth Amendment was adopted, judgments rendered by state courts without proper notice or service of process were binding in the rendering state and were not subject to collateral attack there or elsewhere on due process grounds (Lafayette Ins. Co. v. French, 1856).

This did not mean that state court judgments rendered without notice or service of process were impervious to challenge, however. Under international law at the time the Union was formed, a judgment rendered against a defendant in one state who had not been served with process was void in other states (D'Arcy v. Ketchum, 1851). While the Full Faith and Credit Clause of the Constitution and its implementing statute required courts to recognize judgments rendered elsewhere if the defendant had "full notice" of the action (Mills v. Duryee, 1813), these provisions were not intended to overthrow the international law rule regarding the effect of judgments rendered without jurisdiction. Thus, judgments rendered without jurisdiction or notice were not entitled to full faith and credit in other states (Thompson v. Whitman, 1873; Lafayette Ins. Co. v. French, 1856; D'Arcy v. Ketchum, 1851).[78] In this context, the Supreme Court held that judgments rendered without service of process or notice were contrary to an "immutable principle of natural justice" or the "general law of the land" (Hollingsworth v. Barbour, 1830); "a nullity" (Webster v. Reid, 1851; Shriver Junior's Lessee v. Lynn, 1844); "coram non judice[79] and void" (Boswell's Lessee v. Otis, 1850); or "mere abuse" (D'Arcy v. Ketchum, 1851). Thus, before the adoption of the Fourteenth Amendment Due Process Clause, courts invoked international law, natural law and general principles of justice to bar enforcement of state court judgments rendered without jurisdiction.[80]

But this protection was afforded only outside the rendering state. In other words, no constitutional provision yet barred states from *rendering* judgments without jurisdiction and enforcing them intraterritorially. Although one state court concluded that international law principles applied internally and barred a state legislature from authorizing its courts to bind nonresidents who were not served personally (Beard v. Beard, Ind. 1863), no other state case expressed a similar view, and Whitten offers evidence to suggest that *Beard* would not have been followed in most other states.[81]

Once the Fourteenth Amendment was adopted, however, the Supreme Court quickly recognized that "the validity of [state court] judgments may be *directly* questioned, and their enforcement *in the State* resisted, on the ground that proceedings in a court of justice to determine the personal rights and obligations of parties over whom that court has no jurisdiction do not constitute due process of law" (Pennoyer v. Neff, 1877 (emphasis added)). Not only did the Supreme Court view the Due Process Clause as providing a vehicle for challenging jurisdiction in both the rendering and enforcing states, but it interpreted the words "due process of law" to require that the defendant "be brought within [the court's] jurisdiction by service of process within the State, or his voluntary appearance" (Pennoyer v. Neff, 1877).[82] In other words, the Fourteenth Amendment Due Process Clause was read to limit a state court's territorial jurisdiction and, by requiring in-state service of process in *in personam* cases, to ensure that defendants received notice and an opportunity to be heard before a binding judgment was rendered against them. Since these limitations and requirements applied even if state legislation purported to authorize broader jurisdiction, *Pennoyer* reaffirmed the pre-Fourteenth Amendment understanding that due process restricts the legislature.

Even as the Supreme Court's attention shifted to substantive due process at the turn of the century,[83] it continued to view limitations on jurisdiction, notice and the opportunity to be heard as central to the meaning of procedural due process. In Twining v. New Jersey (1908), for example, the Court reiterated that due process demands that the rendering court have jurisdiction over the parties and that the parties receive notice and an opportunity to be heard. The Court viewed these "fundamental conditions" as "universally prescribed in all systems of law established by civilized countries . . ." (Twining v. New Jersey, 1908). Elaborating on these general requirements, the Court added that as long as

> a court of justice which has jurisdiction, and acts, not arbitrarily, but in conformity with a general law, upon evidence, and after inquiry made with notice to the parties affected and opportunity to be heard, then all the requirements of due process, so far as it relates to procedure in court and methods of trial and character and effect of evidence, are complied with (Twining v. New Jersey, 1908; see also Hooker v. Los Angeles, 1903; Hagar v. Reclamation Dist., 1884).[84]

In the years since *Twining*, the Court has emphasized history less and fairness more in defining due process. If *Murray* defined due process exclusively in terms of historical practice, and *Hurtado* concluded that historical practice was no longer a necessary condition of due process (a practice not recognized at common law might nevertheless satisfy due process), then Powell v. Alabama (1932) no longer considered historical practice to constitute even a sufficient condition.[85] In other words, even a practice that was *accepted* at common law would violate the Due Process Clause if it violated "those 'fundamental principles of liberty and justice which lie at the base of all our civil and political institutions'" (Powell v. Alabama, 1932, quoting Hebert v. Louisiana, 1926). Even though the *Powell* Court conceded that at common law and at the time the Constitution was adopted, a person charged with a felony was not entitled to the assistance of counsel, the Court nevertheless held that the Due Process Clause guaranteed criminal defendants access to appointed counsel because "the right to be heard would be . . . of little avail if it did not comprehend the right to be heard by counsel" (Powell v. Alabama, 1932). Although some have bemoaned the Court's move from history toward a "rather freewheeling search for procedures seen as fundamental by modern judges,"[86] the Court itself has maintained that "'traditional notions of fair play and substantial justice' can be as readily offended by the perpetuation of ancient forms that are no longer justified as by the adoption of new procedures that are inconsistent with the basic values of our constitutional heritage" (Shaffer v. Heitner, 1977).

## NOTES

1. Malinski v. New York, 324 U.S. 401, 414 (1945) (Frankfurter, J., in a separate opinion).

2. The Fifth Amendment Due Process Clause, which regulates the federal government, provides: "[N]or shall any person . . . be deprived of life, liberty or property, without due process of law." U.S. Const. amend. V. The Fourteenth Amendment Due Process Clause, which regulates the states and their political subdivisions, provides: "[N]or shall any State deprive any person of life, liberty, or property without due process of law." U.S. Const. amend. XIV. The Fifth Amendment is written in the passive voice, while the Fourteenth Amendment is written in the active voice. Charles A. Miller, *The Forest of Due Process of Law: The American Constitutional Tradition, in* Nomos XVIII: Due Process 45 n.53 (J. Roland Pennock & John W. Chapman eds., 1977).

3. Substantive due process also bars interference with non-fundamental interests unless a "reasonable justification in the service of a legitimate governmental objective" is established. County of Sacramento v. Lewis, 523 U.S. 833, 846 (1998).

4. Magna Carta art. XXXIX (1215), *quoted in* Rodney L. Mott, Due Process of Law § 1, at 3 (1973). For different translations of the same chapter of the Magna Carta, see The Essential Bill of Rights: Original Arguments and Fundamental Documents 14 (Gordon Lloyd & Margie Lloyd eds., 1998) and Joseph Story, Commentaries on the Constitution of the United States § 923, at 656 (Ronald D. Rotunda & John E. Nowak eds., Carolina Academic Press 1987) (1833).

There is some disagreement about whether the requirements of a jury trial and application of "the law of the land" were conjunctive or disjunctive. Mott concludes that the better translation of the original Latin is "and," but recognizes that the American constitutions followed Coke's translation, which read the word disjunctively. *See* Mott, *supra*, § 1, at 3 n.8. *See also id.* § 13; William Sharp McKechnie, Magna Carta: A Commentary on the Great Charter of King John 381–83 (2d ed. 1914); Hermine Herta Meyer, The History and Meaning of the Fourteenth Amendment: Judicial Erosion of the Constitution Through the Misuse of the Fourteenth Amendment 128 (1977); Ralph U. Whitten, *The Constitutional Limitations on State-Court Jurisdiction: A Historical-Interpretative Reexamination of the Full Faith and Credit and Due Process Clauses (Part Two)*, 14 Creighton L. Rev. 735, 745 (1981) (hereinafter Whitten Part II).

5. McKechnie, *supra* note 4, at 376–81 & 382 n.2; Mott, *supra* note 4, § 1; Frank H. Easterbrook, *Substance and Due Process*, 1982 Sup. Ct. Rev. 85, 95.

6. Meyer, *supra* note 4, at 128–30. *See also* McKechnie, *supra* note 4, at 379 & n.5.

7. McKechnie, *supra* note 4, at 380 & n.1. *See also* Hugh Evander Willis, *Due Process of Law Under the United States Constitution*, 74 U. Pa. L. Rev. 331, 333 (1926).

8. In the reissue of 1225, the Magna Carta was reduced from sixty-three to thirty-seven chapters, and the "law of the land" clause was moved from chapter 39 to chapter 29. Miller, *supra* note 2, at 5.

9. Meyer, *supra* note 4, at 135.

10. *Id.*

11. Easterbrook, *supra* note 5, at 95–96; Whitten Part II, *supra* note 4, at 742–44; Mott, *supra* note 4, § 26; Raoul Berger, Government by Judiciary: The Transformation of the Fourteenth Amendment 197 (1977).

12. Easterbrook, *supra* note 5, at 96; James W. Ely, Jr., *The Oxymoron Reconsidered: Myth and Reality in the Origins of Substantive Due Process*, 16 Const. Comment. 315, 320 (1999); Davidson v. New Orleans, 96 U.S. 97, 101, 102 (1877).

13. For a more thorough treatment of Coke's statement in Bonham's case, see John V. Orth, Due Process of Law: A Brief History 18–32 (2003). Many have argued that any Act of Parliament constitutes due process of law. *See, e.g.*, Lowell J. Howe, *The Meaning of "Due Process of Law" Prior to the Adoption of the Fourteenth Amendment*, 18 Cal. L. Rev. 583, 586 (1930); Willis, *supra* note 7, at 334; Hurtado v. California, 110 U.S. 516, 531 (1884).

14. 2 Edward Coke, The Institutes of the Laws of England 50 (photo. reprint 1986) (Butler & Hargrave eds., 1797) (stating that, "the words, by the law of the land, are rendred without due proces of law").

15. Whitten Part II, *supra* note 4, at 768; Berger, *supra* note 11, at 196. *Cf.* Edward S. Corwin, *The Doctrine of Due Process of Law Before the Civil War*, 24 Harv. L. Rev. 366, 368 (1911) (concluding that Coke misled generations of commentators); Meyer, *supra* note 4, at 138–40 (similar); 2 William Winslow Crosskey, Politics and the Constitution in the History of the United States 1103 (1953) (similar).

16. See The Essential Bill of Rights, *supra* note 4, and The Complete Bill of Rights: The Drafts, Debates, Sources and Origins (Neil H. Cogan, ed., 1997) for the texts of the colonial charters and early laws. *See also* Meyer, *supra* note 4, at 140–46 (discussing colonial charters and laws and state constitutions).

17. Mott, *supra* note 4, § 47, at 123. *Cf.* Whitten Part II, *supra* note 4, at 754, 770.

18. Mott, *supra* note 4, § 48.

19. *Id.* § 51; *see also* Miller, *supra* note 2, at 7.

20. Mott, *supra* note 4, § 54; Whitten Part II, *supra* note 4, at 770–71. *But see* Berger, *supra* note 11, at 194 (stating that due process "quite plainly . . . *did not mean*, in either 1789 or 1866 . . . judicial power to override legislation on substantive or policy grounds"); Corwin, *supra* note 15, at 373.

21. Mott, *supra* note 4, § 5, at 13; Robert Allen Rutland, The Birth of the Bill of Rights: 1776–1791, at 41 (1955).

22. Rutland, *supra* note 21, at 78–79, 100, 107.

23. Mott, *supra* note 4, § 54; Rutland, *supra* note 21, at 41.

24. Mott, *supra* note 4, §§ 7, 9–10, & 54. For a comprehensive discussion of the state constitutions and the different phraseologies used to assure due process, *see id.* §§ 9–11, 67–72; *see also* Easterbrook, *supra* note 5, at 96; Miller, *supra* note 2, at 8–9; Whitten Part II, *supra* note 4, at 748–54.

25. Rutland, *supra* note 21, at 100.

26. Ordinance of 1787, *quoted in* Rutland, *supra* note 21, at 103.

27. Mott, *supra* note 4, § 55.

28. Rutland, *supra* note 21, at 104–05.

29. Corwin, *supra* note 15, at 374–75.

30. Rutland, *supra* note 21, at 107–08.

31. *Id.* at 113–25; Mott, *supra* note 4, § 56.

32. Mott, *supra* note 4, § 56 (citing James Madison's record of the debates which can be found in The Records of the Federal Convention of 1787 (Max Farrand, ed., 1966)).

33. Rutland, *supra* note 21, at 124, 128–30, 133–34.

34. *Id.* at 126–89 (for discussion of ratification debates) & 137 (quoting Philadelphia Indep. Gazetteer, Nov. 1, 1787). *See also* Mott, *supra* note 4, § 58.
35. Mott, *supra* note 4, § 57.
36. Rutland, *supra* note 21, at 146.
37. *Id.* at 180–81.
38. Mott, *supra* note 4, § 58.
39. Rutland, *supra* note 21, at 181, 187–89.
40. *Id.* at 202, 206.
41. Mott, *supra* note 4, § 60 & n.46.
42. U.S. Const. art. III, § 2.
43. U.S. Const. art. VI (stating that "This Constitution, and the Laws of the United States which shall be made in Pursuance thereof; and all Treaties made, or which shall be made, under the Authority of the United States, shall be the supreme Law of the Land").
44. Miller, *supra* note 2, at 10–11. *See also* Bernard H. Siegan, Property Rights: From Magna Carta to the Fourteenth Amendment 107 (2001).
45. Rutland, *supra* note 21, at 207–09.
46. *Id.* at 211–15; Mott, *supra* note 4, § 60.
47. Rutland, *supra* note 21, at 215–16.
48. Mott, *supra* note 4, §§ 61 & 62 & n.66; Rutland, *supra* note 21, at 216–17.
49. Rutland, *supra* note 21, at 217.
50. An early commentary on the Constitution, written by Justice Joseph Story, noted that the words "by the law of the land" in the Magna Carta "mean by due process of law. . . ." Story, *supra* note 4, § 932.
51. Mott, *supra* note 4, § 62, at 159. *Cf.* 2 Crosskey, *supra* note 15, at 1104–07, 1137 (concluding that the Due Process Clause of the Fifth Amendment commanded "appropriate" legal process); Miller, *supra* note 2, at 11 (concluding that "it is difficult to construe [the Due Process Clause of the Fifth Amendment's] general terms with the generality many people . . . have accorded it").
52. Mott, *supra* note 4, § 62.
53. 2 Crosskey, *supra* note 15, at 1102–16, 1137.
54. Easterbrook, *supra* note 5, at 99.
55. This conclusion was consistent with conclusions of state courts interpreting state constitutional Due Process Clauses. *See, e.g.,* Wynehamer v. People, 13 N.Y. 378, 392 (1856) (concluding that state constitutional due process clauses "are imposed by the people as restraints upon the power of the legislature"); *see also* Hoke v. Henderson, 15 N C. 1, 15–16 (1833) (interpreting "law of the land" clause).
56. J. Roland Pennock, *Introduction*, *in* Nomos XVIII: Due Process xvii (J. Roland Pennock & John W. Chapman eds., 1977); 2 Crosskey, *supra* note 15, at 1108–09; Easterbrook, *supra* note 5, at 102.
57. Miller, *supra* note 2, at 13.
58. *See infra* Chapter 2 at text accompanying notes 31 to 44.
59. For example, the abolitionists argued that the Due Process Clause "granted slaves their physical liberty, or at least protected the children of slaves in their natural-born liberty," while the slave owners argued that slaves were property and slave owners had a protected liberty interest in traveling north with their "property." Miller, *supra* note 2, at 14–16. The Supreme Court accepted the slave owners' argument in Dred Scott v. Sandford,

60 U.S. (19 How.) 393, 450 (1856), which decision was repudiated by the Civil War amendments.

60. *See infra* Chapter 2 at text accompanying notes 46 to 49. *See also* Howe, *supra* note 13, at 602–04; Miller, *supra* note 2, at 14.

61. Jacobus tenBroek, The Antislavery Origins of the Fourteenth Amendment 183–87, 209 (1951); Horace Edgar Flack, The Adoption of the Fourteenth Amendment 94 (1908); Mott, *supra* note 4, § 63.

62. Flack, *supra* note 61, at 56–65 (quoting earlier drafts of the Fourteenth Amendment); tenBroek, *supra* note 61, at 187–89 (same).

63. Flack, *supra* note 61, at 57–69; tenBroek, *supra* note 61, at 200–01.

64. tenBroek, *supra* note 61, at 200–16, 220–21.

65. Mott, *supra* note 4, § 65; Berger, *supra* note 11, at 201.

66. Whitten Part II, *supra* note 4, at 805; Mott, *supra* note 4, § 63; tenBroek, *supra* note 61, at 187–90.

67. Cong. Globe, 39th Cong., 1st Sess. 2766 (1866).

68. Cong. Globe, 39th Cong., 1st Sess. 2459 (1866).

69. Berger, *supra* note 11, at 211–13.

70. Meyer, *supra* note 4, at 126–27.

71. *See also* Miller, *supra* note 2, at 17–18; 2 Crosskey, *supra* note 15, at 1119–30, 1135.

72. Black's Law Dictionary 783 (7th ed. 1999).

73. 2 Crosskey, *supra* note 15, at 1140; *see id.* at 1136–41.

74. Pennock, *supra* note 56, at xvii; *see also* Miller, *supra* note 2, at 18.

75. Whitten Part II, *supra* note 4, at 816.

76. *Id.* at 816–17; *see also id.* at 809–17.

77. The Due Process Clause of the Fifth Amendment had been invoked to bar judgments rendered by territorial courts without service of process or notice. Webster v. Reid, 52 U.S. (11 How.) 437, 450 (1851). Interestingly, while counsel in *Webster* invoked due process to bolster the argument that a judgment rendered without service of process or notice was void, the Supreme Court did not explicitly mention due process to support its conclusion that "[n]o person is required to answer in a suit on whom process has not been served, or whose property has not been attached." *Id.* at 459–60. Likewise, while the Supreme Court held that judgments rendered by federal courts without notice or personal service of process upon the defendant were "absolutely void" and "contrary to the first principles of justice," Harris v. Hardeman, 55 U.S. (14 How.) 334, 339–40 (1853), it did not invoke the Fifth Amendment Due Process Clause to support this conclusion.

78. For a comprehensive review of the original meaning of the Full Faith and Credit Clause in Article IV, § 1, and the implementing legislation enacted by Congress in 1790, *see* Ralph U. Whitten, *The Constitutional Limitations on State-Court Jurisdiction: A Historical-Interpretative Reexamination of the Full Faith and Credit and Due Process Clauses (Part One)*, 14 Creighton L. Rev. 499 (1981).

79. Coram non judice means "[o]utside the presence of a judge" or "[b]efore a judge or court that is not the proper one or that cannot take legal cognizance of the matter." Black's Law Dictionary 338 (7th ed. 1999).

80. The Full Faith and Credit Clause did not affirmatively limit state court jurisdiction. *See* Patrick J. Borchers, *Jurisdictional Pragmatism*: International Shoe'*s Half-Buried*

*Legacy*, 28 U.C. Davis L. Rev. 561, 566 (1995) (hereinafter Borchers, *Jurisdictional Pragmatism*).

81. Whitten Part II, *supra* note 4, at 800. *See also* Patrick J. Borchers, *The Death of the Constitutional Law of Personal Jurisdiction: From* Pennoyer *to* Burnham *and Back Again*, 24 U.C. Davis L. Rev. 19, 32 (1990) (concluding that in intrastate cases, "the sole question was whether the court rendering the judgment followed the applicable state statutes") (hereinafter Borchers, *Death of Constitutional Law*); Roger H. Transgrud, *The Federal Common Law of Personal Jurisdiction*, 57 Geo. Wash. L. Rev. 849, 877–78 (1989) (discussing *Beard*).

82. The state court judgment in issue in *Pennoyer* had been entered two years before the ratification of the Fourteenth Amendment, so the Court's due process analysis was dictum. *See* Borchers, *Death of Constitutional Law*, *supra* note 81, at 37–38 (citations omitted); John B. Oakley, *The Pitfalls of "Hit and Run" History: A Critique of Professor Borchers's "Limited View" of* Pennoyer v. Neff, 28 U.C. Davis L. Rev. 591, 632 (1995). The reading proffered in the text—that *Pennoyer* intended the Due Process Clause to provide both a vehicle for challenging a state court's exercise of jurisdiction as well as the content of the jurisdictional rules to be applied—has been referred to as the "expansive" view of *Pennoyer*. Borchers, *Death of Constitutional Law*, *supra* note 81, at 38–39. Borchers posits a more limited reading of *Pennoyer*, pursuant to which the Due Process Clause would provide a vehicle for challenging jurisdiction in all cases, but not the content of the jurisdictional rules to be applied. *Id.* at 40 (under this view, Field "intended for defendants to have at least one chance to ensure that a state followed its own rules of jurisdiction, whatever those rules might be"); *see also* Borchers, *Jurisdictional Pragmatism*, *supra* note 80, at 569. For a scathing critique of the limited view, *see* Oakley, *supra*, at 616–85.

83. *See, e.g.*, Lochner v. New York, 198 U.S. 45 (1905); Allgeyer v. Louisiana, 165 U.S. 578 (1897); *see also* Easterbrook, *supra* note 5, at 104.

84. Crosskey concludes that the *Twining* opinion "undoubtedly discloses the Supreme Court at its worst." 2 Crosskey, *supra* note 15, at 1141; *see id.* at 1141–46 (criticizing *Twining*).

85. Pennock, *supra* note 56, at xvii & xxxi n.5; *see also* Easterbrook, *supra* note 5, at 106 (noting *Powell*'s reliance on cases that "give no support to judicial augmentation of historically recognized procedures").

86. Easterbrook, *supra* note 5, at 107.

# 2

# Preliminaries

***"Appearances in the dark are apt to look different in the light of day."***[1]

Before we begin our analysis of the procedural protections afforded by the Due Process Clauses, we must examine four critical preliminary issues. First, we must consider who qualifies as a "person" protected by due process. Do the Fifth and Fourteenth Amendments protect only individuals or are noncorporeal entities—like corporations, unions, and even governments themselves—also protected? Are *all* individuals considered "persons" within the meaning of the Due Process Clauses or are only American citizens or those admitted for permanent residence protected? Second, since the Due Process Clauses protect persons from only governmental, not private, action, we must next consider who qualifies as a "state" or "government" actor. Put differently, when are private parties sufficiently involved in governmental action to qualify as state actors for constitutional purposes? Third, we must define the interests protected by the Due Process Clauses. Does the word "property" entail anything more than real estate? Is tangible personal property protected? What about non-tangible interests, like employment and reputation? And how broadly are the words "life" and "liberty" read? Finally, we must consider the state of mind that the governmental actor must possess at the time she deprives a person of a protected interest to trigger due process protection. If a state actor's mere negligence causes a person to lose a protected interest, has there been a "deprivation" for due process purposes, or must the state actor actually *intend* to deprive her of a protected interest to trigger due process protection? If negligent acts do not satisfy the state-of-mind requirement, how about grossly negligent or reckless acts? It is to these critically important preliminary issues that we now turn.

## "PERSONS" PROTECTED BY DUE PROCESS

*Webster's Dictionary* defines a "person" as "a human being, whether man, woman or child."[2] Taken at face value, this definition suggests that aliens clandestinely seeking entry into the United States and even enemy combatants are persons, but that corporations, labor unions and school boards are not. As we will see, the Supreme Court's interpretation of the word "person" in the Due Process Clauses varies significantly from this commonsense definition of the word.

### Individuals

Assuming for now that American citizens are "persons" within the meaning of the Due Process Clauses, one must ask whether noncitizens, such as aliens living in the United States and those who have not yet entered the country, also are entitled to due process protections. As early as 1886 (only eleven years after Congress enacted the first immigration law), the Supreme Court stated that the provisions of the Fourteenth Amendment are "universal in their application, to all persons within the territorial jurisdiction, without regard to any differences of race, of color, or of nationality" (Yick Wo v. Hopkins, 1886). Consistent with this statement, the Court has long held that due process protects aliens within this country (Terrace v. Thompson, 1923; Wong Wing v. United States, 1896; Yick Wo v. Hopkins, 1886), even if they are here illegally (Zadvydas v. Davis, 2001; The Japanese Immigrant Case, 1903; Plyler v. Doe, 1982).[3] For example, the Court has recognized that resident aliens cannot be deported without a fair hearing consistent with due process (Wong Yang Sung v. McGrath, 1950; United States *ex rel.* Vajtauer v. Comm'r of Immigr., 1927).

In its most recent decision addressing the due process rights of aliens in the immigration context, the Supreme Court reiterated that "the Fifth Amendment entitles aliens to due process of law in deportation proceedings," but it also emphasized that "Congress may make rules as to aliens that would be unacceptable if applied to citizens" (Demore v. Kim, 2003). Upholding a law that requires the detention of criminal aliens pending removal proceedings—even when the individuals have not been shown to be flight risks or dangerous—the Court concluded that "when the Government deals with deportable aliens, the Due Process Clause does not require it to employ the least burdensome means to accomplish its goal" (Demore v. Kim, 2003). Thus, the conclusion that illegal aliens qualify as "persons" protected by due process does not necessarily mean that they are entitled to the same protections as citizens.[4]

Moreover, the Court has long distinguished between the rights of aliens who have gained entry into the country and those who have not (Landon v. Plasencia, 1982; Kwong Hai Chew v. Colding, 1953). Noncitizens seeking initial entry into the United States have not been treated as "persons" within the meaning of the Fifth Amendment and therefore have no right to due process (Shaughnessy v. United States *ex rel.* Mezei, 1953; United States *ex rel.* Knauff v. Shaughnessy, 1950; Detroit Free Press v. Ashcroft, 6th Cir. 2002 (dicta)). Put differently, "Whatever the procedure authorized by Congress is, it is due process as far as an alien denied entry is concerned" (United States *ex rel.* Knauff v. Shaughnessy, 1950).[5]

Likewise, few, if any, constitutional protections are afforded to enemy aliens whose countries are at war with the United States. In Johnson v. Eisentrager (1950), for example, the Supreme Court concluded that nonresident enemy aliens are not "persons" within the meaning of the Fifth Amendment.[6] Even resident aliens, if they are citizens of a country at war with the United States, may be deported without notice or an opportunity to be heard on the issue of their dangerousness (Ludecke v. Watkins, 1948). Likewise, unlawful combatants, including "those who during time of war pass surreptitiously from enemy territory into our own, discarding their uniforms upon entry, for the commission of hostile acts involving destruction of life or property," can be tried by military commissions for offenses against the law of war without the Fifth and Sixth Amendment guarantees of trial by jury, even if they are American citizens (Ex Parte Quirin, 1942).[7] Thus, without stating that resident enemy aliens and unlawful combatants are not "persons" within the meaning of the Fifth Amendment, the Supreme Court has concluded that they are not entitled to standard Fifth Amendment protections in these contexts.[8]

The extent to which those at war with the United States are protected by due process is a critical issue today, as the United States continues to wage the "war on terrorism" begun in the aftermath of the tragic events of September 11, 2001. Given the ever-changing military target—al Qaeda, the Taliban in Afghanistan, the Baathist regime in Iraq—it is more difficult in this war than in past wars to determine whether a person qualifies as an enemy combatant.[9] In a recent trilogy of cases, the Supreme Court has clarified to some extent the rights of those the government detains as enemy combatants. First, detainees being held within the United States or on an American military base over which the United States has complete jurisdiction and control, such as Guantanamo Bay, may challenge their classification as enemy combatants and the legality of their confinement in federal court. Put differently, the federal district courts have jurisdiction to hear petitions for writs of habeas corpus filed both by American citizens detained as enemy combatants within the United States (Hamdi v. Rumsfeld, 2004; Rumsfeld v. Padilla, 2004)[10] and by aliens captured abroad in connection with hostilities and detained on the American naval base at Guantanamo Bay (Rasul v. Bush, 2004).[11] Second, and more important for our purposes, the Supreme Court has clarified that American citizens detained as enemy combatants within the United States are entitled to certain due process protections: "a citizen-detainee seeking to challenge his classification as an enemy combatant must receive notice of the factual basis for his classification, and a fair opportunity to rebut the Government's factual assertions before a neutral decisionmaker" (Hamdi v. Rumsfeld, 2004, plurality op.). In addition, a citizen challenging classification as an enemy combatant "unquestionably has the right to access to counsel" in connection with such proceedings (Hamdi v. Rumsfeld, 2004, plurality op.).[12]

## Corporations, Partnerships and Unions

The Supreme Court has long treated private corporations as "persons" protected by both the Due Process and Equal Protection Clauses of the Fourteenth Amendment (Metro. Life Ins. Co. v. Ward, 1986; Louis K. Liggett Co. v. Lee, 1933; Grosjean v. Am. Press Co., 1936; Covington & Lexington Tpk. Rd. Co. v. Sandford, 1896). Corporations have also been treated as persons under the Due Process Clause of the Fifth Amendment (United States v. Morton Salt Co., 1950; In re Real Estate Title & Settlement Servs. Antitrust Litig., 3d Cir. 1989; Marshall v. Kleppe, 9th Cir. 1980). In concluding that corporations are persons under the Due Process Clauses, the Court has reasoned that "such corporations are merely associations of individuals united for a special purpose, and permitted to do business under a particular name. . . ." (Pembina Consol. Silver Mining & Milling Co. v. Pennsylvania, 1888). In other words, since the individual shareholders who own the corporation are protected by due process, so is the entity itself.

In states that have adopted the Revised Uniform Partnership Act and in other jurisdictions that treat partnerships as entities distinct from their partners, partnerships may sue and be sued in the name of the partnership (Rev. Unif. Partnership Act § 307(a), 1997). Moreover, under Rule 17(b) of the Federal Rules of Civil Procedure, a partnership or other unincorporated association that lacks such capacity under state law "may sue or be sued in its common name [in federal court] for the purpose of enforcing for or against it a substantive right existing under the Constitution or laws of the United States . . ." (Fed. R. Civ. P. 17(b)). To the extent partnerships, like corporations, are deemed "merely associations of individuals united for a special purpose" (Pembina Consol. Silver Mining & Milling Co. v. Pennsylvania, 1888), they, too, should be protected by the Due Process Clauses. Although there are few decisions directly on point, partnerships have challenged the constitutionality of assertions of personal jurisdiction over them under due process. The courts that have entertained these challenges implicitly have recognized partnerships as "persons" (Sedio, N.V. v. Bell, Kalnick, Klee & Green, N.D. Ill. 1992; Felicia, Ltd. v. Gulf Am. Barge, Ltd., N.D. Ill. 1983).

Like partnerships, labor unions have implicitly been treated as "persons" protected by the Due Process Clauses. Ordinarily unions are unincorporated associations and at common law, they lacked authority to sue and be sued in their own name (United Mine Workers v. Coronado Coal Co., 1922). Today, most states permit unions to sue and be sued in their own name and some federal statutes, including labor and antitrust laws, permit suits against unincorporated labor unions (Textile Workers Union v. Lincoln Mills, 1957; United Mine Workers v. Coronado Coal Co., 1922). Just as courts have entertained jurisdictional challenges made by partnerships, so have they entertained jurisdictional and other due process challenges made by labor unions, implicitly treating them as "persons" entitled to due process (Reed v. Int'l Union of United Auto. Workers, 7th Cir. 1991 (jurisdiction); Cent. Operating Co. v. Util. Workers, 4th Cir. 1974 (notice)).

### States, Municipalities and other Political Subdivisions

States are not "persons" protected by the Fifth or Fourteenth Amendments (Pennsylvania v. New Jersey, 1976 (equal protection); South Carolina v. Katzenbach, 1966 (due process)).[13] Without explicitly reaching the question of whether counties, cities, municipalities or other political subdivisions of the state are persons under the Fourteenth Amendment, the Supreme Court and lower courts have held that these subdivisions may not raise Fourteenth Amendment claims against their own state (City of Newark v. New Jersey, 1923; Hunter v. City of Pittsburgh, 1907; Bd. of Educ. v. Shutz, N.D.N.Y. 2001) or even against another political subdivision of the same state (S. Macomb Disposal Auth. v. Township of Washington, 6th Cir. 1986; City of New Rochelle v. Town of Mamaroneck, S.D.N.Y. 2000).[14] These principles are often couched in terms of a lack of standing (Indian Oasis-Baboquivari Unified Sch. Dist. No. 40 v. Kirk, 9th Cir. 1996). As the Supreme Court once put it, "Being but creatures of the State, municipal corporations have no standing to invoke . . . the provisions of the Fourteenth Amendment of the Constitution in opposition to the will of their creator" (Coleman v. Miller, 1939).[15]

The rationale for this political subdivision standing doctrine is the need for state control over its subdivisions. The Supreme Court has long recognized that municipal corporations are "the instruments of government, created for its purposes" (Trs. of Dartmouth Coll. v. Woodward, 1819), and therefore, "the regulation of municipalities is a matter peculiarly within the domain of the State" (City of Newark v. New Jersey, 1923). As the Sixth Circuit put it, "The relationship between the entities [i.e., political subdivisions within a single state] is a matter of state concern; the Fourteenth Amendment protections and limitations do not apply" (S. Macomb Disposal Auth. v. Township of Washington, 6th Cir. 1986). In determining whether an entity is a political subdivision of the state for these purposes, federal courts look to state law (Delta Spec. Sch. Dist. No. 5 v. State Bd. of Educ., 8th Cir. 1984).

Notwithstanding this substantial body of precedent, numerous courts have permitted political subdivisions to challenge the constitutionality of state action in at least four contexts. First, several courts have held that municipalities and other political subdivisions are "persons" with standing to sue a government *other than* the state of which they are a part (or a political subdivision of that state) for deprivations of a protected interest without due process of law (City of Santa Clara v. Andrus, 9th Cir. 1978 (dicta); Township of River Vale v. Town of Orangetown,

2d Cir. 1968; City of Sault Ste. Marie v. Andrus, D.D.C. 1980). Similarly, the Third Circuit Court of Appeals has held that a school district may raise a due process challenge to a federal court's exercise of personal jurisdiction over it in the absence of minimum contacts (In re Real Estate Title & Settlement Servs. Antitrust Litig., 3d Cir. 1989).[16] Although these decisions recognize municipalities and other political subdivisions as "persons" protected by due process, they may be reconciled with the political subdivision standing cases above because they acknowledge the subdivisions' standing to sue only governments other than their own state or other political subdivisions of the same state.

Second, several courts have permitted political subdivisions to challenge the constitutionality of state laws on Supremacy Clause grounds (Lawrence County v. Lead-Deadwood Sch. Dist. No. 40–1, 1985; Branson Sch. Dist. RE-82 v. Romer, 10th Cir. 1998; Rogers v. Brockette, 5th Cir. 1979). For example, in Lawrence County v. Lead-Deadwood School District No. 40–1 (1985), a school district sought to compel a county of the same state to disburse funds it received from the federal government as directed by a state statute. The county argued that the state statute was invalid under the Supremacy Clause because it was inconsistent with a federal law that left it to the county to determine how to spend the federal funds. Without discussing the school district's standing to sue the county or the county's authority to challenge the constitutionality of a state law, the Supreme Court addressed the merits, recognizing Congress's authority to impose conditions upon the receipt of federal funds and holding that the state law violated the Supremacy Clause. In an earlier case, the Fifth Circuit expressly recognized a municipality's standing to challenge the constitutionality of a state statute on Supremacy Clause grounds, reading the putative standing cases as setting forth a "substantive principle that the Constitution does not interfere with a state's internal political organization," rather than limiting standing, and concluding that *Congress* has authority to interfere with a state's internal political organization (Rogers v. Brockette, 5th Cir. 1979). Similarly, the Tenth Circuit read the standing cases "only for the limited proposition that a municipality may not bring a constitutional challenge against its creating state when the constitutional provision that supplies the basis for the complaint was written to protect individual rights, as opposed to collective or structural rights" (Branson Sch. Dist. RE-82 v. Romer, 10th Cir. 1998). Although these cases provide no support for the proposition that municipalities and other political subdivisions are "persons" within the meaning of the Due Process Clauses, they do recognize that municipalities have standing to sue their own states in some circumstances.

Third, the courts of at least one state have concluded that municipal corporations may press procedural due process claims against a political subdivision of their own state (City of Colorado Springs v. Bd. of County Comm'rs, Colo. Ct. App. 1994 (dicta); City & County of Denver v. Eggert, Colo. 1982).[17] Like the Fifth Circuit in *Rogers*, the Colorado courts read the standing cases as barring municipalities from invoking the Fourteenth Amendment to "impose [substantive] restrictions upon the relationships between one political subdivision of a state and another," but not as limiting their standing to sue or to invoke the procedural protections of the Fourteenth Amendment.

Finally, in Washington v. Seattle School District No. 1 (1982), the United States Supreme Court upheld a school district's equal protection challenge to a state law but failed to expressly address the school district's standing or status as a "person" under the Fourteenth Amendment. By entertaining the challenge, however, the Court implicitly concluded both that the school district had standing to sue its own state and that it was a "person" for purposes of the Fourteenth Amendment. It is difficult to reconcile the Supreme Court's willingness in *Seattle School* to entertain a school district's substantive challenge to a state law under the Fourteenth Amendment with its earlier political subdivision standing cases. Few courts have made much of this seeming departure, however. The Ninth Circuit, for one, has concluded that *Seattle School* "does not constitute binding authority with respect to [political subdivision] standing" because the Supreme Court did not directly address the standing issue (Burbank-Glendale-Pasadena Airport Auth. v. City of Burbank, 9th Cir. 1998; Indian Oasis-Baboquivari Unified Sch. Dist. No. 40 v. Kirk, 9th Cir. 1996).[18]

## STATE ACTION REQUIREMENT

Now that we have a better idea of who can invoke the protections of due process, we consider who is required by the Constitution to provide due process. Like section 1983 of Title 42, which provides a remedy only if a person acting under color of state law deprives someone of a protected right, the Due Process Clauses of the Fifth and Fourteenth Amendments regulate only governmental (or "state") action,[19] not private conduct.[20] The Court has justified strict adherence to the state action requirement by noting that it serves two purposes: to preserve individual freedom by limiting the reach of federal law and federal judicial power; and to avoid imposing liability on the state for conduct for which the state cannot fairly be blamed (Lugar v. Edmondson Oil Co., 1982). On the other hand, the Court carefully scrutinizes nominally private conduct to determine if state action exists to ensure that constitutional standards are followed when the state is in fact responsible for the challenged conduct (Brentwood Acad. v. Tenn. Secondary Sch. Athletic Ass'n, 2001).

State action requires two elements: (1) the claimed deprivation must result from the exercise of a right or privilege having its source in state authority, and (2) the party charged with the deprivation must be a state actor (Am. Mfrs. Mut. Ins. Co. v. Sullivan, 1999; Lugar v. Edmondson Oil Co., 1982). Put differently, the first element asks whether the defendant acted pursuant to state law, and the second element asks whether the defendant can fairly be treated as a state actor. The

Court has recognized that the second element requires a "factbound inquiry" (Edmonson v. Leesville Concrete Co., 1991).

When the plaintiff challenges conduct of a state agency or official, the state action inquiry typically is abbreviated. State employees generally qualify as state actors (Lugar v. Edmondson Oil Co., 1982),[21] as do government-controlled corporations that promote governmental objectives, such as Amtrak (Lebron v. Nat'l R.R. Passenger Corp., 1995). Likewise, official actions of the government, such as legislation, executive orders and court degrees, always constitute state action.[22]

The more difficult cases grapple with the circumstances in which conduct of private parties qualifies as state action. In such cases, courts scrutinize the nature of the relationship between the private party and the government, attempting to determine if "there is a sufficiently close nexus between the State and the challenged action of the regulated entity so that the action of the latter may be fairly treated as that of the State itself" (Jackson v. Metro. Edison Co., 1974). This nexus requirement is designed to ensure that constitutional standards are invoked only when the state is actually responsible for the challenged conduct (Blum v. Yaretsky, 1982). No single fact or circumstance is determinative, although the Court has identified a number of facts that bear on the fairness of such attribution (Brentwood Acad. v. Tenn. Secondary Sch. Athletic Ass'n, 2001).

The required nexus may exist if the private party exercises powers that are "traditionally the exclusive prerogative of the State" (Jackson v. Metro. Edison Co., 1974). Likewise, private parties that use state procedures with the help of state officials qualify as state actors if they are "joint participants" with the state (Tulsa Prof'l Collection Servs. v. Pope, 1988; Lugar v. Edmondson Oil Co., 1982; Burton v. Wilmington Parking Auth., 1961). In addition, private parties that act under the compulsion of state law or state-enforced custom are state actors, as are those that receive significant encouragement from the government (Blum v. Yaretsky, 1982; Adickes v. S.H. Kress & Co., 1970). And nominally private organizations will be treated as state actors when there is "pervasive entwinement of public institutions and public officials in its composition and workings. . . ." (Brentwood Acad. v. Tenn. Secondary Sch. Athletic Ass'n, 2001).

But action by private parties taken pursuant to a state statute does not necessarily qualify as state action, even if the state acquiesces in the private conduct (Flagg Bros., Inc. v. Brooks, 1978). That a private business is subject to extensive state regulation does not necessarily convert its action into state action for constitutional purposes, even if it has monopoly status (Blum v. Yaretsky, 1982; Jackson v. Metro. Edison Co., 1974). Nor does receipt of state funding necessarily justify treatment as a state actor (S.F. Arts & Athletics, Inc. v. United States Olympic Comm., 1987; Rendell-Baker v. Kohn, 1982).

Until recently, the Supreme Court had declined to resolve whether the "exclusive public function" test, the "state compulsion" test, the "nexus" test and the "joint participation" test "are actually different in operation or simply different ways of characterizing the necessarily fact-bound inquiry that confronts the Court in such a situation. . . ." (Lugar v. Edmondson Oil Co., 1982). In 2001, the Court clarified a bit, declaring that state action can be found if one test is met even if the facts do not support a finding of state action under a different test: "Facts that address *any* of these criteria are significant, but no one criterion must necessarily be applied" (Brentwood Acad. v. Tenn. Secondary Sch. Athletic Ass'n, 2001, emphasis added).

The Supreme Court's decision in American Manufacturers Mutual Insurance Co. v. Sullivan (1999) applies a number of these different tests. There, plaintiffs challenged a Pennsylvania workers' compensation law, which permitted an insurer to withhold payment to an injured employee while a disputed medical treatment was being reviewed by a utilization review organization ("URO") to determine whether the treatment was reasonable and necessary. Before an insurer could withhold payment, it had to submit a one-page form to the state Workers' Compensation Bureau, identifying the employee, the date of injury, the medical provider and the challenged treatment. Upon receipt, the Bureau reviewed the form to ensure that all required information was included, notified the parties that URO review had been requested, and forwarded the request for review to a URO comprised of private licensed professionals in the relevant field. At that point, the insurer was authorized to withhold payment.

The Supreme Court conceded that the insurer's challenged action was taken pursuant to state law because it acted with knowledge of and pursuant to the Pennsylvania workers' compensation statute. The Court nevertheless held that the insurer was not a state actor because the alleged unconstitutional conduct was not "fairly attributable to the State" (Am. Mfrs. Mut. Ins. Co. v. Sullivan, 1999).

In determining whether a sufficiently close nexus existed between the state and the insurer's decision to withhold payment, the Court considered whether the state had "exercised coercive power or [had] provided such significant encouragement, either overt or covert," that the conduct should be deemed state action (Am. Mfrs. Mut. Ins. Co. v. Sullivan, 1999). Here, the decision to refer the matter to a URO was made by the private insurer with no direct involvement by the state. While conceding that the state may have encouraged insurers to make referrals by amending the statute to permit them to withhold payment while seeking URO review, the Court viewed that encouragement as too "subtle" to justify a finding of state action. The state did no more than permit a "private choice" (Am. Mfrs. Mut. Ins. Co. v. Sullivan, 1999).

The Court rejected the argument that the insurer's conduct constituted state action because it had to obtain authorization from the Workers' Compensation Bureau before withholding payment. In a prior case, Blum v. Yaretsky (1982), the Court had rejected the notion that the state was responsible for private conduct simply because it required private parties to complete a form if they made a particular decision. "The additional 'paper shuffling' performed by the Bureau here in response to an insurer's request does not alter that conclusion" (Am. Mfrs. Mut. Ins. Co. v. Sullivan, 1999).

The Court also considered the plaintiffs' contention that the insurer's decision constituted state action because it was performing a function "traditionally exclusively reserved to the State" (Am. Mfrs. Mut. Ins. Co. v. Sullivan, 1999). In rejecting this argument, the Court distinguished West v. Atkins (1988), in which it had held that treatment provided to an injured inmate by a private physician under contract with the state constituted state action because the state had a constitutional obligation to provide adequate medical care to inmates and had delegated this exclusive public function to the doctor. The state in *American Manufacturers Mutual*, on the other hand, was not required to provide medical treatment or workers' compensation benefits to injured workers; rather, the state statute imposed that obligation on employers.

In its most recent state action case, the Supreme Court introduced another layer to the state action analysis (Brentwood Acad. v. Tenn. Secondary Sch. Athletic Ass'n, 2001). If a court concludes that the facts support a finding of state action, it must then ask whether these facts are "outweighed in the name of some value at odds with finding public accountability in the circumstances" (Brentwood Acad. v. Tenn. Secondary Sch. Athletic Ass'n, 2001). One such countervailing value might be concern for "an epidemic of unprecedented federal litigation," although the *Brentwood Academy* Court rejected that argument on the facts of the case because the record did not support a finding that such a litigation explosion was likely. Another countervailing value might be the "social utility" of expanding the class of state actors in a case where the claim was "pushing at the edge of the class of possible defendant state actors." Again, however, the Court rejected the argument because the facts of the case were "nowhere near the margin. . . ." (Brentwood Acad. v. Tenn. Secondary Sch. Athletic Ass'n, 2001). The Court cited only one case, Polk County v. Dodson (1981), in which a countervailing value had been found strong enough to overcome a finding of state action. There, a county-employed defense attorney's actions were deemed private because the attorney did not act on the state's behalf, but rather on behalf of the state's adversary. Presumably, in future cases, the Court will be called upon to clarify the parameters of the "countervailing value" analysis.

The state action requirement has been subject to substantial criticism from the academy, and some scholars have suggested that it should be "banished from American law."[23] Notwithstanding the many criticisms, the Supreme Court has steadfastly adhered to the state action requirement, continuing to carefully scrutinize the relationship between the government and private parties to determine whether to characterize the challenged conduct as state action.

## INTERESTS PROTECTED BY DUE PROCESS

Under current Supreme Court case law, every procedural due process case requires application of a two-part test: first, whether the plaintiff has been deprived of a protected "life," "liberty," or "property" interest; and second, if so, whether the procedures in place comport with due process (Mathews v. Eldridge, 1976). Only when protected interests are implicated does the right to "some kind of a hearing" attach (Bd. of Regents v. Roth, 1972). Prior to its decision in *Roth*, the Court employed a unitary concept of "life, liberty or property,"[24] deeming interests to be protected by due process as long as they were important enough to warrant such protection, without regard to whether they were categorized as "life," "liberty," or "property" (Bell v. Burson, 1971; Joint Anti-Fascist Refugee Comm. v. McGrath, 1951, Frankfurter, J., concurring). Since *Roth*, the Court has changed its approach, parsing each word of the clause separately to determine if a protected "life," "liberty," or "property" interest exists before determining the scope of due process protection (Paul v. Davis, 1976; Meachum v. Fano, 1976). The Court has emphasized that the *nature* of the interest at stake, rather than its importance or weight, determines whether it is entitled to due process protection (Bd. of Regents v. Roth, 1972). The Court has made clear that "[the] range of interests protected by procedural due process is not infinite" (Bd. of Regents v. Roth, 1972) and it has "repeatedly rejected 'the notion that *any* grievous loss visited upon a person by the State is sufficient to invoke the procedural protections of the Due Process Clause'" (Ingraham v. Wright, 1977; Meachum v. Fano, 1976, emphasis added). Thus, the Court has rejected the unitary concept of "life, liberty or property" and the importance test.

Scholars have roundly criticized the Court's approach.[25] Professor John Hart Ely has taken the Court to task for adopting a circular definition: "It turns out . . . that whether it's a property interest is a function of whether you're entitled to it, which means the Court has to decide whether you're entitled to it before it can decide whether you get a hearing on the question whether you're entitled to it."[26] Professor Monaghan views the Court's approach in *Roth* as a "break with traditions developed over the last half century which appeared to be firmly embedded in our constitutional order," traditions that protected "all interests valued by sensible men."[27] A return to the traditional method would avoid the difficulty of characterizing interests and focus attention on the severity of the harm suffered by the individual.[28] To date, the Supreme Court has declined to heed the call to resume use of the pre-*Roth* unitary analysis.

Following the Court's lead, we will examine the concepts of life, liberty and property separately, tracing the evolving treatment of these interests before examining the kinds of procedures required to satisfy due process. Since the Court has spent more time attempting to define "property" and "liberty" interests than "life" interests, we will focus our attention on those areas, examining "life" only briefly.

### Life Interests

The Court has declined to define the term "life."[29] Capital punishment may be the only setting in which the government actually proposes to take a person's life. In this context, where the criminal defendant's life is so obviously in jeopardy, the Supreme Court has required numerous procedural protections. Although the Court has developed much of its capital punishment jurisprudence under the Eighth Amendment ban on cruel and unusual punishment,[30] it has also invoked the Due Process Clause, proceeding on the often unstated assumption that the defendant's interest in avoiding the death penalty is a protected life interest (Shafer v. South Carolina, 2001; Simmons v. South Carolina, 1994; Skipper v. South Carolina, 1986).

Only occasionally has the Court explicitly mentioned the life interest in capital punishment cases. In Gardner v. Florida (1977), for example, the Court found that due process was violated when the trial judge who imposed the death sentence relied on a pre-sentence investigation report, which had not been shared with counsel for the defendant. It noted that "this procedure does not satisfy the constitutional command that no person shall be deprived of life without due process of law" (Gardner v. Florida, 1977, plurality op.).

This "original" life interest is entitled to due process protection during the trial and sentencing proceedings, but once a defendant is convicted and sentenced to death, his life interest is limited. While a death row inmate "maintains a residual life interest, e.g., in not being summarily executed by prison guards . . . [he] cannot use his interest in not being executed in accord with his sentence to challenge the clemency determination by requiring the procedural protections he seeks" (Ohio Adult Parole Auth. v. Woodard, 1998). In the Court's view, the death row inmate's original life interest is extinguished by the conviction and death sentence (Ohio Adult Parole Auth. v. Woodard, 1998).

The Court has occasionally considered whether a protected life interest exists beyond the capital punishment setting. In the abortion context, for example, the Court has rejected the view that a fetus is a person who may not be deprived of life without due process of law (Planned Parenthood v. Casey, 1992; Roe v. Wade, 1973). Had it ruled otherwise, laws permitting abortion, even if only to save the mother's life, would have been constitutionally suspect (Roe v. Wade, 1973). In the context of a "right to die" case, the Court stated that "the Due Process Clause protects an interest in life as well as an interest in refusing life-sustaining medical treatment" and it recognized an "unqualified [state] interest in the preservation of human life to be weighed against the constitutionally protected interests of the individual" (Cruzan v. Dir., Mo. Dep't of Health, 1990; see also Washington v. Glucksberg, 1997). In at least two other cases—one involving the murder of a girl by a parolee (Martinez v. California, 1980) and the other involving a fatal car accident (County of Sacramento v. Lewis, 1998)—the Court accepted without discussion that a life interest was at stake.

### Property Interests

The reigning entitlement theory, adopted by the Supreme Court thirty years ago, posits that property interests are not created by the federal Constitution. Rather, property interests "are created and their dimensions are defined by existing rules or understandings that stem from an independent source such as state law—rules or understandings that secure certain benefits and that support claims of entitlement to those benefits" (Bd. of Regents v. Roth, 1972). Certain forms of private property—real estate, chattels and money—have long been recognized as entitled to due process protection (Bd. of Regents v. Roth, 1972).[31] That due process protects a wider range of interests—including various forms of government largess—has been a critical part of the "due process revolution."

Professor Charles Reich's seminal work, *The New Property*, published in 1964, described how various forms of government largess—benefits, jobs, licenses, franchises, subsidies, services and the use of public resources—had become an increasingly large portion of overall wealth in America. For most of our history, individual rights in such largess were limited by legal principles that reserved to the government unfettered control over such wealth.[32] Invoking one of these principles, the right/privilege distinction, courts traditionally held that procedural due process rights attached only when a person was deprived of a "right," but not of a "privilege." Thus, persons could be fired from public employment without due process because the job was a mere privilege, not a "right" protected by the Due Process Clause. As Justice Holmes put it in an infamous case involving a police officer fired for engaging in political activity, "[t]he petitioner may have a constitutional right to talk politics, but he has no constitutional right to be a policeman" (McAuliffe v. Mayor of New Bedford, Mass. 1892).

The Supreme Court's recognition that due process protects individuals from deprivations of governmentally-dispensed wealth varied depending on the type of wealth involved. The Court first protected the types of largess that were intimately bound up with a person's freedom to earn a living, such as occupational licenses[33] and franchises.[34] Over time, and against a backdrop of dramatic social and political change, the Court wrestled with the right/privilege distinction in the context of other forms of largess, including government employment and benefits.

As Professor Cynthia Farina has convincingly demonstrated, the Red Scare and the McCarthy era forced the Court to reconsider the right/privilege distinction and the lack of procedural protections that attended termination of government employment.[35] In 1949, Dorothy Bailey, a government employee who had been dismissed on the basis of unsworn charges made by unnamed informants, challenged her dismissal in court (Bailey v. Richardson, D.C. Cir. 1950). The D.C. Circuit summarily rejected her due process claim, noting that "it has been held repeatedly and consistently that Government employ is not 'property,'" but one judge dissented. Although the Supreme Court affirmed by an equally divided Court (Bailey v. Richardson, 1951, per curiam), "it became increasingly hard for the judiciary to turn away victims of McCarthyism by merely parroting Justice Holmes' facile distinction between 'rights' and 'privileges.'"[36] Over the course of the decade that followed, the Court grew more willing to protect government employees and licensees from adverse employment decisions rendered without appropriate procedural protections,[37] sometimes invoking non-constitutional grounds to support its decision.[38]

In the 1960s, other social and political forces, including the civil rights movement and the growth of the Great Society governmental programs, provided courts with additional opportunities to rethink the kinds of interests deserving of constitutional protection.[39] In Professor Farina's words,

> As modern society became more complex and interdependent, as Americans' collective political choices gave government a more pervasive role in regulating and supporting their individual social and economic lives, the right/privilege distinction became an increasingly inadequate touchstone for determining when the Constitution regulates interactions between government and the citizen.[40]

It was against this backdrop that in 1961, the Court openly questioned the viability of the right/privilege distinction, dismissing the "easy assertion that, because [the government employee] had no constitutional right to be there in the first place, she was not deprived of liberty or property by the Superintendent's action" in revoking the badge required for admittance to the naval facility where she worked (Cafeteria & Rest. Workers Union v. McElroy, 1961; see also Sherbert v. Verner, 1963).

Within years of the Court's decision in *Cafeteria Workers*, Professor Charles Reich published *The New Property*, which illustrated the extent to which increasing amounts of wealth now take the form of government largess, rather than traditional forms of private property. Concerned that recipients of government largess lose autonomy and security due to pervasive regulation and dependency upon government, Reich advocated that certain forms of government largess—including unemployment compensation, public assistance and old age insurance—be deemed to be held as of right. Professor Reich added his voice to those clamoring for an end to the right/privilege distinction.[41]

By the time Goldberg v. Kelly (1970) was argued before the Supreme Court, the right/privilege distinction had so little support that the government actually *conceded* that due process protections extended to public welfare programs

(Goldberg v. Kelly, 1970; Kelly v. Wyman, S.D.N.Y. 1968). Influenced by Professor Reich's work, the *Goldberg* Court explicitly rejected the right/privilege distinction, holding that welfare benefits are "a matter of statutory entitlement for persons qualified to receive them" (Goldberg v. Kelly, 1970).[42] Relying on Reich's premise that "[m]uch of the existing wealth in this country takes the form of rights that do not fall within traditional common-law concepts of property,"[43] the Court characterized welfare entitlements "as more like 'property' than a 'gratuity'" (Goldberg v. Kelly, 1970). By 1972, the Court had "fully and finally rejected the wooden distinction between 'rights' and 'privileges' that once seemed to govern the applicability of procedural due process rights" (Bd. of Regents v. Roth, 1972).[44]

Although language in *Goldberg* suggested that a benefit would be treated as property if its deprivation would cause the recipient "grievous loss" (Goldberg v. Kelly, 1970), the Court soon rejected this importance test, looking instead to state and federal statutory law to determine whether a person has a "legitimate claim of entitlement" to a benefit or other claimed property interest:

> To have a property interest in a benefit, a person clearly must have more than an abstract need or desire for it. He must have more than a unilateral expectation of it. He must, instead, have a legitimate claim of entitlement to it. It is a purpose of the ancient institution of property to protect those claims upon which people rely in their daily lives, reliance that must not be arbitrarily undermined (Bd. of Regents v. Roth, 1972).

As Justice O'Connor later put it, "the distinction between an 'entitlement' and a mere 'expectancy' must necessarily depend on the degree to which the decisionmakers' discretion is constrained by law" (Bd. of Pardons v. Allen, 1987, O'Connor, J., dissenting).[45]

In approaching the entitlement/expectancy question, the Supreme Court has carefully scrutinized statutory language before finding a property interest created by statute, regulation or other source of positive law. For example, in American Manufacturers Mutual Insurance Co. v. Sullivan (1999), the Court acknowledged that employees were entitled to workers' compensation benefits under Pennsylvania law. But the Court scrutinized the statute, noting that employees were entitled to only "reasonable" and "necessary" medical treatment, not all treatment. Thus, employees had to establish that the treatment sought was reasonable and necessary *before* their interests qualified as property interests protected by due process.

For a period of years, it appeared that the Court might permit legislatures to restrict property rights by conditioning their grant on a specified procedural mechanism for their removal, one that might not comply with minimum due process requirements. In his plurality opinion in Arnett v. Kennedy (1974), Chief Justice Rehnquist contended that a legislature could delineate the procedural rights available to a government employee removed from her position for cause by incorporating the procedures for removal or suspension into the very statute that created the property interest in the position itself.[46] In his view, the property right created by the statute was defined and restricted by the procedures for removal: "where the grant of a substantive right is inextricably intertwined with the limitations on the procedures which are to be employed in determining that right, a litigant in the position of appellee must take the bitter with the sweet" (Arnett v. Kennedy, 1974, plurality op.).[47]

Justice Rehnquist's opinion in *Arnett* garnered only two additional votes, and six Justices specifically rejected the "bitter with the sweet" theory in that case. Although the theory gained additional support in the years following *Arnett* (Bishop v. Wood, 1976; Goss v. Lopez, 1975, Powell, J., dissenting), a majority of the Court has since clearly rejected it. In Vitek v. Jones (1980), for example, the Court stated that because "minimum [procedural] requirements [are] a matter of federal law, they are not diminished by the fact that the State may have specified its own procedures that it may deem adequate for determining the preconditions to adverse official action" (*see also* Logan v. Zimmerman Brush Co., 1982). And in Cleveland Board of Education v. Loudermill (1985), an eight-Justice majority of the Court explicitly rejected the "bitter with the sweet" approach, noting that it:

> misconceives the constitutional guarantee. . . . The point is straightforward: the Due Process Clause provides that certain substantive rights—life, liberty, and property—cannot be deprived except pursuant to constitutionally adequate procedures. The categories of substance and procedure are distinct. Were the rule otherwise, the Clause would be reduced to a mere tautology. "Property" cannot be defined by the procedures provided for its deprivation any more than can life or liberty. The right to due process "is conferred, not by legislative grace, but by constitutional guarantee. While the legislature may elect not to confer a property interest in [public] employment, it may not constitutionally authorize the deprivation of such an interest, once conferred, without appropriate procedural safeguards" (Cleveland Bd. of Educ. v. Loudermill, 1985, quoting Arnett v. Kennedy, 1974, Powell, J., concurring in part and concurring in the result in part).[48]

Thus, Chief Justice Rehnquist's "attempted due process counterrevolution" failed.[49] While state legislatures and Congress retain substantial discretion to create and define substantive rights, it is a body of federal constitutional law, not legislation, that determines the nature and sufficiency of the procedural protections that secure those rights. Likewise, federal constitutional law determines whether a state-created substantive interest "rises to the level of a 'legitimate claim of entitlement' protected by the Due Process Clause" (Memphis Light, Gas & Water Div. v. Craft, 1978).

Over the years, the Court has found a wide range of property interests that qualify as entitlements, including mere possessory interests in chattels (Fuentes v. Shevin, 1972), intangible interests such as causes of action (Logan v. Zimmerman Brush Co., 1982), the right of an employer to discharge an employee for cause

(Brock v. Roadway Express, Inc., 1987), a child's entitlement to a public school education (Goss v. Lopez, 1975), and continued gas and electric service conditioned upon payment of proper charges (Memphis Light, Gas & Water Div. v. Craft, 1978). In the sections that follow, we will trace the Court's treatment of three important and pervasive property interests: professional licenses, government benefits and public employment.

### *The "Old Property": Professional Licenses*

Long before the due process revolution of the early 1970s, the Supreme Court recognized a property interest in professional licenses entitled to due process protection (Dent v. West Virginia, 1889; Goldsmith v. United States Bd. of Tax Appeals, 1926). These interests came under siege during the Red Scare, and the Court at that time characterized a license to practice medicine as "a privilege granted by the State under its substantially plenary power to fix the terms of admission" (Barsky v. Bd. of Regents, 1954).[50] By the late 1950s, however, it declined to decide whether the practice of law was a "right" or a "privilege," concluding that regardless of the characterization, a "person cannot be prevented from practicing except for valid reasons. Certainly the practice of law is not a matter of the State's grace" (Schware v. Bd. of Bar Examiners, 1957; Willner v. Comm. on Character & Fitness, 1963). Although licenses may be revoked or suspended, state laws typically create "a clear expectation of continued enjoyment of a license absent proof of culpable conduct" (Barry v. Barchi, 1979).

Over the years, the Supreme Court has held that a variety of professional and other occupational licenses qualify as property protected by the Due Process Clause, including licenses to practice medicine (Withrow v. Larkin, 1975; Dent v. West Virginia, 1889) and law (In Re Ruffalo, 1968; Willner v. Comm. on Character & Fitness, 1968)[51] and to serve as harness race horse trainers (Barry v. Barchi, 1979).[52] In addition to professional and occupational licenses, the Court has recognized that driver's licenses qualify as property interests protected by due process (Illinois v. Batchelder, 1983; Mackey v. Montrym, 1979), relying in one case on the fact that the "continued possession" of a driver's license "may become essential in the pursuit of a livelihood" (Bell v. Burson, 1971).

### *The "New Property": Government Benefits*

Unlike professional licenses, government benefits have been treated as protected property interests only since the early 1970s. Before then, the Court treated benefits as privileges, or "unaccrued" property rights, not entitled to due process protection (Flemming v. Nestor, 1960).

In a single paragraph of the pathbreaking case of Goldberg v. Kelly (1970), the Supreme Court dramatically departed from that course, holding that welfare benefits qualify as a property interest entitled to due process protection. Recognizing that "such benefits are a matter of statutory entitlement for persons qualified to receive them," the Court flatly rejected the argument that "public assistance benefits are 'a "privilege" and not a "right"'" (Goldberg v. Kelly, 1970). In a footnote, the Court noted that welfare entitlements are "more like 'property' than a 'gratuity,'" adding that "[m]uch of the existing wealth in this country takes the form of rights that do not fall within traditional common-law concepts of property" (Goldberg v. Kelly, 1970).

In the years following *Goldberg*, the Supreme Court has recognized a protected property interest in Medicare and Medicaid benefits (O'Bannon v. Town Ct. Nursing Ctr., 1980),[53] Social Security benefits (Califano v. Yamasaki, 1979; Mathews v. Eldridge, 1976),[54] food stamps (Atkins v. Parker, 1985) and veteran's benefits for death or disability (Walters v. Nat'l Ass'n of Radiation Survivors, 1985). The Court has declined to determine whether "applicants for benefits, as distinct from those already receiving them, have a legitimate claim of entitlement" protected by due process (Lyng v. Payne, 1986; Walters v. Nat'l Ass'n of Radiation Survivors, 1985). Dissenting from a denial of certiorari, Justices O'Connor, Brennan and Marshall noted that "[o]ne would think that where state law creates an entitlement to general assistance based on certain substantive conditions, there . . . results a property interest that warrants at least some procedural safeguards" (Gregory v. Town of Pittsfield, 1985, O'Connor, J., dissenting from denial of certiorari). Most (if not all) federal courts addressing the issue have agreed, rejecting the distinction between applicants and recipients (Mallette v. Arlington County Employees' Supplemental Ret. Sys. II, 4th Cir. 1996; Lewis v. N.M. Dep't of Health, D.N.M. 2000). Some state courts, however, have relied on it (Gregory v. Town of Pittsfield, Me. 1984; Sumpter v. White Plains Hous. Auth., N.Y. 1972; Zobriscky v. Los Angeles County, Cal. Ct. App. 1972).

Recently, courts have begun to pay much closer attention to the precise statutory language at issue to determine if government benefits qualify as protected property interests (Am. Mfrs. Mut. Ins. Co. v. Sullivan, 1999). For example, in Colson v. Sillman (2d Cir. 1994), the Second Circuit Court of Appeals considered a due process challenge to the administration of a county program that provided medical services to physically disabled children under New York's Public Health Law. Applicants claimed that the county and the state had violated their due process rights by failing to provide timely written notice of the outcome of their applications and an administrative appeals process. In determining whether the applicants had a "claim of entitlement" to the benefits or merely a "unilateral expectation," the court examined the statute that created the program to determine the degree of discretion retained by the disbursing agency. The Public Health Law provided: "The [state] department [of health] shall on its own initiative provide, within the limits of the appropriations made therefor, such medical service for children with physical disabilities as in the judgment of the commissioner is needed" (N.Y. Pub. Health L. § 2582(1) (McKinney, 1993)). Since the statute gave the state and its Department of Health "virtually total discretion," the applicants had no claim of entitlement to the benefits running against the state and hence no protected property interest (Colson v. Sillman, 2d Cir. 1994).

Professor Richard Pierce predicted that the Supreme Court would employ similar reasoning to dramatically alter the conception of government benefits as protected property interests when it was called upon to review the federal statute that overhauled the welfare system in 1996.[55] The Personal Responsibility and Work Opportunity Reconciliation Act of 1996[56] was designed to "end welfare as we know it." Like the New York Public Health Law at issue in *Colson*, the 1996 Welfare Amendments conferred discretion on state agencies that administer the program and authorized them to limit benefits based on potential fiscal constraints.[57] The statute expressly stated that it creates no entitlement to welfare benefits.[58] In a 1996 essay predicting a "due process counterrevolution," Professor Pierce anticipated that when the "inevitable" constitutional challenge to the 1996 Welfare Amendments reached the Supreme Court, it would "adopt the Second Circuit's reasoning in *Colson* to hold that neither welfare benefits nor Medicare benefits are property interests protected by due process. That series of opinions will signal the end of the largest single battle in the due process counterrevolution."[59]

Professor Cynthia Farina has taken issue with Pierce's prediction, arguing that even if the 1996 Welfare Amendments themselves create no protected property interest in welfare benefits, the state laws and regulations that implement the federal law do. The 1996 Welfare Amendments require states to adopt "objective criteria" for determining eligibility and for delivery of benefits.[60] Since under *Roth*, a property interest is created when positive law constrains the discretion of a disbursing agency, the state laws implementing the 1996 Welfare Amendments, which set forth the objective eligibility criteria, should create property interests entitled to due process protections.[61] To date, Professor Pierce's prediction has not been realized.

### *Public Employment*

While early cases held that "government employment, in the absence of legislation, can be revoked at the will of the appointing officer" (Cafeteria & Rest. Workers Union v. McElroy, 1961),[62] the Supreme Court has since recognized that public employees with claims of entitlement to continued employment have a protected property interest in their positions (LaChance v. Erickson, 1998; Fed. Deposit Ins. Corp. v. Mallen, 1988).[63] The seminal cases in this area are Board of Regents v. Roth (1972) and Perry v. Sindermann (1972). In *Roth*, an assistant professor was hired to teach at a state university for a single academic year. By February of that year, he was notified that he would not be rehired for the next year. The state law that governed employment of faculty at state universities provided for tenure only after four years of employment. The law contained no eligibility standards for renewal of one-year contracts, leaving such decisions to the "unfettered discretion of university officials" (Bd. of Regents v. Roth, 1972). The Court rejected the professor's claim that the university deprived him of liberty and property without due process by failing to provide him with prior notice of the reasons for nonrenewal and an opportunity to heard. The Court eschewed reliance on the "wooden distinction between 'rights' and 'privileges' that once seemed to govern the applicability of procedural due process rights" (Bd. of Regents v. Roth, 1972). Noting that property interests are created not by the Constitution, but by "existing rules or understandings that stem from an independent source such as state law," the Court considered whether Mr. Roth had a "legitimate claim of entitlement" to his position. While his one-year appointment secured his interest in employment for that one year, it made no provision for contract renewal; the terms of his appointment "secured absolutely no interest in re-employment for the next year." Thus, while he "surely had an abstract concern in being rehired, . . . he did not have a *property* interest sufficient to require the University authorities to give him a hearing when they declined to renew his contract of employment" (Bd. of Regents v. Roth, 1972).

Perry v. Sindermann (1972), a companion case to *Roth*, also considered whether a state college professor had a protected property interest in his position. Like Mr. Roth, Mr. Sindermann lacked formal tenure and had no contractual right to re-employment. Unlike Roth, however, Sindermann alleged that the college had a *de facto* tenure system, reflected in the college's Faculty Guide and the guidelines promulgated by the Coordinating Board of the state college and university, and that he had acquired a protected property interest in his position thereunder (Perry v. Sindermann, 1972). Rejecting the proposition that the absence of an explicit contractual provision necessarily forecloses the possibility of a property interest in re-employment, the Court recognized that "[a] teacher . . . who has held his position for a number of years, might be able to show from the circumstances of this service—and from other relevant facts—that he has a legitimate claim of entitlement to job tenure" (Perry v. Sindermann, 1972). If Sindermann could prove the legitimacy of his claim of entitlement to continued employment, his interest would be constitutionally protected.

Even before *Roth* and *Sindermann*, the Supreme Court had recognized that tenured professors at public universities have interests in their positions protected by due process (Slochower v. Bd. of Higher Educ., 1956). Since *Roth* and *Sindermann*, the Court has made clear that teachers, professors and other public employees who lack tenure or even contracts for a specified term nevertheless have a protected interest if their employer makes an express or implied promise of continued employment (Cleveland Bd. of Educ. v. Loudermill, 1985; Connell v. Higgenbotham, 1971). While a mere subjective "expectancy" is not protected by procedural due process, an employee must be afforded the opportunity to prove that she has a legitimate claim of entitlement to continued employment in light of the practices and policies of, and the statutes or ordinances governing, the public employer (Bishop v. Wood, 1976; Perry v. Sindermann, 1972). Without a legitimate claim of entitlement to continued employment, however, public employees appointed for short, fixed terms with no right of renewal have no property interest sufficient to require their employer to provide a hearing before declining to renew the contract (Bd. of Regents v. Roth, 1972).[64] The Supreme Court has assumed without deciding that tenured public employees have a protected interest in not being subject to discipline short of termination, such as a suspension without pay (Gilbert v. Homar, 1997)[65] and that students enrolled at public universities have a property right in continued enrollment (Regents of Univ. of Mich. v. Ewing, 1985).

Now that we have explored the Supreme Court's treatment of property interests over time, let us consider its treatment of liberty interests. As we will see, while the Court has expanded the category of property interests that qualify for due process protection by recognizing some forms of "new property," it has narrowed the scope of protected liberty interests.

### Liberty Interests

The Supreme Court has declined to define liberty with "any great precision" (Bolling v. Sharpe, 1954). While "liberty" has always encompassed freedom from bodily restraint and punishment (Hamdi v. Rumsfeld, 2004; Ingraham v. Wright, 1977; Rochin v. California, 1952), the Court has made clear since the turn of the twentieth century that the term covers much more (Allgeyer v. Louisiana, 1897; Bolling v. Sharpe, 1954).

> Without doubt, it denotes not merely freedom from bodily restraint but also the right of the individual to contract, to engage in any of the common occupations of life, to acquire useful knowledge, to marry, establish a home and bring up children, to worship God according to the dictates of his own conscience, and generally to enjoy those privileges long recognized . . . as essential to the orderly pursuit of happiness by free men (Meyer v. Nebraska, 1923).

Thus, over the course of the first quarter of the twentieth century, the Supreme Court extended the liberty interest to protect against not only procedural irregularities in criminal trials, as the framers intended, but also to preserve other forms of negative liberty, or freedom from governmental restraint.[66]

As with protected property interests, liberty interests "must rise to more than 'an abstract need or desire,' and must be based on more than 'a unilateral hope.' Rather, an individual claiming a protected [liberty] interest must have a legitimate claim of entitlement to it" (Ky. Dep't of Corr. v. Thompson, 1989). The Court has identified two sources of the liberty interests protected by the Fourteenth Amendment: the Due Process Clause itself and state law (Sandin v. Conner, 1995; Meachum v. Fano, 1976). Several Justices have strenuously disagreed with this analysis, arguing that

> Neither the Bill of Rights nor the laws of sovereign States create the liberty which the Due Process Clause protects. . . . [A]ll men [are] endowed by their Creator with liberty as one of the cardinal inalienable rights. It is that basic freedom that the Due Process Clause protects, rather than the particular rights or privileges conferred by specific laws or regulations (Meachum v. Fano, 1976, Stevens, J., dissenting).[67]

During the first quarter of the twentieth century, the Court's recognition of constitutionally-created "liberty" was quite expansive. As the discussion that follows will illustrate, however, in the last three decades, the Court has cut back substantially on the liberty interests protected by due process, especially vis-à-vis prisoners. Professor Monaghan has suggested that the Court altered its approach to the content and meaning of "liberty" in the face of significant pressure to keep suits against state government out of the federal courts: "Rather than facing the balancing question at the merits stage, the Court struck a compromise at the definitional stage."[68] The section that follows traces the effect of this definitional shift in three areas: reputation; prisoners' rights; and parole, probation and clemency.

### *Reputation*

The Supreme Court's willingness to treat reputation as a protected liberty interest has changed over the course of the last fifty years, increasing at the height of the due process revolution and waning substantially toward the end of the twentieth century and into the twenty-first. During the Red Scare, the Court recognized the grievous injury a person would suffer if labeled "communist" or "subversive" by the government. For example, in Wieman v. Updegraff (1952), the Court recognized that exclusion from public employment on disloyalty grounds imposed "a badge of infamy." Likewise, in Joint Anti-Fascist Refugee Committee v. McGrath (1951), three members of the five-Justice majority expressed the view that due process barred the government from condemning a group as "communist" without notice and the opportunity to be heard.

Two decades later, in Wisconsin v. Constantineau (1971), the Supreme Court applied these principles beyond the communism context, broadly stating that procedural due process protections must be provided "where a person's good name, reputation, honor, or integrity is at stake." There, the Court struck down a state statute, pursuant to which the chief of police had posted a notice in liquor stores, forbidding the sale of alcohol to named individuals because of their prior excessive drinking. The Court recognized that the posting imposed "such a stigma or badge of disgrace that procedural due process requires notice and an opportunity to be heard" (Wisconsin v. Constantineau, 1971). In a number of different contexts, the Court recognized a liberty interest in one's reputation or good name (Goss v. Lopez, 1975; Jenkins v. McKeithen, 1969).

Yet the Court's acknowledgment of a liberty interest in reputation was never so expansive as to recognize that "a person is deprived of 'liberty' when he simply is not rehired in one [government] job but remains as free as before to seek another" (Bd. of Regents v. Roth, 1972).[69] The stigma would have to be substantial enough that it "foreclosed his freedom to take advantage of other employment opportunities" (Bd. of Regents v. Roth, 1972; Hampton v. Mow Sun Wong, 1976). As long as there was no public disclosure of the reasons for the discharge, no liberty interest was implicated when a public employee was discharged from a position that was terminable at will (Bishop v. Wood, 1976; see also Bd. of Curators v. Horowitz, 1978).

Only five years after deciding *Constantineau*, the Supreme Court in Paul v. Davis (1976) cut back on the due process protections afforded to reputation even when the government publicly stigmatizes someone. While conceding that its prior decisions had "pointed out the frequently drastic effect of the 'stigma' which may result from defamation by the government," the Supreme Court rejected the proposition that "reputation alone, apart from some more tangible interests such as employment, is either 'liberty' or 'property' by itself sufficient to invoke the procedural protection of the Due Process Clause" (Paul v. Davis, 1976). In *Paul*, the Court considered an effort by local law enforcement officials to reduce shoplifting by circulating to merchants a flyer listing the names of individuals "known to be active in this criminal field." While acknowledging that the Red Scare line of cases "recognized the serious damage that could be inflicted by branding a government employee as 'disloyal,'" the *Paul* Court noted that the branding or defamation in those cases was accompanied by a loss of government employment (Paul v. Davis, 1976). Conceding that the *Constantineau* opinion contained language that could be taken to mean that defamation by a government actor, without more, implicated procedural due process protections, the *Paul* Court declined to read *Constantineau* that broadly. Since the posting at issue in *Constantineau* significantly altered the plaintiff's status as a matter of state law (by depriving her of a pre-existing right to purchase alcohol),

> It was that alteration of legal status which, combined with the injury resulting from the defamation, justified the invocation of procedural safeguards. The "stigma" resulting from the defamatory character of the posting was doubtless an important factor in evaluating the extent of harm worked by that act, but we do not think that such defamation, standing alone, deprived Constantineau of any "liberty" protected by the procedural guarantees of the Fourteenth Amendment (Paul v. Davis, 1976; see also Owen v. City of Independence, 1980).

In an effort to synthesize the "reputation as liberty" cases with the property cases discussed in the "Property Rights" section of this chapter, the Court generalized that "interests attain . . . constitutional status by virtue of the fact that they have been initially recognized and protected by state law. . . ." (Paul v. Davis, 1976).[70] Since state law did not provide Mr. Davis with any "legal guarantee of present enjoyment of reputation" that had been altered by distribution of the shoplifting flyer, the interest in reputation was not deemed a "liberty" interest protected by the Due Process Clause. Thus, in the words of Professor Monaghan, *Paul* "radically reorient[ed] thinking about the nature of the 'liberty' protected by the due process clause" by narrowly defining the class of liberty interests created by the Due Process Clause itself, focusing instead on state law as a source of liberty.[71]

Since Paul v. Davis (1976), the Supreme Court has cut back even further on the due process protections afforded to reputation. In Siegert v. Gilley (1991), the Court considered a claim by a clinical psychologist who resigned from St. Elizabeth's Hospital, a federal government hospital, after receiving notice that he was about to be terminated for poor performance. Following his resignation, he began working in Bremerhaven, an American army hospital in Germany, which required that he be "credentialed" to maintain his position. Mr. Siegert signed a Credential Information Request Form, asking St. Elizabeth's to provide Bremerhaven with information regarding his job performance. Upon receipt of a scathing, allegedly defamatory evaluation from his prior supervisor at St. Elizabeth's, the Army Credentials Committee denied Mr. Siegert the credentials sought. His federal employment was terminated shortly thereafter. When he brought a claim against his former supervisor alleging a deprivation of his "liberty interests," the Court held that the plaintiff "failed to allege the violation of a clearly established constitutional right" because of "the lack of any constitutional protection for the interest in reputation" (Siegert v. Gilley, 1991). As Justice Marshall noted in dissent, since "the injury to Siegert's reputation caused him to lose the benefit of *eligibility for future government employment,*" his liberty interest would have been protected under *Paul* (Siegert v. Gilley, 1991, Marshall, J., dissenting). The *Siegert* majority did not address Marshall's contention directly, noting only that the "alleged defamation was not uttered incident to the termination of Siegert's employment by the hospital. . . ." (Siegert v. Gilley, 1991). Thus, *Siegert* may stand for the proposition that "reputational injury deprives a person of liberty only when combined with loss of *present* employment, not *future* employment" (Siegert v. Gilley, 1991, Marshall, J., dissenting) or it may limit even more dramatically the constitutional protection for reputation.[72]

The Court did not resolve this issue in its most recent decision regarding reputation, Connecticut Department of Public Safety v. Doe (2003). There, the Court upheld Connecticut's "Megan's Law," which required the state to publicize the name, address and photograph of all convicted sex offenders upon their release into the community. The Court rejected the argument that the law deprived a sex offender of a protected liberty interest—"his reputation combined with the alteration of his status under state law—without notice or a meaningful opportunity to be heard" (Conn. Dep't of Pub. Safety v. Doe, 2003). The Court found it unnecessary to determine whether the plaintiff had a protected liberty interest in reputation because even if he did, due process would not have entitled him to a hearing on the issue of his current dangerousness since that fact was irrelevant under the Connecticut statute, which required public disclosure regarding *all* sex offenders.

### *Prisoners' Rights*

At one time, it was believed that a criminal conviction deprived a person of all liberty interests, reducing her to a "slave of the State" (Ruffin v. Commonwealth, Va. 1871). While the Supreme Court has repeatedly recognized that "a valid criminal conviction and sentence extinguish a defendant's otherwise protected right to be free from confinement" (Hewitt v. Helms, 1983, Blackmun, J., concurring in part and dissenting in part), it also has recognized that inmates retain a residuum of liberty; they are not "wholly stripped of constitutional protections when [they are] imprisoned for crime" (Wolff v. McDonnell, 1974). The Due Process Clause, as an independent source of liberty, protects only the prisoners' most basic liberty interests (Hewitt v. Helms, 1983). The inmates' residual liberty interest is not infringed by prison conditions that are "within the normal limits or range of custody which the conviction has authorized the State to impose" (Meachum v. Fano, 1976; see also Montanye v. Haymes, 1976). Only " 'consequences visited on the prisoner [that] are qualitatively different from the punishment characteristically suffered by a person convicted of crime' may invoke the protections of the Due Process Clause . . . in the absence of a state-created right" (Ky. Dep't of Corr. v. Thompson, 1989).

Only rarely has the Court found that the Due Process Clause itself confers a liberty interest upon inmates.[73] In Vitek v. Jones (1980), for example, the Court held that even independent of state law, a transfer to a mental hospital implicated a liberty interest protected by due process itself because "the loss of liberty produced by an involuntary commitment is more than a loss of freedom from confinement." Because a prisoner transferred to a mental hospital would suffer adverse social consequences and the indignity of compelled treatment, the Court concluded that "a convicted felon . . . is entitled to the benefit of procedures appropriate in the circumstances before he is found to have a mental disease and transferred to a mental hospital" (Vitek v. Jones, 1980).[74] Likewise, in Washington v. Harper (1990), the Court found that the inmate "possesse[d] a significant liberty interest in avoiding the unwanted administration of antipsychotic drugs under the Due Process Clause of the Fourteenth Amendment" itself.[75]

The Court has recognized that in addition to the basic and few liberty interests created by the Due Process Clause itself, the states through enactment of statutory or regulatory measures may create liberty interests to which constitutional due process protections extend (Hewitt v. Helms, 1983). For example, in Wolff v. McDonnell (1974), the Court considered whether prisoners' interests in their "good-time" credits for satisfactory behavior were entitled to due process protection. Recognizing that the "Constitution itself does not guarantee good-time credit," the Court looked to state law as the source of the liberty interest (Wolff

v. McDonnell, 1974). Once a state creates the right to "good-time" credits and recognizes their deprivation as a sanction for serious misconduct in prison, "the prisoner's interest has real substance and is sufficiently embraced within Fourteenth Amendment 'liberty' to entitle him to those minimum procedures appropriate under the circumstances and required by the Due Process Clause to insure that the state-created right is not arbitrarily abrogated" (Wolff v. McDonnell, 1974; see also Superintendent v. Hill, 1985).[76] Likewise, due process protections must be afforded to prisoners before they are placed in solitary confinement as a sanction for serious misconduct (Wolff v. McDonnell, 1974).

Following *Wolff*, the Court began to focus more on the statutory or regulatory language adopted by the state and less on the nature of the interest at stake. Rather than asking whether the inmate had suffered a "grievous loss" of liberty (Morrissey v. Brewer, 1972) or whether the inmate's claimed liberty interest was one of "real substance" (Wolff v. McDonnell, 1974), the Court considered whether the state had "plac[ed] substantive limitations on official discretion" (Ky. Dep't of Corr. v. Thompson, 1989; Olim v. Wakinekona, 1983). Although a state could do this in a number of ways, the most common way was by "establishing 'substantive predicates' to govern official decision-making and, further, by mandating the outcome to be reached upon a finding that relevant criteria have been met" (Ky. Dep't of Corr. v. Thompson, 1989). The state statute or regulation had to contain "explicitly mandatory language" (Ky. Dep't of Corr. v. Thompson, 1989; Hewitt v. Helms, 1983). Thus, if a statute or regulation narrowly cabined the authority of prison officials to change a condition of confinement or impose some other restraint, the inmate acquired "a kind of right to avoid it" (Sandin v. Conner, 1995, Breyer, J., dissenting). Applying this approach, the Court concluded that the state had created a protected liberty interest by defining specific substantive predicates for transfers from the general prison population to administrative segregation, which precluded transfers without appropriate procedural protections (Hewitt v. Helms, 1983).

Scrutinizing a different state law, the Court concluded that inmates in that state had no protected liberty interest in visitation by friends and family members. The Due Process Clause itself did not create a liberty interest in "unfettered visitation" and the prison regulations at issue did not include mandatory language requiring admission of visitors if certain "substantive predicates" were met (Ky. Dep't of Corr. v. Thompson, 1989).

Nor do inmates have a liberty interest in remaining in the prison to which they are initially confined (Meachum v. Fano, 1976). The Due Process Clause itself does not protect against an inmate's intrastate transfer to a higher security prison because her conviction has "sufficiently extinguished the defendant's liberty interest to empower the State to confine [her] in *any* of its prisons" (Meachum v. Fano, 1976). Unless state law confers a right on the prisoner to remain in the prison to which she is initially confined subject to transfer only for acts of misconduct, no liberty interest is implicated when an intrastate transfer is made (Meachum v. Fano, 1976; Montanye v. Haymes, 1976). Since the state law at issue in *Meachum* permitted transfer "for whatever reason or for no reason at all," no liberty interest was created (Meachum v. Fano, 1976). Likewise, since an inmate "has no justifiable expectation that he will be incarcerated in any particular State" and since state prison regulations "place[d] no substantive limitations on official discretion" to make transfers, even an interstate transfer (from a Hawaiian prison to one on the mainland) failed to deprive an inmate of a protected liberty interest (Olim v. Wakinekona, 1983).

More recently, the Court has rejected the search for mandatory statutory language and specific substantive predicates in determining whether state law confers a liberty interest on inmates (Sandin v. Conner, 1995). In *Sandin*, the Court expressed concern that the "search for mandatory language" approach had created disincentives for states to codify their prison management procedures and had resulted in federal courts micro-managing routine prison management. In place of this approach, the *Sandin* Court opted to return to an examination of the nature of the interest at stake:

> Following *Wolff*, we recognize that States may under certain circumstances create liberty interests which are protected by the Due Process Clause. But these interests will be generally limited to freedom from restraint which, while not exceeding the sentence in such an unexpected manner as to give rise to protection by the Due Process Clause of its own force, nonetheless imposes atypical and significant hardship on the inmate in relation to the ordinary incidents of prison life (Sandin v. Conner, 1995).

In other words, only extreme changes in the conditions of confinement—those that impose "atypical and significant hardship"—implicate a protected liberty interest, triggering due process protection.

Since the conditions of disciplinary segregation at issue in *Sandin* were (in the view of the majority) similar to those of administrative segregation, to which any inmate could have been transferred in the prison authorities' total discretion, the transfer to disciplinary segregation did "not present a dramatic departure from the basic conditions of [the inmate's] indeterminate sentence" (Sandin v. Conner, 1995). Thus, considering the nature of the inmate's hardship, the Court held that his "discipline in segregated confinement did not present the type of atypical, significant deprivation in which a State might conceivably create a liberty interest" (Sandin v. Conner, 1995). Even though the alleged misconduct underlying the transfer to disciplinary segregation would be considered by the parole board, "the chance that a finding of misconduct will alter the balance [of decision-making] is simply too attenuated to invoke the procedural guarantees of the Due Process Clause" (Sandin v. Conner, 1995). Hence, no protected liberty interest was implicated by the finding of misconduct or the transfer to disciplinary segregation.

In dissent, Justice Ginsburg chastised the *Sandin* majority for setting forth a new test without offering any guidance as to what it means: "The Court ventures no examples, leaving consumers of the Court's work at sea, unable to fathom what would constitute an 'atypical, significant deprivation,' and yet not trigger protection under the Due Process clause directly" (Sandin v. Conner, 1995, Ginsburg, J., dissenting). Justice Breyer noted that lower federal courts might read *Sandin* "as offering significantly less protection against deprivation of liberty" (Sandin v. Conner, 1995, Breyer, J., dissenting).[77] Professor Pierce, in agreement, has described *Sandin* as "[t]he first major battle of the due process counterrevolution of the 1990s [that] has already been fought and won."[78]

A review of the decisions by the Courts of Appeals following *Sandin* reveals the prescience of Justice Breyer's prediction. As Judge Posner put it, "the right to litigate disciplinary confinements has become vanishingly small" (Wagner v. Hanks, 7th Cir. 1997). As a preliminary matter, there is some uncertainty as to "which prison or part of a prison is to provide the standard of comparison" (Brown v. Plaut, D.C. Cir. 1997), with at least one court suggesting that the proper standard for comparison may be the most restrictive prison in the nation (Wagner v. Hanks, 7th Cir. 1997).[79] Some of the Courts of Appeals have scrutinized changes in conditions of confinement quite closely, paying attention to the duration and frequency of disciplinary segregation as well as the degree to which special housing conditions vary from other prison conditions.[80] Even following such scrutiny, however, numerous federal courts have concluded that transfers to segregation implicate no protected liberty interest,[81] even where a state-created liberty interest in avoiding segregation previously had been found (Neal v. District of Columbia, D.C. Cir. 1997; Cato v. Rushen, 9th Cir. 1987).

*Sandin* has had an impact on prisoners' rights beyond the disciplinary segregation context. One federal Court of Appeals has held that removal of an inmate from a residential community release program did not implicate a state-created liberty interest even though the inmate's life in prison was "fundamentally different" from his life at the halfway house because his "return to prison did not impose atypical and significant hardship on him in relation to the ordinary incidents of prison life" (Asquith v. Dep't of Corr., 3d Cir. 1999; see also Porter v. Soice, 6th Cir. 2001). Other lower courts have used similar reasoning to conclude that the loss of work release privileges (Kitchen v. Upshaw, 4th Cir. 2002; Dominique v. Weld, 1st Cir. 1996)[82] or commissary privileges (Malchi v. Thaler, 5th Cir. 2000; Thomas v. Ramos, 7th Cir. 1997) or the opportunity to earn good-time credits while in segregation (Luken v. Scott, 5th Cir. 1995)[83] or a transfer from a psychiatric treatment facility to a regular prison (Walsh v. Corcoran, 4th Cir. 2000) or placement in physical restraints (Key v. McKinney, 8th Cir. 1999) implicates no protected liberty interest, although not all courts agree. Likewise, as we will see in the section that follows, the Supreme Court has invoked *Sandin* to conclude that there is no protected life or liberty interest at stake in petitions for executive clemency (Ohio Adult Parole Auth. v. Woodard, 1998). Several lower courts have read *Sandin* more narrowly, concluding that it does not apply to pretrial detainees, who retain a liberty interest in not being placed in disciplinary segregation (Benjamin v. Fraser, 2d Cir. 2001) or to prospective parolees, whose expectation of release is constitutionally protected if the state parole statute employs mandatory language (McQuillion v. Duncan, 9th Cir. 2002; Ellis v. District of Columbia, D.C. Cir. 1996).

### *Parole, Probation and Clemency*

At the height of the due process revolution, the Supreme Court considered whether due process protections apply to parole revocations. The Court quickly dismissed the argument that due process did not apply because parole was a "privilege," not a "right," flatly rejecting the right/privilege distinction (Morrissey v. Brewer, 1972). Recognizing that revocation of parole "deprives an individual, not of the absolute liberty to which every citizen is entitled, but only of the conditional liberty properly dependent on observance of special parole restrictions," the Court nevertheless concluded that a protected liberty interest was at stake: "the liberty of a parolee, although indeterminate, includes many of the core values of unqualified liberty and its termination inflicts a 'grievous loss' on the parolee and often on others. . . . By whatever name, the liberty is valuable and must be seen as within the protection of the Fourteenth Amendment" (Morrissey v. Brewer, 1972). A year later, the Court held that revocation of probation, like revocation of parole, implicates a protected liberty interest (Gagnon v. Scarpelli, 1973).[84] The Court has treated release from prison under a pre-parole program as similar enough to parole to qualify as a liberty interest entitled to the procedural protections outlined in *Morrissey* (Young v. Harper, 1997).

*Morrissey* and *Scarpelli* left open the question whether inmates have a constitutionally protected liberty interest in an initial parole determination. In Greenholtz v. Inmates of the Nebraska Penal & Correction Complex (1979), the Court addressed the issue, noting that "[t]here is no constitutional or inherent right of a convicted person to be conditionally released before the expiration of a valid sentence." Nor does the mere presence of a parole system itself give rise to a constitutionally protected liberty interest. Rejecting the argument that the parole revocation decision protected in *Morrissey* and the parole determination at issue in *Greenholtz* implicate the same conditional liberty interest, the Court noted two important distinctions. First, parolees live outside the prison, enjoying the freedom to be with family and friends, while inmates merely hoping for parole are confined and subject to all of the restraints inherent in prison life. Second, the decisions whether to grant parole and to revoke it are based on different factors and are made from different perspectives, one largely predictive and the other largely retrospective (Greenholtz v. Inmates of the Neb. Penal & Corr. Complex, 1979). Notwithstanding its rejection of the argument that the state creates a reasonable entitlement whenever it provides for the possibility of parole, the Court begrudgingly accepted the inmates' argument that the mandatory language of the state parole statute at issue created a legitimate "expectancy of release . . . entitled to some measure of constitutional protection" (Greenholtz v. Inmates of the Neb. Penal & Corr. Complex, 1979).[85] Nearly a decade later, the Court followed *Greenholtz*, finding another state statute's mandatory language had created a constitutionally protected liberty interest in parole release (Bd. of Pardons v. Allen, 1987).

Pardon and commutation decisions have traditionally been within the executive's discretion and have not been the subject of judicial review (Ohio Adult Parole Auth. v. Woodard, 1998; Conn. Bd. of Pardons v. Dumschat, 1981). The Court has held that an inmate has "'no constitutional or inherent right' to commutation of his sentence" (Conn. Bd. of Pardons v. Dumschat, 1981). The inmate's expectation that his sentence would be commuted, based upon the practice of the Board of Pardons, was not entitled to constitutional protection in the absence of a statute or rule creating an entitlement. And since the state statute at issue gave the Board of Pardons "unfettered discretion" to commute sentences, no state-created liberty interest was implicated (Conn. Bd. of Pardons v. Dumschat, 1981). Following *Dumschat* and Sandin v. Conner (1995), the Court in Ohio Adult Parole Authority v. Woodard (1998) declined to find a protected life or liberty interest at stake in petitions for executive clemency, concluding that "the availability of clemency, or the manner in which the State conducts clemency proceedings, does not impose 'atypical and significant hardship on the inmate in relation to the ordinary incidents of prison life'" (Ohio Adult Parole Auth. v. Woodard, 1998). Thus, *Sandin* has affected the Court's decision making beyond the "nature of confinement" context.

As we have seen, the post-*Roth* Court has rejected a unitary concept of protected interests. Instead, the Court has treated life, liberty and property interests separately and has relied on positive law as the exclusive source of property rights. State action that results in the loss of a protected life, liberty or property interest, so defined, does not necessarily qualify as a "deprivation," however. As we will see in the next section of this chapter, the state of mind of the state actor is relevant.

## STATE OF MIND REQUIREMENT

In Parratt v. Taylor (1981), the Supreme Court held that even a negligently caused loss amounted to a deprivation for due process purposes. In a separate opinion, Justice Powell disagreed, positing that a negligent act by a state actor does not work a deprivation of property "in the *constitutional sense*. . . . A 'deprivation' connotes an intentional act denying something to someone, or, at the very least, a deliberate decision not to act to prevent a loss" (Parratt v. Taylor, 1981, Powell, J., concurring in the result). Several years later, a majority of the Court in Daniels v. Williams (1986) adopted Justice Powell's position, overruling *Parratt* "to the extent that it states that mere lack of due care by a state official may 'deprive' an individual of life, liberty, or property under the Fourteenth Amendment" (Daniels v. Williams, 1986; see also Davidson v. Cannon, 1986). In so ruling, the Court expressed concern about trivializing the meaning of the Due Process Clause and opening the federal courts to a flood of litigation in the absence of an "affirmative abuse of power" (Daniels v. Williams, 1986). The *Daniels* Court declined to consider whether "something less than intentional conduct, such as recklessness or 'gross negligence,' is enough to trigger the protections of the Due Process Clause" (Daniels v. Williams, 1986; compare Canton v. Harris, 1989).

In County of Sacramento v. Lewis (1998), a substantive due process case, the Court added that the appropriate level of culpability is "a matter for closer calls" While deliberate indifference may be actionable in cases where state officials have time to make unhurried judgments, such as when prison officials ignore the medical needs of patients in their care, that standard "is sensibly employed only when actual deliberation is practical" (County of Sacramento v. Lewis, 1998). When, on the other hand, fast action is critical, such as when prison officials seek to quell a riot or when law enforcement officers engage in a high-speed chase, "a much higher standard of fault than deliberate indifference has to be shown for officer liability" (County of Sacramento v. Lewis, 1998).

## CONCLUSION

Since deciding Board of Regents v. Roth (1972), the Court has engaged in a bifurcated procedural due process analysis, asking first whether a protected interest is implicated and if so, deciding what process is due. The Court examines life, liberty and property interests separately. It looks to legislation and other sources of positive law for the definition and scope of protected property interests. It looks to legislation as the primary source of liberty interests as well, although it acknowledges that the Due Process Clause itself creates and preserves some liberty interests. In the last quarter-century or so, the Court has narrowed the category of protected liberty interests, especially in cases involving reputation and conditions of confinement for prisoners. Once a protected interest is identified, the Court applies federal constitutional law to determine the procedural protections that must be afforded, having rejected the theory that the state may limit the scope of a state-created right by defining the procedures for its deprivation.

Mere negligence by the state does not result in a "deprivation" for constitutional purposes. To deprive a person of a protected interest, the government must act intentionally, or in cases where deliberation is feasible, with deliberate indifference.

## NOTES

1. Joint Anti-Fascist Refugee Comm. v. McGrath, 341 U.S. 123, 171 (1951) (Frankfurter, J., concurring).

2. Webster's encyclopedic Unabridged Dictionary 1074 (new rev. ed. 1996).

3. In some cases, this promise of constitutional protection proves hollow, however. For example, in Terrace v. Thompson, 263 U.S. 197 (1923), while the Court stated that aliens are entitled to the protections of the Fourteenth Amendment, it nevertheless upheld the constitutionality of a state statute that barred aliens from owning land.

4. As the Court itself explained it, "[t]he alien . . . has been accorded a generous and ascending scale of rights as he increases his identity with our society. Mere lawful presence in the country creates an implied assurance of safe conduct and gives him certain rights; they become more extensive and secure when he makes preliminary declaration of intention to become a citizen, and they expand to those of full citizenship upon naturalization." Johnson v. Eisentrager, 339 U.S. 763, 770 (1950).

5. *See also* Benitez v. Wallis, – U.S. –, 124 S. Ct. 1143 (2004) (granting *certiorari* to decide whether aliens who have been apprehended at the border and denied admission to the United States may be detained indefinitely).

6. Some courts have read Johnson v. Eisentrager (1950) more broadly, as standing for the proposition that aliens outside the territorial limits of the United States, whether enemy aliens or not, are not entitled to Fifth Amendment protections. *See, e.g.*, United States v. Verdugo-Urzuidez, 494 U.S. 259, 269 (1990); Al Odah v. United States, 321 F.3d 1134, 1140–41 (D.C. Cir. 2003), *rev'd sub nom.* Rasul v. Bush, – U.S. –, 124 S. Ct. 2686 (2004).

7. The President has designated six non-American detainees, including one Australian and two British terrorism suspects, to be tried before military tribunals with only restricted access to civilian counsel. Neil A. Lewis, *Six Detainees Soon May Face Military Trials*, N.Y. Times, July 4, 2003, at A1 & A11; Adam Liptak, *Tribunals Move from Theory to Reality*, N.Y. Times, July 4, 2003, at A11.

8. When unlawful combatants are criminally prosecuted in federal court, they are entitled to Fifth Amendment protections. *See, e.g.*, United States v. Lindh, 212 F. Supp. 2d 541, 564–68 (E.D. Va. 2002) (reviewing Lindh's claim that he was the victim of impermissible selective prosecution in violation of the Fifth Amendment's Equal Protection Clause).

9. *See, e.g.*, David Cole, *Enemy Aliens*, 54 Stan. L. Rev. 953, 984 (2002) (stating that "outside of a declared war against an identifiable nation, aliens living among us are entitled to . . . due process"); Liptak, *supra* note 7, at A11 (discussing Professor Eric Freedman's concern that the six detainees designated for trial before military tribunals "do not fit within the narrow historical category of unlawful enemy combatant for whom such trials might be appropriate"); Hamdi v. Rumsfeld, 337 F.3d 335 (4th Cir. 2003) (debating, in concurring and dissenting opinions, whether Yaser Hamdi was afforded meaningful judicial review of his claim that he was not an enemy combatant), *vacated,* – U.S. –, 124 S. Ct. 2633 (2004).

10. In Rumsfeld v. Padilla, – U.S. –, 124 S. Ct. 2711 (2004), the Supreme Court held that the proper respondent in such an action is the person with immediate physical custody over the detainee. Jurisdiction is proper only in the district in which the detainee is confined.

11. In Hamdi v. Rumsfeld, – U.S. –, 124 S. Ct. 2633 (2004), a plurality of the Court left open the possibility that the due process to which a citizen-detainee seeking to challenge his classification as an enemy combatant is entitled could be provided in "an appropriately authorized and properly constituted military tribunal." *Id.* at 2651.

12. Dissenting in part, Justice Souter, joined by Justice Ginsburg, argues that the Authorization for Use of Military Force Resolution, 115 Stat. 224, does not authorize detention of an enemy combatant in these circumstances. Therefore, in Souter's view, Hamdi's detention violates the Non-Detention Act, 18 U.S.C. § 4001(a), which prohibits detention of American citizens "except pursuant to an Act of Congress." Hamdi v. Rumsfeld, – U.S. –, 124 S. Ct. at 2652–59 (2004) (Souter, J., concurring in part, dissenting in part, and concurring in the judgment). Justice Scalia, joined by Justice Stevens, argues that the government may either prosecute a citizen for treason or some other crime, or, in the exigencies of war, suspend the writ of habeas corpus. But absent suspension, "the Executive's assertion of military exigency has not been thought sufficient to permit detention without charge" of an American citizen within the territorial jurisdiction of a federal court. *Id.* at 2660 (Scalia, J., dissenting). Only Justice Thomas argues that "due process requires nothing more than a good-faith executive determination" that the detainee is an enemy combatant. *Id.* at 2680 (Thomas, J., dissenting).

13. The Supreme Court has never explicitly held that the United States is not protected by the Due Process Clauses. Since the Due Process Clauses were designed to protect individuals from arbitrary government action, however, it would be anomalous to conclude that the United States is a "person" protected by due process. *Cf.* Tenn. Valley Auth. v. Whitman, 336 F.3d 1236, 1258–60 (11th Cir. 2003) (assuming without analysis that the Tennessee Valley Authority, a federal agency, is protected by the Due Process Clause of the Fifth Amendment).

14. *See generally* 13A Charles Alan Wright et al., Federal Practice and Procedure § 3531.11 (2d ed. 1984).

15. *See id.* (acknowledging that "[a]t times, this conclusion is expressed as a lack of standing," but concluding that "it would be better left to disposition as a matter of substantive constitutional law").

16. The Ninth Circuit followed this decision in Board of Natural Resources v. Brown, 992 F.2d 937 (9th Cir. 1993), concluding that school districts are "persons" under the Fifth Amendment with standing to challenge a *federal* statute on equal protection grounds. *Id.* at 942–43. In a later opinion, the Ninth Circuit refused to read *Brown* as repudiating the political subdivision standing doctrine and held that an Arizona school district lacked standing to challenge the constitutionality of an Arizona statute on Supremacy Clause grounds. *See* Indian Oasis-Baboquivari Unified Sch. Dist. No. 40 v. Kirk, 91 F.3d 1240, 1242–44 (9th Cir. 1996); *see also* Burbank-Glendale-Pasadena Airport Auth. v. City of Burbank, 136 F.3d 1360, 1363–64 (9th Cir. 1998) (adhering to a per se rule barring political subdivision standing); Palomar Pomerado Health Sys. v. Belshe, 180 F.3d 1104, 1107–08 (9th Cir. 1999), *cert. denied*, 528 U.S. 1074 (2000).

17. *See also* Michael A. Lawrence, *Do "Creatures of the State" Have Constitutional Rights?: Standing for Municipalities to Assert Procedural Due Process Claims Against the State*, 47 Vill. L. Rev. 93 (2002).

18. *See also* United States v. Alabama, 791 F.2d 1450, 1456 n.5 (11th Cir. 1986) (attempting to harmonize *Seattle School* with the conclusion "that a creature of the state

normally has no Fourteenth Amendment rights against its creator"; stating that *Seattle School* recognized that "the Constitution does not interfere with a state's internal political organization" but held that "once a state's political organization is in place, the state may only re-organize that structure . . . consistently with the constitutional guarantee of equal protection"), *cert. denied sub nom.* Bd. of Trs. v. Ala. State Bd. of Educ., 479 U.S. 1085 (1987); Mun. Utils. Bd. v. Ala. Power Co., 934 F.2d 1493 (11th Cir. 1991) (reading *Seattle Schools* as standing for the principle "that states may not circumscribe or rescind delegated authority in such a way that impairs federally protected rights" and permitting municipalities to challenge state legislation as violative of federal antitrust laws), *cert. denied*, 513 U.S. 1148 (1995).

19. The phrase "state action" is used regardless of whether the plaintiff claims a violation of the Fifth Amendment by the federal government or a violation of the Fourteenth Amendment by a state or one of its political subdivisions.

20. Although the state action requirement of the Fourteenth Amendment and the "under color of state law" requirement of section 1983 "denote two separate areas of inquiry," Flagg Bros., Inc. v. Brooks, 436 U.S. 149, 155–56 (1978), if a defendant's conduct constitutes state action for purposes of the Fourteenth Amendment, then it also qualifies as conduct under color of state law for section 1983 purposes. Lugar v. Edmondson Oil Co., 457 U.S. 922, 935 & n.18 (1982); *see also* Nat'l Collegiate Athletic Ass'n v. Tarkanian, 488 U.S. 179, 182 n.4 (1988). *But see* Will v. Mich. Dep't of State Police, 491 U.S. 58, 64, 71 (1989) (holding that neither a state nor a state official acting in her official capacity is a "person" amenable to suit under section 1983); Ngiraingas v. Sanchez, 495 U.S. 182, 192 (1990) (holding that neither the Territory of Guam nor an officer of the Territory acting in her official capacity is a "person" amenable to suit under section 1983).

21. *Cf.* Polk County v. Dodson, 454 U.S. 312, 325 (1981) (holding that "a public defender does not act under color of state law [for § 1983 purposes] when performing a lawyer's traditional functions as counsel to a defendant in a criminal proceeding"); West v. Atkins, 487 U.S. 42, 51 (1988) (declining to create an analogous exception for doctors under contract with the state to provide medical treatment to injured inmates because the doctor's "professional and ethical obligation to make independent medical judgments did not set him in conflict with the State and other prison authorities"). *See also* Nat'l Collegiate Athletic Ass'n v. Tarkanian, 488 U.S. 179, 196 (1988).

22. 3 Ronald D. Rotunda & John E. Nowak, Treatise on Constitutional Law: Substance and Procedure § 10.4, at 344 (3d ed. 1999); Ronald J. Krotoszynski, Jr., *Back to the Briarpatch: An Argument in Favor of Constitutional Meta-Analysis in State Action Determinations*, 94 Mich. L. Rev. 302, 315 (1995).

23. Erwin Chemerinsky, *Rethinking State Action*, 80 Nw. U.L. Rev. 503, 550 (1985). *See also, e.g.*, Kenneth L. Karst & Harold W. Horowitz, Reitman v. Mulkey: *A Telophase of Substantive Equal Protection*, 1967 Sup. Ct. Rev. 39. *Cf.* Charles L. Black, Jr., *The Supreme Court, 1966 Term, Foreword: "State Action," Equal Protection, and California's Proposition 14*, 81 Harv. L. Rev. 69, 100 (1967) (advocating an expansion of the state action concept "to include every form of state fostering, enforcement, and even toleration" of discrimination).

24. Henry Paul Monaghan, *Of "Liberty" and "Property,"* 62 Cornell L. Rev. 405, 409 (1977); Mark Tushnet, *The Newer Property: Suggestion for the Revival of Substantive Due*

*Process*, 1975 Sup. Ct. Rev. 261, 261–62. *See also* Comment, *Entitlement, Enjoyment, and Due Process of Law*, 1974 Duke L.J. 89, 119.

25. *See, e.g.,* John Hart Ely, Democracy and Distrust: A Theory of Judicial Review 19 (1980); 2 Richard J. Pierce, Jr., Administrative Law Treatise §§ 9.3 & 9.4, at 575–76, 578–79 (4th ed. 2002) (describing Ely and Monaghan critiques); Cynthia R. Farina, *Conceiving Due Process*, 3 Yale J.L. & Feminism 189 (1991); Monaghan, *supra* note 24, at 409–10.

26. Ely, *supra* note 25, at 19 (footnote omitted).

27. Monaghan, *supra* note 24, at 409–10.

28. *See, e.g.*, 2 Pierce, *supra* note 25, §§ 9.3 & 9.4, at 575–76, 578–79; Ely, *supra* note 25, at 19.

29. *Accord* 3 Rotunda & Nowak, *supra* note 22, § 17.3, at 8.

30. *See, e.g.,* Buchanan v. Angelone, 522 U.S. 269 (1998); Lockett v. Ohio, 438 U.S. 586 (1978) (plurality op.); Woodson v. North Carolina, 428 U.S. 280 (1976) (plurality op.); Furman v. Georgia, 408 U.S. 238 (1972) (per curiam).

31. *See also* Richard J. Pierce, Jr., *The Due Process Counterrevolution of the 1990s?*, 96 Colum. L. Rev. 1973, 1974 (1996) (describing protected property rights as "only forms of property that are usually the fruits of an individual's labor, such as money, a house, or a license to practice law . . .").

32. Professor Reich described four different legal doctrines that limited individual rights in largess: the right/privilege distinction; the gratuity principle; the whole and the parts (because government could completely withhold a benefit, it could grant it subject to conditions); and internal management (like private businesses, government should have control over its internal management functions). Charles A. Reich, *The New Property*, 73 Yale L.J. 733, 740 (1964).

33. *Id.* at 741 (citing, among others, Willner v. Comm. on Character & Fitness, 373 U.S. 96 (1963); Schware v. Bd. of Bar Examiners, 353 U.S. 232 (1957); Konigsberg v. State Bar, 353 U.S. 252 (1957)).

34. *Id.* at 742 (citing, among others, City of Owensboro v. Cumberland Tel. & Tel. Co., 230 U.S. 58 (1913) (treating a right conferred by ordinance to erect and maintain telephone poles on public streets as a "property right"); Frost v. Corp. Comm'n, 278 U.S. 515, 519–20 (1929) (treating the right to operate a cotton gin as a franchise; "as such it constitutes a property right within the protection of the Fourteenth Amendment")).

35. Cynthia R. Farina, *On Misusing "Revolution" and "Reform": Procedural Due Process and the New Welfare Act*, 50 Admin. L. Rev. 591, 601–04 (1998) (hereinafter Farina, *Misusing Revolution*). Professor Rodney Smolla has argued that the Court did not reject the right/privilege distinction itself, just the terminology. In Smolla's view, the *Roth* entitlement theory is a reincarnation of the right/privilege distinction that *Roth* purported to repudiate. Rodney A. Smolla, *The Reemergence of the Right-Privilege Distinction in Constitutional Law: The Price of Protesting Too Much*, 35 Stan. L. Rev. 69, 69–75 (1982).

36. Farina, *Misusing Revolution*, *supra* note 35, at 601 (footnote omitted).

37. *Id.* at 602 (citing Greene v. McElroy, 360 U.S. 474 (1959) (finding the revocation of a government employee's security clearance based on unsworn accusations by unnamed informants to be of doubtful constitutionality); Slochower v. Bd. of Higher Educ., 350 U.S. 551 (1956) (overturning the discharge of a professor at a state college for invoking the

Fifth Amendment privilege); Barsky v. Bd. of Regents, 347 U.S. 442 (1954) (upholding the suspension of a medical license after conviction for contempt of court)). *See also* Speiser v. Randall, 357 U.S. 513 (1958) (invalidating a statutory provision that denied veterans a property tax exemption unless they proved that they did not advocate the overthrow of the government by force).

38. Farina, *Misusing Revolution*, *supra* note 35, at 602 n.79 (citations omitted). *See also* William W. Van Alstyne, *The Demise of the Right-Privilege Distinction in Constitutional Law*, 81 Harv. L. Rev. 1439, 1445–58 (1968) (describing five different doctrinal means by which the Supreme Court "circumvent[ed] the harsh consequences of the right-privilege distinction as applied to private interests in the public sector" before rejecting the distinction outright).

39. Farina, *Misusing Revolution*, *supra* note 35, at 602–03. *See also* Peter N. Simon, *Liberty and Property in the Supreme Court: A Defense of* Roth *and* Perry, 71 Cal. L. Rev. 146, 149 (1983) (noting that an "enormous increase in the variety and importance of government benefits [introduced as Great Society programs] added substantial impetus toward extending procedural due process requirements to cover the disbursement of these benefits").

40. Farina, *Misusing Revolution*, *supra* note 35, at 603.

41. Reich, *supra* note 32, at 785–86.

42. Rejection of the right/privilege distinction has not been universally lauded. Professor Pierce, for example, has argued that "by eliminating the distinction between 'rights' and 'privileges,' the Court rejected both the distinction between public and private political spheres and the individualistic liberal political philosophy such a distinction represents." Pierce, *supra* note 31, at 1980. *Cf.* Farina, *Misusing Revolution*, *supra* note 35, at 626–31. *See also* Smolla, *supra* note 35, at 79–80 (viewing this language in *Goldberg* as the "evolutionary link" between the right/privilege distinction and the entitlement theory of *Roth*).

43. Reich, *supra* note 32, at 734–37.

44. The Court has repeatedly reaffirmed this rejection of the right/privilege distinction. *See, e.g.*, Barry v. Barchi, 443 U.S. 55, 64 & n.11 (1979); Shapiro v. Thompson, 394 U.S. 618, 627 n.6 (1969); Bell v. Burson, 402 U.S. 535, 539 (1971).

45. For a defense of the *Roth* test, *see* Simon, *supra* note 39, at 156–74 (defending *Roth* because its definition of property preserves administrators' freedom in making discretionary decisions).

46. In Rehnquist's words, "the very section of the statute which granted [the federal employee] that right [to continued employment subject to removal 'only for such cause as will promote the efficiency of the service'] expressly provided also for the procedure by which 'cause' was to be determined, and expressly omitted . . . procedural guarantees [such as a right to a trial-type adversary hearing]." Arnett v. Kennedy, 416 U.S. 134, 152 (1974) (plurality op.). Judge Stephen Williams has argued that the Court's current entitlements analysis, with its emphasis on individual reliance interests, is defective precisely because it provides no basis for courts, under the guise of due process review, to alter legislatively established procedures. Stephen F. Williams, *Liberty and Property: The Problem of Government Benefits*, 12 J. Legal Stud. 3, 6 (1983).

47. *See also* Frank H. Easterbrook, *Substance and Due Process*, 1982 Sup. Ct. Rev. 85, 95–99 (arguing that the Due Process Clause was intended to require the executive and the judiciary to comply with rules laid down in "law" and to bar judges from proceeding

*ex parte*, but was not intended to restrict the legislature from establishing as law whatever procedures it wished).

48. The Court's substance/process dichotomy has been criticized by some scholars, *see, e.g.*, Easterbrook, *supra* note 47, at 109–19, and defended by others. *See, e.g.,* Simon, *supra* note 39, at 156–78.

49. Pierce, *supra* note 31, at 1986–87.

50. Even though the Court characterized the practice of medicine as a privilege, it nevertheless scrutinized the statutory procedures and substantive standards to determine whether the suspension of a medical license violated either substantive or procedural due process.

51. *But see* Leis v. Flynt, 439 U.S. 438, 442 (1979) (holding that an out-of-state lawyer's interest in appearing *pro hac vice* "is not a right granted either by statute or the Constitution"; "the record here is devoid of any indication that an out-of-state lawyer may claim such an entitlement in Ohio") (per curiam). Some courts have held that once an attorney is granted permission to appear *pro hac vice*, she acquires a limited property interest in that status, which may not be revoked without notice and the opportunity to be heard. *See, e.g.,* Kirkland v. Nat'l Mortgage Network, Inc., 884 F.2d 1367, 1371–72 (11th Cir. 1989); Bank of Haw. v. Kunimoto, 984 P.2d 1198, 1214 (Haw. 1999).

52. *See also* Goldsmith v. United States Bd. of Tax Appeals, 270 U.S. 117 (1926) (holding that a certified public accountant could not be denied permission to practice before the Board of Tax Appeals without notice and an opportunity to be heard); Hornsby v. Allen, 326 U.S. 605 (5th Cir. 1964) (holding that an applicant could not be denied a license to operate a retail liquor store without notice and an opportunity to be heard).

53. The Court has declined to recognize as property the claimed right of Medicaid patients to remain in the nursing home of their choice. O'Bannon v. Town Ct. Nursing Ctr., 447 U.S. 773 (1980).

54. *But see* Richardson v. Wright, 405 U.S. 208 (1972) (declining to decide whether a recipient is entitled to a hearing prior to suspension or termination of disability benefits); Flemming v. Nestor, 363 U.S. 603, 608, 611 (1960) (declining to treat Social Security benefits as "accrued property rights").

55. Pierce, *supra* note 31, at 1989 (predicting that "[t]he next counterrevolutionary decision probably will be issued in the context of welfare benefits; the recent overhaul of the welfare system indicates that this battle already has been joined").

56. Pub. L. No. 104-193, 110 Stat. 2105 (codified in scattered sections throughout 42 U.S.C. (1994 ed. Supp. IV)) (hereinafter "1996 Welfare Amendments").

57. Pierce, *supra* note 31, at 1990; Farina, *Misusing Revolution*, *supra* note 35, at 597 (both describing 1996 amendments); *see* 1996 Welfare Amendments, § 103(a), 110 Stat. at 2113, *codified at* 42 U.S.C. 601(a) (1994 ed. Supp. IV) (noting the purpose is "to increase the flexibility of the States"); *id.* § 103(a), 110 Stat. at 2124, *codified* at 42 U.S.C. § 604(a)(1) (1994 ed. Supp. IV) (permitting states to use federal grants "in any manner that is reasonably calculated to accomplish the purpose of this part"); *id.* § 103(a), 110 Stat. at 2141, *codified at* 42 U.S.C. § 608(b)(4) (1994 ed. Supp. IV) (stating that "[t]he exercise of the authority of this subsection shall be within the sole discretion of the State").

58. 1996 Welfare Amendments, § 103(a), 110 Stat. at 2113 (codified at 42 U.S.C. § 601(b) (1994 ed. Supp. IV)) (providing that the statute "shall not be interpreted to entitle any individual or family to assistance under any State program funded under this part").

The statute enacting the State Children's Health Insurance Program contains a similar disclaimer. See Balanced Budget Act of 1997, Pub. L. No. 105-33, § 4901, 111 Stat. 251, 554 (codified at 42 U.S.C. 1397bb(b)(4)) (1994 ed. Supp. IV).

59. Pierce, *supra* note 31, at 1990.

60. 1996 Welfare Amendments, § 402(a)(1)(B)(iii), 110 Stat. at 2114 (codified at 42 U.S.C. § 602(a)(1)(B)(iii) (1994 ed. Supp. IV)).

61. Farina, *Misusing Revolution*, *supra* note 35, at 618–32. *See also* Randal S. Jeffrey, *The Importance of Due Process Protections After Welfare Reform: Client Stories From New York City*, 66 Alb. L. Rev. 123 (2002); Weston v. Cassata, 37 P.3d 469, 477 (Colo. Ct. App. 2001) (concluding that welfare recipients have a "property right that cannot be compromised without procedural due process protections" notwithstanding the inclusion of statutory "no entitlement" language), *cert. denied*, 536 U.S. 923 (2002); State *ex rel.* K.M. v. W. Va. Dep't of Health & Human Res., 575 S.E.2d 393, 409 (W. Va. 2002) (similar).

62. Cafeteria & Rest. Workers Union v. McElroy, 367 U.S. 886, 896 (1961) (citing, among others, Parsons v. United States, 167 U.S. 324, 331–34 (1897); Keim v. United States, 177 U.S. 290, 293–94 (1900); Taylor & Marshall v. Beckham, 178 U.S. 548, 575–78 (1900)). *See also* In Re Sawyer, 124 U.S. 200 (1888).

63. The Court has also noted that dismissal from public employment based upon an unsupported charge that could wrongfully injure the employee's reputation may implicate a protected liberty interest. *See infra* "Liberty Interests" section of this chapter, subsection "Reputation."

64. Likewise, public employment during a probationary period may not qualify as a property interest. Codd v. Velger, 429 U.S. 624, 628 n.2 (1977). *Cf.* Perri v. Aytch, 724 F.2d 362, 365–66 (3d Cir. 1983) (holding that where personnel regulations provided that probationary employees could be dismissed "for just cause only," probationer had a protected property interest in her position).

65. *See also* Fed. Deposit Ins. Corp. v. Mallen, 486 U.S. 230, 240 (1988). *Compare* Williams v. Pa. State Police, 108 F. Supp. 2d 460, 470 (E.D. Pa. 2000) (holding that a public employee's placement on restricted duty "does not rise to the level of a *constitutional* deprivation"), *with* Wozniak v. Conry, 236 F.3d 888, 890 (7th Cir. 2001) (holding that a "dramatic change of duties [for a tenured faculty member] affected his 'property' within the meaning of the due process clause").

66. Williams, *supra* note 46, at 20; Monaghan, *supra* note 24, at 411–13; see *also* Isaiah Berlin, *Two Concepts of Liberty*, in Isaiah Berlin, Four Essays on Liberty 121–23 (1960) (discussing negative liberty).

67. *See also* Greenholtz v. Inmates of the Neb. Penal & Corr. Complex, 442 U.S. 1, 22 (1979) (Marshall, J., dissenting in part) (opining that "*all* prisoners potentially eligible for parole have a liberty interest of which they may not be deprived without due process, regardless of the particular statutory language that implements the parole system"); Ky. Dep't of Corr. v. Thompson, 490 U.S. 454, 466–68 (1989) (Marshall, J., dissenting) (positing that a liberty interest is implicated when a prisoner suffers a "grievous loss" or is singled out for disparate treatment); Sandin v. Conner, 515 U.S. 472, 489–90 (1995) (Ginsburg, J., dissenting).

68. Monaghan, *supra* note 24, at 429.

69. *Cf.* Codd v. Velger, 429 U.S. 624, 633 n.3 & 638 n.11 (1977) (Stevens, J., dissenting) (reading *Roth* as distinguishing between two "quite different interests" protected by

due process: the individual's interest in her reputation and good name, and her interest in avoiding a "stigma or other disability" that would foreclose employment opportunities).

70. In a footnote to this passage, the majority acknowledged that interests guaranteed by the Bill of Rights and incorporated into the Fourteenth Amendment were likewise protected. Paul v. Davis, 424 U.S. 693, 710 n.5 (1976). The dissent took issue with the majority's contention that only interests with pre-existing legal protection qualify as "liberty" interests protected by due process: "the content of 'liberty' in [the Due Process Clauses of the Fifth and Fourteenth Amendments] has never been thought to depend on recognition of an interest by the State or Federal Government, and has never been restricted to interests explicitly recognized by other provisions of the Bill of Rights." *Id.* at 722 n.10 (Brennan, J., dissenting).

71. Monaghan, *supra* note 24, at 424.

72. For Courts of Appeals decisions applying *Siegert, see, e.g.*, Advanced Mgmt. Tech., Inc. v. Fed. Aviation Admin., 211 F.3d 633, 637 (D.C. Cir. 2000); Hason v. Davis, 210 F.3d 354 (2d Cir. 2000); Renaud v. Wyo. Dep't of Family Servs., 203 F.3d 723, 727 (10th Cir. 2000); WMX Techs., Inc. v. Miller, 197 F.3d 367, 373 (9th Cir. 1999); Cypress Ins. Co. v. Clark, 144 F.3d 1435, 1437 (11th Cir. 1998); Ludwig v. Bd. of Trs., 123 F.3d 404, 410 (6th Cir. 1997); Waddell v. Forney, 108 F.3d 889, 896 (8th Cir. 1997); Jackson v. Long, 102 F.3d 722, 730 (4th Cir. 1996); Kelly v. Borough of Sayreville, 107 F.3d 1073, 1077–78 (3d Cir. 1997); Aversa v. United States, 99 F.3d 1200, 1214–15 (1st Cir. 1996); Vander Zee v. Reno, 73 F.3d 1365, 1369–79 (5th Cir. 1996); Buckley v. Fitzsimmons, 20 F.3d 789, 797 (7th Cir. 1994); Valmonte v. Bane, 18 F.3d 992, 999–1002 (2d Cir. 1994).

73. Outside the prison context, the Court has found other liberty interests that derive directly from the Constitution. *See, e.g.*, Santosky v. Kramer, 455 U.S. 745, 753 (1982) (discussing "[t]he fundamental liberty interest of natural parents in the care, custody, and management of their child"); Lassiter v. Dep't of Soc. Servs., 452 U.S. 18, 27 (1981) (holding that a parent's right to the companionship and custody of her children is a protected liberty interest).

74. The Court also found a liberty interested conferred by state law because the state law and practice at issue created an "'objective expectation' . . . that a prisoner would not be transferred unless he suffered from a mental disease or defect that could not be adequately treated in the prison." Vitek v. Jones, 445 U.S. 480, 489–90 (1980). *See also* Beierle v. Zavares, No. 99-1383, 2000 U.S. App. LEXIS 13916 (10th Cir. June 12, 2000) (concluding that prisoners have a liberty interest in not being branded as sex offenders); Kirby v. Siegelman, 195 F.3d 1285, 1291 (11th Cir. 1999) (same).

75. The Court also concluded that state law created "a right to be free from the arbitrary administration of antipsychotic medication." Washington v. Harper, 494 U.S. 210, 221 (1990). *See also* Sell v. United States, 539 U.S. 166 (2003) (citing *Harper* for the proposition that "an individual has a 'significant' constitutionally protected 'liberty interest' in 'avoiding the unwanted administration of antipsychotic drugs'"); Mills v. Rogers, 457 U.S. 291, 299 (1982) (assuming without deciding that "the Constitution recognizes a liberty interest in avoiding the unwanted administration of antipsychotic drugs") (footnote omitted); Bell v. Wolfish, 441 U.S. 520, 535 (1979) (holding that the Due Process Clause itself protects pretrial detainees from punishment prior to an adjudication of guilt).

76. The Court disavowed the suggestion that the same due process protections extend to cases involving the imposition of lesser penalties, such as the loss of privileges. Wolff v.

McDonnell, 418 U.S. 539, 571 n.19 (1974). *See also* Baxter v. Palmigiano, 425 U.S. 308, 323 (1975) (declining to decide whether an inmate may be deprived of privileges without due process protections).

77. *See also The Supreme Court, 1994 Term—Leading Cases*, 109 Harv. L. Rev. 111, 147 (1995) (noting that "*Sandin*'s principal effect was to send a thinly veiled message to lower courts that they have free rein to reject constitutional liberty-interest claims by prisoners") (footnote omitted).

78. Pierce, *supra* note 31, at 1988.

79. *See* Hatch v. District of Columbia, 184 F.3d 846, 851, 856 (D.C. Cir. 1999) (surveying different approaches to the comparative baseline taken in different circuits); Austin v. Wilkinson, 189 F. Supp. 2d 719, 739 (N.D. Ohio 2002) (surveying different approaches; concluding that "the better approach is to compare the range of prison conditions experienced by the plaintiffs against the complete range of prison conditions experienced by a broad range of similarly situated inmates").

80. *See, e.g.*, Sims v. Artuz, 230 F.3d 14, 22–24 (2d Cir. 2000); *Hatch*, 184 F.3d at 854–58; Neal v. District of Columbia, 131 F.3d 172, 175 (D.C. Cir. 1997); Keenan v. Hall, 83 F.3d 1083, 1089 (9th Cir. 1996) (remanding for "case by case, fact by fact consideration"). *Cf.* Luken v. Scott, 71 F.3d 192 (5th Cir. 1995), *cert. denied sub nom.* Luken v. Johnson, 517 U.S. 1196 (1996) (treating issue summarily); Rodgers v. Singletary, 142 F.3d 1252, 1253 (11th Cir. 1998) (per curiam) (same); May v. Baldwin, 109 F.3d 557, 565 (9th Cir. 1997) (same).

81. *See, e.g.,* Torres v. Fauver, 292 F.3d 141, 149–51 (3d Cir. 2002); Resnick v. Hayes, 213 F.3d 443, 448 (9th Cir. 2000) (reviewing transfer to segregation of inmate who was convicted but not yet sentenced); Robinson v. Shewalter, No. 00-3211, 2000 U.S. App. LEXIS 31942, *7 (6th Cir. Dec. 6, 2000); *Rodgers*, 142 F.3d at 1253; *Neal*, 131 F.3d at 175 (reviewing incarceration in protective custody); Thomas v. Ramos, 130 F.3d 754, 759–62 (7th Cir. 1997); *May*, 109 F.3d at 565; *Luken*, 71 F.3d at 193. *But see Sims*, 230 F.3d at 23 (finding that lengthy sentences in disciplinary segregation were "atypical" enough to implicate a protected liberty interest); Tellier v. Fields, 280 F.3d 69, 79–81 (2d Cir. 2000) (similar); Pifer v. Marshall, 1998 U.S. App. LEXIS 3189, *6 (9th Cir. Feb. 24, 1998) (remanding case involving segregated confinement in California prison for over 11 years); Austin v. Wilkinson, 189 F. Supp. 2d 719, 740 (N.D. Ohio 2002) (concluding that conditions at Ohio's "supermax" prison "are atypical and impose a significant hardship"); Koch v. Lewis, 216 F. Supp. 2d 994, 1002 (D. Ariz. 2001) (holding that five and a half years of confinement in the most secure super-maximum security prison in the country gives rise to a protected liberty interest under *Sandin*), *appeal dismissed*, 335 F.3d 993 (9th Cir. 2003).

82. *But see* Friedl v. City of New York, 210 F.3d 79, 84 (2d Cir. 2000) (concluding that "[p]risoners on work release have a liberty interest in continued participation in such programs"); Segreti v. Gillen, 259 F. Supp. 2d 733, 737–38 (N.D. Ill. 2003) (similar).

83. *See also* Malchi v. Thaler, 211 F.3d 953, 959 (5th Cir. 2000) (concluding that a change in an inmate's good-time earning status did not implicated a protected liberty interest). The Courts of Appeals have not read *Sandin* as retreating from *Wolff* and have continued to treat *already-earned* good-time credits as liberty interests entitled to procedural protection. McGuinness v. DuBois, 75 F.3d 794, 797 n.3 (1st Cir. 1996); *see also Malchi*, 211 F.3d at 957–58.

84. Only a few years after *Morrissey*, the Court appeared to narrow the scope of the parolee's liberty interest. In Moody v. Daggett, 429 U.S. 78 (1976), the Court held that if the parole board issued a warrant for a parole violation but did not execute it—because the parolee has been incarcerated after conviction for a different offense committed while on parole—no hearing was required until after the new sentence was served and the parolee was taken into custody upon execution of the parole violator warrant. "With only a prospect of future incarceration [for the parole violation] which is far from certain, we cannot say that the parole violator warrant has any present or inevitable effect upon the liberty interests which *Morrissey* sought to protect." *Id.* at 87.

85. Four dissenting Justices in *Greenholtz* rejected the proposition that the availability of due process protections depends upon the particular wording of the state statute governing parole, maintaining instead that the mere presence of a parole system creates a protected liberty interest. *See* Greenholtz v. Inmates of the Neb. Penal & Corr. Complex, 442 U.S. 1, 18–20 (1979) (Powell, J., concurring in part and dissenting in part); *id.* at 22 (Marshall, J., dissenting in part). *See also* Meachum v. Fano, 427 U.S. 215, 230, 233 (1979) (Stevens, J., dissenting).

# 3

# Notice and the Opportunity to Be Heard

***"[T]he two central concerns of procedural due process [are] the prevention of unjustified or mistaken deprivations and the promotion of participation and dialogue by affected individuals in the decisionmaking process."*** [1]

If a state actor deprives a person of life, liberty or property while acting with the requisite state of mind, due process must be afforded. But what do the enigmatic words "due process" mean? In this chapter, we will address the central procedural protections afforded by due process: notice and the opportunity to be heard. We will consider *when* notice and an opportunity to be heard must be afforded in relation to the threatened deprivation. Once the timing issue has been addressed, we will evaluate the benefits of various procedural protections and explore the circumstances in which they have been required or deemed unnecessary as a matter of due process. Finally, we will explore the availability of a damages remedy for procedural due process violations.

## TIMING AND FORM OF THE HEARING

The Fifth and Fourteenth Amendments protect people from deprivations of life, liberty or property without due process of law. Once it is determined that a protected interest in life, liberty or property is implicated, the critical question becomes what process is due. But when statutes or regulations that affect the interests of many people are enacted, due process does not guarantee each affected individual an opportunity to be heard (Bowles v. Willingham, 1944; see also Atkins v. Parker, 1985). As Justice Holmes explained:

> Where a rule of conduct applies to more than a few people it is impracticable that every one should have a direct voice in its adoption. The Constitution does not require all public acts to be done in town meeting or an assembly of the whole. General statutes within the

> state power are passed that affect the person or property of individuals, sometimes to the point of ruin, without giving them a chance to be heard. Their rights are protected in the only way that they can be in a complex society, by their power, immediate or remote, over those who make the rule (Bi-Metallic Investment Co. v. State Bd., 1915).

In other cases, when the government deprives specific individuals of protected interests, due process generally requires notice and the opportunity for some kind of hearing. The nature and scope of the procedural protections required by due process are a question of federal law, unaffected by state legislative efforts to define the procedures that govern deprivations of state-created rights (Cleveland Bd. of Educ. v. Loudermill, 1985; Vitek v. Jones, 1980). Although the Supreme Court has consistently held that "*some kind of hearing* is required *at some time* before a person is finally deprived of his . . . interests" (Wolff v. McDonnell, 1974, emphasis added), this statement fails to grapple with the critical due process issues—the timing of the hearing in relation to the deprivation and the form the hearing must take.

The timing issues are straightforward to state but sometimes difficult to decide: under what circumstances must the government afford an interested party an opportunity to be heard *before* it acts, and, alternatively, when does a postdeprivation hearing satisfy due process? If no prior hearing is required, how promptly must the postdeprivation hearing be provided to satisfy due process?

In terms of the form of the hearing, the Court has noted that "[t]he formality and procedural requisites for the hearing can vary, depending upon the importance of the interests involved and the nature of the subsequent proceedings" (Boddie v. Connecticut, 1971). With regard to both timing and the form of the hearing, the Court has consistently maintained the difficulty of defining due process with any degree of precision (Lassiter v. Dep't of Soc. Servs., 1981) and has frequently reiterated that the demands of due process are flexible (Ingraham v. Wright, 1977):

> The very nature of due process negates any concept of inflexible procedures universally applicable to every imaginable situation. "'Due process,' unlike some legal rules, is not a technical conception with a fixed content unrelated to time, place and circumstances." It is "compounded of history, reason, the past course of decisions. . . ." (Cafeteria & Rest. Workers Union v. McElroy, 1961, quoting Joint Anti-Fascist Refugee Comm. v. McGrath, 1951, Frankfurter, J., concurring).

Two landmark cases, Goldberg v. Kelly (1970) and Mathews v. Eldridge (1976), provide the backdrop for our analysis of both the timing and form of hearing issues. Let us first examine these seminal cases and then explore these two critical due process issues in greater detail.

## The Landmark Cases

### *Goldberg v. Kelly (1970)*

In the landmark case of Goldberg v. Kelly (1970), the Court considered "whether the Due Process Clause requires that the [welfare] recipient be afforded an evidentiary hearing *before* the termination of benefits." After concluding that the benefits at issue were statutory entitlements protected by due process, the Court considered "the extent to which procedural due process must be afforded the recipient" (Goldberg v. Kelly, 1970). Foreshadowing the balancing test that it would later adopt in Mathews v. Eldridge (1976), the Court stated that the procedural protections required would depend upon whether the claimant's interest in avoiding the loss of benefits outweighed the government's interest in summary adjudication. After emphasizing the unique financial needs of welfare recipients, the Court concluded that "the interest of the eligible recipient in uninterrupted receipt of public assistance, coupled with the State's interest that his payments not be erroneously terminated, clearly outweighs the State's competing concern to prevent any increase in its fiscal and administrative burdens" (Goldberg v. Kelly, 1970). Conceding that the government may terminate some benefits without affording a prior evidentiary hearing in exigent circumstances, the Court nevertheless concluded that "when welfare is discontinued, only a pretermination evidentiary hearing provides the recipient with procedural due process" (Goldberg v. Kelly, 1970).

The Court next considered the specific procedural protections required by due process in this context. Since the statute at issue assured the recipient a posttermination "fair hearing," the sole function of the pretermination hearing was to reduce the risk of an erroneous termination of benefits by providing a preliminary check on the validity of the termination decision. In this context, a complete record and a comprehensive opinion were not required. Recognizing the shared interest in "a relatively speedy resolution of questions of eligibility," the Court concluded that only "minimum procedural safeguards" were required at the pretermination hearing (Goldberg v. Kelly, 1970).

Having said that, the Court went on to require a full-blown evidentiary hearing. It held that a welfare recipient threatened with termination of benefits is entitled to

> timely and adequate notice detailing the reasons for a proposed termination, and an effective opportunity to defend by confronting any adverse witnesses and by presenting his own arguments and evidence orally. These rights are important in cases such as those before us, where recipients have challenged proposed terminations as resting on incorrect or misleading factual premises or on misapplications of rules or policies to the facts of particular cases (Goldberg v. Kelly, 1970).[2]

While not requiring the appointment of counsel for all recipients threatened with termination, the Court held that recipients must be allowed to bring retained counsel with them to the hearing. The Court required that the decisionmaker's conclusion rest solely on the evidence adduced at the hearing. To demonstrate compliance with this requirement, the decisionmaker had to state the reasons for her decision and the evidence relied on. Finally, the Court noted the importance of an impartial decisionmaker.

Although the Court extended *Goldberg* to other contexts in the years immediately following the decision (Fuentes v. Shevin, 1972; Bell v. Burson, 1971), it soon realized that government agencies could not operate effectively if they had to provide trial-type hearings whenever they made a decision affecting a person's eligibility for benefits or status.[3] Only six years later, in Mathews v. Eldridge (1976), the Court adopted a balancing test to determine both the timing and nature of the hearing required by due process, the application of which has often yielded a preliminary hearing with fewer procedural protections than were required by *Goldberg*.

### *Mathews v. Eldridge (1976)*

*Eldridge* involved a decision by the Social Security Administration to terminate Mr. Eldridge's disability benefits. Rather than seeking reconsideration of the agency's decision, Mr. Eldridge filed suit in federal district court, challenging the constitutional validity of the administrative procedures established by the Secretary of Health, Education and Welfare ("HEW")[4] for determining whether a recipient of disability benefits had a continuing disability. He argued that under Goldberg v. Kelly (1970), he was entitled to an evidentiary hearing *before* the termination of benefits. Reiterating its earlier statements regarding the flexibility of due process (Morrissey v. Brewer, 1972), the Supreme Court identified three factors to be considered in determining the timing and nature of the hearing required:

> First, the private interest that will be affected by the official action; second, the risk of an erroneous deprivation of such interest through the procedures used, and the probable value, if any, of additional or substitute procedural safeguards; and finally, the Government's interest, including the function involved and the fiscal and administrative burdens that the additional or substitute procedural requirement would entail (Mathews v. Eldridge, 1976).

Before applying the test, the Court described the "elaborate" administrative procedures that the HEW Secretary had implemented. Under these procedures, a disability recipient and her doctors were periodically asked to provide information to the participating state agency concerning the recipient's current condition. Whenever the agency tentatively concluded that she was no longer disabled, the recipient was informed that benefits might be terminated, provided with a summary of the evidence underlying the decision, and afforded an opportunity to review the medical reports and other evidence in her file. She was also permitted to respond in writing and to submit additional evidence (Mathews v. Eldridge, 1976). If the state agency made a final determination that the recipient was no longer disabled and if that determination was accepted by the Social Security Administration ("SSA"), disability benefits were terminated and the SSA notified the recipient in writing of the decision and informed her of the basis for the decision and of her right to seek *de novo* reconsideration by the state agency. If, upon reconsideration, the state agency upheld its decision and the SSA concurred, the recipient then had a right to an evidentiary hearing before an administrative law judge.

Since the procedures provided for retroactive payments to workers whose disabilities were ultimately found to have extended beyond the termination date, the Court concluded that the worker's "sole interest is in the uninterrupted receipt of this source of income pending final administrative decision on his claim" (Mathews v. Eldridge, 1976). In an effort to distinguish *Goldberg*, the *Eldridge* Court noted that since eligibility for disability benefits was not based on financial need and since recipients of such benefits might have income or support from a variety of other sources, a temporary deprivation of disability benefits would not deprive an eligible worker "'of the very means by which to live while he waits'" (Mathews v. Eldridge, 1976, quoting Goldberg v. Kelly, 1970). Thus, the potential deprivation in *Eldridge* was considered to be less severe than in *Goldberg*.

In addition to assessing the severity of the claimant's injury, the Court recognized that "'the possible length of wrongful deprivation of . . . benefits [also] is an important factor in assessing the impact of official action on the private interests'" (Mathews v. Eldridge, 1976, quoting Fusari v. Steinberg, 1975). Recognizing that more than a year could pass between the time a recipient's benefits were terminated and her posttermination evidentiary hearing and conceding that the hardship imposed upon the recipient might be "significant," the Court nevertheless maintained that "the disabled worker's need is likely to be less than that of a welfare recipient" because in addition to possible private resources, the terminated disability recipient would become eligible to receive other forms of government assistance if her income fell below the subsistence level (Mathews v. Eldridge, 1976). Given these potential sources of income, the Court saw "less reason here than in *Goldberg* to depart from the ordinary principle, established by our decisions, that something less than an evidentiary hearing is sufficient prior to adverse administrative action" (Mathews v. Eldridge, 1976).

In gauging the risk of erroneous deprivation and the probable value of additional procedural safeguards, the Court began by clarifying the nature of the relevant inquiry. In the disability benefits context, the disabled worker "must demonstrate by means of 'medically acceptable clinical and laboratory diagnostic techniques' . . . that he is unable 'to engage in any substantial gainful activity by reason of any *medically determinable* physical or mental impairment. . . .'"

(Mathews v. Eldridge, 1976, quoting 42 U.S.C. § 423(d), emphasis added). The Court viewed the medical assessment of the worker's condition as "a more sharply focused and easily documented decision than the typical determination of welfare entitlement" because the ultimate decision would turn on unbiased medical reports by doctors, whose credibility and veracity would not routinely be questioned (Mathews v. Eldridge, 1976). Hence, because the written medical reports upon which the agency's decisions were based were presumed to be reliable, the "potential value of an evidentiary hearing, or even oral presentation to the decisionmaker, is substantially less in this context than in *Goldberg*" (Mathews v. Eldridge, 1976). The Court further noted that the doctors (whose opinions were central to the ultimate determination) were able to communicate effectively in writing, unlike the welfare recipients whose benefits were at stake in *Goldberg*.

The final factor the Court considered was the public interest, including "the administrative burden and other societal costs" that would result from a decision recognizing a constitutional right to an evidentiary hearing before termination of disability benefits (Mathews v. Eldridge, 1976). The Court identified as the "most visible burden" the "incremental cost resulting from the increased number of hearings and the expense of providing benefits to ineligible recipients pending decision" (Mathews v. Eldridge, 1976). Eschewing any effort to quantify this cost, the Court nevertheless concluded that "the ultimate additional cost in terms of money and administrative burden would not be insubstantial" and might ultimately be borne by "deserving" recipients of government benefits, whose benefits might be reduced (Mathews v. Eldridge, 1976).

In the end, the Court questioned the appropriateness of transplanting wholesale judicial procedures to the administrative context. The essence of due process is notice and an opportunity to be heard, with procedures "tailored, in light of the decision to be made, to 'the capacities and circumstances of those who are to be heard. . . .'" (Mathews v. Eldridge, 1976, quoting Goldberg v. Kelly, 1970). Expressing a willingness to give "substantial weight" to the good-faith judgment made by administrators of social welfare programs, the Court concluded that "an evidentiary hearing is not required prior to the termination of disability benefits and that the present administrative procedures fully comport with due process" (Mathews v. Eldridge, 1976).

The Supreme Court has applied the *Eldridge* balancing test to determine both the timing and the nature of the hearing required in a wide variety of contexts, including cases involving deprivations of liberty (Hamdi v. Rumsfeld, 2004; Parham v. J.R., 1979; Smith v. Org. of Foster Families for Equal. & Reform, 1977). In recent years, however, the Court has held that the *Eldridge* test does not govern the constitutionality of state procedural rules that are part of the criminal process (Medina v. California, 1992).[5] In fact, the Court has held that apart from incorporating the specific guarantees enumerated in the Bill of Rights, the Due

Process Clause " 'has limited operation' " in the criminal context (Medina v. California, 1992, quoting Dowling v. United States, 1990).[6]

With these background cases in mind, let us now turn to the question of when an opportunity for a hearing must be provided relative to the deprivation of a protected interest by the state.

## Timing of the Hearing

As a general rule, due process guarantees notice and an opportunity to be heard *before* the government may deprive a person of a protected interest (United States v. James Daniel Good Real Prop., 1993; Mullane v. Cent. Hanover Bank & Trust Co., 1950). In fact, the Court has recognized that the opportunity for a prior hearing is a "root requirement" of due process (Cleveland Bd. of Educ. v. Loudermill, 1985; Boddie v. Connecticut, 1971). Thus, the Court has held that due process requires an opportunity to be heard *before* the government deprives a welfare recipient of benefits (Goldberg v. Kelly, 1970), *before* it terminates an employee for cause (Cleveland Bd. of Educ. v. Loudermill, 1985), *before* it seizes real estate liable to forfeiture (United States v. James Daniel Good Real Prop., 1993), and *before* it revokes parole or probation (Gagnon v. Scarpelli, 1973; Morrissey v. Brewer, 1972).

Against this backdrop requirement of a prior hearing, the Court has employed three strands of analysis that justify governmental action *without* a prior hearing in specified circumstances. First, in a line of cases that pre-dates *Eldridge*, the Court has dispensed with the obligation to provide a prior hearing where the need for immediate action is pressing. Thus, the Court has announced an exigent circumstances exception to the prior hearing requirement. Second, since adopting the *Eldridge* balancing test, the Court has attempted to meld the exigent circumstances analysis into the more general *Eldridge* analysis. As we will see, in some cases, the governmental interest in prompt action is so strong that the balance counsels in favor of summary action without a prior hearing. Third, the Court has recognized that when the deprivation is caused by random or unauthorized governmental action, it would be impractical, if not impossible, for the government to provide a predeprivation hearing. In these instances, when no prior opportunity to be heard is required, a prompt, postdeprivation hearing or a common-law tort remedy satisfies due process.

Let us explore these exceptions, keeping in mind the overarching principle that some form of hearing is required *before* an individual is *finally* deprived of a protected interest. As the *Eldridge* Court put it,

> The "right to be heard before being condemned to suffer grievous loss of any kind, even though it may not involve the stigma and hardships of a criminal conviction, is a principle basic to our society." The fundamental requirement of due process is the opportunity to be

heard "at a meaningful time and in a meaningful manner" (Mathews v. Eldridge, 1976, quoting Joint Anti-Fascist Refugee Comm. v. McGrath, 1951, Frankfurter, J., concurring, and Armstrong v. Manzo, 1965, emphasis added).

### *Exigent Circumstances*

The Supreme Court has often noted that in "rare and extraordinary" situations, the government may immediately seize property without affording the owner an opportunity for a prior hearing (Bd. of Regents v. Roth, 1972; Boddie v. Connecticut, 1971). Before the Court announced the *Eldridge* balancing test, it identified three factors that distinguish these exceptional situations from other cases:

> First, in each case, the seizure has been directly necessary to secure an important governmental or general public interest. Second, there has been a special need for very prompt action. Third, the State has kept strict control over its monopoly of legitimate force: the person initiating the seizure has been a government official responsible for determining, under the standards of a narrowly drawn statute, that it was necessary and justified in the particular instance (Fuentes v. Shevin, 1972).

Several governmental interests have been found sufficiently important and pressing to justify immediate seizure. For instance, the Court has permitted a deprivation of property without a prior opportunity to be heard when necessary to protect public health or safety. In North American Cold Storage Co. v. City of Chicago (1908), for example, the Court upheld a municipal ordinance that authorized members of the health department to enter the premises of cold storage companies and, without notice or the opportunity to be heard, to seize and destroy food that had decayed or otherwise become unsafe for human consumption. Relying on the "right and duty" of the government to protect the lives and health of its citizens, the Court upheld the summary action, noting that the owner of the property would have a right to a postseizure hearing (N. Am. Cold Storage Co. v. City of Chicago, 1908).

The Court employed similar reasoning to uphold the pre-hearing seizure of "misbranded" food supplements (Ewing v. Mytinger & Casselberry, Inc., 1950) and the issuance of immediate orders to cease surface mining operations upon a finding by the Secretary of the Interior that such operations would create an immediate danger to public health or safety (Hodel v. Va. Surface Mining & Reclamation Ass'n, 1981). Likewise, it upheld the prompt suspension of a bank president upon his indictment, invoking the need to protect depositors' interests and to maintain public confidence in banking institutions (Fed. Deposit Ins. Corp. v. Mallen, 1988).[7]

National security interests, too, have been deemed sufficiently important to justify summary action to be followed by a postseizure hearing. For example, in Central Union Trust Co. v. Garvan (1921), the Court upheld the constitutionality of a federal wartime statute that authorized the Alien Property Custodian to seize property owned by or for the benefit of an enemy of the United States. Citing urgent security interests, the Court emphasized the need for immediate action, relying on a postseizure hearing to afford the property owner an opportunity to contest the seizure. And the Court has upheld the summary seizure of property to collect the internal revenue of the United States (Phillips v. Comm'r, 1931; Bowles v. Willingham, 1944).

Even when the governmental interest is significant, notice may be dispensed with only if the need for immediate action is pressing. This requirement will be satisfied if the government establishes a risk that the property at issue will be removed, concealed or destroyed if advance warning is provided. For example, in Calero-Toledo v. Pearson Yacht Leasing Co. (1974), the Court upheld seizure without notice or prior hearing of a yacht that had been used to transport illegal drugs. Noting that the forfeiture statute fostered a public interest in preventing the continued illegal use of property, the Court then addressed the special need for prompt action: "the property seized—as here, a yacht—will often be of a sort that could be removed to another jurisdiction, destroyed, or concealed, if advance warning of confiscation were given" (Calero-Toledo v. Pearson Yacht Leasing Co., 1974; see also United States v. $8,850 in United States Currency, 1983). In a later forfeiture case involving real property, the Court concluded that due process demanded notice and an opportunity for a prior hearing because the government had no pressing need for prompt action. The property could not be hidden, and the government could obtain a *lis pendens*, or a notice informing the public that the property was the subject of litigation, to prevent it from being sold (United States v. James Daniel Good Real Prop., 1993).

### *Application of* Eldridge *Balancing Test*

Since deciding Mathews v. Eldridge in 1976, the Court has applied the balancing test to determine not only the procedural protections that must be afforded in a given case, but also *when* an opportunity to be heard must be provided relative to the deprivation. As we shall see, cases involving exigent circumstances may now be analyzed under the *Eldridge* test, which takes into account the government's interest, including the financial and administrative burden involved in affording a prior opportunity to be heard.

In evaluating the private interest at stake, the Court has considered the severity, length and finality of the deprivation (Gilbert v. Homar, 1997; Logan v. Zimmerman Brush Co., 1982; Mackey v. Montrym, 1979). In the prison context, for example, the right to be free from confinement is extinguished by a lawful conviction and sentence, so the prisoner has only a limited liberty interest at stake (Hewitt v. Helms, 1983). On the other hand, when citizen-detainees accused of being enemy combatants challenge their detention and contest their classification as enemy combatants, their "interest is being free from physical detention" is "substantial" and "fundamental" (Hamdi v. Rumsfeld, 2004, plurality op.). In the employment context, while the Court has repeatedly recognized the severity of depriving a person of her livelihood in public employment cases (Fed. Deposit Ins. Corp. v. Mallen, 1988; Brock v. Roadway Express, Inc., 1987), it has distinguished between terminations and temporary suspensions. An employee who is temporarily suspended without pay has a substantial interest at stake (Barry v. Barchi, 1979), but the loss of income is relatively insubstantial compared with the loss suffered by an employee who is actually terminated (Gilbert v. Homar, 1997). The Court has drawn a similar distinction between temporary suspensions from school and expulsions (Goss v. Lopez, 1975), and has emphasized the severity of an order permanently terminating parental rights (Santosky v. Kramer, 1982; Armstrong v. Manzo, 1965). Lower courts have distinguished between employees who are fired from their government positions and those who retain the same title and salary but are assigned to perform less appealing work (Wozniak v. Conry, 7th Cir. 2001).

Some deprivations, even if temporary or brief, may impose tremendous hardship, such as the termination of electrical, gas or water service (Memphis Light, Gas & Water Div. v. Craft, 1978), the termination of welfare benefits (Goldberg v. Kelly, 1970), the garnishment of wages (Sniadach v. Family Finance Corp., 1969), the repossession of a household stove (Fuentes v. Shevin, 1972), or even the attachment of real property (Connecticut v. Doehr, 1991).

In addition to assessing the severity, length and finality of the deprivation, the Court has considered whether and to what extent the individual can be made whole if she prevails at the final hearing. Thus, while lost wages or withheld benefits can be recouped if the individual prevails (Gilbert v. Homar, 1997; Mathews v. Eldridge, 1976), collateral losses, such as inconvenience suffered, lost clients or lost business, will not be compensated (Mackey v. Montrym, 1979; Barry v. Barchi, 1979; Dixon v. Love, 1976). While utility service that is terminated may be restored following a hearing, the "cessation of essential services for any appreciable time works a uniquely final deprivation" (Memphis Light, Gas & Water Div. v. Craft, 1978; see also Connecticut v. Doehr, 1991, plurality op.). And rarely can persons deprived of liberty interests be made whole after the fact (Ingraham v. Wright, 1977, Stevens, J., dissenting, and White, J., dissenting).

The Court has also considered whether the claimant has a present entitlement to the property at issue. In one recent case, the state withheld monies from a public works contractor because one of its subcontractors failed to comply with certain requirements of the state labor code (Lujan v. G&G Fire Sprinklers, Inc., 2001). Consistent with the labor code, the contractor then deducted that amount from the monies owed to the subcontractor. No pre- or postdeprivation hearing was provided; the contractor's sole remedy under the statute was a lawsuit against the government for breach of contract, which could be assigned to the subcontractor. In upholding the constitutionality of the statute, a unanimous Supreme

Court distinguished other due process cases in which the claimant was "presently entitled either to exercise ownership dominion over real or personal property, or to pursue a gainful occupation. Unlike those claimants, [the subcontractor] has not been denied any present entitlement" (Lujan v. G&G Fire Sprinklers, Inc., 2001). It had only its claim that it had complied with the labor code and that it was entitled to full payment.[8]

Finally, in cases where the private interest is rooted in history, the scope of the interest may be subject to historical limitations (Ingraham v. Wright, 1977). For example, while children have a liberty interest in personal security that is implicated when a public school teacher engages in corporal punishment, that interest is qualified by the teacher's historical right to engage in "some limited corporal punishment [when] necessary in the course of a child's education" (Ingraham v. Wright, 1977).

Even when the private interest is substantial, the Court will uphold deprivations without the opportunity for a prior hearing if the other *Eldridge* factors are weightier. Governmental interests in public health, safety and welfare weigh heavily in this balance. In the prison context, for example, the Court has held that state officials may transfer an inmate from the general prison population to administrative segregation without first conducting a hearing if there is an urgent need to preserve the safety of other inmates and prison staff, as in the case of a prison riot (Hewitt v. Helms, 1983), or if the inmate is likely to attempt to intimidate potential witnesses or fabricate an alibi (Hughes v. Rowe, 1980). Likewise, students who pose an immediate danger to others or who threaten to disrupt the academic process may be removed from school summarily (Goss v. Lopez, 1975). And in employment cases, the Court has emphasized the need for immediate action when the employee occupies a position of "great public trust and high public visibility" (Gilbert v. Homar, 1997). Thus, the Court has upheld the immediate suspension without pay of a state university police officer upon his arrest on a felony drug charge (Gilbert v. Homar, 1997) and of a bank president upon his indictment for making false statements to the FDIC (Fed. Deposit Ins. Corp. v. Mallen, 1988). On the other hand, when the employee's position is less visible, the governmental employer may share the employee's interest in avoiding disruption and may benefit by keeping a qualified employee on the job, thereby reducing the need to train a new one pending a final decision (Cleveland Bd. of Educ. v. Loudermill, 1985).

Other governmental interests deemed sufficiently compelling to justify summary action include maintenance of the integrity of state-supervised harness horse racing (Barry v. Barchi, 1979) and the safety of public roads and highways (Brock v. Roadway Express, Inc., 1987; Mackey v. Montrym, 1979; Dixon v. Love, 1976). While a governmental interest in cost containment may be considered, "it does not justify denying a hearing meeting the ordinary standards of due process" (Goldberg v. Kelly, 1970; see also Bell v. Burson, 1971). And when the state already claims to provide an immediate postdeprivation hearing, it cannot argue that the administrative or financial costs of providing a predeprivation hearing in its place would be prohibitive (Connecticut v. Doehr, 1991).

In assessing the risk of erroneous deprivation and the likely value of any additional procedural protections, the Court has focused on the limited goal of preliminary predeprivation hearings: to ensure that reasonable grounds exist to support the proposed governmental action (Cleveland Bd. of Educ. v. Loudermill, 1985; Mackey v. Montrym, 1979). When a state official has been arrested or indicted, the *ex parte* finding of probable cause that supports the arrest or indictment provides that assurance and therefore is sufficient to support an immediate suspension from employment without a prior hearing (Gilbert v. Homar, 1997; Fed. Deposit Ins. Corp. v. Mallen, 1988). The Court has also viewed the risk of erroneous deprivation to be low when the relevant facts are within the personal knowledge of an impartial government official or readily ascertainable by her (Mackey v. Montrym, 1979). Thus, the Court found that an independent official's determination that a racehorse had been drugged was sufficiently reliable to support the suspension of the horse's trainer without a prior formal hearing (Barry v. Barchi, 1979). On the other hand, the risk of erroneous deprivation is higher when the decisionmaker must rely on the reports and advice of others (Goss v. Lopez, 1975) and when witnesses with knowledge of the relevant facts have a personal interest in the outcome of the proceeding (Parham v. J.R., 1979).

The narrower the decisionmaker's discretion and the more objective the criteria that cabin her discretion, the smaller the risk of erroneous deprivation and the less the need for a prior evidentiary hearing. Thus, a scheme that required the Secretary of State to revoke a driver's license if it had been suspended three times in ten years was constitutional even though it afforded no prerevocation hearing (Dixon v. Love, 1977). Likewise, the Court upheld the issuance of an *ex parte* sequestration order upon proof of a debt, a vendor's lien, and the debtor's delinquency, since these are "ordinarily uncomplicated matters that lend themselves to documentary proof" (Mitchell v. W.T. Grant Co., 1974). On the other hand, when factual disputes need to be resolved, the decisionmaker's discretion is broad, or the availability of relief turns upon proof of "fault," the person to be affected should be afforded an opportunity to be heard before the deprivation takes place (Connecticut v. Doehr, 1991; Cleveland Bd. of Educ. v. Loudermill, 1985; Mitchell v. W.T. Grant Co., 1974).

Even when decisions are based largely on objective criteria, if the underlying data is computer-generated, the risk of computer error needs to be taken into account in assessing the risk of erroneous deprivation (Memphis Light, Gas & Water Div. v. Craft, 1978).

In addition to weighing the factors prescribed by the *Eldridge* balancing test, the Court has considered the availability and effectiveness of any postdeprivation process. The Court in *Eldridge* itself went so far as to say that "[a] claim to a predeprivation hearing as a matter of constitutional right rests on the proposition that full relief cannot be obtained at a postdeprivation hearing" (Mathews v. Eldridge, 1976). In a number of cases, the Court has so found. In Logan v. Zimmerman Brush Co. (1982), for example, the Court reinforced its conclusion that a predeprivation hearing was required by noting that the only postdeprivation process available was an independent tort action, which it described as a "lengthy and speculative process." Likewise, the Court in *Memphis Light* held that the opportunity to seek an injunction against termination of electrical service was an inadequate substitute for a pretermination hearing because it was "likely to be too bounded by procedural constraints and too susceptible of delay" and too costly a vehicle to remedy a utility billing dispute (Memphis Light, Gas & Water Div. v. Craft, 1978). And in North Georgia Finishing, Inc. v. Di-Chem, Inc. (1975), the Court noted the lack of an opportunity for an early postdeprivation hearing in support of its conclusion that a statute authorizing pre-judgment garnishment violated the Due Process Clause. In at least one case, the Court found a postdeprivation remedy inadequate because it placed the burden of proof on the party whose liberty interest was affected (Armstrong v. Manzo, 1965).

In other cases, the availability of effective postdeprivation remedies has proven determinative. In Mackey v. Montrym (1979) and Mitchell v. W.T. Grant Co. (1974), for instance, in support of its conclusion that no prior hearing was required, the Court cited the immediate availability of a postdeprivation hearing that could be initiated simply by asking for it.[9] In Ingraham v. Wright (1977), it held that the common-law remedies for excessive corporal punishment themselves constituted due process; "where the State has preserved what 'has always been the law of the land,' the case for administrative safeguards is sufficiently less compelling."[10] And in Lujan v. G&G Fire Sprinklers, Inc. (2001), the Court held that an ordinary breach of contract suit adequately protects the property interests of a subcontractor denied payment under a government contract when the sub has no present entitlement to payment, just its contention that it complied with the contract.

Justice Stevens has argued that since a damages remedy is more likely to make a person completely whole when she suffers a loss of property than a loss of liberty, the availability of a postdeprivation remedy is more likely to satisfy due process in the property context (Ingraham v. Wright, 1977, Stevens, J., dissenting; *cf.* Fuentes v. Shevin, 1972).

### *Timeliness of Postdeprivation Hearing*

When the balance of interests justifies the deprivation of a protected interest without a prior opportunity to be heard, due process demands a prompt postdeprivation hearing. Likewise, where the balance justifies action after only informal proceedings that find probable cause, a full hearing must be available promptly after the temporary deprivation occurs (Barry v. Barchi, 1979). An unjustified delay in conducting a postdeprivation hearing can result in a constitutional violation (Brock v. Roadway Express, Inc., 1987; Cleveland Bd. of Educ. v. Loudermill, 1985), and the Court has been especially leery of statutes that fail, on their face, to assure a prompt postdeprivation hearing (Barry v. Barchi, 1979). But mere delay in reaching a final decision caused by thorough procedures does not necessarily violate due process, even if the delay lasts as long as nine months (Cleveland Bd. of Educ. v. Loudermill, 1985) or eighteen months (United States v. $8,850 in United States Currency, 1983). "Little can be said on when a delay becomes presumptively improper, for the determination necessarily depends on the facts of the particular case" (United States v. $8,850 in United States Currency, 1983). Some opinions have vaguely required only that the hearing be held "within a reasonable time" following the initial deprivation (Hewitt v. Helms, 1983).

In determining whether a delay is constitutionally permissible, the Court has applied a variant of the *Eldridge* analysis: "it is appropriate to examine the importance of the private interest and the harm to this interest occasioned by delay; the justification offered by the Government for delay and its relation to the underlying governmental interest; and the likelihood that the interim decision may have been mistaken" (Fed. Deposit Ins. Corp. v. Mallen, 1988).

In this context, the Court has recognized that even the temporary loss of one's livelihood can cause severe hardship, not only in terms of lost income but also in terms of lost clients (Barry v. Barchi, 1979). Furthermore, a deprivation of property other than wages can cause substantial hardship (United States v. $8,850 in United States Currency, 1983). But other concerns may outweigh the private interest, as they did in *Mallen*, where the Court held that a postsuspension hearing within ninety days satisfied due process, notwithstanding the severity of the deprivation suffered by a bank president who was summarily suspended (Fed. Deposit Ins. Corp. v. Mallen, 1988).

The same governmental interests that justify a deprivation without a prior hearing may justify some delay in providing the postdeprivation hearing. For example, in *Mallen*, the government's interest in the integrity of the banking industry justified both the immediate suspension of the bank president upon his indictment and whatever postsuspension delay was necessary to gather and weigh the evidence to determine whether he could be returned to his position without threatening the depositors' interests or compromising public confidence in the bank (Fed. Deposit Ins. Corp. v. Mallen, 1988). Likewise, administrative necessity justified a month-long delay in providing a hearing to a person who sought to recoup an impoundment fee he had paid to retrieve his car, which had been towed by the city (City of Los Angeles v. David, 2003).

More generally, when the government deprives a person of a protected interest under exigent circumstances, that preliminary decision is made hastily. Afterwards, the government may need some time to gather facts to determine whether it should even seek to make the deprivation permanent. In cases where the government has seized property liable to forfeiture, the pendency of related criminal or administrative proceedings may also justify some delay in the commencement of civil forfeiture proceedings (United States v. $8,850 in United States Currency, 1983).

Finally, in assessing the likelihood that the deprivation was erroneous, the Court has stressed the relevance of predeprivation probable cause-type determinations by independent decisionmakers, such as indictments or arrests in the public employment context. These determinations demonstrate that the deprivation was not arbitrary (Fed. Deposit Ins. Corp. v. Mallen, 1988).

### *Random and Unauthorized Conduct*

In certain situations, the Court has held that postdeprivation tort remedies are all the process that is due because they are the only remedies the state can be expected to provide (Zinermon v. Burch, 1990). The leading case in this area is Parratt v. Taylor (1981). There, the Court considered a claim by an inmate who had mail-ordered hobby materials valued at $23.50. When the prison lost the hobby materials, which had arrived at the prison but had not been delivered to the inmate, he sued under section 1983, alleging that he had been deprived of property without due process of law. Noting that the state had deprived the inmate of property by losing his hobby kit, the question was whether in so doing, the prison had violated the Due Process Clause (Parratt v. Taylor, 1981).

The Court framed the issue as "whether the tort remedies which [the state] provides as a means of redress for property deprivations satisfy the requirements of procedural due process" (Parratt v. Taylor, 1981).[11] The Court noted that in most cases in which it had required a predeprivation hearing, the challenged action had been taken pursuant to an established procedure and "process" could have been afforded before the deprivation occurred. But the exigent circumstance cases recognize that "either the necessity of quick action by the State or the impracticality of providing any meaningful predeprivation process, when coupled with the availability of some meaningful means by which to assess the propriety of the State's action at some time after the initial taking, can satisfy the requirements of procedural due process" (Parratt v. Taylor, 1981). Stating that due process requires "some kind of hearing . . . at some time before a State *finally* deprives a person of his property interests," the Court rejected the proposition that the hearing always must precede the initial deprivation of property (Parratt v. Taylor, 1981, emphasis added). When an inmate's property is lost through a random and unauthorized act—rather than as a result of an established state procedure—it would be impracticable or even impossible for the state to provide a meaningful predeprivation hearing. In such cases, due process requires only a meaningful postdeprivation hearing (Parratt v. Taylor, 1981). On the other hand, when the state deprives a person of property pursuant to an established state procedure, a postdeprivation remedy ordinarily does *not* satisfy due process (Logan v. Zimmerman Brush Co., 1982). In *Parratt*, a tort remedy against the state was found adequate, even though it did not provide for punitive damages, trial by jury or an action against individual state employees (Parratt v. Taylor, 1981; see also Ingraham v. Wright, 1977). The Court has described *Parratt* as "a special case of the general *Mathews v. Eldridge* analysis. . . ." (Zinermon v. Burch, 1990).[12]

Several Justices concurring in *Parratt* emphasized that its logic applies only to cases involving deprivations of property, not life or liberty, and only to cases involving negligent, not intentional, conduct (Parratt v. Taylor, 1981, Blackmun, J., concurring). These qualifications were considered by the full Court in subsequent cases.

Just three years after deciding *Parratt*, the Court considered whether its logic applied to intentional, but unauthorized, deprivations of property (Hudson v. Palmer, 1984). Since "[t]he state can no more anticipate and control in advance the random and unauthorized intentional conduct of its employees than it can anticipate similar negligent conduct," the Court concluded that the reasoning of *Parratt* extends to intentional conduct (Hudson v. Palmer, 1984). Thus, the Court held "that an unauthorized intentional deprivation of property by a state employee does not constitute a violation of the procedural requirements of the Due Process Clause of the Fourteenth Amendment if a meaningful postdeprivation remedy for the loss is available" (Hudson v. Palmer, 1984).

Although some of the Courts of Appeals had initially limited *Parratt* to deprivations of property, the Supreme Court has extended it to unauthorized deprivations of liberty as well. In Zinermon v. Burch (1990), the plaintiff alleged that administrators and doctors at a state mental hospital deprived him of liberty without due process of law by admitting him as a "voluntary" mental patient—without the procedural safeguards that precede an involuntary commitment—when he lacked the competency to give informed consent. Rejecting the plaintiff's argument that "postdeprivation tort remedies are *never* constitutionally adequate for a deprivation of liberty," the Court found no support in the case law for a "categorical distinction" between deprivations of property and liberty (Zinermon v. Burch, 1990).

In addition to holding that *Parratt* may apply to deprivations of liberty, the Court in *Zinermon* helped clarify the circumstances in which a postdeprivation remedy may satisfy due process under *Parratt* and *Hudson*. *Parratt* and *Hudson* apply only if three conditions are met: (1) the deprivation of liberty or property is unpredictable; (2) predeprivation process would be impracticable or impossible; and (3) the challenged conduct is unauthorized (Zinermon v. Burch, 1990). In *Zinermon*, none of these conditions were present: the state could have foreseen that an incompetent person might request treatment and that state officials might not initiate involuntary commitment proceedings; the state could have limited or guided the hospital's authority to admit mental patients without the benefit of involuntary commitment procedures; and the state had delegated to hospital personnel the authority to effect the very deprivation complained of by the plaintiff.

As demonstrated above, state actors may deprive people of protected interests without a prior hearing where the need for immediate governmental interest is great, the private interest is insignificant, the risk of erroneous deprivation is low, or the postdeprivation procedures available are deemed adequate. With all this attention paid to the exceptions, however, it is important not to lose sight of the forest for the trees: as a general rule, due process guarantees notice and an opportunity to be heard *before* the government may deprive a person of a protected interest.

Now that we have an understanding of when an opportunity to be heard must be provided, let us consider the form that the hearing must take.[13]

## Nature of the Hearing

While the adversary process is generally regarded as the best means of ascertaining the truth and minimizing error (Mackey v. Montrym, 1979), the Court has often held that "something less than an evidentiary hearing is sufficient prior to adverse administrative action" (Mathews v. Eldridge, 1976). In this section, we will explore the benefits and occasional drawbacks of various procedural protections and identify the circumstances in which each has been required. The Court has often applied the *Eldridge* test to determine not only when a hearing is required, but also the nature of the hearing and the procedural protections it must afford.

### *Impartiality and Qualifications of the Decisionmaker*

When the late Judge Friendly compiled a prioritized list of elements of a fair hearing, he listed an unbiased tribunal first.[14] Likewise, Professors Redish and Marshall posit that an independent adjudicator is necessary to ensure that other core due process values are served.[15] This neutrality requirement "safeguards the two central concerns of procedural due process, the prevention of unjustified or mistaken deprivations and the promotion of participation and dialogue by affected individuals in the decisionmaking process" (Marshall v. Jerrico, Inc., 1980). A person will accept the legitimacy of a decision depriving her of a protected interest only if the decisionmaker is, and appears to be, independent and impartial. The Court has recognized a presumption of impartiality, which may be rebutted by a showing of a conflict of interest or other reason for disqualification. The burden of proving such a conflict is borne by the party that raises it (Schweiker v. McClure, 1982).

While the general requirement of an impartial decisionmaker is universally accepted (Schweiker v. McClure, 1982; Marshall v. Jerrico, Inc., 1980), two issues have arisen: (1) what kinds of interests or involvements in the case will so compromise the decisionmaker's neutrality as to disqualify her from serving? and (2) must the decisionmaker be a judicial officer, and if not, what qualifications must she have? Let us consider these issues in turn.

Prior involvement in a case, or employment by the state actor involved, will not necessarily bar a person from serving as the decisionmaker (Washington v. Harper, 1990; Goldberg v. Kelly, 1970). Thus, the Court has held that a decision to subject an inmate to involuntary treatment with anti-psychotic drugs can be made by a committee of medical professionals who have treated or diagnosed the inmate in the past as long as they are not involved, at the time of the hearing, in her current treatment or diagnosis (Washington v. Harper, 1990). Likewise, in Schweiker v. McClure (1982), the Court held that a hearing to review denial of a Medicare claim made by a government-appointed insurance carrier can be conducted by a hearing officer appointed by the carrier, even if she is a current carrier employee. And in Vitek v. Jones (1980), the Court held that members of the prison or hospital administration can make the decision to transfer a prisoner to a mental hospital as long as they are independent (see also Wolff v. McDonnell, 1974; Morrissey v. Brewer, 1972).

The Court has offered two reasons to support its conclusion that employment by the state actor, in and of itself, does not disqualify someone from serving as a decisionmaker. First, "it is only by permitting persons connected with the institution to make these decisions that courts are able to avoid 'unnecessary intrusion into either medical or correctional judgments'" (Washington v. Harper, 1990). Thus, respect for institutional autonomy has influenced the Court's assessment of independence. Second, the scientific literature suggests that outside decisionmakers are no more rigorous in scrutinizing proposed government action than insiders. Regarding decisions to administer anti-psychotic drugs to inmates against their will, for example, the literature indicated "that outside decisionmakers concur with the treating physician's decision to treat a patient involuntarily in most, if not all, cases" (Washington v. Harper, 1990). Thus, employees of the relevant agency are deemed capable of independent judgment as long as their own decisions, recommendations, or diagnoses are not the subject of review.

Even members of an administrative agency that has investigated a matter are not necessarily disqualified from then adjudicating the same matter (Withrow v. Larkin, 1975).

> The mere exposure to evidence presented in nonadversary investigative procedures is insufficient in itself to impugn the fairness of the Board members at a later adversary hearing. Without a showing to the contrary, state administrators "are assumed to be men [and women] of conscience and intellectual discipline, capable of judging a particular controversy fairly on the basis of its own circumstances" (Withrow v. Larkin, 1975, quoting United States v. Morgan, 1941).

Just as a judge who issues an arrest warrant may later preside over the trial of the individual charged, so too may agencies that investigate and approve the filing of charges then participate in the hearings that follow (Withrow v. Larkin, 1975).[16] There is no logical inconsistency between finding probable cause upon a review of only some of the evidence and later finding no violation of the law upon a review of all of the evidence. The Court declined to assume that the risk of bias in this circumstance was intolerably high.

On the other hand, when review of an initial decision is undertaken, the person whose decision is under review may not serve as the factfinder or decisionmaker (Withrow v. Larkin, 1975). In *Morrissey*, the Court explained this policy, concluding that a parole officer who recommends revocation of parole may not conduct the hearing to determine whether parole should be revoked. Even assuming that the supervising parole officer bears no ill will toward the parolee that would destroy her neutrality, "there should be an uninvolved person to make this . . . evaluation of the basis for believing the conditions of parole have been violated. The officer directly involved in making recommendations cannot always have complete objectivity in evaluating them," since prior interactions and possible friction between the officer and the parolee may influence the officer's judgment (Morrissey v. Brewer, 1972). Likewise, a judge who indicts a person under a state law that authorizes judges to serve as one-person grand juries cannot then preside over the trial of the individual indicted (In re Murchison, 1955).[17]

In one anomalous case, the Court upheld the constitutionality of a scheme that vested decision-making authority in a person who may have been directly involved in the case. In Goss v. Lopez (1975), the Court held that school principals or other disciplinarians may render short suspension decisions even if "the disciplinarian himself has witnessed the conduct forming the basis for the charge." Without specifically explaining this departure from standard due process requirements, the Court emphasized the high volume of short suspensions from school, the need for flexibility and informality, and the utility of the disciplinary process as a teaching tool.

Even decisionmakers with no prior involvement in a case may lack the requisite neutrality if they have a financial interest that would impair their judgment. In Tumey v. Ohio (1927), for example, the Court struck down as unconstitutional a local ordinance that authorized direct compensation to the decisionmaker only if the defendant was convicted. "[I]t certainly violates the Fourteenth Amendment, and deprives a defendant in a criminal case of due process of law, to subject his liberty or property to the judgment of a court the judge of which has a direct, personal, substantial, pecuniary interest in reaching a conclusion against him in his case" (Tumey v. Ohio, 1927).

The financial stake need not be as direct as it was in *Tumey* to disqualify the decisionmaker. In Ward v. Village of Monroeville (1972), for example, the Court held that another local ordinance violated due process even though it authorized no personal payment to the mayor/decisionmaker. Since the mayor was responsible for village finances and since traffic fines and court costs contributed a substantial fraction of the village's total revenue, the mayor could not sit as a judge in these cases. Applying a test laid out in *Tumey*, the Court concluded that the situation would "'offer a possible temptation to the average [person] as a judge to forget the burden of proof required to convict the defendant, or . . . might lead him not to hold the balance nice, clear and true between the State and the accused'" (Ward v. Village of Monroeville, 1972, quoting Tumey v. Ohio, 1927).[18] The Court has declined, however, "to read *Tumey* as constitutionalizing any rule that a decision rendered by a judge with 'the slightest pecuniary interest' constitutes a violation of the Due Process Clause" (Aetna Life Ins. Co. v. LaVoie, 1986).

While the law regarding disqualifying financial or personal interests applies with equal force to administrative decisionmakers or private parties performing adjudicative functions delegated by the legislature (Concrete Pipe & Prods. v. Constr. Laborers Pension Trust, 1993; Gibson v. Berryhill, 1973), the Court has limited the "rigid requirements" of *Tumey* and *Ward* to officials performing judicial or quasi-judicial functions. Noting that constitutional issues would be raised if those acting in prosecutorial or plaintiff-like capacities were motivated by financial interest, the Court has declined to specify the limits on financial or personal interest for those acting in non-judicial capacities (Marshall v. Jerrico, Inc., 1980; see also Young v. United States *ex rel.* Vuitton et Fils S.A., 1987).

Like financial interests, institutional loyalty may cast doubt on a decisionmaker's neutrality, although the Court has required proof that neutrality has in fact been compromised. In Parham v. J.R. (1979), for example, the Court considered a claim that hospital administrators were insufficiently "neutral and detached" to decide whether to admit juveniles to mental health care facilities because of institutional pressure to admit children whether or not they needed hospital care. Finding no evidence to support the charge, the Court stated that "such cases, if they are found, can be dealt with individually" (Parham v. J.R., 1979). Likewise, in Schweiker v. McClure (1982), the Court considered the assertion that decisionmakers appointed by insurance carriers to review denials of Medicare payments by the carriers themselves were, "for reasons of psychology, institutional loyalty, or carrier coercion, . . . reluctant to differ with carrier determinations" (Schweiker v. McClure, 1982; see also Walters v. Nat'l Ass'n of Radiation Survivors, 1985). While finding no evidence to support the charge, the Court intimated that proof of such pressure would disqualify a decisionmaker. In Ford v. Wainwright (1986), the Court held that a state statute that gave the executive branch exclusive responsibility to determine whether a prisoner sentenced to death was sane provided inadequate assurances of accuracy: "The commander of the State's corps of prosecutors cannot be said to have the neutrality that is necessary for reliability in the factfinding proceeding." Likewise, in Hamdi v. Rumsfeld

(2004), a plurality of the Court held than an American citizen may not be detained upon the executive's determination that he is an enemy combatant; due process assures the detainee an opportunity to challenge that classification "before a neutral decisionmaker."

In addition to determining when prior involvement or financial interest compromises the neutrality that due process demands, the Court has grappled with the qualifications that the decisionmaker must possess. Ordinarily, the decisionmaker need not be a judicial officer or even have legal training (Washington v. Harper, 1990; Schweiker v. McClure, 1982). In the parole revocation context, for example, the Court held that traditional parole boards, with non-judicial and non-lawyer members, may make final revocation decisions; the "granting and revocation of parole are matters traditionally handled by administrative officers" (Morrissey v. Brewer, 1972). Likewise, in the Medicare context, the Court has held that due process does not require that hearing officers be attorneys or that final review of decisions denying payment be made by judges or other persons with legal training (Schweiker v. McClure, 1982). Even in criminal cases that carry imprisonment as a possible sanction, the Court has upheld the constitutionality of a two-tier trial court system with non-lawyer judges adjudicating cases in the first tier as long as defendants have an appeal as of right with a *de novo* trial before a law-trained judge and as long as the lay judge is neutral (North v. Russell, 1976; see also Shadwick v. City of Tampa, 1972).

The Court has been particularly accepting of non-judicial decisionmakers in cases involving admissions to, or treatment in, mental health care facilities (Washington v. Harper, 1990; Vitek v. Jones, 1980; Sec'y of Pub. Welfare v. Institutionalized Juveniles, 1979). Psychologists, psychiatrists and other health care providers may be better equipped to make these decisions, which turn on proper diagnosis and treatment needs, since "'neither judges nor administrative hearing officers are better qualified than psychiatrists to render psychiatric judgments'" (Parham v. J.R., 1979). In upholding a scheme that vested decision-making authority in a committee comprised of a psychiatrist, a psychologist and the associate superintendent of the treatment facility, the Court also emphasized that medical professionals would accommodate the state's interests "in providing appropriate medical treatment to reduce the danger that an inmate suffering from a serious mental disorder represents to himself or others" (Washington v. Harper, 1990). While the Court acknowledged

> the fallibility of medical and psychiatric diagnosis, [it did] not accept the notion that the shortcomings of specialists can always be avoided by shifting the decision from a trained specialist using the traditional tools of medical science to an untrained judge or administrative hearing officer after a judicial-type hearing. Even after a hearing, the nonspecialist decisionmaker must make a medical-psychiatric decision. Common human experience and scholarly opinions suggest that the supposed protections of an adversary proceeding to

determine the appropriateness of medical decisions for the commitment and treatment of mental and emotional illness may well be more illusory than real (Parham v. J.R., 1979, quoted in Washington v. Harper, 1990).

### Notice of Proposed Action

In the landmark decision, Mullane v. Central Hanover Bank & Trust Co. (1950), the Supreme Court announced that "[a]n elementary and fundamental requirement of due process in any proceeding which is to be accorded finality is notice reasonably calculated, under all the circumstances, to apprise interested parties of the pendency of the action and afford them an opportunity to present their objections." This statement identifies the two essential characteristics of notice: it must inform the individual of the threatened deprivation and it must be given in time to afford her an opportunity to defend. Thus, when the government provides an individual with notice of the grounds for its proposed action, she has an opportunity to marshal evidence and prepare her case in anticipation of a hearing. In assessing the adequacy of the notice provided, the Court considers the education, experience and resources of the person facing the deprivation as well as the importance of the interest at stake (Memphis Light, Gas & Water Div. v. Craft, 1978).

The Court has frequently restated the fundamental requirement of notice in a wide range of contexts, including cases involving the termination of welfare benefits (Goldberg v. Kelly, 1970), public school suspensions (Goss v. Lopez, 1975), pre-trial detention of accused juvenile offenders (Schall v. Martin, 1984; In re Gault, 1967), detention of citizen-enemy combatants (Hamdi v. Rumsfeld, 2004, plurality op.), the loss of "good-time" credits (Wolff v. McDonnell, 1974), administrative segregation from the general prison population (Hewitt v. Helms, 1983), parole revocation (Morrissey v. Brewer, 1972), termination of parental rights (Stanley v. Illinois, 1972; Armstrong v. Manzo, 1965), and termination of electrical service by a public utility (Memphis Light, Gas & Water Div. v. Craft, 1978).

As we will see in Chapter 4, which analyzes the notice requirement in greater detail, the Court has occasionally upheld very limited notice, including notice provided just hours before the hearing (Greenholtz v. Inmates of the Neb. Penal & Corr. Complex, 1979) or even at the hearing itself (Goss v. Lopez, 1975). In an exceptional case, Lehr v. Robertson (1983), the Court upheld the constitutionality of a statute that authorized the adoption of a child without *any* notice to the biological father. The statute at issue required notice to men whose names were listed on the putative father registry[19] and six other categories of putative fathers, including those whose paternity had been established and those who lived with the child and held themselves out as the child's father. The state legislature had concluded that a more open-ended notice requirement would unduly complicate the adoption process and cause other deleterious effects. Given the ease with which the biological father could have placed his name on the putative father registry and the weakness of the liberty interest at stake—the father and child never had a significant relationship—the Court concluded that the state's statutory scheme satisfied due process (Lehr v. Robertson, 1983). Perhaps *Lehr* should be read to stand for the proposition that unwed fathers who fail to acknowledge paternity early in the child's life have no protected liberty interest at stake and therefore are not entitled to any due process protections.[20] If *Lehr* is not so read, it is an aberrational case that dispenses with the need for *any* notice before a hearing.

### *Opportunity to Submit Evidence*

The Court has frequently stated that "the fundamental requisite of due process of law is the opportunity to be heard" (Grannis v. Ordean, 1914, quoted in Ford v. Wainwright, 1986). A defendant may not be deprived of the opportunity to be heard as a mere punishment for contempt of court (Hammond Packing Co. v. Arkansas, 1909; Hovey v. Elliott, 1897).[21] When a decisionmaker must resolve contested issues to render a decision, she benefits when all interested parties are afforded the opportunity to offer probative information. The parties may have access to information unavailable to others and they have the incentive to search for information that bolsters their position. Without the benefit of this party-provided evidence, the decisionmaker is much more likely to reach an erroneous decision (Ford v. Wainwright, 1986). Therefore, due process typically guarantees an opportunity to present evidence before a final decision is made.

The Court has been especially vigilant about protecting the right of individuals convicted of capital offenses to offer evidence. For example, in Jurek v. Texas (1976), the Court scrutinized a death penalty statute to ensure that it provided the defendant with the opportunity "to bring before the jury at the separate sentencing hearing whatever mitigating circumstances relating to the individual defendant [as] can be adduced." Likewise, when a convicted felon is sentenced to death and his sanity at the time of execution is called into question,

> [A]ny procedure that precludes the prisoner or his counsel from presenting material relevant to his sanity or bars consideration of that material by the factfinder is necessarily inadequate. "[T]he minimum assurance that the life-and-death guess will be a truly informed guess requires respect for the basic ingredient of due process, namely, an opportunity to be allowed to substantiate a claim before it is rejected" (Ford v. Wainwright, 1986, quoting Solesbee v. Balkcom, 1950, Frankfurter, J., dissenting).

Thus, a prisoner facing execution must be afforded an opportunity to present reports by psychiatrists who have concluded that she is not competent to suffer execution (Ford v. Wainwright, 1986). And when the state contends that a defendant in a capital case is likely to be a menace if sentenced to prison rather than death, due process requires that the defendant be permitted to offer evidence on the issue of his future dangerousness (Skipper v. South Carolina, 1986). It is an "elemental due process requirement that a defendant not be sentenced to death 'on the basis of information which he had no opportunity to deny or explain'" (Skipper v. South Carolina, 1986, quoting Gardner v. Florida, 1977).

Of course, the right to present evidence is not limited to capital cases. In Cleveland Board of Education v. Loudermill (1985), for example, the Supreme Court held that government employees are entitled to an opportunity to present their side of the story before being terminated, barring exigent circumstances. In Memphis Light, Gas & Water Division v. Craft (1978), the Court held that public utility customers who believe they are being overcharged or charged for services not rendered must be afforded an opportunity for informal consultation with utility company personnel empowered to correct any mistakes before termination of service. In Hewitt v. Helms (1983), the Court held that prisoners transferred to administrative segregation pending an investigation of disciplinary charges are entitled to present their views to the prison decisionmaker, ordinarily in writing, on whether they should remain in segregation pending completion of the investigation. And in Hamdi v. Rumsfeld (2004), a plurality of the Court held that "a citizen-detainee seeking to challenge his classification as an enemy combatant must receive . . . a fair opportunity to rebut the Government's factual assertions. . . ."

Laws creating irrebuttable presumptions deprive individuals of the opportunity to be heard on the matter and to present evidence to rebut the presumption. For example, in Stanley v. Illinois (1972), the Court struck down a state statutory scheme that denied unmarried fathers the opportunity to be heard on their fitness as parents before their children were removed from their custody. The state had presumed that all unmarried fathers were unqualified to raise their children. "It insists on presuming rather than proving [the father's] unfitness solely because it is more convenient to presume than to prove. Under the Due Process Clause that advantage is insufficient to justify refusing a father a hearing when the issue at stake is the dismemberment of his family" (Stanley v. Illinois, 1972). Because the right to the custody and companionship of one's child is a protected liberty interest and because some unmarried fathers are fit to parent their children, the Court held that they are entitled to a hearing on the issue, with the attendant right to offer evidence of their fitness (Stanley v. Illinois, 1972). Likewise, in Vlandis v. Kline (1973), the Court invalidated a state law that irrebuttably presumed that individuals who applied to a state university from outside the state were nonresidents for tuition purposes. "[S]tandards of due process require that the State allow such an individual the opportunity *to present evidence* showing that he is a bona fide resident entitled to the in-state rates" (Vlandis v. Kline, 1973; see also Cleveland Bd. of Educ. v. LaFleur, 1974; Bell v. Burson, 1971).[22]

In another irrebuttable presumption case, Michael H. v. Gerald D. (1989), the Court considered the constitutionality of a state statute that conclusively presumed that a child born to a married woman living with her husband is a child of the marriage. The putative father, who had engaged in an adulterous relationship with the child's mother at the time of conception, argued that he had a procedural due process right to attempt to establish his paternity. A plurality of the Court declined to view the case as raising any question of procedural due process, concluding instead that the case turned on the "fit" between the classification drawn by the statute and the policy it purported to serve, a substantive due process question (Michael H. v. Gerald D., 1989). But five Justices agreed that "the flaw inhering in a conclusive presumption that terminates a constitutionally protected interest without any hearing whatsoever is a *procedural* one": "the State has declared a certain fact relevant, indeed controlling, yet has denied a particular class of litigants a hearing to establish that fact. This is precisely the kind of flaw that procedural due process is designed to correct" (Michael H. v. Gerald D., 1989, Brennan, J., dissenting). Four of these five justices concluded that the statute at issue was invalid because it denied the putative father an opportunity to establish his paternity, while the fifth Justice concluded that the biological father had been given a fair opportunity to seek visitation rights (Michael H. v. Gerald D., 1989, Stevens, J., concurring in the judgment). Thus, a majority of the Court concluded that the putative father was constitutionally entitled to present evidence of his relationship with the child before a court could deny him visitation rights.

Due process protects the right to submit evidence only with respect to facts that are relevant to the outcome. In a recent decision upholding Connecticut's Megan's Law, the Supreme Court held that procedural due process does not guarantee convicted sex offenders released into the community an opportunity to prove that they are no longer dangerous where a statute requires the disclosure of their names, addresses and photographs regardless of current dangerousness. "Plaintiffs who assert a right to a hearing under the Due Process Clause must show that the facts they seek to establish in that hearing are relevant under the statutory scheme" (Conn. Dep't of Pub. Safety v. Doe, 2003).

### Opportunity to Appear in Person Before Decisionmaker

The right to offer evidence is broader than the right to appear in person before the decisionmaker. In some cases, the Court has held that due process guarantees the individual an opportunity to submit evidence in writing, but not orally or in person. What difference does the mode of presentation make and in what circumstances has the right to appear in person been recognized?

In Goldberg v. Kelly (1970), the Court identified three advantages afforded by personal appearance in support of its conclusion that a welfare recipient threatened with termination of benefits is entitled to "an effective opportunity to defend . . . by presenting his own arguments and evidence orally" when factual issues are in dispute. First, a poorly educated or unskilled individual may not be able to communicate effectively in writing, but she may be able to present her case effectively if afforded an opportunity to appear before the decisionmaker in person. Since many welfare recipients are poorly educated and lack the resources to obtain professional help, the Court concluded that written submissions are an inadequate substitute for the opportunity to appear in person. Second, oral presentations allow much greater flexibility, permitting the individual to mold her argument to the issues deemed important by the decisionmaker. A personal appearance permits give-and-take between the individual and the decisionmaker. Third, written submissions are ineffective in cases where credibility and veracity are at issue, as they are in welfare cases (Goldberg v. Kelly, 1970). Thus, personal appearances improve the accuracy of factfinding by ensuring that the decisionmaker receives complete information from the parties and is able to assess the veracity of the witnesses.

In addition to reducing the risk of error, an appearance by the person whose interest is at stake "'[promotes] participation and dialogue in . . . the decisionmaking process' by ensuring that individuals adversely affected by governmental action may confront the ultimate decisionmaker and thus play some part in formulating the ultimate decision" (United States v. Raddatz, 1980, Marshall, J., dissenting). Fairness and human dignity are advanced when the factfinder hears live testimony from the person whose protected interest is at stake.[23]

Beyond the welfare context, the Court has held that parolees and probationers are entitled to appear in person at both the initial probable cause and final revocation hearings and to speak on their own behalf (Gagnon v. Scarpelli, 1973; Morrissey v. Brewer, 1972). Even in the initial parole determination context, the inmate is entitled to appear before the parole board in person to ensure that the records it has before it are his and to "present any special considerations demonstrating why he is an appropriate candidate for parole" (Greenholtz v. Inmates of the Neb. Penal & Corr. Complex, 1979).[24] Likewise, a juvenile facing pre-trial detention has a right to speak on her own behalf (or through her parent or counsel) and to challenge any information supporting, or recommendation of, pre-trial detention (Schall v. Martin, 1984).

But due process does not guarantee an opportunity to appear in person before the decisionmaker when the probable value of a personal appearance is low. In Mathews v. Eldridge (1976), for example, the Court upheld an administrative scheme that afforded disability recipients the right to submit written evidence, but denied them the opportunity to appear in person before the decisionmaker before benefits were terminated. The Court distinguished *Goldberg*, noting that the critical issues in disability cases are the recipient's physical or mental condition, "a more sharply focused and easily documented decision than the typical determination of welfare entitlement" (Mathews v. Eldridge, 1976). Moreover, the state agency charged with administration of the disability program rarely questions the credibility or veracity of the medical specialists upon whom it relies for evaluation of recipients' medical conditions. Because the experts' written reports are presumed to be reliable and because the medical experts are able to communicate effectively in writing, the "potential value of an evidentiary hearing, or even oral presentation to the decisionmaker, is substantially less in this context than in *Goldberg*" (Mathews v. Eldridge, 1976; see also Dixon v. Love, 1977; Wozniak v. Conry, 7th Cir. 2001).

The Court has also dispensed with the right to appear in person before the decisionmaker in cases in which the government's interest outweighs the private interests at stake. For example, in pre-*Sandin* prison cases involving transfers to more restrictive quarters for administrative, rather than punitive, reasons—to protect the safety of other inmates and prison staff pending a hearing on disciplinary charges, for example—"the Due Process Clause requires only an informal nonadversary review of evidence. . . ." (Hewitt v. Helms, 1983). The inmate is entitled to present her views to the decisionmaker, but "ordinarily a written statement by the inmate will accomplish this purpose" (Hewitt v. Helms, 1983). In holding that due process does not guarantee an opportunity to appear in person in this context, the Court downplayed the significance of the inmate's private interest, noting that she was "merely transferred from one extremely restricted environment to an even more confined situation" (Hewitt v. Helms, 1983). The government's interest in segregating the inmate, on the other hand, was deemed to be "of great importance" and "weighty" because the transfer was made to preserve institutional security and safety and to prevent intimidation of prospective witnesses. In a dissenting opinion, Justice Stevens argued that due process assures inmates an opportunity to present their views in person because they often have little education and are poorly equipped to express themselves effectively in writing (Hewitt v. Helms, 1983, Stevens, J., dissenting).[25]

Even when the right to appear in person and to testify orally is protected, as it is in criminal cases, the right may be restricted to testifying before a magistrate, rather than the judge who will decide the motion (United States v. Raddatz, 1980). Acknowledging the difficulty a judge will have in making credibility determinations on the cold record, the Supreme Court nevertheless concluded that due process is satisfied as long as the judge retains discretion to "hear the witnesses live to resolve conflicting credibility claims" (United States v. Raddatz, 1980). As Justice Blackmun noted in his concurrence, when the judge adopts the magistrate's proposed result, she serves as a

> "backup" jurist whose review serves to enhance reliability and benefit the defendant. Respondent was afforded procedures by which a neutral decisionmaker, after seeing and hearing the witnesses, rendered a decision. After the decisionmaker found against him, respondent received a second turn, albeit on a cold record, before another neutral decisionmaker (United States v. Raddatz, 1980, Blackmun, J., concurring).

Even the majority conceded that "serious questions" would be raised if the judge were to *reject* the magistrate's proposed findings on credibility and substitute her own appraisal without seeing or hearing the witnesses whose credibility was at issue (United States v. Raddatz, 1980).

In some contexts—including criminal cases, prison disciplinary hearings and deportation hearings—due process requires the availability of an interpreter to assure that the opportunity to appear in person and be heard is meaningful for non-English speakers (Gonzales-Perez v. Harper, 8th Cir. 2001; Nazarova v. INS, 7th Cir. 1999).[26] In criminal cases, an indigent defendant who has obvious difficulty with the English language has a due process right to a court-appointed interpreter, but only if she requests one or if the state is otherwise put on notice of a significant language barrier (Luna v. Black, 8th Cir. 1985; United States v. Carrion, 1st Cir. 1973; United States *ex rel.* Negron v. State, 2d Cir. 1970). Non-indigent criminal defendants, represented by retained counsel, who do not speak English have a right to an interpreter, but not necessarily a court-appointed one (United States v. Martinez, 5th Cir. 1980). In some deportation cases or portions of cases, the need for an interpreter may be so strong that the government must bear the cost of providing one (Nazarova v. INS, 7th Cir. 1999; United States v. Leon-Leon, 9th Cir. 1994).[27]

### *Opportunity to Call Witnesses*

The right to call witnesses to testify on one's behalf is "basic to a fair hearing" (Wolff v. McDonnell, 1974). In the criminal context, this right is specifically protected by the Sixth Amendment, which guarantees the accused "the right . . . to have compulsory process for obtaining witnesses in his favor. . . ." (U.S. Const. amend. VI; see also Chambers v. Mississippi, 1973). Beyond the criminal context, the Due Process Clause ordinarily guarantees the right to call witnesses, especially when a loss of physical liberty is threatened. Thus, for example, the Court has recognized a due process right to call witnesses when an individual faces indefinite commitment under a sex offenders statute (Specht v. Patterson, 1967), revocation of parole (Morrissey v. Brewer, 1972) or probation (Gagnon v. Scarpelli, 1973), or an involuntary transfer from a prison to a mental hospital (Vitek v. Jones, 1980). The Court has even recognized that the right to offer oral testimony may be "essential" in some cases involving property interests (Fed. Deposit Ins. Corp. v. Mallen, 1988; see also Elliott v. Weinberger, 9th Cir. 1975).

Due process does not guarantee a right to call witnesses in all situations, however, and in some cases, the right may be qualified. In determining whether an opportunity to call witnesses in a given context is protected and to what extent, the Court has applied the *Eldridge* balancing test, weighing the significance of the private interest at stake, the administrative burden of providing an opportunity to call witnesses, and the risk of erroneous deprivation in the absence of oral testimony.

In the prison discipline context, the Court has relied most heavily on the first two of these factors to limit the right of inmates to call witnesses. When a prisoner is accused of a disciplinary infraction and faces a loss of good-time credits, the threatened deprivation does not work any immediate change in her physical liberty; the good-time credits may be restored and even if they are not, the loss may not affect the actual date of parole. Thus, the threatened sanction does not necessarily result in a loss of physical liberty, as it does in the parole or probation revocation contexts (Wolff v. McDonnell, 1974). More important, the Court noted the "very different stake the State has in the structure and content of the prison disciplinary hearing" (Wolff v. McDonnell, 1974). In the "tightly controlled" prison environment, tension between guards and inmates is "unremitting." When inmates bring charges against other inmates or testify against them at disciplinary hearings,

> [r]etaliation is much more than a theoretical possibility; and the basic and unavoidable task of providing reasonable personal safety for guards and inmates may be at stake, to say nothing of the impact of disciplinary confrontations and the resulting escalation of personal antagonisms on the important aims of the correctional process (Wolff v. McDonnell, 1974).

In this unique context, the Court held that due process requires an opportunity for the inmate to "call witnesses and present documentary evidence in his defense when permitting him to do so will not be unduly hazardous to institutional safety or correctional goals" (Wolff v. McDonnell, 1974). While recognizing that "[o]rdinarily, the right to present evidence is basic to a fair hearing," the Court qualified the right to call witnesses from the prison population, vesting substantial discretion in prison officials to refuse to call witnesses or provide access to witnesses from whom written statements are sought when the potential for disruption or reprisal, or the need for swift punishment, so dictates (Wolff v. McDonnell, 1974; see also Vitek v. Jones, 1980).[28]

In the school discipline context, too, the Court relied upon the brevity of the suspensions in issue and the enormous administrative cost of requiring adversarial hearings to conclude that due process does not require that "hearings in connection with short suspensions . . . afford the student the opportunity . . . to call his own witnesses to verify his version of the incident" (Goss v. Lopez, 1975). While declining to characterize 10-day school suspensions as *de minimis*, the Court conceded that "[l]onger suspensions or expulsions for the remainder of the school term, or permanently, may require more formal procedures" (Goss v. Lopez, 1975). The private interest at stake in the short suspension context is outweighed by the strain on administrative resources: "Brief disciplinary suspensions are almost countless. To impose in each such case even truncated trial-type procedures might overwhelm administrative facilities in many places, and, by diverting resources, cost more than it would save in educational effectiveness" (Goss v. Lopez, 1975). Formalizing the process might also destroy its effectiveness as a teaching tool.

In other contexts, the Court has focused more on the unlikelihood that witness testimony will reduce the risk of an erroneous deprivation. In determining the procedural protections that must be afforded when an inmate applies for parole, for instance, the Court considered whether a formal hearing, with the opportunity to call witnesses, would reduce the risk of error. In making this judgment, the Court distinguished the parole release context from the parole revocation context, in which due process guarantees a qualified right to call witnesses. In the parole revocation context, the factfinder must determine whether the parolee violated the conditions of her parole, a retrospective factual question on which witness testimony may well prove helpful. In the parole release context, on the other hand, the board must make a subjective appraisal of the inmate's readiness for release based on her behavior record and the gravity of the offense committed (Greenholtz v. Inmates of the Neb. Penal & Corr. Complex, 1979). Since the parole release decision is made largely on the basis of the inmate's prison record, due process is satisfied as long as she has an opportunity to ensure that the prison records before the board are in fact hers and to present any special considerations supporting her request for release (Greenholtz v. Inmates of the Neb. Penal & Corr. Complex, 1979). "Procedures designed to elicit specific facts, such as those required in [the parole revocation context] are not necessarily appropriate to [an initial] parole determination" (Greenholtz v. Inmates of the Neb. Penal & Corr. Complex, 1979).

### *Opportunity to Confront and Cross-Examine Adverse Witnesses*

The Court has frequently recognized the importance of cross-examination in the truth-seeking process:

> Certain principles have remained relatively immutable in our jurisprudence. One of these is that where governmental action seriously injures an individual, and the reasonableness of the action depends on fact findings, the evidence used to prove the Government's case must be disclosed to the individual so that he has an opportunity to show that it is untrue. While this is important in the case of documentary evidence, it is even more important where the evidence consists of the testimony of individuals whose memory might be faulty or who, in fact, might be perjurers or persons motivated by malice, vindictiveness, intolerance, prejudice, or jealousy. We have formalized these protections in the requirements of confrontation and cross-examination (Greene v. McElroy, 1959).

The late Professor Wigmore noted that "no safeguard for testing the value of human statements is comparable to that furnished by cross-examination. . . ."[29]

In criminal prosecutions, the right to confront and cross-examine adverse witnesses is guaranteed by the Sixth Amendment.[30] In other contexts, the Court has often recognized these rights "where important decisions turn on questions of fact" (Goldberg v. Kelly, 1970), especially in cases where an individual faces a loss of physical liberty. Thus, in juvenile delinquency proceedings (In re Gault, 1967), in sentencing proceedings under sex offender statutes (Specht v. Patterson, 1967), in parole (Morrissey v. Brewer, 1972) and probation revocation hearings (Gagnon v. Scarpelli, 1973), in hearings held to determine whether a prisoner should be transferred to a mental hospital (Vitek v. Jones, 1980), and in proceedings to determine whether a prisoner facing execution is sane (Ford v. Wainwright, 1986, plurality op.), the Court has held that due process guarantees a right to confront and cross-examine adverse witnesses. On the other hand, government employees facing termination for cause are not entitled to confront or cross-examine adverse witnesses unless they dispute the facts proffered to support their discharge (Cleveland Bd. of Educ. v. Loudermill, 1985).

Like the right to call witnesses, the availability and extent of the right to confront and cross-examine adverse witnesses depends upon the *Eldridge* factors: the significance of the private interest at stake; the governmental interest, including the administrative burden of affording an opportunity to confront and cross-examine witnesses, and the risk of erroneous deprivation in the absence of confrontation and cross-examination.

In the parole and probation revocation contexts, the Court has recognized the significance of the individual's liberty interest in freedom from bodily restraint, but has also considered the governmental need to protect the safety of informants. Thus, the right to cross-examine witnesses in the revocation context is a qualified one: the parolee or probationer may confront and question anyone who has provided adverse information against her *unless* the hearing officer determines that the informant would face a risk of harm if her identity were disclosed (Gagnon v. Scarpelli, 1973; Morrissey v. Brewer, 1972; see also Vitek v. Jones, 1980).

The governmental interest in institutional security counsels against cross-examination even more strongly in the prison discipline context. When an inmate seeks to cross-examine an accuser unknown to her, the mere disclosure of the accuser's identity "may pose a high risk of reprisal within the institution" (Wolff v. McDonnell, 1974). Even when the inmate knows the accuser, the risk of lingering resentment may be substantial. Emphasizing the "considerable potential for havoc inside the prison walls," the increased length and unwieldiness of proceedings that afford a right to cross-examine, and an adequate basis for decision without cross-examination, the Court held that due process does not require an opportunity to cross-examine adverse witnesses in this context (Wolff v. McDonnell, 1974). Prison officials have discretion to determine the cases in which a right to cross-examine should be afforded and need not provide a statement of reasons explaining why that opportunity is denied (Baxter v. Palmigiano, 1976).

Other governmental interests have affected the *Eldridge* balance in different contexts. For example, the government's interest in avoiding the cost of protracted proceedings supported the Court's holding that due process does not require an opportunity to confront and cross-examine adverse witnesses in connection with short suspensions from school (Goss v. Lopez, 1975) or criminal sentencing when the judge relies on a written sentencing report (Williams v. New York, 1949). Likewise, the interest in maintaining a healthy parent-child relationship counsels against recognition of a right to cross-examine witnesses when a parent seeks to have a child committed to a mental health care facility (Parham v. J.R., 1979).

> Since the parents can and usually do play a significant role in the treatment while the child is hospitalized and even more so after release, there is a serious risk that an adversary confrontation will adversely affect the ability of the parents to assist the child while in the hospital. Moreover, it will make his subsequent return home more difficult (Parham v. J.R., 1979).

In addition to considering the private and governmental interests at stake, the Court has weighed the risk of erroneous deprivation and the likelihood that affording a right to confront and cross-examine would reduce that risk. In cases where the facts at issue are objective or lend themselves to documentary proof, the Court has been most willing to relax these rights. For example, in Mathews v. Eldridge (1976), the Court noted that decisions regarding eligibility for disability benefits are likely to turn on "unbiased medical reports by physician specialists," whose credibility is not likely to be challenged. Thus, because the risk of error is low, the potential value of a predeprivation evidentiary hearing, with the attendant right of cross-examination, is reduced (see also Dixon v. Love, 1977).

On the other hand, when the issues are subjective or complex or the motives or credibility of the witness may be questioned, an opportunity to cross-examine will reduce the risk of an erroneous deprivation. For example, in Ford v. Wainwright (1986), the Court recognized a right to cross-examine psychiatric experts when the sanity of a prisoner facing execution was called into question:

> Cross-examination of the psychiatrists, or perhaps a less formal equivalent, would contribute markedly to the process of seeking truth in sanity disputes by bringing to light the bases for each expert's beliefs, the precise factors underlying those beliefs, any history of error or caprice of the examiner, any personal bias with respect to the issue of capital punishment, the expert's degree of certainty about his or her own conclusions, and the precise meaning of ambiguous words used in the report. Without some questioning of the experts concerning their technical conclusions, a factfinder simply cannot be expected to evaluate the various opinions, particularly when they are themselves inconsistent (Ford v. Wainwright, 1986, plurality op.).

Finally, the Court has considered the nature of the hearing and the decision to be made in determining whether due process guarantees a right to confront and cross-examine adverse witnesses. For example, in Brock v. Roadway Express, Inc. (1987), the Court found that due process did not guarantee a right to confront and cross-examine witnesses during an administrative investigation culminating in an order that temporarily deprived a party of property. In *Brock*, the Court considered the constitutionality of a federal statute, the Surface Transportation Assistance Act of 1982, which protects truck drivers from being fired in retaliation for refusing to operate unsafe vehicles. Section 405 of the statute (49 U.S.C. § 31105) authorizes the Department of Labor to conduct a preliminary investigation of challenged discharges. If the Secretary finds reasonable cause to believe that a driver has been discharged in violation of the statute, she must order the employer to reinstate the driver. At this point, the employer may request an evidentiary hearing and a final decision by the Secretary. An employer challenged the constitutionality of the statute, arguing that the failure to provide an evidentiary hearing and to allow cross-examination of adverse witnesses *before* issuance of the temporary reinstatement order deprived it of property without due process. Since cross-examination would "extend . . . inordinately the period in which the employee must suffer unemployment" without increasing the reliability of the preliminary reasonable cause finding, the Court held that "cross-examination of the employee's witnesses need not be afforded *at this stage of the proceedings*" (Brock v. Roadway Express, Inc., 1987, plurality op.). Focusing on the preliminary nature of the reasonable cause finding, the Court added that "[f]inal assessments of the credibility of supporting witnesses are appropriately reserved for the administrative law judge, before whom an opportunity for complete cross-examination of opposing witnesses is provided" (Brock v. Roadway Express, Inc., 1987, plurality op.; see also Cleveland Bd. of Educ. v. Loudermill, 1985). Dissenting Justices argued that since the disputed issues were factual and the final hearing might not be held promptly, due process required an opportunity to test the strength of the evidence through confrontation and cross-examination *before* issuance of the reinstatement order (Brock v. Roadway Express, Inc., 1987, Brennan, J., concurring in part and dissenting in part; Stevens, J., dissenting in part). They chastised the majority for minimizing "the critical role that cross-examination plays in accurate factfinding.

### *A Decision Based on the Evidence and Supported by a Statement of Reasons*

It has long been recognized that courts and other decisionmakers may take judicial or administrative notice of matters of common knowledge and indisputable fact in order to save the time and other resources that would be expended if evidence were offered to prove them (Ohio Bell Tel. Co. v. Pub. Utils. Comm'n, 1937).[31] But proof is required as to matters not universally agreed upon. For example, while a court may take judicial notice of the fact that Confederate money depreciated during the Civil War, evidence is required to prove the extent of the depreciation at a given time and place (Ohio Bell Tel. Co. v. Pub. Utils. Comm'n, 1937). Even when judicial or administrative notice is taken, moreover, litigants are free to dispute the matter by evidence if they believe it is disputable (Ohio Bell Tel. Co. v. Pub. Utils. Comm'n, 1937).

Except as to matters subject to judicial or administrative notice, courts and other decisionmakers are required to base their decisions only on the evidence offered at the hearing (Ohio Bell Tel. Co. v. Pub. Utils. Comm'n, 1937; United States v. Abilene & S. Ry. Co., 1924). This general due process requirement discourages arbitrary decisionmaking and protects the right to confront and cross-examine witnesses. For if decisionmakers could base their decisions on evidence not offered at the hearing, there would be no opportunity to challenge the accuracy of the information relied upon, to rebut it, or to cross-examine the individuals providing it. Presumably, it was for these reasons that the Supreme Court in Goldberg v. Kelly (1970) held that "the decisionmaker's conclusion . . . must rest solely on the legal rules and evidence adduced at the hearing" (see also Sheppard v. Maxwell, 1966).

These principles are not necessarily violated if the decisionmakers meet with proponents of the government's position before the hearing (Washington v. Harper, 1990). "Absent evidence of resulting bias, or evidence that the actual decision is made before the hearing, allowing respondent to contest the staff's position at the hearing satisfies the requirement that the opportunity to be heard 'must be granted at a meaningful time and in a meaningful manner'" (Washington v. Harper, 1990, quoting Armstrong v. Manzo, 1965).

The Court has crafted an exception from the general rule that decisionmakers must base their decisions only on evidence presented at the hearing. Since inmates in the prison disciplinary context have no general right to confront and cross-examine adverse witnesses (Wolff v. McDonnell, 1974), the main premise for limiting factfinders to the evidence offered does not obtain in prison discipline cases (Baxter v. Palmigiano, 1976):

> Due to the peculiar environment of the prison setting, it may be that certain facts relevant to the disciplinary determination do not come to light until after the formal hearing. It would be unduly restrictive to require that such facts be excluded from consideration, inasmuch as they may provide valuable information with respect to the incident in question and may assist prison officials in tailoring penalties to enhance correctional goals (Baxter v. Palmigiano, 1976).

Even if due process permits the prison decisionmaker to consider evidence not offered at the hearing, it nevertheless requires that there be some evidence to support the decision reached. In a variety of contexts, including the prison discipline context, the Court has recognized that a decision that deprives a person of a protected interest violates due process if it is not supported by any evidence

(Superintendent v. Hill, 1985; Douglas v. Buder, 1973; United States *ex rel.* Vajtauer v. Comm'r of Immigr., 1927). "This standard is met if 'there was some evidence from which the conclusion of the administrative tribunal could be deduced. . . .'" (Superintendent v. Hill, 1985).[32]

To ensure compliance with the general rule that the decisionmaker base his decision only on the evidence presented at the hearing, the *Goldberg* Court held that he "should state the reasons for his determination and indicate the evidence he relied on, though his statement need not amount to a full opinion or even formal findings of fact and conclusions of law" (Goldberg v. Kelly, 1970). Since a reviewing court would be unable to determine if the decisionmaker's findings were supported by the evidence if the evidence relied upon were unknown, the written statement facilitates appellate review or judicial review of agency decisionmaking (Black v. Romano, 1985; Specht v. Patterson, 1967; Ohio Bell Tel. Co. v. Pub. Utils. Comm'n, 1937).

This "statement of reasons" requirement not only facilitates appellate or judicial review, but also furthers other purposes. First, "the provision for a written record helps to insure that administrators, faced with possible scrutiny by state officials and the public, and perhaps even the courts, . . . will act fairly" (Wolff v. McDonnell, 1974). Second, a written record assures that if a decision rendered in one context has collateral consequences, at least the nature of the original proceeding will be well understood. For example, a finding by a prison adjustment committee that an inmate violated a disciplinary rule may not only result in the loss of good-time credits, but it may also support a transfer decision by the warden or a parole denial by the parole board. "Written records of proceedings will thus protect the inmate against collateral consequences based on a misunderstanding of the nature of the original proceeding" (Wolff v. McDonnell, 1974).

The Court has not offered a clear explanation of when due process requires a statement of reasons for a decision that results in a deprivation of a protected interest (Black v. Romano, 1985, Marshall, J., concurring). While the post-*Goldberg* Court has suggested that situations requiring a statement of reasons "are the exception rather than the rule" (Harris v. Rivera, 1981, per curiam), it has nevertheless required a written statement of reasons in a variety of contexts beyond the termination of welfare benefits. For example, even as the Court excepted prison adjustment committees from the general rule requiring decisionmakers to base their decisions only on the evidence presented, it explicitly required them to provide a written statement of the evidence relied on and the reasons for the disciplinary action taken (Baxter v. Palmigiano, 1976; Wolff v. McDonnell, 1974).[33] Likewise, when a prisoner is transferred to a mental hospital, the factfinder must provide a written statement of the evidence relied on and the reasons for transferring the inmate (Vitek v. Jones, 1980). And in the parole and probation revocation contexts, both the independent officer who conducts the preliminary hearing and the board that conducts the final revocation hearing must state the reasons for their decisions and indicate the evidence relied upon (Gagnon v. Scarpelli, 1973; Morrissey v. Brewer, 1972).[34]

In the parole and probation revocation contexts, the Court has read the statement requirement narrowly. Thus, it has held that due process does not require the parole board or other factfinder to demonstrate on the record that it considered alternatives to incarceration or to explain its reasons for rejecting them (Black v. Romano, 1985).

> [T]he fairness guaranteed by due process does not require a reviewing court to second-guess the factfinder's discretionary decision as to the appropriate sanction. . . . [A] general requirement that the factfinder elaborate upon the reasons for a course *not taken* would unduly burden the revocation proceeding without significantly advancing the interests of the probationer (Black v. Romano, 1985, emphasis added).

Nor need the parole board, when reviewing an application for parole, "specify the particular 'evidence' in the inmate's file or at his interview on which it rests the discretionary determination that an inmate is not ready for conditional release" (Greenholtz v. Inmates of the Neb. Penal & Corr. Complex, 1979). As long as the board informs the inmate "in what respects he falls short of qualifying for parole," no further process is due (Greenholtz v. Inmates of the Neb. Penal & Corr. Complex, 1979).

Likewise, when prison officials deny an inmate the opportunity to call witnesses at a disciplinary hearing, the

> prison officials may be required to explain in a limited manner, the reason why witnesses were not allowed to testify, but . . . they may do so either by making the explanation a part of the "administrative record" in the disciplinary proceeding, or by presenting testimony in court if the deprivation of a "liberty" interest is challenged because of that claimed defect in the hearing. In other words, the prison officials may choose to explain their decision at the hearing, or they may choose to explain it "later" (Ponte v. Real, 1985).

The Court has declined to require *any* statement of reasons when a board of pardons denies an application for commutation of a sentence (Conn. Bd. of Pardons v. Dumschat, 1981) or when a state judge conducting a bench trial acquits a criminal defendant (Harris v. Rivera, 1981). Since the commutation process is entirely discretionary and inmates have no right to have their sentences commuted, the "state cannot be required to explain its reasons for a decision when it is not required to act on prescribed grounds" (Conn. Bd. of Pardons v. Dumschat, 1981). Likewise, since review of state criminal judgments in federal habeas corpus proceedings is available only if federal constitutional rights were violated and since an inconsistent verdict (acquitting one defendant but convicting another) is not necessarily unconstitutional, state judges are not required to offer an explanation of inconsistencies between bench trial verdicts (Harris v. Rivera, 1981).

In an effort to make sense of this uneven line of cases, Justice Marshall has posited that the *Eldridge* balancing test governs the written statement requirement, just as it governs other procedural due process issues:

> When written reasons would contribute significantly to the "fairness and reliability" of the process by which an individual is deprived of liberty or property, reasons must be given in this form unless the balance between the individual interest affected and the burden to the government tilts against the individual. Whether written reasons would make such a contribution in any particular case depends on a variety of factors, including the nature of the decisionmaking tribunal, the extent to which other procedural protections already assure adequately the fairness and accuracy of the proceedings, and the nature of the question being decided (Black v. Romano, 1985, Marshall, J., concurring).

### *Right to Counsel*

The Sixth Amendment to the Constitution guarantees the accused in all criminal prosecutions "the Assistance of Counsel for his defence" (U.S. Const. amend. VI).[35] The Due Process Clause, too, guarantees a right to counsel in certain situations. Before exploring those situations, let us first consider how the introduction of counsel may change the nature of a proceeding. From the perspective of the person whose interest is at issue, counsel may be necessary to make the right to be heard a meaningful one (Powell v. Alabama, 1932). As the Court noted in Goldberg v. Kelly (1970), "Counsel can help delineate the issues, present the factual contentions in an orderly manner, conduct cross-examination, and generally safeguard the interests of the recipient." In addition, counsel can explain the intricacies of the law to an untrained litigant, make a skilled inquiry into the facts, and insist that procedural protections be afforded (In re Gault, 1967).

Not all of the effects of participation by counsel are salutary, however. For example, participation by counsel may delay or lengthen the proceedings. Delay may be the inevitable by-product of an attorney's careful scrutiny of the government's proof, or it may be the intentional goal of an attorney serving her client's best interests. If the state's adversary is represented by counsel, the government may provide one for itself (Gagnon v. Scarpelli, 1973). With counsel appearing on both sides, a short and amicable conference may turn into a protracted, adversarial hearing.

In addition to causing delay, the introduction of counsel increases the government's cost in providing a hearing. Obviously, in cases where the government provides appointed counsel for its adversary, the cost increases. But even in cases where the individual is represented by retained counsel, if that attorney is provided by a legal services organization supported by public funds, such representation increases the government's cost as well.[36] The introduction of counsel also increases the length of the record and makes judicial review more likely, both of which increase the financial cost to the state (Gagnon v. Scarpelli, 1973). Finally, the nature of the hearing may change when counsel appear, as the decisionmaker becomes more self-conscious of its judicial or quasi-judicial role (Gagnon v. Scarpelli, 1973; Walters v. Nat'l Ass'n of Radiation Survivors, 1985). With these benefits and costs in mind, let us now consider the case law addressing the due process right to counsel.

Given the magnitude of the government's financial cost in providing appointed counsel, the Court has required a compelling private interest and a significant risk of erroneous deprivation before concluding that due process requires appointed counsel. In determining when these factors of the *Eldridge* balancing test outweigh the government's interest in avoiding the financial cost, the Court has announced two conditions: generally the litigant must face a loss of physical liberty and she must be unable to exercise her rights without assistance by counsel (Lassiter v. Dep't of Soc. Servs., 1981). Put differently, the Court has identified a presumption against appointed counsel unless the litigant's physical liberty is at stake.

In criminal cases in which the accused faces a risk of imprisonment, the Court has relied on due process in addition to the Sixth Amendment to find a right to appointed counsel. In Specht v. Patterson (1967), for example, the Court held that due process guarantees a right to counsel to persons convicted of a sex offense who, under a sex offenders statute, face an indeterminate sentence of from one day to life if they are found to be habitual offenders. Likewise, in Douglas v. California (1963), the Court relied on both the Equal Protection and Due Process Clauses to hold that an indigent criminal defendant is entitled to appointed counsel to pursue a first appeal of a criminal conviction.[37] In Evitts v. Lucey (1985), it held that due process guarantees effective assistance of counsel on the first appeal of right. Before 1963, when the Court incorporated the Sixth Amendment right to counsel into the Due Process Clause of the Fourteenth Amendment (Gideon v. Wainwright, 1963), the Court held that the Due Process Clause itself guaranteed indigent, illiterate defendants a right to appointed counsel in a capital case (Powell v. Alabama, 1932). In addition to emphasizing the risk of incarceration or death faced by the defendants, the Court emphasized the inability of "the ignorant and illiterate, or those of feeble intellect" to present an effective defense without the assistance of counsel (Powell v. Alabama, 1932).

Beyond the criminal context, too, the Court has imposed the same two conditions—loss of physical liberty and inability to exercise one's rights without assistance—in determining whether a due process right to appointed counsel exists. For example, the Court has recognized a right to appointed counsel in juvenile delinquency proceedings if a determination of delinquency "may result in commitment to an institution in which the juvenile's freedom is curtailed" (In re Gault, 1967; see also Schall v. Martin, 1984; Kent v. United States, 1966). In addition to the threatened loss of physical liberty, the Court emphasized the child's need for counsel:

"The most informal and well-intentioned of judicial proceedings are technical; few adults without legal training can influence or even understand them; *certainly children cannot.* Papers are drawn and charges expressed in legal language. Events follow one another in a manner that appears arbitrary and confusing to the uninitiated. Decisions, unexplained, appear too official to challenge. But with lawyers come records of proceedings; records make possible appeals . . . ." (In re Gault, 1967, quoting President's Comm'n on Law Enforcement & Admin. of Justice, The Challenge of Crime in a Free Society 86 (1967), emphasis added).

In addition to the delinquency context, four of the five Justices who reached the merits in Vitek v. Jones (1980) concluded that an indigent prisoner facing an involuntary transfer to a mental hospital is entitled to appointed counsel at the pre-transfer hearing. Although the prisoner's liberty interest is already seriously compromised by her conviction and sentence of imprisonment, the transfer to a mental hospital would expose her to involuntary psychiatric treatment. In addition to this loss of physical liberty, the *Vitek* plurality stressed the stigma suffered by persons who are classified as mentally ill and the mentally ill prisoner's need for assistance. "A prisoner thought to be suffering from a mental disease or defect requiring involuntary treatment probably has an even greater need for legal assistance [than illiterate and uneducated prisoners], for such a prisoner is more likely to be unable to understand or exercise his rights" (Vitek v. Jones, 1980, plurality op.).[38]

While the Court has been willing to generalize about the inability of juveniles and mentally ill patients to exercise their procedural rights without counsel and the concomitant risk of erroneous deprivation, it declined to make such a generalization in two other cases, holding only that states should determine, on a case-by-case basis, whether individuals need legal assistance. In the first such case, Gagnon v. Scarpelli (1973), the Court held that state authorities that administer the parole and probation systems should decide, on a case-by-case basis, whether indigent parolees or probationers are entitled to appointed counsel at revocation hearings.[39] Since parole and probation revocation proceedings place the individual at risk of losing her physical liberty, the Court focused on the needs of probationers and parolees for assistance. It recognized that "the effectiveness of the [constitutionally-secured procedural] rights . . . may in some circumstances depend on the use of skills which the probationer or parolee is unlikely to possess" and that "the unskilled or uneducated probationer or parolee may well have difficulty in presenting his version of a disputed set of facts where the presentation requires the examining or cross-examining of witnesses or the offering or dissecting of complex documentary evidence" (Gagnon v. Scarpelli, 1973). But parolees and probationers who are convicted of crimes committed while on parole or probation, and those who admit the charges against them, likely may not need such assistance. In light of the "direct costs and serious collateral disadvantages" associated with appointed counsel and the likely change in the nature of the proceedings when counsel are introduced,[40] the Court stated that due process requires appointed counsel only when the state concludes that the individual parolee or probationer cannot fairly present her version of a disputed fact without the assistance of a trained advocate (Gagnon v. Scarpelli, 1973).[41]

Likewise, in Lassiter v. Department of Social Services (1981), the Court declined to hold that due process requires appointed counsel for all indigent parents facing termination of their parental rights. Starting with the presumption against appointed counsel unless the litigant's physical liberty is at stake, the Court focused not only on the litigant's ability to put on her defense, but also on the Mathews v. Eldridge factors. Positing that the "net weight" of these factors could overcome the presumption against appointed counsel, the Court noted that a parent's interests in her child and in the accuracy and justice of a decision to terminate her parental rights are commanding. The state shares the parent's interest in a correct decision. The inability of some parents to understand and refute expert medical and psychiatric testimony, and their uncommon difficulty dealing with life in general and the stress of the termination hearing in particular, could, but would not always, combine to make the risk of an erroneous deprivation of parental rights insupportably high. The state's pecuniary interest in avoiding the costs of appointed counsel ordinarily would not be significant enough to overcome the private interests at stake (Lassiter v. Dep't of Soc. Servs., 1981).

The *Eldridge* factors would overcome the presumption against appointed counsel when the "parent's interests were at their strongest, the State's interests were at their weakest, and the risks of error were at their peak," and in that case, due process would require appointed counsel (Lassiter v. Dep't of Soc. Servs., 1981). But because the "factors will not always be so distributed," due process does not require appointment of counsel in all parental rights termination proceedings. Therefore, entitlement to appointed counsel in termination cases should be determined on a case-by-case basis in the trial court, subject to appellate review (Lassiter v. Dep't of Soc. Servs., 1981). Some state courts have extended *Lassiter*'s reasoning beyond the termination of parental rights context, holding that due process may require the appointment of counsel to represent indigent parents in dependency and neglect proceedings as well (Wofford v. Eid, Fla. Dist. Ct. App. 1996; Watson v. Div. of Family Servs., Del. 2002).[42]

Even in circumstances where no right to appointed counsel exists, due process may require a right to retained counsel (Goldberg v. Kelly, 1970). Since the government's financial burden is lower if counsel is retained, a private interest less compelling than loss of physical liberty, when coupled with a genuine risk of erroneous deprivation, may suffice to tip the balance in favor of a due process right to retained counsel. On the other hand, if the government has an interest that would be frustrated by the presence of counsel, the balance may tip the other way.

In the prison discipline context in particular, the Court has held that the government's interest outweighs the other factors, resulting in a denial of the right to counsel (Baxter v. Palmigiano, 1976; Wolff v. McDonnell, 1974). In these cases, the Court emphasized the increased costs to the state and other negative consequences that would result if counsel were introduced:

> The insertion of counsel into the disciplinary process would inevitably give the proceedings a more adversary cast and tend to reduce their utility as a means to further correctional goals. There would also be delay and very practical problems in providing counsel in sufficient numbers at the time and place where hearings are to be held. At this stage of the development of these procedures we are not prepared to hold that inmates have a right to either retained or appointed counsel in disciplinary proceedings (Wolff v. McDonnell, 1974).[43]

Similar concerns led the Court to hold that students threatened with short suspensions from school are not entitled to the opportunity to secure counsel (Goss v. Lopez, 1975).

Finally, if other procedural safeguards reduce the need for counsel, the balance of interests may support a denial of access to counsel. In Walters v. National Ass'n of Radiation Survivors (1985), the Court held that veterans seeking Veterans' Administration benefits may be denied any realistic opportunity to obtain counsel by a statute that limits attorneys' fees in such cases to ten dollars. In upholding the fee-limiting statute, the Court emphasized both the government's interest in preserving a non-adversarial, informal decision-making process and the numerous "substitute safeguards" that exist. For example, various veterans' organizations provide the free assistance of trained service agents to veterans filing benefits claims, and agency decisionmakers are obligated under governing regulations to assist claimants in developing their claims and to resolve all reasonable doubts in favor of claimants. In these circumstances, "the need for counsel is considerably diminished" (Walters v. Nat'l Ass'n of Radiation Survivors, 1985; cf. Middendorf v. Henry, 1976).

### *Standard of Proof*

Courts typically apply one of three standards of proof in any given case: proof by a preponderance of the evidence; proof by clear and convincing evidence; or proof beyond a reasonable doubt. The standard of proof not only allocates the risk of error between the litigants, but indicates the relative importance of the ultimate decision to be made (Addington v. Texas, 1979). Put differently, "a standard of proof represents an attempt to instruct the factfinder concerning the degree of confidence our society thinks he should have in the correctness of factual conclusions for a particular type of adjudication" (In re Winship, 1970, Harlan, J., concurring).

In determining whether due process requires a heightened standard of proof, the Court has emphasized four factors: the nature of the private interest at stake; the standard of proof applied by a majority of states in that kind of case; the role of the state in the litigation; and the nature of the issues to be decided in the proceeding. In civil cases involving monetary disputes between private parties, society has little concern in the outcome because the private interest is strictly a financial one. Therefore, in litigation between private parties where only property is at stake, courts apply the preponderance of the evidence standard and litigants share the risk of error roughly equally (Addington v. Texas, 1979). When, on the other hand, the state is a contestant and the private interests at stake involve liberty interests that are "particularly important" and "more substantial than mere loss of money," the Court has held that due process requires a heightened standard of proof (Addington v. Texas, 1979, quoted in Santosky v. Kramer, 1982; see also Cruzan v. Dir., Mo. Dep't of Health, 1990). Even when the liberty interest is precious, however, the Court has declined to interpret the Due Process Clause as requiring a more exacting standard of proof unless a majority of states have adopted such a standard in that kind of case (Rivera v. Minnich, 1987). Finally, the court has considered the nature of the issue to be decided and its susceptibility to proof by objective fact. Let us now examine the cases in which the Court has considered these factors to determine when due process requires a more exacting standard of proof.

The "beyond a reasonable doubt" standard is designed to minimize the risk of an erroneous judgment as much as possible. The party with the burden of proof assumes almost the entire risk of error (Addington v. Texas, 1979). Before the *Eldridge* balancing test was announced, the Court held that due process requires application of the "beyond a reasonable doubt" standard in criminal and juvenile delinquency cases (In re Winship, 1970). In reaching this conclusion, the Court explicitly considered two of the factors mentioned above: the enormity of the defendant's interest in her freedom and reputation and the "virtually unanimous adherence to the reasonable-doubt standard in common-law jurisdictions" (In re Winship, 1970). The Court held that the "Due Process Clause protects the accused against conviction except upon proof beyond a reasonable doubt of every fact necessary to constitute the crime with which he is charged" (In re Winship, 1970).[44] The same considerations compelled the conclusion that juveniles charged with violations of the criminal law are entitled to the proof beyond a reasonable doubt standard (In re Winship, 1970).

In civil commitment cases, too, the gravity of the private interest at stake and the adoption by many states of heightened standards of proof led the Court to conclude that due process will not tolerate application of the preponderance standard (Addington v. Texas, 1979). As in criminal cases, the liberty interest at stake in commitment cases is very important: the individual's freedom from bodily restraint and from the stigma associated with an involuntary commitment. At that time, only two states had by statute or judicial opinion permitted involuntary commitment by a "preponderance of the evidence" standard, while a majority had adopted a heightened standard of proof (Addington v. Texas, 1979). These factors counseled against the preponderance standard. On the other hand, the state's legitimate interest in providing care for citizens with serious mental and emotional problems and its interest in protecting the community from those with dangerous propensities counseled against the "beyond a reasonable doubt" standard (Addington v. Texas, 1979). Searching for "a middle level of burden of proof that strikes a fair balance between the rights of the individual and the legitimate concerns of the state," the Court held that the standard of proof must be "equal to or greater than the 'clear and convincing' standard . . . to meet due process guarantees" (Addington v. Texas, 1979).[45]

In explaining why the "beyond a reasonable doubt" standard is not required in the civil commitment context, the *Addington* Court attempted to distinguish *Winship*, relying on the nature of the private interests at stake, the practices of the states in the criminal and civil commitment contexts, respectively, and the nature of the issues to be decided. Regarding the private interests at stake, the Court noted that the mentally ill are in need of treatment, so the release of a truly mentally ill person may be worse for the individual than the failure to convict the guilty. In addition, it recognized that the "beyond a reasonable doubt" standard has historically been reserved for criminal cases (Addington v. Texas, 1979). Finally, the Court noted that the nature of the inquiry in the two contexts is quite different. In criminal cases, the central question is a factual one: did the accused commit the crime? In civil commitment cases, on the other hand, in addition to ascertaining the facts, the decisionmaker must attempt to determine whether the individual is mentally ill and dangerous to herself or others. Since psychiatric diagnosis is far from certain and expert witnesses may have difficulty offering definite conclusions, the state might never be able to prove beyond a reasonable doubt that the individual is mentally ill and likely to be dangerous (Addington v. Texas, 1979; *cf.* Cooper v. Oklahoma, 1996).

Like the freedom from bodily restraint and stigma at issue in civil commitment cases, the right to parent one's child is a liberty interest sufficiently important to require the protection of a heightened standard of proof. In Santosky v. Kramer (1982), the Court required a finding of neglect by at least clear and convincing evidence before a state may irrevocably terminate a biological parent's rights in her children. In reaching its decision, the Court applied the *Eldridge* balancing test, noting that "in any given proceeding, the minimum standard of proof tolerated by the due process requirement reflects not only the weight of the private and public interests affected, but also a societal judgment about how the risk of error should be distributed between the litigants" (Santosky v. Kramer, 1982). In proceedings brought to terminate parental rights, all three *Eldridge* factors counsel in favor of a rigorous standard of proof. The parent's invaluable interest in the companionship and custody of her child is in jeopardy of irrevocable termination. The risk of erroneous factfinding in termination proceedings is significant given the imprecise substantive standards to be applied, the value-laden judgment to be made, the disparity between the resources available to the parent and the state, and the state's ability to bring multiple termination proceedings if the first is unsuccessful. And the state's urgent interest in the welfare of the child demands accurate factfinding, for the state has no interest in separating children from fit parents. Finally, a heightened standard of proof reduces the risk of mistake without imposing substantial administrative or fiscal burdens on the state (Santosky v. Kramer, 1982). Noting that a majority of states require a more exacting standard of proof in termination cases, the Court held that the preponderance standard is unconstitutional. In this context, "'the individual should not be asked to share equally with society the risk of error when the possible injury to the individual is significantly greater than any possible harm to the state'" (Santosky v. Kramer, 1982, quoting Addington v. Texas, 1979).

The Court has declined to extend *Santosky* to the paternity context, holding that application of the "preponderance of the evidence" standard of proof satisfies due process in the paternity context (Rivera v. Minnich, 1987). In reaching this decision, the Court again scrutinized the nature of the private interests at stake, the practices of the several states, and the state's role as litigant. In analyzing the private interests at stake, the Court noted that the putative father's interest in avoiding financial responsibility for another man's child and the mother's interest in holding the father financially responsible for his own child are "relatively equal. . . . Each would suffer in a similar way the consequences of an adverse ruling; thus it is appropriate that each share roughly equally the risk of an inaccurate factual determination" (Rivera v. Minnich, 1987). Thus, the Court ignored the psychological and emotional interests and social stigma at stake in a paternity suit and viewed the private (financial) interests to be in equipoise.

In addition to scrutinizing the private interests at stake, the Court emphasized that a majority of American jurisdictions view paternity suits as civil and apply the preponderance standard of proof (Rivera v. Minnich, 1987). A legislative judgment that is consistent with both the traditional and current practices of most states is "entitled to a powerful presumption of validity when it is challenged under the Due Process Clause of the Fourteenth Amendment" (Rivera v. Minnich, 1987). Noting that due process has been held to require a heightened standard of proof only when a majority of jurisdictions have adopted one, the Court held that the preponderance standard, which normally applies in civil cases involving monetary disputes between private parties, should govern in paternity cases as well (Rivera v. Minnich, 1987).

Finally, the Court noted that in all of the cases in which it had held that due process requires a heightened standard of proof—*Winship*, *Addington*, and *Santosky*—the state had been a contestant (Rivera v. Minnich, 1987). Because the state's resources are superior to virtually any individual's, this factor militates in favor of a heightened standard of proof in criminal, civil commitment and termination cases. Furthermore, the state can bring multiple suits to terminate a parent's rights, if the first suit is unsuccessful. In paternity suits, on the other hand, the "principal adversaries are the mother and the putative father, each of whom has an extremely important, but nevertheless relatively equal, interest in the outcome" (Rivera v. Minnich, 1987). And the entry of a final judgment bars a second paternity suit. Thus, there is no "'striking asymmetry in [the parties'] litigation options'" (Rivera v. Minnich, 1987, quoting Santosky v. Kramer, 1982).

Whereas in most of the standard of proof cases the Court has emphasized the significance of the private interest and the standard of proof applied by most states, in Washington v. Harper (1990), the Court focused on the malleability of the issue to be decided by the factfinder. There, the Court considered the standard of proof required when the state seeks to administer anti-psychotic medication to prisoners against their will. Even though the prisoner has a significant liberty interest at stake and even though the state is a litigant in the proceedings, the *Harper* Court summarily rejected the contention that the standard of proof should be by clear and convincing evidence. The Court dealt with the issue in a single sentence, stating, "This standard is neither required nor helpful when medical personnel are making the judgment required by the regulations here" (Washington v. Harper, 1990, citing Vitek v. Jones, 1980). Although the sentence itself is somewhat cryptic, the Court's citation to Vitek v. Jones (1980) and *Vitek*'s citation to Addington v. Texas (1979) help explain the Court's concern with a heightened standard of proof in this context. *Vitek* and *Addington* noted that the issue of mental illness "'turns on the *meaning* of the facts which must be interpreted by expert psychiatrists and psychologists,'" rather than exclusively on the underlying facts themselves (Vitek v. Jones, 1980, quoting Addington v. Texas, 1979, emphasis added). While it is appropriate to require prosecutors to meet the "beyond a reasonable doubt" standard in criminal cases, where they can readily prove what the defendant did, in forced treatment cases, the state would have a difficult time establishing the prisoner's mental illness and dangerousness to a high degree of certainty because psychiatric diagnosis is tentative and indeterminate. Although plausible, even this explanation is not entirely satisfactory, however, because the *Addington* Court itself held that due process requires application of the "clear and convincing evidence" standard in civil commitment cases even though the issue there, as in *Harper*, concerns the mental condition of the state's adversary.

In sum, due process may require a heightened standard of proof when the liberty interest at stake is significant, a majority of states apply a heightened standard of proof in the given context, the issues to be decided are factual in nature, and the state itself is a litigant.

### *Judicial Review of Agency Decisions*

Due process does not guarantee judicial review of all agency decisions. In fact, in deciding whether judicial review is available, due process often operates in the background because the federal Administrative Procedure Act (the "APA") guarantees persons adversely affected or aggrieved by federal agency action a right to judicial review unless another statute precludes it or the agency action is committed to agency discretion by law (5 U.S.C. §§ 701(a)(2), 702).[46]

When is agency action "committed to agency discretion by law"? If a statute confers power on an agency but provides no substantive standards on which a court could base its review, then the action is committed to the complete discretion of the agency and judicial review is proscribed (Webster v. Doe, 1988; Heckler v. Chaney, 1985). In other words, agency action is committed to agency discretion only where the mandate is so broad or the discretion so explicit that "there is no law [for a court] to apply" (Webster v. Doe, 1988; Citizens to Preserve Overton Park, Inc. v. Volpe, 1971). The Court has described section 701(a)(2) as "a very narrow exception," available only in "rare instances" (Citizens to Preserve Overton Park, Inc. v. Volpe, 1971).

Under the APA, there is a strong presumption in favor of judicial review (INS v. St. Cyr, 2001; McNary v. Haitian Refugee Ctr., Inc., 1991), although both the strength and scope of the presumption have been weakened in recent years.[47] Judicial review should be denied only upon a showing by clear and convincing evidence that Congress intended to deny such review (Bowen v. Mich. Acad. of Family Physicians, 1986; Abbott Labs. v. Gardner, 1967; Rusk v. Cort, 1962). Such clear and convincing evidence exists "whenever the congressional intent to preclude judicial review is 'fairly discernible in the statutory scheme'" (Block v. Cmty. Nutrition Inst., 1984). In making this judgment, courts consider specific statutory language; legislative history that is a reliable indicator of Congressional intent; contemporaneous judicial construction barring review and Congressional acquiescence in it; the collective import of legislative and judicial history of the statute; and inferences of intent drawn from the statutory scheme as a whole (Block v. Cmty. Nutrition Inst., 1984).

Even where a statute expressly bars judicial review of individual agency decisions, there continues to be a presumption in favor of judicial review of general agency policy, practice, regulation or methodology (McNary v. Haitian Refugee Ctr., Inc., 1991; Bowen v. Mich. Acad. of Family Physicians, 1986; Johnson v. Robison, 1974).[48] Likewise, even where Congress intends to preclude judicial review by committing a matter to an agency's discretion, it does not necessarily intend to bar review of constitutional claims (Webster v. Doe, 1988). Where Congress intends to preclude judicial review of constitutional claims, its intent must be clear (Webster v. Doe, 1988, citing Johnson v. Robison, 1974).[49]

What if Congress, expressly and unambiguously, seeks to preclude judicial review of a constitutional challenge to agency action? Would due process nevertheless require judicial review? The issue has not been squarely decided (*cf.* Barsky v. Bd. of Regents, 1954, Black, J., dissenting; St. Joseph Stock Yards Co. v. United States, 1936, Brandeis, J., concurring). There is no constitutional right to judicial review unless the challenged action arguably infringes a constitutional right.[50] Therefore, unless the challenged agency action implicates a constitutional right, courts defer to Congress regarding the availability of judicial review.[51]

The Court has held that a statute that restricts judicial review of the constitutionality of an administrative determination to a single court comports with due process "so long as it affords to those affected a reasonable opportunity to be heard and present evidence" (Yakus v. United States, 1944). But the Court has repeatedly stated that a "serious constitutional question" would arise if a statute were construed to deny *any* judicial forum for constitutional claims (Webster v. Doe, 1988; Bowen v. Mich. Acad. of Family Physicians, 1986; Johnson v. Robison, 1974; see also INS v. St. Cyr, 2001; Calcano-Martinez v. INS, 2001). In particular, "[w]here a determination made in an administrative proceeding is to play a critical role in the subsequent imposition of a criminal sanction, there must be *some* meaningful review of the administrative proceeding" (United States v. Mendoza-Lopez, 1987).

Due process would not be the only potential constitutional impediment to a denial of judicial review of constitutional claims; arguably Article III of the Constitution would bar Congress from limiting the jurisdiction of the federal courts in this manner[52] and, in challenges to the legality of executive detention, the Suspension Clause (U.S. Const. art. I, § 9, cl. 2) would bar Congress from repealing habeas jurisdiction (INS v. St. Cyr, 2001).[53] Because the Supreme Court has never interpreted a statute to deprive a person of the ability to obtain judicial consideration of a credible claim that agency action violated her constitutional rights,[54] the due process issue has not been squarely decided.

### *Access to the Courts*

In earlier subsections of the section of this chapter entitled "Nature of the Hearing," we focused on the due process protections that the government must provide when it threatens to deprive a person of life, liberty or property, through either administrative or judicial action. In those cases, the government initiates the action and the individual is in a defensive posture, seeking to avoid loss of a protected interest. In the last subsection, we considered the role due process plays when the individual takes the offensive and seeks judicial review of administrative action. Here, we recognize that due process issues arise in two additional variations in which the individual, rather than the government, initiates the action: (1) after the government has deprived an individual of liberty or property by convicting and sentencing her, the prisoner seeks access to the judicial system to appeal her conviction or to petition for a writ of habeas corpus but is stymied by a lack of access to legal materials, assistance or other necessary resources; or (2) an individual seeks to initiate a civil judicial proceeding but is unable to pay state-imposed access fees. Does due process guarantee a right of access to the courts in these contexts?

The Supreme Court first recognized a constitutional right of access to the courts in the criminal context, relying on the Equal Protection Clause and the Suspension Clause, which protects the "privilege of the Writ of Habeas Corpus," as well as the Due Process Clause. The Court has recently acknowledged that the constitutional basis of the right of access to the courts remains unsettled, noting that it has grounded the right in the Privileges and Immunities Clause, the First Amendment Petition Clause, the Fifth Amendment Due Process Clause, and the Fourteenth Amendment Due Process and Equal Protection Clauses (Christopher v. Harbury, 2002).

Two themes pervade the Supreme Court's right of access decisions in the criminal context: equal access to criminal justice for rich and poor and the need to vindicate fundamental, constitutionally protected rights. The Court has noted that in this context,

> "[D]ue process and equal protection principles converge." The equal protection concern relates to the legitimacy of fencing out would-be appellants based solely on their inability to pay core costs. The due process concern homes in on the essential fairness of the state-ordered proceedings anterior to adverse state action (M.L.B. v. S.L.J., 1996, quoting Bearden v. Georgia, 1983; *see also* Smith v. Robbins, 2000).[55]

The Court has also described the relationship between due process and the right of access in this way: "The right of access to the courts . . . is founded in the Due Process Clause and assures that no person will be denied the opportunity to present to the judiciary allegations concerning violations of fundamental constitutional rights" (Wolff v. McDonnell, 1974).

In defining the inmate's right of access to the courts, the Supreme Court has barred prison officials from interfering with efforts by prisoners to seek redress in the courts; it has invalidated financial obstacles that impede access to the courts by indigent prisoners, such as filing fees and transcript costs; and it has required states to provide professional or other legal assistance and access to legal materials. Let us consider these aspects of the right of access in the criminal context before turning to the civil cases.

The first access decisions required the state to do no more than remove obstacles that frustrated prisoners' efforts to appeal their convictions or file petitions for a writ of habeas corpus (Cochran v. Kansas, 1942; Ex Parte Hull, 1941). In these cases, prison officials had literally interfered with prisoners' efforts to challenge their convictions by refusing to notarize their petitions for writs of habeas corpus unless the papers had been reviewed and approved by the legal investigator to the parole board (Ex Parte Hull, 1941), and by preventing other inmates from perfecting their appeals (Cochran v. Kansas, 1942). Declaring such interference unconstitutional, the Court stated simply that "the state and its officers may not abridge or impair petitioner's right to apply to a federal court for a writ of habeas corpus" (Ex Parte Hull, 1941; see also Cochran v. Kansas, 1942).

A decade later, the Court recognized that filing fees and transcript costs could impede an inmate's ability to seek appellate review as much as the direct interference suffered in *Hull* and *Cochran*. In the landmark case of Griffin v. Illinois (1956), an indigent criminal defendant challenged a state statute that required litigants seeking an appeal to furnish the appellate court with a bill of exceptions or certified report of the trial proceedings. Since a stenographic transcript of the trial proceedings was necessary to prepare these documents and since the indigent petitioners could not afford to obtain the transcript, they contended that the state court's failure to provide them with a transcript violated both the Due Process and Equal Protection Clauses by denying them the opportunity to appeal solely because of poverty. Recognizing that the federal Constitution does not require the states to provide a right to appellate review, a plurality of the Court nevertheless held that the Due Process and Equal Protection Clauses bar states from granting appellate review "in a way that discriminates against some convicted defendants on account of their poverty" (Griffin v. Illinois, 1956, plurality op.; see also Eskridge v. Wash. State Bd. of Prison Terms & Parole, 1958, per curiam). Noting the country's dedication to equal justice to all in the administration of the criminal law, the Court held that "[d]estitute defendants must be afforded as adequate appellate review as defendants who have money enough to buy transcripts" (Griffin v. Illinois, 1956).[56]

The right to a transcript announced in *Griffin*, and the underlying right of access to the appellate process, is not limited to cases in which the defendant has been convicted of a felony or faces imprisonment (Mayer v. City of Chicago, 1971; Williams v. Oklahoma City, 1969). The Court rejected the argument that the defendant's "interest in a transcript is outweighed by the State's fiscal and other interests in not burdening the appellate process" when the defendant faces only a fine (Mayer v. City of Chicago, 1971). Revealing that the right to a transcript is not predicated on an *Eldridge*-like balance, the Court stated, "*Griffin* does not represent a balance between the needs of the accused and the interests of society; its principle is a flat prohibition against pricing indigent defendants out of as effective an appeal as would be available to others able to pay their own way" (Mayer v. City of Chicago, 1971; see also Roberts v. LaVallee, 1967, per curiam; Long v. Dist. Ct., 1966, per curiam).

Like rules requiring indigent prisoners to obtain trial transcripts they cannot afford, rules requiring payment of unaffordable filing fees can interfere with their right of access to the appellate process. In a pair of cases decided shortly after *Griffin*, the Supreme Court invalidated filing fees that barred indigent defendants access to the courts to appeal their criminal convictions. In the first of these cases, Burns v. Ohio (1959), the state argued that *Griffin* was not controlling because it involved a financial impediment to an appeal as of right, while *Burns* involved a fee that made an application for discretionary review by the state supreme court unaffordable. The Court rejected the argument, noting that it "misses the crucial significance of *Griffin*" (Burns v. Ohio, 1959). Because a defendant with resources could apply for leave to appeal to the state supreme court, an indigent defendant could not be denied that opportunity (Burns v. Ohio, 1959). "The imposition by the State of financial barriers restricting the availability of appellate review for indigent criminal defendants has no place in our heritage of Equal Justice Under Law" (Burns v. Ohio, 1959). The second case, Smith v. Bennett (1961), held that a state law that required payment of a $4.00 fee to file an application for a writ of habeas corpus deprived indigent prisoners of equal protection of the laws by impeding their ability to exercise their "state right to sue for [their] liberty. . . ."

Beyond requiring waiver of filing fees and transcript costs, the Court has relied on *Griffin*'s reasoning, and on both the Equal Protection Clause and the "guarantees of fair procedure inherent in the Due Process Clause" (Douglas v. California, 1963, Harlan, J., dissenting), to impose affirmative obligations on the state "to assist inmates in the preparation and filing of meaningful legal papers by providing prisoners with adequate law libraries or adequate assistance from persons trained in the law" (Bounds v. Smith, 1977). Since deciding *Bounds*, the Court has disclaimed any general requirement that "the State . . . enable the prisoner to *discover* grievances, and to *litigate effectively* once in court" (Lewis v. Casey, 1996).

Notwithstanding this disclaimer, the Court has held that when prisoners wish to pursue first appeals of their criminal convictions, the right of access includes a right to appointed counsel (Douglas v. California, 1963; Evitts v. Lucey, 1985). Relying heavily on *Griffin*, the Court stated, "where the merits of *the one and only appeal* an indigent has as of right are decided without benefit of counsel, we think an unconstitutional line has been drawn between rich and poor" (Douglas v. California, 1963).[57]

The Court has declined to extend the reasoning of *Griffin* and *Douglas* to require appointed counsel for discretionary appeals to the state supreme court, applications for review by the United States Supreme Court (Ross v. Moffitt, 1974) or collateral attacks on convictions or sentences (Murray v. Giarratano, 1989; Pennsylvania v. Finley, 1987; Johnson v. Avery, 1969). In concluding that the right of access encompasses a right to appointed counsel only for a first appeal as of right, the Court has emphasized a difference in the posture of cases that it rejected as meaningless in *Burns*, one of the early filing fee cases. By the time a criminal defendant pursues a discretionary appeal, he

> will have, at the very least, a transcript or other record of trial proceedings, a brief on his behalf in the Court of Appeals setting forth his claims of error, and in many cases an opinion by the Court of Appeals disposing of his case. These materials, supplemented by

> whatever submission respondent may make *pro se*, would appear to provide the [state supreme court] with an adequate basis for its decision to grant or deny review (Ross v. Moffitt, 1974).

In these circumstances, the need for appointed counsel should be less pronounced. In any event, since review by the state supreme court is intended to address matters of significant public interest rather than to correct results in individual cases, a failure to appoint counsel to assist an indigent defendant with a discretionary appeal does not deprive him of "an adequate opportunity to present his claims fairly in the context of the State's appellate process" (Ross v. Moffitt, 1974).

Finding that "[p]ostconviction relief is even further removed from the criminal trial than is discretionary direct review," the Court has held that due process does not guarantee the indigent criminal defendant a right to appointed counsel in state postconviction proceedings (Pennsylvania v. Finley, 1987), even if the defendant faces a death sentence (Murray v. Giarratano, 1989).[58]

Even when it is not required to appoint counsel to represent inmates, however, the state must "shoulder affirmative obligations to assure all prisoners meaningful access to the courts" (Bounds v. Smith, 1977). When, for example, the state does not provide appointed counsel or an alternate means of legal assistance, it must permit inmates to help one another with the preparation of petitions for postconviction relief (Johnson v. Avery, 1969; see also Wolff v. McDonnell, 1974). Providing adequate law libraries is another constitutionally acceptable method to assure meaningful access to the courts (Bounds v. Smith, 1977). Prison officials have discretion in devising a program that satisfies the requirement of meaningful access (Murray v. Giarratano, 1989; Bounds v. Smith, 1977), and while economic factors may be considered, "the cost of protecting a constitutional right cannot justify its total denial" (Bounds v. Smith, 1977; see also Younger v. Gilmore, 1971, per curiam; Lewis v. Casey, 1996).

In the civil context, the Court has recognized a right of access to the courts only if two conditions are met: (1) the case affects a fundamental family relationship; and (2) the state judicial apparatus is the only mechanism available to obtain the relief sought. The first case in which the Court extended a due process right of access to the civil justice system, Boddie v. Connecticut (1971), illustrates these conditions well. In *Boddie*, the Court held that, consistent with due process, the state cannot bar indigent claimants from filing for divorce simply because they cannot afford the filing fees. The Court began by noting that most due process cases address defendants' rights because once a plaintiff initiates suit, "the judicial proceeding becomes the only effective means of resolving the dispute at hand and denial of a defendant's full access to that process raises grave problems for its legitimacy" (Boddie v. Connecticut, 1971). Plaintiffs, on the other hand, typically have alternate means of resolving disputes available and need not seek access to the judicial process. But since the state has monopoly power to enter divorce decrees, a statute that requires payment of a filing fee to commence civil litigation in effect deprives indigent claimants of the opportunity to be heard on their divorce claims. Rejecting the state's financial interest in recoupment of costs through imposition of fees, the Court concluded that due process requires that indigent claimants be afforded an opportunity to commence divorce litigation (Boddie v. Connecticut, 1971).

The *Boddie* Court declined to

> decide that access for all individuals to the courts is a right that is, in all circumstances, guaranteed by the Due Process Clause of the Fourteenth Amendment so that its exercise may not be placed beyond the reach of any individual, for . . . in the case before us this right is the exclusive precondition to the adjustment of a fundamental human relationship. The requirement that these appellants resort to the judicial process is entirely a state-created matter (Boddie v. Connecticut, 1971).

Thus, the Court refrained from addressing the broader access question by focusing on two unique features of the *Boddie* case itself: the fundamental nature of the relationship at stake and the state's monopoly power to legally alter it.

Just two years after deciding *Boddie*, the Court was forced to address the broader access question. In United States v. Kras (1973), an indigent man challenged the constitutionality of the Bankruptcy Act, which required the payment of fees upon filing a petition in bankruptcy and barred the court from discharging the bankrupt unless the filing fees were paid in full. He filed for bankruptcy but was unable to pay the fees, even in installments. The Court attempted to distinguish *Boddie* in two ways. First, since state courts have exclusive authority to grant a divorce, resort to the judicial process in *Boddie* was "'no more voluntary in a realistic sense than that of the defendant called upon to defend his interests in court'" (United States v. Kras, 1973, quoting Boddie v. Connecticut, 1971). While federal courts have exclusive authority to grant discharges in bankruptcy, bankruptcy is not the sole means by which a debtor may adjust her legal relationship with her creditors. At least in theory, she may negotiate with her creditors to relieve her debt burden. The passage of time may provide the protection of the statute of limitations. Thus, "*Boddie*'s emphasis on exclusivity finds no counterpart in the bankrupt's situation" (United States v. Kras, 1973). Second, whereas lack of access to the courts in *Boddie* affected fundamental interests in marriage and free association, *Kras* involved only a statutory interest in elimination of debt burden (United States v. Kras, 1973). Thus, *Kras* read *Boddie* narrowly, requiring a right of access to the civil justice system only in cases affecting fundamental relationships over which the state has exclusive power.

The Court has adhered to *Kras*, continuing to read *Boddie* narrowly. Thus, when indigent welfare recipients sought judicial review of agency determinations that their benefits should be reduced, the Supreme Court held that due process did not require waiver of the $25 appellate court filing fee (Ortwein v. Schwab, 1973). An interest in increased welfare payments "has far less constitutional significance than the interest of the *Boddie* appellants" (Ortwein v. Schwab, 1973). Moreover, the recipients had already received the pretermination evidentiary hearings required by Goldberg v. Kelly (1970). Thus, even though the recipients had no opportunity to seek review of the agency determination without payment of filing fees, the Court found that the pretermination hearing itself qualified as an alternative to adjudication (Ortwein v. Schwab, 1973).

In the paternity context, on the other hand, the Court invalidated a state statute that required the party seeking blood tests to pay for them (Little v. Streater, 1981). Unlike *Griffin*, *Mayer* and *Boddie*, wherein the Court declined to weigh the state's costs against the individual's right of access, the *Little* Court applied the *Eldridge* balancing test. The Court considered the constitutional significance of the private interests at stake, the relative weakness of the state's monetary interest in avoiding the expense of blood tests, the difficulty a parent would have in denying a charge of paternity without access to blood tests, and the concomitant risk of an erroneous result without scientific evidence. Placing great weight on the importance of the parent-child relationship at stake and the state's pervasive involvement in the "quasi-criminal" paternity proceedings, the Court held that the statute denied indigent parties a meaningful opportunity to be heard in violation of the Due Process Clause (Little v. Streater, 1981). Distinguishing *Ortwein* and *Kras*, the Court noted that those decisions "emphasized the availability of other relief and the less 'fundamental' character of the private interests at stake than those implicated in *Boddie*. Because appellant has no choice of an alternative forum and his interests, as well as those of the child, are constitutionally significant, this case is comparable to *Boddie* rather than to *Kras* and *Ortwein*" (Little v. Streater, 1981).

The same factors were determinative in M.L.B. v. S.L.J. (1996), where the Court held that indigent parents whose parental rights have been terminated may not be deprived of the opportunity to appeal the termination decree because of an inability to pay transcript preparation fees. After reviewing its prior right of access cases and noting its reluctance to extend *Griffin* to many civil cases, the Court nevertheless noted that it has "consistently set apart from the mine run of cases those involving state controls or intrusions on family relationships" (M.L.B. v. S.L.J., 1996). Emphasizing the primacy of the parent-child relationship and the "unique kind of deprivation" that a termination order works, the Court also distinguished the case from other civil cases by noting that the parent had not initiated the underlying action. Rather, she was "endeavoring to defend against the State's destruction of her family bonds. . . . Like a defendant resisting criminal conviction, she seeks to be spared from the State's devastatingly adverse action" (M.L.B. v. S.L.J., 1996). Thus, the Court relied on both the importance of the interest at stake and the exclusive state power to terminate it in holding that the state may not withhold a trial transcript from an indigent parent who seeks to appeal from an order terminating her parental rights (M.L.B. v. S.L.J., 1996).

In its most recent decision on a constitutional right of access to the courts, Christopher v. Harbury (2002), the Supreme Court distinguished between two categories of access claims: those that look forward to future litigation to be brought once a condition that has frustrated the preparation and filing of a suit is removed (as all of the foregoing cases had), and those that look backward, seeking recovery for a claim forever lost due to prior official acts that "caused the loss or inadequate settlement of a meritorious case, the loss of an opportunity to sue, or the loss of an opportunity to seek some particular order of relief. . . ." (Christopher v. Harbury, 2002). In both categories of cases, the "very point of recognizing any access claim is to provide some effective vindication for a separate and distinct right to seek judicial relief for some wrong" (Christopher v. Harbury, 2002). And in both categories of cases, the plaintiff must allege the elements of the underlying cause of action, whether anticipated or lost. "[W]hen the access claim . . . looks backward, the complaint must [also] identify a remedy that may be awarded as recompense but not otherwise available in some suit that may yet be brought" (Christopher v. Harbury, 2002).

> And because these backward-looking cases are brought to get relief unobtainable in other suits, the remedy sought must itself be identified to hedge against the risk that an access claim be tried all the way through, only to find that the court can award no remedy that the plaintiff could not have been awarded on a presently existing claim (Christopher v. Harbury, 2002).

If a denial-of-access complaint fails to state the underlying claim for relief or to describe the remedy uniquely available in the access claim, the complaint must be dismissed (Christopher v. Harbury, 2002).

## DAMAGES REMEDY FOR A PROCEDURAL DUE PROCESS VIOLATION

If a state actor deprives a person of a protected interest without due process of law, ordinarily the affected person may bring an action to recover money damages under 42 U.S.C. § 1983.[59] Section 1983 creates "a species of tort liability" in favor of persons deprived of constitutional rights (Imbler v. Pachtman, 1976). Government officials performing discretionary functions are entitled to a qualified immunity defense unless their conduct violated "clearly established statutory or constitutional rights of which a reasonable person would have known" (Harlow v. Fitzgerald, 1982, quoted in Conn v. Gabbert, 1999).

The basic purpose of a section 1983 damages award is to compensate the person for injuries caused by the deprivation (Carey v. Piphus, 1978). If the plaintiff would have suffered the same loss had a hearing been held, then she cannot prove that the procedural due process violation caused her injury. Carey v. Piphus (1978) illustrates this point. There, students were suspended for twenty days without the "more formal procedures" required by Goss v. Lopez (1975). Alleging a violation of their procedural due process rights, the students filed suit, seeking damages under section 1983. The Court held that to recover damages suffered as a result of the suspensions themselves, the students would have to prove that they would not have been suspended if proper hearings had been held. Otherwise, "the failure to accord procedural due process could not properly be viewed as the cause of the suspensions" (Carey v. Piphus, 1978). The Court rejected the argument that plaintiffs were entitled to more than nominal damages to compensate them for the "'injury . . . "inherent in the nature of the wrong,"' even if their suspensions were justified and even if they fail to prove that the denial of procedural due process actually caused them some real, if intangible, injury" (Carey v. Piphus, 1978).

The *Carey* Court acknowledged that a person may suffer mental or emotional distress as a result of the government's failure to deal with her fairly, even if the deprivation is justified, and held that such injury is compensable under section 1983. But the plaintiff can recover only if she proves her mental or emotional distress and convinces the trier of fact that she suffered the distress because of the lack of due process, not because of the justified deprivation (Carey v. Piphus, 1978).

Compensatory damages may include out-of-pocket losses, other financial harms, injury to reputation, and pain and suffering. The measure of compensatory damages is the plaintiff's actual loss, not the importance or abstract value of the constitutional right at issue (Memphis Cmty. School Dist. v. Stachura, 1986). Punitive damages are available in a section 1983 action "when the defendant's conduct is shown to be motivated by evil motive or intent, or when it involves reckless or callous indifference to the federally protected rights of others" (Smith v. Wade, 1983). In the absence of proof of actual injury, the plaintiff is nevertheless entitled to recover nominal damages "[b]ecause the right to procedural due process is 'absolute' . . . and because of the importance to organized society that procedural due process be observed" (Carey v. Piphus, 1978).

Reasonable attorneys' fees are available to a prevailing party under 42 U.S.C. § 1988[60] and may exceed the amount of the damages recovered (City of Riverside v. Rivera, 1986). A party that recovers only nominal damages is a prevailing party under 42 U.S.C. § 1988, but "[w]hen a plaintiff recovers only nominal damages because of his failure to prove an essential element of his claim for monetary relief, the only reasonable fee is usually no fee at all" (Farrar v. Hobby, 1992).

Although section 1983 ordinarily provides a civil remedy to persons deprived of protected interests without due process of law, a state prisoner who claims she was deprived of good-time credits without due process of law may not employ section 1983 to seek restoration of the credits and a determination that she is entitled to immediate release or a speedier release; habeas corpus, with its exhaustion of state remedies requirement, is the exclusive remedy in these circumstances (Preiser v. Rodriguez, 1973). Nor may a prisoner seek damages under section 1983 for a deprivation of good-time credits without due process of law if a judgment in her favor would imply the invalidity of the punishment imposed, unless she can demonstrate that the punishment has already been invalidated (Heck v. Humphrey, 1994; Edwards v. Balisok, 1997).[61] This rule obtains because "the hoary principle that civil tort actions are not appropriate vehicles for challenging the validity of outstanding criminal judgments applies to § 1983 damages actions that necessarily require the plaintiff to prove the unlawfulness of his conviction or confinement" (Heck v. Humphrey, 1994). But a prisoner may bring a section 1983 action to challenge only the conditions, rather than the fact or duration, of her confinement, without first satisfying the "favorable termination" requirement of *Heck* (Muhammad v. Close, 2004).

## CONCLUSION

When a protected interest is at stake and the government acts with the requisite state of mind, it must afford the affected person due process of law. In determining both the timing and the nature of the procedural protections required, the Court has applied the *Eldridge* balancing test, weighing the private interest at stake, the government's interest, including the burdens it would suffer if required to provide additional procedural safeguards, and the risk of erroneous deprivation if additional protections are not afforded. Generally speaking, the state must provide notice and an opportunity to be heard before it deprives a person of a protected interest. The hearing may be postponed, however, when the need for immediate action is great, such as when public safety and health are threatened, or when a prior hearing would be impracticable, such as when the government conduct is random and unauthorized. The nature of the hearing, too, depends upon the balance of the *Eldridge* factors, with the Court requiring the most protections when precious liberty interests are at stake, the individual lacks the ability to present her position in writing, and disputed issues of fact exist. A damages remedy is available for violations of due process, but the plaintiff must prove actual injury to recover more than nominal damages.

## NOTES

1. Marshall v. Jerricho, Inc., 446 U.S. 238, 242 (1980).

2. The Court declined to consider whether due process would be satisfied by an opportunity for only written submissions if there were no factual issues in dispute. Goldberg v. Kelly, 397 U.S. 254, 268 n.15 (1970).

3. 2 Richard J. Pierce, Jr., Administrative Law Treatise § 9.3, at 571 (4th ed. 2002); *id.* § 9.4, at 582–83. *See also* Henry J. Friendly, *"Some Kind of Hearing,"* 123 U. Penn L. Rev. 1267, 1299–1301 (1975) (criticizing *Goldberg* for requiring almost all elements of a judicial trial).

4. In 1979, Congress enacted legislation to divide the Department of Health, Education and Welfare into two separate departments, the Department of Health and Human Services and the Department of Education. 20 U.S.C. § 3401 *et seq.*

5. In *Medina*, the Court noted that it had relied on the *Eldridge* balancing test in only two criminal law cases: United States v. Raddatz, 447 U.S. 667 (1980), in which it rejected a due process challenge to a provision of the Federal Magistrates Act that authorizes federal judges to decide motions to suppress on the basis of a record of an evidentiary hearing conducted by a magistrate, and Ake v. Oklahoma, 470 U.S. 68 (1985), in which it held that due process requires that indigent capital defendants in specified circumstances be provided access to the assistance of a psychiatrist. Medina v. California, 505 U.S. 437, 444 (1992). Without disturbing the holdings of those cases, the *Medina* Court questioned whether *Eldridge* "was essential to the results reached in those cases." *Id. Cf. id.* at 453 (O'Connor, J., concurring in the judgment) (concluding that *Eldridge* continues to provide "a useful guide in due process cases"); Burns v. United States, 501 U.S. 129, 148 (1991) (Souter, J., dissenting) (arguing that the *Eldridge* framework is "a general approach for determining the procedures required by due process whenever erroneous governmental action would infringe an individual's protected interest"; maintaining that *Eldridge* should be applied to determine whether a judge must provide notice of her intent to depart from federal sentencing guidelines).

Rather than apply the *Eldridge* balancing test to gauge the validity of state criminal procedural rules, the Court has applied a test announced in Patterson v. New York, 432 U.S. 197 (1977), decided one year after *Eldridge*. Recognizing the state's authority to regulate procedures under which its criminal laws are carried out, the *Patterson* Court held that a state's decision "is not subject to proscription under the Due Process Clause unless 'it offends some principle of justice so rooted in the traditions and conscience of our people as to be ranked as fundamental.'" *Id.* at 201–02 (quoting Speiser v. Randall, 357 U.S. 513, 523 (1958)) (other citations omitted). "Traditionally, due process has required that only the most basic procedural safeguards be observed; more subtle balancing of society's interests against those of the accused have [sic] been left to the legislative branch." *Id.* at 210. *Cf.* Allen v. Illinois, 478 U.S. 364, 375 (1986) (holding that the privilege against self-incrimination "has no place among the procedural safeguards discussed in *Mathews v. Eldridge*, which are designed to enhance the reliability of [the factfinding] process"; "due process does not independently require application of the privilege"). The *Patterson* test is less intrusive than *Eldridge* and more deferential to the states' legislative judgment on matters of criminal procedure. *Medina*, 505 U.S. at 446.

6. *See also* City of W. Covina v. Perkins, 525 U.S. 234, 246 (1999) (Thomas, J., concurring in the judgment) (arguing that the Fourth Amendment, rather than the Due Process Clause, defines the process that is due when the government seizes property in the context of a criminal case). *But see* United States v. James Daniel Good Real Prop., 510 U.S. 43, 49–52 (1993) (holding that both due process and the Fourth Amendment place restrictions on seizures conducted for purposes of civil forfeiture); Chambers v. Mississippi, 410 U.S. 284, 294 (1973) (stating in criminal case that "the rights to confront and cross-examine witnesses and to call witnesses in one's own behalf have long been recognized as essential to due process"); Sheppard v. Maxwell, 384 U.S. 333, 362 (1966) (holding that due process "requires that the accused receive a trial by an impartial jury free from outside influences"; concluding that pervasive prejudicial publicity and courtroom disruption by the media resulted in a denial of due process); Pate v. Robinson, 383 U.S. 375 (1966) (holding that due process requires procedures adequate to protect a criminal defendant's right not to be tried or convicted while incompetent to stand trial); Brady v. Maryland, 373 U.S. 83, 87 (1963) (holding that "the suppression by the prosecution of evidence favorable to an accused upon request violates due process where the evidence is material either to guilt or to punishment, irrespective of the good faith or bad faith of the prosecution").

7. *See also* Fahey v. Mallonee, 332 U.S. 245, 253 (1947) (upholding the appointment of a conservator to take possession of a savings and loan association without notice or prior hearing; citing "the delicate nature of the institution and the impossibility of preserving credit during an investigation").

8. Even if the claimant has a present entitlement to the property, she may not be entitled to a prior hearing if someone else with a current interest in the same property, such as a vendor with a vendor's lien, seeks a pre-judgment writ of sequestration. Mitchell v. W.T. Grant Co., 416 U.S. 600 (1974).

9. The *Mitchell* Court also noted that the availability of a damages award, for harm suffered as a result of a wrongfully issued writ of sequestration, helped to minimize the risk of erroneous deprivation. Mitchell v. W.T. Grant Co., 416 U.S. 600, 610 (1974).

10. *See also* Henry Paul Monaghan, *Of "Liberty" and "Property,"* 62 Cornell L. Rev. 405, 431 (1977) (stating that "prior hearings might well be dispensed with in many circumstances in which the state's conduct . . . would constitute a common-law tort").

11. Professor Richard Fallon has argued that *Parratt* involved substantive, rather than procedural, due process rights and "should be viewed as having introduced an abstention doctrine involving a class of non-fundamental substantive due process rights." Richard H. Fallon, Jr., *Some Confusion About Due Process, Judicial Review, and Constitutional Remedies*, 93 Colum. L. Rev. 309, 312 (1993); *see also id.* at 339–55. Fallon further argued that the Court's later decision in Hudson v. Palmer, 468 U.S. 517 (1984), "reflects a similar confusion of substantive and procedural due process." Fallon, *supra*, at 342.

12. The Court explained: "*Parratt* is not an exception to the *Mathews* balancing test, but rather an application of that test to the unusual case in which one of the variables in the *Mathews* equation—the value of predeprivation safeguards—is negligible in preventing the kind of deprivation at issue." Zinermon v. Burch, 494 U.S. 113, 129 (1990).

13. The late Judge Henry Friendly compiled a list of eleven elements of a fair hearing, including an unbiased tribunal; notice of the proposed action and the grounds for it; an opportunity to present reasons why the proposed action should not be taken (orally or in writing); the right to call witnesses; the right to know the evidence against one; the right to

have a decision based only on the evidence presented; the right to counsel; the making of a record; a written statement of reasons; public attendance; and judicial review. As Judge Friendly himself explained, not all factors are required in every case and fewer are needed in cases where the governmental action threatened or taken is less severe. Friendly, *supra* note 3, at 1278–79.

14. *Id.* at 1279.

15. Martin H. Redish & Lawrence C. Marshall, *Adjudicatory Independence and the Values of Procedural Due Process*, 95 Yale L.J. 455, 475–503 (1986).

16. *See also* Gibson v. Berryhill, 411 U.S. 564, 578–79 (1973) (declining to decide whether the Board of Optometry was disqualified to decide a case because it had filed a civil complaint against the optometrists appearing before it); FTC v. Cement Inst., 333 U.S. 683, 700–01 (1948) (holding that the FTC was not disqualified to hear a price-fixing case even though FTC members had previously testified that the use of the multiple basing-point delivered-price system at issue restrained trade in violation of the Sherman Act; "the fact that the Commission had entertained such views as the result of its prior *ex parte* investigations did not necessarily mean that the minds of its members were irrevocably closed on the subject" of the basing-point system); NLRB v. Donnelly Garment Co., 330 U.S. 219, 236–37 (1947) (stating that "[c]ertainly it is not the rule of judicial administration that . . . a judge is disqualified from sitting in a retrial because he was reversed on earlier rulings. We find no warrant for imposing upon administrative agencies a stiffer rule, whereby examiners would be disentitled to sit because they ruled strongly against a party in the first hearing").

17. The facts of *Murchison* were particularly troubling: the trial judge who convicted the person he had charged with contempt announced that he was relying in part on the attitude the defendant had exhibited before the secret "grand jury," which attitude was not reflected in the record. Thus, the defendant was deprived of an opportunity to confront and cross-examine a witness with direct knowledge of the defendant's conduct before the "grand jury," the trial judge. In re Murchison, 349 U.S. 133, 138–39 (1955). The Court later limited the reach of *Murchison*: "Plainly enough, *Murchison* has not been understood to stand for the broad rule that the members of an administrative agency may not investigate the facts, institute proceedings, and then make the necessary adjudications." Withrow v. Larkin, 421 U.S. 35, 53 (1975).

18. *See also* Marshall v. Jerrico, Inc., 446 U.S. 238, 243 n.2 (1980) (identifying other cases that follow the principles of *Ward* and *Tumey*); Connally v. Georgia, 429 U.S. 245 (1977) (per curiam) (holding that a system that compensated justices of the peace only if they issued a search warrant, but not if they denied one, violated due process); Gibson v. Berryhill, 411 U.S. 564 (1973) (affirming a finding of a disqualifying pecuniary interest).

19. The state maintained a putative father registry, which recorded the names and addresses of men who filed a notice of intent to claim paternity of a child born out of wedlock. Lehr v. Robertson, 463 U.S. 248, 250 n.4 (1983).

20. The Court noted that it was "not assessing the constitutional adequacy of New York's procedures for terminating a developed relationship. [The biological father] has never had any significant custodial, personal, or financial relationship with [the child], and he did not seek to establish a legal tie until after she was two years old." *Id.* at 262 (footnote omitted). The dissent countered that the father had not been given an opportunity to demonstrate his efforts to maintain a relationship with the child. *Id.* at 270–71 (White, J., dissenting). Justice

White further argued that the biological father "either had an interest protected by the Constitution or he did not. If the entry of the adoption order in this case deprived [him] of a constitutionally protected interest, he is entitled to notice and an opportunity to be heard before the order can be accorded finality." *Id.* at 268 (White, J., dissenting).

21. On the other hand, when a party fails to produce information sought in discovery that is relevant to the outcome of the case, the court may strike the defendant's answer and enter a default judgment against her, not only as punishment but on the presumption "that the refusal to produce evidence material to the administration of due process was but an admission of the want of merit in the asserted defense." Hammond Packing Co. v. Arkansas, 212 U.S. 322, 351 (1909). *See also* Ins. Corp. of Ir. v. Compagnie des Bauxites de Guinee, 456 U.S. 694, 705–07 (1982) (holding that due process is not violated when a court, as a sanction for failure to comply with a discovery order seeking information regarding the defendant's contacts with the forum, proceeds as though jurisdiction had been established).

22. *Cf.* Weinberger v. Salfi, 422 U.S. 749 (1975) (declining to apply *Stanley*, *Vlandis* and *LaFleur* irrebuttable presumption analysis to duration-of-relationship requirements for Social Security survivor benefits).

23. For the classic scholarly treatment of dignity theory, see Jerry L. Mashaw, *Administrative Due Process: The Quest for a Dignitary Theory*, 61 B.U. L. Rev. 885 (1981); Jerry L. Mashaw, *The Supreme Court's Due Process Calculus for Administrative Adjudication in* Mathews v. Eldridge: *Three Factors in Search of a Theory of Value*, 44 U. Chi. L. Rev. 28 (1976); Jerry L. Mashaw, Due Process in the Administrative State (1985).

24. *See also* Vitek v. Jones, 445 U.S. 480, 494–96 (1980) (holding that an inmate threatened with transfer to a mental hospital is entitled to appear in person before the decisionmaker); Goss v. Lopez, 419 U.S. 565, 582 (1975) (holding that a student facing a short suspension is entitled to "an opportunity to explain his version of the facts at this discussion" with the school disciplinarian); Londoner v. City of Denver, 210 U.S. 373, 385–86 (1908) (holding that a taxpayer challenging a local assessment is entitled to an opportunity for a hearing at which she may support her objections with oral argument and proof).

25. *Cf.* Koch v. Lewis, 96 F. Supp. 2d 949, 964 (D. Ariz. 2000) (stating that after Sandin v. Conner, 515 U.S. 472 (1995), "distinguishing between disciplinary and administrative actions for the purposes of defining the level of process owed a prisoner is problematic, if not inappropriate").

26. In criminal cases, the Sixth Amendment right to confront and cross-examine witnesses also requires the availability of an interpreter when the defendant faces a significant language barrier. *See, e.g.*, United States v. Martinez, 616 F.2d 185, 188 (5th Cir. 1980); United States v. Carrion, 488 F.2d 12, 14 (1st Cir. 1973) (per curiam), *cert. denied*, 416 U.S. 907 (1974).

27. In addition to the due process and Sixth Amendment rights to an interpreter in the contexts discussed above, a federal statute enacted in 1978, the Court Interpreters Act, requires federal courts to appoint interpreters when the presiding judicial officer determines that a non-English speaking (or hearing-impaired) party or witness otherwise would have difficulty understanding the proceedings or communicating with counsel. 28 U.S.C. § 1827(d).

28. Prison officials also have discretion "to limit access to other inmates to collect statements or to compile other documentary evidence." Wolff v. McDonnell, 418 U.S. 539,

566 (1974). The Court encouraged, but did not require, prison authorities to state their reasons for refusing to permit an inmate to call witnesses in her defense. *Id.*; Baxter v. Palmigiano, 425 U.S. 308, 322 (1976); *see also* Ponte v. Real, 471 U.S. 491, 497 (1985) (holding that prison officials may be required to explain why witnesses were not allowed to testify, but not requiring a contemporaneous explanation).

29. 5 John H. Wigmore, Evidence in Trials at Common Law § 1367 (James H. Chadbourn rev. 1974).

30. "In all criminal prosecutions, the accused shall enjoy the right . . . to be confronted by the witnesses against him; [and] to have compulsory process for obtaining witnesses in his favor. . . ." U.S. Const. amend. VI. *See also* Chambers v. Mississippi, 410 U.S. 284, 294 (1973) (grounding these rights in due process). *Cf.* Williams v. New York, 337 U.S. 241, 249–52 (1949) (finding no due process violation when the judge sentenced the defendant to death in reliance upon a sentencing report, which contained information from witnesses whom the defendant had no opportunity to confront or cross-examine).

31. *See also* Jack H. Friedenthal et al., Civil Procedure 304 (3d ed. 1999); Friendly, *supra* note 3, at 1287.

32. The standard in criminal cases is even more rigorous. *See, e.g.*, Jackson v. Virginia, 443 U.S. 307, 318 (1979) (stating that due process is violated unless "record evidence could reasonably support a finding of guilt beyond a reasonable doubt") (footnote omitted).

33. The Court has recognized that when personal or institutional safety is threatened, the written statement "may properly exclude certain items of evidence, but in that event the statement should indicate the fact of the omission." Wolff v. McDonnell, 418 U.S. 539, 565 (1974). The written statement need not include the board's reasons for refusing to call a witness requested by the inmate. Ponte v. Real, 471 U.S. 491, 496 (1985). *See supra* Chapter 3, section entitled "Timing and Form of the Hearing," subsection entitled "Nature of the Hearing," paragraph entitled "Opportunity to Call Witnesses."

34. "This requirement is not limited to explanations for substantive decisions on the merits, for record explanations must also be provided at stages of the hearing that are integral to assuring fair and accurate determinations on the merits." Black v. Romano, 471 U.S. 606, 618 (1985) (Marshall, J., concurring). *See also* Schall v. Martin, 467 U.S. 253, 275–77 (1984) (requiring a judge to state the facts and reasons supporting a decision to order pre-trial detention of an accused juvenile offender); Specht v. Patterson, 386 U S. 605, 610 (1967); Kent v. United States, 383 U.S. 541, 561 (1966) (holding that a juvenile court that waives its jurisdiction and decides that a juvenile should be prosecuted as an adult must provide a statement of reasons, including a statement of the relevant facts).

35. *See also* Alabama v. Shelton, 535 U.S. 654, 658 (2002); Argersinger v. Hamlin, 407 U.S. 25, 37 (1972); Gideon v. Wainwright, 372 U.S. 335 (1963) (holding that indigent criminal defendants are entitled to appointed counsel; holding that the Sixth Amendment right to counsel is applicable to the states through the Due Process Clause of the Fourteenth Amendment); Johnson v. Zerbst, 304 U.S. 458, 463 (1938). *But see* Texas v. Cobb, 532 U.S. 162 (2001) (holding that the Sixth Amendment right to counsel attaches only to charged offenses, and not to factually related uncharged crimes); Scott v. Illinois, 440 U.S. 367, 373–74 (1979) (holding that a trial of an indigent defendant without appointed counsel does not violate the Sixth Amendment as long as imprisonment is not imposed upon conviction).

36. Friendly, *supra* note 3, at 1288.

37. *But see* Murray v. Giarratano, 492 U.S. 1 (1989) (plurality op.) (holding that indigent death row inmates seeking state postconviction relief have no constitutional right to appointed counsel); Pennsylvania v. Finley, 481 U.S. 551, 555 (1987) (declining to hold that "prisoners have a constitutional right to counsel when mounting collateral attacks upon their convictions") (citation omitted); Ross v. Moffitt, 417 U.S. 600 (1974) (holding that neither equal protection nor due process requires a state to provide an indigent criminal defendant with appointed counsel for a discretionary appeal of his conviction to the state supreme court or for a petition for certiorari to the United States Supreme Court, where the state has already provided appointed counsel for the defendant's first appeal as of right); Johnson v. Avery, 393 U.S. 483, 488 (1969) (stating that "[i]t has not been held that there is any general obligation of the courts, state or federal, to appoint counsel for prisoners who indicate, without more, that they wish to seek [collateral] post-conviction relief"). The Supreme Court has recently agreed to decide whether due process guarantees access to appointed counsel in a discretionary first appeal by an indigent criminal defendant convicted by a guilty plea. Kowalski v. Tesmer, – U.S. –, 124 S. Ct. 1144 (2004). *See also infra* Chapter 3, section entitled "Timing and Form of the Hearing," subsection entitled "Nature of the Hearing," paragraph entitled "Access to the Courts."

38. Justice Powell provided a fifth vote for the more limited proposition that "qualified and independent assistance must be provided to an inmate who is threatened with involuntary transfer to a state mental hospital," Vitek v. Jones, 445 U.S. 480, 497 (1980) (Powell, J., concurring in part), while declining to require that such assistance always be provided by a licensed attorney. Powell's position was adopted by a majority of the Court in Washington v. Harper, 494 U.S. 210 (1990), where the Court held that prisoners seeking to avoid unwanted treatment with anti-psychotic drugs are not entitled to appointed counsel. "Given the nature of the decision to be made [which involved a medical judgment], we conclude that the provision of an independent lay adviser who understands the psychiatric issues involved is sufficient protection." *Id.* at 236.

39. The Court did not decide "whether a probationer or parolee has a right to be represented at a revocation hearing by retained counsel in situations other than those where the State would be obliged to furnish counsel for an indigent." Gagnon v. Scarpelli, 411 U.S. 778, 784 n.6 (1973). *Cf.* Morrissey v. Brewer, 408 U.S. 471, 489 (1972) (declining to decide "whether the parolee is entitled to the assistance of retained counsel or to appointed counsel if he is indigent") (footnote omitted).

40. The Court noted that if counsel appeared, the hearing body might "become more akin to that of a judge at a trial, and less attuned to the rehabilitative needs of the individual probationer or parolee. In the greater self-consciousness of its quasi-judicial role, the hearing board may be less tolerant of marginal deviant behavior and feel more pressure to reincarcerate than to continue nonpunitive rehabilitation." *Scarpelli*, 411 U.S. at 787–88.

41. While declining to formulate detailed guidelines for use by state officials, the Court did offer some guidance:

> Presumptively, it may be said that counsel should be provided in cases where, after being informed of his right to request counsel, the probationer or parolee makes such a request, based on a timely and colorable claim (i) that he has not committed the alleged violation of the conditions upon which he is at liberty; or (ii) that, even if the violation is a matter of public record or is uncontested, there are substantial reasons which justified or mitigated the violation and make revocation inappropriate, and that the reasons are complex or otherwise difficult to develop or present. In passing on a request for the

appointment of counsel, the responsible agency also should consider, especially in doubtful cases, whether the probationer appears to be capable of speaking effectively for himself. In every case in which a request for counsel at a preliminary or final hearing is refused, the grounds for refusal should be stated succinctly in the record.

*Id.* at 790–91.

42. *See generally* Patricia C. Kussmann, Annotation, *Right of Indigent Parent to Appointed Counsel in Proceeding for Involuntary Termination of Parental Rights*, 92 A.L.R.5th 379 (2002).

43. Recognizing that illiterate inmates might need assistance, or that other inmates might need help if their cases raised particularly complex issues, the Court held that such inmates "should be free to seek the aid of a fellow inmate, or if that is forbidden, to have adequate substitute aid in the form of help from the staff or from a sufficiently competent inmate designated by the staff." Wolff v. McDonnell, 418 U.S. 539, 570 (1974). The Court reaffirmed *Wolff* two years later, holding that due process does not require access to counsel in prison disciplinary hearings even when an inmate is charged with conduct punishable as a crime under state law. Baxter v. Palmigiano, 425 U.S. 308, 314–15 (1976).

44. The state is required to prove beyond a reasonable doubt only those facts necessary to constitute the crime charged; it is constitutional to impose upon the defendant the burden of proving an affirmative defense that does not negate any of the facts of the crime. Patterson v. New York, 432 U.S. 197, 206–07, 210 (1977). Likewise, it is constitutional to require the sentencing judge to impose a mandatory minimum sentence if she finds, by only a preponderance of the evidence, that an aggravating factor, which is not an element of the crime charged, is established. McMillan v. Pennsylvania, 477 U.S. 79 (1986). But due process requires that "'any fact (other than prior conviction) that increases the maximum penalty for a crime must be . . . proven beyond a reasonable doubt.'" Apprendi v. New Jersey, 530 U.S. 466, 476 (2000) (quoting Jones v. United States, 526 U.S. 227, 243 n.6 (1999)); *see also* Blakely v. Washington, No. 02-1632, 2004 U.S. LEXIS 4573 (U.S. June 24, 2004); Harris v. United States, 536 U.S. 545 (2002); United States v. Cotton, 535 U.S. 625 (2002).

45. The Court distinguished the "clear and convincing evidence" standard of proof required in *Addington* from the "clear, unequivocal, and convincing evidence" standard required in deportation and denaturalization cases. *See* Woodby v. INS, 385 U.S. 276 (1966); Schneiderman v. United States, 320 U.S. 118 (1943). "The term 'unequivocal,' taken by itself, means proof that admits of no doubt, a burden approximating, if not exceeding, that used in criminal cases." Addington v. Texas, 441 U.S. 418, 432 (1979). That standard is appropriate in deportation and denaturalization cases, where the issues are factual and the consequences to the individual are drastic. But the *Addington* Court declined to require that standard in commitment cases, where the ultimate decision turns less on objective facts, and more on the subtleties of psychiatric diagnosis. *Id.* at 432. Neither *Woodby* nor *Schneiderman* explicitly held that the "clear, unequivocal, and convincing evidence" standard of proof was required by due process.

In Jones v. United States, 463 U.S. 354, 366–68 (1983), the Court upheld the constitutionality of the indefinite commitment of a criminal defendant who was acquitted by reason of insanity, under a statute that required him to affirmatively establish his insanity by only a preponderance of the evidence. Rejecting the contention that due process required proof of insanity by clear and convincing evidence, the Court distinguished *Addington* in three respects. First, in *Jones*, the defendant himself, rather than the state, advanced insanity as a defense, so the risk of an erroneous finding of mental illness was reduced. Second, while in *Addington* the person committed would suffer from the stigma associated with civil commitment, the defendant in *Jones* would be stigmatized by the criminal verdict itself; "the commitment causes little additional harm in this respect." *Id.* at 367 n.16. Third, "the proof that [the defendant] committed a criminal act as a result of mental illness eliminates the risk that he is being committed for mere 'idiosyncratic behavior.' A criminal act by definition is not 'within a range of conduct that is generally acceptable.'" *Id.* at 367 (citations omitted).

46. *See also* 5 U.S.C. § 704 (stating that "[a]gency action made reviewable by statute and final agency action for which there is no other adequate remedy in a court are subject to judicial review"). The scope of judicial review is set out in 5 U.S.C. § 706. For a more thorough discussion of judicial review of agency action, see 3 Pierce, *supra* note 3, §§ 17.2–17.9.

47. *Id.* § 17.7. Throughout the nineteenth century, there had been a presumption of *un*reviewability. *See, e.g.*, Martin v. Mott, 25 U.S. (12 Wheat.) 19, 29 (1827), discussed in 3 Pierce, *supra* note 3, § 17.5.

48. *Cf.* Heckler v. Ringer, 466 U.S. 602 (1984) (concluding that plaintiffs' challenge to a policy adopted by the Secretary of Health and Human Services regarding Medicare benefits for a specified surgical procedure was "inextricably intertwined" with their individual claims for benefits; holding that the statute required plaintiffs to exhaust their administrative remedies before seeking judicial review).

49. The Supreme Court has held that there is a presumption *against* judicial review when an agency declines to take enforcement action. "[A]n agency's decision not to prosecute or enforce . . . is a decision generally committed to an agency's absolute discretion." Heckler v. Chaney, 470 U.S. 821, 831 (1985). *Cf.* Yick Wo v. Hopkins, 118 U.S. 356 (1886) (holding that a city's practice of enforcing a statute against only Chinese subjects violated the Equal Protection Clause). The lower federal courts disagree on the scope of the presumption of unreviewability of agency inaction. 3 Pierce, *supra* note 3, § 17.7.

50. Richard J. Pierce, Jr., et al., Administrative Law and Process § 5.2, at 125 (3d ed. 1999) (hereinafter Pierce, Administrative Law and Process). *See also, e.g.*, Czerkies v. United States Dep't of Labor, 73 F.3d 1435, 1441 (7th Cir. 1996) (en banc).

51. Pierce, Administrative Law and Process, § 5.2, at 125.

52. 3 Pierce, *supra* note 3, § 17.9, citing Henry M. Hart, Jr., *The Power of Congress to Limit the Jurisdiction of Federal Courts: An Exercise in Dialectic*, 66 Harv. L. Rev. 1362 (1953).

53. The Suspension Clause provides: "The Privilege of the Writ of Habeas Corpus shall not be suspended, unless when in Cases of Rebellion or Invasion the public Safety may require it." U.S. Const. art. I, § 9, cl. 2.

54. 3 Pierce, *supra* note 3, § 17.9.

55. The *M.L.B.* Court noted that most of the decisions in the right of access line of cases "'rest on an equal protection framework,'" M.L.B. v. S.L.J., 519 U.S. 102, 120 (1996) (quoting Bearden v. Georgia, 461 U.S. 660, 665 (1983)), but did not disavow the Due Process Clause as an alternate source of the right. *See also id.* at 129 (Kennedy, J., concurring in the judgment) (positing that "due process is quite a sufficient basis for

our holding"); *id.* at 130 (Thomas, J., dissenting) (chastising the majority for "carrying forward the ambiguity in the cases on which it relies"); Evitts v. Lucey, 469 U.S. 387, 403–05 (1985) (noting the significant role the Due Process Clause plays in right of access cases); Logan v. Zimmerman Brush Co., 455 U.S. 422, 430 n.5 (1982) (describing relationship between right of access cases and procedural due process).

56. *Accord* Lane v. Brown, 372 U.S. 477 (1963) (holding that the state had denied an indigent defendant a right secured by the Fourteenth Amendment by refusing to provide him with a transcript of a *coram nobis* hearing, which was required to appeal the denial of the writ). The state need not provide a complete verbatim transcript in every case in which an indigent files an appeal; the state "may find other means of affording adequate and effective appellate review to indigent defendants." *Griffin*, 351 U.S. at 20 (plurality op.). *See also* Draper v. Washington, 372 U.S. 487, 495 (1963) (noting that "[a]lternative methods of reporting trial proceedings are permissible if they place before the appellate court an equivalent report of the events at trial from which the appellant's contentions arise"). But the state must provide a transcript when one is necessary to assure the indigent defendant as effective an appeal as a defendant with financial resources can obtain. Mayer v. City of Chicago, 404 U.S. 189, 195 (1971).

57. The right to appointed counsel on a first appeal of right "does not include the right to bring a frivolous appeal and, concomitantly, does not include the right to counsel for bringing a frivolous appeal." Smith v. Robbins, 528 U.S. 259, 278 (2000) (footnote omitted). The Court has held that a criminal defendant who makes a preliminary showing that her sanity at the time of the offense is likely to be a significant factor at trial is entitled to a psychiatrist's assistance at the government's expense if she cannot otherwise afford such assistance. Ake v. Oklahoma, 470 U.S. 68, 83 (1985).

58. Whether or not they are entitled to appointed counsel, inmates "must have a reasonable opportunity to seek and receive the assistance of attorneys. Regulations and practices that unjustifiably obstruct the availability of professional representation or other aspects of the right of access to the courts are invalid." Procunier v. Martinez, 416 U.S. 396, 419 (1974). A rule that barred law students and paralegals from conducting attorney/client interviews in prison, for example, was invalidated because it inhibited professional representation of inmates by increasing its cost and deterring some attorneys from representing indigent inmates. The burden was not outweighed by any legitimate interest of penal administration. *Id.* at 420–22.

59. Section 1983 provides:

> Every person who, under color of any statute, ordinance, regulation, custom, or usage, of any State or Territory or the District of Columbia, subjects, or causes to be subjected, any citizen of the United States or other person within the jurisdiction thereof to the deprivation of any rights, privileges, or immunities secured by the Constitution and laws, shall be liable to the party injured in an action at law, suit in equity, or other proper proceeding for redress. . . .

42 U.S.C. § 1983.

60. Section 1988 provides in pertinent part:

> In any action or proceeding to enforce a provision of sections [1983 and other specified civil rights statutes], the court, in its discretion, may allow the prevailing party, other than the United States, a reasonable attorney's fee as part of the costs, except that in any action brought against a judicial officer for

an act or omission taken in such officer's judicial capacity such officer shall not be held liable for any costs, including attorney's fees, unless such action was clearly in excess of such officer's jurisdiction.

28 U.S.C. § 1988.

61. The Prison Litigation Reform Act of 1995 further limits prisoners' right to sue under section 1983 to challenge prison conditions by requiring that they first exhaust administrative remedies. 42 U.S.C. § 1997e. The Supreme Court has held that "§ 1997e(a)'s exhaustion requirement applies to all prisoners seeking redress for prison circumstances or occurrences," including those who challenge only a single incident involving a particular inmate, rather than general prison conditions. Porter v. Nussle, 534 U.S. 516, 520 (2002).

5

# Due Process Limitations on the Binding Effect of Judgments

***"It is a violation of due process for a judgment to be binding on a litigant who was not a party or a privy and therefore has never had an opportunity to be heard."*** [1]

Even before the Fourteenth Amendment was adopted, the United States Supreme Court held that a person cannot be bound by a judgment unless she is served with process or voluntarily defends the action (D'Arcy v. Ketchum, 1851). In its most famous statement of this principle, the Supreme Court in Hansberry v. Lee (1940) declared:

> It is a principle of general application in Anglo-American jurisprudence that one is not bound by a judgment *in personam* in a litigation in which he is not designated as a party or to which he has not been made a party by service of process. A judgment rendered in such circumstances is not entitled to . . . full faith and credit . . .; and judicial action enforcing it against the person or property of the absent party is not that due process which the Fifth and Fourteenth Amendments require.

The Court has noted a direct connection between this due process protection and the opportunity to be heard:

> The opportunity to be heard is an essential requisite of due process of law in judicial proceedings. And as a State may not, consistently with the Fourteenth Amendment, enforce a judgment against a party named in the proceedings without a hearing or an opportunity to be heard, so it cannot, without disregarding the requirement of due process, give a conclusive effect to a prior judgment against one who is neither a party nor in privity with a party therein (Richards v. Jefferson County, 1996).

In neither case would it be fair to bind a person by a judgment unless she (or someone looking out for her interests) had an opportunity to be heard.[2] Put differently, the Constitution protects each person's own day in court.[3]

While the Court has steadfastly adhered to this principle in the years following *D'Arcy* and *Hansberry*, it has recognized a number of circumstances in which persons who are not formal parties to a litigation may nevertheless be bound by the judgment. In fact, the *Hansberry* Court itself noted that:

> members of a class not present as parties to the litigation may be bound by the judgment where they are in fact adequately represented by parties who are present, or where they actually participate in the conduct of the litigation in which members of the class are present as parties, or where the interests of the members of the class, some of whom are present as parties, is joint, or where for any other reason the relationship between the parties present and those who are absent is such as legally to entitle the former to stand in judgment for the latter (Hansberry v. Lee, 1940).

In this chapter, we will examine the dynamic relationship between preclusion principles, which permit a nonparty to be bound by a judgment in certain circumstances and the Due Process Clauses, which exert a check on preclusion principles to protect the nonparty's opportunity to be heard.

## BACKGROUND PRECLUSION PRINCIPLES

Before we begin our examination of this due process protection, let us first consider what it means to be bound by a judgment. A person who is bound by a judgment is not free to challenge it in a collateral, or separate, proceeding. Two legal doctrines—claim preclusion and issue preclusion (also known as res judicata and collateral estoppel)—preclude such collateral attacks. To illustrate claim preclusion principles, we will consider the case of a plaintiff suing to recover money damages for injuries suffered in a car accident allegedly caused by the defendant's negligence. Imagine that she offers only her own testimony at trial to prove the defendant's negligence and the jury disbelieves her and the court renders judgment against her. If she later sues a second time on the same claim, hoping to offer the testimony of several eyewitnesses to prove the defendant's negligence this time around, she will be barred from doing so. The doctrine of claim preclusion ordinarily denies a party who has had a full opportunity to present her claim in court a second chance to present the same claim. According to the Second Restatement of Judgments, if the plaintiff loses the first suit, the judgment rendered against her "bars another action by the plaintiff on the same claim" (Restatement (Second) of Judgments § 19, 1982; see also § 17(2)). To be accorded preclusive effect, the judgment must be valid, final and on the merits.[4] This aspect of claim preclusion—referred to as "bar" because it bars the plaintiff from bringing multiple suits on the same claim—protects the defendant from the potential harassment of repetitive suits on the same claim.

But what if the plaintiff wins the first suit? What if initially she sued only for the broken arm she suffered as a result of the accident, and now, after winning that first suit, she sues the same defendant a second time to recover for the broken leg suffered in the same accident?[5] Claim preclusion precludes relitigation of the same claim whether the plaintiff *wins or loses* the first suit. Thus, even if the plaintiff wins the first suit, she "cannot thereafter maintain an action on the original claim or any part thereof . . ." (Restatement (Second) of Judgments § 18(1), 1982). This aspect of claim preclusion—referred to as merger—promotes efficiency by preventing the plaintiff from "splitting her claim" by bringing only part of it in the first action and then, after winning, seeking to litigate a second part of the same claim in a separate law suit. The entire claim is merged into the judgment in the first action and the underlying claim is extinguished. Although different jurisdictions define the scope of the claim differently,[6] the Second Restatement of Judgments defines the claim broadly so that a valid and final judgment precludes "all rights of the plaintiff to remedies against the defendant with respect to all or any part of the transaction, or series of connected transactions, out of which the action arose" (Restatement (Second) of Judgments § 24(1), 1982). Thus, the plaintiff would be precluded from suing a second time for damages suffered in a single car accident.

Now let us assume that the plaintiff seeks damages for all of her injuries in the context of a single suit and obtains a judgment against the defendant. Can the defendant collaterally attack the judgment by raising defenses to the plaintiff's claim, either in a new action that the defendant initiates to challenge the judgment or in the context of an action by the plaintiff to enforce the judgment against him? Claim preclusion applies to plaintiffs and defendants alike, precluding the defendant from collaterally attacking a judgment against him by "avail[ing] himself of defenses he might have interposed, or did interpose, in the first action" (Restatement (Second) of Judgments § 18(2), 1982). As the Comments to the Restatement make clear, "It is immaterial whether the defendant had a defense to the original action if he did not rely on it, or if he did rely on it and judgment was nevertheless given against him" (Restatement (Second) of Judgments § 18 cmt. a, 1982). Thus, win or lose, plaintiff or defendant, each party is afforded one good "crack at the apple"—one full and fair opportunity to present her claim or defense—but only one. Second chances ordinarily are not permitted.[7]

Now let us assume that the plaintiff has two claims against the defendant, which arise out of different transactions. Imagine, for example, that in January, the defendant agreed to buy a car from the plaintiff and in February, the defendant agreed to buy a motorcycle from her.[8] Now imagine that the plaintiff sues the defendant, seeking specific performance of the February agreement. If the undisputed facts prove that the defendant was under the age of majority at the time the agreement was made and lacked capacity to enter into an enforceable agreement, the court will grant summary judgment to her on that ground. If the plaintiff later sues the defendant for damages for breach of the January agreement, the doctrine of claim preclusion will not prevent her from suing the same defendant a second time to present the second claim because it arises from a separate transaction. But even if the second *claim* is not precluded, the doctrine of issue preclusion will bar the parties from relitigating an *issue* of fact or law that was "actually litigated and determined by a valid and final judgment" in the first action if the determination was "essential to the judgment" (Restatement (Second) of Judgments § 27, 1982). Thus, the judgment in the first suit will bar the plaintiff from relitigating the question of the defendant's age and capacity at the time the agreement was made. By preventing different judges or juries from reaching different conclusions on the same issue, the doctrine of issue preclusion preserves public confidence in the judiciary.

All that we have said so far about the binding effect of a judgment applies when successive suits are filed within the same jurisdiction. If successive suits are filed in courts of the same state, the judge-made preclusion law of that state will determine the preclusive effect of the judgment rendered in the first suit. Likewise, if successive suits arising under federal law are filed in federal district courts (in the same or different districts), federal preclusion law will determine the preclusive effect of the judgment.

But what if the first suit is filed in one state's court (forum 1 or F1) and the second suit is filed in a different state's court (forum 2 or F2)? Or what if the second suit is filed in federal court? Now the obligation to accord the first judgment preclusive effect derives from the federal Constitution and/or federal statute. The Full Faith and Credit Clause of the Constitution requires each state to give the "judicial Proceedings" of other states full faith and credit (U.S. Const. art. IV, § 1). A federal statute, moreover, requires state and federal courts to give state court judgments "the same full faith and credit . . . as they have by law or usage in the courts of such State . . . from which they are taken" (28 U.S.C. § 1738). The Supreme Court has interpreted the statute to require the F2 court to give the F1 judgment the same preclusive effect that it would receive in the F1 (or rendering) court. Put differently, to the extent that the two jurisdictions' preclusion laws vary, the F2 court is required to apply the preclusion law of F1, rather than its own, to determine the preclusive effect of the prior state court judgment (Matsushita Elec. Indus. Co. v. Epstein, 1996; Marrese v. Am. Acad. of Orthopaedic Surgeons, 1985).

Although neither the Constitution nor the federal statute explicitly requires state courts to give federal judgments full faith and credit, it is well established that state courts are required to do so (Semtek Int'l Inc. v. Lockheed Martin Corp., 2001; Stoll v. Gottlieb, 1938). If F1 is a federal district court sitting in diversity—in other words, the suit is between citizens of different states and the federal court applies state substantive law—federal common law determines the claim preclusive effect of its judgment (Semtek Int'l Inc. v. Lockheed Martin Corp., 2001). Since federal common law ordinarily requires that the judgment receive the same preclusive effect that it would have received had it been rendered by a state court in the state in which the rendering federal court sits (Semtek Int'l Inc. v. Lockheed

Martin Corp., 2001), the result is the same as what would have occurred under the Full Faith and Credit Clause or statute had F1 been a state court.

Now that we have a better understanding of what it means to say a party is bound by a judgment, we are ready to explore the role that due process plays in limiting the binding effect of judgments.

## LACK OF PERSONAL JURISDICTION

Before the ratification of the Fourteenth Amendment, there was no federal constitutional vehicle for directly challenging the authority of a state court to enter a judgment against a party who was not served with process while physically present in the state or otherwise subject to the court's jurisdiction. Thus, if the highest court of the rendering state concluded that jurisdiction was available (even if the defendant had not been served with process), the defendant was bound by the judgment rendered against him and had no opportunity to avoid enforcement of the judgment within the rendering state. While the full faith and credit statute ordinarily required F2 courts to recognize F1 judgments, "a judgment rendered in one State, assuming to bind the person of a citizen of another, was void within the foreign State, when the defendant had not been served with process or voluntarily made defence, because neither the legislative jurisdiction, nor that of courts of justice, had binding force" (D'Arcy v. Ketchum, 1851). In other words, the Supreme Court interpreted the Full Faith and Credit Clause and implementing statute as excepting judgments rendered by courts that lacked personal jurisdiction over the defendant (W. Union Tel. Co. v. Pennsylvania, 1961).

Following ratification of the Fourteenth Amendment in 1868, the Supreme Court held that due process bars a state from *rendering* a judgment against a party over whom the court has not acquired jurisdiction and provides a vehicle for resisting enforcement of the judgment even in the rendering state. In the landmark case of Pennoyer v. Neff (1877), the Supreme Court stated:

> Since the adoption of the Fourteenth Amendment to the Federal Constitution, the validity of such judgments [i.e., judgments rendered without personal jurisdiction over the defendant] may be directly questioned, and their enforcement in the State resisted, on the ground that proceedings in a court of justice to determine the personal rights and obligations of parties over whom that court has no jurisdiction do not constitute due process of law.

The availability of a collateral attack in these circumstances gives "teeth" to the due process protection against assertions of jurisdiction over persons who lack sufficient connection to the forum state.[9] If lack of jurisdiction were not a constitutionally prescribed exception to standard preclusion principles, then a defendant who defaulted (because she was not subject to jurisdiction in the forum state) would not be permitted to raise lack of jurisdiction as a defense in a collateral attack on the judgment; her jurisdictional defense would have merged into the judgment. Thus, the Constitution spares the defendant the obligation to appear in the very place that she contends is too inconvenient for her to attend to preserve her jurisdictional challenge.

If the defendant appears, however, in the first proceeding and contests personal jurisdiction, she will be precluded from later collaterally attacking the judgment for lack of jurisdiction (Ins. Corp. of Ir., Ltd. v. Compagnie des Bauxites de Guinee, 1982; Baldwin v. Iowa State Traveling Men's Assoc., 1931). Because she had a full and fair opportunity to litigate the issue of her amenability to jurisdiction in the rendering court, the doctrine of issue preclusion, backed up by the Full Faith and Credit Clause, bars her from relitigating the same issue in a collateral proceeding. Viewed through the due process lens, this result makes sense, as the defendant had an opportunity to be heard on the issue and therefore should be bound by the judgment. Likewise, if a defendant appears in a proceeding and *fails* to challenge personal jurisdiction, she will not be permitted to collaterally attack the judgment later on the theory that the rendering court lacked jurisdiction over her because she had an *opportunity* to be heard on the issue—even if she did not seize it. Thus, due process affords a collateral attack to a person who is beyond the court's jurisdiction only if she does not appear in the rendering court.[10]

## ORDINARILY NONPARTIES ARE NOT BOUND

If a party to an action who has not been brought within the court's jurisdiction cannot be bound by the judgment, it follows *a fortiori* that a *nonparty* to the action, who had *no* opportunity to be heard, cannot be bound either. Although the Supreme Court has acknowledged exceptions to this general rule (in circumstances to be discussed shortly), it has consistently recognized the role that due process plays in protecting nonparties from judgments rendered in their absence. Three recent Supreme Court decisions illustrate this fundamental due process protection.

### Martin v. Wilks (1989)

Martin v. Wilks (1989) involved a lawsuit by seven African-American plaintiffs against the City of Birmingham, Alabama, and the Jefferson County Personnel Board, alleging that the defendants had engaged in racially discriminatory hiring and promotion practices in violation of Title VII of the Civil Rights Act.[11] Ultimately the parties entered into a consent decree that required the defendants to take specified steps to increase the number of African-Americans hired as firefighters and promoted within the department. After the consent decree was entered, a group of white firefighters filed another suit against the City and the Board, claiming that they were denied promotions in favor of less qualified minority candidates in violation of federal law. A group of African-American individuals, including Martin, intervened to defend the consent decree, pursuant to which the challenged promotion decisions had been made. Conceding that they had made race-conscious employment decisions, the City and the Board nevertheless moved to dismiss the action as an impermissible collateral attack on the consent decree. Put differently, they argued that their conduct was not actionable because the consent decree required them to take race into account. The question before the Court was whether the white firefighters, who had not participated in the action in which the consent decree was entered, nevertheless were barred from challenging employment decisions made pursuant to it.

Starting with the "deep-rooted historic tradition that everyone should have his own day in court," the Court concluded that "a person cannot be deprived of his legal rights in a proceeding to which he is not a party" (Martin v. Wilks, 1989). Since the white firefighters were not parties to the action in which the decree was entered, they were not bound by it. The *Martin* petitioners argued that since the white firefighters were aware of the earlier litigation but nevertheless "chose to pass up an opportunity to intervene, they should not be permitted to later litigate the issues in a new action" (Martin v. Wilks, 1989). Rejecting this argument, the Court noted that intervention under the Federal Rules of Civil Procedure is permissive, not mandatory, so a nonparty who declines to intervene is not bound by the judgment. "Joinder as a party, rather than knowledge of a lawsuit and an opportunity to intervene, is the method by which potential parties are subjected to the jurisdiction of the court and bound by a judgment or decree" (Martin v. Wilks, 1989).

## Baker v. General Motors Corp. (1998)

The Supreme Court reaffirmed this principle a decade later in Baker v. General Motors Corp. (1998). *Baker* involved a long-time General Motors ("GM") employee, Ronald Elwell, who studied vehicular fires and helped GM redesign its fuel lines. Over the course of his career, Elwell often helped GM lawyers defend the company against products liability actions. The employment relationship soured, however, when Elwell testified in one case that the fuel system of a GM pickup truck was inferior in comparison to other trucks. Elwell later sued GM for wrongful discharge, among other claims. The parties ultimately settled the claim and agreed to entry of a permanent injunction enjoining Elwell from testifying against GM in any litigation. A Michigan state court entered the injunction. In a private settlement agreement, the parties agreed that if a court ordered Elwell to appear and testify, GM would not seek to have him held in contempt.

When Kevin and Steven Baker sued GM in Missouri, claiming that a faulty fuel pump in a GM truck caused an engine fire that killed their mother, they sought to call Elwell as a witness at trial. GM objected, arguing that the Michigan injunction barred his testimony. The federal district court hearing the case declined to enforce the Michigan injunction, allowing the Bakers to call Elwell as a witness. On appeal, the Eighth Circuit Court of Appeals reversed, holding that Elwell's testimony should not have been admitted.

The Supreme Court unanimously reversed the Eighth Circuit's judgment, citing Martin v. Wilks (1989) for the proposition that

> Michigan's judgment . . . cannot reach beyond the Elwell-GM controversy to control proceedings against GM brought in other States, *by other parties*, asserting claims the merits of which Michigan has not considered. Michigan has no power over those parties, and no basis for commanding them to become intervenors in the Elwell-GM dispute. Most essentially, Michigan lacks authority to control courts elsewhere by precluding them, in actions brought by *strangers to the Michigan litigation*, from determining for themselves what witnesses are competent to testify and what evidence is relevant and admissible in their search for the truth (Baker v. Gen. Motors Corp., 1998, emphasis added).

Conceding that the Michigan injunction could bar Elwell from volunteering to testify against GM, the Court held that Michigan could not determine evidentiary issues in a suit "brought by parties who were not subject to the jurisdiction of the Michigan court." Because the Bakers were not parties to the Michigan action, they were not bound by the injunction (Baker v. Gen. Motors Corp., 1998).

### Nelson v. Adams USA, Inc. (2000)

In another unanimous decision rendered just two years later, the Supreme Court in Nelson v. Adams USA, Inc. (2000) again had occasion to emphasize the protection nonparties have against the binding effect of judgments. Ohio Cellular Products Corp. ("OCP") filed a lawsuit against Adams USA, Inc. ("Adams"), alleging patent infringement. The district court ultimately dismissed OCP's claim because the patents had been anticipated by prior art and were therefore invalid. Donald Nelson, OCP's president and sole shareholder, had deceitfully withheld the prior art from the Patent and Trademark Office. In light of this inequitable conduct, which was chargeable to OCP, the court ordered OCP to pay Adams's substantial costs and attorneys' fees. Adams feared that it would be unable to collect this award because OCP's counsel had warned that OCP would be liquidated if it were subject to a substantial judgment for fees. In an effort to protect its judgment, Adams moved to amend its pleading to add Nelson, personally, as a party from whom fees could be collected and simultaneously moved for an amended judgment, subjecting Nelson to liability as soon as he was joined. The district court granted the motion to amend and altered the judgment at the same time. Concluding that the postjudgment joinder did not prejudice Nelson, the Court of Appeals for the Federal Circuit affirmed.

Before the Supreme Court, Nelson challenged only the portion of the order that altered the judgment to make him personally liable without an opportunity to be heard. The Court began its opinion by examining Rule 15 of the Federal Rules of Civil Procedure, which governs amendments. If leave to amend a pleading to join a party is granted, Rule 15(a) affords the newly joined party at least "10 days after service of the amended pleading" in which to file a responsive pleading (Fed. R. Civ. P. 15(a)). This opportunity to respond, the Court noted, is "fundamental to due process" (Nelson v. Adams USA, Inc., 2000). Yet Nelson was afforded *no* opportunity to respond to the amended pleading. In fact, no amended pleading was ever filed or served. "Instead," Justice Ginsburg wrote, "judgment was entered against him the moment permission to amend the pleading was granted" (Nelson v. Adams USA, Inc., 2000). Thus the process both failed to comply with Rule 15 and violated the Due Process Clause, which protected Nelson's "right to have time and opportunity to respond to the claim once Adams gained leave to sue [him] in his individual capacity. . . ." (Nelson v. Adams USA, Inc., 2000). Even if Nelson would have had no better defense against the charge of inequitable conduct than OCP had offered, he nevertheless was entitled to "the actual opportunity to defend that due process affords every party against whom a claim is stated" (Nelson v. Adams USA, Inc., 2000).[12]

*Martin*, *Baker* and *Nelson* all stand for the proposition that only parties—those actually joined and served with process—may be bound by a judgment in an action. But does this due process imperative admit any exceptions? Are not absent class members bound by a judgment rendered against the class in a class action? Are not beneficiaries of a trust bound when the trustee litigates a claim on behalf of the trust? It is to these questions that we now turn.

## NONPARTIES WHO MAY BE BOUND

In Hansberry v. Lee (1940), the Supreme Court identified three circumstances in which nonparties to an action may be bound by a judgment: the absentee is adequately represented by a party to the action; she actually participates in the litigation; or she shares a joint interest with a party to the litigation. We will begin with an analysis of *Hansberry* itself and then consider in greater depth these circumstances in which nonparties may be bound by judgments rendered in their absence.

### The Landmark Case of Hansberry v. Lee (1940)

*Hansberry* involved a pair of lawsuits brought to enforce racially restrictive covenants that barred landowners in a Chicago neighborhood called South Park from selling or leasing their property to African-Americans.[13] By their terms, the covenants were binding only if signed by owners of ninety-five percent of the property in the South Park subdivision. In the first suit, Olive Burke sued on behalf of herself and other similarly situated property owners to enforce the racially restrictive covenant. Although denominated a class action, it appears that no notice was provided to the absent class members (Lee v. Hansberry, Ill. 1939, Shaw, J., dissenting). Burke and the defendants stipulated that ninety-five percent of the South Park property owners had signed the restrictive covenants even though only fifty-four percent in fact had signed. On these stipulated facts, an Illinois state court enforced the restrictive covenant, rejecting the defendants' argument that it would be unjust to do so in light of the changed demographic make-up of the neighborhood. The Illinois Court of Appeals affirmed (Burke v. Kleiman, Ill. App. Ct. 1934).

As Professor Allen Kamp's history of *Hansberry* reveals, in the years following *Burke*, Chicago's black population continued to grow and its demand for housing increased. At the same time, the white population in South Park declined and property owners who wanted to rent or sell found few white tenants or buyers. Faced with the choice between financial loss or violation of a racially restrictive covenant, white property owners in South Park chose to violate the covenant and rent or sell to African-Americans. One of these white property owners was Mr. Burke, whose wife Olive had been the successful plaintiff in Burke v. Kleiman (Ill. App. Ct. 1934). When Mr. Burke arranged a dummy transaction to sell his property to an African-American, Carl Hansberry (father of playwright Lorraine Hansberry), a second lawsuit was filed in Illinois state court to enforce the restrictive covenant in South Park, this time to enjoin the sale to Hansberry.[14] The defendants, Burke and Hansberry, argued that the covenant was unenforceable because fewer than ninety-five percent of the property owners in the neighborhood had signed it. Although the Illinois trial court found that only fifty-four percent in fact had signed, it nevertheless concluded that the defendants were precluded from raising this defense because they were bound by the judgment rendered in *Burke*. As absent class members (ostensibly represented by Ms. Burke), they were bound by the determination in *Burke* that ninety-five percent of the property owners had signed the restrictive covenant.[15] The Illinois Supreme Court affirmed (Lee v. Hansberry, Ill. 1939).

The United States Supreme Court reversed, holding that it would violate due process to bind Burke and Hansberry by the judgment rendered in *Burke* even though it technically had been denominated a class action. Recognizing that "[s]tate courts are free to attach such descriptive labels to litigations before them as they may choose and to attribute to them such consequences as they think appropriate under state constitutions and laws," the Court nevertheless required that class action judgments comport with federal constitutional requirements if they are to bind absent class members: "the interests of those not joined [must be] of the same class as the interests of those who are, and . . . the latter [must] fairly represent the former in the prosecution of the litigation of the issues in which all have a common interest. . . ." (Hansberry v. Lee, 1940). In language that will serve as our guide in determining when class members and other nonparties may be bound by a judgment, the Court went on to note that

> members of a class not present as parties to the litigation may be bound by the judgment where they are in fact adequately represented by parties who are present, or where they actually participate in the conduct of the litigation in which members of the class are present as parties, or where the interest of the members of the class, some of whom are present as parties, is joint, or where for any other reason the relationship between the parties present and those who are absent is such as legally to entitle the former to stand in judgment for the latter (Hansberry v. Lee, 1940).

Thus, adequate representation of, or actual participation by, those not technically joined would justify binding them by the judgment, as would a joint interest between the nonparty and a litigant.

In applying these principles to determine whether Burke and Hansberry were bound by the judgment in Burke v. Kleiman (Ill. App. Ct. 1934), the Court quickly disposed of the argument that Burke and Hansberry shared a joint interest with the litigants in *Burke* that would justify binding them by the judgment. Without addressing whether Mr. and Ms. Burke themselves held their property jointly, the Court noted that the "restrictive agreement did not purport to create a joint obligation or liability" because the promises "were the several obligations of the signers and those claiming under them" (Hansberry v. Lee, 1940). Thus, no joint interest justified binding Mr. Burke and his buyer, Mr. Hansberry, by the judgment rendered in *Burke*. The Court did not even mention the possibility that Mr. Burke might actually have participated in the *Burke* action (given his wife's role as plaintiff and named class representative).

Instead, the central focus of *Hansberry* was the failure of Ms. Burke to adequately represent property owners, like Mr. Burke and his successor, Mr. Hansberry, who opposed enforcement of the restrictive covenant. "Because of the dual and potentially conflicting interests of those who are putative parties to the agreement in compelling or resisting its performance, it is impossible to say, solely because they are parties to it, that any two of them are of the same class" (Hansberry v. Lee, 1940). Since Ms. Burke's interests were not "necessarily or even probably the same as those whom [she was] deemed to represent," her appointment as class representative did "not afford that protection to absent parties which due process requires" (Hansberry v. Lee, 1940).

Nor had the defendants in *Burke* represented Mr. Burke and Mr. Hansberry. Although they may have shared an interest in opposing the covenant, the court had not certified a defendant class and the *Burke* defendants did not purport to represent the interests of like-minded property owners who opposed enforcement of the covenant.

With *Hansberry* as our guide, let us explore in greater depth the circumstances in which persons not parties to an action may, consistent with due process, be bound by the judgment: if they actually controlled the litigation; if they had a joint interest with a party to the action; or if they were adequately represented by a party to the action.

### Persons Who Control the Litigation

*Hansberry* recognized that class members may be bound by a judgment "where they actually participate in the conduct of the litigation. . . ." (Hansberry v. Lee, 1940). More broadly, it is well accepted that a nonparty who controls a party's presentation in litigation may be bound by the judgment (for issue preclusion purposes) to the same extent as the party (Restatement (Second) of Judgments § 39, 1982).[16] In such cases, the nonparty has "effectively enjoyed his day in court" (Gonzalez v. Banco Cent. Corp., 1st Cir. 1994).

A person has control of litigation when she has "effective choice as to the legal theories and proofs to be advanced" and has "control over the opportunity to obtain review" (Restatement (Second) of Judgments § 39 cmt. c, 1982; see also Becherer v. Merrill Lynch, Pierce, Fenner & Smith, Inc., 6th Cir. 1999). The court must consider "the totality of the circumstances to determine whether they justify a reasonable inference of a nonparty's potential or actual involvement as a decisionmaker in the earlier litigation" (Gonzalez v. Banco Cent. Corp., 1st Cir. 1994). Mere payment of a party's attorneys' fees, or reimbursement of the damages awarded against a party, or appearance as *amicus curiae*, or retention of the attorney who represented a litigant in the prior suit, will not give rise to an inference of control (Restatement (Second) of Judgments § 39, Reporter's Note on cmt. c, 1982; Drummond v. United States, 1945; Benson & Ford, Inc. v. Wanda Petroleum Co., 5th Cir. 1987).

Some courts impose an additional requirement, binding a nonparty who asserted control only if she had a financial or proprietary interest in the litigation (Va. Hosp. Ass'n v. Baliles, 4th Cir. 1987). Professors Wright and Miller posit that such an interest in the outcome may explain the nonparty's incentive to control the suit and to litigate vigorously, but they question whether the interest requirement serves any independent purpose.[17] The Second Restatement of Judgments has abandoned the interest test (Restatement (Second) of Judgments § 39 cmt. a, 1982).

The Supreme Court applied the control theory in Montana v. United States (1979). There, a contractor on a federal project, Peter Kiewit Sons' Company, sued in state court to challenge a Montana law that imposed a gross receipts tax upon contractors of public, but not private, construction projects. Less than a month after Kiewit filed this first action in state court, the United States filed a second action in federal district court to challenge the constitutionality of the same tax. The federal action was stayed pending resolution of the state court action. The state trial court upheld the constitutionality of the tax, as did the Montana Supreme Court on appeal. But what effect, if any, would this judgment have on the United States in its federal action? Could the government be precluded from relitigating the issue of the constitutionality of the tax in the federal proceeding even though it had not been a party to the first action?

Although nonparties ordinarily are not bound by judgments rendered in their absence, the policies underlying preclusion law counsel in favor of binding them if they "assume control over litigation in which they have a direct financial or proprietary interest and then seek to redetermine issues previously resolved. . . [T]he persons for whose benefit and at whose direction a cause of action is litigated cannot be said to be 'strangers to the cause . . .'" (Montana v. United States, 1979). Here, the United States government's control over the *Kiewit* litigation was undisputed. It had directed Kiewit to file the action, reviewed the complaint before it was filed, paid Kiewit's attorneys' fees, and when Kiewit lost in the trial court, directed it to appeal. The United States also had filed an *amicus* brief in the Montana Supreme Court in connection with Kiewit's appeal. "Thus, although not a party, the United States plainly had a sufficient 'laboring oar' in the conduct of the state-court litigation to actuate principles of estoppel" (Montana v. United States, 1979). While no due process issue was presented in *Montana*—the nonparty to be bound by the judgment, the United States, is not protected by the Due Process Clause[18]—the reasoning in *Montana* strongly suggests that, consistent with due process, a nonparty may be bound by a judgment as long as she exercised sufficient control over the underlying litigation.

The lower courts have applied *Montana*'s reasoning in a variety of settings to bind nonparties who controlled the litigation. For example, courts have held that an insurance company was bound by a judgment against its insured;[19] the president and sole shareholder of a corporation was bound by a judgment against the company;[20] an attorney was bound by a judgment rendered against her client;[21] a manufacturer was bound by a judgment rendered against the distributor of its product where the manufacturer had actively conducted the defense in the prior litigation;[22] and, in what appears to have been a much closer call, an employer was bound by a judgment rendered against its employees because it had paid substantial expenses incurred by the employees in connection with the earlier litigation and had participated in a number of depositions taken in that action.[23]

In some cases, the courts explicitly addressed the due process issue that lurks in all cases in which a nonparty is bound, holding that it comports with due process to bind a nonparty who controlled the prior litigation (Alman v. Danin, 1st Cir. 1986; Nabisco, Inc. v. Amtech Int'l, Inc., S.D.N.Y. 2000). The Sixth Circuit Court of Appeals was most explicit:

[M]inimum standards of due process require that, in order to be claim precluded, a nonparty must (A) have actual control over the first litigation, (B) be able to hold the first party or its attorney legally accountable for the result in the first action, or (C) be able to rescind its express or implied consent to being represented by the first party if it deems its interests diverge sufficiently early in the litigation (Becherer v. Merrill Lynch, Pierce, Fenner & Smith, Inc., 6th Cir. 1999).

## "Joint" Interests

The *Hansberry* Court recognized that it would comport with due process to bind a nonparty to a judgment not only if she controlled the earlier litigation, but alternatively if she and the party to the earlier action shared a "joint" interest. *Hansberry* offered no citations for this proposition and failed to define "joint" interest, a matter governed by state property law. Without immersing ourselves in the intricacies of property law, we will expand upon *Hansberry*'s observation and explore the two general rules governing the effect a judgment has on a nonparty who shares a joint property interest with a litigant: first, successors in interest are bound by judgments both for and against the person from whom they acquire the property; and second, concurrent property owners ordinarily are not bound by judgments for or against the person with whom they share an interest in property.

### *Successors in Interest*

Whether they are purchasers, heirs, assignees or other transferees, persons who succeed to another's property are bound by any judgment rendered either for or against the person from whom they acquire the property. This principle is not limited to *in rem* or *quasi-in-rem* proceedings. The Second Restatement of Judgments states the proposition this way: "A judgment in an action that determines interests in real or personal property . . . [h]as preclusive effects upon a person who succeeds to the interest of a party to the same extent as upon the party himself" (Restatement (Second) of Judgments § 43(1)(b), 1982). This principle is consistent with the commonsense proposition that a person can transfer no greater property interest than she has (Postal Tel. Cable Co. v. City of Newport, 1918; Capital Inv. Corp. v. King County, Wash. Ct. App. 2002). According to Professors Wright and Miller, the justification for binding the successor is not that the litigant adequately represented the successor's interests, but rather that the victor in the litigation is entitled to finality. It would be unfair to deprive her of the victory through the mere expedient of a postjudgment transfer of the property.[24] But if finality for the victor were an adequate justification for binding nonparties, this rationale might apply far more broadly to extinguish the rights of other nonparties to litigate autonomously. Perhaps finality justifies preclusion of nonparty successors in interest (but not other nonparties) because in the property context alone, the victor may have believed she was litigating a claim to the property itself (binding on all), rather than a claim against a particular person.

This explanation is bolstered by the qualification that successors in interest are bound only if the underlying action affected the property itself and not merely the personal rights of the litigants (Restatement (Second) of Judgments § 43 cmt. a, 1982). Thus, judgments entered in suits to quiet title and other judgments that affect title to property are binding on successors (Ward v. Davis, Ark. 1989). Judgments that determine only personal rights are not binding on successors, however. In Southcenter Joint Venture v. National Democratic Policy Committee (Wash. 1989), for example, the owner of a private shopping mall sued a political organization to bar it from soliciting contributions and selling literature in the mall. The mall owner lost, when the trial court held that the political organization had a constitutional right to solicit contributions. Subsequently, a new owner purchased the mall from the unsuccessful litigant and brought its own suit against the same organization to enjoin solicitations in the mall. The Washington Supreme Court rejected the political organization's contention that the successor mall owner was collaterally estopped from relitigating the issues raised in the earlier suit. Conceding that the plaintiff "did acquire the mall from a party to the prior action" and noting "that a successor in interest to a party to an action that determines interests in property is subject to the preclusive effects of that action," the court nevertheless held that the mall owner was not bound because the "previous action involved a 'personal' right, as opposed to a 'property' right. . . . This is because such a right [i.e., the political organization's free speech right to solicit contributions and sell literature in the mall] is not unique to the particular shopping mall involved, nor does it affect the title thereto" (Southcenter Joint Venture v. Nat'l Democratic Policy Comm., Wash. 1989).

In cases where it is difficult to determine whether the earlier claim affected the property or only the personal rights of the litigants, Professors Wright and Miller suggest that

> substantial weight should be given to the reasonable expectations of the victor that a judgment would protect against relitigation by any future adversary. Weight also must be given to the nature of the rights asserted and adjudicated; a limitation on use of property, for example, may be treated differently than a question of title.[25]

Since the doctrine of claim preclusion bars litigation not only of theories advanced or claims to the property that actually were raised but also of theories and claims that might have been raised, both the litigant and the successor in interest to the subject property are bound in this way by the judgment affecting the property (Restatement (Second) of Judgments § 43 cmt. b, 1982). Thus, when one corporation sued another for breach of a contract to sell real property, the plaintiff's successor in interest was precluded from later suing the defendant's successor in interest for a *prima facie* tort arising out of the same failed real estate transaction (Williams v. Rape, Mo. App. 1999).

All that we have said so far explains why a successor in interest may be bound by a judgment affecting property if the judgment was rendered *before* the transfer of the property to the successor. But what if the litigation affecting the property is commenced, and the judgment is rendered, *after* the successor acquires the property? Or what if the litigation is commenced before the transfer but the judgment is rendered only after the successor acquires the property? It is to these questions that we now turn.

The United States Supreme Court has held that it would violate due process to bind a successor in interest by a judgment rendered in an action commenced after the transfer of the subject property (Postal Tel. Cable Co. v. City of Newport, 1918). Since the reason for binding a successor is that "the estoppel runs with the property," in the Court's words, "it follows that nothing which the grantor can do or suffer after he has parted with the title can affect rights previously vested in the grantee, for there is no longer privity between them" (Postal Tel. Cable Co. v. City of Newport, 1918). Therefore, just as a state cannot enforce a judgment against an original party unless the person is afforded notice and an opportunity to be heard, "so it cannot, without disregarding the requirement of due process, give a conclusive effect to a prior judgment against one who is neither a party nor in privity with a party therein" (Postal Tel. Cable Co. v. City of Newport, 1918).[26] Thus, a judgment rendered in an action commenced after the transfer of the property is not binding on the successor to the subject property.

Ordinarily, a successor in interest is bound by a judgment affecting the property rendered after the transfer if the action was pending at the time of the transfer (Golden State Bottling Co. v. NLRB, 1973; Restatement (Second) of Judgments § 44, 1982). The rationale for this rule is clearest when the successor was aware of the pending litigation at the time she acquired the property and forewent the opportunity to seek a substitution of parties or to intervene in, or otherwise participate in, the litigation. In such a case, the successor consents to representation of her interest by the transferor (Restatement (Second) of Judgments § 44 cmt. a, 1982). The rationale is more complicated when the successor was not aware of the pending litigation at the time she acquired the property. On the one hand, there is reluctance to bind her, given that she had no opportunity to participate in the litigation. On the other hand, if she is not bound, she may compel the opposing party to relitigate a claim that the opponent believed had been resolved once and for all in the suit against the transferor. According to a Comment to the Second Restatement:

> When the equities are in this balance, the burden is properly placed on the successor. Aside from whatever weight may be given to the principle of *caveat emptor* are the

considerations that the successor usually has an express or implied right of indemnity against the transferor for loss resulting from the judgment; the successor changed the status quo regarding ownership and may justly be burdened with losses which might be expected possibly to result; and, if the rule were otherwise, the stabilizing effect of a judgment concerning the property could indefinitely be postponed by successive transfers (Restatement (Second) of Judgments § 44 cmt. a, 1982).[27]

The rule as applied to unaware successors in interest seems in tension with Martin v. Wilks (1989), which held that nonparties may not be bound by a judgment rendered in their absence even if they were aware of the earlier litigation and could have intervened.

### *Concurrent Property Owners*

As a general rule, a judgment rendered against a property owner is not binding on other persons who have a concurrent ownership interest in the same property (Restatement (Second) of Judgments § 54, 1982). In other words, simply because people choose to own property together does not mean that they will adequately represent each other's interests. In fact, as a Comment to the Restatement recognizes, the relationship between co-owners is a potential source of ongoing conflict, so their interests may be adverse rather than identical or co-extensive (Restatement (Second) of Judgments § 54 cmt. a, 1982).

Of course, if the co-owners have another relationship from which preclusion may arise, then a judgment for or against one of them will be binding on the other (Restatement (Second) of Judgments § 54(1), 1982). For example, if one owner brings a lawsuit to enjoin a neighboring property owner from trespassing upon the plaintiff's land owned with another, ordinarily the co-owner of the property will not be bound by the judgment. But if the nonparty co-owner controls the litigation brought by the named co-owner, then she *will* be bound—not because she is a co-owner of the property but because she exercised control over the litigation (Restatement (Second) of Judgments § 54(1) & cmt. b, 1982).

## Persons Adequately Represented by Parties

In addition to those who exercise control over litigation and those who succeed to property held by a litigant, nonparties whose interests are adequately represented by a litigant may, consistent with due process, be bound by a judgment (Martin v. Wilks, 1989; Hansberry v. Lee, 1940). In what circumstances are the interests of the representative sufficiently aligned with those of the absent person to justify this exception from the general rule that only parties are bound? It is to this question that we now turn.

### *Formal Legal Relationships*

The law recognizes a number of formal legal relationships wherein one person represents the interests of another, who, while not technically a party to the lawsuit, will be bound by the judgment. For example, the trustee of an estate represents the interests of the beneficiaries, who are bound by a judgment rendered by or against the trustee (Restatement (Second) of Judgments § 41(a), 1982; Kerrison v. Stewart, 1876). Likewise, an executor, administrator or guardian represents the interests of others, who are bound by a judgment rendered by or against the fiduciary (Restatement (Second) of Judgments § 41(c), 1982; Sea-Land Servs., Inc. v. Gaudet, 1974). In these cases, due process is satisfied even though the nonparty has no personal opportunity to be heard because an opportunity is afforded to her representative (Harris County v. Carmax Auto Superstores, Inc., 5th Cir. 1999).

Professor John McCoid has posited that "consent and/or necessity are the principal supports of all res judicata privity categories based on representation. . . ."[28] Where a person selects a representative by contract—such as where a principal designates an agent to represent her—the justification for binding the absent party is consent. In other cases, where the court appoints a representative to enable litigation to go forward—such as where the court appoints a guardian to represent an infant or a class member to represent a large class of absentees—the justification is necessity. The infant is incapable of representing herself, and the class members are too numerous to join individually as parties, so appointment of a representative must be made if the litigation is to proceed.[29]

### *Class Actions*

In the class action context, an absent class member may be bound by the judgment only if her interests were adequately represented by the class representative (Hansberry v. Lee, 1940; Smith v. Swormstedt, 1854). In the years since *Hansberry*, the courts have attempted to define "adequacy of representation" in the class action context and have considered whether due process requires more than mere adequacy of representation before a class member may be bound by a judgment rendered in her absence. One of the thorniest issues, whether due process requires notice to individual class members in (b)(1) and (b)(2) and hybrid class actions, was addressed in Chapter 4 and will not be revisited here. Instead, we will focus on three other due process issues that arise in the class action setting: (1) whether a judgment is binding on absent class members who lack minimum contacts with the forum state; (2) whether due process guarantees absent class members an opportunity to opt out; and (3) the circumstances in which absent class members may collaterally attack a judgment on the theory that the representation was inadequate.

### *Lack of Personal Jurisdiction Over Absent Class Members*

As discussed in the earlier section of this chapter entitled "Lack of Personal Jurisdiction," a person is not bound by a judgment rendered by a court that lacked personal jurisdiction over her. But does this due process protection extend to absent class members? This issue was raised in Phillips Petroleum Co. v. Shutts (1985),[30] where the defendant challenged entry of a judgment against it on behalf of a nationwide class, arguing that the state court could not assert jurisdiction over the claims of the absent class members unless they affirmatively consented to jurisdiction or had minimum contacts with the rendering state. The Supreme Court conceded several well-established points: first, that the claims of the class members were property interests protected by due process; and second, that due process protects a *defendant* from the entry of a judgment against her unless she has sufficient minimum contacts with the state such that an assertion of jurisdiction would comport with traditional notions of fair play and substantial justice or unless she consents to the court's jurisdiction.

But the Court rejected the argument that it would violate due process to assert jurisdiction over the claims of absent plaintiff class members who lack minimum contacts with the forum state. Because the burdens placed upon an absent class action plaintiff "are not of the same order or magnitude" as those placed upon a defendant, the due process protections afforded to class action plaintiffs are not identical to those afforded to defendants. Unlike defendants, absent class action plaintiffs need not retain attorneys to represent them, travel to the forum, participate in discovery, or risk entry of a judgment requiring them to pay damages or costs or to comply with an injunction (Phillips Petroleum Co. v. Shutts, 1985).

Not only are absent class action plaintiffs spared these burdens, but they receive protection from the court and the class representative, who are required by the procedural rules governing class actions to look out for the interests of the absent class members. For example, before certifying the class, the court must assess the adequacy of representation and the degree of commonality among the claims of the absent class members and the named representative ( Fed. R. Civ. P. 23(a)), and before approving a settlement of a class action, the court must assess its fairness (Fed. R. Civ. P. 23(e)).[31]

Since the burdens borne by absent class action plaintiffs are fewer than those borne by defendants in non-class actions,[32] the Due Process Clause affords each group differing degrees of protection. Rejecting the defendant's argument regarding personal jurisdiction, the Court held:

> [A] forum State may exercise jurisdiction over the claim of an absent class-action plaintiff, even though that plaintiff may not possess minimum contacts with the forum which would support personal jurisdiction over a defendant. If the forum State wishes to bind an absent plaintiff concerning a claim for money damages or similar relief at law, it must provide

minimal procedural due process protection. The plaintiff must receive notice plus an opportunity to be heard and participate in the litigation, whether in person or through counsel. The notice must be the best practicable. . . . Additionally, we hold that due process requires at a minimum that an absent plaintiff be provided with an opportunity to remove himself from the class by executing and returning an "opt out" or "request for exclusion" form to the court. Finally the Due Process Clause of course requires that the named plaintiff at all times adequately represent the interests of the absent class members (Phillips Petroleum Co. v. Shutts, 1985).[33]

Under *Shutts*, then, the procedural protections afforded by Rule 23 (and state law analogues) are an adequate substitute for the protection that due process otherwise provides by limiting the jurisdictional reach of the forum (In re Real Estate Title & Settlement Servs. Antitrust Litig., 3d Cir. 1989).

In a footnote to this seminal passage, the *Shutts* Court limited its holding to class actions that "seek to bind known plaintiffs concerning claims wholly or predominately for money judgments," specifically disclaiming any view regarding mandatory or hybrid class actions or defendant class actions (Phillips Petroleum Co. v. Shutts, 1985). This footnote raises the critical issue of whether absent class members in mandatory or hybrid class actions, or unknown class members, must be subject to the court's personal jurisdiction in order to be bound by a class action judgment.[34]

As might be expected given the lack of guidance from the Supreme Court on this issue, the lower courts are divided.[35] Several courts have held that in mandatory class actions, and other class actions with unknown class members, due process is satisfied even if absent class members lack minimum contacts with the forum state as long as other due process protections are afforded them, such as notice and adequate representation. For example, in an opinion later vacated by the Supreme Court, the Fifth Circuit held that *Shutts* does not apply to limited fund class actions, concluding that "minimum contacts or consent to jurisdiction are not necessary in equitable class actions" (In re Asbestos Litig., 5th Cir. 1996). Similarly, the Second Circuit has concluded that *Shutts* does not apply directly to unknown plaintiff class members and that a class action settlement is binding on unknown absent class members over whom the court may lack personal jurisdiction (In re Agent Orange Prod. Liab. Litig., 2d Cir. 1993). Applying an analysis more like Mathews v. Eldridge (1976) than *Shutts*, the Second Circuit concluded that whatever marginal gains might have been realized by affording the class members greater procedural protections were outweighed by society's interest in the efficient and fair resolution of the large-scale class action.[36]

Other courts have read *Shutts* differently, concluding that due process bars the certification of mandatory class actions unless the absent class members are subject to the court's personal jurisdiction.[37] To understand their position, let us first spell out something that these courts inferred from *Shutts*: it is constitutional to bind absent class members in a (b)(3)-type class action even if they lack minimum contacts with the forum state because they have the option to opt out. If they choose not to exercise that option, they are deemed to have waived their jurisdictional defense and to have consented to jurisdiction.[38] But in mandatory class actions certified under Rule 23(b)(1) or (b)(2), or the state-law analogues, one cannot infer a waiver. Therefore, at least one court has held that "a mandatory class action would violate the constitutional rights of those persons who have insufficient contacts to allow the court to exercise personal jurisdiction over them" (Waldron v. Raymark Indus., Inc., N.D. Ga. 1989).

The Third Circuit refrained from addressing this issue directly, but nevertheless concluded that it would violate due process to enjoin absent class members who lacked minimum contacts with the forum from bringing individual suits following settlement of a mandatory class action that involved both equitable and monetary claims. The Third Circuit distinguished *Shutts*, noting that the class members before it had not been afforded an opportunity to opt out and yet would have been denied an opportunity left open to the class members in *Shutts* to attack the class action judgment collaterally (on inadequacy of representation grounds) in the forum of their choice (In re Real Estate Title & Settlement Servs. Antitrust Litig., 3d Cir., 1989).[39]

Until the Supreme Court resolves this issue, there will be substantial uncertainty regarding the binding effect of mandatory class action judgments rendered without personal jurisdiction over absent plaintiff class members.

### *Denial of Right to Opt Out*

At least in cases in which absent plaintiff class members lack minimum contacts with the forum state, due process requires that known class members be afforded an opportunity to opt out if their claims are "wholly or predominately" for money damages (Phillips Petroleum Co. v. Shutts, 1985). But it is not clear whether due process guarantees a right to opt out to class members who seek declaratory or injunctive relief, and if so, whether this protection is enjoyed only by absent class members who lack minimum contacts with the forum state or by *all* absent class members regardless of connection to the forum state.[40] Put differently, the *Shutts* Court declined to address whether class members in mandatory or hybrid class actions are entitled to an opportunity to opt out, and if so, in what circumstances. In a later case, Ortiz v. Fibreboard Corp. (1999), the Supreme Court recognized the "serious constitutional concerns that come with any attempt to aggregate individual tort claims on a limited fund rationale" and commented that "[t]he inherent tension between representative suits and the day-in-court ideal is only magnified if applied to damage claims gathered in a mandatory class," but decided the case on other grounds (Ortiz v. Fibreboard Corp., 1999).[41]

As might be expected, the lower courts have had to address the circumstances in which due process guarantees class members an opportunity to opt out of the class. In mandatory class actions filed under Rule 23(b)(2) or a state-law analogue, most (if not all) courts agree that absent class members are bound by a judgment denying or granting injunctive relief even if they are denied an opportunity to opt out (Robinson v. Metro-North Commuter R.R., 2d Cir. 2001; Brown v. Ticor Title Ins. Co., 9th Cir. 1992).[42]

There is less agreement on the applicability of *Shutts* to limited-fund class actions and (b)(2) class actions in which the class seeks both injunctive and monetary relief: does due process permit absent class members to be bound by a judgment that resolves monetary claims without affording them an opportunity to opt out? In the context of an appeal from an order denying Rule 23(b)(2) class certification, the Fifth Circuit adopted a bright-line rule distinguishing between claims for money damages that are wholly incidental to claims for injunctive or declaratory relief, and claims for money damages that are not wholly incidental (Allison v. Citgo Petroleum Corp., 5th Cir. 1998; see also Smith v. Texaco, Inc., 5th Cir. 2001). If the class seeks injunctive relief and wholly incidental monetary relief,[43] the class action may be certified under Rule 23(b)(2) notwithstanding the lack of an opt-out right; but if the claims for monetary relief predominate and are not merely incidental, then Rule 23(b)(2), which denies class members an opt-out right, may not be employed (Allison v. Citgo Petroleum Corp., 5th Cir. 1998). This bright-line rule eliminates the risk that absent class members will be deprived of their claims without the procedural protections that due process assures (Robinson v. Metro-North Commuter R.R., 2d Cir. 2001). The Seventh Circuit likewise has held that Rule 23(b)(2) may not be used when the class seeks non-incidental monetary relief (Jefferson v. Ingersoll Int'l Inc., 7th Cir. 1999).[44] While neither *Allison* nor *Jefferson* arose in the context of a collateral attack, both suggest that class members cannot be bound by a judgment that resolves non-incidental monetary claims unless they have been afforded an opportunity to opt out.[45]

The Second and Ninth Circuits have rejected a *per se* rule that would guarantee class members the right to opt out whenever the class action purports to resolve *any* monetary claims (Molski v. Gleich, 9th Cir. 2003; Robinson v. Metro-North Commuter R.R., 2d Cir. 2001).[46] Furthermore, these courts have declined to follow *Allison*, which permits certification of a non-op-out class only if the monetary relief sought is wholly incidental. Rather, the Second and Ninth Circuits have engaged in a case-specific, fact-based analysis to determine whether opt-out rights must be provided.

Where the monetary damages sought by the class are substantial, the Ninth Circuit has held that due process requires the right to opt out even if the class is certified under Rule 23(b)(1) or (b)(2) (Molski v. Gleich, 9th Cir. 2003; Brown v. Ticor Title Inc. Co., 9th Cir. 1992). Put differently, a judgment may not bind absent class members and preclude them from later suing to recover substantial monetary damages unless they were afforded an opportunity to opt out of the class action (Frank v. United Airlines, Inc., 9th Cir. 2000; Brown v. Ticor Title Ins. Co., 9th Cir. 1992). Several other of the Circuit Courts of Appeals appear to agree.[47]

Other courts have concluded that absent class members may be bound by judgments in mandatory class actions that resolve their monetary claims as long as due process is assured through some alternative mechanism. For example, the Fifth Circuit has held that absent plaintiff class members in a mandatory limited-fund class action may be bound by a judgment that forecloses their claims for money damages as long as they were adequately represented in the class action (In re Asbestos Litig., 5th Cir. 1996), but this decision was reversed on other grounds by *Ortiz*.[48] Likewise, the Third Circuit has held that absent class members may be bound even if they were denied an opportunity to opt out "as long as they had minimum contacts with the forum state and they were not otherwise denied due process" (Grimes v. Vitalink Communications Corp., 3d Cir. 1994).[49]

In 1993, the Supreme Court granted a writ of certiorari to decide whether, consistent with due process, class members who are denied an opportunity to opt out nevertheless may be bound by a judgment that resolves their monetary claims (Ticor Title Ins. Co. v. Brown, 1993). The Court ultimately dismissed the writ as improvidently granted (Ticor Title Ins. Co. v. Brown, 1994).[50] Again, a lack of guidance from the Supreme Court leaves the scope of due process protection in this context uncertain. Judgments resolving monetary claims in class actions may be vulnerable to collateral attack if the absent class members are denied an opportunity to opt out.

### *Inadequate Representation*

While doubt remains whether absent class members are bound by the judgment if they are denied an opportunity to opt out of the class action, it has long been established that absent class members are not bound by a class action judgment if the representation of the class was inadequate (Hansberry v. Lee, 1940). As the Court has reiterated, the "named plaintiff [must] *at all times* adequately represent the interests of the absent class members" (Phillips Petroleum Co. v. Shutts, 1985, emphasis added). Likewise, section 42 of the Second Restatement of Judgments recognizes that class members are not bound by judgments if "there was such a substantial divergence of interest between [the representative] and the members of the class . . . that he could not fairly represent them . . ." or if "[t]he representative failed to prosecute or defend the action with due diligence and reasonable prudence, and the opposing party was on notice of facts making that failure apparent" (Restatement (Second) of Judgments §§ 42(1)(d) & (e), 1982).

In assessing the adequacy of representation when making the initial class certification decision, courts examine the qualifications of class counsel, the commonality of interests between the named representative and the absent class members, and the risk of collusion (Brown v. Ticor Title Ins. Co., 9th Cir. 1992), as well as "'structural assurance of fair and adequate representation for the diverse groups and individuals affected,'" such as the use of subclasses with separate representation for groups with potentially conflicting interests (Ortiz v. Fibreboard Corp., 1999, quoting Amchem Prods., Inc. v. Windsor, 1997). In the settlement class action context, the Supreme Court has made clear that courts must scrutinize the adequacy of representation with "undiluted, even heightened, attention. . . ." (Amchem Prods., Inc. v. Windsor, 1997).

But if the court may certify a class action only if it concludes that the named representative and her counsel will adequately represent the class, are the class members bound by this judicial determination of adequacy? Put differently, are absent class members free to collaterally attack a class action judgment on the theory that their interests were *not* in fact adequately represented, or does issue preclusion bind them by the finding that the representation was adequate? The language in *Shutts* that the "named plaintiff [must] *at all times* adequately represent the interests of the absent class members" suggests that absent class members are free to collaterally attack a class action judgment for inadequate representation even if the adequacy issue was litigated at the outset (Phillips Petroleum Co. v. Shutts, 1985, emphasis added). The Second Restatement's backward-looking assessment of the diligence with which the representative prosecuted the action reinforces this suggestion, and a Comment to section 41 states this conclusion explicitly: if the interests of the representative and the class have diverged or the representative has failed to prosecute the action diligently, "the represented person may avoid being bound either by appearing in the action before rendition of the judgment *or* by attacking the judgment by subsequent proceedings" (Restatement (Second) of Judgments § 41 cmt. a, 1982, emphasis added).[51] While the Restatement is clear on this point, the lower courts are not in complete agreement.[52]

Some courts in collateral proceedings have examined the adequacy of representation without even mentioning issue preclusion (Stephenson v. Dow Chem. Co., 2d Cir. 2001; In re Agent Orange Prod. Liab. Litig., 2d Cir. 1993; Gonzales v. Cassidy, 5th Cir. 1973), while others have expressly concluded that issue preclusion (or the related doctrine of law of the case) does not preclude absent class members from challenging the adequacy of representation in a collateral proceeding (State v. Homeside Lending, Inc., Vt. 2003; Battle v. Liberty Nat'l Life Ins. Co., N.D. Ala. 1991; Research Corp. v. Edward J. Funk & Sons Co., N.D. Ind. 1971).

Two powerful arguments support the conclusion that issue preclusion does not bar relitigation of the adequacy of representation. First, the issue determined at the outset of the underlying class action—whether the representative and her lawyer will adequately represent the class—and the issue raised in the collateral attack—whether the class representative and her attorney in fact adequately represented the interests of the class throughout the litigation—are different issues.

As the Fifth Circuit put it, the latter question "requires a hindsight approach to the issue of adequate representation, and in no way reflects on the [certifying] court's conclusion that [the named representative] would adequately represent the class" (Gonzales v. Cassidy, 5th Cir. 1973).[53] Second, even if objectors appear in the underlying class action and contest the adequacy of representation provided by the representative, the objectors themselves are not class representatives and therefore a finding of adequacy rendered against them cannot bind the absent class members (Epstein v. MCA, Inc., 9th Cir. 1997 (withdrawn)).[54]

Other courts, however, have refused to "second-guess a prior decision that counsel adequately represented a class" (Brown v. Ticor Title Ins. Co., 9th Cir. 1992). For example, the Third and Ninth Circuit Courts of Appeals have concluded that class members are bound by a determination in the underlying class action that the representation was adequate and may not collaterally attack the judgment on a theory of inadequate representation (Epstein v. MCA, Inc., 9th Cir. 1999; Grimes v. Vitalink Communications Corp., 3d Cir. 1994).[55] The Ninth Circuit has permitted a limited collateral review only to consider whether "the *procedures* in the prior litigation afforded the party against whom the earlier judgment is asserted a 'full and fair opportunity' to litigate the claim or issue," but not to examine whether the representation in fact was adequate (Epstein v. MCA, Inc., 9th Cir. 1999, emphasis added). In an earlier case in which a class member was represented by his own counsel at the fairness hearing, the Ninth Circuit refused to consider his collateral challenge to the adequacy of representation because he "was adequately represented by virtue of his own participation in the class action" (Dosier v. Miami Valley Broad. Corp., 9th Cir. 1981; see also King v. S. Cent. Bell Tel. & Tel. Co., 6th Cir. 1986).

Three Supreme Court Justices—Justices Ginsburg, Stevens and Souter—have noted that the named representative's duty to adequately represent the interests of the absent class members is a continuing one (Matsushita Elec. Indus. Co. v. Epstein, 1996, Ginsburg, J., concurring in part and dissenting in part). While the trial court that certifies the class has initial responsibility to ensure that due process is satisfied, "[f]inal judgments . . . remain vulnerable to collateral attack for failure to satisfy the adequate representation requirement. A court conducting an action cannot predetermine the res judicata effect of the judgment; that effect can be tested only in a subsequent action" (Matsushita Elec. Indus. Co. v. Epstein, 1996, Ginsburg, J., concurring in part and dissenting in part). A majority of the Court, however, declined to address the due process claim.[56] More recently, an evenly divided Court affirmed a Second Circuit judgment permitting a collateral attack by absent class members who claimed their interests were not adequately represented (Dow Chem. Co. v. Stephenson, 2003), but such an affirmance has no precedential effect (Neil v. Biggers, 1972). Until a majority of the Court reaffirms that adequacy of representation may be challenged collaterally, there will be some doubt (at least in some circuits) regarding the scope of due process protection afforded to absent class members.

In conclusion, absent class members may be bound by a judgment even if they lack minimum contacts with the forum state as long as they receive notice, an opportunity to be heard, an opportunity to opt out, and adequate representation at all times. Moreover, absent class members may be bound by a judgment denying or granting injunctive relief even if they are denied an opportunity to opt out. But in limited-fund and (b)(2) class actions in which the class seeks both injunctive and monetary relief, due process may require an opportunity to opt out, at least if the absent class members lack minimum contacts with the forum state. Since due process assures adequate representation of the absent class members at all times, the better view is that absent class members may collaterally attack the class action judgment and avoid its binding effect by demonstrating that the representation actually provided was not adequate.

### *Representation by the Government*

Beyond the class action context, the Second Restatement of Judgments provides that a nonparty may be bound by a judgment where "[a]n official or agency invested by law with authority to represent the person's interests" was a litigant (Restatement (Second) of Judgments § 41(1)(d), 1982). In some instances, the public official's authority to bring or defend litigation on behalf of the public (or a group of public citizens) is exclusive. In other words, *only* the government may sue to protect a particular interest and private individuals lack standing to bring these claims. In these instances, the question of whether the private individuals are bound by the judgment rendered in their absence is beside the point, as any suit they might try to bring on their own would be dismissed for lack of standing (Restatement (Second) of Judgments § 41 cmt. d, 1982; 18A Wright et al., Fed. Practice & Procedure § 4458.1, 2d ed. 2002).

In other contexts, both government actors and individual members of the public have standing to seek redress. But if the government brings or defends litigation, are members of the public bound by the judgment or do they retain an individual right to litigate on their own behalf? Is it constitutional to bind private citizens on the theory that the government represented their interests in the prior litigation?

It is well accepted that when the government litigates common public rights, private citizens who assert only a diffuse interest shared with the general public are bound by the judgment (City of Tacoma v. Taxpayers of Tacoma, 1958). Similarly, when the state brings suit in its capacity as *parens patriae*, advancing both the rights of its citizens and its own sovereign or quasi-sovereign interest (Alfred L. Snapp & Son, Inc. v. Puerto Rico *ex rel.* Barez, 1982)—to protect its citizens from air or water pollution, for example—the state is presumed to represent the interests of all its citizens (Envtl. Def. Fund v. Higginson, D.C. Cir. 1979). In such cases, too, the represented citizens are bound by the judgment (Alaska Sport Fishing Ass'n v. Exxon Corp., 9th Cir. 1994).

Just as it is well accepted that members of the public with diffuse general interests are bound by judgments to which the government is a party, it is also well accepted that when private parties have legal rights that are distinct from the general public interests at stake in the litigation involving the government, the private parties are not precluded from pressing their own claims in separate litigation (Williamson v. Bethlehem Steel Corp., 2d Cir. 1972; 18A Wright et al., Fed. Practice & Procedure § 4458.1, 2d ed. 2002). The Supreme Court emphasized this point in Richards v. Jefferson County (1996), holding that taxpayers may not be deprived of their own day in court if they seek to challenge, on federal constitutional grounds, a taxation scheme that "attempt[s] to levy personal funds. . . ."[57]

On a related note, the state may not sue as *parens patriae* to assert the private rights of private citizens (Satsky v. Paramount Communications, Inc., 10th Cir. 1993). If it sues as *parens patriae* to raise common public rights, the judgment does not preclude private parties from later suing to recover for injuries to purely private interests, which the state lacked standing to raise in the prior action (Satsky v. Paramount Communications, Inc., 10th Cir. 1993).[58]

The more difficult cases are those in which the private citizens have individual *interests* distinct from those of the general population but do not have distinct *legal rights*. For example, in Southwest Airlines Co. v. Texas International Airlines, Inc. (5th Cir. 1977), the court considered whether a group of airlines with distinct pecuniary interests were bound by a judgment against the cities of Dallas and Fort Worth. The dispute there began when the Civil Aeronautics Board ("CAB") required the cities to designate a single airport in the area for CAB-approved service. The cities agreed to build a new airport equidistant between them and adopted an ordinance requiring a gradual transition of CAB service from Love Field and other local airports to the new regional airport. Southwest Airlines was a non-CAB-certified airline providing intrastate commercial service out of Love Field pursuant to a certificate issued by a state aeronautical agency. The cities filed suit against Southwest, seeking a declaration that they had authority to exclude the airline from Love Field pursuant to the ordinance. The federal court rendered judgment for Southwest, concluding that the state aeronautical agency, rather than the cities, had authority to control intrastate service from Love Field. Eight other airlines, all certified by the CAB, filed suit against Southwest in state court, seeking to enforce the cities' ordinance against it. The suit was removed to federal court, and the issue was whether the airlines were free to relitigate the enforceability of the ordinance against Southwest notwithstanding the cities' prior unsuccessful efforts.

On appeal from a preliminary injunction enjoining the airlines' lawsuit, the Fifth Circuit recognized that the CAB carriers had pecuniary interests that were distinct from the interests of the general public, but also noted that they suffered no "private legal wrong independent from the violation of the ordinance" (S.W. Airlines Co. v. Tex. Int'l Airlines, Inc., 5th Cir. 1977). Moreover, they sought only the relief already denied to the cities, namely, the exclusion of Southwest from Love Field. Relying upon a tentative draft of the Second Restatement of Judgments for guidance, the court stated that "[p]ermission to relitigate appears reserved for the private plaintiff who would vindicate a breach of duty owed specifically to the plaintiff or who would recover under a 'statutory system of remedies [that] may contemplate enforcement of private interests both by a public agency and the affected private parties'" (S.W. Airlines Co. v. Tex. Int'l Airlines, Inc., 5th Cir. 1977). Since no duty was owed specifically to the airlines and the ordinance contemplated only public enforcement, the court concluded that the airlines "received adequate representation in the earlier litigation and should be bound by the judgment in that litigation" (S.W. Airlines Co. v. Tex. Int'l Airlines, Inc., 5th Cir. 1977; see also Washington v. Wash. State Commercial Passenger Fishing Vessel Ass'n, 1979; Rynsburger v. Dairymen's Fertilizer Coop., Inc., Cal. Ct. App. 1968).

Rejecting the argument that it would violate due process to bind the airlines by the judgment, the Fifth Circuit concluded that the airlines' legal interests "precisely coincide[d] with those of the cities and the regional airport board" and the quality of the legal representation provided by the cities' counsel satisfied due process. In addition, the airlines had followed the litigation closely, attending hearings in the case and submitting *amicus* briefs (S.W. Airlines Co. v. Tex. Int'l Airlines, Inc., 5th Cir. 1977).[59]

A similar rationale may justify preclusion of citizen suits following environmental litigation by the government. In fact, in this context, several statutes permit the filing of citizen suits only if the government has not yet *commenced* litigation or administrative proceedings (42 U.S.C. § 7604(b)(1)(B); 42 U.S.C. § 11046(e)). If the government has commenced action and is diligently prosecuting it, the private suit to enforce the statute will be dismissed. Thus, private suits are barred even though the government's suit has not yet gone to judgment and standard claim preclusion principles do not apply.[60]

### *Virtual Representation*

Some courts have bound persons who were not made parties to a lawsuit on a theory of virtual representation. According to this amorphous preclusion theory, "a person may be bound by a judgment even though not a party if one of the parties to the suit is so closely aligned with his interests as to be his virtual representative" (Monfils v. Taylor, 7th Cir. 1998; see also Klugh v. United States, 4th Cir. 1987). The virtual representation theory is sometimes referred to as de facto representation or representation by proxy (Gonzalez v. Banco Cent. Corp., 1st Cir. 1994).[61]

One of the most widely cited cases to invoke a virtual representation theory is Aerojet-General Corp. v. Askew (5th Cir. 1975). There, a private corporation sued two state agencies in federal court seeking specific performance of a contract pursuant to which the agencies had granted the corporation the option to purchase state-owned land at a specified price. After the contract had been executed but before the suit was filed, the state legislature enacted a law requiring state agencies to offer state-owned land to the county in which the land was located before selling it to private parties. In the action, the state agencies argued that the option contract was not valid, but failed to raise the state statute as a defense to the private corporation's claim. Judgment was rendered in favor of the private corporation. When the state agencies declined to transfer title to the corporation following judgment, the clerk of the federal district court, acting as commissioner, executed a deed to the land in favor of the corporation. Pursuant to a writ of mandamus issued by the Florida Supreme Court in a subsequent suit commenced by the county, the state agencies executed a deed to the same property in favor of the county.

Given these competing deeds to the same tract of land, the corporation sought to enforce the first (federal) judgment against both the state agencies and the county and to preclude them from raising the state statute as a defense. The county conceded that the prior judgment precluded the state agencies from now arguing that the state statute compelled them to offer the land to the county, but it argued that it could not be bound because it had not been a party to the first suit and its interests had not been represented by the state agencies. The Fifth Circuit Court of Appeals rejected this argument, stating that "a person may be bound by a judgment even though not a party if one of the parties to the suit is so closely aligned with his interests as to be his virtual representative" (Aerojet-Gen. Corp. v. Askew, 5th Cir. 1975). Offering little analysis on this issue, the court noted only that the state agencies clearly would have preferred to transfer the land to the county rather than to the corporation and would not have been prejudiced had they raised the state statute as an alternative to their defense that the option agreement was unenforceable. Noting that the question of virtual representation is one of fact, the court of appeals affirmed the trial court's conclusion that the county "'was in such close relationship to the parties to the first lawsuit . . . that its interests . . . were represented in that proceeding'" (Aerojet-Gen. Corp. v. Askew, 5th Cir. 1975).

In determining whether or not to bind a nonparty on a virtual representation theory, courts consider whether the party to the first suit and the nonparty to be bound share identical interests; whether the party to the first suit had a strong incentive to protect the interests of the nonparty; whether the nonparty participated in the prior litigation, or appeared to consent or acquiesce to be bound; whether the nonparty engaged in tactical maneuvering in an effort to avoid being bound; whether the nonparty had actual or constructive notice of the earlier suit;

and the nature of the issue (Bittinger v. Tecumseh Prods. Co., 6th Cir. 1997; Tyus v. Schoemehl, 8th Cir. 1996; Gonzalez v. Banco Cent. Corp., 1st Cir. 1994).[62] Courts are more willing to invoke virtual representation to bind nonparties regarding public law issues, where the number of potential plaintiffs with standing otherwise might be limitless, than private law issues (Niere v. St. Louis County, 8th Cir. 2002; Tyus v. Schoemehl, 8th Cir. 1996; L.A. Branch NAACP v. L.A. Unified Sch. Dist., 9th Cir. 1984).

Some courts have employed the virtual representation theory liberally, applying it as long as the nonparty to be bound had a "substantial relationship" with a party to the first suit or the nonparty's interests were "closely aligned" with those of the party (Tyus v. Schoemehl, 8th Cir. 1996; see also Sondel v. N.W. Airlines, Inc., 8th Cir. 1995; NAACP v. Hunt, 11th Cir. 1990). These courts emphasize the salutary effects of preclusion law, including the conservation of judicial resources; the protection of defendants from vexatious, repetitive lawsuits; and its equitable nature.

Other courts, including the Fifth Circuit Court of Appeals (which decided *Aerojet-General*), apply the doctrine more narrowly, requiring an express or implied legal relationship that renders the party to the first suit accountable to the nonparty before the latter may be bound by the judgment (Becherer v. Merrill Lynch, Pierce, Fenner & Smith, Inc., 6th Cir. 1999; Collins v. E.I. DuPont de Nemours & Co., 3d Cir. 1994; Pollard v. Cockrell, 5th Cir. 1978). The First Circuit employs virtual representation to bind a nonparty only if the interests of the party to the prior suit and the nonparty are identical; the nonparty had actual or constructive notice of the prior litigation; and the balance of the equities tips in favor of preclusion (Gonzalez v. Banco Cent. Corp., 1st Cir. 1994). The Fourth Circuit applies virtual representation only when the party to the first suit was accountable to the nonparty and had at least the tacit approval of the court to represent the interests of the nonparty, whose identity must have been known at the time of the first suit (Wise v. City of Norfolk, 4th Cir. 2000; Klugh v. United States, 4th Cir. 1987). And the Sixth and Seventh Circuits take a "dim view" of the virtual representation theory outside the formal class action context (Debraska v. City of Milwaukee, 7th Cir. 1999; Bittinger v. Tecumseh Prods. Co., 6th Cir. 1997), concluding that it "cannot override an individual's right to his own day in court unless the facts show a strong reason why the first litigant was, in effect, a real representative (not a virtual one) of the second" (Perry v. Globe Auto Recycling, Inc., 7th Cir. 2000).

This narrow view of virtual representation is better tailored to protect nonparties' due process rights than the broader view. In fact, the narrow view may be required by the Supreme Court's decision in Richards v. Jefferson County (1996), which called into question the use of virtual representation to bind nonparties who lack a formal legal relationship with a party to the prior suit. There, the City of Birmingham, its acting director of finance, and three taxpayers sued Jefferson County, Alabama, in state court to challenge a county occupation tax on state and federal constitutional grounds. After the Alabama Supreme Court upheld the constitutionality of the tax, two private employees filed another action to challenge the tax. The county argued that this subsequent suit was barred by the judgment in the first action. While recognizing that state courts generally are free to develop their own preclusion principles, the Supreme Court nevertheless noted that "extreme applications of the doctrine of res judicata may be inconsistent with a federal right that is 'fundamental in character'" (Richards v. Jefferson County, 1996; Postal Tel. Cable Co. v. City of Newport, 1918). In other words, due process checks a state's authority to bind nonparties by a judgment rendered in their absence.

Noting that nonparties may be bound by a judgment if they are "in privity"[63] with a person who was a party to the action, the Court declined to invoke that exception here for two reasons. First, the parties to the first action failed to provide the plaintiffs in the second action with any notice of the pendency of an action that could have resolved their legal rights. This failure troubled the Court because "the right to be heard ensured by the guarantee of due process 'has little reality or worth unless one is informed that the matter is pending and can choose for himself whether to appear or default, acquiesce or contest'" (Richards v. Jefferson County, 1996). Second, even if adequate representation might cure a lack of notice (which the Court appeared to doubt),[64] the judgment in the first suit could not bind the plaintiffs here because the first action was not "'devised and applied . . . to insure that those present [were] of the same class as those absent and that the litigation [was] so conducted as to insure the full and fair consideration of the common issue'" (Richards v. Jefferson County, 1996, quoting Hansberry v. Lee, 1940). Neither the plaintiffs nor the court in the first action took steps to protect the interests of the absent private taxpayers. Because the plaintiffs in the first and second suits were "mere 'strangers' to one another," the Court was unable to conclude that the plaintiffs in the first suit "provided representation sufficient to make up for the fact that [the plaintiffs in the second action] neither participated in nor had the opportunity to participate in" the first action (Richards v. Jefferson County, 1996).

*Richards* and South Central Bell Telephone Co. v. Alabama (1999),[65] a case decided a few years later that relied heavily upon *Richards*, stand for the proposition that mere identity of interests between a litigant and a nonparty is insufficient to justify binding the nonparty by the judgment rendered against the litigant, at least where the nonparty has a legally protected interest at stake. These decisions cast doubt on the constitutionality of a liberal use of virtual representation theory to bind nonparties with legally protected interests to judgments rendered in their absence unless a party to the earlier action was accountable to them.

## Special Remedial Schemes

The Supreme Court has recognized the constitutionality of special remedial schemes that are expressly designed to foreclose successive lawsuits by nonparties (Martin v. Wilks, 1989). In bankruptcy proceedings, for example, "proof of claim must be presented to the Bankruptcy Court for administration, or be lost. . . ." (NLRB v. Bildisco & Bildisco, 1984).[66] Likewise, in the probate context, nonclaim statutes require creditors to file claims against decedents' estates within a specified period of time, or they too are lost (Tulsa Prof. Collection Servs., Inc. v. Pope, 1988).

Discussing such legislative schemes in Martin v. Wilks (1989), the Court commented that "legal proceedings may terminate preexisting rights if the scheme is otherwise consistent with due process." In other words, as long as the notice provided to creditors satisfies the *Mullane* standard (described earlier in Chapter 4) and the creditors are afforded an opportunity to present their claims, due process is satisfied. In these contexts, it is the systemic need for finality (In re Edwards, 7th Cir. 1992) and the government's "legitimate interest in the expeditious resolution" of the bankruptcy, probate or trust proceedings that purportedly justifies binding nonparties (Tulsa Prof. Collection Servs., Inc. v. Pope, 1988).

In recent years, courts and scholars have debated whether two relatively new remedial schemes—adopted by Congress in the employment discrimination and environmental clean-up contexts—comport with due process. In an effort to "overturn" Martin v. Wilks (1989) and to ensure the finality of civil rights consent decrees consistent with due process,[67] Congress amended the Civil Rights Act in 1991 to foreclose collateral attacks on judgments and consent decrees rendered in employment discrimination cases by nonparties. The amended statute bars collateral challenges by those who received actual notice of the proposed judgment or decree and a reasonable opportunity to object to it, and by those "whose interests were adequately represented by another person who had previously challenged the judgment or order on the same legal grounds and with a similar factual situation. . . ." (42 U.S.C. § 2000e-2(n)(1)(B)(ii)).[68] In gauging the adequacy of representation under the second prong, courts are guided by the body of law developed in the class action context (Rutherford v. City of Cleveland, 6th Cir. 1998; H.R. Rep. No. 40(I), 102nd Cong., 1st Sess. 57, 1991).

While some prominent scholars have concluded that "[t]he preclusion theories adopted [by the statute] are consistent with due process,"[69] others have questioned the constitutionality of both prongs of the statute.[70] First, the provision that binds those who receive notice of the proposed settlement has been criticized because it appears to sanction notice by publication rather than require individual notice by mail to employees whose names and addresses are known, as *Mullane* demands.[71] In fact, the House Report that accompanied the bill states that the notice "need not come from a party or from the court" but "[i]nstead, it may come from any source . . ." (H.R. Rep. 40(I), 102d Cong., 1st Sess. 56, 1991). Although the statute purports to bind only those who actually receive notice, other legislation has been struck down as violative of due process where it failed to "contain a provision making it reasonably probable that notice" would be received by the interested party (Wuchter v. Pizzutti, 1928). Moreover, the notice required by the first prong to bind a nonparty may come late in the litigation, only after a settlement has been reached. Thus, the absentees are denied a full opportunity to participate in the litigation, including an opportunity to take discovery.[72] For these reasons, at least one court has expressed concern that the "perfunctory process employed . . . belittles our notion of fairness" (Edwards v. City of Houston, 5th Cir. 1996).

Second, the provision that purports to bind absentees whose interests have been represented by another objector creates a *de facto* class action even though the absentees receive none of the procedural protections that Rule 23 guarantees. For example, nothing in the statute requires the court to scrutinize the adequacy of the representation at the outset of the case or to provide notice to the absentees, and even the purported representatives are afforded only "a reasonable opportunity to present objections," rather than a full and fair opportunity to litigate the case.[73] In Professor Laycock's view, "[t]he difference between the right to make the original parties prove their case and the limited right to object to a presumptive settlement is the difference between due process and an ineffectual formality."[74]

In the environmental area, Congress amended the Comprehensive Environmental Response, Compensation and Liability Act ("CERCLA") in 1986 to protect parties who settle their liabilities with the United States or a state in an administratively or judicially approved settlement from contribution claims by other potentially responsible parties ("PRPs") (42 U.S.C. §§ 9613(f)(2), 9622(h)(4)).[75] These sections, which deprive nonparties to the settlement of their contribution claims against the settling parties, are designed to foster settlements and to provide settling parties with a measure of finality (United States v. Cannons Eng'g Corp., 1st Cir. 1990; United States v. SCA Servs. of Ind., Inc., N.D. Ind. 1993). Other sections of the statute require that notice of proposed administrative settlements be published in the Federal Register and that nonparties be afforded an opportunity to comment on both administrative and judicial settlements before final approval (42 U.S.C. §§ 9622(d)(2)(B), 9662(i)).

The Supreme Court has not yet addressed the constitutionality of these amendments to CERCLA. Some lower courts have upheld them, concluding that nonparties' contribution claims may be extinguished by a settlement if the nonparties were afforded an opportunity to be heard before the settlement was approved (Kelley *ex rel.* Mich. Dep't of Envtl. Quality v. Wagner, E.D. Mich. 1996). But other courts have noted that it would violate due process to extinguish contribution claims of nonparties who were denied procedural protections (Gen. Time Corp. v. Bulk Materials, Inc., M.D. Ga. 1993; CPC Int'l, Inc. v. Aerojet-Gen. Corp., W.D. Mich. 1991). At least one court has upheld the preclusive effect of a settlement where the nonparties received only constructive notice through publication of the proposed settlement in the Federal Register rather than actual notice (United States v. Serafini, M.D. Pa. 1992), while at least one other court has questioned whether constructive notice is sufficient (Gen. Time Corp. v. Bulk Materials, Inc., M.D. Ga. 1993).

While Martin v. Wilks (1989) stated that special remedial schemes designed to foreclose successive suits by nonlitigants can terminate preexisting rights, it required that such schemes otherwise comport with due process. At least as to PRPs whose liability is clear and whose whereabouts are known, due process requires actual notice and an opportunity to be heard under the Supreme Court's decisions in Mullane v. Central Hanover Bank & Trust Co. (1950) and Tulsa Professional Collection Services, Inc. v. Pope (1988). Thus, the constructive notice afforded by publication in the Federal Register would appear to be inadequate as to known PRPs.[76] Moreover, just as the Civil Rights Act of 1991 may be susceptible to constitutional challenge because it purports to bind nonparties who are afforded only a limited opportunity to object to a consent decree rather than participate fully in the litigation, so too CERCLA may violate due process to the extent it purports to cut off the contribution rights of PRPs who are afforded only a limited opportunity to object to a settlement between the government and another PRP.[77]

## CONCLUSION

Ordinarily, a person may not be bound by a judgment unless she was a party to the action in which the judgment was rendered. Put differently, the doctrines of claim preclusion and issue preclusion cannot be invoked to bar a person from litigating a claim or an issue that was previously litigated to judgment unless she was a party to the prior action. The Due Process Clause imposes these limits on the binding effect of judgments to protect the opportunity to be heard.

The Supreme Court has long recognized exceptions to the general rule that nonparties may not be bound by judgments rendered in their absence. A person who controls a party's presentation in litigation may be bound by the judgment (at least for issue preclusion purposes) to the same extent as a party. Likewise, a person who succeeds to another's property (whether by purchase, inheritance or otherwise) may be bound by a judgment rendered for or against the prior owner. In addition, persons whose interests are adequately represented by a party to a lawsuit may be bound by the judgment, at least where the absentee and the litigant are in a legal relationship that renders the litigant accountable to the nonparty. This representation exception has been invoked in the class action context to bind absent class members by judgments rendered in their absence; in the context of litigation brought by or against governmental officials who purport to represent the public interest; and more generally whenever a party's interests are so aligned with the interests of an absentee that she may be deemed to be a "virtual representative."

Participation, joint interest and adequate representation are not the only recognized exceptions to the "day in court" ideal. The Supreme Court has also acknowledged the constitutionality of remedial schemes expressly designed to foreclose successive lawsuits by nonparties. These schemes are constitutional only if interested persons are afforded adequate notice and an opportunity to participate in the action.

## NOTES

1. Parklane Hosiery Co. v. Shore, 439 U.S. 322, 327 n.7 (1979) (citations omitted).

2. *Cf.* Patrick Woolley, *Rethinking the Adequacy of Adequate Representation*, 75 Tex. L. Rev. 571 (1997) (hereinafter Woolley, *Rethinking Adequacy*) (concluding that, as a general rule, due process guarantees absent class members an opportunity to be heard and to participate, even if they decline to opt out).

3. For criticism of the ways in which courts and scholars use the "day in court" ideal to justify limitations on nonparty preclusion, *see* Robert G. Bone, *Rethinking the "Day in Court" Ideal and Nonparty Preclusion*, 67 N.Y.U. L. Rev. 193 (1992).

4. The Second Restatement eschews the "on the merits" terminology "because of its possibly misleading connotations." Restatement (Second) of Judgments § 19 cmt. a (1982); *see also id.* cmt. b. A valid and final judgment will be accorded preclusive effect as long as "there was an opportunity to get to the merits." Charles Alan Wright & Mary Kay Kane, The Law of Federal Courts § 100A, at 726–27 (6th ed. 2002). *See also* Jack H. Friedenthal et al., Civil Procedure § 14.7 (3d ed. 1999) (stating that a judgment must be valid, final and on the merits to be given preclusive effect and exploring each of these requirements).

5. Restatement (Second) of Judgments § 24 cmt. c, illus. 1 (1982).

6. For example, the majority rule bars a plaintiff from splitting a claim into separate actions for personal injury and property damage arising from a single car accident. *See, e.g.*, Mason v. Parker, 695 N.E.2d 70 (Ill. App. Ct.), *appeal denied*, 705 N.E.2d 439 (Ill. 1998); Peterson v. Temple, 918 P.2d 413 (Or. 1996). The minority rule permits the plaintiff to file separate actions to recover for personal injury and property damage. *See, e.g.*, Childers v. F.A.F. Motor Cars, Inc., 319 S.E.2d 90 (Ga. Ct. App. 1984) (relying upon a statute that created separate causes of action for property damage and personal injury arising from car accidents). *See also* Andrea G. Nadel, Annotation, *Simultaneous Injury to Person and Property as Giving Rise to Single Cause of Action—Modern Cases*, 24 A.L.R. 4th 646 (1983).

7. For exceptions to these general rules of claim preclusion, *see* Restatement (Second) of Judgments §§ 20, 26 (1982).

8. This example is modeled after *id.* § 27 cmt. d, illus. 10.

9. *See infra* Chapter 6 for a full discussion of the limits on state court jurisdiction imposed by the Due Process Clauses.

10. 2 Robert C. Casad & William B. Richman, Jurisdiction in Civil Actions § 6–2 (3d ed. 1998).

11. For a more thorough treatment of the officially sanctioned racial discrimination that prompted the underlying suit in *Martin*, see Samuel Issacharoff, *When Substance Mandates Procedure:* Martin v. Wilks *and the Rights of Vested Incumbents in Civil Rights Consent Decrees*, 77 Cornell L. Rev. 189, 194–97 (1992).

12. Because Nelson was the president and sole shareholder of OCP, and because he apparently participated in the litigation and controlled OCP's litigation strategy, he might have been in privity with OCP. *See infra* section entitled "Nonparties Who May Be Bound," subsection entitled "Persons Who Control the Litigation." If he were in privity, the doctrine of issue preclusion would have barred him from relitigating the findings made during the litigation between OCP and Adams. Nelson v. Adams USA, Inc., 529 U.S. 460, 472 n.5 (2000). But judgment still could not have been rendered against him personally without affording him an opportunity to defend, including an opportunity to contest the claim that he had participated in the litigation and controlled OCP. *Id.* at 466, 468, 472; *see also* Zenith Radio Corp. v. Hazeltine Research, Inc., 395 U.S. 100, 110–11 (1969).

13. Judicial enforcement of racially restrictive covenants was declared unconstitutional in Shelley v. Kraemer, 334 U.S. 1, 20 (1948) (holding "that in granting judicial enforcement of the restrictive agreements . . ., the States have denied petitioners the equal protection of the laws"). For an interesting and more comprehensive discussion of the facts underlying the *Hansberry* decision, see Allen R. Kamp, *The History Behind* Hansberry v. Lee, 20 U.C. Davis L. Rev. 481 (1987).

14. *See id.* at 486–88.

15. Since the issue of the percentage of property owners who signed the covenant had not actually been litigated in *Burke* (but rather was stipulated), issue preclusion would not have prevented relitigation of this issue even if the parties to the two actions had been identical unless they clearly had intended the issue to be foreclosed in other litigation. *See* 18A Charles Alan Wright et al., Fed. Practice & Procedure § 4443, at 252–53 & n.6 (2d ed. 2002). *Accord* Kamp, *supra* note 13, at 490. *See also* In re Graham, 973 F.2d 1089, 1097 (3d Cir. 1992) (stating that "the intent of the parties concerning the preclusive effect of agreed facts or claims is also relevant").

16. Since the person to be bound was not a party to the underlying action, her claim was not before the court and therefore the doctrine of claim preclusion ordinarily would not apply. Restatement (Second) of Judgments § 39 cmt. b (1982); 18A Wright, *supra* note 15, § 4451, at 369. *Accord* Montana v. United States, 440 U.S. 147, 154 (1979). *Cf.* Gonzalez v. Banco Cent. Corp., 27 F.3d 751, 757 (1st Cir. 1994); Charter Oak Fire Ins. Co. v. Sumitomo Marine & Fire Ins. Co., 750 F.2d 267, 270 (3d Cir. 1984).

17. 18A Wright et al., *supra* note 15, § 4451, at 370, 382–84.

18. *See* note 13 following Chapter 2. Although the United States is not a "person" protected by due process, the Supreme Court and the lower federal courts have held that it is protected from the binding effect of judgments to the same extent as private parties who are protected by due process. *See, e.g.*, Cappaert v. United States, 426 U.S. 128, 146 (1976) (concluding that the United States was not bound by a prior judgment because it "was not made a party . . . nor was [it] in privity with" a party to the prior action); United States v. Texas, 158 F.3d 299, 305 (5th Cir. 1998) (same); United States v. Perchitti, 955 F.2d 674, 677 (11th Cir. 1992) (stating that "[t]he United States is entitled to its full day in court"); United States v. Monroe Serv. Co., 901 F.2d 610, 613 (7th Cir. 1990).

19. *See, e.g.*, *Charter Oak Fire Ins. Co.*, 750 F.2d at 270; Iacaponi v. New Amsterdam Cas. Co., 379 F.2d 311, 312 (3d Cir. 1967) (per curiam), *cert. denied*, 389 U.S. 1054 (1968).

20. *See, e.g.,* Alman v. Danin, 801 F.2d 1, 3–5 (1st Cir. 1986); Kreager v. Gen. Elec. Co., 497 F.2d 468, 472 (2d Cir.), *cert. denied*, 419 U.S. 861 (1974). *See also* Restatement (Second) of Judgments § 59(3)(a) (1982). *Cf.* J.M.S. & Assocs., Inc. v. Eastman Kodak Co., 156 F.3d 1230 (6th Cir. 1998) (table) (per curiam; unpublished opinion) (holding that a corporation was bound by a judgment rendered in an action filed by its president and sole shareholder in his individual capacity even though he controlled the corporation, rather than vice versa); Kaplan v. First Options of Chi., Inc., 143 F.3d 807, 815–16 (3d Cir. 1998) (holding that the sole shareholder of a corporation was not bound by an arbitration award against the company even though he controlled the prior proceeding because he had withheld consent to be bound personally by the award).

21. Phelps v. Hamilton, 122 F.3d 1309, 1319 (10th Cir. 1997); Krislov v. Aetna Plywood, Inc., 1999 U.S. Dist. LEXIS 19626, at *15–16 (N.D. Ill. Dec. 16, 1999), *aff'd sub nom.* Montgomery v. Aetna Plywood, Inc., 231 F.3d 399 (7th Cir. 2000), *cert. denied,* 532 U.S. 1038 (2001). *Cf.* Aziz v. Pa. State Univ., 1998 U.S. Dist. LEXIS 18612, at *7 (E.D. Pa. Nov. 17, 1998), *aff'd without published op.*, 189 F.3d 463 (3d Cir. 1999) (holding that under Pennsylvania law, an attorney is not deemed to be in privity with her client because the attorney must represent the client's, rather than her own, interests).

22. Bros, Inc. v. W.E. Grace Mfg. Co., 261 F.2d 428, 430–32 (5th Cir. 1958).

23. Iowa Elec. Light & Power Co. v. Mobile Aerial Towers, Inc., 723 F.2d 50, 52 (8th Cir. 1983).

24. 18A Wright et al., *supra* note 15, § 4462, at 659–60.

25. *Id.* at 662–63.

26. *See also* Restatement (Second) of Judgments § 44 cmt. f (1982); 18A Wright et al., *supra* note 15, § 4462, at 665–69.

27. The Second Restatement admits two exceptions to this general rule regarding pending actions. First, if "[a] procedure exists for notifying potential successors in interest of pending actions concerning property, the procedure was not followed, and the successor did not otherwise have knowledge of the action," then the successor is not bound. Restatement (Second) of Judgments § 44(1) (1982). In such a case, the successor is entitled to assume that she would have been notified had there been a pending action with respect to the property, and because she was not so notified, she should not be bound unless she otherwise learned of the action. *Id.* § 44 cmt. c. Second, the successor is not bound by the judgment if "[t]he opposing party in the action knew of the transfer to the successor and knew also that the successor was unaware of the pending action." *Id.* § 44(2). In such a case, the opposing party both knows that the successor has not consented to be represented by the transferor and has the means to protect her own interest in repose by notifying the transferee of the pending litigation. 18A Wright et al., *supra* note 15, § 4462, at 672–73 (footnote omitted).

28. John C. McCoid, *A Single Package for Multiparty Disputes*, 28 Stan. L. Rev. 707, 716 (1976).

29. In certain circumstances, a nonparty may be bound by the judgment even though the litigant did not purport to represent the nonparty's interest. In these cases, the substan-

tive law dictates that the relationship between the litigant and the nonparty is such that it is fair to bind the nonparty, such as where the nonparty succeeds to the litigant's interest in property, discussed above, or where a nonparty indemnitor had notice of an action against the litigant-indemnitee. *See* Restatement (Second) of Judgments §§ 43–44, 57 & 62 (1982).

30. For a thorough analysis of *Shutts*, see Arthur R. Miller & David Crump, *Jurisdiction and Choice of Law in Multistate Class Actions After* Phillips Petroleum Co. v. Shutts, 96 Yale L.J. 1 (1986). *See generally* 1 Alba Conte & Herbert B. Newberg, Newberg on Class Actions §§ 1.15 (4th ed. 2002).

31. *See* 7B Wright et al., *supra* note 15, §§ 1797 & 1797.1. A 2003 amendment to Rule 23(e) explicitly requires the court to determine if the settlement, dismissal or compromise is "fair, reasonable and adequate." Fed. R. Civ. P. 23(e)(1)(C).

32. Professor Monaghan has noted the Court's lack of concern "with the monitoring or participation burdens placed on nonresident class members. . . ." Henry Paul Monaghan, *Antisuit Injunctions and Preclusion Against Absent Nonresident Class Members*, 98 Colum. L. Rev. 1148, 1157 (1998).

33. For the argument that under *Shutts*, class members "have a procedural right to be heard and participate" in class action litigation, see Woolley, *Rethinking Adequacy*, *supra* note 2, at 580–81.

34. Another issue left open by the *Shutts* Court—whether absent class members must have minimum contacts with the forum state if the judgment exposes them to liability for costs or fees—has been answered affirmatively by the Vermont Supreme Court in State v. Homeside Lending, Inc., 826 A.2d 997, 1008 (Vt. 2003).

35. *Shutts* involved a class action filed in state court and thus involved due process protections afforded by the Fourteenth Amendment. The post-*Shutts* class actions filed in federal court have involved due process protections under the Fifth Amendment. To the extent that *Shutts* concluded that state courts may bind absent class members by a judgment even if they lack minimum contacts with the forum state, it follows *a fortiorari* that federal courts, too, may enter binding judgments against class members who lack minimum contacts with the state in which the federal court sits. 7A Wright et al., *supra* note 15, § 1757.

The harder question is if state courts *cannot* bind absent class members who lack minimum contacts (because, for instance, they were not afforded an opportunity to opt out), may federal courts nevertheless bind absent class members in similar circumstances? This question is complicated because the restrictions on a state court's personal jurisdiction imposed by the Fourteenth Amendment are not co-extensive with the restrictions on a federal court's personal jurisdiction imposed by the Fifth Amendment, and yet, in many cases, Rule 4(k)(1)(A) of the Federal Rules of Civil Procedure directs federal courts to employ state long-arm statutes to obtain personal jurisdiction over non-resident defendants, rendering this difference in potential jurisdictional reach irrelevant. *See generally infra* Chapter 6, section entitled "Due Process Limitations on Assertions of Personal Jurisdiction by Federal Courts." For discussions of this issue in the class action context, *see, e.g.,* 7B Wright et al., *supra* note 15, § 1789, at 254–55; Miller & Crump, *supra* note 30, at 29–31; Monaghan, *supra* note 32, at 1153 n.19; Carlough v. Amchem Prods., Inc., 10 F.3d 189, 199 (3d Cir. 1993).

36. Several commentators have suggested that due process in the mandatory class action context should be gauged by balancing competing interests. *See, e.g.*, Miller &

Crump, *supra* note 30, at 55–56; Brief of Amicus Curiae Public Citizen, Ticor Title Ins. Co. v. Brown, 510 U.S. 810 (1993) (No. 92-1988). *Cf.* Mark C. Weber, *Preclusion and Procedural Due Process in Rule 23(b)(2) Class Actions*, 21 U. Mich. J. L. Ref. 347, 387–94 (1988).

37. *See also* Miller & Crump, *supra* note 30, at 52 (positing that if *Shutts* is a case about distant forum abuse, then it does not abolish all mandatory class actions but "prohibits only those mandatory actions that are brought in inappropriate forums").

38. *See* Krell v. Prudential Ins. Co. of Am., 148 F.3d 283, 306 (3d Cir. 1998) (inferring tacit consent to jurisdiction from the class members' receipt of notice, an opportunity to be heard and an opportunity to opt out), *cert. denied sub nom.* Krell v. Prudential Ins. Co of Am., 525 U.S. 1114 (1999). *See also* Miller & Crump, *supra* note 30, at 16, 52 (positing that "[t]he right to opt out is essential to the Supreme Court's inference of consent, and that reasoning, in turn, is essential to the Court's validation of jurisdiction over members who have no affiliation with a distant forum") (footnote omitted); John E. Kennedy, *The Supreme Court Meets the Bride of Frankenstein*: Phillips Petroleum Co. v. Shutts *and the State Multistate Class Action*, 34 Kan. L. Rev. 255, 278–84, 290–95 (1985) (criticizing the Court's treatment of absent class members as plaintiffs and its consent rationale).

39. *See also* Carlough v. Amchem Prods., Inc., 10 F.3d 189, 200–01 (3d Cir. 1993) (holding that the district court violated due process by enjoining absent class members from pursuing monetary claims outside the confines of a class action because it lacked personal jurisdiction over them and the class members had not yet received notice or an opportunity to opt out).

40. *See* Miller & Crump, *supra* note 30, at 52–55; *see also* Monaghan, *supra* note 32, at 1173–75; Woolley, *Rethinking Adequacy*, *supra* note 2, at 602 (stating that "it would be wrong to conclude that class members who have minimum contacts with the forum have a constitutionally protected right to opt out").

41. The Court later recognized "at least a substantial possibility" that "in actions seeking monetary damages, classes can be certified only under Rule 23(b)(3), which permits opt-out, and not under Rules 23(b)(1) and (b)(2), which do not." Ticor Title Ins. Co. v. Brown, 511 U.S. 117, 121 (1994) (per curiam). *See infra* note 50.

42. *See also* 5 Alba Conte & Herbert B. Newberg, Newberg on Class Actions § 16:17, at 213–14, 216–17 (4th ed. 2002).

43. Incidental damages are "damages that flow directly from liability to the class *as a whole* on the claims forming the basis of the injunctive or declaratory relief. . . . Ideally, incidental damages should be only those to which class members automatically would be entitled once liability to the class (or subclass) as a whole is established." Allison v. Citgo Petroleum Corp., 151 F.3d 402, 415 (5th Cir. 1998) (citations omitted).

44. *See also* Blair v. Equifax Check Servs., Inc., 181 F.3d 832, 839 (7th Cir. 1999) (asking "[i]f damages are at issue, how can Rule 23(b)(2) be used to avoid opt-outs and notice?"). *Cf.* Williams v. Burlington N., Inc., 832 F.2d 100, 104 (7th Cir. 1987).

45. "By limiting (b)(2) certification to claims involving no more than incidental damages, the standard [adopted in *Allison*] forecloses (b)(2) class certifications of all claims that include compensatory damages (or punitive damages) even if the class-wide injunctive relief is the 'form of relief in which the plaintiffs are primarily interested.'" Robinson v. Metro-North Commuter R.R., 267 F.3d 147, 163 (2d Cir. 2001), *cert. denied*, 535 U.S. 951 (2002). For further discussion of *Allison, see*, *e.g.*, *id.* at 163 & n.8; Warnell v. Ford Motor

Co., 189 F.R.D. 383, 388–89 (N.D. Ill. 1999) (concluding that "[a]ny statements about Rule 23 in *Allison* are . . . dicta"); Lesley Frieder Wolf, Note, *Evading Friendly Fire: Achieving Class Certification After the Civil Rights Act of 1991,* 100 Colum. L. Rev. 1847, 1858–61 (2000) (reading *Allison* and *Jefferson* as "effectively eliminat[ing] the possibility of (b)(2) certification whenever plaintiffs request money damages"; critiquing *Allison*'s per se rule); Nikaa Baugh Jordan, Comment, Allison v. Citgo Petroleum: *The Death Knell for the Title VII Class Action?*, 51 Ala. L. Rev. 847, 867–81 (2000).

46. This is consistent with the view of almost all of the other Courts of Appeals, which have concluded that "monetary relief may be obtained in a (b)(2) class action so long as the predominant relief sought is injunctive or declaratory." *Allison*, 151 F.3d at 411 (supporting citations and footnote omitted).

47. *See, e.g., Robinson*, 267 F.3d at 166 (stating that "certification of a claim for non-incidental damages under Rule 23(b)(2) poses a due process risk because this provision does not expressly afford the procedural protections of notice and opt out"); Jefferson v. Ingersoll Int'l Inc., 195 F.3d 894, 898 (7th Cir. 1999); Eubanks v. Billington, 110 F.3d 87, 95 (D.C. Cir. 1997).

48. *See also* Wetzel v. Liberty Mut. Ins. Co., 508 F.2d 239, 256–57 (3d Cir.) (holding that members of a mandatory class can be bound by a judgment, even if they were denied notice and an opportunity to opt out, as long as their interests were adequately represented), *cert. denied*, 421 U.S. 1011 (1975).

49. *See also* In re Drexel Burnham Lambert Group, 960 F.2d 285, 292 (2d Cir. 1992) (holding that a right to opt out is not required when the court has personal jurisdiction over the absent class members), *cert. denied sub nom.* Hart Holding Co. v. Drexel Burnham Lambert Group, 506 U.S. 1088 (1993); White v. Nat'l Football League, 822 F. Supp. 1389, 1410, 1412 (D. Minn. 1993) (holding that "where a class action involves claims for money damages, mandatory non-opt-out class certification remains proper as long as the class claims for equitable or injunctive relief predominate over the claims for damages"; "where sufficient alternative procedural safeguards are employed, opt-out rights are not constitutionally required"), *aff'd*, 41 F.3d 402 (8th Cir. 1994), *cert. denied*, 515 U.S. 1137 (1995); In re Real Estate Title & Settlement Servs. Antitrust Litig., MDL No. 633, 1986 U.S. Dist. LEXIS 24435 (E.D. Pa. June 10, 1986) (holding that absent class members in a hybrid class action need not be afforded an opportunity to opt out as long as they are adequately represented, receive notice of the proposed settlement and the court reviews its fairness), *aff'd without op.*, 815 F.2d 695 (3d Cir. 1987), *cert. denied sub nom.* Arizona v. Chi. Title Ins. Co., 485 U.S. 909 (1988); In re Asbestos Sch. Litig., 620 F. Supp. 873 (E.D. Pa. 1985) (holding that absent class members may be precluded from pursuing punitive damages claims outside the confines of a class action as long as notice and adequate representation are provided to class members). *Cf.* In re Real Estate Title & Settlement Servs. Antitrust Litig., 869 F.2d 760, 762 (3d Cir.) (holding that it would violate due process to enjoin absent class members from relitigating monetary claims purportedly settled in the class action since they were denied an opportunity to opt out and lacked minimum contacts with the forum), *cert. denied sub nom.* Chi. Title Ins. Co. v. Tucson Unified Sch. Dist., 493 U.S. 821 (1989).

50. The Court held that the constitutional question raised "may be entirely hypothetical," Ticor Title Ins. Co. v. Brown, 511 U.S. 117, 118 (1994) (per curiam), because there "is at least a substantial possibility" that "in actions seeking monetary damages, classes

can be certified only under Rule 23(b)(3), which permits opt-out, and not under Rules 23(b)(1) and (b)(2), which do not." *Id.* at 121. That nonconstitutional issue could not be raised in the context of *Ticor*, however, because the absent class members were bound by the determination in the underlying class action that the class was properly certified under Rules 23(b)(1)(A) and 23(b)(2). *Id.* In a subsequent case, the Court granted certiorari "to decide whether [a state court's] approval of the class action and the settlement agreement . . ., without affording all class members the right to exclude themselves from the class or the agreement, violated the Due Process Clause of the Fourteenth Amendment" but again dismissed the writ as improvidently granted. Adams v. Robertson, 520 U.S. 83, 85 (1997) (per curiam).

51. *See also* Restatement (Second) of Judgments § 42 cmt. a (1982) (stating that "the adequacy of the representation can be established in the action itself only with respect to such of the represented persons who have had opportunity to be heard on the representation question. As to others, the question can be concluded only if and when a person allegedly represented challenges the judgment's effect on him").

52. The scholars are also in disagreement. *Compare, e.g.*, Monaghan, *supra* note 32, at 1200 and Patrick Woolley, *The Availability of Collateral Attack for Inadequate Representation in Class Suits*, 79 Tex. L. Rev. 383, 388, 391 (2000) *with* Marcel Kahan & Linda Silberman, Matsushita *and Beyond: The Role of State Courts in Class Actions Involving Exclusive Federal Claims*, 1996 Sup. Ct. Rev. 219, 264 and William T. Allen, *Finality of Judgments in Class Actions: A Comment on* Epstein v. MCA, Inc., 73 N.Y.U. L. Rev. 1149, 1163–64 (1998). *See generally* Rhonda Wasserman, *Dueling Class Actions*, 80 B.U. L. Rev. 461, 494–97 (2000).

53. This argument is more persuasive in the context of class actions that go to trial than in the context of settlement class actions. Kahan & Silberman, *supra* note 52, at 268–69.

54. *Accord* Monaghan, *supra* note 32, at 1199; Wasserman, *supra* note 52, at 504–06.

55. In an earlier case, the Third Circuit denied issue preclusive effect to a determination regarding the adequacy of representation where the basis of the first court's decision was unclear. In re Real Estate Title & Settlement Servs. Antitrust Litig., 869 F.2d 760, 764 n.1 (3d Cir.), *cert. denied sub nom.* Chi. Title Ins. Co. v. Tucson Unified Sch. Dist., 493 U.S. 821 (1989). *See also* Frank v. United Airlines, Inc., 216 F.3d 845, 850, 852 (9th Cir. 2000) (permitting a collateral attack on the basis of inadequate representation where the parties to the underlying class action, settled thirty years earlier, had "stipulated to class certification" and had settled the action after judgment without judicial approval), *cert. denied*, 532 U.S. 914 (2001).

56. In a footnote, the majority declined to address the due process claim because it was "outside the scope of the question presented in this Court." Matsushita Elec. Indus. Co. v. Epstein, 516 U.S. 367, 379 n.5 (1996). In the same footnote, the Court commented that the absent class members sought to collaterally attack the class action settlement "in spite of the Chancery Court's express ruling, following argument on the issue, that the class representatives fairly and adequately protected the interests of the class." *Id.*

57. In *Richards*, the City of Birmingham and the acting director of its finance department challenged the constitutionality of a county occupation tax. "Even if we were to assume . . . that by suing in his official capacity, the finance director intended to represent the pecuniary interests of all city taxpayers, and not simply the corporate interests of the city itself, he did not purport to represent the pecuniary interests of *county* taxpayers

like petitioners." Richards v. Jefferson County, 517 U.S. 793, 801–02 (1996). The Court declined to decide "whether public officials are always constitutionally adequate representatives of all persons over whom they have jurisdiction when, as here, the underlying right is personal in nature." *Id.* at 802 n.6.

58. The United States government's representation of Native Americans may be *sui generis* and more akin to representation based upon a formal legal relationship described above than the more common representation of the general public by the government. The Supreme Court has referred to Native Americans as "dependents" and "wards" of the government and has concluded that when the United States purports to represent their interests, the judgment binds not only the United States, but also the Native Americans. *See, e.g.*, Nevada v. United States, 463 U.S. 110, 135, 142 (1983); Arizona v. California, 460 U.S. 605, 615, 626–27 & n.20 (1983); Heckman v. United States, 224 U.S. 413, 444–46 (1912). The Court has reaffirmed this conclusion even where the Native Americans have unique legal interests not shared by the general public, *see, e.g.*, *Heckman*, 224 U.S. at 444–46, and even where the government purports to represent both Native Americans and other competing interests in the same litigation. *Nevada*, 463 U.S. at 135, 142–43; *Arizona*, 460 U.S. at 627. The Court has rejected the argument that preclusion in the face of such a conflict of interest violates due process. *Nevada*, 463 U.S. at 135 n.15, 144 n.16.

59. *See also* In re Engelhard & Sons Co., 231 U.S. 646, 651 (1914) (concluding that "[t]he city was the proper party . . . as representative of all interested," including both the public at large and the subscribers to telephone service, who had a personal pecuniary interest in the suit by the telephone company challenging a rate ordinance enacted by the city).

60. For a thorough discussion of the statutory and constitutional issues that arise when successive suits to enforce the Clear Air Act are filed by the government and private parties, see William V. Luneburg, *Claim Preclusion, Full Faith and Credit, and Clear Air Act Enforcement: The Ghosts of* Gwaltney, 10 Widener L. Rev. 113 (2003).

61. For a discussion of the history of virtual representation doctrine and its role in nonparty preclusion law, see Bone, *supra* note 3, at 203–18.

62. *See also* 18A Wright et al., *supra* note 15, § 4457, at 521–24.

63. "The concept of 'privity' refers to a cluster of relationships . . . under which the preclusive effects of a judgment extend beyond a party to the original action and apply to persons having specified relationships to that party. . . ." Restatement (Second) of Judgments intro. at 1 (1982). The terms "privity" and "privies" have been criticized as "conclusory and analytically unsound." Montana v. United States, 440 U.S. 147, 154 n.5 (1979) (citations omitted). The Second Restatement of Judgments abandons the "privity" nomenclature, focusing instead on the nature of the relationship between the party to the action and the person to be bound. *See* Restatement (Second) of Judgments intro. & §§ 34–61 (1982).

64. The *Richards* Court cited three cases that suggest that notice and adequate representation are independent due process requirements. Richards v. Jefferson County, 517 U.S. 793, 801 (1996) (citing *Hansberry*, 311 U.S. at 40 (stating that in determining whether it is constitutional to bind a person by a judgment, the court must examine whether she "has been afforded such *notice* and opportunity to be heard as are requisite to the due process which the Constitution prescribes") (emphasis added); Eisen v. Carlisle & Jacquelin, 417 U.S. 156, 176–77 (1974) (rejecting the view "that adequate representation,

rather than notice, is the touchstone of due process in a class action and therefore satisfies Rule 23" and stating that "this view has little to commend it"); Mullane v. Cent. Hanover Bank & Trust Co., 339 U.S. 306, 318 (1950) (requiring notice "reasonably calculated to reach" those with an interest in the action).

65. In South Central Bell Telephone Co. v. Alabama, 526 U.S. 160 (1999), the Court relied heavily on *Richards* to conclude that South Central Bell Telephone Co. was not precluded from challenging an Alabama tax even though another company had previously challenged the same tax on the same grounds and had lost. The earlier suit had not been conducted as a class action and the parties had not been in privity with one another. *Id.* at 168.

66. In a footnote to this passage, the Court added that "a plan of reorganization is binding upon *all* creditors once the plan is confirmed, whether or not the claim was presented for administration." NLRB v. Bildisco & Bildisco, 465 U.S. 513, 529 n.10 (1984) (citations omitted) (emphasis added).

67. H.R. Rep. No. 40(I), 102d Cong., 1st Sess. at 49–50 (1991).

68. Another section of the statute, which provides that "[n]othing in this subsection shall be construed to . . . (D) authorize or permit the denial to any person of the due process of law required by the Constitution," 42 U.S.C. § 2000e-2(n)(2)(D), begs the constitutional question. Marjorie A. Silver, *Fairness and Finality: Third-Party Challenges to Employment Discrimination Consent Decrees After the 1991 Civil Rights Act*, 62 Fordham L. Rev. 321, 362 n.250 (1993).

69. 18A Wright et al., *supra* note 15, § 4452, at 411; *see also* Owen M. Fiss, *The Allure of Individualism*, 78 Iowa L. Rev. 965 (1993); Susan S. Grover, *The Silenced Majority:* Martin v. Wilks *and the Legislative Response*, 1992 U. Ill. L. Rev. 43; Silver, *supra* note 68.

70. *See, e.g.*, Douglas Laycock, *Due Process of Law in Trilateral Disputes*, 78 Iowa L. Rev. 1011, 1023–28 (1993); *see also* Issacharoff, *supra* note 11, at 194, 230.

71. Laycock, *supra* note 70, at 1024; Issacharoff, *supra* note 11, at 227; Woolley, *Rethinking Adequacy*, *supra* note 2, at 623. *Cf.* Silver, *supra* note 68, at 362–63 & n.253 (concluding that the statute "governs only persons who *actually* receive notice, and does not present the question of the adequacy of notice that was sent but never received"); *id.* at 365 (stating that "the *Mullane* standards for notice are not constitutionally required for purposes of notifying nonparties to the litigation").

72. Laycock, *supra* note 70, at 1024–25; *see also* Silver, *supra* note 68, at 365–66; Woolley, *Rethinking Adequacy*, *supra* note 2, at 623–24.

73. Laycock, *supra* note 70, at 1020–21, 1024–25. *See also* Weber, *supra* note 36, at 349 (arguing that it "almost certainly" violates due process to bind absent class members without notice). *Cf.* Silver, *supra* note 68, at 367–68 (arguing that "adequacy of representation without notice . . . is constitutionally sufficient to bar subsequent challenges . . . when legislated as part of a statutory scheme like Title VII").

74. Laycock, *supra* note 70, at 1026; *see also id.* at 1023–28.

75. Several courts have read § 9613(f)(2) broadly, concluding that it protects from contribution claims not only parties who settle with the United States or a state, but also parties who settle with municipalities or other private parties. *See, e.g.*, United States v. SCA Servs. of Ind., Inc., 827 F. Supp. 526, 532 (N.D. Ind. 1993); Allied Corp. v. Acme Solvent Reclaiming, Inc., 771 F. Supp. 219, 222 (N.D. Ill. 1990); City of New York v. Exxon Corp.,

697 F. Supp. 677, 685 (S.D.N.Y. 1988). *But see* Comerica Bank-Detroit v. Allen Indus., Inc., 769 F. Supp. 1408, 1413 (E.D. Mich. 1991).

76. See Chapter 4 of this volume. *Accord* John M. Hyson, *CERCLA Settlements, Contribution Protection and Fairness to Non-Settling Responsible Parties*, 10 Vill. Envtl. L.J. 277, 339 (1999); Christopher D. Man, *The Constitutional Rights of Nonsettling Potentially Responsible Parties in the Allocation of CERCLA Liability*, 27 Envtl. L. 375, 396–97 (1997).

77. *See, e.g.*, Man, *supra* note 76, at 399 (stating that "CERCLA fairness hearings, by themselves, fail to provide sufficient protection to nonsettling parties"); *see generally id.* at 380–401 (concluding that CERCLA settlement provisions violate due process). *See also* McDermott, Inc. v. AmClyde, 511 U.S. 202, 213–15 (1994) (in admiralty context, concluding that a model like CERCLA, which deprives non-settling defendants of a right to seek contribution, "is likely to lead to inequitable apportionments of liability"; incentive to settlement that this model affords "comes at too high a price in unfairness") (footnote omitted).

# 4

# The Form and Extent of Notice

*"The right to a hearing is meaningless without notice."*[1]

*"Notice by publication is a poor and sometimes a hopeless substitute for actual service of notice."*[2]

As we have seen in Chapter 3, the Due Process Clauses ordinarily require that the government afford a person notice and an opportunity to be heard before it deprives her of a protected interest. But what form must the notice take? What efforts must the government make to ensure that it has identified all persons who might have a protected interest? What efforts must the government make to locate and notify persons that it has identified as having a protected interest? And how much notice must the government provide a person before it takes action against her? It is to these issues that we now turn.

## NOTICE REQUIREMENTS BEFORE 1950

An inherent conflict exists between the interest of an individual whose life, liberty or property may be affected by governmental action and who therefore wants the best possible personal notice of the impending action and the government's interest in the quick and inexpensive resolution of claims. This conflict may be pronounced when the individual's identity is difficult to ascertain or her interest is remote or contingent. In such cases, the government may prefer to provide only notice by publication, rather than personal service. But notice by publication—notice published in the back pages of a newspaper—is unlikely to provide actual notice to the individual.

Prior to the Supreme Court's decision in Mullane v. Central Hanover Bank & Trust Co. in 1950, this conflict between the interests of the individual and the state was often resolved in favor of the government, especially in *in rem* actions—those resolving competing claims to property.[3] The United States Supreme Court upheld notice by publication in *in rem* proceedings (even though it rarely, if ever, provided actual notice) for a number of reasons: *in rem* proceedings created no personal liability; nonresidents with potential interests in forum property could not be served with process within the territorial limits of the state; nonresident owners were presumed to have left their property in the care of a person under a duty to notify them of actions placing it at risk; and the state had a powerful interest in clearing title to property within its borders (see, e.g., Longyear v. Toolan, 1908; Ballard v. Hunter, 1907; Winona & St. Peter Land Co. v. Minnesota, 1895).[4]

During the nineteenth and early twentieth centuries, the Supreme Court rarely had occasion to discuss the form that notice had to take in *in personam* actions—actions seeking to impose personal liability—because its personal jurisdiction jurisprudence (to be discussed more fully in Chapter 6) ensured, as a practical matter, that defendants in such actions received notice through personal service of process. In Pennoyer v. Neff (1877), for example, the Court held that a civil defendant had to be personally served with process in the forum state in order to be brought within the court's jurisdiction. As long as due process required in-hand personal service to obtain personal jurisdiction, there was no need to consider the form that substituted service—a method of service other than personal service—might take in *in personam* cases.[5] Put differently, the Court had little occasion to explore notice as an independent due process requirement since an exercise of jurisdiction itself assured personal service, the "gold standard" of notice.

Once the Supreme Court held that a person might be subject to *in personam* jurisdiction even in the absence of in-state personal service if she had minimum contacts with the forum state (Int'l Shoe Co. v. Washington, 1945), it became necessary to consider the form of notice required in such cases. Put differently, once the exercise of personal jurisdiction no longer depended upon in-state personal service, the question became what other forms of notice would satisfy due process.

Before addressing this question generally, the Supreme Court focused on the limited circumstance in which a state implied consent to suit from a person's use of state highways and authorized service of process upon a state official (as agent for the defendant) in actions that arose out of car accidents within the forum state. In such cases, the Court held that due process requires that the state statute "contain a provision making it reasonably probable that notice of the service on the [state official] will be communicated to the non-resident defendant who is sued" (Wuchter v. Pizzutti, 1928). Thus, it was not enough that the defendant actually received notice; the government had to adopt a formal mechanism to ensure that notice was provided.

## THE LANDMARK CASE OF MULLANE V. CENTRAL HANOVER BANK & TRUST CO. (1950)

In Mullane v. Central Hanover Bank & Trust Co. (1950), the Supreme Court addressed in a more general way the form and extent of notice required by due process in the absence of personal service of process. Fifty years after it was decided, *Mullane* continues to be the leading case on the constitutionally required form and extent of notice.

*Mullane* considered the constitutionality of notice provided to beneficiaries of a common trust fund set up pursuant to legislation that permitted the pooling of several participating trusts into a single common trust for investment administration. The legislation required the trustee of the common trust fund to make an accounting twelve to eighteen months after the establishment of the fund and every three years thereafter. Once a court approved the accounting, no claim could be brought against the trustee regarding any matter set forth in the accounting.

In January 1946, when Central Hanover Bank and Trust Company set up a common trust fund under this legislation, it mailed a copy of the judicial settlement and notice provisions of the law to each income or principal beneficiary in any of the participating trusts whose name and address were known to it. In March 1947, Central Hanover petitioned the court for judicial approval of its first accounting as common trustee. Pursuant to the enabling legislation, the bank provided notice by publication to the beneficiaries of the trust. The notice, published once a week for four successive weeks in a local newspaper, stated the name and address of the bank, the name and date of establishment of the common trust fund, and a list of the all of the participating trusts that made up the common trust fund. Individual beneficiaries were not named, however. Upon the filing of the petition for the settlement of accounts, the court appointed separate guardians to represent the income and principal beneficiaries of the common trust fund. Kenneth Mullane, who was appointed to represent the income beneficiaries, appeared specially, claiming that the notice provided and the statutory provisions for notice were inadequate to afford due process. The New York courts rejected Mullane's constitutional challenge and accepted the accounts.

On appeal, the United States Supreme Court reversed. While it might have upheld notice by publication on the theory that such notice traditionally was employed in *in rem* actions, the Court declined to classify the instant action as an *in rem* action or to distinguish among *in personam*, *in rem*, or *quasi-in-rem* actions. In an important step toward its landmark jurisdictional decision in Shaffer v. Heitner (1977),[6] the Court stated that

> the requirements of the Fourteenth Amendment . . . do not depend upon a classification for which the standards are so elusive and confused generally and which, being primarily for

> state courts to define, may and do vary from state to state. . . . [W]e do not rest the power of the State to resort to constructive service in this proceeding upon how its courts or this Court may regard this historical antithesis (Mullane v. Cent. Hanover Bank & Trust Co., 1950).

Thus, the Court declined to uphold service by publication by characterizing the action as an *in rem* action affecting only property located within the forum state, rather than the personal rights of the beneficiaries.

Eschewing this easy way out, the Court directly addressed the question whether the notification scheme sanctioned by the state accorded beneficiaries "full opportunity to appear and be heard" (Mullane v. Cent. Hanover Bank & Trust Co., 1950). Noting that "[m]any controversies have raged about the cryptic and abstract words of the Due Process Clause," the Court made clear that "at a minimum they require that deprivation of life, liberty or property by adjudication be preceded by notice and opportunity for hearing appropriate to the nature of the case" (Mullane v. Cent. Hanover Bank & Trust Co., 1950). But what form must the notice take?

The Court described in-state personal service as "the classic form of notice always adequate in any type of proceeding" (Mullane v. Cent. Hanover Bank & Trust Co., 1950). Noting that in-state personal service would be impossible in many cases involving beneficiaries living outside the state, the Court quickly added that "[a] construction of the Due Process Clause which would place impossible or impractical obstacles in the way could not be justified" (Mullane v. Cent. Hanover Bank & Trust Co., 1950). Instead, the Court introduced a balancing test that would weigh the state's interest in settling the accounts on the common trust fund against the individual's interest in being heard. Declining to adopt any specific formula to achieve balance, the Court offered "a few general principles" gleaned from precedent:

> An elementary and fundamental requirement of due process in any proceeding which is to be accorded finality is notice reasonably calculated, under all the circumstances, to apprise interested parties of the pendency of the action and afford them an opportunity to present their objections. The notice must be of such nature as reasonably to convey the required information and it must afford a reasonable time for those interested to make their appearance. . . .
>
> But when notice is a person's due, process which is a mere gesture is not due process. The means employed must be such as one desirous of actually informing the absentee might reasonably adopt to accomplish it. The reasonableness and hence the constitutional validity of any chosen method may be defended on the ground that it is in itself reasonably certain to inform those affected, or, where conditions do not reasonably permit such notice, that the form chosen is not substantially less likely to bring home notice than other of the feasible and customary substitutes (Mullane v. Cent. Hanover Bank & Trust Co., 1950).

Thus, due process requires notice that is reasonably likely to reach interested parties, or, if no such method is available, then notice that is at least as effective as the customary substitutes.[7]

The Court then applied this disjunctive test to assess the constitutionality of the notice provided to the beneficiaries of the common trust fund. The advertisements in small print in the back pages of the newspaper were unlikely to reach local beneficiaries, let alone those living in another state or abroad, especially since they did not include the beneficiaries' names. Nor was publication reinforced by other steps likely to attract their attention, such as the steps taken in *in rem* or *quasi-in-rem* cases—seizure of personal property or entry upon land. Thus, the notice was not reasonably likely to reach interested parties (Mullane v. Cent. Hanover Bank & Trust Co., 1950).

But was it at least as effective as the customary substitutes? As to those beneficiaries whose interests or whereabouts the bank could not ascertain with due diligence, publication was constitutionally acceptable because it was "not reasonably possible or practicable to give more adequate warning" (Mullane v. Cent. Hanover Bank & Trust Co., 1950). Publication was even deemed acceptable as to those beneficiaries whose interests were conjectural or future or whose identities did not routinely come to the bank's knowledge. Noting that ordinary standards of diligence might require more extensive efforts in other circumstances, the Court acceded to the state's judgment that here it was too expensive and burdensome for the bank to track the interests of beneficiaries with remote future or contingent interests and to provide them with more certain notice. Thus, the Court upheld the sufficiency of the publication notice provided to beneficiaries whose interests or addresses were unknown to the bank (Mullane v. Cent. Hanover Bank & Trust Co., 1950).

But the bank had names and addresses for the present income beneficiaries, so there was no reason to dispense with "a serious effort to inform them personally of the accounting, at least by ordinary mail to the record addresses" (Mullane v. Cent. Hanover Bank & Trust Co., 1950). "Where the names and post-office addresses of those affected by a proceeding are at hand, the reasons disappear for resort to means less likely than the mails to apprise them of its pendency" (Mullane v. Cent. Hanover Bank & Trust Co., 1950). Even though service by mail was itself less likely than personal service to actually notify the known beneficiaries, it was acceptable in this case because all of the income beneficiaries had an identical interest in the integrity of the fund and the fidelity of the trustee. Thus, in these circumstances, "reasonable risks that notice might not actually reach every beneficiary [were] justifiable" (Mullane v. Cent. Hanover Bank & Trust Co., 1950).

While *Mullane* made clear that notice by publication was not sufficient on the facts of the case to satisfy due process, it left open many questions. Would notice by publication be sufficient in *in rem* and *quasi-in-rem* proceedings? In other contexts? How much effort would the government have to expend to identify, locate and notify persons with protected interests, especially in actions that involved few claimants with identical interests? And what if efforts to afford individual notice were unsuccessful? It is to those issues that we now turn.

## NOTICE REQUIRED IN ACTIONS AFFECTING REAL PROPERTY

Just years after deciding *Mullane*, the Supreme Court had occasion to address the first of these questions, quickly putting to rest the idea that notice by publication would suffice in actions affecting real property. In Walker v. City of Hutchinson (1956), the Court held that notice by publication was inadequate to protect the rights of property owners whose land was condemned by the city. Beginning with the proposition that "due process requires that an owner whose property is taken for public use must be given a hearing in determining just compensation," the Court noted that "[t]he right to a hearing is meaningless without notice" (Walker v. City of Hutchinson, 1956).

The city argued that service by publication was constitutionally sufficient because the action was *in rem*, invoking Huling v. Kaw Valley Railway & Improvement Co. (1889), which had upheld notice by publication in a condemnation proceeding against a nonresident property owner on the theory that service by publication constituted due process in *in rem* actions. The *Walker* Court distinguished *Huling*, noting that it had involved a nonresident property owner while Walker was a forum resident. While formally declining to "consider the extent to which *Mullane* [had] undermined the reasoning of the *Huling* decision," the *Walker* Court implicitly rejected *Huling* and the notion that notice by publication was constitutionally sufficient in *in rem* actions (Walker v. City of Hutchinson, 1956).

Applying *Mullane* to an action affecting real property, the *Walker* Court reiterated the problems with notice by publication, noting that it "rarely informs a landowner of proceedings against his property" (Walker v. City of Hutchinson, 1956). Since the city had the property owner's name in its official records, there was no reason why it could not provide him with "direct notice" of the action to condemn his property and determine his compensation.

In subsequent cases, the Court has continued to require notice by mail in condemnation proceedings, holding that notice by publication, even when accompanied by posting of the notice, is constitutionally inadequate. In Schroeder v. City of New York (1962), for example, the Court considered a challenge to a statute that permitted New York City to condemn land required for its water system. The statute required notice by publication and posting of handbills in the vicinity of the real estate to be taken. Although twenty-two notices were posted on trees and poles along a seven- or eight-mile stretch of the river the waters of which were to be diverted, no notice was posted on Ms. Schroeder's property, which she occupied only two months a year. Furthermore, the notice that was published and posted failed to include Ms. Schroeder's name, even though "her name and address were readily ascertainable from both deed records and tax rolls" (Schroeder v. City of New York, 1962). Ms. Schroeder did not see the notice in the newspaper or on the posted handbills and sued for damages suffered as a result of the city's taking of her land. The Court relied on *Mullane* for the "general rule that . . . notice by publication is not enough with respect to a person whose name and address are known or very easily ascertainable and whose legally protected interests are directly affected by the proceedings in question" (Schroeder v. City of New York, 1962). The posted handbills did not satisfy the "personal notice" required by *Mullane* because "no such sign was placed anywhere on the appellant's property, or ever seen by her" (Schroeder v. City of New York, 1962).

In a later case, Greene v. Lindsey (1982), the Court made clear that even a notice posted directly on a person's property could be insufficient to satisfy due process. *Greene* involved forcible entry and detainer actions filed by the local housing authority against tenants in a public housing project, seeking repossession of the apartments. In each of the cases on appeal, notice had been posted on the tenant's door pursuant to a statute that authorized posting of the notice "in a conspicuous place on the premises" (Greene v. Lindsey, 1982, quoting Ky. Rev. Stat. § 454.030). The tenants claimed that they never saw the posted summonses and only learned of the eviction proceedings when they were served with writs of possession, which had been executed after default judgments were rendered against them and their time to appeal had lapsed. The tenants commenced a class action in federal court, challenging the constitutionality of the notice procedure. The housing authority defended the form of notice employed, arguing that because the action to recover possession of the apartment was an *in rem* action, notice by posting was "*ipso facto* constitutionally adequate" (Greene v. Lindsey, 1982).

As in *Mullane*, the Supreme Court declined to resolve the constitutional issue by resort to the *in rem/in personam* dichotomy. Noting that the tenants had been deprived of a significant interest in property—the right to remain in their homes—the Court refused to accept that "because the action is *in rem*, it is only necessary to serve notice 'upon the thing itself'" (Greene v. Lindsey, 1982). Instead, the Court focused on the realities of the case, asking whether the form of notice employed was reasonably likely to inform the tenants of the pendency of the proceedings.

Proceeding from the presumption noted in *Mullane* that actions that "physically disturb" one's property will come to the owner's attention, the *Greene* Court went so far as to accept that this presumption is "particularly well founded where notice is posted at a residence" (Greene v. Lindsey, 1982). But even while conceding that posting notice on the door of a person's home would, in many or perhaps most instances, constitute not only a constitutionally acceptable means of service, but indeed a singularly appropriate and effective way of ensuring that a person who cannot conveniently be served personally is actually apprised of proceedings against him" (Greene v. Lindsey, 1982),

the Court nevertheless held that the notices posted on the tenants' doors in *Greene* failed to provide them with notice sufficient to satisfy due process:

> As the process servers were well aware, notices posted on apartment doors in the area where these tenants lived were "not infrequently" removed by children or other tenants before they could have their intended effect. Under these conditions, notice by posting on the apartment door cannot be considered a "reliable means of acquainting interested parties of the fact that their rights are before the courts" (Greene v. Lindsey, 1982).

As in *Mullane*, the Court considered the particular circumstances of the case in assessing the adequacy of the notice provided and again extolled the efficacy of the mails in achieving actual notice (Greene v. Lindsey, 1982).

Read together, *Walker*, *Schroeder* and *Greene* extend the *Mullane* standard to govern the constitutionality of notice in actions affecting real property. These cases clearly reject the notion that notice by publication is constitutionally adequate in *in rem* actions where the names and addresses of those interested in real property are known or "easily ascertainable" (Schroeder v. City of New York, 1962). Moreover, *Walker*, *Schroeder* and *Greene* have been extended to govern *in rem* admiralty actions. Thus, notice satisfying the *Mullane* standard must be afforded to anyone with a known interest in the vessel. While in many admiralty cases, notice by posting on the ship will be constitutionally adequate as the owner is usually in charge of the vessel, such notice does not satisfy due process where the owner cannot reasonably be presumed to receive it (Ehorn v. Sunken Vessel Known as the "Rosinco," 7th Cir. 2002; MacDougalls' Cape Cod Marine Serv., Inc. v. One Christina 40' Vessel, 1st Cir. 1990).

But what interests other than ownership entitle one to notice? And what is meant by "easily ascertainable"? How much effort must the government expend to identify parties with protected interests at stake? We now turn to these issues.

## THE EXTENT OF THE OBLIGATION TO IDENTIFY PARTIES WITH PROTECTED INTERESTS

Mennonite Board of Missions v. Adams (1983) addressed the constitutionality of a statutory notice scheme that authorized the sale of real property on which the payment of taxes had been delinquent for fifteen months or longer. Consistent with the real property cases discussed above, the statute required notice by certified mail to the owner of the property at her last known address. In addition, the county auditor was required to post notice in the county courthouse and to publish notice. Under the state law, however, because mortgagees—lenders with a security interest in the property—had no title to the mortgaged property, they were not considered owners and therefore were not entitled to notice by mail under the statute. Once notice was provided to the owner, the property was sold at public auction.

In *Mennonite Board of Missions*, a mortgagee challenged the constitutionality of this notice scheme in the context of a purchaser's action to quiet title to property purchased at the public auction. *Mullane* had made clear that an *owner* of property is entitled to notice by mail or in-hand personal service; but what about a mortgagee? Does due process guarantee a mortgagee notice meeting the *Mullane* standard?

Starting with the proposition that a mortgagee has a substantial, legally protected property interest in real estate, the *Mennonite* Court applied *Mullane* to hold that a mortgagee "is entitled to notice reasonably calculated to apprise him of a pending tax sale" (Mennonite Bd. of Missions v. Adams, 1983). Clearly, under *Mullane*, notice by publication would not do:

> When the mortgagee is identified in a mortgage that is publicly recorded, constructive notice by publication must be supplemented by notice mailed to the mortgagee's last known available address, or by personal service. But unless the mortgagee is not reasonably identifiable, constructive notice alone does not satisfy the mandate of *Mullane* (Mennonite Bd. of Missions v. Adams, 1983).

Here, county records identified the mortgagee by name, county and state, but did not include its street address. The Court assumed that "the mortgagee's address could have been ascertained by reasonably diligent efforts," but specifically declined to impose an obligation "to undertake extraordinary efforts to discover the identity and whereabouts of a mortgagee whose identity is not in the public record" (Mennonite Bd. of Missions v. Adams, 1983). In a strongly worded dissent, Justice O'Connor chastised the majority for transforming *Mullane*'s flexible balancing test into an unyielding requirement that notice by mail or personal service be provided whenever a party has any legally protected property interest at stake (Mennonite Bd. of Missions v. Adams, 1983, O'Connor, J., dissenting).

While *Mennonite* made clear that mortgagees are entitled to notice by mail or personal service if they are reasonably identifiable, it clarified neither the nature of an interest that entitles one to notice under *Mullane* nor the extent of the obligation to identify those with protected interests (Mennonite Bd. of Missions v. Adams, 1983, O'Connor, J., dissenting).

The Court returned to these issues in Tulsa Professional Collection Services, Inc. v. Pope (1988), a case that arose in the context of a probate proceeding. A hospital that had provided medical care to the decedent immediately before her death had assigned its claim for payment to a subsidiary, which served as a collection agency for the hospital. The subsidiary-creditor challenged a statutory notice scheme, which authorized the executor of the decedent's estate to publish notice in a local newspaper for two consecutive weeks to advise the decedent's creditors that they had to present their claims to the executor within two months of the date of first publication or their claims would be barred forever. The state courts upheld the "short-term nonclaim" statute (as such provisions are called) against a due process challenge, concluding that neither *Mullane* nor *Mennonite* required more than notice by publication because the nonclaim statute was nothing more than a self-executing statute of limitations.

On appeal, the Supreme Court reversed. Beginning with *Mennonite*'s statement that "'actual notice is a minimum constitutional precondition to a proceeding which will adversely affect the liberty or property interests of *any* party . . . if its name and address are reasonably ascertainable'" (Tulsa Prof'l Collection Servs., Inc. v. Pope, 1988, quoting Mennonite Bd. of Missions v. Adams, 1983, emphasis added), the Court asked two preliminary questions: first, whether the hospital's subsidiary had an interest that was protected by the Constitution, and second, whether there was sufficient state action to implicate the Fourteenth Amendment. As to the first question, the Court relied on *Mullane* itself for the proposition that a claim, like the subsidiary's claim against the estate for an unpaid bill, is "'a species of property protected by the Fourteenth Amendment's Due Process Clause'" (Tulsa Prof'l Collection Servs., Inc. v. Pope, 1988). As to the second question, while the Court conceded that the state's involvement in the mere running of a statute of limitations is ordinarily insufficient to constitute state action (Texaco, Inc. v. Short, 1982), it declined to characterize the short-term nonclaim statute as a "self-executing" statute of limitations.[8] Here, the time bar was activated only after probate proceedings were commenced and the state court appointed an executor. The nonclaim statute further required the executor to file with the court copies of the notice and proof of publication. Since state involvement in the process was "pervasive and substantial," the Court found that state action existed and the Due Process Clause was implicated (Tulsa Prof'l Collection Servs., Inc. v. Pope, 1988).

With these preliminary issues out of the way, the Court engaged in the balancing of the individual and state interests advocated by *Mullane* to assess the adequacy of published notice in this context. On the one hand, a creditor may not know of the debtor's death or the institution of probate proceedings. Thus the creditor's need for actual notice may be substantial. On the other hand, "the State undeniably has a legitimate interest in the expeditious resolution of probate proceedings" (Tulsa Prof'l Collection Servs., Inc. v. Pope, 1988). In deciding the case in favor of the subsidiary-creditor, the Court concluded that the state could assure actual notice "to known or reasonably ascertainable creditors" without compromising its own goals (Tulsa Prof'l Collection Servs., Inc. v. Pope, 1988).

Notice by mail would be an inexpensive and efficient means of providing actual notice. While reiterating *Mullane*'s disavowal of "any intent to require 'impracticable and extended searches . . . in the name of due process,'" the *Tulsa* Court nevertheless held that executors must make

> "reasonably diligent efforts" to uncover the identities of creditors. For creditors who are not "reasonably ascertainable," publication notice can suffice. Nor is everyone who may conceivably have a claim properly considered a creditor entitled to actual notice. Here, as in *Mullane*, it is reasonable to dispense with actual notice to those with mere "conjectural" claims (Tulsa Prof'l Collection Servs., Inc. v. Pope, 1988, quoting Mennonite Bd. of Missions v. Adams, 1983).

Noting that it had required actual notice to creditors in the bankruptcy setting, where the need for prompt administration of claims is also high (Bank of Marin v. England, 1966; City of New York v. N.Y., N.H. & H. R.R., 1953), the Court declined to create an exception from the actual notice requirement for probate proceedings without a greater showing that the obligation to provide such notice would be "so burdensome or impracticable as to warrant reliance on publication notice alone" (Tulsa Prof'l Collection Servs., Inc. v. Pope, 1988).

Because the record did not reveal whether the executrix of the estate in issue knew of the hospital subsidiary's identity as a creditor or reasonably could ascertain it, the Court remanded for further proceedings. The Court offered only the slightest clue as to the meaning of "reasonably ascertainable": the executrix "of course was aware that her husband endured a long stay at [the hospital], but it is not clear that this awareness translates into knowledge of [the subsidiary's] claim" (Tulsa Prof'l Collection Servs., Inc. v. Pope, 1988). Thus, the Court remanded for further proceedings "to determine whether 'reasonably diligent efforts' would have identified [the subsidiary] and uncovered its claim." If the executrix reasonably could have ascertained the identity of the subsidiary, it was entitled to "'notice by mail or other means as certain to ensure actual notice'" (Tulsa Prof'l Collection Servs., Inc. v. Pope, 1988, quoting Mennonite Bd. of Missions v. Adams, 1983).

The nature of the obligation to identify and notify those with interests at stake has arisen in many contexts, including the tax sale, probate and bankruptcy settings. With the limited guidance offered by the Supreme Court in *Mullane* and its progeny, the lower federal courts and the state courts have had to make difficult judgments regarding the adequacy of notice afforded in these and other contexts. Although we cannot survey all of the different notice issues that have arisen in recent years, we offer below a smattering of some of the more interesting ones.

When the government brings a foreclosure action for nonpayment of taxes, it must provide notice by mail or actual notice to reasonably identifiable property owners (Mennonite Bd. of Missions v. Adams, 1983). But what if the owner of the property is deceased? Must the government make efforts to notify the heirs or future purchasers? The Second Circuit Court of Appeals has held that when the record owner is deceased and a foreclosure notice mailed to her is not returned by the post office as undeliverable, the government is not obligated to identify and notify the distributees of the decedent's estate. It might be burdensome for the government to locate them since their names are not recorded in the land records and the government reasonably can expect that the administrator of the estate "would place something on the land record to put the world on notice of the owner's death and would also obtain mail addressed to their decedent" (Bender v. City of Rochester, 2d Cir. 1985). On the other hand, the Eighth Circuit has held that when the government initiates proceedings to demolish a home titled in the name of a person known to be deceased, due process requires it to attempt to notify the decedent's heirs if their names and addresses are reasonably ascertainable and may also require it to file and record with the county a notice that the property has been declared a nuisance to protect the interests of prospective purchasers (Kornblum v. St. Louis County, 8th Cir. 1995).

In addition to owners and first mortgagees, many others may be affected by a tax sale of real property, including second mortgagees,[9] occupants,[10] lessees,[11] holders of mineral leases,[12] concurrent owners,[13] judgment creditors,[14] holders of easements[15] and land sale contract purchasers.[16] Legislatures and courts have struggled to determine whether any or all of these parties are entitled to notice under *Mullane* and *Mennonite,* weighing the government's interest in its tax sale program and its need to provide marketable title, the burden of identifying those with unrecorded property interests, and the interests of parties who may be affected by tax sales.[17] There is a growing consensus that local governments must examine both the records of the tax collector and the land records to identify those with protected property interests who are entitled to notice of a tax sale.[18]

Some jurisdictions have responded to this notice quandary by enacting "request-notice" statutes, which permit interested parties to file a request for notice of tax proceedings.[19] Municipalities and other governmental bodies then mail individual notice to all interested parties who have filed such requests before conducting a tax sale. But is due process satisfied if the government provides individual notice only to those who request it and relies on notice by publication to notify other reasonably identifiable parties with legally protected interests who do not request notice under the statute?

The Supreme Court in *Mennonite* declined to address this issue[20] and the lower federal courts and state courts are not in agreement on this issue. Some courts have held that request-notice statutes relieve the government of an obligation to provide notice to interested parties who decline to request it (Elizondo v. Read, Ind. 1992; Bankers Life Co. v. Regotti, La. Ct. App. 1987; In re Tax Foreclosure No. 35, N.Y. App. Div. 1987; see also In re ISCA Enters., N.Y. 1991). These courts conclude that the state's "crucial stake in collecting delinquent taxes through tax sales" and its "substantial interest in avoiding the costly and time-consuming burden of ascertaining the identity and location of any party with a legally protected interest by resorting to a title search for each delinquent parcel" outweigh the interests of those with property rights that will be adversely affected by the tax sale because such parties "must assume the blame for not having received such notice" if they fail to request it (In re Tax Foreclosure No. 35, N.Y. App. Div. 1987).

Other courts have held that request-notice statutes do not relieve the government of its obligation under *Mullane* and *Mennonite* to provide notice by mail to mortgagees and other reasonably identifiable parties with legally protected interests even if such parties fail to request that notice be mailed to them (Bank of W. Baton Rouge v. Stewart, La. Ct. App. 2001; Sunburst Bank v. Patterson, Tenn. Ct. App. 1997; Island Fin., Inc. v. Ballman, Md. Ct. Spec. App. 1992; Town of Phillipsburg v. Block 22, N.J. Super. Ct. Ch. Div. 1987). As the Fifth Circuit Court of Appeals put it, enactment of a statute that prospectively shifts the burden of providing actual notice in every case to the would-be recipient does not satisfy the government's obligation to take reasonably diligent efforts to ascertain the identity of property owners (Small Engine Shop, Inc. v. Cascio, 5th Cir. 1989).

Beyond the real estate context, too, questions arise regarding the extent of the government's obligation to identify and notify property owners whose interests are threatened. For example, when the government proposes to sell an abandoned car, it must notify the owner and lien holders of record. But what if the owner transfers title to the car and the new owner fails to register with the state? At least one court has held that only the registered owner is entitled to notice unless the government knows the identity of the real owner and could notify her by an inexpensive and efficacious means (Schluga v. City of Milwaukee, 7th Cir. 1996).

In the partnership tax context, when the Internal Revenue Service (the "IRS") audits a partnership, it is required by statute to notify those partners that own at least a one percent share in the partnership. The Tax Equity and Fiscal Responsibility Act (the "Act") does not require the government to provide personal notice to the small-share partners (26 U.S.C. § 6223(b)(1)) because it requires a designated general partner, the "tax matters partner," to keep all other partners informed of the proceedings (26 U.S.C. § 6223(g)). Likewise, if one of the partners listed on the partnership tax return is itself a partnership, the Act does not require the IRS to provide notice to the "indirect" partners of this "pass-through partnership" because the Act requires the pass-through partnership to forward notices to the indirect partners (26 U.S.C. § 6223(h)). The lower federal courts have held that this statutory notice scheme comports with due process because "the government could conclude that it is 'reasonably certain' that tax matters partners [and pass-through partnerships] would carry out their statutory duty to pass on notices to other partners" (Walthall v. United States, 9th Cir. 1997; see also Kaplan v. United States, 7th Cir. 1998; Goldman v. Comm'r, U.S. Tax Ct. 1996).

Finally (for our purposes), the bankruptcy context is fertile ground for debating the extent of the obligation to identify creditors and others interested in bankruptcy proceedings. It is well accepted that both secured and unsecured creditors[21] and equity security holders[22] have property interests that are protected by due process. Known creditors are entitled to personal notice by mail of the date by which they must file their claims against the debtor (City of New York v. N.Y., N.H. & H.R.R. Co., 1953; Chemetron Corp. v. Jones, 3d Cir. 1995). But where the trustee cannot reasonably ascertain the identity of creditors, due process requires only notice by publication (In re Provident Hosp., Inc., 4th Cir. 1991). When creditors who were not notified of the bar date seek to file late claims, courts must ascertain whether or not they were known or unknown creditors. If they were known creditors who were not notified, due process bars the discharge of their claims and demands that they be permitted to file late claims (In re Maya Constr. Co., 9th Cir. 1996; United States v. Cardinal Mine Supply Inc., 6th Cir. 1990; In re Spring Valley Farms, Inc., 11th Cir. 1989; In re U.S.H. Corp. of N.Y., Bankr. S.D.N.Y. 1998). If, on the other hand, they were unknown creditors (or creditors with potential claims whom the court deems to be "unknown"), their claims are foreclosed as long as notice by publication was provided (City of New York v. N.Y., N.H. & H.R.R. Co., 1953; In re Trans World Airlines Inc., 3d Cir. 1996; Chemetron Corp. v. Jones, 3d Cir. 1995; In re Chi., M., St. P. & Pac. R.R., 7th Cir. 1992).

Assuming the government identifies a person as having a protected interest, what efforts must it make to ensure that the person actually receives notice? We now turn to the extent of the obligation to notify persons already identified as having legally protected interests.

## THE EXTENT OF THE OBLIGATION TO NOTIFY PARTIES WITH PROTECTED INTERESTS

*Mullane* itself made clear that notice by publication does not constitute due process as to known persons whose whereabouts are known. But *Mullane* and its progeny have not read the Due Process Clause as requiring in-hand personal service either. Rather, the Supreme Court has consistently held that service by mail is ordinarily sufficient (Tulsa Prof'l Collection Servs., Inc. v. Pope, 1988; Mullane v. Cent. Hanover Bank & Trust Co., 1950) and the lower federal courts have upheld notice by fax transmission in a variety of contexts (Wilkens v. Johnson, 5th Cir. 2001; St. Joseph Lease Capital Corp. v. Comm'r, 4th Cir. 2000; In re Virtual Vision, Inc., 9th Cir. 1997).[23] Indeed, several courts have even upheld service by e-mail where a foreign defendant was not subject to service of process using traditional means within the United States (Rio Props., Inc. v. Rio Int'l Interlink, 9th Cir. 2002; In re Int'l Telemedia Assocs., Bankr. N.D. Ga. 2000).[24]

But what if a notice sent by mail is returned as undeliverable? Or what if the intended recipient is incarcerated and mail sent to the prison does not actually reach the prisoner? Or what if she is a fugitive from justice whose whereabouts are unknown? Put more generally, must the intended recipient actually *receive* notice, or is it sufficient that the government takes steps reasonably calculated to reach her? And if steps reasonably calculated to provide notice are adequate, how do we determine what steps satisfy this standard?

The Court provided limited guidance regarding the extent of the obligation to notify in Robinson v. Hanrahan (1972), which involved an effort by the state to seize an automobile allegedly used in an armed robbery. The owner of the car was arrested, charged with the crime and incarcerated in the local jail awaiting trial. Nevertheless, the state mailed notice of the forfeiture proceeding to him at his home address (the address on file with the secretary of state), rather than at the jail. He did not receive notice of the proceeding until after his release, by which time the car had already been forfeited and sold by the state. Reviewing the adequacy of the notice provided, the Supreme Court summarily concluded that the government's efforts to provide notice were not reasonably calculated to apprise the owner of the pendency of the forfeiture proceedings where it knew that he "was not at the address to which the notice was mailed and, moreover, knew also that [he] could not get to that address since he was at that very time confined in the [local] jail" (Robinson v. Hanrahan, 1972). With one exception,[25] the federal Courts of Appeals have consistently followed *Robinson*, holding that a notice mailed to a person at an address at which the government knows her not to be fails to satisfy the *Mullane* requirement that notice be "reasonably calculated" to reach her.[26]

But what if the notice *is* reasonably calculated to reach the intended recipient but does not? Language in *Mullane* suggested that actual receipt of notice is not constitutionally required, as long as the means employed are "reasonably calculated, under all the circumstances, to apprise interested parties of the pendency of the action. . . ." (Mullane v. Cent. Hanover Bank & Trust Co., 1950). In fact, the *Mullane* Court accepted as constitutional the possibility that some of the known beneficiaries would not actually receive notice because others with identical interests would: "under such circumstances reasonable risks that notice might not actually reach every beneficiary are justifiable" (Mullane v. Cent. Hanover Bank & Trust Co., 1950). *Mullane* left open the question, however, whether actual receipt of notice is required to satisfy due process in cases where no other person with identical interests is notified.

Language in *Mennonite* appeared to require actual notice in such circumstances: "Notice by mail or other means as certain to ensure *actual notice* is a minimum constitutional precondition to a proceeding which will adversely affect the liberty or property interests of *any* party . . . if its name and address are reasonably ascertainable" (Mennonite Bd. of Missions v. Adams, 1983).[27] In a footnote, the *Mennonite* Court elaborated: "Our cases have required the State to make efforts to provide *actual notice* to all interested parties comparable to the efforts that were previously required only in *in personam* actions" (Mennonite Bd. of

Missions v. Adams, 1983). The Court in *Tulsa* continued to employ the phrase "actual notice."

But did the Court intend the phrase "actual notice" to mean actual *receipt* of notice, or did it use this phrase simply to distinguish notice by mail and other forms of personalized notice from notice by publication? This ambiguity and the resultant uncertainty caused the lower federal courts and the state courts to wrestle with the question whether a person who does not actually receive notice can be deprived of liberty or property if the government takes steps reasonably calculated to notify her; and if so, what measures short of in-hand personal service are deemed "reasonably calculated" to notify an identifiable person (*Cf.* Weng v. United States, 2d Cir. 1998; Whiting v. United States, 1st Cir. 2000; United States v. Minor, 4th Cir. 2000).

The United States Supreme Court resolved these issues in its most recent notice case, holding that actual receipt of notice is not constitutionally required (Dusenbery v. United States, 2002). The Court applied the *Mullane* test, rather than the Mathews v. Eldridge (1976) balancing test urged by the petitioner,[28] to test the adequacy of the notice provided. In other words, the Court asked whether the method used was "'reasonably calculated, under all the circumstances, to apprise interested parties of the pendency of the action and afford them an opportunity to present their objections'" (Dusenbery v. United States, 2002, quoting Mullane v. Cent. Hanover Bank & Trust Co., 1950).

The *Dusenbery* Court considered the adequacy of notice provided by the Federal Bureau of Investigation (the "FBI") to a federal prisoner of his right to challenge the administrative forfeiture of nearly $22,000 in cash seized from his home during the execution of a search warrant years earlier. The FBI had sent multiple letters of its intention to forfeit the cash by certified mail to the prisoner; the letters were sent care of the prison in which he was incarcerated, to the residence where he had been arrested, and to an address in the town where his mother lived. It also published notice for three consecutive weeks in a newspaper of general circulation in the judicial district in which the forfeiture proceeding was brought. When the FBI received no response within the time allotted, it declared the items administratively forfeited. Nearly five years later, the prisoner raised a due process challenge to the adequacy of the notice provided, arguing "that the notice was insufficient because due process generally requires 'actual notice' to interested parties prior to forfeiture, which he [took] to mean actual receipt of notice" (Dusenbery v. United States, 2002).

The Court disagreed, noting that its prior cases had not required actual receipt of notice or verification of delivery but rather had accepted as constitutionally sufficient any method of notice that was "'reasonably certain to inform those affected'" (Dusenbery v. United States, 2002, quoting Mullane v. Cent. Hanover Bank & Trust Co., 1950). The method employed by the FBI—certified mail sent to the prison—satisfied that test. The Court rejected the argument made by Justice Ginsburg in dissent that the notice provided by the FBI was constitutionally flawed because it was "'substantially less likely to bring home notice' than a 'feasible substitute'"—i.e., the method now used by the Bureau of Prisons, which requires prisoners to sign log books acknowledging delivery (Dusenbery v. United States, 2002, Ginsburg, J., dissenting, quoting Mullane v. Cent. Hanover Bank & Trust Co., 1950). This method does not improve the reliability of the delivery procedures leading up to the prisoner's receipt, the majority argued, and even if it did, the availability of new, improved procedures does not "necessarily demonstrate the infirmity of those that were replaced" (Dusenbery v. United States, 2002).

In short, even if a prisoner does not actually receive notice of the forfeiture, he is not deprived of property without due process as long as the method of notice employed is reasonably calculated to apprise him of the threatened action.

In other contexts beyond the forfeiture setting, including real estate foreclosures,[29] class actions,[30] other civil litigation,[31] and the employee benefits context,[32] courts have upheld the constitutionality of notice reasonably calculated to reach the intended recipient even if she does not actually receive it.

Notice by regular mail has been deemed constitutionally adequate, even though notice by certified mail, return receipt requested, may be preferred because it provides proof of receipt (United States v. Warner, 8th Cir. 2002; Armendariz-Mata v. United States Dep't of Justice, 5th Cir. 1996; United States v. Orellana, 1st Cir. 1996; Weigner v. City of New York, 2d Cir. 1988).[33]

Ordinarily the adequacy of notice is gauged as of the time it was sent (Garcia v. Meza, 7th Cir. 2000; Sarit v. United States Drug Enforcement Admin., 1st Cir. 1993). But where the mailed notice is returned to the sender as undeliverable, the sender may no longer assume that the mail has reached its intended recipient (Torres v. $36,256.80 United States Currency, 2d Cir. 1994). Due process may require follow-up efforts to locate and notify the intended recipient, especially if she is in government custody,[34] has multiple residences,[35] or has provided the government with a change of address.[36] If, however, the intended recipient voluntarily moves and the government has no knowledge of her new address, mailed notice to her former address may satisfy due process even if it is returned as undeliverable (Madewell v. Downs, 8th Cir. 1995; Sarit v. United States Drug Enforcement Admin., 1st Cir. 1993). Likewise, if notice is mailed to the intended recipient's home address but is returned because it does not state the apartment number or the correct zip code, due process is satisfied as long as the sender had no reason to know that detail (Bass v. DEA, 8th Cir. 2002; Peters v. Nat'l R.R. Passenger Corp., D.C. Cir. 1992).

If *no* notice is provided and a default judgment is nevertheless rendered against a person, the defendant's motion to set aside the default judgment must be granted even if she is unable to establish a meritorious defense to the underlying action (Peralta v. Heights Med. Ctr., Inc., 1988). Only that relief "wipe[s] the slate clean" and restores the defendant "to the position he would have occupied had due process of law been accorded to him in the first place" (Armstrong v. Manzo, 1965).[37]

## THE SOPHISTICATION OF THE PERSON RECEIVING THE NOTICE

The government must provide notice meeting the *Mullane* standard even if the person to be notified has independent knowledge of the proceedings. As early as 1953, in the context of bankruptcy proceedings, the United States Supreme Court held that a creditor could not be deprived of its lien against a bankrupt without notice even if the creditor had independent knowledge of the reorganization proceedings (City of New York v. N.Y., N.H. & H. R.R., 1953). "[E]ven creditors who have knowledge of a reorganization have a right to assume that the statutory 'reasonable notice' will be given them before their claims are forever barred" (City of New York v. N.Y., N.H. & H. R.R., 1953).

The Court reiterated this point more recently in Mennonite Board of Missions v. Adams (1983), in the context of a tax sale of delinquent real estate. Personal service or mailed notice to the mortgagee was required even though sophisticated creditors would have the means to discover on their own whether real estate taxes had been paid and whether tax sale proceedings were likely to be initiated. Not all mortgagees are sophisticated, the Court noted, and even if they are, a person's ability to look out for her own interests does not relieve the state of its constitutional obligation to provide notice. In short, "[n]otice by mail or other means as certain to ensure actual notice is a minimum constitutional precondition to a proceeding which will adversely affect the liberty or property interests of *any* party, whether unlettered or well versed in commercial practice, if its name and address are reasonably ascertainable" (Mennonite Bd. of Missions v. Adams, 1983).

While the Court has declined to relieve the government of the obligation to notify sophisticated creditors, it has nevertheless required it to make "particularly extensive efforts to provide notice . . . when the State is aware of a party's inexperience or incompetence" (Mennonite Bd. of Missions v. Adams, 1983). In Covey v. Town of Somers (1956), for example, a town had initiated proceedings to foreclose tax liens on real property owned by a mentally incompetent woman. Pursuant to the relevant statute, the town provided the owner with notice by mail, a means that the Court has extolled in many other cases. But here, because the property owner "was known by the officials and citizens of the Town . . . to be a person without mental capacity to handle her affairs or to understand the meaning of any notice served upon her" and because no guardian had been appointed to protect her interests, the Court held that notice by mail was inadequate to satisfy due process (Covey v. Town of Somers, 1956). Thus, the adequacy of notice provided must be assessed in light of the individual's actual needs and circumstances rather than against the needs of the "ordinary" person or creditor (Covey v. Town of Somers, 1956).

In Memphis Light, Gas & Water Division v. Craft (1978), the Court again assessed the adequacy of the notice provided in light of the recipient's relative lack of sophistication and experience. There, the Court considered the constitutional adequacy of the notice that a public utility provided to customers before terminating service for nonpayment. The notice had warned the customer in issue that if she did not pay her bill, her electrical service would be terminated, but it did not "advise [her] of the availability of a procedure for protesting a proposed termination of utility service as unjustified" (Memphis Light, Gas & Water Div. v. Craft, 1978). That the customer made repeated efforts to resolve what she thought was a double-billing problem demonstrated that "she was not adequately notified of the procedures" available to resolve such disputes (Memphis Light, Gas & Water Div. v. Craft, 1978). In a footnote, the Court conceded that in other circumstances, the "skeletal" notice provided might have been adequate. "Here, however, the notice is given to thousands of customers of various levels of education, experience, and resources. Lay consumers of electric service . . . should be informed clearly of the availability of an opportunity to present their complaint" (Memphis Light, Gas & Water Div. v. Craft, 1978). Thus, the government was required to ensure that the notice provided was sufficient in light of the intended recipient's lack of sophistication.

## NOTICE IN THE CLASS ACTION CONTEXT

A class action is a suit filed by one or more individuals on behalf of a larger group of people who are not formally made parties to the suit. Whether the named representative wins, loses or settles the class action, the absent class members are bound by the judgment as long as the procedural rules and due process are satisfied (Hansberry v. Lee, 1940; Fed. R. Civ. P. 23(c)). Does due process demand that each class member receive personal notice of the action? Before addressing this question, it will help to understand a bit more about the different kinds of class actions available. We will focus on Rule 23 of the Federal Rules of Civil Procedure, which governs the certification of class actions in federal district courts and which has served as a model for many state class action rules.[38]

### Rule 23's Classification Scheme and Notice Requirements

If the prerequisites of Rule 23(a) are met,[39] Rule 23(b) authorizes certification of a class action in four different circumstances:

- where the prosecution of separate suits by individual class members would create a risk of inconsistent adjudications that would establish incompatible standards of conduct for the defendant (Fed. R. Civ. P. 23(b)(1)(A));
- where an individual suit by one class member would impair or impede the ability of non-party class members to protect their own interests (Fed. R. Civ. P. 23(b)(1)(B));
- where the defendant has acted or refused to act on grounds generally applicable to the class, making injunctive or declaratory relief with respect to the entire class an appropriate remedy (Fed. R. Civ. P. 23(b)(2)); and
- if legal and factual questions common to all class members predominate over individual questions and a class action is superior to other available methods for resolving the controversy (Fed. R. Civ. P. 23(b)(3)).

Rule 23 requires that in class actions maintained under Rule 23(b)(3), "the court must direct to class members the best notice practicable under the circumstances, including individual notice to all members who can be identified through reasonable effort" (Fed. R. Civ. P. 23(c)(2)(B)). The notice must state in "plain, easily understood language" the nature of the action; the definition of the class; the claims, defenses and issues raised; that class members have a right to opt out of the action or to enter an appearance through counsel if they choose not to opt out; and the binding effect of the judgment (Fed. R. Civ. P. 23(c)(2)(B)).

In addition to this mandatory notice provision for (b)(3) class actions, Rule 23(c)(2)(A) permits the court to "direct appropriate notice to the class" in any class action certified under Rule 23(b)(1) or (2)[40] and Rule 23(d)(2) permits the court to order notice to some or all of the absent class members in other circumstances. Although acknowledging that "[m]embers of classes certified under Rules 23(b)(1) or (b)(2) have interests that may deserve protection by notice," the 2003 Advisory Committee Notes add that "[t]he authority to direct notice to class members in a (b)(1) or (b)(2) class action should be exercised with care" (Fed. R. Civ. P. 23(c)(2) 2003 advisory committee's note).

The 1966 Advisory Committee Notes stated that the mandatory notice required by Rule 23(c)(2), coupled with the discretionary notice contemplated by Rule 23(d)(2), "is designed to fulfill requirements of due process to which the class action procedure is of course subject" (Fed. R. Civ. P. 23(d)(2) 1966 advisory committee's note (citing, among others, Hansberry v. Lee, 1940 and Mullane v. Cent. Hanover Bank & Trust Co., 1950)).

## Due Process Notice Requirements in the Class Action Context

But what does due process require? The Supreme Court has offered only limited guidance on the form and extent of notice required in the class action context. In Eisen v. Carlisle & Jacquelin (1974), the Court held, in the context of a class action certified under Rule 23(b)(3), that "[i]ndividual notice must be sent to all class members whose names and addresses may be ascertained through reasonable effort," even if the class has millions of members with small claims and the cost of sending individual notice to each would be prohibitive (Eisen v. Carlisle & Jacquelin, 1974). While noting that the notice requirements of Rule 23(c)(2) are designed to satisfy the demands of due process, the *Eisen* Court grounded its holding in Rule 23, rather than the Due Process Clause itself.[41] In a case decided a year later, Sosna v. Iowa (1975), the Court noted in passing that the "notice problems" raised in *Eisen* "are not present" in a class action certified under Rule 23(b)(2).

In Phillips Petroleum Co. v. Shutts (1985), the Court again addressed notice requirements in the class action context, this time grounding its decision explicitly in the Due Process Clause of the Fourteenth Amendment. It held that in actions seeking money damages, absent class members who are beyond the court's jurisdictional reach

> must receive notice plus an opportunity to be heard and participate in the litigation, whether in person or through counsel. The notice must be the best practicable, "reasonably calculated, under all the circumstances, to apprise interested parties of the pendency of the action and afford them an opportunity to present their objections." The notice should describe the action and the plaintiffs' rights in it (Phillips Petroleum Co. v. Shutts, 1985).

The Court limited its holding "to those class actions which seek to bind known plaintiffs concerning claims wholly or predominately for money judgments," expressing no view on the extent or form of notice required in class actions seeking equitable relief (Phillips Petroleum Co. v. Shutts, 1985; see also Ortiz v. Fibreboard Corp., 1999).

With this limited guidance, the lower federal courts and state courts have had to address a variety of notice issues in the class action context.

### *Notice Requirements in (b)(1) and (b)(2) Class Actions*

Perhaps most interesting is the issue alluded to in *Sosna* and expressly left unresolved by *Shutts*, namely, whether due process requires individual notice to class members in actions certified under Rule 23(b)(1) or (b)(2) or their state law analogues. Under Rule 23, notice to absent class members in Rule 23(b)(1) and (b)(2) class actions is merely discretionary. The theory is that generally these classes are more cohesive and homogeneous so class members have little incentive to opt out. Furthermore, because there are few individual defenses or issues in (b)(1) or (b)(2) class actions, there is less reason for class members to participate personally in the litigation.[42]

But does Rule 23 comport with due process? Although several pre-*Eisen* cases held that "pre-judgment notice is required in all representative actions,"[43] including those certified pursuant to Rule 23(b)(1) or (b)(2), most lower courts addressing this issue since *Eisen* have held that due process does not require individual notice in (b)(1) or (b)(2) class actions seeking only injunctive and declaratory relief (or even back pay, deemed to be an equitable remedy).[44] In hybrid class actions certified under Rule 23(b)(2)—where the class seeks both injunctive and monetary relief—many courts have held that due process requires notice if the judgment is to be accorded claim preclusive effect.[45] This conclusion is consistent with the 2003 Advisory Committee Notes to Rule 23(c)(2), which state that "[i]f a Rule 23(b)(3) class is certified in conjunction with a (b)(2) class, the (c)(2)(B) notice requirements must be satisfied as to the (b)(3) class" (Fed. R. Civ. P. 23(c)(2) 2003 advisory committee's note). Some courts have required precertification notice to prospective members of a mandatory class action proposed to be certified under Rule 23(b)(1) to inform them of the opportunity to oppose certification.[46]

### *The Extent of the Obligation to Identify and Notify Absent (b)(3) Class Members*

In class actions certified under Rule 23(b)(3), class members whose identities are known are entitled to notice by first-class mail even if it is time-consuming and expensive to cull their names and addresses from available business or public records (Eisen v. Carlisle & Jacquelin, 1974; Twigg v. Sears, Roebuck & Co., 11th Cir. 1998; In re Nissan Motor Corp. Antitrust Litig., 5th Cir. 1977). Notice by certified mail, on the other hand, is not required to satisfy either Rule 23 or due process (Zimmer Paper Prods., Inc. v. Berger & Montague, P.C., 3d Cir. 1985). Where a defendant can identify the absent class members more efficiently or inexpensively than the class representative, the court may order the defendant to do so, but in such cases, the court has discretion to require the plaintiff representative to bear the expense of the defendant's labor if it is substantial because it is the plaintiff who derives the benefit (Oppenheimer Fund, Inc. v. Sanders, 1978). In class actions filed under the Age Discrimination in Employment Act (rather than pursuant to Rule 23), the names and addresses of prospective class members may be available through pre-trial discovery (Hoffmann-La Roche Inc. v. Sperling, 1989).

In class actions brought under the federal securities laws, the obligation to provide notice is complicated by the fact that stock is often purchased through a broker who may be listed as the record owner. In such cases, where the stock is held in "street name," class counsel must reimburse the brokerage firms for the administrative costs they incur in searching their records to find the names and addresses of the beneficial owners and must also send the brokerage firms postage-paid copies of the notice to be forwarded to the beneficial owners identified in those searches (In re Victor Techs. Secs. Litig., 9th Cir. 1986).

Difficulties arise when class actions are certified under Rule 23(b)(3) and large numbers of class members are unknown. Examples include class actions filed on behalf of persons who ingested or were exposed to deleterious substances (such as Agent Orange, asbestos and Fen-Phen) or who purchased defective consumer products. While some class members may be identifiable from military, employment, prescription or warranty registration records, many other class members will remain unknown. In some such cases, lower courts have authorized notice to be provided by advertisements published in newspapers and magazines, aired on the radio and television, disseminated on the Internet and, in a class action filed on behalf of users of dairy products, printed on milk cartons (In re Arizona Dairy Prods. Litig., D. Ariz. 1975).[47] In a class action brought on behalf of all people who had been exposed to asbestos occupationally or whose spouses or household members had been exposed to asbestos occupationally (including those who did not even know of the exposure), however, the United States Supreme Court recognized without resolving "the gravity of the question whether class action notice sufficient under the Constitution and Rule 23 could ever be given to legions so unselfconscious and amorphous" (Amchem Prods., Inc. v. Windsor, 1997).

### *Information that Must Be Included in the Notice to Satisfy Due Process*

While acknowledging that "[w]hat due process requires by way of notice in any particular case may vary," the Second Circuit recently stated that class action notices ordinarily

> should: (1) describe succinctly and simply the substance of the action and the position of the parties; (2) identify the opposing parties, class representatives, and counsel; (3) indicate the relief sought; (4) explain any special risks of being a class member, such as being bound by the judgment; (4) describe clearly the procedures and deadlines for opting out; and (6) note the right of any class member to appear in the action through counsel (Robinson v. Metro-North Commuter R.R., 2d Cir. 2001).

These requirements are similar to those mandated by amended Rule 23(c)(2), which took effect in December 2003 (Fed. R. Civ. P. 23(c)(2)(B)).[48]

Stated more generally, the notice must describe the substantive claims brought on behalf of the class and must contain sufficient information to enable class members to decide whether to remain class members and be bound by the final judgment or to opt out of the action (Twigg v. Sears, Roebuck & Co., 11th Cir. 1998; Kyriaki v. W. Elec. Co., 3d Cir. 1981). If the class members will be subject to liability for costs or fees in excess of their expected recovery, the notice must inform them of this exposure to comport with due process (State v. Homeside Lending, Inc., Vt. 2003). The notice also should inform class members if a partial settlement of the claims has been achieved (In re Nissan Motor Corp. Antitrust Litig., 5th Cir. 1977). In class actions involving large numbers of Spanish-speaking class members, some courts have ordered notice in both English and

Spanish (Walters v. Reno, 9th Cir. 1998; Montelongo v. Meese, 5th Cir. 1986; Ruiz v. McKaskle, 5th Cir. 1984), although it does not appear that due process requires bilingual notice (Nazarova v. INS, 7th Cir. 1999).

### *The Effect of a Judgment on a (b)(3) Class Member Who Does Not Receive Actual Notice*

Language in Phillips Petroleum Co. v. Shutts (1985) suggests that the judgment is not binding unless the class member actually *receives* notice: "If the forum state wishes to bind an absent plaintiff concerning a claim for money damages or similar relief at law, . . . [t]he plaintiff must *receive* notice. . . ." (Phillips Petroleum Co. v. Shutts, 1985). On the other hand, *Shutts* immediately adds that "[t]he notice must be the best practicable, 'reasonably calculated, under all the circumstances, to apprise interested parties of the pendency of the action. . . .' " (Phillips Petroleum Co. v. Shutts, 1985, quoting Mullane v. Cent. Hanover Bank & Trust Co., 1950). This reliance on *Mullane* suggests that class members need not actually receive notice to be bound.

Professors Wright and Miller posit that *Shutts* should be read to permit the binding of absent class members who do not actually receive notice as long as the court adopted a reasonable notice scheme fully meeting the *Mullane* standard.[49] Several courts have concurred, holding that due process is satisfied even if a class member does not receive actual notice as long as the notice provided was reasonably calculated to reach her.[50] A class member who does not receive actual notice of the action may have a claim against class counsel for breach of fiduciary duty or negligence in providing notice (Peters v. Nat'l R.R. Passenger Corp., D.C. Cir. 1992; Zimmer Paper Prods., Inc. v. Berger & Montague, P.C., 3d Cir. 1985).

This issue is particularly salient in class actions in which many class members are unknown and notice by publication is relied upon. A due process requirement that class members actually *receive* notice would mean that many class members in such actions would not be bound by the class action judgment. At least one court has expressed doubt as to whether *Shutts* even applies to class actions filed on behalf of unknown class members and has held that in such cases, absent class members are bound by the judgment even if they do not receive individual notice of the action.[51] As noted above, the Supreme Court has questioned (but has not decided) whether constitutionally adequate notice can be afforded to a class of unknown or unknowing class members (Amchem Prods., Inc. v. Windsor, 1997).

### *Notice of Class Action Settlement*

According to amended Rule 23(e), "The court must direct notice in a reasonable manner to all class members who would be bound by a proposed settlement, voluntary dismissal, or compromise" (Fed. R. Civ. P. 23(e)(1)(B)). According to the 2003 Advisory Committee Notes, "Reasonable settlement notice may require individual notice in the manner required by Rule 23(c)(2)(B) for certification notice to a Rule 23(b)(3) class . . . if class members are required to take action—such as filing claims—to participate in the judgment, or if the court orders a settlement opt-out opportunity under Rule 23(e)(3)" (Fed. R. Civ. P. 23(e)(1) 2003 advisory committee's note).

Notice under Rule 23(e) "need only satisfy the 'broad "reasonableness" standards imposed by due process'" (Petrovic v. Amoco Oil Co., 8th Cir. 1999, quoting Grunin v. Int'l House of Pancakes, 8th Cir. 1975). To comport with due process, the notice of settlement must inform class members that the class action is pending and that their claims may be adjudicated as a part of it (King v. S. Cent. Bell Tel. & Tel. Co., 6th Cir. 1986). The notice must set forth the terms of the proposed settlement and the options open to the class in sufficient detail to permit absent class members to determine the potential costs and benefits involved or at least whether additional investigation is warranted (Petrovic v. Amoco Oil Co., 8th Cir. 1999; Maywalt v. Parker & Parsley Petroleum Co., 2d Cir. 1995; Weinberger v. Kendrick, 2d Cir. 1982; Reynolds v. Nat'l Football League, 8th Cir. 1978). The notice need not include a specific formula by which individual monetary awards will be calculated or distributed (Petrovic v. Amoco Oil Co., 8th Cir. 1999; In re Agent Orange Prod. Liab. Litig., 2d Cir. 1987; In re Corrugated Container Antitrust Litig., 5th Cir. 1981), nor need it disclose that the class representatives oppose the settlement (Maywalt v. Parker & Parsley Petroleum Co., 2d Cir. 1995). The notice must be neutral; it may not express an opinion on the merits of the proposed settlement (Handschu v. Special Servs. Div., 2d Cir. 1986; In re Traffic Exec. Ass'n, 2d Cir. 1980).

## AMOUNT OF NOTICE REQUIRED

In cases in which due process assures an opportunity to be heard before a person may be deprived of a protected interest and where the person's name and address are known, the question becomes *how much* notice is required? *Mullane* itself stated only that "[t]he notice must . . . afford a reasonable time for those interested to make their appearance" (Mullane v. Cent. Hanover Bank & Trust Co., 1950). In determining how much time is "reasonable," it is helpful to note the different functions that notice serves: it informs the recipient of the upcoming hearing; it affords her time to travel to the site of the hearing, to arrange her affairs so that she may attend, to retain counsel and to marshal evidence in her favor; it clarifies the issues to be addressed at the hearing; and it accommodates prospective witnesses (Memphis Light, Gas & Water Div. v. Craft, 1978; Wolff v. McDonnell, 1974; In re Gault, 1967; Roller v. Holly, 1900).

While the Supreme Court has consistently declined to adopt a rigid formula for gauging the constitutionality of notice, it has offered some guidance on the amount of notice required in specific contexts. For instance, in Roller v. Holly (1900), the Court held that five days' notice did not constitute due process in a foreclosure action where the defendant was served in Virginia and ordered to appear in Texas. In child delinquency proceedings, written notice of the charges must be given "at the earliest practicable time" and "sufficiently in advance of scheduled court proceedings so that reasonable opportunity to prepare will be afforded. . . ." (In re Gault, 1967). Oral notice to a juvenile's mother that a hearing would be held the next day did not comport with due process (In re Gault, 1967). In state disbarment proceedings, the respondent must know the precise nature of the charges before the proceedings commence; charges may not be added after testimony has been elicited at the hearing (In re Ruffalo, 1968).

In the tense and highly charged prison disciplinary context, on the other hand, one day's notice may be sufficient. In that context, due process requires that an inmate receive advance written notice of the claimed violation at least twenty-four hours before her appearance before the disciplinary committee (Wolff v. McDonnell, 1974). Likewise, while school children are entitled to notice of the accusations against them and an opportunity to respond to those charges before they are suspended, "There need be no delay between the time 'notice' is given and the time of the hearing" (Goss v. Lopez, 1975). In most cases, the school disciplinarian may discuss the alleged misconduct with the student within minutes of its occurrence (Goss v. Lopez, 1975).

Finally, in the employment context, where public employees are entitled to notice of the charges against them and some form of a hearing before they are terminated without pay (Cleveland Bd. of Educ. v. Loudermill, 1985), lower federal courts have held that notice of the charges may be provided to the employee at the *Loudermill* hearing itself or just a day or two before (Panozzo v. Rhoads, 7th Cir. 1990; Riggins v. Bd. of Regents, 8th Cir. 1986; Kelly v. Smith, 11th Cir. 1985; Brasslett v. Cota, 1st Cir. 1985).[52]

Taken together, these cases suggest that in determining the amount of notice required by due process, courts must balance the individual's need for time to prepare for the hearing, the likelihood that additional time will yield more information and more accurate decisions, and the government's interest in prompt action. This balancing approach is consistent with the Court's more general due process analysis announced in Mathews v. Eldridge (1976) and described in detail in Chapter 3.

## CONCLUSION

Since the Supreme Court decided Mullane v. Central Hanover Bank & Trust Co. in 1950, it has consistently maintained that due process requires "notice reasonably calculated, under all the circumstances, to apprise interested parties of the pendency of the action and afford them an opportunity to present their objections." Where the names and addresses of parties with constitutionally protected interests are known, due process requires notice by first-class mail or a more reliable means. On the other hand, where the identities of the interested parties are unknown or their interests are merely conjectural or future, notice by publication is sufficient.

Due process is satisfied even if the interested party does not actually receive notice as long as steps reasonably calculated to reach her are taken. Reasonably diligent efforts must be made to uncover the identities of interested parties with present interests.

In class actions involving claims of known parties for wholly or predominately money judgments, due process requires notice that meets the *Mullane* standard. In hybrid class actions, too, in which the class seeks both injunctive and monetary relief, due process may require notice if the judgment is to be accorded claim preclusive effect.

## NOTES

1. Walker v. City of Hutchinson, 352 U.S. 112, 115 (1956).

2. City of New York v. N.Y., N.H. & H. R.R., 344 U.S. 293, 296 (1953).

3. *See infra* Chapter 6, section entitled "Traditional Bases for Personal Jurisdiction," subsection entitled "State Sovereignty and the Physical Presence Requirement."

4. *See also* Frank S. Alexander, *Tax Liens, Tax Sales, and Due Process*, 75 Ind. L.J. 747, 765 (2000) (identifying three rationales that supported notice by publication in proceedings to enforce delinquent property taxes at the turn of the nineteenth century); Joshua Siebert, *Here's Your Hat, What's Your Hurry?: Why "Caretaker Theory" Has Overstayed Its Welcome in Due Process Jurisprudence*, 64 U. Pitt. L. Rev. 589, 591–95 (2003) (tracing the history of the caretaker theory).

5. See 1 Robert C. Casad & William B. Richman, Jurisdiction in Civil Actions § 2–7[1] (3d ed. 1998). *In personam* jurisdiction refers to a court's power to enter a binding judgment against a defendant personally, rather than one that affects only her property interests.

6. *Shaffer* is discussed more fully in Chapter 6, section entitled "The Modern Formula," subsection entitled "The Breakthrough Cases," paragraph entitled "*Shaffer v. Heitner* (1977)."

7. *See* 1 Casad & Richman, *supra* note 5, § 2–7[3][a] (describing *Mullane*'s "disjunctive test").

8. For scholarly commentary distinguishing long-term nonclaim statutes and concluding that they are self-executing statutes of limitations, *see* Debra A. Falender, *Notice to Creditors In Estate Proceedings: What Process Is Due?*, 63 N.C. L. Rev. 659, 676–77 (1985); Thomas L. Waterbury, *Notice to Decedents' Creditors*, 73 Minn. L. Rev. 763, 771 (1989).

9. *See, e.g.*, Island Fin., Inc. v. Ballman, 607 A.2d 76, 79 (Md. Ct. Spec. App. 1992) (stating that second mortgagees have a constitutionally protected property interest); Bankers Life Co. v. Regotti, 518 So. 2d 563, 568 (La. Ct. App. 1987) (same); Mid-State Homes, Inc. v. Portis, 652 F. Supp. 640, 645 (W.D. La. 1987) (same).

10. *See, e.g.*, In re Application for Tax Deed, 675 N.E.2d 285 (Ill. App. Ct.) (holding that an occupant with no ownership interest is entitled to notice of a tax sale under state

law), *appeal denied*, 679 N.E.2d 380 (1997) (table). *See also* Alexander, *supra* note 4, at 787–88, 805–06 (stating that occupants have property interests deserving of protection but noting the difficulty of identifying them if their leases are unrecorded; suggesting that copies of the notice addressed to "occupant" be mailed to and posted on the property).

11. *See, e.g.*, Sallie v. Tax Sale Investors, Inc., 998 F. Supp. 612, 618–19 (D. Md. 1998) (holding that a tenant with an unrecorded leasehold interest is not entitled to notice by mail of a tax sale but is entitled to notice of eviction following the sale and expiration of the redemption period); Nelson v. Forbes, 545 N.W.2d 576, 582 (Iowa Ct. App. 1996) (stating that under state law, "a leasehold interest is a right sufficient to confer on the tenant the right to redeem" and holding that lessee "should have been served with the redemption expiration notice").

12. *See, e.g.*, Davis Oil Co. v. Mills, 873 F.2d 774, 787–89 (5th Cir. 1989) (recognizing that a mineral lease is a legally protected property interest but holding that holders of such leases are not entitled to notice when the underlying property is foreclosed because it would be too burdensome to search the conveyance records to identify them).

13. *See, e.g.*, Olson v. Town of Fitzwilliam, 702 A.2d 318, 320–21 (N.H. 1997) (holding, on statutory grounds, that the government had to mail the notice of an impending tax lien to both tenants in common and that a notice sent to one did not bind the other); Magee v. Amiss, 502 So. 2d 568, 571–72 (La. 1987) (holding that the former wife had an interest in real property acquired by her husband during the marriage, which entitled her to notice by mail or other means reasonably certain to provide actual notice of the impending sheriff's sale). *See also* Alexander, *supra* note 4, at 784–85.

14. *See, e.g.*, Verba v. Ohio Cas. Ins. Co., 851 F.2d 811, 815–17 (6th Cir. 1988) (holding that the filing of a certificate of judgment creates a specific judicial lien on the real property of the judgment debtor, which lien is a property interest protected by due process; holding that a lien holder whose identity and address are a matter of public record is entitled to personal notice). *See also* Alexander, *supra* note 4, at 786.

15. *See id.* at 788–89 (stating that "easements and covenants are substantial real property interests" but noting that ordinarily tax sales do not adversely affect such interests).

16. *See, e.g.*, Gainer v. Brown, 558 N.E.2d 867, 871 (Ind. Ct. App. 1990) (stating that "a vendee under a recorded land contract is entitled to the same protection accorded to the mortgagee in *Mennonite*"); In re Foreclosure of Tax Liens, 316 N.W.2d 362, 365 (Wis. 1982) (stating that "under a land contract, both the vendor and vendee have an interest in the land" entitling them to notice of a tax sale). *See also* Alexander, *supra* note 4, at 785–86.

17. *See id.* at 768–69, 783–89.

18. *Id.* at 791.

19. *Id.* at 769; Siebert, *supra* note 4, at 606 n.130.

20. The *Mennonite* Court declined to consider the constitutionality of an amendment to the state statute adopted after the tax sale in issue occurred, which provides for notice by certified mail to mortgagees who request notice of tax sale proceedings. Mennonite Bd. of Missions v. Adams, 462 U.S. 791, 793 n.2 (1983).

21. *See, e.g.*, Tulsa Prof'l Collection Servs., Inc. v. Pope, 485 U.S. 478, 485 (1988) (expressing "little doubt" that an unsecured claim is "is property protected by the Fourteenth Amendment"); United States v. Sec. Indus. Bank, 459 U.S. 70, 74–78 (1982) (concluding that a security interest is property for purposes of the Fifth Amendment); *Mullane*,

339 U.S. at 313 (noting that a potential claim against a trustee is a property interest protected by due process). *See also* Russell A. Eisenberg & Frances Gecker, *Due Process and Bankruptcy: A Contradiction in Terms?*, 10 Bankr. Dev. J. 47, 71–72 (1993–94); Robert M. Lawless, *Realigning the Theory and Practice of Notice in Bankruptcy Cases*, 29 Wake Forest L. Rev. 1215, 1226 (1994).

22. Lawless, *supra* note 21, at 1226–27. *See also* In re Brooks Fashion Stores, Inc., 124 B.R. 436, 443 (Bankr. S.D.N.Y. 1991) (noting that the legislative history of the Bankruptcy Code states that "due process will certainly require notice to all creditors and equity security holders") (citation omitted).

23. *See also* Fed. R. Civ. P. 5(b)(2)(D) (authorizing service of pleadings and other papers (other than the original complaint) by electronic means if consented to in writing by the person served).

24. *See also* Yvonne A. Tamayo, *Are You Being Served?: E-Mail and (Due) Service of Process*, 51 S.C. L. Rev. 227 (2000); Harold K. Don, Jr., *Trends in Pennsylvania Civil Practice and Procedure*, 71 Pa. B. Ass'n Q. 47, 49 (2000).

25. United States v. Donovan, 33 Fed. Appx. 823, 825–26 (7th Cir. 2002) (upholding notice that was sent to the claimant's home rather than the prison in which he was incarcerated because he failed to take any steps signaling his intent to contest the forfeitures of which he was aware). *See also* People *ex rel.* Devine v. $30,700.00 United States Currency, 766 N.E.2d 1084, 1093–95 (Ill. 2002) (holding that notice mailed to the claimant's residence satisfied due process even though he was incarcerated at the time because the agency providing the notice did not know of his arrest and incarceration on charges unrelated to the seizure of the property at issue).

26. *See, e.g.*, Alli-Ballogun v. United States, 281 F.3d 362, 369 (2d Cir. 2002); United States v. Minor, 228 F.3d 352, 357–59 (4th Cir. 2000); Krecioch v. United States, 221 F.3d 976, 981 (7th Cir. 2000); United States v. One Toshiba Color T.V., 213 F.3d 147, 156 (3d Cir. 2000); United States v. Libretti, No. 99-8047, 2000 U.S. App. LEXIS 2499, at *7–8 (10th Cir. Feb. 17, 2000); Small v. United States, 136 F.3d 1334, 1337 (D.C. Cir. 1998); Armendariz-Mata v. United States Dep't of Justice, 82 F.3d 679 (5th Cir. 1996); United States v. Combs, No. 95-50471, 1996 U.S. App. LEXIS 26739, at *4–5 (9th Cir. Oct. 9, 1996) (mem.). *See also* United States v. McGlory, 202 F.3d 664, 672–74 (3d Cir. 2000) (en banc) (holding that due process requires that when a person is incarcerated, the forfeiting agency must mail notice of a forfeiture proceeding to her at the place of confinement and cannot delegate its responsibility to another governmental agency).

27. The Second Circuit Court of Appeals read this language in *Mennonite* as "add[ing] rigor to the *Mullane* standard." Bender v. City of Rochester, 765 F.2d 7, 10 (2d Cir. 1985).

28. *See* Chapter 3, section entitled "Timing and Form of the Hearing," subsection entitled "The Landmark Cases," paragraph entitled "*Mathews v. Eldridge* (1976)" for a discussion of Mathews v. Eldridge, 424 U.S. 319 (1976).

29. *See, e.g.*, Weigner v. City of New York, 852 F.2d 646, 649 (2d Cir. 1988) (stating that "the state's obligation to use notice 'reasonably certain to inform those affected' does not mean that all risk of non-receipt must be eliminated"), *cert. denied*, 488 U.S. 1005 (1989); Farbotko v. Clinton County, 168 F. Supp. 2d 31, 37–38 (N.D.N.Y. 2001).

30. *See, e.g.*, Peters v. Nat'l R.R. Passenger Corp., 966 F.2d 1483, 1486–87 (D.C. Cir. 1992); In re Cherry's Petition to Intervene, 164 F.R.D. 630, 635–37 (E.D. Mich. 1996). *See also* the section entitled "Notice in the Class Action Context" of this chapter.

31. *See, e.g.*, United States v. Warner, 32 Fed. Appx. 190, 191 (8th Cir. 2002) (per curiam).

32. *See, e.g.*, Lepre v. Dep't of Labor, 275 F.3d 59 (D.C. Cir. 2001).

33. *Cf.* Alexander, *supra* note 4, at 805 (recommending the use of registered mail or certified mail, return receipt requested).

34. *See, e.g.*, Foehl v. United States, 238 F.3d 474, 479–80 (3d Cir. 2001); Small v. United States, 136 F.3d 1334, 1337–38 (D.C. Cir. 1998); Boero v. Drug Enforcement Admin., 111 F.3d 301, 307 (2d Cir. 1997); Armendariz-Mata v. United States Dep't of Justice, 82 F.3d 679, 683 (5th Cir. 1996); Torres v. $36,256.80 United States Currency, 25 F.3d 1154, 1161 (2d Cir. 1994). *But see* United States v. Donovan, 33 Fed. Appx. 823, 825–26 (7th Cir. 2002) (upholding notice that was sent to claimant's home rather than prison where he was incarcerated because he failed to take any steps signaling his intent to contest the forfeitures of which he was aware).

35. United States v. Rodgers, 108 F.3d 1247, 1251, 1253 (10th Cir. 1997). *But see* Wilson v. City of New Orleans, Civ. Action No. 00-3115, 2002 U.S. Dist. LEXIS 1283, at *11–15 (E.D. La.) (in a condemnation action, holding that notice mailed to the address recorded in the tax rolls was constitutionally adequate even when it was returned as undeliverable and the government was aware that the property owner had multiple residences), *aff'd without op.*, 51 Fed. Appx. 929 (5th Cir. 2002).

36. *See, e.g.*, Sicari v. Comm'r, 136 F.3d 925, 929 (2d Cir. 1998); Hoffman v. State, 871 P.2d 27, 31 (N.M. Ct. App. 1994); *see also* Alexander, *supra* note 4, at 792–93 (noting that "[t]here is wide variance . . . in interpreting the scope of the government's duty when notice is mailed to the last known address . . . and is returned as undeliverable").

37. Several of the federal Courts of Appeals have upheld forfeitures that were preceded by inadequate notice where the claimant either admitted that the assets were forfeitable or had no defense to the forfeiture. *See, e.g.*, United States v. Poe, No. 99-5089, 2000 U.S. App. LEXIS 1905, at *7 (6th Cir. Feb. 7, 2000); United States v. Gagliardi, No. 98-1078, 1999 U.S. App. LEXIS 14780, at *11 (1st Cir. June 24, 1999); Adames v. United States, 171 F.3d 728 (2d Cir. 1999); United States v. Deninno, 103 F.3d 82, 86 (10th Cir. 1996). Where the statute of limitations would bar the government from filing a new forfeiture proceeding, however, a forfeiture preceded by inadequate notice is "void and must be vacated." Clymore v. United States, 164 F.3d 569, 573 (10th Cir. 1999). *Accord* Juda v. Nerney, No. 99-2070, 2000 U.S. App. LEXIS 6914, at *9–10 (10th Cir. Apr. 17, 2000); Kadonsky v. United States, 216 F.3d 499, 505–07 (5th Cir. 2000), *cert. denied*, 531 U.S. 1176 (2001); United States v. One Toshiba Color T.V., 213 F.3d 147, 156 (3d Cir. 2000); United States v. Marolf, 173 F.3d 1213, 1217 (9th Cir. 1999). *But see* United States v. Dusenbery, 201 F.3d 763, 768 (6th Cir.) (stating that "inadequate notices should be treated as voidable, not void"), *cert. denied*, 531 U.S. 925 (2000). Two of the Courts of Appeals would nevertheless permit the government to seek to quiet title to the seized property in a civil equitable proceeding. *See* Alli-Balogun v. United States, 281 F.3d 362, 372 (2d Cir. 2002); United States v. Clymore, 245 F.3d 1195, 1200–03 (10th Cir. 2001). The Civil Asset Forfeiture Reform Act of 2000 permits the government to file a new forfeiture proceeding notwithstanding the expiration of the statute of limitations if an administrative forfeiture is set aside because of inadequate notice. 18 U.S.C. § 983(e)(2).

38. American Bar Association Section of Litigation, Survey of State Class Action Law: A Report of the State Laws Subcommittee of the Class Actions and Derivative Suits Committee (1999).

39. A class action may be certified only if "(1) the class is so numerous that joinder of all members is impracticable, (2) there are questions of law or fact common to the class, (3) the claims or defenses of the representative parties are typical of the claims or defenses of the class, and (4) the representative parties will fairly and adequately protect the interests of the class." Fed. R. Civ. P. 23(a).

40. In August 2001, the Civil Rules Advisory Committee published for public comment an amendment to Rule 23 that would have required notice "calculated to reach a reasonable number of class members" in (b)(1) and (b)(2) class actions. Following publication of this proposal, the Committee received many comments expressing concern that such a requirement would make it too expensive to file many civil rights actions. The Advisory Committee abandoned the requirement in favor of an amendment to Rule 23(c)(2) that merely authorizes the court to direct appropriate notice in a (b)(1) or (b)(2) class action. *See* Proposed Amendments to the Federal Rules of Civil Procedure, transmitted to Congress March 2003, Changes Made After Publication and Comment, at 34, 38.

41. For a discussion of Justice Powell's reliance on due process to support his reading of Rule 23(c)(2) in *Eisen*, *see* Kenneth W. Dam, *Class Action Notice: Who Needs It?*, 1974 Sup. Ct. Rev. 97, 109–11.

42. 7B Charles Alan Wright et al., Federal Practice and Procedure § 1786 (2d ed. 1986). *See also, e.g.,* Samuel Issacharoff, *Preclusion, Due Process, and the Right to Opt Out of Class Actions*, 77 Notre Dame L. Rev. 1057, 1073 (2002); Allison v. Citgo Petroleum Corp., 151 F.3d 402, 413 (5th Cir. 1998); Johnson v. Gen. Motors Corp., 598 F.2d 432, 437 (5th Cir. 1979); Wetzel v. Liberty Mut. Ins. Co., 508 F.2d 239, 248–49, 256–57 (3d Cir.), *cert. denied*, 421 U.S. 1011 (1975); In re Cherry's Petition to Intervene, 164 F.R.D. 630, 635 (E.D. Mich. 1996); Fed. R. Civ. P. 23(c)(2) advisory committee's notes.

43. *See, e.g.*, Schrader v. Selective Serv. Sys., 470 F.2d 73, 75 (7th Cir.) (citations omitted), *cert. denied*, 409 U.S. 1085 (1972), *questioned in* Bijeol v. Benson, 513 F.2d 965 (7th Cir. 1975); Zeilstra v. Tarr, 466 F.2d 111, 113 (6th Cir. 1972); Eisen v. Carlisle & Jacquelin, 391 F.2d 555, 564–65 (2d Cir. 1968); Zachary v. Chase Manhattan Bank, 52 F.R.D. 532, 535 (S.D.N.Y. 1971) (mem.); Pasquier v. Tarr, 318 F. Supp. 1350, 1352 (E.D. La. 1970), *aff'd on other grounds*, 444 F.2d 116 (5th Cir. 1971) (per curiam). *See also* Mark C. Weber, *Preclusion and Procedural Due Process in Rule 23(b)(2) Class Actions*, 21 U. Mich. J. L. Reform 347, 393 (1988) (concluding that "[d]ue process requires individual notice to all reasonably identifiable class members in binding Rule 23(b)(2) actions . . . ."); Patrick Woolley, *Rethinking the Adequacy of Representation*, 75 Tex. L. Rev. 571, 600 (1997) (arguing that due process requires that (b)(2) class members receive notice and an opportunity to be heard if they are to be bound).

44. *See, e.g.*, Stoetzner v. United States Steel Corp., 897 F.2d 115, 119 (3d Cir. 1990); Johnson v. Gen. Motors Corp., 598 F.2d 432, 433 (5th Cir. 1979); Elliott v. Weinberger, 564 F.2d 1219, 1228–29 (9th Cir. 1977), *aff'd in part, rev'd in part sub nom.* Califano v. Yamasaki, 442 U.S. 682 (1979); Larionoff v. United States, 533 F.2d 1167, 1186 (D.C. Cir. 1976), *aff'd*, 431 U.S. 864 (1977); *Wetzel*, 508 F.2d at 252–53, 255–57; Stolz v. United Bhd. of Carpenters, 620 F. Supp. 396 (D. Nev. 1985). *See also* 7B Wright, *supra* note 42, § 1786, at 191 & n.9; *id.* at 41 & n.9 (2002 pocket part).

45. *See, e.g.*, Molski v. Gleich, 318 F.3d 937, 952–53 (9th Cir. 2003); Robinson v. Metro-North Commuter R.R., 267 F.3d 147, 165 (2d Cir. 2001), *cert. denied*, 535 U.S. 951 (2002); Frank v. United Airlines, Inc., 216 F.3d 845 (9th Cir. 2000), *cert. denied*, 532 U.S. 914 (2001); Wright v. Collins, 766 F.2d 841, 847 (4th Cir. 1985); Kyriazi v. W. Elec. Co.,

647 F.2d 388, 394 (3d Cir. 1981); Penson v. Terminal Transp. Co., 634 F.2d 989, 994 (5th Cir. 1981); *Johnson*, 598 F.2d at 433; Bogard v. Cook, 586 F.2d 399, 408–09 (5th Cir. 1978), *cert. denied*, 444 U.S. 883 (1979); In re Cherry's Petition to Intervene, 164 F.R.D. 630, 635 (E.D. Mich. 1996). *But see* Fowler v. Birmingham News Co., 608 F.2d 1055, 1059 (5th Cir. 1979) (concluding that an absent class member's claim was barred by the judgment in a prior (b)(2) class action even though notice was provided only by posting on a bulletin board in the work place).

Rather than requiring notice to be provided in hybrid (b)(2) class actions, many courts simply have declined to certify a class action under Rule 23(b)(2) if the monetary claims predominate over the claims for equitable relief. *See* Issacharoff, *supra* note 42, at 1068–73 & nn.58–59 (describing the predominance test and how it has been applied by various courts). *See also* Chapter 5, section entitled "Nonparties Who May Be Bound," subsection entitled "Persons Adequately Represented by Parties," paragraph entitled "*Class Actions*"; 1 Alba Conte & Herbert Newberg, Newberg on Class Actions § 4.14, at 93–94 (4th ed. 2002) (describing the predominance test but suggesting that it is counter-productive for courts to expend time resolving this "largely discretionary question").

46. *See, e.g.,* In re Temple, 851 F.2d 1269, 1272 (11th Cir. 1988); In re N. Dist. of Cal., Dalkon Shield IUD Prods. Liab. Litig., 693 F.2d 847, 857 (9th Cir. 1982), *cert. denied sub nom.* A.H. Robins v. Abed, 459 U.S. 1171 (1983). *Cf.* In re Integra Realty Res., Inc., 262 F.3d 1089, 1109 (10th Cir. 2001) (upholding the adequacy of pre-certification notice in a 23(b)(1) defendant class action where copies of the motion to certify were served on all members of the class known at the time and strenuous arguments against certification were presented).

47. *See, e.g.*, In re Agent Orange Prod. Liab. Litig., 818 F.2d 145, 167–69 (2d Cir. 1987), *cert. denied sub nom.* Adams v. United States, 484 U.S. 1004 (1988); Macarz v. Transworld Sys., Inc., Case No. 3:97CV2194 (JBA), 2001 U.S. Dist. LEXIS 18005, at *9 (D. Conn. May 11, 2001); In re Diet Drugs Prods. Liab. Litig., 99-20593, 2000 U.S. Dist. LEXIS 12275, at *101–20 (E.D. Pa. Aug. 28, 2000); In re Silicone Gel Breast Implant Prods. Liab. Litig., No. CV 92-P-10000-S, 1994 WL 114580, at *6 & Exhibit C (N.D. Ala. Apr. 1, 1994); Carlough v. Amchem Prods., Inc., 158 F.R.D. 314, 320–29 (E.D. Pa. 1993). *See also* Katherine Kinsella, *Providing the Courts with Quantifiable Notice Results*, 11 Newsletter of the Am. Bar Ass'n, Section of Litig., Comm. on Class Actions & Derivative Suits 3 (2000/01).

48. *Cf.* Arthur R. Miller & David Crump, *Jurisdiction and Choice of Law in Multistate Class Actions After* Phillips Petroleum Co. v. Shutts, 96 Yale L.J. 1, 22–23 (1986) (describing potential conflict between completeness and comprehensibility in class action notices; stating a preference for "a short notice written in clear English").

49. 7B Wright, *supra* note 42, § 1789, at 255–56. *See also* Miller & Crump, *supra* note 48, at 20 (stating that "the most appropriate reading of *Shutts* may be that class members constitutionally may be included if first-class mail is directed to them and is not returned as undeliverable").

50. *See, e.g.*, In re Integra Realty Res., Inc., 262 F.3d 1089, 1110–11 & n.18 (10th Cir. 2001); Silber v. Mabon, 18 F.3d 1449, 1451, 1454 (9th Cir. 1994); Peters v. Nat'l R.R. Passenger Corp., 966 F.2d 1483, 1486–87 (D.C. Cir. 1992); In re Agent Orange Prod. Liab. Litig., 818 F.2d 145, 168 (2d Cir. 1987), *cert. denied sub nom.* Adams v. United States, 484

U.S. 1004 (1988); In re Gen. Elec. Capital Corp., MDL 1192, 2000 U.S. Dist. LEXIS 4808, at *16–17 (N.D. Ill. Mar. 9, 2000).

51. According to the Second Circuit Court of Appeals, *Shutts* " 'is limited to those class actions which seek to bind known plaintiffs concerning claims wholly or predominantly for money judgments,' and 'intimates no view concerning other types of class actions.' As such, 'Shutts does not apply directly to classes of unknown plaintiffs.' " In re Agent Orange Prod. Liab. Litig., 996 F.2d 1425, 1435 (2d Cir. 1993) (citations omitted), *cert. denied sub nom.* Ivy v. Diamond Shamrock Chems. Co., 510 U.S. 1140 (1994), *overruled in part on other grounds by* Syngenta Crop Prot., Inc. v. Henson, 537 U.S. 28 (2002). In a case like *Agent Orange*, in which a large number of the class members are not only unknown but unknowing (because they are not even aware of their injuries), the Second Circuit concluded that due process requires "fair and just recovery procedures," rather than individual notice and opt-out rights. *Id. See also* Susan P. Koniak, *Feasting While the Widow Weeps:* Georgine v. Amchem Products, Inc., 80 Cornell L. Rev. 1045, 1086–93 (1995) (discussing the Second Circuit's decision and drawing the distinction between unknown and unknowing class members).

52. *Cf.* Morton v. Beyer, 822 F.2d 364, 369–71 (3d Cir. 1987) (noting that "advance notice is not a *per se* requirement of due process" but holding that advance notice is required where the incident that precipitated the suspension occurred six months earlier and the employee did not know the specific charges to which he should respond; "presentation of adverse evidence within minutes of ineffective notice simply does not comport with the due process requirements set forth in *Loudermill*").

# 6

# Due Process Limitations on Personal Jurisdiction

***"[P]roceedings in a court of justice to determine the personal rights and obligations of parties over whom that court has no jurisdiction do not constitute due process of law."*** [1]

If the principal procedural protections afforded by due process are notice and the opportunity to be heard, protection from litigation in a distant and inconvenient forum is an important corollary. Even if a defendant receives personal notice and is promised a full opportunity to present evidence to an impartial decisionmaker and to cross-examine the witnesses against her, these protections may prove illusory if the defendant is summoned to appear in a distant forum with which she has no connection. If the inconvenience of defending there is sufficiently great, the defendant may default and the court will render judgment against her without having afforded her a meaningful opportunity to defend on the merits. Even if the defendant is able to appear, she may be seriously disadvantaged if compelled to defend in a distant state: she may not be able to subpoena important witnesses to appear and testify; she may not be able to obtain jurisdiction over potential third-party defendants onto whom she otherwise would seek to shift all or a portion of her liability; and she may be subject to the less favorable laws of the forum state, which a court in her home state (or an alternate forum) would not apply.[2] To ensure, then, that the defendant's opportunity to be heard is a meaningful one, due process shields her from suit in a state with which she has "no contacts, ties, or relations" (Shaffer v. Heitner, 1977; Int'l Shoe Co. v. Washington, 1945). In other words, the Due Process Clause limits the reach of the court's personal jurisdiction. Because the plaintiff consents to jurisdiction by filing suit in the forum state, the focus ordinarily is on the defendant's amenability to jurisdiction.[3]

Of course, the Due Process Clauses do not explicitly mention limitations on personal jurisdiction. Therefore, we will begin by considering when and why the United States Supreme Court first concluded that the Due Process Clauses constrain personal jurisdiction, and whether this due process protection is properly classified as procedural. Next, we will consider the Supreme Court's early jurisdictional decisions, which barred states from asserting jurisdiction over people and property outside their territorial limits, and the exceptions to this strict territorial rule that the Court was forced to acknowledge as the demands of a developing national economy and an itinerant population grew. Then we will examine the breakthrough cases, in which the Court dramatically shifted the focus of its jurisdictional jurisprudence from state sovereignty and territoriality to "minimum contacts," fairness and reasonableness, and the subsequent cases that reflect the Court's ongoing ambivalence about the importance of state lines in jurisdictional analysis.

Once the current minimum contacts framework for gauging the constitutionality of jurisdiction has been introduced, we will analyze several of the most important doctrinal refinements that the Court has made in recent years. Then we will examine how the lower federal courts have struggled to adapt these jurisdictional principles to the unique demands of the Internet. Finally, we will consider whether the restrictions imposed by the Due Process Clauses of the Fifth and Fourteenth Amendments are identical, and if not, why and in what circumstances and respects the federal courts have broader rein in exercising personal jurisdiction.

## CONSTITUTIONAL SOURCE OF PROTECTION AGAINST LITIGATION IN AN INCONVENIENT FORUM

Since the Due Process Clauses do not explicitly mention any limitation on personal jurisdiction, one wonders when and why these clauses were interpreted to limit personal jurisdiction and whether this protection from litigation in a distant forum is a procedural one. We begin with an examination of these preliminary questions.

### Full Faith and Credit Clause or Due Process Clause?

Before the Fourteenth Amendment was adopted, the federal Constitution did not limit state court jurisdiction. The limitations that did exist derived from international law. These international jurisdictional limitations did not directly limit a state court's exercise of jurisdiction, but rather permitted other states to decline to enforce a judgment rendered without proper jurisdiction. Thus, jurisdictional issues often were raised collaterally, when a winning plaintiff (i.e., a judgment creditor) sought to enforce a state court judgment in another state and the losing defendant (i.e., a judgment debtor) claimed the judgment was unenforceable because the rendering court lacked personal jurisdiction over her. In such cases, the judgment creditor would invoke Article IV, section one of the Constitution which provides that "Full Faith and Credit shall be given in each State to the public Acts, Records and judicial Proceedings of every other State" (U.S. Const. art.

IV, § 1). This clause of the Constitution and the full faith and credit statute, which requires all courts in the United States to give state court judgments "the same full faith and credit . . . as they have by law or usage in the Courts of such State . . . from which they are taken" (28 U.S.C. § 1738), dictates that judgments rendered in one state be recognized in other states and in the federal courts.[4] Ordinarily, then, parties could not collaterally attack the merits of one state's judgment in another state's courts (M'Elmoyle v. Cohen, 1839).

But the Supreme Court recognized early on that full faith and credit was "applicable only when the court rendering the judgment had jurisdiction of the parties. . . ." (Pennoyer v. Neff, 1877). In other words, courts in other states could inquire into the jurisdiction of the court that rendered the judgment (D'Arcy v. Ketchum, 1851). If the rendering court lacked jurisdiction over the defendant, the judgment would not be entitled to full faith and credit. In this way, the Full Faith and Credit Clause (or more accurately, international law left undisturbed by the Full Faith and Credit Clause) restricted state court jurisdiction, but only indirectly: one could avoid enforcement of a judgment rendered without jurisdiction, but only in the courts of another state or in federal court. Neither international law nor full faith and credit provided a vehicle for directly challenging jurisdiction in the courts of the state that rendered the judgment.[5]

The Due Process Clause of the Fourteenth Amendment provides that vehicle. Pennoyer v. Neff (1877) was decided less than a decade after the ratification of the Fourteenth Amendment. Holding that the judgment of a court that lacked jurisdiction was not entitled to full faith and credit, the *Pennoyer* Court went on to note that the Due Process Clause itself restricted state court jurisdiction:

> Since the adoption of the Fourteenth Amendment to the Federal Constitution, the validity of such judgments may be directly questioned, and their enforcement in the State resisted, on the ground that proceedings in a court of justice to determine the personal rights and obligations of parties over whom that court has no jurisdiction do not constitute due process of law (Pennoyer v. Neff, 1877).

In other words, upon adoption of the Fourteenth Amendment, a defendant could challenge the constitutionality of a state court's attempt to exercise jurisdiction over her in the rendering court itself, or, if she failed to appear in the initial action, she could seek to avoid enforcement of a judgment rendered against her without jurisdiction even in the rendering state (Riverside & Dan River Cotton Mills v. Menefee, 1915).[6] A judgment rendered in violation of the Due Process Clause was not entitled to full faith and credit elsewhere (Hanson v. Denckla, 1958).

Scholars have questioned the role due process plays in limiting state court jurisdiction[7] and some have even suggested that "much of the current confusion could be relieved if we stopped thinking of federal limitations on state court jurisdiction in terms of due process."[8] Hermine Meyer argued that as originally conceived by the framers, the Due Process Clause of the Fourteenth Amendment left the states free to apply whatever procedures they chose as long as they applied them evenhandedly to blacks and whites alike.[9] While refuting this contention, Ralph Whitten nevertheless questions whether *Pennoyer*'s incorporation of international territorial rules of jurisdiction into due process can be justified as within the original meaning of the clause.[10] The late Max Rheinstein, too, questioned whether jurisdictional limits derive from due process, arguing instead that the Law of Nations (as it was understood in the late eighteenth century) limited state court jurisdiction and that these limitations were "implied" in the Full Faith and Credit Clause.[11] Roger Transgrud also argues that restrictions on state court jurisdiction over noncitizens derive not from the Due Process Clause, but from the Full Faith and Credit Clause, which required the development of federal common law rules to govern jurisdiction.[12] And Patrick Borchers argues that even the *Pennoyer* Court may not have intended to constitutionalize limits on personal jurisdiction.[13]

Notwithstanding doubt within the academy about the propriety of invoking due process to limit state court jurisdiction, the Supreme Court has steadfastly maintained that the Due Process Clauses are the "only [constitutional] source of the personal jurisdiction requirement. . . ." (Ins. Corp. of Ir. v. Compagnie des Bauxites de Guinee, 1982). In light of the Court's unwavering conclusion that constitutional limits on personal jurisdiction derive from due process, we will proceed to analyze the substantial body of jurisdictional doctrine that the Court has developed under the Due Process Clause of the Fourteenth Amendment. Before doing so, however, we will first address whether due process limits on state court jurisdiction are substantive or procedural.

## Substantive Due Process or Procedural Due Process?

Although the Supreme Court has repeatedly invoked the Due Process Clause of the Fourteenth Amendment to limit the authority of a state court to assert personal jurisdiction over a nonresident defendant, it has not clarified whether the limitation is substantive or procedural. Numerous scholars have classified the constitutional limits on personal jurisdiction as substantive.[14] This classification makes sense from a *Lochnerian* perspective:[15] if substantive due process bars a state from interfering with a person's liberty to contract (even if the person has close connections with the state), then surely it would bar a state from interfering with the liberty of a person who had little or no connection with the state. And just as substantive due process would limit the reach of a state's legislative jurisdiction (a topic we will discuss more fully in the next chapter), it would limit the territorial reach of a state's judicial jurisdiction. In other words, substantive due process would limit a state's authority to deprive a litigant of liberty (by compelling her to appear and defend in its courts) or property (by entering a judgment against her) if she lacked sufficient connection with the state.

Wendy Collins Perdue argues that the substantive due process classification "eliminates an anomaly that would otherwise exist"—namely, that a court's exercise of jurisdiction can deprive a defendant of liberty *even before* judgment is rendered or enforced. "If personal jurisdiction is a substantive due process right, . . . then the mere existence of a proceeding in an improper forum is itself a taking of liberty regardless of whether it results later in a taking of property."[16]

Notwithstanding these reasons for treating due process restrictions on personal jurisdiction as substantive, we have chosen to include the topic in this volume on procedural due process for three reasons. First, like the procedural due process rights of notice and the opportunity to be heard, the personal jurisdiction protection goes not to the substantive merits of the claim, but to the fairness of the adjudicatory process. If the defendant is sued in a very inconvenient place—and either cannot afford to defend there or cannot put on an adequate defense there—she may be deprived of a meaningful opportunity to defend, which is a core procedural due process requirement.[17] Thus, one can conceive of constitutional limits on personal jurisdiction as procedural in nature.

Second, since the Supreme Court rejected substantive due process as a basis for invalidating New Deal social legislation, it has softened restrictions on personal jurisdiction "so as to make [them] appear to be founded on that concept of procedural due process to which the Court continued to adhere."[18] Thus, the Court frequently invokes the language of procedural due process in discussing limits on state court jurisdiction: individuals must have "*fair warning* that a particular activity may subject [them] to the jurisdiction of a foreign sovereign" (Burger King Corp. v. Rudzewicz, 1985; Shaffer v. Heitner, 1977); defendants must "*reasonably anticipate* being haled into court there" (Calder v. Jones, 1984; World-Wide Volkswagen Corp. v. Woodson, 1980, emphasis added); "[w]hen a corporation 'purposefully avails itself of the privilege of conducting activities within the forum State,' it has *clear notice* that it is subject to suit there" (World-Wide Volkswagen Corp. v. Woodson, 1980, emphasis added); the "requirement of *fair notice* . . . includes *fair warning* that a particular activity may subject a person to the jurisdiction of a foreign sovereign" (Shaffer v. Heitner, 1977, Stevens, J., concurring in the judgment, emphasis added).[19] Thus, the Court's jurisdictional language is redolent of procedural due process.

Finally, as a practical matter, the legal academy treats constitutional limits on personal jurisdiction as procedural rather than substantive. Just consider the casebooks used to teach American law students: all of the leading Civil Procedure casebooks cover the topic of personal jurisdiction at length (often treating notice and jurisdiction in tandem), while none of the leading Constitutional Law casebooks mention personal jurisdiction even though all of them discuss substantive due process at length.[20] Since we are treating the core procedural due process protections of notice and the opportunity to be heard in this volume, it makes sense to include the closely related subject of constitutional limits on personal jurisdiction.

## TRADITIONAL BASES FOR PERSONAL JURISDICTION

Until the middle of the twentieth century, when the Supreme Court developed the modern test for gauging the constitutionality of an assertion of state court jurisdiction, the Court employed three traditional bases for jurisdiction: state sovereignty, domicile and consent. We will briefly explore these traditional theories of jurisdiction before moving on to the modern approach.

### State Sovereignty and the Physical Presence Requirement

In 1877, the Supreme Court decided Pennoyer v. Neff (1877),[21] a landmark case that identified state sovereignty as the source of both the authority to exercise state court jurisdiction and the restrictions on that authority. In determining the scope of state court jurisdiction, the Supreme Court applied "two well-established principles of public law"—"that every State possesses exclusive jurisdiction and sovereignty over persons and property within its territory" and that "no State can exercise direct jurisdiction and authority over persons or property without its territory" (Pennoyer v. Neff, 1877). Under the first public law principle, state sovereignty justified assertions of jurisdiction over all persons and property found within the territorial limits of the state. As long as the defendant was served with process while physically present within the territorial limits of the state, the state could acquire *in personam* jurisdiction, or jurisdiction to enter a binding judgment against her personally. Service by publication, or some other form of constructive service, or even personal service beyond the state's borders, was "unavailing" (Pennoyer v. Neff, 1877).

Under the second public law principle announced in *Pennoyer*, limits on state court jurisdiction over nonresidents were necessary to preserve the sovereignty of other states. "[A]ny direct exertion of authority" over nonresidents "would be deemed an encroachment upon the independence of the State in which the persons [were] domiciled" (Pennoyer v. Neff, 1877). Thus, under *Pennoyer*'s sovereignty theory, states lacked jurisdiction over nonresidents who could not be found and served within the borders of the state even if they had caused harm to state citizens.

In addition to justifying assertions of *in personam* jurisdiction over persons found within the state's borders, the sovereignty principle also supported jurisdiction over property located within the state. In disputes involving title to or ownership of real property, courts could exercise *in rem* jurisdiction, or jurisdiction over the property itself,[22] as long as the property was located within the state borders and was subject to state control. In such cases, since the judgment would not require anyone to pay money or to engage in, or refrain from engaging in, any conduct, the court did not need *in personam* jurisdiction over those claiming ownership interests in the property. In other words, even if claimants to the real property resided out-of-state and were not amenable to in-hand personal service within the state, the state could adjudicate their interests in the property because the property itself was subject to the state's sovereign power. A judgment *in rem* was binding on the entire world and personal service of process on interested parties was not required: "Substituted service by publication, or in any other authorized form, . . . may answer in all actions which are substantially proceedings *in rem*" (Pennoyer v. Neff, 1877).

The *Pennoyer* Court acknowledged that the personal service requirement for *in personam* jurisdiction limited the ability of a state court to acquire jurisdiction over nonresidents who might have wronged state citizens. But the Court discussed another type of jurisdiction—*quasi-in-rem* jurisdiction[23]—that might afford a means of obtaining jurisdiction over nonresidents who owned property in the state. Since the sovereignty theory posited that a state had jurisdiction over all property within its borders, a state court could seize a defendant's in-state property—even if the lawsuit was unrelated to the property—and use it as a "hook" for exercising jurisdiction over the defendant. If the defendant appeared in the action and defended on the merits, he would be deemed to have submitted to the court's *in personam* jurisdiction (Pennoyer v. Neff, 1877; Cooper v. Reynolds, 1870).[24] If, on the other hand, the owner defaulted, a judgment could be rendered against him, but only "'to the extent of such property, and [could not] have the effect of a conclusive judgment *in personam*'" (Pennoyer v. Neff, 1877; Picquet v. Swan, C.C.D. Mass. 1828). In other words, the judgment could not require the defendant to pay any more than the value of the in-state property since the court had jurisdiction only over the property, not the defendant himself.

*Pennoyer* imposed an important limitation on the use of *quasi-in-rem* jurisdiction: the property had to be "brought under the control of the court by attachment or some other equivalent act" at the time the suit was commenced because the court's authority to "inquire into and determine [the property owner's] obligations at all is only incidental to its jurisdiction over the property" (Pennoyer v. Neff, 1877). Thus, even if the defendant owned property at the time the suit was commenced, if the property was not attached at the outset, *quasi-in-rem* jurisdiction was unavailable and any judgment rendered was subject to collateral attack.

Courts had little difficulty applying the *Pennoyer* framework to acquire *in rem* or *quasi-in-rem* jurisdiction when the defendant owned real property in the state because the property was immovable and easy to locate. But the Supreme Court did not limit the application of property-based assertions of jurisdiction to real estate, accepting that states had sovereign power over personal property and even intangible property such as bank deposits, bonds and insurance coverage (Harris v. Balk, 1905). Tangible personal property was subject to the sovereign power of whatever state could seize it, and when an intangible property interest was embodied in a writing—such as an insurance policy—courts typically treated the situs of the property as the place where the writing could be found (First Trust Co. v. Matheson, Minn. 1932).

But some intangible property interests were not embodied in a writing. The Supreme Court addressed such an interest in Harris v. Balk (1905), where a creditor, Epstein, wished to sue his debtor, Balk, in Maryland but could not obtain *in personam* jurisdiction over him because Balk lived in North Carolina. Epstein decided to proceed by attaching Balk's property and obtaining *quasi-in-rem* jurisdiction. But what property did Balk own in Maryland? As it turned out, Harris, another North Carolinian, owed Balk \$180. When Harris, Balk's debtor, traveled from North Carolina to Maryland, Epstein served him with a writ of garnishment (used to attach property held by a third party), thereby attempting to seize Balk's property—the debt that Harris owed to Balk. The Maryland court entered a judgment for \$180 in Epstein's favor. Balk later challenged the validity of the Maryland judgment, claiming that the Maryland court lacked *quasi-in-rem* jurisdiction because the situs of the debt between two North Carolinians was in North Carolina and not in Maryland, where Harris had strayed only temporarily. The Supreme Court rejected this contention, holding that the Maryland judgment was valid and binding on Balk because "the obligation of the debtor [Harris] to pay his debt clings to and accompanies him wherever he goes" (Harris v. Balk, 1905). So when Harris went to Maryland, it was as though he carried Balk's property in his pocket. Balk's property was subject to *quasi-in-rem* jurisdiction in Maryland upon personal service of the writ of garnishment upon Harris.

The attachment of the defendant's intangible property would support *quasi-in-rem* jurisdiction only if the defendant's ownership of the property was conceded (as it was in *Harris*: Harris conceded that he owed Balk the \$180). If, on the other hand, the defendant's entitlement to the property was in issue, then proceedings would be required to adjudicate his personal rights and *in personam* jurisdiction would be necessary (N.Y. Life Ins. Co. v. Dunlevy, 1916).

The New York Court of Appeals extended the logic of Harris v. Balk (1905) to permit *quasi-in-rem* jurisdiction in a New York court in a case against a Canadian driver who caused a car accident in Vermont (Seider v. Roth, 1966). How was this jurisdictional feat accomplished? The Canadian driver had purchased an insurance policy, issued in Canada, which contractually obligated the insurer to defend the insured in any automobile negligence action and to indemnify him in the event judgment was rendered against him. When the New York plaintiffs sued the driver in New York seeking to attach his "property" there, the court concluded that the insurer owed the driver a "debt" as soon as the accident occurred. Since the insurance company did business in New York, it was subject to service of process there. Just as personal service of the writ of garnishment on Harris gave the Maryland court *quasi-in-rem* jurisdiction over Balk's property, in-state service of the warrant of attachment on the insurer gave the New York court *quasi-in-rem* jurisdiction over the driver's property. As the New York Court of Appeals concluded, "Jurisdiction is properly acquired by this attachment since the policy obligation is a debt owed to the defendant by the insurer, the latter being regarded as a resident of this State. . . ." (Seider v. Roth, N.Y. 1966). Thus, the state's sovereignty over the insurer and the debt the insurer owed the driver gave it jurisdiction to adjudicate the damages claim against the Canadian driver (but only up to the policy limits). New York, one of only three states ever to permit *Seider* jurisdiction,[25] limited its availability to cases arising in New York or brought by New York plaintiffs (Donawitz v. Danek, N.Y. 1977; Simpson v. Loehmann, N.Y. 1967; Minichiello v. Rosenberg, 2d Cir. 1968). The demise of *quasi-in-rem* jurisdiction in general and *Seider* jurisdiction in particular will be discussed in the section of this chapter entitled, "The Modern Formula: Minimum Contacts and Reasonableness Factors."

### Consent

Like physical presence within the forum state, consent was a traditional basis for personal jurisdiction. Indeed, *Pennoyer* itself acknowledged that states could require nonresidents doing business within the state to appoint local agents to receive service of process for claims relating to the business conducted within the state (Pennoyer v. Neff, 1877).

Consent to jurisdiction could be express or implied. A party could expressly consent to jurisdiction by entering into a contract and agreeing to adjudicate disputes before a particular court (The Bremen v. Zapata Off-Shore Co., 1972) or by appointing an agent for receipt of service of process in a particular jurisdiction (Nat'l Equip. Rental, Ltd. v. Szukhent, 1964). The Court even held that a party would be bound by a forum-selection clause buried in pages of fine print in a form contract drafted by her adversary (Carnival Cruise Lines, Inc. v. Shute, 1991).

A party could impliedly consent to a state court's jurisdiction by making a general appearance in court (i.e., an appearance that did not challenge the court's jurisdiction) (McDonald v. Mabee, 1917; Cooper v. Reynolds, 1870) or by presenting a claim for adjudication there (Adam v. Saenger, 1938). Likewise, a party would be deemed to have waived the opportunity to object to the court's jurisdiction over her if she failed to present the defense in a timely manner.[26]

In the years following *Pennoyer*, as more and more business was conducted by corporations and other incorporeal business entities, states experimented with the concept of consent in an effort to obtain jurisdiction over the foreign businesses that caused harm to their citizens. Because corporations were not deemed to be citizens protected by the Privileges and Immunities Clause of the Constitution (Paul v. Virginia, 1869),[27] states could exclude foreign corporations from their borders entirely or permit them to do business within the state only "upon such terms and conditions as those States may think proper to impose" (Paul v. Virginia, 1869; see also Lafayette Ins. Co. v. French, 1856). States seized this opportunity to impose conditions, enacting statutes that required foreign corporations to appoint in-state agents for service of process—in other words, to expressly consent to jurisdiction in the state—in consideration for the privilege of conducting business within the state (Pa. Fire Ins. Co. v. Gold Issue Mining & Milling Co., 1917).

Recognizing that foreign corporations might do business within the state without making the requisite appointment, some states went further, deeming foreign corporations that did business in the state to have appointed a local employee, or even the secretary of state or state superintendent of insurance, as their agent for service of process for all claims arising out of their business within the state.[28] The Supreme Court upheld the validity of these implied consent statutes, noting that they authorized service of process upon the corporation's agent only within the territorial limits of the forum state (St. Clair v. Cox, 1882; Lafayette Ins. Co. v. French, 1856). Thus, while the states struggled to obtain jurisdiction over foreign corporations doing business with their citizens, the Court invoked the fiction of consent to reconcile the states' efforts with the concern for state sovereignty articulated in *Pennoyer*.

The construction of an interstate railroad system and the invention of the automobile and the telephone in the years following *Pennoyer* resulted in a dramatic increase in interstate travel and commerce by individuals as well as corporations. Since natural persons *were* citizens entitled to the protections of the Privileges and Immunities Clause of the Constitution, they could *not* be required to appoint an in-state agent for receipt of service of process as a condition to entry into the state, and the Supreme Court initially declined to permit states to employ implied consent statutes to gain jurisdiction over individuals who did business in other states (Flexner v. Farson, 1919).

Yet as individuals drove into other states and caused accidents there, the states sought to provide a local forum for their citizens to sue the nonresident motorists who caused the accidents. Adapting the express consent statutes that first had been used to acquire jurisdiction over foreign corporations, the states enacted statutes that required nonresident motorists to consent to jurisdiction by appointing a state official as their agent for receipt of service of process for claims relating to the operation of a motor vehicle within the state. Recognizing the need for public safety and "[t]he power of a State to regulate the use of motor vehicles on its highways," the Court upheld such an express consent statute (Kane v. New Jersey, 1916).

Realizing that many nonresident motorists would fail to make the requisite appointment of an agent, states soon adopted implied consent statutes, deeming nonresident motorists who used the public highways of the state to have appointed a state official as their agent for service of process for suits arising out of automobile accidents. Purporting to rely on *Kane* for the questionable proposition that states could exclude nonresidents who failed to appoint a local agent, the Court went on to hold that states could "declare that the use of the highway by the non-resident is the equivalent of the appointment of the registrar as agent on whom process may be served" (Hess v. Pawloski, 1927). Thus, the Court upheld the constitutionality of a nonresident motorist implied consent statute.

More recently, the Court has held that participation as a member of a corporation's board of directors does not imply consent to jurisdiction in the state in which the corporation is chartered unless the state enacts a statute that treats the acceptance of the directorship as consent to jurisdiction (Shaffer v. Heitner, 1977). A number of states have enacted statutes that treat acceptance of a directorship in a local corporation as consent to jurisdiction,[29] and their constitutionality has been upheld (Armstrong v. Pomerance, Del. 1980; Swenson v. Thibaut, N.C. Ct. App. 1978).

In the years following *Pennoyer*, consent statutes permitted states to exercise jurisdiction over defendants who could not be served while physically present in the state, but the physical presence requirement itself was not rejected: because the state official or resident employee was served while present in the state, the Court was able to reconcile the consent statutes with *Pennoyer*'s in-state personal service requirement and the sovereignty rationale for jurisdiction.

## Domicile

But in the early part of the twentieth century, as states attempted to assert jurisdiction over domiciliaries, or permanent residents, who were temporarily absent from the state, the Court had to massage the sovereignty rationale to permit jurisdiction over domiciliaries who were not subject to personal service within the state. A pair of cases decided in the first half of the twentieth century developed domicile as a basis for jurisdiction. In Blackmer v. United States (1932), the Court upheld the enforceability of a federal subpoena served on an American citizen in France. Because Mr. Blackmer remained an American citizen, "[h]e continued to owe allegiance to the United States" and "the United States retained its authority over him. . . ." (Blackmer v. United States, 1932). Synthesizing the sovereignty and domicile rationales for jurisdiction, the Court added: "Nor can it be doubted that the United States possesses the power inherent in sovereignty to require the return to this country of a citizen, resident elsewhere, whenever the public interest requires it. . . ." (Blackmer v. United States, 1932). Because due process required notice and because notice in this situation had to be communicated abroad to be effective, the Court found no impediment to service of the subpoena beyond the territorial limits of the country. Although *Blackmer* involved the authority of the United States to compel a citizen to testify as a witness rather than a state's authority to compel a domiciliary to defend an action as a party, the case laid the groundwork for state court jurisdiction over domiciliaries who could not be served while present in the state.

In fact, less than a decade later, the Court in Milliken v. Meyer (1940) explicitly extended the reasoning of *Blackmer* to assertions of state court jurisdiction over domiciliaries residing elsewhere. *Milliken* involved the validity of a judgment entered by a Wyoming court against a Wyoming domiciliary living in Colorado. The defendant had been personally served with process in Colorado but had not appeared and judgment had been rendered against him by the Wyoming court. He later challenged the validity of the Wyoming judgment in a Colorado court, contending that the Wyoming court lacked jurisdiction over him and therefore that the judgment was not entitled to full faith and credit in Colorado. The United States Supreme Court upheld the jurisdiction of the Wyoming court, declaring unequivocally:

> Domicile in the state is alone sufficient to bring an absent defendant within the reach of the state's jurisdiction for purposes of a personal judgment by means of appropriate substituted service. Substituted service in such cases has been quite uniformly upheld where the absent defendant was . . . personally served without the state (Milliken v. Meyer, 1940).

Conceding that *Pennoyer* had "intimat[ed]" that substituted service would be inadequate in these circumstances, the Court held that such service was constitutional as long as it was "reasonably calculated to give [the defendant] actual notice of the proceedings and an opportunity to be heard" (Milliken v. Meyer, 1940). In other words, as long as the due process notice requirement was satisfied, the Court was not concerned that constitutional restrictions on state court jurisdiction would be violated by an assertion of jurisdiction over a domiciliary who could not be served while physically present in the state. Thus, the Court's insistence on in-state personal service wavered.

### The Problem with Corporations

Traditionally, corporations were subject to jurisdiction only in the state of incorporation because they were believed to have "no legal existence out of the boundaries of the sovereignty by which [they were] created" (Bank of Augusta v. Earle, 1839). As corporations engaged in more and more interstate commerce and caused injury to increasing numbers of people beyond their states of incorporation, this limitation proved unacceptable. But states had difficulty applying *Pennoyer*'s in-hand service requirement to corporations because it was hard to determine when the corporation itself was "present" within the territorial limits of the state and which employees of the corporation qualified as agents for purposes of service of process. In an effort to afford their citizens an opportunity to sue corporations created under the laws of other states, state legislatures enacted the express and implied consent statutes described above. But what if a state legislature had not enacted an implied consent statute and the corporation had not given its express consent?

The courts concluded that a foreign corporation that had not consented to jurisdiction could be sued outside its state of incorporation "only if it [was] doing business within the State in such manner and to such extent as to warrant the inference that it [was] present there" (Phil. & Reading Ry. Co. v. McKibbin, 1917; see also Int'l Harvester Co. v. Kentucky, 1914). Thus, a finding that a corporation was "doing business" within a state supported jurisdiction on two theories: first, the corporation would be considered "present" there and, second, if the state had an implied consent statute, the corporation would be deemed to have consented to jurisdiction there. Although the "doing business" test was used to determine both corporate presence and consent, a finding that the corporation was present within the state would support jurisdiction over it even with respect to claims that were unrelated to the business conducted there, while the corporation would be deemed to have consented to suit only for claims related to the business conducted within the forum state.[30] Courts expended considerable energy attempting to define and apply the elusive criteria for "doing business" (Shaffer v. Heitner, 1977).

## THE MODERN FORMULA: MINIMUM CONTACTS AND REASONABLENESS FACTORS

As we have seen, in the decades following *Pennoyer*, the states frequently asserted jurisdiction over residents of other states, arguably interfering with the sovereignty and "exclusive" jurisdiction of the states in which the defendants resided. In upholding the consent, domicile and "doing business" bases for jurisdiction developed by the state legislatures and courts, the United States Supreme Court acquiesced in the erosion of the strict in-hand personal service requirement. But it was not until the Court decided International Shoe Co. v. Washington (1945) that it finally rejected the "presence" requirement and dramatically changed its conception of jurisdictional authority and limits.

### The Breakthrough Cases

In a pair of cases decided thirty years apart—International Shoe Co. v. Washington (1945) and Shaffer v. Heitner (1977)—the Supreme Court transformed the focus of jurisdictional analysis from physical presence and state sovereignty to fairness and reasonableness. In lieu of the presence test, the *International Shoe* Court adopted a more flexible "minimum contacts" test, which considers whether the defendant has sufficient connection to the state to make an assertion of jurisdiction over her fair and reasonable. *Shaffer* extended the reach of the minimum contacts test, concluding that even defendants who own property within a state are protected from assertions of jurisdiction unless they have sufficient connection to the state to satisfy the minimum contacts test.

### *International Shoe Co. v. Washington (1945)*

The Supreme Court's decision in *International Shoe* rejected *Pennoyer*'s physical presence requirement in favor of a more flexible approach that considered the fairness of an exercise of jurisdiction in light of the defendant's contacts with the forum state. The case involved an effort by the state of Washington to compel a foreign corporation to make payments to the state unemployment compensation fund. The corporation, the International Shoe Co., was a Delaware corporation with its principal place of business in St. Louis, Missouri. The company manufactured and sold shoes. It had no offices in Washington and maintained no inventory there, but it employed more than ten salespeople who resided in Washington and who solicited orders for the purchase of shoes within the state. The state personally served the notice of assessment on one of the salespeople in the state of Washington and sent a copy by registered mail to the company at its headquarters in St. Louis. The company claimed that an assertion of personal jurisdiction over it in Washington State would deprive it of due process.

The Washington Supreme Court upheld jurisdiction on the theory that "the regular and systematic solicitation of orders in the state by [the company's] salesmen, resulting in a continuous flow of [the company's] product into the state, was sufficient to constitute doing business in the state so as to make [the company] amenable to suit in its courts" (Int'l Shoe Co. v. Washington, 1945). In other words, the company did enough business in the state to manifest its "presence" there for jurisdictional purposes.

In a single paragraph in *International Shoe*, the United States Supreme Court rejected the presence test and offered a more realistic, flexible gauge for assessing amenability to suit:

> Historically the jurisdiction of courts to render judgment *in personam* is grounded on their de facto power over the defendant's person. Hence his presence within the territorial jurisdiction of a court was prerequisite to its rendition of a judgment personally binding him. But now that the *capias ad respondendum* has given way to personal service of summons or other form of notice, due process requires only that in order to subject a defendant to a judgment *in personam*, if he be not present within the territory of the forum, he have certain minimum contacts with it such that the maintenance of the suit does not offend "traditional notions of fair play and substantial justice" (Int'l Shoe Co. v. Washington, 1945, quoting Milliken v. Meyer, 1940).

The Court noted that since corporations are incorporeal, the only way they can manifest their presence is through the activities carried on in their behalf by their agents. Thus, it begs the question to ask whether a corporation is present, "[f]or the terms 'present' or 'presence' are used merely to symbolize those activities of the corporation's agent within the state which courts will deem to be sufficient to satisfy the demands of due process" (Int'l Shoe Co. v. Washington, 1945). Rather than focus on "presence," the Court considered the extent of the corporation's in-state activities and the inconvenience it would suffer if required to defend in the courts of the forum state.

In elaborating upon the new "minimum contacts" test, the *International Shoe* Court emphasized the importance of two key variables: the amount of contact the defendant had with the forum state and the degree of relatedness between the claim sued upon and the contacts. When both variables were high—when the defendant had "continuous and systematic" contacts with the forum state and those contacts "[gave] rise to the liabilities sued on"—the case for jurisdiction was very strong. On the other hand, when both variables were low—the corporation's agent had engaged in only a single or isolated act on the corporation's behalf within the forum state and the claim was unrelated to that activity—jurisdiction was unavailable. In other cases, the answers were less categorical, depending upon "the quality and nature of the activity in relation to the fair and orderly administration of the laws which it was the purpose of the due process clause to insure" (Int'l Shoe Co. v. Washington, 1945). Although the *International Shoe* case involved jurisdiction over a corporation, the opinion suggested that the minimum contacts standard would govern the availability of jurisdiction over individuals as well.

Applying the minimum contacts test to the activities of the International Shoe Co., the Court concluded that its business in Washington State was "systematic and continuous throughout the years," resulting in a "large volume of interstate business. . . ." (Int'l Shoe Co. v. Washington, 1945). Since the obligation sued upon—the company's obligation to contribute to the unemployment compensation fund—arose directly out of its in-state activities, the Court concluded that an assertion of jurisdiction over the company was "reasonable and just." The Court added that service by registered mail to the company's home office was adequate because it was "reasonably calculated to apprise [the company] of the suit" (Int'l Shoe Co. v. Washington, 1945). Thus, in-hand personal service within the territory of the state was not required.

*International Shoe* thus rejected the second of the public law principles announced in *Pennoyer*—that "no State can exercise direct jurisdiction and authority over persons or property without its territory" (Pennoyer v. Neff, 1877). A state *can* exercise jurisdiction over a person without its territory as long as the defendant has sufficient minimum contacts with the forum state. But what about the continued viability of the first public law principle announced in *Pennoyer*—that "every State possesses exclusive jurisdiction and sovereignty over persons and property within its territory" (Pennoyer v. Neff, 1877)? Put differently, if physical presence was no longer necessary to establish jurisdiction, was it nevertheless sufficient?

Even after *International Shoe* rejected the physical presence requirement for *in personam* jurisdiction, courts continued to assume that a state could assert jurisdiction over all property within its territory regardless of whether the owner of that property had minimum contacts with the forum. In other words, courts continued to use *in rem* and *quasi-in-rem* jurisdiction to adjudicate claims against individuals who owned property in the state, up to the value of the property.[31] The next breakthrough case that we will consider, Shaffer v. Heitner (1977), questioned the constitutionality of this approach and rejected the property prong of the first public law principle announced in *Pennoyer*. According to *Shaffer*, states do *not* necessarily have jurisdiction over property within their territory.

### *Shaffer v. Heitner (1977)*

The plaintiff, Mr. Heitner, owned one share of stock in the Greyhound Corporation, a Delaware corporation with its principal place of business in Phoenix, Arizona. Heitner contended that the officers and directors of Greyhound had breached their fiduciary duty to the company by causing it to engage in conduct that resulted in civil and criminal liability in Oregon. Heitner initiated a shareholder's derivative action, or a suit filed by a shareholder on behalf of the company, against the officers and directors in state court in Delaware, seeking damages for the harm caused to the company as a result of the breach of duty.

The defendants were nonresidents of Delaware, but many of them owned Greyhound stock. A Delaware statute deemed the situs of stock in Delaware corporations to be in Delaware, regardless of where the stock certificates were located (Del. Code Ann. tit. 8, § 169). Relying on Harris v. Balk (1905) for the proposition that the presence of a defendant's intangible property in a state would support an assertion of *quasi-in-rem* jurisdiction up to the value of the property attached, and aware of *Pennoyer*'s requirement that the property be attached at the commencement of the action, Heitner filed a motion for an order of sequestration (similar to attachment) to seize the defendants' Greyhound stock at the same time that he filed the complaint. The judge signed the sequestration order on the same day, even though the defendants had not been afforded notice or the opportunity to be heard on the motion. The court-appointed sequestrator seized the defendants' stock by placing "stop transfer" orders on the books of the company.

The defendants, who received notice of the action by certified mail and by publication in a Delaware newspaper, made a special appearance to challenge the court's action and authority. The defendants made three arguments: first, the stock was not capable of attachment in Delaware; second, the *ex parte* sequestration order, pursuant to which their property had been seized without notice, violated due process; and third, because they lacked minimum contacts with Delaware, they were not subject to jurisdiction there even if the property was located there.

The Supreme Court addressed only the third argument. Noting that assertions of *in rem* and *quasi-in-rem* jurisdiction affect the interests of people in the property attached, the Court concluded:

> [I]n order to justify an exercise of jurisdiction *in rem*, the basis for jurisdiction must be sufficient to justify exercising "jurisdiction over the interests of persons in a thing." The standard for determining whether an exercise of jurisdiction over the interests of persons is consistent with the Due Process Clause is the minimum-contacts standard elucidated in *International Shoe* (Shaffer v. Heitner, 1977).

In other words, the mere presence of property within the territorial limits of a state was no longer sufficient to support an exercise of jurisdiction over that property and the defendant's interest in it unless the defendant had minimum contacts with the state. Just as *International Shoe* had rejected the second of the public law principles announced in *Pennoyer*, *Shaffer* rejected the first: the physical presence of a defendant was no longer necessary to acquire jurisdiction over her, and the physical presence of property within a state was no longer sufficient.

The *Shaffer* Court was not concerned that its holding would invalidate all assertions of *in rem* and *quasi-in-rem* jurisdiction. To the contrary, since the defendant's ownership of property in a state is a contact among the defendant, the forum and the litigation, the Court noted that "when claims to the property itself are the source of the underlying controversy between the plaintiff and the defendant, it would be unusual for the State where the property is located not to have jurisdiction" (Shaffer v. Heitner, 1977). Thus, in *in rem* cases, where the plaintiff seeks a judgment that "affects the interests of all persons in designated property," and in true *quasi-in-rem* cases, where the plaintiff seeks "to secure a pre-existing claim in the subject property and to extinguish or establish the nonexistence of similar interests of particular persons," jurisdiction should be available even if the minimum contacts test applies (Shaffer v. Heitner, 1977). The defendant's claim to the in-state property evinces an expectation that she will benefit from the state's protection of the property. In addition, the state has powerful interests in assuring the marketability of local property and in providing a mechanism for the resolution of disputes regarding such property (Shaffer v. Heitner, 1977).

Jurisdiction may even be available in some cases involving attachment jurisdiction—the kind of *quasi-in-rem* jurisdiction in which "the plaintiff seeks to apply what he concedes to be the property of the defendant to the satisfaction of a claim against him" (Shaffer v. Heitner, 1977). If, for example, a plaintiff sues an absentee land owner claiming that she was injured on the defendant's land, the presence of the defendant's in-state property may be sufficient to establish *quasi-in-rem* jurisdiction of the attachment variety.

But in the majority of attachment jurisdiction cases—where the property seized is entirely unrelated to the plaintiff's claim—*Shaffer*'s holding would effect an important change:

> [A]lthough the presence of the defendant's property in a State might suggest the existence of other ties among the defendant, the State, and the litigation, the presence of the property alone would not support the State's jurisdiction. If those other ties did not exist, cases over which the State is now thought to have jurisdiction could not be brought in that forum (Shaffer v. Heitner, 1977).

In other words, the mere presence of property within the forum state would not guarantee the availability of *quasi-in-rem* jurisdiction. Rather, "all assertions of state-court jurisdiction," including *in rem* and *quasi-in-rem* jurisdiction, "must be evaluated according to the standards set forth in *International Shoe* and its progeny" (Shaffer v. Heitner, 1977).

### The Role of State Sovereignty

While it is fair to say that *International Shoe* and *Shaffer* de-emphasized state sovereignty and physical presence and focused instead on the fairness of jurisdiction, this conclusion elides the Court's ongoing ambivalence about the role of state sovereignty and interstate federalism in jurisdictional analysis.

Even after *International Shoe*'s seismic shift in focus,[32] the Court twice again invoked the sovereignty rationale to explain why state court jurisdiction is limited. In Hanson v. Denckla (1958), for example, the Court concluded that restrictions on personal jurisdiction "are more than a guarantee of immunity from inconvenient or distant litigation. They are a consequence of territorial limitations on the power of the respective States" (Hanson v. Denckla, 1958). Later, the Court explained that the minimum contacts test not only "protects the defendant against the burdens of litigation in a distant or inconvenient forum," but "acts to ensure that the States through their courts, do not reach out beyond the limits imposed on them by their status as coequal sovereigns in a federal system" (World-Wide Volkswagen Corp. v. Woodson, 1980). In elucidating this interstate federalism/sovereignty rationale, the Court went on to note:

> The Framers . . . intended that the States retain many essential attributes of sovereignty, including . . . the sovereign power to try causes in their courts. The sovereignty of each State, in turn, implied a limitation on the sovereignty of all its sister States—a limitation express or implicit in both the original scheme of the Constitution and the Fourteenth Amendment (World-Wide Volkswagen Corp. v. Woodson, 1980).

Thus, the Court resurrected sovereignty and interstate federalism as rationales for limiting state court jurisdiction.

This resurrection was short-lived, however. Only two years later, the Court retreated, stating that due process limitations on state court jurisdiction "represent[ ] a restriction on judicial power not as a matter of sovereignty, but as a matter of liberty" (Ins. Corp. of Ir. v. Compagnie des Bauxites de Guinee, 1982). In a footnote to this passage, the Court recognized that in the past, it had stated that limitations on state court jurisdiction "reflect[ed] an element of federalism and the character of state sovereignty vis-à-vis other States." In an effort to resolve this tension, the Court added:

> The restriction on state sovereign power described in *World-Wide Volkswagen Corp.* . . . must be seen as ultimately a function of the individual liberty interest preserved by the Due Process Clause. That Clause is the only source of the personal jurisdiction requirement and the Clause itself makes no mention of federalism concerns (Ins. Corp. of Ir. v. Compagnie des Bauxites de Guinee, 1982).[33]

Even *Ireland* did not bring the sovereignty pendulum to a comfortable resting point, however. As certain as the *Ireland* Court sounded about the demise of the sovereignty rationale for limiting state court jurisdiction, the Court again hinted at its relevance in Burnham v. Superior Court (1990), where a unanimous Court upheld transient jurisdiction and a plurality invoked sovereignty, territoriality and tradition to justify an assertion of jurisdiction over a defendant served while physically present in the forum state regardless of fairness.

The minimum contacts test itself captures the Court's ambivalence about the role of state sovereignty in jurisdictional analysis: by asking about the defendant's connection with a particular state, the test emphasizes the ongoing relevance of state lines; but by framing the ultimate inquiry in terms of "fair play and substantial justice," the test highlights the importance of fairness and reasonableness. Until the Court resolves *why* due process restrains state court jurisdiction, its jurisdictional jurisprudence is likely to remain confused. It is with this caveat that we now turn to refinements in the Court's jurisdictional doctrine.

## Doctrinal Refinements

The breakthrough cases described above set forth the core principles of the Supreme Court's personal jurisdiction jurisprudence. But in the years since *International Shoe*, the Court has clarified and applied the minimum contacts test in a variety of circumstances, offering guidance on how the test should be employed and when jurisdiction should be available.

### *Reasonableness Factors*

In its 1980 decision in World-Wide Volkswagen Corp. v. Woodson (1980), the Court added another important layer to current jurisdictional analysis by requiring consideration of a host of "reasonableness factors" in addition to the defendant's contacts with the forum state. The Court began by noting that the minimum contacts requirement "protects the defendant against the burdens of litigating in a distant or inconvenient forum," and then added that the protection against inconvenience is "typically described in terms of 'reasonableness' or 'fairness'" (World-Wide Volkswagen Corp. v. Woodson, 1980). Then, in a remarkable feat of judicial legerdemain, the Court explained that in assessing reasonableness or fairness, courts should not focus exclusively on the defendant's burden, but should also consider

> other relevant factors, including the forum State's interest in adjudicating the dispute; the plaintiff's interest in obtaining convenient and effective relief, at least when that interest is not adequately protected by the plaintiff's power to choose the forum; the interstate judicial system's interest in obtaining the most efficient resolution of controversies; and the shared interest of the several States in furthering fundamental substantive social policies (World-Wide Volkswagen Corp. v. Woodson, 1980).

Thus, through an odd syllogism of sorts, the Court formalized consideration of a host of factors in addition to the burden on the defendant.

The *World-Wide Volkswagen* Court did not explain the relationship between these reasonableness factors and the minimum contacts analysis.[34] In a later case, however, the Court clarified how minimum contacts and the reasonableness factors should be synthesized to determine the overall constitutionality of an assertion of jurisdiction:

> Once it has been decided that a defendant purposefully established minimum contacts within the forum State, these contacts may be considered in light of other factors [i.e., the reasonableness factors] to determine whether the assertion of personal jurisdiction would comport with "fair play and substantial justice." . . . These considerations sometimes serve to establish the reasonableness of jurisdiction upon a lesser showing of minimum contacts than would otherwise be required. On the other hand, where a defendant who purposefully has directed his activities at forum residents seeks to defeat jurisdiction, he must present a compelling case that the presence of some other considerations would render jurisdiction unreasonable (Burger King Corp. v. Rudzewicz, 1985).

Thus, once the plaintiff proves the existence of minimum contacts, the burden of proof shifts to the defendant to demonstrate the unreasonableness of an exercise of jurisdiction.[35]

A sliding scale of reasonableness applies depending upon the strength of the defendant's contacts with the forum: the weaker the plaintiff's showing of minimum contacts, the less a defendant needs to offer in terms of unreasonableness to defeat jurisdiction. Conversely, a strong showing of reasonableness may bolster borderline contacts to support jurisdiction (Ticketmaster-N.Y., Inc. v. Alioto, 1st

Cir. 1994). If the defendant proves that an exercise of jurisdiction would be fundamentally unfair in light of the reasonableness factors, an assertion of jurisdiction will be unconstitutional even if the defendant has minimum contacts with the forum state (Asahi Metal Indus. Co. v. Superior Ct., 1987; Metro. Life Ins. Co. v. Robertson-Ceco Corp., 2d Cir. 1996). In Asahi Metal Industry Co. v. Superior Court (1987), for example, the Supreme Court held that it would be unreasonable and hence unconstitutional for a California court to exercise jurisdiction over a Japanese valve manufacturer whose product was incorporated into motorcycles sold in California.

Let us now examine the five reasonableness factors in turn, to see how each has been interpreted and applied. The first factor, the burden on the defendant, is "always a primary concern" (World-Wide Volkswagen Corp. v. Woodson, 1980). When minimum contacts are established, however, the plaintiff's interest and the forum state's interest in the exercise of jurisdiction may justify even onerous burdens on the defendant (Asahi Metal Indus. Co. v. Superior Ct., 1987). Courts have been particularly sensitive to the burdens borne by alien defendants, who may have to travel great distances to defend in American courts and who may be unaccustomed to our legal system and our language.[36] Inconvenience to American defendants, on the other hand, can sometimes be alleviated by a change in venue (Burger King Corp. v. Rudzewicz, 1985; cf. Ticketmaster-N.Y., Inc. v. Alioto, 1st Cir. 1994).

The second factor, the forum state's interest in adjudicating the dispute, counsels in favor of jurisdiction when the plaintiff resides in or has other significant ties to the state (Burger King Corp. v. Rudzewicz, 1985; McGee v. Int'l Life Ins. Co., 1957), the claim arises in the forum state (Keeton v. Hustler Magazine, Inc., 1984), or forum law governs the dispute (Burger King Corp. v. Rudzewicz, 1985).[37] According to the Supreme Court in *Asahi*, the forum's "legitimate interests in the dispute [are] considerably diminished" if the plaintiff does not reside there (Asahi Metal Indus. Co. v. Superior Ct., 1987; see also Fields v. Sedgwick Associated Risks, Ltd., 9th Cir. 1986). The state has an interest in providing a local forum to its residents even if they are large corporations with the resources to litigate elsewhere (Burger King Corp. v. Rudzewicz, 1985).

The third factor, the "plaintiff's interest in obtaining convenient and effective relief," counsels in favor of jurisdiction when the plaintiff resides in or is domiciled in the forum state or if the wrong occurs there (Nowak v. Tak How Invs., Ltd., 1st Cir. 1996). In *Asahi*, once the plaintiff had settled with the defendants and all that remained in the California court was the Taiwanese defendant Cheng Shin's indemnity claim against the Japanese third-party defendant Asahi, the Court noted that "Cheng Shin has not demonstrated that it is more convenient for it to litigate its indemnification claim against Asahi in California rather than in Taiwan or Japan" (Asahi Metal Indus. Co. v. Superior Ct., 1987).

The fourth reasonableness factor, "the interstate judicial system's interest in obtaining the most efficient resolution of controversies" (World-Wide Volkswagen Corp. v. Woodson, 1980), concerns the forum's ability to compel witnesses to appear in its courts and to compel the production of physical evidence (Fields v. Sedgwick Associated Risks, Ltd., 9th Cir. 1986). For example, in *Burger King*, the Court considered (although ultimately dismissed) the defendant's argument that litigation in the forum state would impair his ability to call out-of-state witnesses or authenticate corporate documents (Burger King Corp. v. Rudzewicz, 1985). In addition, the interstate judicial system has an interest in adjudication by a court that can obtain jurisdiction over all parties to the dispute. If the forum state cannot bind all necessary parties and resolve the entire controversy, then litigation in other fora may follow, with the associated costs and risk of inconsistent judgments (Nowak v. Tak How Invs., Ltd., 1st Cir. 1996).[38]

The final reasonableness factor is "the shared interest of the several States in furthering fundamental substantive social policies" (World-Wide Volkswagen Corp. v. Woodson, 1980). When two or more American states have an interest in the outcome of a dispute, the "potentially conflicting 'fundamental substantive social policies' can usually be accommodated through choice-of-law rules rather than through outright preclusion of jurisdiction in one forum" (Burger King Corp. v. Rudzewicz, 1985). On the other hand, when one of the parties is an alien and a foreign country has an interest in furthering its social policy, this reasonableness factor typically counsels against jurisdiction. As the Court explained in *Asahi*, the interests of other nations

> as well as the Federal Government's interest in its foreign relations policies, will be best served by . . . an unwillingness to find the serious burdens on an alien defendant outweighed by minimal interests on the part of the plaintiff or the forum State. "Great care and reserve should be exercised when extending our notions of personal jurisdiction into the international field" (Asahi Metal Indus. Co. v. Superior Ct., 1987, quoting United States v. First Nat'l City Bank, 1965, Harlan, J., dissenting; cf. Nowak v. Tak How Invs., Ltd., 1st Cir. 1996).

### General v. Specific Jurisdiction

The distinction between general and specific jurisdiction, first drawn by Professors von Mehren and Trautman in 1965,[39] was incorporated into Supreme Court jurisdictional jurisprudence twenty years later (Calder v. Jones, 1984). A court exercises specific jurisdiction over a defendant when the claim sued upon arises out of or relates to the defendant's contacts with the forum state. A court exercises general jurisdiction over a defendant when the claim sued upon does not arise out of or relate to the defendant's contacts with the forum state (Helicopteros Nacionales de Colombia v. Hall, 1984). As Mary Twitchell put it, specific jurisdiction is dispute-specific, based only on affiliations between the claim and the forum, while general jurisdiction is dispute-blind, based on all of the defendant's ties to the forum without regard to the nature of the dispute.[40] Although not expressly discussed in *International Shoe*, the general/specific jurisdiction distinction was alluded to even then, when the Court emphasized the importance of the relationship between the claim sued upon and the in-state contacts (Int'l Shoe Co. v. Washington, 1945).

In-state personal service and domicile (or place of incorporation and principal place of business for corporations) support general jurisdiction over a defendant (Burnham v. Superior Ct., 1990; Milliken v. Meyer, 1940), as does consent in some circumstances.[41] When general jurisdiction is based on the defendant's contacts with the forum state, the amount of contact required is quite high: the defendant must have "continuous and systematic" contacts with the forum state (Helicopteros Nacionales de Colombia v. Hall, 1984). This stringent test was satisfied in Perkins v. Benguet Consolidated Mining Co. (1952). There, a shareholder of the Benguet Consolidated Mining Co. filed suit in an Ohio state court, seeking dividends and damages from Benguet for its alleged failure to issue stock certificates to her. Benguet, a company organized under the laws of the Philippine Islands, owned and operated gold and silver mines in the Philippines. The company's operations in the Philippines were completely halted during World War II, when the Japanese occupied the Islands. During that period, the president of the company moved to Ohio, where he maintained two active bank accounts with company funds, drew and distributed salary checks to himself and two other company employees, held directors' meetings, employed a local bank to serve as transfer agent for the company's stock and oversaw the rehabilitation of the company's Philippines properties. In the Court's view:

> [H]e carried on in Ohio a continuous and systematic supervision of the necessarily limited wartime activities of the company. . . . While no mining properties in Ohio were owned or operated by the company, many of its wartime activities were directed from Ohio and were being given the personal attention of its president in that State at the time he was served with summons (Perkins v. Benguet Consol. Mining Co., 1952).

Thus, it concluded that it would not violate due process for Ohio to exercise jurisdiction over the company even on a claim that did not arise in Ohio or relate to the company's activities there.

The only other post-*International Shoe* case decided by the Supreme Court that considered the availability of general jurisdiction based on contacts was Helicopteros Nacionales de Colombia v. Hall (1984). There, the Court considered the constitutionality of an assertion of jurisdiction by a Texas court over a Colombian company, Helicol, that provided helicopter transportation services in Peru. One of the defendant's helicopters crashed in Peru, killing four Americans, who were working on a pipeline construction project there. Their survivors filed wrongful death actions against Helicol and two other defendants in Texas.[42]

In considering whether Helicol was subject to jurisdiction in Texas, the Court examined four contacts the Colombian company had with the state: (1) it sent its chief executive officer to Texas to negotiate the contract for the provision of helicopter service to the pipeline project; (2) it accepted checks drawn on a Texas bank account; (3) over a seven-year period, it purchased $4,000,000 in helicopters, equipment and accessories from Bell Helicopter in Texas; and (4) it sent its pilots to Texas for training and other personnel there for technical consultation.

The wrongful death claim did not arise out of the defendant's contacts with Texas since both the accident and the pilot's negligence occurred in Peru. But surely the claim was related to the defendant's contacts with Texas—Helicol had purchased in Texas the very helicopter that crashed; the pilot whose negligence caused the crash had been trained in Texas; and the contract for helicopter service had been negotiated in Texas (Helicopteros Nacionales de Colombia v. Hall, 1984, Brennan, J., dissenting). Nevertheless, because the plaintiffs conceded that the claims did not arise out of or relate to the defendant's contacts with Texas, the Court considered only whether Helicopteros's contacts with Texas were sufficiently "continuous and systematic" to support general jurisdiction. It specifically declined to consider

> (1) whether the terms "arising out of" and "related to" describe different connections between a cause of action and a defendant's contacts with a forum, and (2) what sort of tie between a cause of action and a defendant's contacts with a forum is necessary to a determination that either connection exists (Helicopteros Nacionales de Colombia v. Hall, 1984).[43]

Easily concluding that the contract negotiation session and receipt of the Texas-drawn checks failed to qualify as "continuous and systematic" contacts, the Court then considered the purchases of the helicopters in Texas and the Texas training. Relying on a pre-*International Shoe* opinion, Rosenberg Bros. & Co. v. Curtis Brown Co. (1923), the Court held that "mere purchases, even if occurring at regular intervals, are not enough to warrant a State's assertion of *in personam* jurisdiction over a nonresident corporation in a cause of action not related to those purchase transactions" (Helicopteros Nacionales de Colombia v. Hall, 1984). In dissent, Justice Brennan criticized the majority's failure to ascertain whether *Rosenberg*'s narrow view of jurisdiction comported with an expansive national economy and its refusal to consider the availability of specific jurisdiction (Helicopteros Nacionales de Colombia v. Hall, 1984, Brennan, J., dissenting).

With only *Perkins* and *Helicopteros* as guidance from the Court on the availability of contacts-based general jurisdiction, the lower federal courts and the state courts have struggled with three issues: first, whether a court gauging the availability of general jurisdiction must consider the reasonableness factors identified in *World-Wide Volkswagen*; second, the proper dividing line between general and specific jurisdiction, or, put differently, when a claim arises out of or relates to the defendant's in-state contacts; and third, the amount of contact required to meet the "continuous and systematic contacts" standard for general jurisdiction.

The Supreme Court added the reasonableness factors to the jurisdictional analysis in the context of a specific jurisdiction case and it has not clarified whether these factors also apply in general jurisdiction cases. Neither of the Court's two general jurisdiction cases addressed the applicability of the reasonableness factors to the general jurisdiction analysis: *Perkins* was decided before the Court had added this layer of analysis, and the *Helicopteros* Court did not address the reasonableness factors, having concluded that continuous and systematic contacts did not exist. Every federal circuit court that has considered this issue has required that assertions of general jurisdiction be reasonable in light of the reasonableness factors,[44] as have many state courts.[45]

On the second question regarding the proper dividing line between specific and general jurisdiction, the Supreme Court has expressly "decline[d] to reach the question[ ] . . . whether the terms 'arising out of' and 'related to' describe different connections between a cause of action and a defendant's contacts with a forum" (Helicopteros Nacionales de Colombia v. Hall, 1984). Scholars have staked out competing positions on this issue. For example, Lea Brilmayer argues:

> A contact is related to the controversy if it is the geographical qualification of a fact relevant to the merits. A forum occurrence which would ordinarily be alleged as part of a comparable domestic complaint is a related contact. In contrast, an occurrence in the forum State of no relevance to a totally domestic cause of action is an unrelated contact, a purely jurisdictional allegation with no substantive purpose.[46]

Since Brilmayer's definition of related contacts is narrow, so is her vision of specific jurisdiction.

Mary Twitchell advocates a far more expansive view of specific jurisdiction, one that would include "all exercises of jurisdiction based even remotely on the nature of the claim presented."[47] Thus, she argues that specific jurisdiction should apply when the defendant has engaged in conduct in the forum state that is similar to the conduct underlying the claim, even if the claim did not arise out of the in-state conduct. She would reserve general jurisdiction for "exercises of jurisdiction that are truly dispute-blind."[48]

The practical difference between these two perspectives is well illustrated by the following hypothetical. Imagine that a manufacturer markets its product in all fifty states, and a consumer who purchases and uses the product in State A is injured by the allegedly defective product in State A, but sues the defendant in State B.[49] Applying Brilmayer's substantive relevance test, specific jurisdiction would be unavailable even though the defendant markets the same product in both states because the sales in State B have no bearing on the substantive merits of the claim.[50] Applying Twitchell's connectedness test, specific jurisdiction should be considered because of "the similarity between the manufacturer's conduct in the forum and the conduct underlying the plaintiff's cause of action."[51]

Like the scholars, the lower courts have struggled to find the proper dividing line between specific and general jurisdiction. In cases strikingly similar to the hypothetical, most courts have held that specific jurisdiction is unavailable since the claim does not arise out of the in-state sales.[52] Few courts concluded that specific jurisdiction should be considered because the claim relates to the in-state sales.[53] In cases involving slightly different facts—patent infringement actions filed against defendants who sell other non-infringing products in the forum state—some courts have treated the sales of the other products as sufficiently closely related to the claim to support specific jurisdiction.[54]

More generally, the lower courts have found specific jurisdiction only when the defendant's forum activity "caused" the plaintiff's harm, but they have applied a number of different causation tests. Some courts, most notably the Ninth Circuit Court of Appeals, have adopted a permissive "but for" test for distinguishing between specific and general jurisdiction cases: "a claim arises out of the forum-related activities if it would not have happened but for the forum-related activities."[55] In the Ninth Circuit's view, the "but for" test "preserves the essential distinction between general and specific jurisdiction" without unduly restricting the availability of jurisdiction in cases where purposeful availment is established (Shute v. Carnival Cruise Lines, 9th Cir. 1990).

Other courts have rejected a "but for" test as lacking a limiting principle and have adopted a more restrictive standard, such as a proximate cause standard.[56] According to the First Circuit, the proximate cause standard is more likely than a "but for" test to enable defendants to anticipate the conduct that will subject them to jurisdiction in a given state (Nowak v. Tak How Invs., Ltd., 1st Cir. 1996).

The Sixth and Seventh Circuits apply tests that are less restrictive than the proximate cause test, but somewhat more limited than the "but for" test. According to the Seventh Circuit, a claim arises from forum contacts if it "lies in the wake of the commercial activities by which the defendant submitted to the jurisdiction" of local courts.[57] The Sixth Circuit test requires that the claim have a "substantial connection with" the defendant's in-state activities (Dean v. Motel 6 Operating L.P., 6th Cir. 1998; Kerry Steel, Inc. v. Paragon Indus., Inc., 6th Cir. 1997).

As to the third issue—the amount of contact necessary to satisfy the "continuous and systematic" contacts requirement for general jurisdiction—the lower federal courts and the state courts agree on some general principles. For example, advertising in the forum state, even when combined with employment of sales people in the state, is usually not enough activity to support general jurisdiction.[58] Likewise, the mere listing of a company's securities on a stock exchange in the forum state does not subject the company to general jurisdiction there (Wiwa v. Royal Dutch Petroleum Co., 2d Cir. 2000; Celi v. Canadian Occidental Petroleum Ltd., E.D.N.Y. 1992). On the other hand, a defendant that conducts an integral part of its business in the forum state will usually be subject to general jurisdiction there.[59] Apart from these few points of agreement, the cases are all over the lot, with different courts reaching opposite conclusions on similar facts.[60] As Bruce Posnak argued in 1990, the "Court should take the next opportunity to explain what constitutes 'substantial' contacts in this context."[61] To date, the Court has failed to provide such guidance.

### *Purposeful Availment*

In the years following *International Shoe*, the Court continued to expand the scope of state court jurisdiction over nonresidents, in light of the fundamental transformation of the economy and the availability of modern transportation and communication systems. Given the decreased burdens faced by defendants with access to these modern conveniences, the Court made clear that even a single contact with the forum state could support specific jurisdiction, as when an insurance company issues a life insurance contract to a forum resident (McGee v. Int'l Life Ins. Co., 1957).

Not all post-*Shoe* cases have supported this trend, however. Although the Court has focused less on state sovereignty and more on fairness since *International Shoe*, it has occasionally emphasized the role that the minimum contacts test plays in preserving interstate federalism (World-Wide Volkswagen Corp. v. Woodson, 1980; Hanson v. Denckla, 1958). To ensure that states respect the sovereignty of other states and limit their jurisdictional reach accordingly, the Court has incorporated into the minimum contacts test a "purposeful availment" requirement.

The Court first introduced the phrase "purposeful availment" into the jurisdictional lexicon in Hanson v. Denckla (1958). There, the Supreme Court considered whether a Florida court had jurisdiction over a Delaware trust company, which had been named trustee in a trust instrument executed in Delaware by Dora Donner, a Pennsylvania domiciliary. The trust assets, though intangible, were assumed to be located in Delaware. Some years later, Mrs. Donner moved to Florida, where she later died. When Mrs. Donner's daughters commenced litigation in Florida challenging the validity of the trust, the trustee's amenability to suit there became an issue. Noting that the Delaware trust company had not solicited any business in Florida and had no other contacts there, the Supreme Court addressed the relevance of Mrs. Donner's residence there:

> The unilateral activity of those who claim some relationship with a nonresident defendant cannot satisfy the requirement of contact with the forum State. . . . [I]t is essential in each case that there be some act by which the defendant purposefully avails itself of the privilege of conducting activities within the forum state, thus invoking the benefits and protections of its laws (Hanson v. Denckla, 1958).

Thus, Mrs. Donner's move to Florida did not support an assertion of jurisdiction over the Delaware trust company because it had not purposefully affiliated itself in any way with Florida.

The purposeful availment requirement ensures that the defendant is not subject to jurisdiction on the basis of random, fortuitous or attenuated contacts or due to the unilateral activity of the plaintiff or a third party. Rather, the defendant herself must establish a "substantial connection" with the forum state (Burger King Corp. v. Rudzewicz, 1985). Physical presence within the state is not required, however. And entering into a contract with a forum resident is not, in and of itself, enough to subject one to jurisdiction. Rather, in contracts cases, in assessing minimum contacts and purposeful availment, courts evaluate the "prior negotiations and contemplated future consequences, along with the terms of the contract and the parties' actual course of dealing. . . ." (Burger King Corp. v. Rudzewicz, 1985).

In products liability cases, the mere foreseeability that one's product may find its way to the forum state and cause harm there is not enough to subject one to jurisdiction (World-Wide Volkwagen Corp. v. Woodson, 1980). But foreseeability is not irrelevant either: "the foreseeability that is critical to due process analysis is not the mere likelihood that a product will find its way into the forum State. Rather it is that the defendant's conduct and connection with the forum State are such that he should reasonably anticipate being haled into court there" (World-Wide Volkswagen Corp. v. Woodson, 1980). In other words, if the defendant purposefully avails herself of the benefits of doing business in the forum state, she should not be surprised if she is required to defend suits arising from that conduct in its courts.

In later cases, the Court framed this foreseeability analysis in terms of "fair warning":

> By requiring that individuals have "fair warning that a particular activity may subject [them] to the jurisdiction of a foreign sovereign," the Due Process Clause "gives a degree of predictability to the legal system that allows potential defendants to structure their primary conduct with some minimum assurance as to where that conduct will and will not render them liable to suit" (Burger King Corp. v. Rudzewicz, 1985, quoting Shaffer v. Heitner, 1977, Stevens, J., concurring in the judgment, and World-Wide Volkswagen v. Woodson, 1980).

Fair warning is assured when the defendant purposefully directs her activities at forum residents and the litigation arises out of or relates to those activities (Burger King Corp. v. Rudzewicz, 1985).

The Court has invoked the purposeful availment requirement in many cases since *Hanson*, both in upholding jurisdiction and in striking it down. For example, the Court upheld jurisdiction in New Hampshire over the publisher of a nationally-distributed magazine, which had purposefully directed its product at New Hampshire by making regular monthly sales of thousands of magazines (Keeton v. Hustler Magazine, Inc., 1984). Likewise, it upheld jurisdiction in Florida over a Michigan businessman who had entered into a long-term franchise agreement with Burger King Corp., a Florida corporation headquartered in Florida, which agreement contained a Florida choice-of-law clause (Burger King Corp. v. Rudzewicz, 1985). On the other hand, the Supreme Court held that Oklahoma lacked jurisdiction over a New York retail automobile dealer that did no business in Oklahoma. The unilateral activity of the plaintiffs, who had purchased the car in New York and had driven it to Oklahoma, where it was involved in an accident, could not be imputed to the defendant, which had not purposefully availed itself of the privileges and benefits of Oklahoma law (World-Wide Volkswagen Corp. v. Woodson, 1980). Likewise, a man who bought his child a one-way airplane ticket to California and permitted her to move there to live with his ex-wife was not found to have purposefully availed himself of the benefits and protections of California law and could not be sued there for child support (Kulko v. Superior Ct., 1978).

The Court has had the most difficulty applying the purposeful availment test in the products liability context. These cases are often referred to as "stream-of-commerce" cases because the manufacturer places its product into the stream of commerce knowing that someone in the chain of distribution of the final product—a distributor or a retail dealer, perhaps—will sell the product to consumers. The issue in these stream-of-commerce cases is which actors in the chain of distribution are subject to jurisdiction in the state in which the product fails and how much direct contact with that state they must have to be subject to suit there. It is to these cases that we now turn.

### *Stream-of-Commerce Theory*

As in other cases, the key jurisdictional issue in the stream-of-commerce cases is purposeful availment. The leading Supreme Court stream-of-commerce cases illustrate two distinct fact patterns that commonly arise in products liability cases, both of which raise vexing questions of purposeful availment. In the first fact pattern, illustrated by World-Wide Volkswagen Corp. v. Woodson (1980), the plaintiff purchases a product in one state and suffers injury when the product fails in another state to which she has taken it. In the second fact pattern, illustrated by Asahi Metal Industry Co. v. Superior Court (1987), the plaintiff purchases a product and suffers injury in the same state but the defendant itself did not sell the product there. As we will see, the defendant's position in the chain of distribution and its level of expectation that the product would be sold to consumers in the forum state are important factors in determining whether jurisdiction is available in these stream-of-commerce cases.

*World-Wide Volkswagen* involved a lawsuit filed by Harry and Kay Robinson, who had been involved in a terrible car accident in Oklahoma. A year or so before the accident, while living in New York, they had purchased an Audi automobile from a local dealer, Seaway Volkswagen, in Massena, New York. The Robinsons later drove the car to Oklahoma, where it was hit from behind and caught on fire. The Robinsons filed suit in state court in Oklahoma, claiming that a design defect in the car's gas tank caused their injuries. The plaintiffs named four defendants: the manufacturer of the car, Audi; its importer, Volkswagen; the Northeast regional distributor, World-Wide Volkswagen; and the retail dealer, Seaway. World-Wide Volkswagen and Seaway challenged the Oklahoma court's jurisdiction over them.[62]

Applying the purposeful availment requirement in the stream-of-commerce context, the Court noted that the mere forseeability that the car would find its way to Oklahoma and cause harm there was not enough to support jurisdiction. After all, the car was brought to Oklahoma by the *plaintiffs'* unilateral activity. Since neither Seaway nor World-Wide Volkswagen sold any cars outside the New York/New Jersey/Connecticut tri-state area, they had not purposefully availed themselves of the privilege of conducting business in Oklahoma (World-Wide Volkswagen Corp. v. Woodson, 1980).

In dicta, the Court suggested that the case for jurisdiction over the manufacturer or national distributor of the car would have been stronger:

> [I]f the sale of a product of a manufacturer or distributor such as Audi or Volkswagen is not simply an isolated occurrence, but arises from the efforts of the manufacturer or distributor to serve, directly or indirectly, the market for its product in other States, it is not unreasonable to subject it to suit in one of those States if its allegedly defective merchandise has there been the source of injury to its owner or to others. The forum state does not exceed its powers under the Due Process Clause if it asserts personal jurisdiction over a corporation that delivers its products into the stream of commerce with the expectation that they will be purchased by consumers in the forum State (World-Wide Volkswagen Corp. v. Woodson, 1980).

In other words, even if the particular product that failed had been brought into the forum state by the plaintiff, the manufacturer would be subject to jurisdiction there if it sold the same product in the forum state.

But what if the defendant manufacturer does not control the product's sale to consumers in the forum state? This issue, which typically arises when a component part is incorporated into another manufacturer's product, was addressed by the Supreme Court in *Asahi*. There, the plaintiff suffered injury in a motorcycle accident in California. He claimed that the rear tire exploded because the tube was defective and named Cheng Shin Rubber Industrial Co., the Taiwanese tube manufacturer, as a defendant (Asahi Metal Indus. Co. v. Superior Court, 1987). Cheng Shin, in turn, impleaded Asahi Metal Industry Co., the Japanese company that had manufactured the tube's valve assembly. Asahi challenged the California court's jurisdiction over it, claiming that it sold valve assemblies to Cheng Shin in Taiwan and that it never contemplated suit in California.

A unanimous Court held that jurisdiction over Asahi in California would be unconstitutional and eight Justices agreed that it would be unreasonable in light of the *World-Wide Volkswagen* reasonableness factors discussed earlier in this chapter in the section entitled "The Modern Formula," subsection entitled "Doctrinal Refinements, paragraph entitled "Reasonableness Factors." But the Justices had difficulty determining whether minimum contacts existed. Four Justices concluded that Asahi had minimum contacts with California. Writing for them, Justice Brennan invoked the language from *World-Wide Volkswagen* quoted above to demonstrate that the Court had "preserved the stream-of-commerce theory" of jurisdiction. He concluded that a defendant that places goods in the stream of commerce knowing that the final product is marketed in the forum state has minimum contacts there because it benefits economically from the retail sales of its product in the forum state and cannot be surprised by the possibility of litigation there. Thus, even though Asahi did not control the distribution system that carried its product into California, it knew that products incorporating its valve assemblies were being sold in California and it benefitted from those sales (Asahi Metal Indus. Co. v. Superior Ct., 1987, Brennan, J., concurring in part and concurring in the judgment).

Justice Stevens adopted a less categorical approach, examining the volume, value and hazardous character of the product to determine whether a manufacturer purposefully availed itself of the forum's market. "In most circumstances," he concluded, "a regular course of dealing that results in deliveries of over 100,000 units annually over a period of several years would constitute 'purposeful availment' even though the item delivered to the forum state was a standard product marketed throughout the world" (Asahi Metal Indus. Co. v. Superior Ct., 1987, Stevens, J., concurring in part and concurring in the judgment). Thus, Stevens appeared to agree that Asahi had purposefully availed itself of the California market and therefore had minimum contacts with the state.

Four other Justices concluded that Asahi lacked minimum contacts with California because it had not taken any action that was purposefully directed toward the forum state. In a plurality opinion, Justice O'Connor staked out this position:

> The placement of a product into the stream of commerce, without more, is not an act of the defendant purposefully directed toward the forum State. Additional conduct of the defendant may indicate an intent or purpose to serve the market in the forum State, for example, designing the product for the market in the forum State, advertising in the forum State,

establishing channels for providing regular advice to customers in the forum State, or marketing the product through a distributor who has agreed to serve as the sales agent in the forum State. But a defendant's awareness that the stream of commerce may or will sweep the product into the forum State does not convert the mere act of placing the product into the stream into an act purposefully directed toward the forum State (Asahi Metal Indus. Co. v. Superior Ct., 1987, plurality op.).

Since Asahi had not controlled the distribution system that brought its valve assemblies to California or otherwise directed its product to California, the plurality concluded that Asahi lacked minimum contacts with the state.

Given this lack of consensus among members of the Court, the lower federal courts and the state courts have struggled to apply the purposeful availment requirement in the stream-of-commerce context. A number of courts, including the Fifth, Seventh and Eighth Circuit Courts of Appeals, have concluded that the plurality opinion in *Asahi* is not controlling. These courts have continued to rely on *World-Wide Volkswagen* for the proposition that a manufacturer that places its product into the stream of commerce knowing that it will be sold to consumers in the forum state is subject to jurisdiction there.[63] Other courts, including the First and Fourth Circuit Courts of Appeals, have treated the *Asahi* plurality opinion as binding and have embraced the requirement that additional conduct evincing an intent to serve the forum state must be proven.[64] Yet other courts, including the Second, Third, Sixth, Ninth, Eleventh and Federal Circuit Courts of Appeals, have declined to choose between the competing standards, concluding in specific cases that the result would be the same regardless of the test applied.[65] This lack of consistency among the lower courts is likely to persist at least until the Court decides another stream-of-commerce case.

### *Effects Test*

Dicey jurisdictional issues arise not only regarding defendants who place their products in the stream of commerce, but also regarding defendants who cause an effect in the forum state. The "effects" test derives from the Restatement (Second) of Conflict of Laws, which provides:

A state has power to exercise judicial jurisdiction over an individual who causes effects in the state by an act done elsewhere with respect to any claim arising from these effects unless the nature of the effects and of the individual's relationship to the state make the exercise of such jurisdiction unreasonable (Restatement (Second) of Conflict of Laws § 37 (1971)).

The Supreme Court first invoked the "effects" test to support a finding of jurisdiction in Calder v. Jones (1984).[66] There, actress Shirley Jones, a California resident whose television career was centered in California, filed a libel action against the National Enquirer, a Florida corporation that publishes a nationally-distributed magazine, its distributor, its editor, and the reporter who wrote the allegedly libelous article. The article stated that Ms. Jones's heavy drinking in California prevented her from fulfilling her professional obligations. Both the editor and the reporter challenged the California court's jurisdiction over them. In upholding jurisdiction, the United States Supreme Court noted that "the brunt of the harm, in terms both of [plaintiff's] emotional distress and the injury to her professional reputation, was suffered in California. . . . Jurisdiction over [the editor and the reporter] is therefore proper in California based on the 'effects' of their Florida conduct in California" (Calder v. Jones, 1984). Rejecting the defendants' argument that they lacked control over the magazine's circulation and had no direct economic stake in its California sales, the Court noted that "their intentional, and allegedly tortious, actions were expressly aimed at California" (Calder v. Jones, 1984). The defendants wrote and edited an article "that they knew would have a potentially devastating impact upon [Jones]. And they knew that the brunt of that injury would be felt by [her] in the State in which she lives and works and in which the National Enquirer has its largest circulation." Thus, they should have anticipated being haled into court in California (Calder v. Jones, 1984).

The Supreme Court has not invoked the "effects" test since deciding *Calder*, but the lower courts are frequently called upon to apply it. The Seventh Circuit Court of Appeals has read *Calder* broadly, concluding that "the state in which the victim of a tort suffers the injury may entertain a suit against the accused tortfeasor" (Janmark, Inc. v. Reidy, 7th Cir. 1997). The other federal courts of appeals have declined to read the "effects" test as standing for the broad proposition that any action with foreseeable effects in the forum state gives rise to specific jurisdiction.[67] Instead, they have applied it only if the defendant expressly aims its tortious conduct at the forum state or engages in wrongful conduct that specifically targets a known forum resident.[68] Several courts have clarified that even when the effects of the defendant's conduct are felt in the forum state, the plaintiff must demonstrate that the defendant purposefully availed itself of the privilege of conducting activities in the forum state (Panda Brandywine Corp. v. Potomac Elec. Power Co., 5th Cir. 2001; Wallace v. Herron, 7th Cir. 1985). The courts have not limited the effects test to libel cases,[69] and have applied it in other cases involving intentional conduct, including copyright and trademark infringement,[70] tortious interference with contractual relations,[71] interference with prospective economic advantage[72] and fraud.[73]

## Jurisdiction in Cyberspace

With the advent of the Internet, courts have had to consider the extent to which activities in cyberspace affect the jurisdictional calculus.[74] To date, the Supreme Court has not addressed this issue. Several early decisions by lower courts upheld jurisdiction over a defendant that maintained a passive web site on the theory that by advertising its product on the Internet, the defendant purposefully availed itself of the privilege of conducting activities in the forum state (Maritz, Inc. v. Cybergold, Inc., E.D. Mo. 1996; Inset Systems, Inc. v. Instruction Set, Inc., D. Conn. 1996). "[O]nce posted on the Internet, unlike television and radio advertising, the advertisement is available continuously to any Internet user" (Inset Systems, Inc. v. Instruction Set, Inc., D. Conn. 1996). More recently, the trend has been against jurisdiction based solely on passive web sites (Millennium Enters., Inc. v. Millennium Music, LP, D. Or. 1999).

Many courts, including the Fourth,[75] Fifth,[76] Ninth[77] and Tenth[78] Circuit Courts of Appeals, apply a "sliding scale" analysis developed by a federal district court in the case of Zippo Manufacturing Co. v. Zippo Dot Com, Inc. (W.D. Pa. 1997). The *Zippo* court concluded that the availability of jurisdiction should be "directly proportionate to the nature and quality of commercial activity that an entity conducts over the Internet" (Zippo Mfg. Co. v. Zippo Dot Com, Inc., W.D. Pa. 1997). When a defendant "clearly does business over the Internet," jurisdiction should be available, just as it is whenever an entity intentionally reaches into other states to conduct business.[79] On the other hand, when a defendant merely posts information on a web site accessible to browsers in the forum state, jurisdiction should not be available. In the *Zippo* court's words, "A passive web site that does little more than make information available to those who are interested in it is not grounds for the exercise of personal jurisdiction" (Zippo Mfg. Co. v. Zippo Dot Com, Inc., W.D. Pa. 1997).[80] In between these extremes are cases involving interactive web sites, which enable users to exchange information with the host computer. "In these cases, the exercise of jurisdiction is determined by examining the level of interactivity and commercial nature of the exchange of information that occurs on the Web site" (Zippo Mfg. Co. v. Zippo Dot Com, Inc., W.D. Pa. 1997).

Courts have struggled to determine when maintenance of an interactive web site constitutes purposeful availment. A growing number of courts have concluded that maintenance of an interactive web site alone is not sufficient, requiring "'deliberate action' within the forum state in the form of transactions between the defendant and residents of the forum or conduct of the defendant purposefully directed at residents of the forum state."[81] Thus, even a web site that invites prospective purchasers to place orders over the Internet may not constitute purposeful availment in the absence of actual sales to forum residents or intentional targeting of forum residents. This "web site plus" rule modifies or at least clarifies *Zippo*'s guidance regarding interactive web sites.

Although the issue of personal jurisdiction over Internet actors may arise in a wide variety of cases, most commonly it arises in defamation cases in which an allegedly defamatory article is posted to the Internet,[82] patent infringement cases in which a web site is used to market goods that allegedly infringe a patent,[83] and trademark infringement cases in which a web site allegedly infringes a registered trademark.[84]

There is likely to be some uncertainty about the availability of jurisdiction based on Internet activity at least until the Supreme Court addresses the issue. In the meantime, the *Zippo* test and the "web site plus" rule offer some guidance both to courts and to those that maintain web sites.

Another jurisdictional issue that has arisen in cyberspace is the constitutionality of the *in rem* provision in the federal Anticybersquatting Consumer Protection Act (the "ACPA"), 15 U.S.C. § 1125(d)(2)(A). The ACPA amended the Lanham Act to protect owners of registered trademarks from "cybersquatters" who sought to benefit unfairly from the value of another's trademark by registering an Internet domain name similar to it (FleetBoston Fin. Corp. v. fleetbostonfinancial.com, D. Mass. 2001). The *in rem* provision of the ACPA authorizes a trademark owner to bring an *in rem* action against an infringing Internet domain name itself in the judicial district in which the registrar, registry or other authority that assigned or registered the domain name is located if *in personam* jurisdiction over the person using the infringing domain name is not available.

At least two district courts and one court of appeals have upheld the constitutionality of this provision, viewing actions under the statute as true *in rem* actions because they purport to adjudicate the rights of all interested claimants to a disputed mark.[85] The district courts have read Shaffer v. Heitner (1977) narrowly, concluding that due process requires that the defendant have minimum contacts with the forum state only in cases of attachment jurisdiction, not in cases of true *in rem* jurisdiction,[86] while the Fourth Circuit Court of Appeals concluded that registration of the domain name within the judicial district satisfied the minimum contacts test.[87] Thus, these courts have upheld jurisdiction as long as the registry, registrar or other authority that registered the domain name was located in the judicial district. At least five federal district courts have rejected an interpretation of the statute that would authorize jurisdiction in any district in which the plaintiff deposits documents with the court establishing control over the registration and use of the domain name, expressing concern that jurisdiction under that interpretation would be unconstitutional.[88]

### *Quasi-in-rem* Jurisdiction Today

Questions about the scope and meaning of Shaffer v. Heitner (1977) have arisen beyond the cyberspace context. Before the Supreme Court decided *Shaffer*, courts exercised jurisdiction over defendants that lacked minimum contacts with the state as long as they owned property within the state. Employing *quasi-in-rem* jurisdiction, courts seized the defendant's property and exercised jurisdiction up to the value of the property attached. In *Shaffer*, the Supreme Court held that the constitutionality of *all* assertions of jurisdiction—including *in rem* and *quasi-in-rem* jurisdiction—must be gauged by the minimum contacts test. Under *Shaffer*, a defendant who lacks minimum contacts with the forum state may not be compelled to defend there even if she possesses property in the state that can be seized and brought under the court's control.

Immediately following *Shaffer*, several courts concluded that *Seider* jurisdiction—*quasi-in-rem* jurisdiction obtained through garnishment of a nonresident driver's insurance policy to facilitate adjudication of a personal injury or wrongful death claim against her—remained viable notwithstanding *Shaffer*.[89] Taking a realistic view of insurance litigation, the courts noted that the insurers controlled the litigation, selected the defendant's attorney and faced the potential of a money judgment against them. Since the only property of the defendant's at risk was an insurance policy designed for the sole purpose of protecting her from just such a claim, the courts held that the *Seider* procedure comported with "traditional notions of fair play and substantial justice."[90]

The Supreme Court rejected this reasoning and invalidated *Seider* jurisdiction in Rush v. Savchuk (1980). If the obligation of an insurer to defend and indemnify the insured is treated as the defendant's property, and if the property is deemed to be located wherever the insurer is subject to *in personam* jurisdiction, then the debt is "present" in all fifty states simultaneously if the insurer does business throughout the country. "It is apparent," the Court concluded, "that such a 'contact' can have no jurisdictional significance" (Rush v. Savchuk, 1980). Even if the insurer's obligation to the defendant were deemed to be "*a* contact between the defendant and the forum," in the absence of additional contacts among the defendant, the litigation and the forum, jurisdiction would be unavailable under *Shaffer*. Since the individual defendant has no control over the insurer's decision to do business in the forum state, "it cannot be said that the *defendant* engaged in any purposeful activity related to the forum state that would make the exercise of jurisdiction fair, just, or reasonable merely because his insurer does business there" (Rush v. Savchuk, 1980).

Finally, the Court rejected the argument that the *Seider* attachment procedure is the "functional equivalent of a direct action against the insurer." First, since the state's ability to exercise jurisdiction over the driver is "analytically prerequisite to the insurer's entry into the case as a garnishee," the Court declined to treat the driver as a "nominal" defendant whose amenability to jurisdiction could be ignored. Second, the Court questioned the assumption that the driver has no real stake in the litigation, noting that she may have noneconomic interests that might be affected by the litigation (Rush v. Savchuk, 1980).

If assertions of *quasi-in-rem* jurisdiction must comport with the *International Shoe* test and if application of that test spells the demise of *Seider* jurisdiction, then under what circumstances is *quasi-in-rem* jurisdiction ever available? Put differently, since a court can acquire *in personam* jurisdiction over a defendant who has minimum contacts with the forum state, why would it ever exercise *quasi-in-rem* jurisdiction?

In a national survey of states regarding their post-*Shaffer* use of *quasi-in-rem* jurisdiction, Michael Mushlin concluded that most states no longer use it at all.[91] A small number of states have actually abolished the use of *quasi-in-rem* jurisdiction, either by amending their statute or rule to eliminate this jurisdictional option[92] or by declaring unconstitutional a provision that previously had authorized it (City Suburban Agency, Inc. v. Dade Helicopter Servs., Inc., Mich. Ct. App. 1985). A larger number of states still have statutes on the books that authorize *quasi-in-rem* jurisdiction when the defendant is a nonresident of the state, but have not relied on these statutes or at least have not judicially approved of their use since *Shaffer*.[93]

Notwithstanding this general trend, approximately ten states, including New York, continue to employ *quasi-in-rem* jurisdiction.[94] In New York, the courts employ *quasi-in-rem* jurisdiction because the state long-arm statute does not authorize *in personam* jurisdiction to the full limits of the federal constitution. In the words of the New York Court of Appeals, "a situation can occur in which the necessary contacts to satisfy due process are present, but in personam jurisdiction will not be obtained in this State because the statute does not authorize it" (Banco Ambrosiano, S.p.A. v. Artoc Bank & Trust Ltd., N.Y. 1984; see also Intermeat, Inc. v. Am. Poultry, Inc., 2d Cir. 1978). This situation is exemplified by Banco Ambrosiano, S.p.A. v. Artoc Bank & Trust Ltd. (N.Y. 1984), which involved a $15 million loan made by an Italian banking corporation to the defendant, a banking corporation organized under the laws of the Bahamas. The transaction was negotiated entirely outside of New York, but the funds were deposited in a New York bank account and were to be repaid to another New York bank account. When the defendant failed to repay the loan, the plaintiff initiated suit in New York by attaching an account maintained by the defendant in a New York correspondent bank. The defendant was not authorized to do business in New York and its only contact with the state was maintenance of the attached account.

Proceeding on the assumption that the long-arm statute did not authorize *in personam* jurisdiction in New York because the defendant had not "transact[ed] any business within the state,"[95] the New York Court of Appeals nevertheless found that the defendant had minimum contacts with the state because the very account used to obtain *quasi-in-rem* jurisdiction over the defendant was the one through which it had effectuated the loan transaction and the one it used regularly in its international banking business (Banco Ambrosiano, S.p.A. v. Artoc Bank & Trust Ltd., N.Y. 1984). The court noted that the state long-arm statute

> does not provide for in personam jurisdiction in every case in which due process would permit it. Thus, a "gap" exists in which the necessary minimum contacts, including the presence of the defendant's property within the State, are present, but personal jurisdiction is not authorized by [the long-arm statute]. It is appropriate, in such a case, to fill that gap utilizing quasi-in-rem principles (Banco Ambrosiano, S.p.A. v. Artoc Bank & Trust Ltd.,

N.Y. 1984; see also Intermeat, Inc. v. Am. Poultry Inc., 2d Cir. 1978; Drexel Burnham Lambert, Inc. v. D'Angelo, S.D.N.Y. 1978).

In the post-*Shaffer* era, *quasi-in-rem* jurisdiction has been upheld on at least three other theories first suggested by Linda Silberman in her seminal analysis of *Shaffer*.[96] First, relying on a footnote in *Shaffer*,[97] several courts have upheld the use of *quasi-in-rem* jurisdiction when no other forum is available to the plaintiff,[98] exercising what has been called jurisdiction by necessity (Helicopteros Nacionales de Colombia v. Hall, 1984). Second, several courts have concluded that *Shaffer* does not "requir[e] the same minimum contacts for the exercise of quasi in rem jurisdiction as are required for the assertion of in personam jurisdiction" (Cameco Indus., Inc. v. Mayatrac, S.A., D. Md. 1992; Feder v. Turkish Airlines, S.D.N.Y. 1977). Since the judgment in a *quasi-in-rem* case is limited to the value of the property attached, due process may require fewer contacts between the defendant and the forum than would be required in an *in personam* action (Cameco Indus., Inc. v. Mayatrac, S.A., D. Md. 1992).[99] Third, several courts have read *Shaffer* as barring *quasi-in-rem* jurisdiction only "in cases where the presence in the forum of the property providing the basis for jurisdiction was entirely fortuitous."[100] These courts have held that *quasi-in-rem* jurisdiction can be exercised over a corporation that "purposefully" maintains a bank account in the forum state even though the plaintiff claims no pre-existing interest in the property seized. Because maintenance of the account is "voluntary, purposeful and directly related to [the defendant's] general business operations," these courts concluded that it does not offend "'traditional notions of fair play and substantial justice' to hold that [the defendant] has subjected the monies in the account to quasi in rem jurisdiction" in the forum state (Cameco Indus., Inc. v. Mayatrac, S.A., D. Md. 1992). This reading of *Shaffer* has been called into question by the Second Circuit Court of Appeals (O'Connor v. Lee-Hy Paving Corp., 2d Cir. 1978).

In federal court, Rule 4(n)(2) limits the use of *quasi-in-rem* jurisdiction to cases in which "personal jurisdiction over a defendant cannot, in the district where the action is brought, be obtained with reasonable efforts by service of summons in any manner authorized by this rule" (Fed. R. Civ. P. 4(n)(2)). The Advisory Committee Notes state that Rule 4(n)(2) is intended to limit the use of *quasi-in-rem* jurisdiction to cases involving exigent circumstances.

### Transient Jurisdiction Revisited

Under the first public law principle announced in *Pennoyer*—that every State possesses exclusive jurisdiction over people and property within its territory—a state could assert jurisdiction over a person who was served while physically present in the state, even if there only temporarily or transiently. This form of jurisdiction, referred to as transient or tag jurisdiction, has been criticized as unfair because it subjects a defendant who may have very little contact with the forum state to jurisdiction even on claims that are unrelated to the in-state contact.[101]

After the Supreme Court decided Shaffer v. Heitner (1977), holding that *all* assertions of jurisdiction must be gauged by the minimum contacts test, the continued viability of transient jurisdiction was questioned. After all, a defendant who was present in a state only fleetingly likely would not have minimum contacts sufficient to support jurisdiction. A number of lower courts concluded that transient jurisdiction—jurisdiction based solely on personal service while present in the state—was no longer constitutional after *Shaffer*.[102] Not all courts agreed, however. Some courts concluded that because *International Shoe* required minimum contacts only if the defendant "be not present within the territory of the forum," transient jurisdiction survived.[103]

In 1990, the Supreme Court resolved this conflict, upholding transient jurisdiction and concluding that a state court may assert jurisdiction over a defendant who is personally served while transiently present in the state, even if the claim is unrelated to her in-state activities (Burnham v. Superior Ct., 1990). *Burnham* involved a couple that spent most of their married lives together in New Jersey. When they separated, the wife, Francie, moved to California. She sued her husband, Dennis, for divorce in California, and served him while he was in the state on business and visiting their children. Dennis challenged jurisdiction, arguing that he lacked minimum contacts with California.

The Supreme Court unanimously upheld jurisdiction, although the Justices did not agree on the rationale. Writing for a plurality of the Court, Justice Scalia relied heavily on the traditional acceptance of transient jurisdiction by American courts, particularly in 1868, when the Fourteenth Amendment was adopted. Scalia noted that acceptance of transient jurisdiction was not merely longstanding, but also continuing:

> Jurisdiction based on physical presence alone constitutes due process because it is one of the continuing traditions of our legal system that define the due process standard of "traditional notions of fair play and substantial justice." That standard was developed by *analogy* to "physical presence," and it would be perverse to say it could now be turned against that touchstone of jurisdiction (Burnham v. Superior Ct., 1990, plurality op., citations omitted).

Distinguishing *Shaffer* as a case involving jurisdiction over an *absent* defendant, Justice Scalia argued that *Shaffer* "stands for nothing more than the proposition that when the 'minimum contact' that is a substitute for physical presence consists of property ownership it must, like other minimum contacts, be related to the litigation." In other words, the constitutionality of assertions of both *quasi-in-rem* and *in personam* jurisdiction must be measured by the same standard, the minimum contacts test, when the defendant cannot be served while present in the state. But *Shaffer*'s logic does not require "that physically present defendants . . . be treated identically to absent ones." *International Shoe* itself confined the minimum contacts test to cases in which "the defendant 'be not present within the territory of the forum,' and nothing in *Shaffer* expands that requirement beyond that." More generally, Justice Scalia rejected the *Shaffer* Court's willingness to conduct an independent inquiry into the fairness of transient jurisdiction, noting that "its validation is its pedigree" (Burnham v. Superior Ct., 1990, plurality op.).

Writing for himself and three other Justices, Justice Brennan concurred in the judgment, agreeing that "the Due Process Clause of the Fourteenth Amendment generally permits a state court to exercise jurisdiction over a defendant if he is served with process while voluntarily present in the forum State." He did not agree, however, that the practice was constitutional simply because it had a historical pedigree. Indeed, he questioned transient jurisdiction's pedigree, noting that the practice "was rather weakly implanted in American jurisprudence" at the time the Fourteenth Amendment was adopted. But he noted that current defendants are on notice that they may be subject to jurisdiction if "tagged" in a state because of the general acceptance by American courts of transient jurisdiction in the past century (Burnham v. Superior Ct., 1990, Brennan, J., concurring in the judgment).

In addition to history, Justice Brennan considered the fairness of transient jurisdiction gauged by contemporary standards. In his view, *Shaffer*'s "critical insight" was "that all rules of jurisdiction, even ancient ones, must satisfy contemporary notions of due process." He concluded that transient jurisdiction is fair because transient defendants avail themselves of benefits whenever they visit a state, including the protections provided by the local police, fire and emergency medical personnel and the use of local highways and courts. Given modern modes of transportation and means of communication, the burdens borne by transient defendants are slight, and any burdens that do arise can be ameliorated by a change of venue, a *forum non conveniens* dismissal, or other procedural tools. "For these reasons, as a rule the exercise of personal jurisdiction over a defendant based on his voluntary presence in the forum will satisfy the requirements of due process" (Burnham v. Superior Ct., 1990, Brennan, J., concurring in the judgment).

Justice White, who concurred in the judgment and portions of Justice Scalia's opinion, wrote separately, noting that until it can be shown that transient jurisdiction is arbitrary in many instances, "claims in individual cases that the rule would operate unfairly as applied to the particular nonresident involved need not be entertained" (Burnham v. Superior Ct., 1990, White, J., concurring in part and concurring in the judgment).[104] Justice Stevens, also concurring in the judgment, viewed the case as a "very easy" one, given the historical evidence marshaled by Justice Scalia, the considerations of fairness identified by Justice Brennan, and the common sense displayed by Justice White (Burnham v. Superior Ct., 1990, Stevens, J., concurring in the judgment).

Notwithstanding the differing rationales expressed in these four opinions, the Justices unanimously agreed that states may assert jurisdiction over persons who are served while physically present in the state, even if only temporarily. Thus, transient jurisdiction is alive and well notwithstanding the criticisms that have been leveled against it.

## DUE PROCESS LIMITATIONS ON ASSERTIONS OF PERSONAL JURISDICTION BY FEDERAL COURTS

It is the Due Process Clause of the Fifth Amendment, rather than the Fourteenth Amendment or Article III of the Constitution, that limits the personal jurisdictional reach of the federal district courts (Omni Capital Int'l, Ltd. v. Rudolf Wolff & Co., 1987; Ins. Corp. of Ir., Ltd. v. Compagnie des Bauxites de Guinee, 1982). But are the limits imposed by the Fifth Amendment the same as those imposed by the Fourteenth Amendment? Put differently, are there circumstances in which a federal district court may exercise personal jurisdiction over a defendant who would not be subject to jurisdiction in the state courthouse next door? As we will see, because of the interplay between the Constitution and Rule 4 of the Federal Rules of Civil Procedure, which authorizes service of process in the federal district courts, the answer to this question depends in part on the basis for the district court's subject matter jurisdiction in a given case.[105]

Before a court may exercise personal jurisdiction over a defendant, she must receive notice of the action and have a constitutionally sufficient relationship with the forum and "there also must be a basis for the defendant's amenability to service of summons. Absent consent, this means there must be authorization for service of summons on the defendant" (Omni Capital Int'l, Ltd. v. Rudolf Wolff & Co., 1987). Rule 4 provides this authorization and fixes the territorial limits of the federal courts' personal jurisdiction in the first instance.

Rule 4 authorizes service of process upon individuals, corporations and partnerships pursuant to state law (Fed. R. Civ. P. 4(e)(1), 4(h)(1)). While these portions of Rule 4 speak only to service and not amenability to jurisdiction, Rule 4(k)(1) goes further, providing that service of a summons upon a defendant establishes jurisdiction over her if she would have been subject to jurisdiction in a state court in the state in which the district court sits, or if a federal statute so authorizes (Fed. R. Civ. P. 4(k)(1)).[106] With respect to claims arising under federal law, Rule 4(k)(2) further provides that service is effective to establish jurisdiction over a defendant "who is not subject to the jurisdiction of the courts of general jurisdiction of any state" if the exercise of jurisdiction is consistent with the Constitution and federal law (Fed. R. Civ. P. 4(k)(2)). This provision was added in 1993 to ensure that a nonresident alien defendant whose contacts with the United States as a whole are sufficient to support jurisdiction under the Fifth Amendment, but whose contacts with any single state are insufficient to support jurisdiction under the Fourteenth Amendment, is subject to the federal court's personal jurisdiction (Fed. R. Civ. P. 4 advisory committee's note). As Leslie Kelleher put it, "the provision is a general long-arm statute for federal cases which allows jurisdiction to be asserted to the full extent permissible under the Fifth Amendment of the Constitution."[107]

Before we address the full breadth of personal jurisdiction permissible under the Fifth Amendment in federal question cases, let us first consider how Rule 4(k), together with the Constitution, constrains the exercise of jurisdiction when the district court sits in diversity or entertains a federal claim arising under a law that does *not* authorize nationwide service of process. In these cases, Rule 4(k)(1)(A) authorizes the district court to exercise personal jurisdiction over the defendant if a "court of general jurisdiction in the state in which the district court is located" could exercise jurisdiction (Fed. R. Civ. P. 4(k)(1)(A)). Since the Due Process Clause of the Fourteenth Amendment would determine the outer limits of the state court's personal jurisdictional reach, it likewise determines the outer limits of the federal court's jurisdictional reach in these cases (Burger King Corp. v. Rudzewicz, 1985; Keeton v. Hustler Magazine, Inc., 1984).[108] Although it may seem anomalous that Fourteenth Amendment due process standards would limit a federal court's jurisdictional reach in a federal question case,[109] this result follows from the lack of a nationwide service of process statute for certain federal causes of action (which Congress can rectify) and Rule 4(k)(1)(A)'s incorporation of state jurisdictional standards in such cases (Akro Corp. v. Luker, Fed. Cir. 1995; DeJames v. Magnificence Carriers, Inc., 3d Cir. 1981).

The more interesting issue arises when a federal statute authorizes nationwide (or even worldwide) service of process. For example, the Securities Exchange Act of 1934 authorizes service of process "in any . . . district of which the defendant is an inhabitant or wherever the defendant may be found" (15 U.S.C. § 78aa). Like other statutes authorizing nationwide service of process, this statute (coupled with Rule 4(k)(1)(D)) has often been interpreted to permit a federal district court to assert personal jurisdiction over a defendant served anywhere in the country (United Liberty Life Ins. Co. v. Ryan, 6th Cir. 1993; Briesch v. Automobile Club, D. Utah 1999). In enacting nationwide service statutes, Congress recognized that judicial economy would be achieved if all facets of a complex case impacting the national economy could be litigated in a single proceeding regardless of where individual defendants might be located (Oxford First Corp. v. PNC Liquidating Corp., E.D. Pa. 1974).

But are assertions of jurisdiction under these statutes consistent with the Due Process Clause of the Fifth Amendment? Put more concretely, if a defendant resides in New York and engages in securities fraud in New York, is it constitutional for a district court in Alaska to assert personal jurisdiction over her?

A related Fifth Amendment issue arises in federal question cases under Rule 4(k)(2), where a nonresident alien defendant lacks sufficient contacts with any state in the union but has contacts with the country as a whole. Is it constitutional to gauge the foreign defendant's amenability to suit in federal court on the basis of her aggregated contacts with the United States?

Twice, the Supreme Court has expressly declined to decide the appropriate standard for gauging the constitutionality of assertions of jurisdiction by federal district courts under the Fifth Amendment Due Process Clause (Omni Capital Int'l, Ltd. v. Rudolf Wolff & Co., 1987; Asahi Metal Indus. Co. v. Superior Ct., 1987). In the absence of guidance from the Supreme Court, the lower federal courts have applied three main approaches in determining whether an assertion of personal jurisdiction in a federal question case under a nationwide service of process statute comports with the Fifth Amendment Due Process Clause.[110]

First, most courts—including the Courts of Appeals for the First, Second, Fifth, Sixth, Seventh, Ninth and Eleventh Circuits—have asked whether the defendant's contacts with the United States as a whole, when aggregated, are sufficient to render jurisdiction constitutional.[111] Under this approach, federal courts apply a unique federal standard to gauge the constitutionality of assertions of personal jurisdiction in federal question cases, rather than the standard developed under the Fourteenth Amendment to limit state court jurisdiction, which logically should not limit federal judicial power.

Some courts have invoked a sovereignty rationale to support this majority "aggregated contacts" rule: because the judicial power exercised by federal district courts is not limited by the boundaries of the district or the state, but rather is "co-extensive with the boundaries of the United States, due process requires only that a defendant in a federal suit have minimum contacts with the United States, 'the sovereign that has created the court'" (FTC v. Jim Walter Corp., 5th Cir. 1981). The Supreme Court's conclusion in *Insurance Corp. of Ireland* (1982) that "[t]he personal jurisdiction requirement . . . represents a restriction on judicial power not as a matter of sovereignty, but as a matter of individual liberty," may have weakened the sovereignty rationale (Willingway Hosp. v. Blue Cross & Blue Shield, S.D.Ga. 1994).[112] But the Court's more recent decision in Burnham v. Superior Court (1990), which continues to emphasize sovereignty and territoriality, suggests that the federal government's sovereignty over the territory of the United States will continue to bolster the majority "aggregated contacts" rule (Busch v. Buchman, Buchman & O'Brien, 5th Cir. 1994; Brown v. C.D. Smith Drug Co., D. Del. 1999).

Second, several district courts have applied the *International Shoe* minimum contacts test, asking whether the defendant has sufficient contacts with the district or the state in which the federal court sits to render the assertion of jurisdiction consistent with "traditional notions of fair play and substantial justice" (Wichita Fed. Sav. & Loan Ass'n v. Landmark Group, Inc., D. Kan. 1987; see also Doll v. James Martin Assocs., E.D. Mich. 1984; Bolton v. Gramlich, S.D.N.Y. 1982). If it would be unfair to require a defendant who lacks contacts with the state to defend a suit in state court, then it would be equally unfair, in these courts' view, to require the defendant to defend the action in the federal court next door. According to Robert Casad, this view is not widely accepted today.[113]

Finally, a few courts ask, more broadly, whether an assertion of jurisdiction comports with basic "fairness." These courts reject both of the categorical approaches described above: they refuse to conclude that the Fifth Amendment necessarily is satisfied whenever a defendant served pursuant to a nationwide service statute has sufficient contacts with the United States as a whole, and they decline to apply Fourteenth Amendment standards to gauge the constitutionality of a federal court's assertion of personal jurisdiction. Rather than following either of these categorical approaches, these courts focus on the overall fairness of subjecting the defendant to jurisdiction in the federal court, examining not only the defendant's contacts with the forum, but also the inconvenience the defendant would suffer in defending away from home, the effect a dismissal would have on judicial economy, the probable situs of the discovery proceedings in the case and the likelihood that discovery would be taken away from the defendant's home or place of business in all events; the nature of the defendant's conduct and its impact beyond the borders of her home state; and the likelihood that "Congress's purpose in expanding personal jurisdiction would not be advanced by extending jurisdiction in a particular case" (Willingway Hosp. v. Blue Cross & Blue Shield, S.D. Ga. 1994; see also Republic of Panama v. BCCI Holdings (Luxembourg) S.A., 11th Cir. 1997; Oxford First Corp. v. PNC Liquidating Corp., E.D. Pa. 1974). This approach is consistent with the views of Maryellen Fullerton, who argues that a defendant's residence in, or contacts with, the United States does not necessarily make it reasonable for all federal district courts to exercise personal jurisdiction over him. In her view, "[a] defendant must be afforded the opportunity to demonstrate that the location of the litigation is fundamentally unfair to him," in light of the inconvenience he would suffer, his expectations, if any, that litigation would be commenced in this forum, and the federal interests in maintaining the suit there.[114]

## CONCLUSION

For 130 years, the Supreme Court has read the Due Process Clause of the Fourteenth Amendment as limiting the reach of state court jurisdiction. Early decisions emphasized each state's sovereignty over people and property within its borders but not beyond. As the national economy and the needs of an itinerant population grew in the early part of the twentieth century, the Court came to accept the constitutionality of alternatives to in-state personal service. In 1945, the Supreme Court decided the breakthrough case of International Shoe Co. v. Washington (1945), shifting the focus of jurisdictional analysis from sovereignty and physical presence to minimum contacts and fairness.

Since 1945, the Supreme Court has held that a state may exercise personal jurisdiction over a nonresident defendant who has sufficient minimum contacts with the state such that an assertion of jurisdiction over her comports with traditional notions of fair play and substantial justice. In gauging whether the defendant's contacts with the state are sufficient to support jurisdiction, courts assess the volume of the defendant's contacts with the forum, the degree to which the claim sued upon arises out of or relates to the in-state contacts, and the purposefulness of those contacts. Since 1980, the Court has broadened the analysis further, examining not only the defendant's contacts with the forum state and the burden she would suffer if compelled to defend there, but also a number of other factors that affect the overall reasonableness of an exercise of jurisdiction, including the forum state's interest, the plaintiff's interest, the interstate judicial system's interest in efficiency and the states' shared interest in furthering substantive social policies (World-Wide Volkswagen Corp. v. Woodson, 1980).

## NOTES

1. Pennoyer v. Neff, 95 U.S. 714, 733 (1877).

2. *See* Rhonda Wasserman, *The Subpoena Power*: Pennoyer'*s Last Vestige*, 74 Minn. L. Rev. 37, 60–62 (1989). *See also* Riverside & Dan River Cotton Mills v. Menefee, 237 U.S. 189, 193 (1915).

3. *Cf.* Phillips Petroleum Co. v. Shutts, 472 U.S. 797, 812–14 (1985) (concluding that due process is satisfied even if absent plaintiff class members lack minimum contacts with the state and fail to affirmatively request inclusion in the class as long as they receive notice and an opportunity to opt out); Patrick J. Borchers, *The Death of the Constitutional Law of Personal Jurisdiction: From* Pennoyer *to* Burnham *and Back Again*, 24 U.C. Davis L. Rev. 19, 96 (1990) (hereinafter Borchers, *Death of Constitutional Law*) (noting that "*both* of the parties have a constitutional right to litigate and to protect their property interests at stake in the litigation"); Linda S. Mullenix, *Class Actions, Personal Jurisdiction, and Plaintiffs' Due Process: Implications for Mass Tort Litigation*, 28 U.C. Davis L. Rev. 871, 874 (1995) (referring to plaintiffs' due process rights as "the most compelling jurisdictional issue" of our time, especially in the mass tort litigation context).

4. The full faith and credit statute was first enacted by the act of May 26, 1790, 1 Stat. 122 (1790).

5. Ralph U. Whitten, *The Constitutional Limitations on State-Court Jurisdiction: A Historical-Interpretative Reexamination of the Full Faith and Credit and Due Process Clauses (Part I)*, 14 Creighton L. Rev. 499, 580 (1981) (noting that the "international rules of jurisdiction . . . were conceived of as rules governing the relations of sovereigns with each other, not as rules limiting the legislative authority of a sovereign to bind its own courts internally"). *But see* Beard v. Beard, 21 Ind. 321, 327 (1863) (stating that a judgment rendered against a nonresident upon constructive notice "was not obtained by due process of law" and was not enforceable even in the rendering state).

6. For further discussion of *Pennoyer*, including a far less expansive reading of *Pennoyer*, see note 82 following Chapter 1 and the accompanying text.

7. *See, e.g.*, Patrick J. Borchers, Pennoyer's *Limited Legacy: A Reply to Professor Oakley*, 29 U.C. Davis L. Rev. 115, 118 (1995) (positing that "the fundamental role of the Due Process Clause as a limitation on jurisdiction remained in doubt for four decades after *Pennoyer*," and arguing that "there is no historical impediment to rejecting it as the source of jurisdictional law"); Patrick J. Borchers, *Jurisdictional Pragmatism*: International Shoe*'s Half-Buried Legacy*, 28 U.C. Davis L. Rev. 561, 564 (1995) (hereinafter Borchers, *Jurisdictional Pragmatism*) (arguing that "the Due Process Clause places almost no limitations on personal jurisdiction"); Borchers, *Death of Constitutional Law*, *supra* note 3, at 20, 88–89 (arguing that the Supreme Court should "abandon the notion that state court personal jurisdiction is a matter of constitutional law" and positing that nothing in the history of the Fourteenth Amendment suggests that the Due Process Clause was intended to limit state court jurisdiction); Stephen E. Gottlieb, *In Search of the Link Between Due Process and Jurisdiction*, 60 Wash. U. L.Q. 1291, 1337 (1983) (positing that "due process . . . poorly explains the pattern of jurisdictional rules"); Max Rheinstein, *The Constitutional Bases of Jurisdiction*, 22 U. Chi. L. Rev. 775, 791 (1955) (arguing that territorial limits on state court jurisdiction do not derive from the Due Process Clause of the Fourteenth Amendment); Roger H. Transgrud, *The Federal Common Law of Personal Jurisdiction*, 57 Geo. Wash. L. Rev. 849, 882 (1989) (arguing that "the Supreme Court could have applied its federal common law of jurisdiction to intrastate cases without relying on the Due Process Clause"). *But see* John B. Oakley, *The Pitfalls of "Hit and Run" History: A Critique of Professor Borchers's "Limited View" of* Pennoyer v. Neff, 28 U.C. Davis L. Rev. 591, 753 (1995) (arguing that 120 years of consistent precedent supports "the basic idea that the Due Process Clause limits state court personal jurisdiction").

8. Robert C. Casad, *Personal Jurisdiction in Federal Question Cases*, 70 Tex. L. Rev. 1589, 1591 (1992).

9. Hermine Herta Meyer, The History and Meaning of the Fourteenth Amendment: Judicial Erosion of the Constitution Through the Misuse of the Fourteenth Amendment 126–27 (1977); *see also* Ralph U. Whitten, *The Constitutional Limitations on State Court Jurisdiction: A Historical-Interpretative Reexamination of the Full Faith and Credit and Due Process Clauses (Part II)*, 14 Creighton L. Rev. 735, 805–08, 811–12 (1981) (hereinafter Whitten II).

10. *Id.* at 808, 818, 821, 835.

11. Rheinstein, *supra* note 7, at 796, 802, 812, 816.

12. Transgrud, *supra* note 7, at 852, 858–71.

13. *See, e.g.*, Borchers, *Death of Constitutional Law*, *supra* note 3, at 24; Borchers, *Jurisdictional Pragmatism*, *supra* note 7, at 566–68; endnote 82 following Chapter 1.

14. *See, e.g.*, Borchers, *Death of Constitutional Law*, *supra* note 3, at 90 n. 469 (noting the awkwardness of the characterization issue); Richard H. Fallon, Jr., *Some Confusion About Due Process, Judicial Review, and Constitutional Remedies*, 93 Colum. L. Rev. 309, 317–18 (1993); Wendy Collins Perdue, *Sin, Scandal, and Substantive Due Process: Personal Jurisdiction and* Pennoyer *Reconsidered*, 62 Wash. L. Rev. 479, 508 & n.183 (1987). *See also* Kevin M. Clermont, Civil Procedure: Territorial Jurisdiction and Venue 22 (1999) (stating that "[j]urisdictional restrictions are rather substantive compared to the other procedural dictates of due process"). Justice Field, the author of Pennoyer v. Neff, 95 U.S. 714 (1877), the landmark case that first noted that due process restricts state court jurisdiction,

was a "pioneer and prophet" of substantive due process doctrine. Perdue, *supra*, at 503 (footnote omitted).

15. *See* Lochner v. New York, 198 U.S. 45 (1905).

16. Perdue, *supra* note 14, at 508 n.183.

17. *Accord* Whitten II, *supra* note 9, at 837 (noting that it is "possible to reason that a place of trial which does not impose relatively enormous burdens upon the defendant is essential to afford him an adequate opportunity to defend"). *See also* Peter N. Simon, *Liberty and Property in the Supreme Court: A Defense of* Roth *and* Perry, 71 Cal. L. Rev. 145, 148 (1983) (stating that "[a]s early as the decision in *Pennoyer v. Neff*, the due process guarantee was viewed as providing *procedural* protection of traditional property. . . .") (footnote omitted) (emphasis added); *id.* at 176; Borchers, *Jurisdictional Pragmatism*, *supra* note 7, at 578–79, 582 (concluding that "personal jurisdiction is a subject whose dimensions are almost completely procedural"); Martin H. Redish & Eric J. Beste, *Personal Jurisdiction and the Global Resolution of Mass Tort Litigation: Defining the Constitutional Boundaries*, 28 U.C. Davis L. Rev. 917, 922 & n.16 (1995) (arguing that jurisdictional doctrine is properly viewed as a subpart of procedural due process analysis).

18. Rheinstein, *supra* note 7, at 790 (footnote omitted).

19. *See also* Courtland H. Peterson, *Proposals of Marriage Between Jurisdiction and Choice of Law*, 14 U.C. Davis L. Rev. 869, 880–81 (1981) (noting that the minimum contacts test for personal jurisdiction "was mainly, although perhaps not exclusively, designed to protect the defendant from *unfair surprise* with respect to the forum in which he might be summoned to defend") (emphasis added).

20. One leading casebook, William Cohen & Jonathan D. Varat, Constitutional Law: Cases and Materials 473 (11th ed. 2001), devotes a paragraph to personal jurisdiction.

21. The brief description of the case that follows fails to mention the colorful personalities of the players and the fascinating story of deception that underlies *Pennoyer*. For an entertaining account of this background, *see* Perdue, *supra* note 14, at 480–90.

22. "A judgment *in rem* affects the interests of all persons in designated property." Hanson v. Denckla, 357 U.S. 235, 246 n.12 (1958).

23. "A judgment *quasi in rem* affects the interests of particular persons in designated property." *Id.* at 246 n.12.

24. Some states afford the defendant in a *quasi-in-rem* action an opportunity to defend on the merits while still limiting her liability to the value of the property seized. This opportunity is referred to as a limited appearance. Jack H. Friedenthal et al., Civil Procedure § 3.27, at 191 (3d ed. 1999).

25. New Hampshire and Minnesota also permitted *Seider* jurisdiction. See Savchuk v. Rush, 272 N.W.2d 888 (Minn. 1978) (en banc) (upholding the garnishment of a nonresident defendant's insurance policy as a means of obtaining jurisdiction), *rev'd*, 444 U.S. 320 (1980); Forbes v. Boynton, 313 A.2d 129 (N.H. 1973) (upholding the use of *Seider* jurisdiction in a suit by a New Hampshire resident against a New York resident); *but see* Camire v. Scieszka, 358 A.2d 397 (N.H. 1976) (rejecting *Seider* jurisdiction on the facts of the case).

26. *See, e.g.*, Fed. R. Civ. P. 12(h)(1); Fla. R. Civ. P. 1.140(b); N.J. Court Rules, 1969 R. 4:6–7; Or. R. Civ. P. 21 (G)(1); Wis. Stat. § 802.06(8)(a). *See also* Ins. Corp. of Ir. v. Compagnie des Bauxites de Guinee, 456 U.S. 694, 704 (1982).

27. The Privileges and Immunities Clause provides: "The Citizens of each State shall be entitled to all Privileges and Immunities of Citizens in the several States." U.S. Const. art. IV, § 2.

28. *Pennoyer* acknowledged this possibility, too, adding that a state could

> require a non-resident entering into a partnership or association within its limits, or making contracts enforceable there, to appoint an agent or representative in the State to receive service of process . . . and provide, upon their failure, to make such appointment or to designate such place that service may be made upon a public officer designated for that purpose . . . .

*Pennoyer*, 95 U.S. at 735.

29. *See, e.g.*, 10 Del. C. § 3114 (2000); N.C. Gen. Stat. § 1–75.4(8) (2000).

30. Friedenthal, et al., *supra* note 24, § 3.7, at 111.

31. *See, e.g.*, Lebowitz v. Forbes Leasing & Fin. Corp., 456 F.2d 979 (3d Cir.), *cert. denied*, 409 U.S. 843 (1972), *overruled by* Jonnet v. Dollar Sav. Bank, 530 F.2d 1123 (3d Cir. 1976); Great Am. Ins. Co. v. Louis Lesser Enters., Inc., 353 F.2d 997, 1007 (8th Cir. 1965); United States v. Balanovski, 236 F.2d 298, 302 (2d Cir. 1956); ABKCO Ind., Inc. v. Apple Films, Inc., 350 N.E.2d 899, 900 (N.Y. 1976); Fairchild Engine & Airplane Corp. v. Bellanca Corp., 137 A.2d 248, 250 (Pa. 1958). *But see* U.S. Indus., Inc. v. Gregg, 540 F.2d 142, 154 (3d Cir. 1976) (concluding that *International Shoe* governs the constitutionality of assertions of *quasi-in-rem* jurisdiction); Jonnet v. Dollar Sav. Bank, 530 F.2d 1123, 1130 (3d Cir. 1976) (Gibbons, C.J., concurring) (arguing that *International Shoe* should govern the constitutionality of assertions of *quasi-in-rem* jurisdiction).

32. The *International Shoe* Court itself may have been ambivalent about jettisoning the sovereignty rationale as it acknowledged that reasonableness should be assessed "in the context of our federal system of government." Int'l Shoe Co. v. Washington, 326 U.S. 310, 317 (1945). *See also* Wasserman, *supra* note 2, at 57 & n.94 (identifying other language in *International Shoe* that suggested the continued viability of the sovereignty rationale).

33. A rich academic literature debates the role of interstate federalism in restricting state court jurisdiction. *See, e.g.*, Dan Braveman, *Interstate Federalism and Personal Jurisdiction*, 33 Syracuse L. Rev. 533 (1982); Harold L. Korn, *The Development of Judicial Jurisdiction in the United States, Part I*, 65 Brook. L. Rev. 935 (1999); Harold S. Lewis, Jr., *The Three Deaths of "State Sovereignty" and the Curse of Abstraction in the Jurisprudence of Personal Jurisdiction*, 58 Notre Dame L. Rev. 699 (1983); Martin H. Redish, *Due Process, Federalism, and Personal Jurisdiction: A Theoretical Evaluation*, 75 Nw. U.L. Rev. 1112 (1981).

34. Because the *World-Wide Volkswagen* Court concluded that the defendants lacked minimum contacts with Oklahoma, it had no occasion to apply the reasonableness factors it had identified earlier in its opinion. *See* World-Wide Volkswagen Corp. v. Woodson, 444 U.S. 286, 294, 298–99 (1980).

35. 4 Charles Alan Wright & Arthur R. Miller, Federal Practice and Procedure § 1067.6, at 538–53 (3d ed. 2002); 1 Robert C. Casad & William B. Richman, Jurisdiction in Civil Actions § 2–5[d][ii] (3d ed. 1998).

36. *See, e.g. Asahi*, 480 U.S. at 114; Amoco Egypt Oil Co. v. Leonis Navigation Co., 1 F.3d 848, 852 (9th Cir. 1993); Fields v. Sedgwick Associated Risks, Ltd., 796 F.2d 299, 302 (9th Cir. 1986). *Cf.* Nowak v. Tak How Invs., Ltd., 94 F.3d 708, 718 (1st Cir. 1996) (rejecting the argument that a Hong Kong defendant's burden would be especially burdensome).

37. *Cf.* 1 Casad & Richman, *supra* note 35, § 2–5[d][vii] (arguing that choice of law is relevant to the fourth reasonableness factor, efficiency).

38. *See id.* § 2–5[d][vii].

39. Arthur T. von Mehren & Donald T. Trautman, The Law of Multistate Problems: Cases and Materials on Conflict of Laws 654 (1965); Arthur T. von Mehren & Donald T. Trautman, *Jurisdiction to Adjudicate: A Suggested Analysis*, 79 Harv. L. Rev. 1121, 1136 (1966).

40. Mary Twitchell, *The Myth of General Jurisdiction*, 101 Harv. L. Rev. 610 (1988).

41. *See id.* at 614 & n.19, 621, 634 (noting that voluntary appearance at trial and appointment of a local agent for receipt of process support general jurisdiction).

42. For a more complete factual history and an interesting critique of the Supreme Court's jurisdictional jurisprudence, see Louise Weinberg, *The Helicopter Case and the Jurisprudence of Jurisdiction*, 58 S. Cal. L. Rev. 913 (1985).

43. *See also* Carnival Cruise Lines, Inc. v. Shute, 499 U.S. 585, 588–89 (1991) (declining to address the nexus required for a claim to "arise out of or relate to" forum contacts).

44. Metro. Life Ins. Co. v. Robertson-Ceco Corp., 84 F.3d 560, 573 (2d Cir. 1996). *See, e.g.*, Gator.com v. L.L. Bean, Inc., 341 F.3d 1072, 1080 (9th Cir. 2003); Wiwa v. Royal Dutch Petroleum Co., 226 F.3d 88, 99 (2d Cir. 2000); Donatelli v. Nat'l Hockey League, 893 F.2d 459, 465 (1st Cir. 1990); Bearry v. Beech Aircraft Corp., 818 F.2d 370, 377 (5th Cir. 1987).

45. *See, e.g.*, BE&K Constr. Co. v. United Bhd. of Carpenters, 688 So. 2d 246, 250 (Ala.), *cert. denied*, 521 U.S. 1118 (1997); Reyes v. Marine Mgmt. & Consulting, Ltd., 586 So. 2d 103, 109, 111 (La. 1991) (requiring consideration of the reasonableness factors, but concluding that a demonstration of continuous and systematic contacts creates a heavier presumption in favor of jurisdiction than does a few purposeful contacts in a specific jurisdiction case). *Cf.* Anthem Ins. Cos. v. Tenet Healthcare Corp., 730 N.E.2d 1227, 1236 (Ind. 2000) (stating that reasonableness factors are part of the analysis in a general jurisdiction case, but concluding that a finding of continuous and systematic contacts "ensures that jurisdiction over a particular defendant is reasonable").

46. Lea Brilmayer, *How Contacts Count: Due Process Limitations on State Court Jurisdiction*, 1980 Sup. Ct. Rev. 77, 82 (hereinafter Brilmayer, *How Contacts Count*).

47. Twitchell, *supra* note 40, at 613.

48. *Id.*

49. *Id.* at 660–62 (using a similar hypothetical involving an automobile manufacturer that sells similar cars in both the forum state and the state in which the accident occurs).

50. *See* Lea Brilmayer, *Colloquy: Related Contacts and Personal Jurisdiction*, 101 Harv. L. Rev. 1444, 1460 (1988) (questioning "why a defective product sent into the state but causing no injury is as strong a basis for jurisdiction as a defective product sent into the state that does cause injury"); Twitchell, *supra* note 40, at 660–61 (applying Brilmayer's substantive relevance test to a similar hypothetical).

51. Twitchell, *supra* note 40, at 661.

52. *See, e.g.*, Kuenzle v. HTM Sport-Und Freizeitgerate AG, 102 F.3d 453, 456–57 (10th Cir. 1996); Bearry v. Beech Aircraft Corp., 818 F.2d 370, 373 (5th Cir. 1987); Glater v. Eli Lilly & Co., 744 F.2d 213, 216 (1st Cir. 1984); Jones v. N. Am. Aerodynamics, Inc., 594 F. Supp. 657, 662 (D. Me. 1984); Ex Parte Newco Mfg. Co., 481 So. 2d 867, 869 (Ala. 1985).

53. *See, e.g.*, Ticketmaster-N.Y., Inc. v. Alioto, 26 F.3d 201, 206 (1st Cir. 1994) (arguing that the "or relates to" language "portends added flexibility and signals a relaxation of the applicable standard"); Vencedor Mfg. Co. v. Gougler Indus., Inc., 557 F.2d 886, 889 (1st Cir. 1977) (holding that the defendant's sales of the same or similar products to other purchasers in the jurisdiction "are also 'related' to the present cause of action").

54. *See, e.g.*, B & J Mfg. v. Solar Indus., 483 F.2d 594, 598 (8th Cir. 1973), *cert. denied*, 415 U.S. 918 (1974); *see also* Akro Corp. v. Luker, 45 F.3d 1541, 1547–48 (Fed. Cir. 1995); Nova Biomedical Corp. v. Moller, 629 F.2d 190, 195–96 & n.9 (1st Cir. 1980).

55. Omeluk v. Langsten Slip & Batbyggeri A/S, 52 F.3d 267, 271–72 (9th Cir. 1995). *See also* Bancroft & Masters, Inc. v. Augusta Nat'l, Inc., 223 F.3d 1082, 1088 (9th Cir. 2000); Prejean v. Sonatrach, Inc., 652 F.2d 1260, 1270 n.21 (5th Cir. 1981); Lanier v. Am. Bd. of Endodontics, 843 F.2d 901, 908–09 (6th Cir.), *cert. denied*, 488 U.S. 926 (1988); Tatro v. Manor Care, Inc., 625 N.E.2d 549, 553–54 (Mass. 1994). For a thorough discussion of the "but for" test for relatedness, as well as alternatives to that test, see Flavio Rose, *Related Contacts and Personal Jurisdiction: The "But For" Test*, 82 Cal. L. Rev. 1545 (1994).

56. *See, e.g.*, Songbyrd, Inc. v. Grossman, 206 F.3d 172, 181 (2d Cir. 2000) (concluding that a "but for" connection is "too tenuous" to support specific jurisdiction); Nowak v. Tak How Invs., Ltd., 94 F.3d 708, 715–16 (1st Cir. 1996) (rejecting the "but for" test, but not requiring strict adherence to a proximate cause standard in every case). *See also* Pearrow v. Nat'l Life & Accident Ins. Co., 703 F.2d 1067, 1069 (8th Cir. 1983); Gelfand v. Tanner Motor Tours, Ltd., 339 F.2d 317, 321–22 (2d Cir. 1964).

57. The Seventh Circuit often applies this test in determining whether the Illinois long-arm statute, which requires that the cause of action "arise from" the defendant's contacts, is satisfied. *See, e.g.*, Great Lakes Overseas, Inc. v. Wah Kwong Shipping Group, Ltd., 990 F.2d 990, 998 (7th Cir. 1993); Heritage House Rest., Inc. v. Cont'l Funding Group, Inc., 906 F.2d 276, 281 (7th Cir. 1990); John Walker & Sons, Ltd. v. DeMert & Dougherty, Inc., 821 F.2d 399, 403 (7th Cir. 1987); Deluxe Ice Cream Co. v. R.C.H. Tool Corp., 726 F.2d 1209, 1215 (7th Cir. 1984).

58. *See, e.g.*, ESAB Group, Inc. v. Centricut, Inc., 126 F.3d 617, 624–25 (4th Cir. 1997); Pizarro v. Hoteles Concorde Int'l, C.A., 907 F.2d 1256, 1260 (1st Cir. 1990); *Bearry*, 818 F.2d at 376; *Glater*, 744 F.2d at 217; Brokemond v. Marshall Field & Co., 612 N.E.2d 143, 146 (Ind. Ct. App. 1993). *But see* Glover v. W. Air Lines, Inc., 745 P.2d 1365 (Alaska 1987).

59. *See, e.g.*, Wiwa v. Royal Dutch Petroleum Co., 226 F.3d 88, 98 (2d Cir. 2000); Provident Nat'l Bank v. California Fed. Sav. & Loan Ass'n, 819 F.2d 434, 438 (3d Cir. 1987); Reyes v. Marine Mgmt. & Consulting, Ltd., 586 So. 2d 103, 109–11 (La. 1991).

60. *Compare* Kuenzle v. HTM Sport-Und Freizeitgerate AG, 102 F.3d 453, 459 (10th Cir. 1996) (holding that "in the absence of an agency relationship, the acts of a distributor are not ordinarily attributable to a foreign manufacturer for purposes of establishing general jurisdiction"); Conti v. Pneumatic Prods. Corp., 977 F.2d 978, 981 (6th Cir. 1992) (finding that a manufacturer that sold its products in Ohio through two distributors, one of whom had annual sales of $900,000, was not subject to general jurisdiction there); *and* Cascade Corp. v. Hiab-Foco AB, 619 F.2d 36, 37 (9th Cir. 1980) (finding neither general nor specific jurisdiction over a Swedish manufacturer whose products were sold in the forum state through independent distributors); *with* Mich. Nat'l Bank v. Quality Dinette,

Inc., 888 F.2d 462, 465–66 (6th Cir. 1989) (concluding that the Alabama defendants were subject to general jurisdiction in Michigan based upon the regular sales of their products there by an independent sales representative); *and* Ex Parte Newco Mfg. Co., 481 So. 2d 867, 869 (Ala. 1985) (concluding that sales by an independent manufacturer's representative supported an assertion of general jurisdiction).

61. Bruce Posnak, *The Court Doesn't Know Its* Asahi *From Its* Wortman: *A Critical View of the Constitutional Constraints on Jurisdiction and Choice of Law*, 41 Syracuse L. Rev. 875, 886 (1990).

62. The plaintiffs' lawyer believed that juries in the county where the accident happened, Creek County, Oklahoma, would be more sympathetic and generous than would federal juries, drawn from a much wider geographical area. Thus, the plaintiffs fought mightily to keep Seaway and World-Wide Volkswagen in the case. Like plaintiffs, these defendants were New York citizens. The defendants could not remove the suit to federal court if there were New York parties as both plaintiffs and defendants. Charles W. Adams, World-Wide Volkswagen v. Woodson—*The Rest of the Story*, 72 Neb. L. Rev. 1122, 1128–29 (1993).

63. *See, e.g.*, Clune v. Alimak AB, 233 F.3d 538, 542–45 (8th Cir. 2000); Barone v. Rich Bros. Interstate Display Fireworks Co., 25 F.3d 610, 614–15 (8th Cir. 1994); Ruston Gas Turbines, Inc. v. Donaldson Co., 9 F.3d 415, 420 (5th Cir. 1993); Ham v. La Cienega Music Co., 4 F.3d 413, 416 n.11 (5th Cir. 1993); Dehmlow v. Austin Fireworks, 963 F.2d 941, 947 (7th Cir. 1992); Irving v. Owens-Corning Fiberglas Corp., 864 F.2d 383, 385–86 (5th Cir.), *cert. denied*, 493 U.S. 823 (1989).

64. *See, e.g.*, Rodriguez v. Fullerton Tires Corp., 115 F.3d 81, 85 (1st Cir. 1997); Lesnick v. Hollingsworth & Vose Co., 35 F.3d 939, 945–47 (4th Cir. 1994); Boit v. Gar-Tec Prods., Inc., 967 F.2d 671, 682–83 (1st Cir. 1992); Witbeck v. Bill Cody's Ranch Inn, 411 N.W.2d 439, 448 (Mich. 1987); Anderson v. Metro. Life Ins. Co., 694 A.2d 701, 703 (R.I. 1997); CSR Ltd. v. Link, 925 S.W.2d 591, 595–96 (Tex. 1996). *See also* Madara v. Hall, 916 F.2d 1510, 1517 (11th Cir. 1990) (applying the reasoning of the *Asahi* plurality to the libel context).

65. *See, e.g.*, Kernan v. Kurz-Hastings, Inc., 175 F.3d 236, 243–44 (2d Cir. 1999); Pennzoil Prods. Co. v. Colelli & Assocs., Inc., 149 F.3d 197, 206–07 (3d Cir. 1998); Viam Corp. v. Iowa Export-Import Trading Co., 84 F.3d 424, 428 (Fed. Cir. 1996); Tanner v. Illinois Tool Works, Inc., 1996 U.S. App. LEXIS 5378, *7 n.1 (9th Cir. 1996) (mem.); Beverly Hills Fan Co. v. Royal Sovereign Corp., 21 F.3d 1558, 1566 (Fed. Cir. 1994); Vermeulen v. Renault, U.S.A., Inc., 985 F.2d 1534, 1548 (11th Cir. 1993); Tobin v. Astra Pharm. Prods., Inc., 993 F.2d 528, 543–44 (6th Cir. 1993); Morris v. SSE, Inc., 843 F.2d 489, 493–94 & n.5 (11th Cir. 1988).

66. Previously, the Court had declined to uphold jurisdiction on the theory that a father who sent his child to live in California had caused an effect there. Kulko v. Superior Ct., 436 U.S. 84, 96–98 (1978).

67. *See, e.g.*, Bancroft & Masters, Inc. v. Augusta Nat'l Inc., 223 F.3d 1082, 1087 (9th Cir. 2000); Imo Indus., Inc. v. Kiekert AG, 155 F.3d 254, 265 (3d Cir. 1998); ESAB Group, Inc. v. Centricut, Inc., 126 F3d 617, 625–26 (4th Cir. 1997); Far W. Capital, Inc. v. Towne, 46 F.3d 1071, 1079–80 (10th Cir. 1995); Reynolds v. Int'l Amateur Athletic Fed'n, 23 F.3d 1110, 1119–20 (6th Cir. 1994). *See also* Griffis v. Luban, 646 N.W.2d 527, 533–34 (Minn. 2002) (surveying the decisions of the federal courts of appeals after *Calder*).

68. Rippey v. Smith, 16 Fed. Appx. 596, 598 (9th Cir. 2001); Remick v. Manfredy, 238 F.3d 248, 258–59 (3d Cir. 2001); *Bancroft & Masters*, 223 F.3d at 1087–88; *Imo Indus., Inc.*, 155 F.3d at 265–66.

69. *See, e.g.*, Wien Air Alaska, Inc. v. Brandt, 195 F.3d 208, 212 (5th Cir. 1999); Wallace v. Herron, 778 F.2d 391, 395 (7th Cir. 1985).

70. *Bancroft & Masters*, 223 F.3d 1082 (9th Cir. 2000).

71. *Remick*, 238 F.3d 248 (3d Cir. 2001).

72. *Janmark*, 132 F.3d 1200 (7th Cir. 1997).

73. *Rippey*, 16 Fed. Appx. 596 (9th Cir. 2001); *Wien Air Alaska*, 195 F.3d 208 (5th Cir. 1999); Metro. Life Ins. Co. v. Neaves, 912 F.2d 1062, 1065 (9th Cir. 1990).

74. For a thorough compilation of cases addressing this issue, see Richard E. Kaye, Annotation, *Internet Web Site Activities of Nonresident Person or Corporation as Conferring Personal Jurisdiction Under Long-Arm Statutes and Due Process Clause*, 81 A.L.R.5th 41 (2001).

75. ALS Scan, Inc. v. Digital Serv. Consultants, Inc., 293 F.3d 707, 714 (4th Cir. 2002).

76. Mink v. AAAA Dev. LLC, 190 F.3d 333, 336 (5th Cir. 1999).

77. Gator.com v. L.L. Bean, Inc., 341 F.3d 1072, 1079–80 (9th Cir. 2003); Cybersell, Inc. v. Cybersell, Inc., 130 F.3d 414, 419 (9th Cir. 1997).

78. Soma Med. Int'l v. Standard Chartered Bank, 196 F.3d 1292, 1296–97 (10th Cir. 1999).

79. *See, e.g.*, Intercon, Inc. v. Bell Atlantic Internet Solutions, Inc., 205 F.3d 1244, 1247–48 (10th Cir. 2000); CompuServe, Inc. v. Patterson, 89 F.3d 1257, 1263–65 (6th Cir. 1996); *Zippo*, 952 F. Supp. at 1125–26.

80. For cases concluding that a defendant is not subject to jurisdiction on the basis of a passive web site, *see, e.g.*, *Cybersell*, 130 F.3d at 419–20; Revell v. Lidov, 2001 U.S. Dist. LEXIS 3133 (N.D. Tex. Mar. 20, 2001), *aff'd on slightly different grounds*, 317 F.3d 467 (5th Cir. 2002); Bensusan Rest. Corp. v. King, 937 F. Supp. 295, 301 (S.D.N.Y. 1996), *aff'd*, 126 F.3d 25 (2d Cir. 1997). Some courts have held that a defendant that maintains a passive web site is subject to jurisdiction if it also has additional contacts with the forum state. *See, e.g.*, Nissan Motor Co. v. Nissan Computer Corp., 89 F. Supp. 2d 1154, 1159 (C.D. Cal. 2000); Gary Scott Int'l, Inc. v. Baroudi, 981 F. Supp. 714, 717 (D. Mass. 1997); Heroes, Inc. v. Heroes Found., 958 F. Supp. 1, 4–5 (D.D.C. 1996); EDIAS Software Int'l v. BASIS Int'l Ltd., 947 F. Supp. 413, 419–20 (D. Ariz. 1996).

81. Millennium Enters., Inc. v. Millennium Music, LP, 33 F. Supp. 2d 907, 921 (D. Or. 1999) (citations omitted). *See also* Toys "R" Us, Inc. v. Step Two, S.A., 318 F.3d 446, 454 (3d Cir. 2003); Digital Control Inc. v. Boretronics Inc., 161 F. Supp. 2d 1183, 1186–87 (W.D. Wash. 2001); Revell v. Lidov, 2001 U.S. Dist. LEXIS 3133 (N.D. Tex. Mar. 20, 2001); Bedrejo v. Triple E Canada, Ltd., 984 P.2d 739, 742–43 (Mont. 1999).

82. *See, e.g.*, Revell v. Lidov, 317 F.3d 467 (5th Cir. 2002); ALS Scan, Inc. v. Digital Serv. Consultants, Inc., 293 F.3d 707 (4th Cir. 2002); Bochan v. La Fontaine, 68 F. Supp. 2d 692 (E.D. Va. 1999); Barrett v. Catacombs Press, 44 F. Supp. 2d 717 (E.D. Pa. 1999); Blumenthal v. Drudge, 992 F. Supp. 44 (D.D.C. 1998). *See also* Kaye, *supra* note 74, § 8. *Cf.* Gutnick v. Dow Jones & Co., [2001] VSC 305 (S.Ct. of Victoria, Australia, Aug. 28, 2001), *appeal dismissed*, 194 A.L.R. 433 (Austl. 2002).

83. *See, e.g.*, Mink v. AAAA Dev. LLC, 190 F.3d 333 (5th Cir. 1999); ESAB Group, Inc. v. Centricut, Inc., 126 F.3d 617 (4th Cir. 1997); Stomp, Inc. v. NeatO, LLC, 61 F. Supp. 2d 1074 (C.D. Cal. 1999); Edberg v. Neogen Corp., 17 F. Supp. 2d 104 (D. Conn. 1998). *See also* Kaye, *supra* note 74, § 9.

84. *See, e.g.*, Toys "R" Us, Inc. v. Step Two, S.A., 318 F.3d 446 (3d Cir. 2003); Hasbro, Inc. v. Clue Computing, Inc., 994 F. Supp. 34 (D. Mass. 1997); Digital Equip. Corp. v. AltaVista Tech., Inc., 960 F. Supp. 456 (D. Mass. 1997); *Zippo*, 952 F. Supp. 1119 (W.D. Pa. 1997). *See also* Kaye, *supra* note 74, § 10.

85. *See* Porsche Cars N. Am., Inc. v. Porsche.net, 302 F.3d 248, 259–60 (4th Cir. 2002); Cable News Network L.P. v. cnnews.com, 162 F. Supp. 2d 484, 491 (E.D. Va. 2001); Caesars World, Inc. v. caesars-palace.com, 112 F. Supp. 2d 502, 504 (E.D. Va. 2000). *See generally* Thomas R. Lee, In Rem *Jurisdiction in Cyberspace*, 75 Wash. L. Rev. 97 (2000).

86. *Cable News Network*, 162 F. Supp. 2d at 491; *Caesars World*, 112 F. Supp. 2d at 504. *But see* FleetBoston Fin. Corp. v. fleetbostonfinancial.com, 138 F. Supp. 2d 121, 134 (D. Mass. 2001) (declining to "read the holding of *Shaffer* to be limited to type II *quasi in rem* actions").

87. Harrods Ltd. v. Sixty Internet Domain Names, 302 F.3d 214, 224–25 (4th Cir 2002); *See also Porsche Cars*, 302 F.3d at 259–60.

88. *See* Standing Stone Media, Inc. v. Indiancountrytoday.com, 193 F. Supp. 2d 528, 533–34 (N.D.N.Y. 2002); Ford Motor Co. v. Great Domains.com, Inc., 177 F. Supp. 2d 656, 658–59 (E.D. Mich. 2001); *Cable News Network*, 162 F. Supp. 2d at 489 n.15; Mattel, Inc. v. Barbie-Club.com, 00 Civ. 8705 (DLC), 2001 U.S. Dist. LEXIS 5262, at *4–6 (S.D.N.Y. May 1, 2001); *FleetBoston Fin. Corp.*, 138 F. Supp. 2d at 126, 135.

89. *See, e.g.*, O'Connor v. Lee-Hy Paving Corp., 579 F.2d 194 (2d Cir. 1978); Savchuk v. Rush, 272 N.W.2d 888 (Minn. 1978), *rev'd*, 444 U.S. 320 (1980); Alford v. McGaw, 402 N.Y.S.2d 499 (N.Y. App. Div. 1978).

90. *O'Connor*, 579 F.2d at 197–202; *Savchuk*, 272 N.W.2d at 891–93; *Alford*, 402 N.Y.S.2d at 502–03.

91. *See* Michael B. Mushlin, *The New Quasi in Rem Jurisdiction: New York's Revival of a Doctrine Whose Time Has Passed*, 55 Brook. L. Rev. 1059, 1063 (1990); *see also* Holly S. Haskew, Shaffer, Burnham, *and New York's Continued Use of QIR-2 Jurisdiction: A Resurrection of the Power Theory*, 45 Emory L.J. 239, 257 (1996) (identifying ten states that continue to use attachment jurisdiction in some form).

92. *See, e.g.*, Neb. Rev. Stat. § 25–1001 (2001) (authorizing attachment in specified circumstances, but eliminating the defendant's nonresident status as an independent basis for attachment); Vt. R. Civ. P. 4.1 (Reporter's Notes to 1979 Amendment).

93. Mushlin, *supra* note 91, at 1082–87 (concluding that 37 states fall into this category).

94. Haskew, *supra* note 91, at 257 (listing Florida, Louisiana, Maryland, Minnesota, Mississippi, New Hampshire, New York, North Carolina, Pennsylvania, and Utah); *see also* Mushlin, *supra* note 91, at 1098–1103.

95. N.Y. Civ. Prac. L. & R. 302 (McKinney 2001).

96. Linda J. Silberman, Shaffer v. Heitner: *The End of An Era*, 53 N.Y.U. L. Rev. 33, 71–77 (1978); *see also* Haskew, *supra* note 91, at 257–66.

97. *Shaffer*, 433 U.S. at 211 n.37.

98. *See, e.g.*, Excel Shipping Corp. v. Seatrain Int'l S.A., 584 F. Supp. 734, 741 (E.D.N.Y. 1984); Louring v. Kuwait Boulder Shipping Co., 455 F. Supp. 630, 633 (D. Conn. 1977); Rhoades v. Wright, 622 P.2d 343, 347 (Utah 1980), *cert. denied*, 454 U.S. 897 (1981). *Cf.* J.S. Serv. Ctr. Corp. v. Banco Cont'l, 425 N.Y.S.2d 945, 946–47 (N.Y. Sup. Ct. 1980) (concluding that jurisdiction by necessity may be exercised only if the plaintiff has *no* alternate forum available, not even a forum outside the United States).

99. *See also* 4A Charles Alan Wright & Arthur R. Miller, Federal Practice and Procedure § 1072 (3d ed. 2002); Haskew, *supra* note 91, at 261; Silberman, *supra* note 96, at 72.

100. *Cameco Indus.*, 789 F. Supp. at 203. *Accord Feder*, 441 F. Supp. at 1278; Majique Fashions Ltd. v. Warwick & Co., 414 N.Y.S.2d 916 (N.Y. App. Div. 1979). *See also* Silberman, *supra* note 96, at 74.

101. *See, e.g.*, Daniel O. Bernstine, Shaffer v. Heitner: *A Death Warrant for the Transient Rule of In Personam Jurisdiction*, 25 Vill. L. Rev. 38, 61 (1979–80); Lea Brilmayer *et al.*, *A General Look at General Jurisdiction*, 66 Tex. L. Rev. 723, 748–755 (1988); Albert A. Ehrenzweig, *The Transient Rule of Personal Jurisdiction: The "Power" Myth and Forum Conveniens*, 65 Yale L.J. 289 (1956); Donald J. Werner, *Dropping the Other* Shoe: Shaffer v. Heitner *and the Demise of Presence-Oriented Jurisdiction*, 45 Brook. L. Rev. 565 (1979); *The Supreme Court, 1976 Term, Leading Cases*, 91 Harv. L. Rev. 70, 159–60 (1977).

102. *See, e.g.*, Nehemiah v. Athletics Congress, 765 F.2d 42, 46–47 (3d Cir. 1985); Harold M. Pitman Co. v. Typecraft Software Ltd., 626 F. Supp. 305, 312 (N.D. Ill. 1986); Schreiber v. Allis-Chalmers Corp., 448 F. Supp. 1079, 1089 (D. Kan. 1978), *rev'd on other grounds*, 611 F.2d 790 (10th Cir. 1979).

103. *See, e.g.*, Rittenhouse v. Mabry, 832 F.2d 1380 (5th Cir. 1987); Amusement Equip., Inc. v. Mordelt, 779 F.2d 264, 269 (5th Cir. 1985); Moore v. Lindsay, 1989 U.S. Dist. LEXIS 18042 (W.D. Va. 1989); Scholz Research & Dev., Inc. v. Kurzke, 720 F. Supp. 710, 713 (N.D. Ill. 1989).

104. For a critique of Justice White's non-individualized approach to this due process question, *see* Mary Twitchell, Burnham *and Constitutionally Permissible Levels of Harm*, 22 Rutgers L.J. 659 (1991).

105. *See generally* 4 Wright & Miller, *supra* note 35, § 1068.1; 4A *id.* at §1075; 1 Casad & Richman, *supra* note 35, ch. 5; Casad, *supra* note 8.

106. In addition, Rule 4(k)(1) authorizes jurisdiction over a party joined under Rule 14 or Rule 19 who "is served at a place within a judicial district of the United States and not more than 100 miles from the place from which the summons issues," Fed. R. Civ. P. 4(k)(1)(B), or over a defendant "who is subject to the federal interpleader jurisdiction under 28 U.S.C. § 1335. . . ." Fed. R. Civ. P. 4(k)(1)(C).

107. Leslie M. Kelleher, *The December 1993 Amendments to the Federal Rules of Civil Procedure—A Critical Analysis*, 12 Touro L. Rev. 7, 35 (1995). Kelleher maintains that Rule 4(k)(2) is invalid under the Rules Enabling Act because it abridges a substantive right. *See* Leslie M. Kelleher, *Amenability to Jurisdiction As a "Substantive Right": The Invalidity of Rule 4(k) Under the Rules Enabling Act,* 75 Ind. L.J. 1191 (2000).

108. *See also* 4 Wright & Miller, *supra* note 35, § 1068.1, at 592; 4A *id.* § 1075, at 384; Casad, *supra* note 8, at 1595.

109. 4 Wright & Miller, *supra* note 35, § 1068.1, at 598–99.

110. *Cf.* Casad, *supra* note 8, at 1599–1606 (discussing four approaches).

111. *See, e.g.*, ISI Int'l, Inc. v. Borden Ladner Gervais LLP, 256 F.3d 548, 551 (7th Cir. 2001); SEC v. Carrillo, 115 F.3d 1540, 1544 (11th Cir. 1997); United Liberty Life Ins. Co. v. Ryan, 985 F.2d 1320, 1330 (6th Cir. 1993); United Elec. Workers v. 163 Pleasant St. Corp., 960 F.2d 1080, 1085 (1st Cir. 1992); Go-Video, Inc. v. Akai Elec. Co., 885 F.2d 1406, 1414–16 (9th Cir. 1989); FTC v. Jim Walter Corp., 651 F.2d 251, 256 (5th Cir. 1981); Tex. Trading & Milling Co. v. Fed. Republic of Nigeria, 647 F.2d 300, 314–15 (2d Cir. 1981), *cert. denied*, 454 U.S. 1148 (1982). *But see* Republic of Panama v. BCCI Holdings (Luxembourg) S.A., 119 F.3d 935, 945 (11th Cir. 1997).

112. *See also* Whitten II, *supra* note 9, at 850 (concluding that it is "improper" to invoke the sovereign boundaries of the United States to support the constitutionality of nationwide service-of-process statutes).

113. Casad, *supra* note 8, at 1600.

114. Maryellen Fullerton, *Constitutional Limits on Nationwide Personal Jurisdiction in the Federal Courts*, 79 Nw. U. L. Rev. 1, 85 (1984); *see also* Robert A. Lusardi, *Nationwide Service of Process: Due Process Limitations on the Power of the Sovereign*, 33 Vill. L. Rev. 1, 23, 32–38 (1988); Pamela J. Stephens, *The Federal Court Across the Street: Constitutional Limits on Federal Court Assertions of Personal Jurisdiction*, 18 U. Rich. L. Rev. 697 (1984).

# 7

# Due Process Limitations on Choice of Law

In multistate cases—cases in which the parties are from different states or events underlying the claim occurred in more than one state—the forum must choose which state's law should govern. Similar choice-of-law problems arise in cases with connections to more than one country. Ordinarily, when a court in the forum state chooses between the laws of two or more states or countries, it applies its own choice-of-law principles to make this selection. Choice-of-law principles are designed to select the most appropriate law to govern the multistate case and to ensure that the forum in which the suit is filed does not affect the outcome of the case.[1] Many different choice-of-law theories exist[2] and state courts have considerable freedom in selecting the choice-of-law theory to apply, which in turn yields the substantive and procedural law to govern the controversy. The Constitution does impose a modest check, however, on a state's authority to choose its own law to govern the controversy.

The Due Process Clause of the Fourteenth Amendment and the Full Faith and Credit Clause of Article IV of the Constitution provide the primary restrictions on choice of law, although other clauses of the Constitution have relevance as well.[3] After a brief examination of the relationship between full faith and credit and due process in this context, we will focus on the extent to which the Due Process Clause limits state choice-of-law decisions, beginning first with the early Supreme Court decisions and moving on to current standards.

## CONSTITUTIONAL SOURCES OF THE LIMITATIONS ON STATE CHOICE OF LAW

The Due Process Clause of the Fourteenth Amendment does not explicitly regulate state choice of law. Thus, one wonders why it was interpreted to regulate choice of law; how the limitations on choice of law imposed by the Due Process Clause mesh with those imposed by the Full Faith and Credit Clause; and whether the due process protection from the application of unanticipated foreign law is a procedural one. We begin with an examination of these preliminary questions.

### Full Faith and Credit and Due Process Clauses

The Supreme Court has relied on both the Due Process and Full Faith and Credit Clauses to regulate a state's authority to apply its own law to a controversy with which it has little connection (Home Ins. Co. v. Dick, 1930 (due process); Bradford Elec. Light Co. v. Clapper, 1932 (full faith and credit); Watson v. Employers Liab. Assurance Corp., 1954 (both)). Both clauses have relevance in this context, but they monitor different relationships and address different concerns. The Due Process Clause monitors the relationship between the individual and the state. It limits the territorial reach of state power and ensures that the individual is treated fairly in the exercise of that power.[4] If the forum has no connection to the parties or the controversy, application of its law would frustrate the legitimate expectations of the parties.[5] If forum law would impose a burden on a person that another jurisdiction's law would not, the person may be deprived of life, liberty or property without due process of law.[6] The Full Faith and Credit Clause, on the other hand, monitors relationships among the states. It preserves the federal union by requiring each state to respect the sovereignty of other states. If a state applies its own law to a controversy in which another state has a substantially greater interest, it may violate the Full Faith and Credit Clause.[7]

Earlier in our history, the Supreme Court construed the limitations on state choice of law imposed by the Full Faith and Credit Clause as more stringent than those imposed by due process: while it would satisfy due process for a state to apply its own law to a contract made within the state even if it were to be performed elsewhere, it nevertheless would violate the Full Faith and Credit Clause if the foreign state's interests in the controversy were superior to the forum state's interests (Alaska Packers Ass'n v. Indus. Accident Comm'n, 1935). In recent years, however, the Supreme Court has abandoned the full faith and credit balancing test (Franchise Tax Bd. v. Hyatt, 2003) and has repeatedly held that the limits on state choice of law imposed by the Full Faith and Credit and Due Process Clauses of the Constitution are co-extensive (Phillips Petroleum Co. v. Shutts, 1985; Allstate Ins. Co. v. Hague, 1981). Although the Court typically addresses constitutional challenges to choice of law under both the Due Process and Full Faith and Credit Clauses, in its most recent decision, it applied only the Full Faith and Credit Clause (Franchise Tax Bd. v. Hyatt, 2003). The Court's failure to analyze the challenge under the Due Process Clause does not reflect a change in the Court's approach, but rather a peculiarity of the facts underlying the case: since the defendant challenging the constitutionality of Nevada's choice of its own law was the California Franchise Tax Board and since political subdivisions of states are not typically treated as persons protected by due process,[8] it made sense to address the challenge under the Full Faith and Credit Clause alone.

### Substantive or Procedural Due Process?

To the extent that the Due Process Clause limits a state's legislative jurisdiction, is this a substantive or procedural due process protection? As the early due process cases discussed in the next section of this chapter demonstrate, the initial conception was clearly a substantive one. At the same time that the Supreme Court was employing the Due Process Clause to protect the freedom to contract from state regulation, it was applying due process to limit the territorial reach of state law. Even today, it is fair to conceive of the due process limitations on legislative jurisdiction as substantive: regardless of the notice provided and the other procedural protections afforded, it is unreasonable and hence unconstitutional to apply the law of a state that has no connection to or interest in the controversy.[9]

Even though due process limitations on state choice of law are fairly characterized as substantive, we address them here for two reasons. First, in recent years, the Supreme Court has framed the due process analysis in terms of the parties' expectations, shielding the litigants from laws that were not anticipated at the time of the primary conduct (Allstate Ins. Co. v. Hague, 1981; Clay v. Sun Ins. Office, Ltd., 1964). This more procedural conception of due process is distinct from the Court's general substantive due process analysis.[10] Second, since due process limitations on personal jurisdiction and choice of law are closely related and are often addressed together, and since we chose to address constitutional limits on personal jurisdiction in this volume, it makes sense to address due process limits on state choice of law here as well.

## THE EARLY DUE PROCESS CASES

As we shall see, the due process limitations on state choice of law have changed over time against a dynamic social and political landscape. In an effort to understand the legal developments in context, we shall examine the seminal cases in chronological order.

### Constitutional Enshrinement of the Territoriality Principle During the *Lochner* Era

The Supreme Court's earliest decisions in this area were made at the turn of the twentieth century, at a time when the Court was invoking the Due Process Clause to protect private contractual freedom from state regulation.[11] As we shall see, the Court not only invoked due process to protect contractual freedom generally, but it invoked it specifically to restrict the authority of states to regulate extraterritorial contracts and other conduct. Thus, the early cases that invoked due process to limit state choice of law may be viewed as a subset of the *Lochner* era substantive due process cases.

Just as a state's personal jurisdictional reach during this period was limited to persons and property found within the territory of the state, so, too, its legislative jurisdiction, or its authority to regulate conduct by applying its law to a controversy, was bound by the territoriality principle: each state had exclusive authority to regulate conduct within its borders and no authority to regulate conduct beyond them.[12] But what if conduct that occurred in one state gave rise to a claim that was litigated in the courts of another state?

Courts applied a "vested rights" theory, conceiving rights to "vest" under the law of the state in which a central event occurred—in torts cases, the injury; in contracts cases, the making or performance of the contract (Restatement (First) of the Conflict of Laws (1934)). Only the state in which the central event occurred had legislative jurisdiction to apply its law to the controversy. But if suit were filed on the claim in another jurisdiction, the court would enforce the vested right according to the law of the state in which the central event occurred. According to Joseph Beale, the Reporter for the First Restatement of Conflicts, "A right having been created by the appropriate law, the recognition of its existence should follow everywhere. Thus an act valid where done cannot be called into question anywhere."[13] As Justice Holmes put it:

> The theory of the foreign suit is that . . . the act complained of . . . gave rise to an obligation . . ., which, like other obligations, follows the person, and may be enforced wherever the person may be found. But as the only source of this obligation is the law of the place of the act, it follows that that law determines not merely the existence of the obligation, but equally determines its extent (Slater v. Mex. Nat'l R.R. Co., 1904).

As we will see, in three of the leading cases from this period, the Supreme Court enshrined the territoriality principle in the Constitution. And consistent with *Lochner* era jurisprudence, the Court invoked due process to bar states from applying their regulatory laws to contracts made or conduct engaged in outside the state.

The first of these cases, New York Life Insurance Co. v. Dodge (1918), involved a life insurance policy issued to the plaintiff's husband in Missouri. The defendant insurer was a New York corporation licensed to do business in Missouri, where it maintained a local office. The Missouri couple had borrowed against the life insurance policy, signing both the application for the loan and the loan agreement itself in Missouri. Notwithstanding the actual place of signing, the loan agreement stated that it was made and delivered in New York, that payments thereunder were to be made in New York, and that the agreement was made pursuant to New York law (N.Y. Life Ins. Co. v. Dodge, 1918). The Missouri couple pledged the life insurance policy as security for the loan and when they failed to make the required payments, the insurer appropriated the entire reserve value of the policy to satisfy the outstanding obligation and cancelled the policy in accordance with the terms of the loan agreement and New York law.

Upon her husband's death, the plaintiff filed suit against the insurer in a Missouri state court to recover the full amount of the policy, less the amount owed on the loan, the unpaid premiums and interest. The plaintiff relied upon a Missouri nonforfeiture law, which, if applicable, would have required the insurer to use a portion of the reserve to pay premiums on term insurance and would have barred it from cancelling the policy in these circumstances. The insurer argued that application of Missouri law would have deprived it of the full benefit of the loan agreement, thereby depriving it of liberty and property in violation of the Due Process Clause of the Fourteenth Amendment. The Missouri appellate court upheld the constitutionality and application of Missouri law and affirmed a judgment in the plaintiff's favor.

The United States Supreme Court reversed. Although it acknowledged that the original insurance policy was a Missouri contract, the Court treated the loan agreement as a separate transaction—a New York contract, which Missouri "lacked power directly to control" (N.Y. Life Ins. Co. v. Dodge, 1918). "To hold otherwise," the Court continued, "would . . . sanction the impairment of that liberty of contract guaranteed to all by the Fourteenth Amendment" (N.Y. Life Ins. Co. v. Dodge, 1918). Thus, notwithstanding the substantial connections between Missouri and both the underlying insurance policy and the loan agreement and notwithstanding Missouri's interest in protecting its citizens, the Court held that it was unconstitutional for Missouri to apply its law to regulate a loan agreement deemed to have been made in New York.[14] Thus, the Court engrafted the territoriality principle onto the Constitution, thereby providing further due process protection for property and contract rights.

In another insurance case decided a decade later, the Supreme Court again invoked the Due Process Clause to limit a state's authority to regulate out-of-state conduct through the application of its law. Home Insurance Co. v. Dick (1930) involved a fire insurance policy issued in Mexico by a Mexican insurance company on a tugboat owned by Dick, a Texas citizen then residing in Mexico.[15] Dick and a Texas company that had a security interest in the tug were the payees. The policy, which covered the tug only in certain Mexican waters, provided that any suit on the policy had to be brought within one year of the date of damage. This limitation was valid under Mexican law, to which the policy was subject. More than a year after the tug suffered a total loss, Dick commenced an action against the Mexican insurer in a Texas state court, acquiring *quasi-in-rem* jurisdiction by garnishing the obligation undertaken by two New York insurance companies (with local Texas agents) to reinsure part of the risk assumed by the defendant.

The garnishees defended on the theory that Dick's claim was time-barred by the one-year suit provision in the policy. For his part, Dick invoked a Texas statute that barred persons from entering into contracts that limited their right to sue to a period of less than two years. Notwithstanding the garnishees' claim that it would violate due process to apply the Texas statute to a contract made and to be performed outside Texas, the Texas courts applied the Texas statute and entered judgment for Dick against the garnishees.

On appeal, the Supreme Court reversed, concluding that "[t]he Texas statute as here construed and applied deprives the garnishees of property without due process of law" (Home Ins. Co. v. Dick, 1930). Recognizing that a state might proscribe the making of certain contracts within its borders or even prohibit the performance within its borders of contracts made elsewhere if performance would violate its laws, the Court distinguished the facts of the case because "nothing in any way relating to the policy sued on, or to the contracts of reinsurance, was ever done or required to be done in Texas" (Home Ins. Co. v. Dick, 1930). As in *Dodge*, the Court enshrined the territoriality principle in the Constitution, viewing Texas's attempt "to impose a greater obligation than that agreed upon and to seize property in payment of the imposed obligation" as a deprivation of property without due process of law (Home Ins. Co. v. Dick, 1930). The Court viewed as irrelevant Dick's Texas citizenship, the presence of another Texas payee on the policy and Texas's interest in protecting its citizens because it viewed the rights under the policy to have vested in Mexico, where the contract was made.

In Hartford Accident & Indemnity Co. v. Delta & Pine Land Co. (1934), too, the Court continued to adhere to the territoriality principle applied in *Dodge* and *Dick*. There, a Connecticut insurance company had issued a fidelity bond to Delta & Pine, a Mississippi corporation, to protect it from pecuniary losses suffered as a result of fraud or dishonesty by any of its employees "in any position, anywhere." Delta & Pine's Tennessee office had applied for the bond and the defendant insurer had delivered the bond in Tennessee. This suretyship contract required that claims be made within fifteen months of the termination of the suretyship for the defaulting employee, a provision that was enforceable under Tennessee law. The suretyship contract was cancelled in December 1929. In May 1931, Delta & Pine learned that its treasurer had misappropriated money throughout 1929 while working in Mississippi. In June 1931—more than fifteen months after termination of the suretyship contract—Delta & Pine filed a claim and the defendant disclaimed liability. Delta & Pine then filed suit in a Mississippi state court, invoking a Mississippi law that treated "[a]ll contracts of insurance on property, lives or interests" in Mississippi as Mississippi contracts and precluded parties to Mississippi contracts from agreeing to shorten the period in which claims could be brought. Just as the Supreme Court in *Dick* had held that Texas law violated due process when applied to nullify a one-year suit clause in a Mexican insurance policy, in *Delta & Pine* the Court held that the Mississippi statute violated due process by depriving the insurer of the benefit of the fifteen-month suit clause, which was valid under the laws of Tennessee, where the suretyship contract had been made (Hartford Accident & Indem. Co. v. Delta & Pine Land Co., 1934).

Thus, just as the Court was using due process in the *Lochner* line of cases to protect parties' freedom to contract from domestic (i.e., intrastate) regulation, it was using due process to protect freedom to contract from extraterritorial regulation (i.e., regulation by states other than those in which the parties had made their contracts). How would the Court's jurisprudence in this area change once the economic realities of the Depression and other pressures forced it rethink the premises underlying *Lochner*?[16] We turn now to that issue.

## The Shift from Territoriality Toward State Interests During the New Deal Era

As the economy declined, the need for governmental intervention became increasingly apparent. As Lawrence Tribe explains, the premise underlying *Lochner*—that courts that struck down social legislation were merely restoring the "natural" state of affairs—was rejected along with the underlying notion that a "natural" order existed. The "freedom" of contract and property—which the *Lochner* era Court had protected—"came to be seen increasingly as an illusion, subject as it was to impersonal economic forces."[17] Social critics of the 1920s and 1930s recognized the need for legislation to protect the poor and the unemployed and criticized the Supreme Court for its role in stymying governmental efforts to relieve suffering. Political pressure brought to bear on the Court—including President Roosevelt's Court-packing plan—contributed to the timing of the Court's repudiation of *Lochner* and its acceptance of New Deal and other social legislation against substantive due process challenges (W. Coast Hotel Co. v. Parrish, 1937).[18]

Just as the Court was revising its substantive due process jurisprudence more generally, it was rethinking the extent to which due process limited a state's authority to apply its law to contracts made and other conduct engaged in beyond its borders. Thus, as its due process jurisprudence shifted away from substantive protection of contract rights and back toward procedural protections, its scrutiny of state choice-of-law decisions came to focus more on the procedural concerns of the parties' expectations and unfair surprise rather than on the parties' freedom to contract and other substantive economic rights. Furthermore, with its growing acceptance of social legislation generally, the Court became increasingly willing to recognize that states other than those in which the contract was made or the injury occurred might have interests significant enough to render constitutional their exercise of legislative jurisdiction. Thus, the Court moved away from the territorial principle and toward a broader view of legislative jurisdiction. This theoretical shift presaged a parallel shift in state choice-of-law theory generally: while the First Restatement of Conflicts focused principally on territorial factors, most modern choice-of-law theories, including governmental interest analysis, the Second Restatement of Conflicts, and comparative impairment, are designed to further state policies and interests.

This shift in the Court's approach to constitutional limits on choice of law was not sudden, however.[19] As we will see, in Alaska Packers Ass'n v. Industrial

Accident Commission (1935), the Court continued to rely upon the territorial principle but went on to consider the forum state's "interests" in the controversy to justify its exercise of legislative jurisdiction. *Alaska Packers* involved a claim by a Mexican worker hired in California to work temporarily in a salmon canning factory in Alaska, where he was injured. The employee returned to California and sought to recover benefits under the California worker's compensation statute. Both the California and Alaska worker's compensation statutes purported to provide the exclusive remedy in the case. In upholding the application of California law by the California worker's compensation tribunal, the Court began with the territorial principle, noting that "the due process clause denies to a state any power to restrict or control the obligation of contracts executed and to be performed without the state. . . ." (Alaska Packers Ass'n v. Indus. Accident Comm'n, 1935). Since the employee was hired in California, it did not violate due process for California to apply its laws to govern the worker's claim.

While the territorial principle previously adopted by the Court in *Dodge*, *Dick* and *Delta & Pine* thus supported the result in the case, the Court bolstered its conclusion by discussing California's interest in having its law apply in these circumstances: if a Mexican worker hired in California to work temporarily in Alaska were deprived of a remedy in California, he might have no remedy at all because of the difficulties he would face seeking compensation in Alaska. Without a remedy against his employer, the injured worker might become a charge of the state of California. The Court concluded that "California . . . had a legitimate public interest in controlling and regulating this employer-employee relationship in such fashion as to impose a liability upon the employer. . . . [T]he state had as great an interest in affording adequate protection to this class of its population as to employees injured within the state" (Alaska Packers Ass'n v. Indus. Accident Comm'n, 1935; see also Hoopeston Canning Co. v. Cullen, 1943). Thus, while relying upon the territorial principle to decide the case and uphold the application of California law, the Court's discussion of state interests laid the groundwork for a constitutional approach to choice of law that was broader than the narrow territorial principle.

In a second worker's compensation case decided a few years later under the Full Faith and Credit Clause—Pacific Employers Insurance Co. v. Industrial Accident Commission (1939)—the Court upheld the application of the law of the state in which the injury occurred rather than the law of the state where the employment contract was made. Although this result could have been justified under a territorial approach—torts cases traditionally were governed by the place of the injury—earlier Supreme Court cases consistently had applied the *contracts* territorial principle to govern worker's compensation cases (Alaska Packers Ass'n v. Indus. Accident Comm'n, 1935; Bradford Elec. Light Co. v. Clapper, 1932). Rather than holding that the Constitution required the forum to apply the law of the state in which the employment contract was made, the Court recognized "the constitutional authority of [a] state to legislate for the bodily safety and economic protection of employees injured within it. Few matters could be deemed more appropriately the concern of the state in which the injury occurs or more completely within its power" (Pac. Employers Ins. Co. v. Indus. Accident Comm'n, 1939; see also Cardillo v. Liberty Mut. Ins. Co., 1947). Thus, the state's interest in the matter gave it authority to apply its own law.

## THE MID-CENTURY CASES: STATE INTERESTS AND PARTY EXPECTATIONS

By the middle of the twentieth century, the Court had fully incorporated this examination of state interests into its due process analysis.[20] As we will see, the Court also began to expressly consider whether the parties could have expected application of the chosen law, thereby demonstrating concern for the individual litigants and adopting a more procedural conception of the due process protection afforded. Two cases illustrate. The first, Watson v. Employers Liability Assurance Corp. (1954), involved a suit brought by a Louisiana citizen who was injured in Louisiana using a hair care product, the "Toni Home Permanent." (One can only wonder how.) The Toni Co. had manufactured the product in Chicago, Illinois. Toni was a division of Gillette Safety Razor Co., a Delaware corporation with its headquarters in Massachusetts. The plaintiff filed suit in a Louisiana state court against Toni's insurer, the Employers Liability Assurance Corp., relying upon the Louisiana direct action statute, which authorized persons injured in the state to bring suit directly against the tortfeasor's insurer even if the insurance policy barred such direct actions. The defendant insurance company removed the action to federal court and then moved to dismiss, arguing that the policy sued upon contained a no-action clause, which barred suit against the insurer until after judgment had been rendered against the insured. It further argued that the Louisiana law violated due process to the extent that it abrogated the no-suit clause in a policy that had been negotiated, issued and delivered in Massachusetts, where such clauses were enforceable.

Conceding that the policy was issued in Massachusetts, the Court declined to characterize it as a "simple local situation[ ]," noting that the policy protected Gillette and Toni "against damages on account of personal injuries that might be suffered by users of Toni Home Permanents anywhere in the United States, its territories, or in Canada" (Watson v. Employers Liab. Assurance Corp., 1954). Distinguishing *Dick* as a case in which "the subject matter of the contract related in no matter to anything that had been done or was to be done in Texas," and *Delta & Pine* as one in which Mississippi's "activities in connection with the policy were found to be so 'slight' and so 'casual' that Mississippi could not apply its own law in such a way as to enlarge the obligations of the Tennessee contract," the Court discussed Louisiana's various interests in *Watson*:

> Louisiana's direct action statute is not a mere intermeddling in affairs beyond her boundaries which are no concern of hers. Persons injured or killed in Louisiana are most likely to be Louisiana residents, and even if not, Louisiana may have to care for them. Serious injuries may require treatment in Louisiana homes or hospitals by Louisiana doctors. The injured may be destitute. They may be compelled to call upon friends, relatives or the public for help. Louisiana has manifested its natural interest in the injured by providing remedies for recovery of damages. It has a similar interest in policies of insurance which are designed to assure ultimate payment of such damages. Moreover, Louisiana courts in most instances provide the most convenient forum for trial of these cases. . . . What has been said is enough to show Louisiana's legitimate interest in safeguarding the rights of persons injured there. In view of that interest, the direct action provisions here challenged do not violate due process (Watson v. Employers Liab. Assurance Corp., 1954).

Thus, two important facts distinguished *Watson* from *Dick*. First, the injury in *Watson* was sustained in Louisiana, providing that state with a variety of interests, while the loss in *Dick* was suffered in Mexico, giving rise to no Texas interest. Second, the policy in *Watson* protected the insured companies nationwide so arguably the insurers should have realized that a covered loss might arise in Louisiana and they might have to defend such a claim under Louisiana law.[21] The policy in *Dick*, on the other hand, protected the tug only in Mexican waters so the insurers there had no reason to anticipate a suit in Texas or the application of Texas law.

This shift in focus from territoriality to state interests and party expectations is further revealed in Clay v. Sun Insurance Office, Ltd. (1964). There, Clay, a citizen and resident of Illinois, purchased a three-year insurance policy from Sun Insurance Office, a British company licensed to do business in Illinois and Florida, among other states. The policy, which was designated a "Personal Property Floater Policy (World-Wide)," provided worldwide protection against loss or damage to specified personal property. A few months after purchasing the policy, Clay moved to Florida. Two years later, his wife took some insured property from his home in Florida and destroyed it.[22] The policy contained a twelve-month suit clause, which was valid under Illinois law, the state in which the policy was issued. Notwithstanding this clause, Clay filed suit in a federal court in Florida to recover on the policy more than two years after the loss was sustained, relying upon a Florida statute, which rendered void any provision in any contract that limited the time in which to sue to a period shorter than the five-year statute of limitations (Clay v. Sun Ins. Office, Ltd., 1960). The defendant insurer argued that the application of Florida law to an Illinois insurance policy violated the Due Process Clause.[23] The Court of Appeals agreed, relying upon *Dick*, which had held that it violated due process for Texas to apply its law to invalidate a one-year suit provision in a Mexican insurance policy. Unlike the policy at issue in *Dick*, however, which covered the tug only in Mexican waters, the policy at issue in *Clay* involved an "ambulatory contract on which suit might be brought in any one of several States" (Clay v. Sun Ins. Office, Ltd., 1964). The Court went on to elaborate upon the significance of the geographical scope of coverage:

"Insurance companies, like other contractors, do not confine their contractual activities and obligations within state boundaries. They sell to customers who are promised protection in States far away from the place where the contract is made. In this very case the policy was sold to Clay with knowledge that he could take his property anywhere in the world he saw fit without losing the protection of his insurance. . . . The contract did not even attempt to provide that the law of Illinois would govern when suits were filed anywhere else in the country. Shortly after the contract was made, Clay moved to Florida and there he lived for several years. His insured property was there all that time. The company knew this fact. Particularly since the company was licensed to do business in Florida, it must have known it might be sued there. . . ." (Clay v. Sun Ins. Office, Ltd., 1964, quoting Clay v. Sun Ins. Office, Ltd., 1960, Black, J., dissenting).

Thus, the scope of the policy put the insurer on notice that a loss might be suffered in Florida. The insurer could have anticipated the application of Florida law and therefore could not claim unfair surprise. Although the *Clay* Court did not explicitly discuss Florida's interest in the transaction, it did allude to it in distinguishing *Dick* and *Delta & Pine*: "Those were cases where the activities in the State of the forum were thought to be too slight and too casual, as in the *Delta & Pine Land Co.* case, to make the application of local law consistent with due process, or wholly lacking, as in the *Dick* case" (Clay v. Sun Ins. Office, Ltd., 1964). In *Clay*, on the other hand, "[n]o deficiency of that order" was present (Clay v. Sun Ins. Office, Ltd., 1964). Thus, Clay's residence and citizenship in Florida and the fact that the loss was suffered there were contacts with Florida, which gave it an interest in applying its law to the controversy.

*Clay* was decided during a period of great flux in state choice-of-law doctrine. In the years immediately preceding *Clay*, state courts had begun to experiment with modern choice-of-law theories (Haag v. Barnes, N.Y. 1961; Auten v. Auten, N.Y. 1954; W.H. Barber Co. v. Hughes, Ind. 1945). By 1963, the New York Court of Appeals had openly abandoned the territorial *lex loci delicti* rule (Babcock v. Jackson, 1963). By 1977, half the states had abandoned the territorial approach in multistate torts cases.[24] Rejection of the territorial approach in contracts cases was somewhat slower, but by 1984, half the states had abandoned the territorial *lex loci contractus* rule.[25] In place of the territorial approach to choice of law, state courts adopted a variety of modern, policy-based approaches, the malleability of which gave state courts substantial freedom to choose their own law to govern multistate controversies before them. Would the Supreme Court read the Due Process Clause as imposing a check on this freedom? Would the concepts of "state interest" and "party expectations" relied upon in *Watson* and *Clay* replace the territorial principle as the guide, and if so, would they provide a meaningful check? It is to these issues that we now turn.

## THE MODERN CASES

During the 1980s, the Supreme Court decided three cases that announced the current tests for gauging the constitutionality of a state court's choice of its own law. The first two of these cases address the limits imposed by due process on a state court's choice of its own substantive law; the last case considers the limits on a state court's choice of its own procedural law.

### Allstate Insurance Co. v. Hague (1981)

*Allstate* involved an automobile insurance policy issued by the Allstate Insurance Co. to Ralph Hague, a Wisconsin resident who lived just on the Wisconsin side of the border with Minnesota. Hague died when a motorcycle on which he was riding as a passenger was hit by a car in Wisconsin. Both of the drivers involved were Wisconsin residents and neither had valid automobile insurance. Hague, on the other hand, had a policy issued by Allstate on three cars. The policy contained a clause that insured him, up to $15,000 per car, against losses incurred in accidents with uninsured motorists. Minnesota law permitted the $15,000 uninsured motorist coverage on each of the cars to be stacked, providing $45,000 in total coverage, while Wisconsin law disallowed stacking (Allstate Ins. Co. v. Hague, 1981, plurality op.).[26]

Shortly after the accident, Hague's widow moved to Minnesota, where she filed suit against Allstate, seeking a declaration that Minnesota's stacking law governed her claim for the uninsured motorist coverage. Allstate argued that Wisconsin's no-stacking rule governed because "the insurance policy was delivered in Wisconsin, the accident occurred in Wisconsin, and all persons involved were Wisconsin residents at the time of the accident" (Allstate Ins. Co. v. Hague, 1981, plurality op.). Applying Robert Leflar's choice-influencing considerations and the better rule of law[27] to select the governing law, the Minnesota Supreme Court upheld the choice of Minnesota's stacking law, concluding that the choice of forum law did not violate due process.

Declining to comment on the choice-of-law theory applied by the Minnesota Supreme Court, the United States Supreme Court addressed only the constitutional issue. Although the Court concluded that Minnesota's choice of its own substantive law was constitutional, no majority opinion issued. The plurality opinion written by Justice Brennan (joined by Justices White, Marshall and Blackmun) proceeded from the premise "that a set of facts giving rise to a lawsuit, or a particular issue within a lawsuit, may justify, in constitutional terms, application of the law of more than one jurisdiction" (Allstate Ins. Co. v. Hague, 1981, plurality op.). After discussing and attempting to harmonize its prior precedents, the plurality articulated the following standard to assess the constitutionality of a state's choice of law under both the Due Process and Full Faith and Credit

Clauses of the Constitution: "for a State's substantive law to be selected in a constitutionally permissible manner, that State must have a significant contact or significant aggregation of contacts, creating state interests, such that choice of its law is neither arbitrary nor fundamentally unfair" (Allstate Ins. Co. v. Hague, 1981, plurality op.).[28] Three other Justices—Powell, Burger and Rehnquist—accepted this statement as the appropriate constitutional standard (Allstate Ins. Co. v. Hague, 1981, Powell, J., dissenting).

The plurality identified three Minnesota contacts with the parties and the accident, which, in the aggregate, gave Minnesota sufficient interest to apply its own stacking law consistent with due process: Mr. Hague's employment in Minnesota; Allstate's presence in Minnesota; and Mrs. Hague's move to Minnesota before the commencement of the action. We will consider these contacts in turn.

First, Mr. Hague had commuted to and worked in Red Wing, Minnesota, for fifteen years prior to his death. Recognizing that a state's interest in its employees might not be as "substantial" as its interest in its residents, the plurality nevertheless viewed Minnesota's interest in its employee as "important" (Allstate Ins. Co v. Hague, 1981, plurality op.). How did Mr. Hague's employment in Minnesota give the state an interest in applying its stacking law to his widow's claim for uninsured motorist coverage? If Mr. Hague had lived and the more generous stacked coverage would have enabled him to obtain better medical care so that he could have returned to work more quickly, then Minnesota might have had an interest in applying its law to his claim (Allstate Ins. Co. v. Hague, 1981, plurality op.).[29] But Hague did not survive. And it is difficult to view the applicability of Minnesota's stacking law to claims by Minnesota employees as a perquisite that enabled Minnesota to recruit and retain good employees, notwithstanding the plurality's contention that "Minnesota's work force is surely affected by the level of protection the State extends to it, either directly or indirectly" (Allstate Ins. Co. v. Hague, 1981, plurality op.).[30] In short, it is hard to see how Mr. Hague's status as a Minnesota employee gave the state any interest in applying its stacking law to an insurance policy issued in Wisconsin to a Wisconsin citizen killed in Wisconsin.

Second, Allstate did sufficient business in Minnesota to be subject to general jurisdiction there. "By virtue of its presence," the plurality argued,

> Allstate [could] hardly claim unfamiliarity with the laws of the host jurisdiction and surprise that the state courts might apply forum law to litigation in which the company is involved. "Particularly since the company was licensed to do business in [the forum], it must have known that it might be sued there, and that [the forum] courts would feel bound by [forum] law" (Allstate Ins. Co. v. Hague, 1981, plurality op., quoting Clay v. Sun Ins. Office, Ltd., 1960, Black, J., dissenting).

Since the policy provided continental coverage and since Allstate was aware that Mr. Hague worked in Minnesota, it had to have anticipated that Minnesota law might apply if Hague had an accident in Minnesota. Just as the Sun Insurance Office in *Clay* knew that it might have been sued in Florida and would have been subject to Florida law if Clay had suffered a loss there, Allstate knew that it could have been sued in and subject to Minnesota law.

This argument proves too much, however. Allstate presumably did business in all fifty states and Mr. Hague's policy provided him with coverage anywhere in the United States. So at the time it issued the policy, Allstate could have anticipated that Oklahoma law, or California law, or New York law would govern a claim that Hague might bring if he had an accident in one of those states. But what if he did not have an accident in one of those states? While Allstate might have foreseen that a New York court would apply New York law if Hague had an accident in New York, it would *not* have foreseen that Minnesota would apply New York law if Hague had an accident in Wisconsin. Nor would it have foreseen that Minnesota would apply Minnesota law to an accident in Wisconsin.[31] Thus it is hard to see how Allstate's business in Minnesota and its amenability to suit there justified the choice of Minnesota law on the facts of the case.

Third, Hague's widow had moved to Minnesota before she commenced litigation against Allstate and had been appointed personal representative for her late husband's estate by the Minnesota Registrar of Probate. There was no evidence that she moved in anticipation of litigation or in an effort to obtain Minnesota law. Because she was living in Minnesota, that state had an interest in affording her full compensation to keep her off the welfare rolls. Noting that a prior case, John Hancock Mutual Life Insurance Co. v. Yates (1936), had held "that a postoccurrence change of residence to the forum State was insufficient in and of itself to confer power on the forum State to choose its law," the plurality went on to note that "that case did not hold that such a change of residence was irrelevant" where, as here, other local contacts existed (Allstate Ins. Co. v. Hague, 1981, plurality op.). Expressing "no view whether the first two contacts, either together or separately, would have sufficed to sustain the choice of Minnesota law," the plurality concluded that "Minnesota had a significant aggregation of contacts with the parties and the occurrence, creating state interests, such that application of its law was neither arbitrary nor fundamentally unfair" (Allstate Ins. Co. v. Hague, 1981, plurality op.).

Unlike the plurality, Justice Stevens declined to conflate the due process and full faith and credit analyses, viewing the case as raising separate issues under the two clauses: "First, does the Full Faith and Credit Clause *require* Minnesota, the forum State, to apply Wisconsin law? Second, does the Due Process Clause of the Fourteenth Amendment *prevent* Minnesota from applying its own law?" (Allstate Ins. Co. v. Hague, 1981, Stevens, J., concurring in the judgment).[32] Stevens proceeded on the assumption that "a choice-of-law decision would violate the Due Process Clause if it were totally arbitrary or if it were fundamentally unfair to either litigant" (Allstate Ins. Co. v. Hague, 1981, Stevens, J., concurring in the judgment). Because judges are most familiar with forum law and would save time if they were spared the task of discovering and applying the law of other states, he questioned whether "a judge's decision to apply the law of his [or her] own State could ever be described as wholly irrational" (Allstate Ins. Co. v. Hague, 1981, Stevens, J., concurring in the judgment). But even if a state's interest in the efficient operation of its judicial system rendered the choice of its own law presumptively valid, the application of forum law nevertheless would violate due process if it were fundamentally unfair to one of the parties.

Addressing the choice-of-law context specifically, Stevens noted that the application of an otherwise fair and nondiscriminatory rule would violate due process if the litigants, at the time they engaged in their primary conduct, "could not reasonably have anticipated that their actions would later be judged by this rule of law. A choice-of-law decision that frustrates the justifiable expectations of the parties can be fundamentally unfair" (Allstate Ins. Co. v. Hague, 1981, Stevens, J., concurring in the judgment). Here, Stevens concluded that the choice of Minnesota law did not frustrate Allstate's reasonable expectations. Allstate had included neither a choice-of-law clause nor a "no-stacking" provision in the insurance policy. Morever, since the policy provided nationwide coverage and since Allstate did business in Minnesota, it could have anticipated the application of Minnesota law to claims arising under the policy at the time it issued it.

In dissent, Justice Powell (joined by Chief Justice Burger and Justice Rehnquist) agreed with the plurality that "[t]he Court should invalidate a forum State's decision to apply its own law only when there are no significant contacts between the State and the litigation" (Allstate Ins. Co. v. Hague, 1981, Powell, J., dissenting). In his view, "[a] contact, or a pattern of contacts, satisfies the Constitution when it protects the litigants from being unfairly surprised if the forum State applies its own law, and when the application of the forum's law reasonably can be understood to further a legitimate public policy of the forum State" (Allstate Ins. Co. v. Hague, 1981, Powell, J., dissenting).

While agreeing that "no reasonable expectations of the parties were frustrated," Powell concluded that none of the contacts considered by the plurality gave Minnesota an interest in having its stacking law applied to the facts of the case (Allstate Ins. Co. v. Hague, 1981, Powell, J., dissenting). First, while Mr. Hague's status as a Minnesota employee might have supported the application of certain local laws, it did not justify the application of Minnesota's stacking rule because "[n]either the nature of the insurance policy, the events related to the accident, nor the immediate question of stacking coverage is in any way affected or implicated by the insured's employment status" (Allstate Ins. Co. v. Hague, 1981, Powell, J., dissenting). Second, even though Allstate did business in the forum state, that did not give Minnesota an interest in regulating its conduct regarding people and property outside the state. Finally, Mrs. Hague's after-acquired domicile in Minnesota was constitutionally irrelevant. If such post-accident changes were considered, parties would move to obtain better law and the reasonable expectations of their adversaries would be frustrated.

The Supreme Court's decision in *Allstate* raised more questions than it answered. First, what type of interest must a state have to apply its law to a controversy consistent with due process? Does the Constitution require the same type of interest that governmental interest analysis contemplates?[33] The *Allstate* plurality's test purports to require a state interest, but its opinion focuses more on contacts than interests and one is hard-pressed to identify a Minnesota interest furthered by application of its law (except an interest in compensating Mrs. Hague, who moved to Minnesota after the accident occurred). Justice Stevens's due process analysis does not require an examination of the forum state's interest and his full faith and credit analysis requires scrutiny of the forum state's interest only if another state's interest is infringed.[34] Thus, the role of the state interest is ambiguous at best.

Second, what role do *potential* contacts with the forum state play in the due process analysis?[35] All of the participating Justices emphasized Allstate's knowledge that it might have been subject to Minnesota law if Mr. Hague had been involved in an accident there but none seemed bothered by the fact that the accident did not in fact occur there, suggesting that potential contacts may support the choice of a state's law regardless of whether they actually materialize.

Third, how significant are forum contacts that occur after the primary conduct that gives rise to the claim? The plurality acknowledged that John Hancock Mutual Life Insurance Co. v. Yates (1936) stands for the proposition that a post-occurrence move to the forum state, *in and of itself*, will not support the application of forum law, yet it added that *Yates* "did not hold that such a change of residence was irrelevant" (Allstate Ins. Co. v. Hague, 1981, plurality op.). The Court suggested that as long as other forum contacts exist, after-acquired domicile may be considered. But how significant must the other forum contacts be to trigger consideration of after-acquired domicile? And why is it ever fair to consider after-acquired domicile? After all, such a move is made unilaterally, after the conduct giving rise to the claim occurs, and may frustrate the expectations of other parties (Allstate Ins. Co. v. Hague, 1981, Powell, J., dissenting).

Finally, what is the constitutional significance of a defendant's unrelated business contacts with the forum state? Here, the plurality deemed Allstate's business in Minnesota to be relevant. While Minnesota clearly would have been acting constitutionally if it applied its own law to regulate Allstate's dealings with Minnesota citizens in Minnesota, it is not at all clear why Allstate's business dealings in Minnesota justified application of Minnesota law to regulate Allstate's relationship with a Wisconsin citizen in Wisconsin.

In sum, while *Allstate*'s effort to articulate a standard to gauge the constitutionality of a state's choice of law was welcome, ambiguities in the standard and its application left many wondering whether "virtually any old contact will do."[36]

### Phillips Petroleum Co. v. Shutts (1985)

For the first time in decades, the Supreme Court in Phillips Petroleum Co. v. Shutts (1985) held that a state's choice of its own law violated due process.[37] Thus, *Shutts* demonstrated that "any old contact" would *not* suffice to support an assertion of legislative jurisdiction. As we will see, however, the *Shutts* decision did little to answer the questions left open by *Allstate*.

*Shutts* involved a class action filed in a Kansas state court on behalf of a class of property owners against the Phillips Petroleum Co., a Delaware corporation with its principal place of business in Oklahoma. The company leased land from the property owners and extracted natural gas from it, which it sold to customers in interstate commerce. The company paid the property owners a royalty based on the sale price. The company needed permission from the Federal Power Commission ("FPC") to increase prices. When the company proposed a price increase, FPC regulations permitted it to charge its customers the higher price, subject to final FPC approval. If the price increase were disapproved, the company had to pay customers a refund plus interest at a rate specified by FPC regulations.

Because the difference between the last-approved price and the proposed higher price was subject to recoupment by the customers unless final FPC approval was obtained, Phillips Petroleum paid the property owners royalties based on the last-approved price, suspending the royalties owed on the increase. When the price increase was approved, the company paid the property owners the suspended royalties, but without interest. The named representatives filed suit against Phillips Petroleum, alleging that the class members were entitled to interest on the suspended royalty payments. Even though only three percent of the absent class members resided in Kansas and less than one percent of the property was located there, the Kansas trial court applied Kansas case law to hold the company liable to all class members for interest at the rate at which the company would have had to reimburse its customers if the price increase had been disapproved by the FPC. The Kansas Supreme Court affirmed.

In the United States Supreme Court, the company challenged the constitutionality of the application of Kansas interest law to the class claims.[38] The Court began by noting that no constitutional issue would have arisen unless Kansas law conflicted in some material way with the law of a state in which some of the property was located or an absent class member was domiciled. Concluding that Kansas law conflicted with the laws of Texas and Oklahoma, in which most of the land was located, the Court then applied the *Allstate* test: "Kansas must have a 'significant contact or significant aggregation of contacts' to the claims asserted by each member of the plaintiff class, contacts 'creating state interests,' in order to ensure that the choice of Kansas law is not arbitrary or unfair" (Phillips Petroleum Co. v. Shutts, 1985, quoting Allstate Ins. Co. v. Hague, 1981, plurality op.).

The adoption of this test by the seven-member majority in *Shutts* solidified its precedential effect.

The *Shutts* Court concluded that the contacts between the litigation and the forum state were not sufficient to support the choice of Kansas law. No common fund existed in Kansas as there was no identifiable *res* in Kansas and no limited pool of money that might be depleted if all absent class members recovered. Nor had the absent class members evinced an intent to be bound by forum law by not opting out. "Even if one could say that the plaintiffs 'consented' to the application of Kansas law by not opting out, plaintiff's desire for forum law is rarely, if ever, controlling" (Phillips Petroleum Co. v. Shutts, 1985). That the Kansas court had asserted jurisdiction over a nationwide class did not justify the assertion of Kansas law either. Common issues of law are required to certify a class action, but one cannot use the mere certification of a class to "bootstrap" the application of forum law to class claims that have little or no connection to the forum. In short, "[g]iven Kansas' lack of 'interest' in claims unrelated to that State, and the substantive conflict with jurisdictions such as Texas," the Court concluded that the application of Kansas law to all of the claims in the case was "sufficiently arbitrary and unfair as to exceed constitutional limits" (Phillips Petroleum Co. v. Shutts, 1985).

Justice Stevens dissented, finding that the Kansas court's application of general principles of equity and its interpretation of the agreements between the company and the class members "contravened no established legal principles of other States and consequently [could not] be characterized as either arbitrary or fundamentally unfair to Phillips" (Phillips Petroleum Co. v. Shutts, 1985, Stevens, J., concurring in part and dissenting in part). Therefore, in his view, the application of Kansas law did not violate due process.

The very fact that the *Shutts* Court struck down the choice of Kansas law suggested that the constitutional constraints on choice of law were more stringent than many had thought after *Allstate*. But *Shutts* failed to clarify the open issues of the requisite nature of a state interest and the role of potential contacts[39] and cast only dim light on the significance of after-acquired domicile and unrelated business contacts.

In rejecting the argument that the plaintiffs' preference for Kansas law justified its application, the Court noted that the "plaintiff's desire for forum law is rarely, if ever, controlling," even where the plaintiff evinces her desire for forum law by actually moving to the forum state. The Court noted that it had "generally accorded such a move little or no significance" in cases involving after-acquired domicile (Phillips Petroleum Co. v. Shutts, 1985, citing John Hancock Mut. Life Ins. Co. v. Yates, 1936; Home Ins. Co. v. Dick, 1930). In an effort to reconcile this statement and the precedents cited with *Allstate*, the Court noted that in *Allstate*, "the plaintiff's move to the forum was only relevant because it was unrelated and prior to the litigation" (Phillips Petroleum Co. v. Shutts, 1985). Thus, in dicta, the Court intimated that it may be constitutional for a court to consider a party's after-acquired domicile if two conditions are met: first, she moves before filing suit and second, she moves for reasons unrelated to the litigation. While the latter constraint may reduce the incentive to forum-shop (or, more accurately, to home-shop), it does not alleviate the concern for interference with the expectations of other parties.

Regarding unrelated business contacts, the *Shutts* Court acknowledged that Phillips Petroleum owned property in Kansas and conducted substantial business there. But while the *Allstate* Court relied on Allstate's similar unrelated contacts with Minnesota to support the conclusion that the company should have anticipated the application of Minnesota law (even to a claim arising in Wisconsin), the *Shutts* Court noted only that Phillips Petroleum's contacts with Kansas gave Kansas an interest in regulating its conduct *there*, but not its conduct in relation to royalty owners residing elsewhere or property located elsewhere. Thus, *Shutts* suggests that unrelated business contacts with the forum state should not play a role in assessing the constitutionality of a state's application of its own law. Its failure to distinguish *Allstate*, however, leaves some lingering doubt regarding the significance of unrelated contacts.

### Sun Oil Co. v. Wortman (1988)

Like *Shutts*, Sun Oil Co. v. Wortman (1988) involved a class action seeking interest on suspended royalty payments made by the oil company for natural gas extracted from the properties that it leased from the class members. The class representatives filed suit in Kansas, this time against the Sun Oil Co. As in *Shutts*, very little of the leased property was located in Kansas; over ninety percent of it was located in Texas, Oklahoma and Louisiana. Following the Supreme Court's decision in *Shutts*, the trial court declined to apply Kansas substantive law, purporting instead to apply the laws of Texas, Oklahoma and Louisiana, where most of the property was located. Under these states' laws, the trial court held that Sun Oil was liable for interest at the rate specified in the FPC regulations.

Concluding that the *Allstate/Shutts* test for reviewing the constitutionality of a state court's choice of law applied only to substantive law, the trial court applied Kansas's five-year statute of limitations to all of the claims. The Kansas Supreme Court affirmed and Sun Oil sought review by the United States Supreme Court.

The Supreme Court affirmed. Writing for the majority, Justice Scalia proceeded from the assumption that state courts are free to apply their own procedural rules to actions litigated in their courts and spent most of his time addressing the question "whether a statute of limitations may be considered as a procedural matter for purposes of the Full Faith and Credit Clause" (Sun Oil Co. v. Wortman, 1988). Proceeding from the "indisputably correct" premise that statutes of limitations were treated as procedural under international law at the time the Constitution was adopted, Justice Scalia declined to depart from this traditional notion of legislative jurisdiction, eschewing "the enterprise of constitutionalizing choice-of-law rules, with no compass to guide us beyond our own perceptions of what seems desirable. . . . [L]ong established and still subsisting choice-of-law practices that come to be thought, by modern scholars, unwise, do not thereby become unconstitutional" (Sun Oil Co. v. Wortman, 1988).

Separately addressing the argument that it violated due process for Kansas to apply its own statute of limitations to the class claims, Justice Scalia noted that "it matters little" whether constitutional limits on legislative jurisdiction are discussed in the context of the Full Faith and Credit Clause or the Due Process Clause. By the time the Fourteenth Amendment was adopted, the Supreme Court had explicitly approved (under the Full Faith and Credit Clause) the application by the forum court of its own statutes of limitations and that practice has gone "essentially unchallenged" ever since (Sun Oil Co. v. Wortman, 1988). Looking briefly to the modern guideposts of state interest and party expectations, the Court added:

> A State's interest in regulating the workload of its courts and determining when a claim is too stale to be adjudicated certainly suffices to give it legislative jurisdiction to control the remedies available in its courts by imposing statutes of limitations. Moreover, petitioner could in no way have been unfairly surprised by the application to it of a rule that is as old as the Republic. There is, in short, nothing in Kansas' action here that is "arbitrary or unfair," and the due process challenge is entirely without substance (Sun Oil Co. v. Wortman, 1988, quoting Phillips Petroleum Co. v. Shutts, 1985).

While the forum state's interest in protecting its courts from stale claims would justify the application of its own *shorter* statute of limitations, Justice Scalia failed to explain how this interest would justify application of a disinterested forum state's statute of limitations if it were *longer* than the statute in place in the state or states whose substantive law would govern the controversy.[40]

In a concurrence joined by Justices Marshall and Blackmun, Justice Brennan agreed that it is constitutional for a court to apply its own state's statute of limitations, but criticized "[t]he Court's technique of avoiding close examination of the relevant interests by wrapping itself in the mantle of tradition. . . ." (Sun Oil Co. v. Wortman, 1988, Brennan, J., concurring in part and concurring in the judgment). He found even more troubling the majority's "dictum that *any* choice-of-law practice that 'is long established and still subsisting' is constitutional" (Sun Oil Co. v. Wortman, 1988, Brennan, J., concurring in part and concurring in the judgment). In Justice Brennan's view, tradition should not insulate from review practices that would be considered arbitrary or unfair today. He would apply the *Allstate/Shutts* test to gauge the constitutionality of *all* choices of law, including a state court's choice of its own procedural law.

As to purely procedural laws, "the contacts a State has with a dispute by virtue of being the forum always create state procedural interests that make application of the forum's law on purely procedural questions 'neither arbitrary nor fundamentally unfair'" (Sun Oil Co. v. Wortman, 1988, Brennan, J., concurring in part and concurring in the judgment). Statutes of limitations, however, have both substantive and procedural aspects, representing a balance among the state's substantive interest in vindicating substantive claims, its competing substantive interest in providing wrongdoers with repose, and its procedural interest in sparing its courts from stale claims. Justice Brennan engaged in a more thorough examination of this complex mix of interests to conclude that "the contact a State has with a claim simply by virtue of being the forum creates a sufficient procedural interest to make the application of its limitations period to wholly out-of-state claims" consistent with the Constitution (Sun Oil Co. v. Wortman, 1988, Brennan, J., concurring in part and concurring in the judgment).[41]

Scholars have criticized the Court's method of analysis in *Wortman*.[42] Not only did the Court fail to clarify the nature of the state interest required to satisfy due process under the *Allstate/Shutts* test, but it essentially obviated the interest requirement altogether whenever the law chosen is arguably procedural.[43] Thus, it created a potentially enormous exception from the already minimal restrictions on state choice of law imposed by due process under the modern cases. The scope of this exception is potentially broader than even the universe of procedural laws, as *Wortman* arguably immunizes from constitutional scrutiny all traditional choice-of-law rules.[44]

Not only has the Court's mode of analysis been criticized, but the result reached in *Wortman* has been questioned as well. For example, Joseph Singer has questioned the conclusion that Kansas has authority to entertain a claim, and impose liability on the defendant, when the state whose substantive law governs would not permit the claim to be heard in its courts:

> Insisting that Kansas cannot apply its oil and gas law to regulate activities in Texas and then turning around and allowing Kansas to apply its own statute of limitations to create a liability on a Texas gas company that is barred under Texas law seems senseless. Why should a Kansas court protect Texas landowners who have no rights under the law of the only place where they and the defendant have conducted business? If Kansas cannot regulate these activities directly by applying its property and contract law to events and persons in Texas, why should it be able to regulate them indirectly by applying its rules to revise claims the law of the situs has extinguished?[45]

The *Wortman* Court's analysis, which deems constitutional the application of procedural laws, avoids this issue.

## CONCLUSION

Three very modest conclusions emerge regarding the limits imposed by the Due Process Clause of the Fourteenth Amendment on legislative jurisdiction and state choice of law. First, it is now well settled that the standards for gauging the constitutionality of a state's choice of law are the same under both the Due Process Clause of the Fourteenth Amendment and the Full Faith and Credit Clause of Article IV, section 1. Second, when a litigant challenges a state court's choice of a substantive law, the *Allstate/Shutts* test applies: "for a State's substantive law to be selected in a constitutionally permissible manner, that State must have a significant contact or significant aggregation of contacts, creating state interests, such that choice of its law is neither arbitrary nor fundamentally unfair" (Allstate Ins. Co. v. Hague, 1981, plurality op.; Phillips Petroleum Co. v. Shutts, 1985). Third, due process is satisfied whenever a state chooses to apply its own procedural laws in its own courts (Sun Oil Co. v. Wortman, 1988). Beyond these modest conclusions, many issues remain regarding the nature of the state interest required to support application of forum substantive law, the types of contacts that create such an interest, and the scope of the *Wortman* exception for procedural laws.

## NOTES

1. Russell J. Weintraub, *Due Process and Full Faith and Credit Limitations on a State's Choice of Law*, 44 Iowa L. Rev. 449, 449 (1959) (citing Lauritzen v. Larsen, 345 U.S. 571, 591 (1953)).

2. State courts follow a variety of choice-of-law theories, including the traditional *lex loci delicti* and *lex loci contractus* rules included in the First Restatement of the Conflict of Laws (1934); the "most significant relationship" approach included in Second Restatement of the Conflict of Laws (1971); governmental interest analysis; choice-influencing considerations and the "better law" approach; comparative impairment; and the *lex fori* approach. A leading treatise identifies the approach(es) followed in each of the fifty states. *See* Eugene F. Scoles et al., Conflict of Laws §§ 2.20–2.25 (3d ed. 2000).

3. The Privileges and Immunities Clause of Article IV, § 2, bars discrimination on the basis of state citizenship and the Equal Protection Clause of the Fourteenth Amendment bars discrimination more generally. Choice-of-law theories that provide in-state domiciliaries, but not domiciliaries of other states, with the benefit of local law may be scrutinized under these clauses as well. *See, e.g.,* Douglas Laycock, *Equal Citizens of Equal and Territorial States: The Constitutional Foundations of Choice of Law*, 92 Colum. L. Rev. 249, 274–78 (1992); Lea Brilmayer, *Shaping and Sharing in Democratic Theory: Towards a Political Philosophy of Interstate Equality*, 15 Fla. St. U. L. Rev. 389, 409–416 (1987); Douglas Laycock, *Equality and the Citizens of Sister States*, 15 Fla. St. U. L. Rev. 431, 446–48 (1987). *Cf.* Brainerd Currie & Herma Hill Schreter, *Unconstitutional Discrimination in the Conflict of Laws: Privileges and Immunities*, *in* Brainerd Currie, Selected Essays on the Conflict of Laws 445, 503–511 (1963). In addition, the Commerce Clause of Article I, § 8, has some relevance to conflicts of law to the extent that it prohibits extrater-

ritorial regulation by states. *See, e.g.*, Brown- Forman Distillers Corp. v. N.Y. State Liquor Auth., 476 U.S. 573 (1986).

4. *See, e.g.*, Peter Hay, *Full Faith and Credit and Federalism in Choice of Law*, 34 Mercer L. Rev. 709, 716–17 (1983) (describing due process protections as "primarily litigant oriented"); Frederic L. Kirgis, Jr., *The Roles of Due Process and Full Faith and Credit in Choice of Law*, 62 Cornell L. Rev. 94, 95 (1976) (arguing that "due process has a power element as well as a fairness element"); Scoles, *supra* note 2, § 3.20.

5. *See, e.g.*, Weintraub, *supra* note 1, at 455–60 (discussing the role due process plays in protecting litigants from unfair surprise).

6. *See, e.g.*, Robert A. Leflar, *Constitutional Limits on Free Choice of Law*, 28 Law & Contemp. Probs. 706, 711 (1963); Scoles, *supra* note 2, § 3.20.

7. *See, e.g.*, Hay, *supra* note 4, at 717–22 (describing a "negative control" function performed by the Full Faith and Credit Clause to ensure that a state does not interfere with the interests of other states when it applies its law to multistate controversies); Scoles, *supra* note 2, § 3.20. *Cf.* Ralph U. Whitten, *The Constitutional Limitations on State-Court Jurisdiction: A Historical-Interpretative Reexamination of the Full Faith and Credit and Due Process Clauses (Part One)*, 14 Creighton L. Rev. 499, 597–99 & n.439 (1981) (arguing that neither the Full Faith and Credit Clause nor the Due Process Clause should be read to restrict a state's authority to apply its own statutes or common law rules to a dispute).

8. *See* Chapter 2, section entitled "'Persons' Protected by Due Process," subsection entitled "States, Municipalities and Other Political Subdivisions."

9. *See, e.g.*, James A. Martin, *Constitutional Limitations on Choice of Law*, 61 Cornell L. Rev. 185, 185 (1976) (noting that "substantive due process . . . has emerged as the chief doctrinal basis for constitutional conflict-of-law decisions"); Courtland H. Peterson, *Proposals of Marriage Between Jurisdiction and Choice of Law*, 14 U.C. Davis L. Rev. 869, 876 (1981) (suggesting that "due process restraints on choice of law might be suspect because of their substantive flavor").

10. William M. Richman & William L. Reynolds, Understanding Conflict of Laws § 98, at 313 (rev. 3d ed. 2002) (stating that "[t]he Due Process Clause basically protects persons against procedural unfairness. In choice of law, therefore, the focus is on foreseeability and unfair surprise") (footnote omitted); Robert A. Sedler, *Constitutional Limitations on Choice of Law: The Perspective of Constitutional Generalism*, 10 Hofstra L. Rev. 59, 61 (1981) (bemoaning the fact that "the Court's treatment of due process as a limitation on choice of law has generally taken place without regard to the Court's application of substantive due process doctrine in other areas").

11. Richman &. Reynolds, *supra* note 10, § 95; Sedler, *supra* note 10, at 61. *See* Lochner v. New York, 198 U.S. 45 (1905) (holding that a state labor law that limited a bakery employee's work week to sixty hours violated the Due Process Clause by interfering with the right to contract, part of the liberty protected by due process); 1 Lawrence H. Tribe, American Constitutional Law §§ 8-1–8-4 (3d ed. 2000).

12. *See, e.g.*, 3 Joseph H. Beale, A Treatise on the Conflict of Laws §§ 70, 72 (1935) (describing the territorial system); Joseph Story, Commentaries on the Conflict of Laws §§ 18, 20 (1834); Pennoyer v. Neff, 95 U.S. 714, 722 (1878).

13. 3 Beale, *supra* note 12, § 73.

14. In dissent, Justice Brandeis argued that the loan agreement was not an independent contract, but rather the mere performance of acts contemplated by the original policy. He further argued that even if the loan agreement were treated as an independent contract, it

should have been viewed as a Missouri contract. N.Y. Life Ins. Co. v. Dodge, 246 U.S. 357, 381 (1918) (Brandeis, J., dissenting).

15. For a more complete description of Dick's connection to Texas, *see* Jeffrey L. Rensberger, *Who Was Dick?: Constitutional Limitations on State Choice of Law*, 1998 Utah L. Rev. 37 (concluding that Dick was a Texas domiciliary only temporarily present in Mexico at the time the insurance policy issued and the claim arose).

16. For a discussion of the internal and external forces that led to the demise of *Lochner*, *see* 1 Tribe, *supra* note 11, §§ 8-5–8-7.

17. *Id.* § 8-6, at 1358.

18. *Id.* §§ 8-6 & 8-7.

19. The Court continued to rely on the territoriality principle in several cases decided during this period under the Full Faith and Credit Clause. *See, e.g.*, John Hancock Mut. Life Ins. Co. v. Yates, 299 U.S. 178 (1936); Bradford Elec. Light Co. v. Clapper, 286 U.S. 145 (1932).

20. The Court had also incorporated this consideration of state interests into its full faith and credit analysis. *See, e.g.,* Carroll v. Lanza, 349 U.S. 408, 412–13 (1955); *see also* Nevada v. Hall, 440 U.S. 410, 424 (1979).

21. In fact, foreign insurance companies doing business in Louisiana were required by the law to consent to direct actions and the defendant insurer had so consented. Watson v. Employers Liab. Assurance Corp., 348 U.S. 66, 69 (1954).

22. These facts are included in the Supreme Court's earlier decision in the case, Clay v. Sun Ins. Office Ltd., 363 U.S. 207, 208–09 & n.1 (1960), in which the Court declined to reach the constitutional issue until the Florida Supreme Court resolved two predicate issues of state law.

23. The insurer also argued that the Full Faith and Credit Clause required the forum to apply Illinois law to the controversy. Clay v. Sun Ins. Office, Ltd., 377 U.S. 179, 181 (1964).

24. Scoles et al., *supra* note 2, § 2.16.

25. *Id.* § 2.17.

26. Russell Weintraub argues that Wisconsin, like Minnesota, would have permitted stacking by construing ambiguity in the insurance policy against the insurer. *See, e.g.*, Russell J. Weintraub, *Who's Afraid of Constitutional Limits on Choice of Law?*, 10 Hofstra L. Rev. 17, 20–23 (1981) (hereinafter Weintraub, *Who's Afraid?*); Russell J. Weintraub, *The Conflict of Laws Rejoins the Mainstream of Legal Reasoning*, 65 Tex. L. Rev. 215, 233 & n.96 (1986).

27. Robert A. Leflar, *Choice-Influencing Considerations in Conflicts Law*, 41 N.Y.U. L. Rev. 267 (1966); Robert A. Leflar, *Conflicts Law: More on Choice-Influencing Considerations*, 54 Cal. L. Rev. 1584 (1966).

28. In an earlier footnote, the plurality noted that the Court had "taken a similar approach in deciding choice-of-law cases under both the Due Process Clause and the Full Faith and Credit Clause," having abandoned the more exacting "weighing-of-interests" standard under the Full Faith and Credit Clause. Allstate Ins. Co. v. Hague, 449 U.S. 302, 308 n.10 (1981) (plurality op.). *See also* Franchise Tax Bd. v. Hyatt, 538 U.S. 488, 495 (2003) (commenting that the balancing approach previously used in full faith and credit cases "quickly proved unsatisfactory").

29. *See also* Weintraub, *Who's Afraid?*, *supra* note 26, at 28.

30. *See also id.* at 28–29.

31. *See* Lea Brilmayer & Jack Goldsmith, Conflict of Laws: Cases and Materials, Teacher's Manual 42 (5th ed. 2002) (noting "[t]he problem with a foreseeability analysis is that it focuses on the defendant's expectations ex ante, and makes no allowance for what actually happens ex post").

32. In his view, the full faith and credit "inquiry implicates the federal interest in ensuring that Minnesota respect the sovereignty of the State of Wisconsin; the second [due process inquiry] implicates the litigants' interest in a fair adjudication of their rights." Allstate Ins. Co. v. Hague, 449 U.S. 302, 320 (1981) (Stevens, J., concurring in the judgment) (footnote omitted).

33. *See, e.g.*, Peterson, *supra* note 9, at 882; Bruce Posnak, *The Court Doesn't Know Its* Asahi *From Its* Wortman: *A Critical View of the Constitutional Constraints on Jurisdiction and Choice of Law*, 41 Syracuse L. Rev. 875, 881–83 (1990); Lea Brilmayer, Conflict of Laws § 3.2.2 (2d ed. 1995).

34. P. John Kozyris, *Reflections on* Allstate—*The Lessening of Due Process in Choice of Law*, 14 U.C. Davis L. Rev. 889, 896–97 (1981).

35. *See id.* at 900–02 (criticizing the Court's reliance on potential contacts regardless of whether they eventually materialize).

36. Posnak, *supra* note 33, at 882 (footnote omitted).

37. For a more thorough treatment of *Shutts*, see Arthur R. Miller & David Crump, *Jurisdiction and Choice of Law in Multistate Class Actions After* Phillips Petroleum Co. v. Shutts, 96 Yale L.J. 1 (1986).

38. The company also challenged the constitutionality of Kansas's assertion of personal jurisdiction over the absent class members. *See* Chapter 5, section entitled "Nonparties Who May Be Bound," subsection entitled "Persons Adequately Represented by Parties," paragraph entitled "Class Actions," for a discussion of the portion of *Shutts* that upheld jurisdiction.

39. *See, e.g.*, Posnak, *supra* note 33, at 882 (criticizing *Shutts* for failing to "clear any of the 'state interest' muddy water") (footnote omitted); Courtland H. Peterson, *Jurisdiction and Choice of Law Revisited*, 59 U. Colo. L. Rev. 37, 59–60 (1988).

40. *See, e.g.*, Sun Oil Co. v. Wortman, 486 U.S. 717, 737 (1988) (Brennan, J., concurring in part and concurring in the judgment); David E. Seidelson, *1 (*Wortman*) + 1 (*Ferens*) = 6 (Years): That Can't be Right—Can It? Statutes of Limitations and Supreme Court Inconsistency*, 57 Brook. L. Rev. 787, 789–90 (1991); Louise Weinberg, *Choosing Law: The Limitations Debate*, 1991 U. Ill. L. Rev. 683, 698.

41. Regarding the Kansas court's conclusion that Texas, Oklahoma and Louisiana likely would apply the interest rate specified in the FPC regulations in these circumstances, a different majority of the Court held that it does not violate the Constitution for a state court to merely misconstrue the law of another state: "the misconstruction must contradict law of the other State that is clearly established and that has been brought to the court's attention." Sun Oil Co. v. Wortman, 486 U.S. 717, 731 (1988). Kansas's interpretations of Texas, Oklahoma and Louisiana law did not violate this standard.

In a blistering dissent, Justice O'Connor took issue with this portion of the *Wortman* majority opinion, finding that the Kansas court erred in concluding that Texas, Oklahoma and Louisiana would have applied the FPC interest rate rather than the interest rates specified in their prejudgment interest statutes. *Id.* at 743–49 (O'Connor, J., dissenting).

42. *See, e.g.*, Posnak, *supra* note 33; Seidelson, *supra* note 40; Weinberg, *supra* note 40.

43. *See* Posnak, *supra* note 33, at 883.

44. *See* Weinberg, *supra* note 40, at 696–97.

45. Joseph William Singer, *A Pragmatic Guide to Conflicts*, 70 B.U.L. Rev. 731, 816 (1990). *See also* Weinberg, *supra* note 40, at 695–96.

# Bibliographical Essay

## CHAPTER 1: THE HISTORY OF DUE PROCESS

### Primary Materials

Several sources gather and analyze important primary materials. The Lloyds' book gathers the Magna Carta, early colonial charters, original state constitutions, the Articles of Confederation, the plans considered by the framers in drafting the Constitution, early American political writings and important correspondence. For each amendment in the Bill of Rights, including the Fifth Amendment and its Due Process Clause, Neil Cogan's book gathers drafts of the amendment, motions presenting the drafts to Congress, committee reports, analogous provisions from state constitutions and laws and colonial charters, political commentary, correspondence, diaries and material from the state conventions. These works are:

The Complete Bill of Rights: The Drafts, Debates, Sources and Origins (Neil H. Cogan, ed., 1997)

The Essential Bill of Rights: Original Arguments and Fundamental Documents (Gordon Lloyd & Margie Lloyd eds., 1998)

### The Origins of Due Process: Magna Carta and Early English Law

Several books provide helpful insights into the historical antecedents of the Due Process Clauses. Coke provides an extended treatment of the Magna Carta and states his famous equation of the "law of the land" and due process. John Hudson, William McKechnie and Bernard Siegan provide additional analysis of the Magna Carta and place it in broader historical context. John Orth analyzes Dr. Bonham's case in detail. These works are:

Edward Coke, The Institutes of the Laws of England (photo. reprint 1986) (Butler & Hargrave eds., 1797)

John Hudson, The Formation of the English Common Law: Law and Society in England From the Norman Conquest to Magna Carta (1996)

William Sharp McKechnie, Magna Carta: A Commentary on the Great Charter of King John (2d ed. 1914)

John V. Orth, Due Process of Law: A Brief History (2003)

Bernard H. Siegan, Property Rights: From Magna Carta to the Fourteenth Amendment (2001)

## The Federal Constitution and the Fifth Amendment

In addition to Siegan (cited above), several works proved invaluable in tracing the history of the Bill of Rights in general and the Due Process Clause of the Fifth Amendment in particular. Robert Rutland sets out the history of the original Constitution as well as the Bill of Rights. Rodney Mott argues that the Fifth Amendment Due Process Clause was intended to prevent general arbitrary action on the part of the government. William Crosskey contends that the Due Process Clause was not intended to check the substantive fairness of Congressional legislation. Charles Miller, whose chapter traces the history of due process from Magna Carta to the twentieth century, explains why the Fifth Amendment may have employed the phrase "due process" rather than its historical antecedent, "law of the land." Frank Easterbrook argues that the Due Process Clause was intended to bar *ex parte* procedures and to require courts to afford litigants notice and an opportunity to present a defense, but was not intended to invalidate legislation. These works are:

William Winslow Crosskey, Politics and the Constitution in the History of the United States (1953)

Frank H. Easterbrook, *Due Process and Parole Decision-Making*, in Parole in the 1980s 77 (B. Borsage ed. 1981)

Frank H. Easterbrook, *Substance and Due Process*, 1982 Sup. Ct. Rev. 85

Charles A. Miller, *The Forest of Due Process of Law: The American Constitutional Tradition, in* Nomos XVIII: Due Process 3 (J. Roland Pennock & John W. Chapman eds., 1977)

Rodney L. Mott, Due Process of Law (1973)

Robert Allen Rutland, The Birth of the Bill of Rights 1776–1791 (1955)

## Due Process Before the Civil War

In separate articles, Edward Corwin and Lowell Howe examine the pre-Civil War understanding of the phrases "due process of law" and "the law of the land." Ralph Whitten examines colonial laws and constitutions as well as state court decisions interpreting due process before the adoption of the Fourteenth Amendment. David Bodenhamer and Bernard Siegan (cited above) examine the same time frame, the former focusing on criminal justice and the latter focusing on property rights. These works are:

David J. Bodenhamer, Fair Trial: Rights of the Accused in American History (1992)

Edward S. Corwin, *The Doctrine of Due Process of Law Before the Civil War*, 24 Harv. L. Rev. 366 (1911)

Lowell J. Howe, *The Meaning of "Due Process of Law" Prior to the Adoption of the Fourteenth Amendment*, 18 Cal. L. Rev. 583 (1930)

Ralph U. Whitten, *The Constitutional Limitations on State-Court Jurisdiction: A Historical-Interpretative Reexamination of the Full Faith and Credit and Due Process Clauses (Part Two)*, 14 Creighton L. Rev. 735 (1981)

### Adoption of the Fourteenth Amendment

A wealth of scholarship analyzes the Fourteenth Amendment in general and the Due Process Clause in particular (much of it addressing substantive due process and the incorporation debate, which are beyond the scope of this book). Jacobus tenBroek views the Civil War amendments in the context of the abolitionist movement. Horace Flack contends that the Fourteenth Amendment was intended to make the first eight amendments of the Bill of Rights binding upon the states and to give Congress authority to enact direct legislation to secure civil rights. Raoul Berger, Horace Flack, Hermine Herta Meyer, Bernard Siegan (cited above) and Jacobus tenBroek all discuss the drafting of the Fourteenth Amendment and the debates in the Thirty-ninth Congress. Berger and Meyer argue that the states retained power under the Fourteenth Amendment to make their own procedural rules, as long as they applied them equally to all. Ralph Whitten (cited above) argues that the Due Process Clause restricted the legislature as well as the courts. These works are:

Raoul Berger, Government by Judiciary: The Transformation of the Fourteenth Amendment (1977)

Horace Edgar Flack, The Adoption of the Fourteenth Amendment (1908)

Hermine Herta Meyer, The History and Meaning of the Fourteenth Amendment: Judicial Erosion of the Constitution Through Misuse of the Fourteenth Amendment (1977)

Jacobus tenBroek, The Antislavery Origins of the Fourteenth Amendment (1951)

### Procedural Due Process in the Post-Civil War Period

Roald Mykkeltvedt views Powell v. Alabama (1932) as a turning point in the Supreme Court's due process jurisprudence, evincing a new willingness to monitor the fairness of state criminal proceedings. Roland Pennock and Frank Easterbrook (cited above) both comment upon the shift in the Court's due process analysis from a historical approach to a more subjective, fairness-oriented approach. William Crosskey (cited above) criticizes the Court for not reading the Due Process Clause to incorporate all of the "process" guarantees of the first eight amendments, but only those that the Justices themselves desire. These works are:

Roald Y. Mykkeltvedt, The Nationalization of the Bill of Rights: Fourteenth Amendment Due Process and the Procedural Rights (1983)

J. Roland Pennock, *Introduction*, *in* Nomos XVIII: Due Process xv (J. Roland Pennock & John W. Chapman eds., 1977)

## CHAPTER 2: PRELIMINARIES

### "Persons" Protected by Due Process

#### *Individuals*

A rich and growing body of literature discusses the extent to which noncitizens, including illegal aliens, enemy aliens and enemy combatants, enjoy the protections of the Due Process Clauses. In an article critiquing many of the security measures taken by the government in the wake of September 11th, David Cole discusses the due process protections that aliens receive, Congress's plenary power over immigrants, the differential treatment between aliens who enter the United States and those outside our borders, and the qualified rights of enemy aliens. He contends that "outside of a declared war against an identifiable nation, aliens living among us are entitled to . . . due process . . . ." In an earlier article, Cole maintains that the Due Process Clause, read together with the Suspension Clause of Article I of the Constitution, requires federal judicial review of claims that aliens are being removed from the country in violation of federal law.

In a student note, Jim Rosenfeld identifies three distinct phases in the history of aliens' due process rights. Hiroshi Motomura examines the government's differential treatment of citizens and noncitizens and argues that the line between citizen and noncitizen is temporary and porous. In separate articles, Matthew Hall and Mark Jackson describe the government's use of undisclosed evidence in immigration proceedings and debate whether this practice violates due process. In a student note, Alicia Brown discusses the due process rights of aliens, the Supreme Court's decision in Zadvydas v. Davis (2001), and the extent to which the case renders portions of the Patriot Act vulnerable to constitutional challenge.

The Schulhofer, Dempsey and Cole, and Cole books discuss a host of constitutional issues raised by the war on terrorism, including the due process issues surrounding the use of secret evidence, closed immigration hearings and the indefinite detention of aliens. These works are:

Alicia Brown, *Striking a Balance: The Conflict Between Safety and Due Process Rights—The Practical Implications of* Zadvydas v. Davis, 22 J. NAALJ 429 (2002)

David Cole, *Jurisdiction and Liberty: Habeas Corpus and Due Process as Limits on Congress's Control of Federal Jurisdiction*, 86 Geo. L.J. 2481 (1998)

David Cole, *Enemy Aliens*, 54 Stan. L. Rev. 953 (2002)

David Cole, Enemy Aliens: Double Standards and Constitutional Freedoms in the War on Terrorism (2003)

James X. Dempsey & David Cole, Terrorism and the Constitution: Sacrificing Civil Liberties in the Name of National Security (2d ed. 2002)

Matthew R. Hall, *Procedural Due Process Meets National Security: The Problem of Classified Evidence in Immigration Proceedings,* 35 Cornell Int'l L.J. 515 (2002)

D. Mark Jackson, *Exposing Secret Evidence: Eliminating a New Hardship of United States Immigration*, 19 Buff. Pub. Int. L.J. 25 (2000–01)

Hiroshi Motomura, *Immigration and We the People After September 11*, 66 Alb. L. Rev. 413 (2003)

Jim Rosenfeld, *Deportation Proceedings and Due Process of Law*, 26 Colum. Hum. Rts. L. Rev. 713 (1995)

Stephen J. Schulhofer, The Enemy Within: Intelligence Gathering, Law Enforcement, and Civil Liberties in the Wake of September 11 (2002)

### *States, Municipalities and Other Political Subdivisions*

While there is consensus that corporations, partnerships and unions are "persons" protected by due process, there is debate regarding political subdivisions of states. Several scholars have considered whether political subdivisions should have standing to raise constitutional claims against their own states. Michael Lawrence argues that municipalities should have standing to pursue procedural due process claims, rejecting the proposition that municipal corporations have no constitutional rights vis-à-vis their creating states. In a student note, Alexander Willscher rejects the standing rubric, arguing that municipalities fail to state claims under the Fourteenth Amendment and the Contract Clause because those provisions do not protect municipalities. Willscher further argues that Congress lacks authority to grant municipalities an implied cause of action to sue their states. These works are:

Michael A. Lawrence, *Do "Creatures of the State" Have Constitutional Rights?: Standing for Municipalities to Assert Procedural Due Process Claims Against the State*, 47 Vill. L. Rev. 93 (2002)

Alexander Willscher, *The Justiciability of Municipal Preemption Challenges to State Law*, 67 U. Chi. L. Rev. 243 (2000)

## State Action

Many articles review and critique the Supreme Court's difficult body of state action case law, described by the late Charles Black as a "conceptual disaster area." Numerous scholars have recommended that the state action requirement be abolished. Erwin Chemerinsky, for example, argues that the state action requirement is harmful (because it permits infringement of important individual rights by private parties), anachronistic when judged by its original purpose, unnecessary to preserve private autonomy or to safeguard state sovereignty and actually counterproductive to these goals. Kenneth Karst and Harold Horowitz advocate a substantive analysis in lieu of a state action analysis. Other scholars argue that the state action requirement should be retained, but nevertheless critique the current state of the law. Robert Glennon and John Nowak eschew a unitary concept of state action, advocating a balancing test instead, pursuant to which courts would weigh the value of challenged practices against the harm they do to given rights and the value of those rights. Barbara Rook Snyder criticizes the Court for confusing the question whether state action is present with the question whether the state action violates the Fourteenth Amendment. Ronald Krotoszynski recommends adoption of a "meta-analysis": if a defendant does not qualify as a state actor under any of the existing tests, the court should consider whether the defendant qualifies as a state actor nonetheless because she satisfies a sufficient portion of each of the tests. These works are:

Charles L. Black, Jr., *The Supreme Court, 1966 Term—Foreward: "State Action," Equal Protection, and California's Proposition 14*, 81 Harv. L. Rev. 69 (1967)

Erwin Chemerinsky, *Rethinking State Action*, 80 Nw. U. L. Rev. 503 (1985)

Robert J. Glennon, Jr. & John E. Nowak, *A Functional Analysis of the Fourteenth Amendment "State Action" Requirement*, 1976 Sup. Ct. Rev. 221

Kenneth L. Karst & Harold W. Horowitz, Reitman v. Mulkey: *A Telophase of Substantive Equal Protection*, 1967 Sup. Ct. Rev. 39

Ronald J. Krotoszynski, Jr., *Back to the Briarpatch: An Argument in Favor of Constitutional Meta-Analysis in State Action Determinations*, 94 Mich. L. Rev. 302 (1995)

Barbara Rook Snyder, *Private Motivation, State Action and the Allocation of Responsibility for Fourteenth Amendment Violations*, 75 Cornell L. Rev. 1053 (1990)

## Interests Protected by Due Process

An enormous literature explores the meaning of the words "liberty" and "property" in the Due Process Clauses, the reigning entitlement theory and the history of the right/privilege distinction.

### *Right/Privilege Distinction*

In an article tracing the demise of the right/privilege distinction, William Van Alstyne identifies five different devices employed by the Supreme Court that greatly minimized its harsh consequences. After demonstrating how these doctrines rendered the right/privilege distinction inconsequential, Van Alstyne advocates an outright rejection of the distinction, arguing that due process should apply directly to "status interests in the public sector." Charles Reich, too, is highly critical of the right/privilege distinction, arguing that certain forms of government largess, including unemployment compensation, public assistance and Social Security, should be treated as protected property interests. In a later piece, Reich argues that the Due Process Clause assures all persons in the United States minimum subsistence, housing, child care, education, employment, health insurance, retirement benefits and a clean and healthy environment. Rodney Smolla argues that the right/privilege distinction is not in fact dead, but has reemerged under the guise of the entitlement theory. If the entitlement theory is the reincarnation of the right/privilege distinction, Smolla argues it should be subject to the limitations that evolved over time to curtail abuses of that distinction. In separate pieces, Cynthia Farina and Doug Rendleman agree that the entitlement theory resurrects the right/privilege distinction. Rendleman posits that both analyses "formulate a cut-off," identifying those interests that merit due process protection. These works are:

Cynthia R. Farina, *Conceiving Due Process*, 3 Yale J.L. & Feminism 189 (1991)

Charles A. Reich, *The New Property*, 73 Yale L.J. 733 (1964)

Charles A. Reich, *Individual Rights and Social Welfare: The Emerging Legal Issues*, 74 Yale L.J. 1245 (1965)

Charles A. Reich, *Beyond the New Property: An Ecological View of Due Process*, 56 Brook. L. Rev. 731 (1990)

Doug Rendleman, *The New Due Process: Rights and Remedies*, 63 Ky. L.J. 531 (1975)

Rodney A. Smolla, *The Reemergence of the Right-Privilege Distinction in Constitutional Law: The Price of Protesting Too Much*, 35 Stan. L. Rev. 69 (1982)

William W. Van Alstyne, *The Demise of the Right-Privilege Distinction in Constitutional Law*, 81 Harv. L. Rev. 1439 (1968)

### *Entitlement Theory*

Doug Rendleman (cited above) argues that the reigning entitlement theory offers courts a "fresh start . . . to sort out those interests felt to be important enough for due process."

Peter Simon, too, defends the *Roth/Perry* approach to protected interests, arguing that it properly leaves substantive matters to the state legislatures, while reserving procedural matters for the courts.

Other scholars are less sanguine about the entitlement theory. Henry Monaghan describes the analytical shift in the Court's thinking from an approach that took the words "life, liberty or property" as a unitary concept that embraced "all interests valued by sensible men" to an approach that scrutinizes the words in the clause separately, focusing not on the weight of the interest at stake, but rather on its "nature." Mark Tushnet describes the same shift, criticizing the Court's insistence in *Roth* that only property rights created and defined by positive law are entitled to due process protection. John Hart Ely agrees that the result of the analytical shift was a significant, even disastrous, constriction of interests entitled to procedural protection. In separate pieces, Ely and Sylvia Law criticize the entitlement theory because it is circular and forces courts to make premature judgments on the merits just to determine whether a protected interest is implicated (i.e., the court must determine whether one has an entitlement before it can decide whether one is entitled to a hearing on the question of whether one has an entitlement). Law argues that under this approach, due process constrains the state from treating citizens arbitrarily, but, at the same time, allows the state exclusive discretion to define the interests that trigger due process scrutiny. Cynthia Farina (cited above), too, critiques the entitlement theory (and critiques of it) and bemoans the Court's extension of this approach to liberty interests. As a new starting point, she offers "a set of feminist understandings and methods." In separate pieces, Jerry Mashaw and Edward Rubin argue that the positive law approach is incoherent and leads to bizarre conclusions regarding protected interests. Mashaw further maintains that under the Court's approach, "[d]iscretion bounded by standards requires due process; but absolute discretion . . . escapes constitutional notice under the current analysis." Rubin argues that the due process inquiry should focus on the fairness of the governmental action. The student Comment recommends that both the entitlement theory and the present enjoyment requirement be abandoned and replaced by a balancing test.

These works are:

Comment, *Entitlement, Enjoyment, and Due Process of Law*, 1974 Duke L.J. 89

John Hart Ely, Democracy and Distrust: A Theory of Judicial Review (1980)

Sylvia A. Law, *Some Reflections on* Goldberg v. Kelly *at Twenty Years*, 56 Brook. L. Rev. 805 (1990)

Jerry L. Mashaw, *Administrative Due Process: The Quest for a Dignitary Theory*, 61 B.U. L. Rev. 885 (1981)

Jerry L. Mashaw, *Dignitary Process: A Political Psychology of Liberal Democratic Citizenship*, 39 U. Fla. L. Rev. 433 (1987)

Henry Paul Monaghan, *Of "Liberty" and "Property,"* 62 Cornell L. Rev. 405 (1977)

Edward L. Rubin, *Due Process and the Administrative State*, 72 Cal. L. Rev. 1044 (1984)

Peter N. Simon, *Liberty and Property in the Supreme Court: A Defense of* Roth *and* Perry, 71 Cal. L. Rev. 146 (1983)

Mark Tushnet, *The Newer Property: Suggestion for the Revival of Substantive Due Process*, 1975 Sup. Ct. Rev. 261

## Judicial Review of Procedural Protections

Henry Monaghan and Peter Simon (cited above) agree that our legal tradition demands independent judicial scrutiny to gauge the adequacy of procedure. In separate pieces, Douglas Laycock and Frank Michelman reject the argument that the legislature may determine the effective scope of due process by prescribing the procedures that accompany the denial of a protected interest. Martin Redish and Lawrence Marshall, too, critique legislative control over procedure, arguing that such a conception of due process would effectively render the constitutional guarantee "a rubber stamp for all legislative enactments." In stark contrast, Frank Easterbrook argues that the Due Process Clause was not intended to restrict legislative authority to determine the procedures that attend termination of government benefits and employment. He further maintains that because substance and procedure are intimately related, courts that demand procedural protections are vindicating their own view of substantive rights, rather than the legislators' views. Jerry Mashaw (cited above) argues that the Court's approach is incoherent and unworkable because, on the one hand, it "reads statutes as if they established rights that have some independent meaning apart from the legal protections that attend their deprivation," but on the other hand, it maintains that rights derive only from positive law. These works are:

Frank Easterbrook, *Due Process and Parole Decision Making*, in Parole in the 1980s 77 (B. Borsage ed. 1981)

Frank H. Easterbrook, *Substance and Due Process*, 1982 Sup. Ct. Rev. 85

Douglas Laycock, *Due Process and Separation of Powers: The Effort to Make the Due Process Clauses Nonjusticiable*, 60 Tex. L. Rev. 875 (1982)

Frank I. Michelman, *Formal and Associational Aims in Procedural Due Process*, in Nomos XVIII: Due Process 126 (J. Roland Pennock & John W. Chapman eds., 1977)

Martin H. Redish & Lawrence C. Marshall, *Adjudicatory Independence and the Values of Procedural Due Process*, 95 Yale L.J. 455 (1986)

## Liberty

Isaiah Berlin distinguishes between two divergent and irreconcilable concepts of liberty: negative liberty, or freedom from interference with one's activity, and positive liberty, or a right of self-direction, to share in public power by participating in the government and choosing governmental leaders. Henry Monaghan (cited above) argues that the Court in the 1970s "radically reorient[ed] thinking about the nature of the 'liberty' protected by the due process clause" by narrowly restricting the class of interests protected directly by due process. In an article that critiques the entitlement theory, William Van Alstyne argues that freedom from arbitrary adjudicative procedures itself should be treated as a substantive element of protected "liberty," so that "government may not adjudicate the claims of individuals by unreliable means." In other words, the Due Process Clause should provide an "immunity . . . from procedural arbitrariness" or "from unwarranted procedural grossness." Stephen Williams critiques this nonarbitrariness theory as well as the reigning entitlement theory and the importance theory. Relying heavily on the historical meaning of the words "liberty" and "property," Williams offers an alternate approach that would protect only those interests that were entitled to due process protections in 1925–life, negative liberty, and conventional property. In an earlier article, Williams argues that the framers of the Fifth Amendment viewed liberty primarily as freedom from incarceration. These works are:

Isaiah Berlin, *Two Concepts of Liberty, in* Isaiah Berlin, Four Essays on Liberty 118 (1970)

William Van Alstyne, *Cracks In "The New Property": Adjudicative Due Process in the Administrative State*, 62 Cornell L. Rev. 445 (1977)

Stephen F. Williams, *Liberty and Property: The Problem of Government Benefits*, 12 J. Legal Stud. 3 (1983)

Stephen F. Williams, *"Liberty" in the Due Process Clauses of the Fifth and Fourteenth Amendments: The Framers' Intentions*, 53 U. Colo. L. Rev. 117 (1981)

### Due Process Counterrevolution?

Richard Pierce provides a dramatic history of the due process revolution and its aftermath. He argues that the Court's revolutionary decision to recognize government benefits as "property," coupled with its later realization that elaborate procedural protections in all benefits cases cannot be afforded, has resulted in a diminution in protection for even "old" property. His prediction of a dramatic "counterrevolution" in due process has yet to be fully realized. Cynthia Farina critiques Pierce's essay, recounting an alternate history of procedural due process with roots in the McCarthy period and the civil rights movement. In Farina's view, the Court in *Goldberg* conflated three different notions of "entitlement." One of these entitlements—the interest created by regulatory standards that constrain the discretion of government actors—should remain constitutionally protected even after "reform" efforts like the 1996 welfare amendments. Randal Jeffrey builds on Farina's article, arguing that public assistance is property entitled to due process protection even after the 1996 welfare legislation. Rebecca Zietlow expresses concern that the due process counterrevolution will most severely affect the poor and disenfranchised, who lack the financial resources and political power to propose legislation to establish their property and liberty interests.

These works are:

Cynthia R. Farina, *On Misusing "Revolution" and "Reform": Procedural Due Process and the New Welfare Act*, 50 Admin. L. Rev. 591 (1998)

Randal S. Jeffrey, *The Importance of Due Process Protections After Welfare Reform: Client Stories From New York City*, 66 Alb. L. Rev. 123 (2002)

Richard J. Pierce, Jr., *The Due Process Counterrevolution of the 1990's?*, 96 Colum. L. Rev. 1973 (1996)

Rebecca E. Zietlow, *Giving Substance to Process: Countering the Due Process Counterrevolution*, 75 Denv. U.L. Rev. 9 (1997)

## CHAPTER 3: NOTICE AND THE OPPORTUNITY TO BE HEARD

### Critiques of Mathews v. Eldridge (1976)

The Supreme Court's decision in Mathews v. Eldridge (1976) adopts a utilitarian approach, seeking to maximize social welfare by balancing the social value of the claimant's private interest against the social cost of introducing additional procedures. For critical analyses of the *Eldridge* balancing test, see the work of Cynthia Farina, Jerry Mashaw, Charles Koch and Jane Rutherford. Farina criticizes the *Eldridge* balancing test as stacked against the individual, whose interest is denied constitutional protection unless it outweighs the collective good. She further notes the impossibility of applying the balancing test given the inability to quantify many relevant variables.

Jerry Mashaw criticizes *Eldridge* for focusing on questions of adjudicatory technique, rather than on the values underlying due process (such as individual dignity, equality and tradition). In later works, Mashaw elaborates upon the dignitary approach to administrative due process, arguing that it reinforces the view that "process concerns are intimately connected to substantive rights . . . ." Mashaw ultimately maintains that dignitary theory can make only modest demands on the processes of public decisionmaking.

Like Farina and Mashaw, Charles Koch criticizes the *Eldridge* test, asserting that courts lack data about the practical value of procedural elements and that the analysis perceives state and individual interests as being intrinsically adverse. In lieu of a balancing test, Koch urges a system of principles that coordinate important values shared by the community and its members. Stephen Gottlieb agrees that individual rights and community interests are not inherently adverse.

Jane Rutherford critiques the utility, dignity and contract theories, concluding that all three "fail to address adequately the power relationships among individuals, groups, and society." Rutherford offers instead a unified reading of the Fourteenth Amendment that combines substantive and procedural due process with equal protection to balance power, facilitate participation and enhance equality.

Frank Easterbrook defends the *Eldridge* approach to the extent that it requires government employees to keep the substantive promises that government has made and to seek to minimize the sum of error and process costs.

Alexander Aleinikoff critiques balancing as a general method of constitutional interpretation and identifies serious problems in its application as well as more fundamental problems, such as its tendency to undermine the check and validation functions of constitutional law. He expresses concern that in procedural due process cases, balancing spares the Court the need to develop and defend a theoretical understanding of due process.

These works are:

T. Alexander Aleinikoff, *Constitutional Law in the Age of Balancing*, 96 Yale L.J. 943 (1987)

Frank Easterbrook, *Due Process and Parole Decision Making*, in Parole in the 1980s 77 (B. Borsage ed. 1981)

Cynthia R. Farina, *Conceiving Due Process*, 3 Yale J.L. & Feminism 189 (1991)

Stephen E. Gottlieb, *Communities in the Balance: Comments on Koch*, 37 Hous. L. Rev. 711 (2000)

Charles H. Koch, Jr., *A Community of Interest in the Due Process Calculus*, 37 Hous. L. Rev. 635 (2000)

Jerry L. Mashaw, *Administrative Due Process: The Quest for a Dignitary Theory*, 61 B.U. L. Rev. 885 (1981)

Jerry L. Mashaw, *The Supreme Court's Due Process Calculus for Administrative Adjudication in* Mathews v. Eldridge: *Three Factors in Search of a Theory of Value*, 44 U. Chi. L. Rev. 28 (1976)

Jerry L. Mashaw, Due Process in the Administrative State (1985)

Jane Rutherford, *The Myth of Due Process*, 72 B.U. L. Rev. 1 (1992)

## Contract Theory

Contract theory posits that procedural protections can be left to the market, and that people will bargain for process rights if they value them. In a recent work, Robert Bone critiques the ex ante argument, which "holds that a procedure is fair if all parties would have agreed to the procedure had they been able to contract for it in advance of ('ex ante') their dispute." In its place, he offers a "constructivist" approach to procedural fairness that seeks to construct moral principles from established practice. This work is:

Robert G. Bone, *Agreeing to Fair Process: The Problem with Contractarian Theories of Procedural Fairness*, 83 B.U. L. Rev. 485 (2003)

## Elements of a Fair Hearing

Henry Friendly's classic article identifies eleven elements of a fair hearing and the various types of government action that might require some kind of hearing. He argues that fewer procedural protections should be required when the governmental action is less severe. Martin Redish and Lawrence Marshall argue that the flexibility of the Court's approach to due process fails to assure a minimum level of protection independent of legislative control. They argue that there must be a "solid, value-oriented floor serving as the necessary 'ground' for procedural due process," including an independent adjudicator. Edward Rubin focuses on the due process protections required in adjudicative administrative proceedings. He identifies two guiding principles: the principle of rule obedience, which requires government decisionmakers to follow applicable law, and the principle of minimum procedures, which requires that certain minimum procedures be followed in various situations, such as notice, a hearing and an impartial decisionmaker. These works are:

Henry J. Friendly, *"Some Kind of Hearing,"* 123 U. Penn. L. Rev. 1267 (1975)

Martin H. Redish & Lawrence C. Marshall, *Adjudicatory Independence and the Values of Procedural Due Process*, 95 Yale L.J. 455 (1986)

Edward L. Rubin, *Due Process and the Administrative State*, 72 Cal. L. Rev. 1044 (1984)

## Due Process as Management Technique

In a pre-*Eldridge* work, Jerry Mashaw argues that procedural safeguards and appellate checks alone will not assure accurate and timely resolution of social welfare claims. An adversarial process may not make sense in this context because of the large number of claims and the low educational attainment of most claimants. In Mashaw's view, systematic management techniques should be used to "discover errors, identify their causes and implement corrective action." On a related note, Richard Fallon argues that due process law does not operate at the individual level, guaranteeing an effective remedy for every constitutional violation, but rather at the managerial level, creating schemes and incentives to keep the government within the bounds of the law in most cases. He concludes, "For better or for worse, the doctrine reflects an implicit premise that individual fairness must often be sacrificed to the practical needs of the modern administrative state." These works are:

Richard H. Fallon, Jr., *Some Confusions about Due Process, Judicial Review, and Constitutional Remedies*, 93 Colum. L. Rev. 309 (1993)

Jerry L. Mashaw, *The Management Side of Due Process: Some Theoretical and Litigation Notes on the Assurance of Accuracy, Fairness, and Timeliness in the Adjudication of Social Welfare Claims*, 59 Cornell L. Rev. 772 (1974)

## CHAPTER 4: THE FORM AND EXTENT OF NOTICE

### *Mullane* and the Meanings of Notice

Edward Rubin identifies two distinct meanings of notice: notice of the time and place of the hearing, and notice of how the opposing party will proceed. The latter kind of notice facilitates preparation and increases procedural efficiency. In the context of government-initiated litigation, Rubin maintains that notice serves yet another function: it constrains the government's exercise of power by compelling it "to limit itself to the grounds specified in the notice and to subject itself to challenges on those grounds."

Douglas Laycock analyzes *Mullane* and discerns two distinct holdings: persons with protected interests whose names and addresses are easily ascertainable are entitled to notice by mail or some other means reasonably calculated to reach them; and persons whose names and addresses are not easily ascertainable are not entitled to individual notice but to some other due process protection, such as the appointment of a guardian to represent their interests. These works are:

Douglas Laycock, *Due Process of Law in Trilateral Disputes*, 78 Iowa L. Rev. 1011 (1993)

Edward L. Rubin, *Due Process and the Administrative State*, 72 Cal. L. Rev. 1044 (1984)

### Notice by Electronic Means

Yvonne Tamayo considers the feasibility and constitutionality of notice by e-mail or electronic service of process. She argues that electronic service should be permitted in civil cases as long as it is reasonably calculated to apprise the defendant of the action against her. Harold Don focuses on Pennsylvania practice rules that authorize service by electronic means or facsimile transmission. These works are:

Yvonne A. Tamayo, *Are You Being Served?: E-Mail and (Due) Service of Process*, 51 S.C. L. Rev. 227 (2000)

Harold K. Don, Jr., *Trends in Pennsylvania Civil Practice and Procedure*, 71 Pa. B. Ass'n Q. 47 (2000)

### Notice in the Context of Property Tax Sales

Frank Alexander identifies and comprehensively analyzes four issues that arise in determining the form and extent of notice required in the context of property tax sales: first, the point in the tax sale proceedings at which notice must be provided; second, the definition of a legally protected property interest; third, whether a title search must be undertaken to determine the property interests at stake in a given tax proceeding; and fourth, the efforts that must be undertaken to identify the names and addresses of parties with protected interests. Michael Rubin and Keith Carter argue that the reasoning of Mennonite Board of Missions v. Adams (1983) applies not only to tax sales, but to conventional foreclosure sales as well. Focusing on Louisiana law, they address many of the same issues as Alexander and conclude that inferior mortgagees are entitled to notice in conventional foreclosure proceedings. These works are:

Frank S. Alexander, *Tax Liens, Tax Sales, and Due Process*, 75 Ind. L.J. 747 (2000)

Michael H. Rubin & E. Keith Carter, *Notice of Seizure in Mortgage Foreclosures and Tax Sale Proceedings: the Ramifications of* Mennonite, 48 La. L. Rev. 535 (1988)

## Notice in the Bankruptcy Context

In separate articles, Robert Lawless and Russell Eisenberg and Frances Gecker address analogous issues regarding the form and extent of notice required in the bankruptcy context. They note the tension between the obligation to afford notice to the many claimants potentially affected by the bankruptcy of a large corporation and the need to conserve the limited financial resources of the bankruptcy estate. Lawless proposes a short restatement of the law of notice for bankruptcy proceedings. Eric Richards considers whether confirmation of a plan of reorganization may extinguish liens held by creditors with security interests in property of the bankruptcy estate. He concludes that even where a lien holder is aware of the debtor's pending bankruptcy, her lien interests may not be modified unless she receives written notice of the proposed plan of reorganization. These works are:

Russell A. Eisenberg & Frances Gecker, *Due Process and Bankruptcy: A Contradiction in Terms?*, 10 Bankr. Dev. J. 47 (1993–94)

Robert M. Lawless, *Realigning the Theory and Practice of Notice in Bankruptcy Cases*, 29 Wake Forest L. Rev. 1215 (1994)

Eric S. Richards, *Due Process Limitations on the Modification of Liens Through Bankruptcy Reorganization*, 71 Am. Bankr. L.J. 43 (1997)

## Notice in the Probate Context

In an article cited by the Supreme Court in Tulsa Professional Collection Services, Inc. v. Pope (1988), Debra Falender analyzes the notice to which creditors are entitled before their claims against a decedent's estate may be barred. Anticipating the Court's reasoning in *Tulsa*, she concludes that estate creditors have protected property interests and are entitled to actual notice if their names and addresses are known or can be ascertained with reasonable diligence. Falender also discusses long-term nonclaim statutes, which provide that claims against an estate are barred if they are not filed within a specified number of years following the decedent's death. Classifying these statutes as self-executing statutes of limitations because they begin to run upon the death of the decedent and are not triggered by state action, she concludes that they are constitutional even though they do not afford individual notice. In a later piece, Thomas Waterbury analyzes *Pope* and offers proposed amendments to the Uniform Probate Code to bring it into compliance with *Pope*. Like Falender, he concludes that long-term nonclaim statutes are self-executing statutes of limitations. These works are:

Debra A. Falender, *Notice to Creditors In Estate Proceedings: What Process Is Due?*, 63 N.C. L. Rev. 659 (1985)

Thomas L. Waterbury, *Notice to Decedents' Creditors*, 73 Minn. L. Rev. 763 (1989)

## Notice in the Admiralty Context

George Rutherglen describes and distinguishes arrest and attachment, two pre-trial remedies available in admiralty that permit seizure of a vessel without prior notice or hearing and without the posting of a bond to cover the defendant's expenses. Rutherglen describes 1985 amendments to Supplemental Rules B, C and E of the Federal Rules of Civil Procedure, which govern admiralty procedure, to require a prompt postseizure hearing and judicial scrutiny of the complaint before issuance of the writ authorizing seizure. He critiques the amended rules for failing to provide direct notice to the defendant or any notice (in most cases) to third parties with a lien or other interest in the seized property, and for failing to require the posting of a bond. In a later work, Rutherglen revisits these issues. These works are:

George Rutherglen, *The Contemporary Justification for Maritime Arrest and Attachment*, 30 Wm. & Mary L. Rev. 541 (1989)

George Rutherglen, *The Federal Rules for Admiralty and Maritime Cases: A Verdict of Quiescent Years*, 27 J. Mar. L. & Com. 581 (1996)

## Notice in the Class Action Context

The extent of notice required in the class action context is inextricably linked to the preclusive effect of the class action judgment. Thus, readers interested in the notice issue are advised to consult the works cited in the sections of this essay that follow on the preclusive effect of class action judgments.

In separate articles, Abram Chayes and Kenneth Dam criticize the Supreme Court's decision in Eisen v. Carlisle & Jacquelin (1974) as being insensitive to the "pragmatic spirit" of *Mullane*, which did *not* require individual notice to all identifiable parties in interest. Chayes argues that rigid notice requirements may be inappropriate in class actions designed to deter and punish wrongdoing by defendants, rather than to compensate victims. Dam, too, questions whether due process demands individual notice and whether the benefits to the class are sufficiently important to justify notice in all cases.

Courts and scholars have debated whether due process requires notice in mandatory class actions. George Rutherglen argues that notice and an opportunity to opt out should be provided in civil rights class actions brought under Title VII that seek individual compensatory relief in the form of back pay, reinstatement or remedial seniority. He does not reach the question whether due process requires individual notice, but rather argues that portions of hybrid class actions should be certified under Rule 23(b)(3). Addressing the constitutional issue, Mark Weber concludes that "[d]ue process requires individual notice to all reasonably identifiable class members in binding Rule 23(b)(2) actions . . . ." Douglas Laycock (cited above) appears to agree. To preserve due process rights, Weber proposes a revision of Rule 23(b)(2) to eliminate its binding effect on absent class members. Patrick Woolley agrees that only class members who receive notice may be bound by the judgment.

In a later work, George Rutherglen concludes that "[t]he exact dimensions of the constitutional requirement of individual notice remain uncertain . . . ." He notes that if class members do not receive adequate notice, they may still take advantage of a judgment that favors the class, but they may not be bound by a judgment that favors the defendant. In other words, due process may be satisfied by giving more notice to the class or less preclusive effect to the judgment. He favors an amendment to Rule 23 that would require individual notice only when it would be both feasible and effective in protecting the rights of class members. Stephen Yeazell agrees that Rule 23 requires too much notice in some class actions, and not enough in others. Like Rutherglen and Chayes, he argues that "the elaborateness of the notice ought to approximate the issues at stake."

These works are:

Abram Chayes, *Public Law Litigation and the Burger Court*, 96 Harv. L. Rev. 4 (1982)

Kenneth W. Dam, *Class Action Notice: Who Needs It?*, 1974 Sup. Ct. Rev. 97

George Rutherglen, *Better Late than Never: Notice and Opt Out at the Settlement Stage of Class Actions*, 71 N.Y.U. L. Rev. 258 (1996)

George Rutherglen, *Notice, Scope, and Preclusion in Title VII Class Actions,* 69 Va. L. Rev. 11 (1983)

Mark C. Weber, *Preclusion and Procedural Due Process in Rule 23(b)(2) Class Actions*, 21 U. Mich. J.L. Reform 347 (1988)

Patrick Woolley, *Rethinking the Adequacy of Adequate Representation*, 75 Tex. L. Rev. 571 (1997)

Stephen C. Yeazell, *The Past and Future of Defendant and Settlement Classes in Collective Litigation*, 39 Ariz. L. Rev. 687 (1997)

## CHAPTER 5: DUE PROCESS LIMITATIONS ON THE BINDING EFFECT OF JUDGMENTS

### Rationales for Binding Nonparties

The central issue raised in this chapter is whether it is constitutional to bind nonparties by a judgment rendered in their absence, and if so, in what circumstances. John McCoid argues that consent and necessity are the primary rationales for binding nonparties whose interests were represented by others. Rather than enlarge the category of nonparties who may be bound on a privity/representation theory, he advocates mandatory joinder of nonparties whose interests may be affected by the litigation. In his view, a compulsory joinder regime would prevent multiplicity of suits and provide a vehicle for examining convenience issues raised by the party to be joined. James Pielemeister, too, opposes the expansion of nonparty preclusion, positing that persons with protected liberty and property interests generally have a "due process right to an individualized adversarial hearing on the merits. . . ."

Robert Bone questions this "day in court" ideal and rejects aggregation as the optimal solution to repetitive litigation. He challenges on both positive and normative grounds the standard assumption that individuals have a "universal right to make personal litigation strategy choices." He posits that both outcome- and process-oriented participation theories support broader nonparty preclusion rules. Bone maintains that "the extent of an individual's right to participate in litigation should vary with the type of case."

These works are:

Robert G. Bone, *Rethinking the "Day in Court" Ideal and Nonparty Preclusion*, 67 N.Y.U. L. Rev. 193 (1992)

John C. McCoid, *A Single Package for Multiparty Disputes*, 28 Stan. L. Rev. 707 (1976)

James R. Pielemeier, *Due Process Limitations on the Application of Collateral Estoppel Against Nonparties to Prior Litigation*, 63 B.U. L. Rev. 383 (1983)

## Commentary on Martin v. Wilks (1989)

The Supreme Court's decision in Martin v. Wilks (1989) and the subsequent passage of the Civil Rights Act of 1991 provoked a scholarly debate regarding the constitutionality of consent decrees and structural injunctions that purport to bind absent third parties. Owen Fiss views *Martin* as an assault on structural injunctions, rendering them vulnerable to collateral attack by third parties who did not participate in the proceedings that led to their issuance. Reading *Mullane* narrowly, Fiss argues that due process guarantees a "right to have one's interest adequately represented," not a right of direct participation. He therefore concludes that the Civil Rights Act of 1991 comports with due process because it guarantees interest representation. In separate articles, Cynthia Fountaine and Marjorie Silver agree that interest representation is a constitutionally sufficient substitute for notice and an opportunity to be heard. Susan Grover, too, concludes that the Civil Rights Act of 1991 is constitutional and appears to agree that due process guarantees only interest representation.

Not all scholars accept Fiss's interest representation model or the conclusion that the Civil Rights Act of 1991 satisfies due process. For example, Douglas Laycock views *Martin* as part of a "straight and continuous" line of cases, beginning with *Mullane*, that requires not only interest representation, but individual notice to readily identifiable people with legally cognizable claims and the appointment of an independent guardian to represent the interests of those whose identities are not known. Criticizing the Civil Rights Act of 1991, Laycock advocates that "notice be sent early, that those who respond be given the full rights of parties, and that guardians ad litem be appointed for those who cannot respond. . . ." George Strickler, too, emphasizes the need for early notice and a right of full participation (although he concedes that "the number of intervenors can be limited once the court is convinced that persons with claims representative of all those who potentially will be effected by the litigation have been allowed to join"). Laycock's earlier work maintains that persons with arguable legal claims must be afforded notice and an opportunity to join a litigation if the court knows that they will be significantly affected by the proposed decree.

Like Laycock, Susan Sturm rejects the view that due process protects only interest representation, not a right of participation. Unlike Laycock, however, Sturm distinguishes between two different classes of third-party stakeholders that may claim a right to participate at the remedial stage of public law litigation: those asserting legal rights to invalidate a remedy (like the white firefighters in *Martin*) and those seeking to influence the choice of remedy (like children with an interest in the nature of a school desegregation order). Maintaining that participation "plays a crucial role in . . . effective remedial decision making," Sturm posits that the nature of a stakeholder's interest should dictate the form of participation required.

Samuel Issacharoff agrees that the nature of the opportunity to be heard "must be commensurate to the rights at stake." Incumbent public employees, who have protected property interests under Board of Regents v. Roth (1972), must be afforded personal notice, an opportunity to take discovery, subpoena witnesses and appeal an adverse ruling before they may be bound by a judgment or consent decree. Those who only aspire to public employment have no protected property interest under *Roth* and therefore may not be entitled to these procedural protections.

Addressing these issues in the context of class action litigation, Patrick Woolley questions the common wisdom that class members may be bound as long as they are adequately represented in the class action. Put differently, Woolley doubts that "adequate, nonconsensual representation" satisfies due process. Although he recognizes exceptions, he posits that, as a general rule, if the suit will extinguish their claims, absent class members must be afforded an opportunity to participate, including a right to present admissible evidence, take discovery and make nonfrivolous legal arguments that otherwise would not be presented to the court. He concludes that due process ordinarily bars a court from imposing a settlement on class members who wish to pursue their claims independently.

In an article written before Martin v. Wilks (1989) was decided, Larry Kramer describes the dynamics of the consent decree process and suggests an alternative to the collateral attack bar: suits by nonparties seeking to challenge a consent decree should be transferred to the district in which the decree was entered and consolidated with the consent decree proceedings. He nevertheless maintains that the collateral attack bar comports with due process as long as the nonparty is afforded a reasonable period of time in which to intervene in the consent decree proceedings after she learns of the decree. In his view, *Mullane* does not require formal notice from opposing parties in this context.

These works are:

Owen M. Fiss, *The Allure of Individualism*, 78 Iowa L. Rev. 965 (1993)

Cynthia L. Fountaine, *Due Process and the Impermissible Collateral Attack Rule in Employment Discrimination Cases: An Analysis of Section 108 of the Civil Rights Act of 1991*, 58 U. Pitt. L. Rev. 435 (1997)

Susan S. Grover, *The Silenced Majority:* Martin v. Wilks *and the Legislative Response*, 1992 U. Ill. L. Rev. 43

Samuel Issacharoff, *When Substance Mandates Procedure:* Martin v. Wilks *and the Rights of Vested Incumbents in Civil Rights Consent Decrees*, 77 Cornell L. Rev. 189 (1992)

Larry Kramer, *Consent Decrees and the Rights of Third Parties*, 87 Mich. L. Rev. 321 (1988)

Douglas Laycock, *Consent Decrees Without Consent: The Rights of Nonconsenting Third Parties*, 1987 U. Chi. Legal F. 103 (1987)

Douglas Laycock, *Due Process of Law in Trilateral Disputes*, 78 Iowa L. Rev. 1011 (1993)

Marjorie A. Silver, *Fairness and Finality: Third-Party Challenges to Employment Discrimination Consent Decrees After the 1991 Civil Rights Act*, 62 Fordham L. Rev. 321 (1993)

George M. Strickler, Jr., Martin v. Wilks, 64 Tul. L. Rev. 1557 (1990)

Susan P. Sturm, *The Promise of Participation*, 78 Iowa L. Rev. 981 (1993)

Patrick Woolley, *Rethinking the Adequacy of Adequate Representation*, 75 Tex. L. Rev. 571 (1997)

## Hansberry v. Lee (1940) in Context

The seminal case regarding the due process limitations on the binding effect of judgments is Hansberry v. Lee (1940). Allen Kamp puts that case in historical and social context. This work is:

Allen R. Kamp, *The History Behind* Hansberry v. Lee, 20 U.C. Davis L. Rev. 481 (1987)

## Preclusion in the Class Action Context

Arthur Miller and David Crump analyze the many issues raised by the Supreme Court's decision in Phillips Petroleum Co. v. Shutts (1985). They focus on *Shutts*'s recognition of the right to opt out as a due process requirement and consider whether *Shutts* prohibits mandatory class actions, particularly mandatory punitive damages class actions. If *Shutts* is a case about "distant forum abuse," then the right to opt out is required only when class members lack minimum contacts with the forum state. On the other hand, if *Shutts* assures a right to opt out to protect an absent class member's ability to control her own suit, then it could be read to bar all mandatory class actions. Miller and Crump propose a four-factor analysis for determining the propriety of mandatory class actions, which weighs efficiency, equity, the risk of distant forum abuse and an interest in individualized control.

Stephen Safranek questions whether *Shutts* was decided correctly, and posits that the Constitution may require an "opt-in" procedure for plaintiff class actions that lack a unitary interest. He maintains that such a procedure would better protect the liberty of absent class members who do not wish to participate in a class action.

Henry Monaghan focuses on whether absent class members may bring a due process challenge to a class action judgment in a different forum. He reads *Shutts* as recognizing "only a *limited* and *conditional* jurisdiction over nonresident class members" and therefore argues that unless nonresident class members have minimum contacts with the forum state, a state court cannot preclude (or enjoin) them from raising due process challenges to the class action judgment in other jurisdictions. Patrick Woolley agrees that class members who lack "a sufficient nexus with the forum cannot constitutionally be compelled to litigate the adequacy of the representation there." Even if absent class members have minimum contacts with the forum state, Woolley posits that they have a due process right to collaterally attack the class action judgment for inadequate representation "[b]ecause current law imposes no obligation on [them] to raise adequacy objections in the class suit itself. . . ."

Marcel Kahan and Linda Silberman disagree, arguing that because class members who have been afforded notice and an opportunity to opt out are deemed to have consented to the court's jurisdiction, they may be forced to raise whatever objections they have to the adequacy of representation in the context of the class action itself, rather than by way of collateral attack. In their view, at least in the context of state court class action settlements that release exclusive federal claims, a collateral attack should be permitted only if the proponent first raises her objections in the underlying state class action proceeding and then demonstrates that the "structures that state courts employ in settling federal claims do not reasonably protect federal interests." William Allen, too, questions whether members of a (b)(3) class action who decline to opt out may collaterally attack the class action judgment on the theory that the class was not adequately represented.

Like Kahan and Silberman and Allen, Samuel Issacharoff questions Monaghan's assertion that absent class members retain a constitutional right to collaterally attack a class action judgment. He argues that "[s]o long as notice is sufficient and the opportunity to intervene and appeal is protected, it remains unclear why collateral challenge is the preferred mechanism to challenge abuse of class action practice." He views the situs of the challenge as less important than the underlying conditions of adequacy of representation that justify class action treatment. Issacharoff reads Amchem Products, Inc. v. Windsor (1997) and Ortiz v. Fibreboard Corp. (1999) as requiring "capable representation by an agent who must be faithful to the interests of the nonparticipants that are to be . . . bound" and a careful examination of class counsel's incentives to ensure such faithfulness.

In a later work, Issacharoff maintains that a right to opt out is available in a (b)(3) class action, but not in a (b)(1) or (b)(2) class action, because a (b)(3) class action is "merely an aggregation of what might otherwise be self-sustaining individual causes of action," while mandatory class actions "truly inhere in the collective entity of the class." In other words, no individual has an autonomous right to control the claim pursued in a (b)(1) or (b)(2) class action. Issacharoff posits that preclusion should be tailored to the type of class action certified: judgments rendered in mandatory class actions that deny class members an opportunity to opt out should not preclude individual actions for damages. In another work on class action conflicts, Issacharoff stresses the importance of preserving a meaningful right to opt out.

Focusing on Title VII class actions, George Rutherglen agrees that notice and an opportunity to opt out protect the due process rights of absent class members who seek compensatory relief. He posits that "[f]ailure to opt out after having received notice at least approximates actual consent to representation in the class action." He also suggests that district courts should appoint separate counsel to represent each subclass and define classes or subclasses narrowly so that the claims of the representative and the claims of the absent class members are "so similar that they are likely to be asserted with equal strength." In a later work, Rutherglen refines his views, maintaining that due process does not necessarily demand individual notice at the outset of a class action. He posits that different forms of notice provided later in the action can also satisfy due process "if the preclusive effects of the resulting judgment are suitably limited." Rutherglen suggests that Rule 23 should be revised to give class members the "right to receive effective notice later in the proceedings and the right to opt out at the settlement stage of class actions in order to register their dissatisfaction with the performance of the class attorney."

Susan Koniak critiques the settlement that was reviewed in *Amchem* and, like Issacharoff and Rutherglen, she admonishes courts to rigorously assess the adequacy of representation in class actions to ensure due process. She suggests the appointment of guardians or special masters to monitor the adequacy of representation; the use of subclasses; the availability of back-end opt-out rights; and a rule that would bar class counsel from representing competing groups against a common defendant.

Linda Mullenix bemoans the Supreme Court's failure to address the due process rights of absent plaintiff class members in hybrid, limited fund and other mandatory class actions. She notes the inherent tension between providing absent class members with a universal right to opt-out of class actions and the utility of the class action as a litigation aggregation device.

These works are:


William T. Allen, *Finality of Judgments in Class Actions: A Comment on* Epstein v. MCA, Inc., 73 N.Y.U. L. Rev. 1149 (1998)

Samuel Issacharoff, *Class Action Conflicts*, 30 U.C. Davis L. Rev. 805 (1997)

Samuel Issacharoff, *Governance and Legitimacy in the Law of Class Actions*, 1999 Sup. Ct. Rev. 337 (1999)

Samuel Issacharoff, *Preclusion, Due Process, and the Right to Opt Out of Class Actions*, 77 Notre Dame L. Rev. 1057 (2002)

Marcel Kahan & Linda Silberman, Matsushita *and Beyond: The Role of State Courts in Class Actions Involving Exclusive Federal Claims*, 1996 Sup. Ct. Rev. 219

Susan P. Koniak, *Feasting While the Widow Weeps*: Georgine v. Amchem Products, Inc., 80 Cornell L. Rev. 1222 (1995)

Arthur R. Miller & David Crump, *Jurisdiction and Choice of Law in Multistate Class Actions After* Phillips Petroleum Co. v. Shutts, 96 Yale L.J. 1 (1986)

Henry Paul Monaghan, *Antisuit Injunctions and Preclusion Against Absent Nonresident Class Members*, 98 Colum. L. Rev. 1148 (1998)

Linda S. Mullenix, *Class Actions, Personal Jurisdiction, and Plaintiff's Due Process: Implications for Mass Tort Litigation*, 28 U.C. Davis L. Rev. 871 (1995)

George Rutherglen, *Better Late than Never: Notice and Opt Out at the Settlement Stage of Class Actions*, 71 N.Y.U. L. Rev. 258 (1996)

George Rutherglen, *Notice, Scope, and Preclusion in Title VII Class Actions,* 69 Va. L. Rev. 11 (1983)

Stephen J. Safranek, *Do Class Action Plaintiffs Lose Their Constitutional Rights?*, 1996 Wis. L. Rev. 263 (1996)

Patrick Woolley, *The Availability of Collateral Attack for Inadequate Representation in Class Suits*, 79 Tex. L. Rev. 383 (2000)

## CHAPTER 6: DUE PROCESS LIMITATIONS ON PERSONAL JURISDICTION

### Full Faith and Credit or Due Process Clause?

Several scholars criticize the Supreme Court's reliance on the Fourteenth Amendment Due Process Clause to limit state court jurisdiction. Roger Transgrud asserts that due process "is not a sensible basis" for limiting state court jurisdiction. Instead, he maintains that the Full Faith and Credit Clause required the development of federal common law rules to define state court jurisdiction and that the Supreme Court should have grounded such rules on the principle of political consent. Ralph Whitten agrees that the Court "erred in incorporating the jurisdictional standards that had been employed in full faith and credit cases into the due process clause of the fourteenth amendment." But Whitten concludes that Congress alone, rather than the Supreme Court, had authority (granted by the Full Faith and Credit Clause) to modify the jurisdictional rules that had operated between the states in 1787.

Patrick Borchers questions whether Pennoyer v. Neff (1877) was intended to transform limits on state court jurisdiction into constitutional law grounded in due process. He proffers a more limited reading of *Pennoyer*: the Due Process Clause was intended to provide defendants with a vehicle for ensuring that rendering states followed their own jurisdictional rules, "whatever those rules might be," rather than to determine the content of the jurisdictional rules that state courts had to apply.

John Oakley vehemently disputes Borchers's limited reading of *Pennoyer*, carefully analyzing the Court's opinion paragraph by paragraph. He then examines numerous post-*Pennnoyer* decisions to demonstrate that both state courts and the United States Supreme Court itself rejected the limited view and understood *Pennoyer* to have announced constitutional limits on the reach of state court jurisdiction.

These works are:

Patrick J. Borchers, *The Death of the Constitutional Law of Personal Jurisdiction: From* Pennoyer *to* Burnham *and Back Again*, 24 U.C. Davis L. Rev. 19 (1990)

Patrick J. Borchers, *Jurisdictional Pragmatism:* International Shoe*'s Half-Buried Legacy*, 28 U.C. Davis L. Rev. 561 (1995)

Patrick J. Borchers, Pennoyer's *Limited Legacy: A Reply to Professor Oakley*, 29 U.C. Davis L. Rev. 115 (1995)

John B. Oakley, *The Pitfalls of "Hit and Run" History: A Critique of Professor Borchers's "Limited View" of* Pennoyer v. Neff, 28 U.C. Davis L. Rev. 591 (1995)

Roger H. Transgrud, *The Federal Common Law of Personal Jurisdiction*, 57 Geo. Wash. L. Rev. 849 (1989)

Ralph U. Whitten, *The Constitutional Limitations on State-Court Jurisdiction: A Historical-Interpretive Reexamination of the Full Faith and Credit and Due Process Clauses (Parts One and Two)*, 14 Creighton L. Rev. 499 & 735 (1981)

## Pennoyer v. Neff (1877) in Context

Wendy Collins Perdue provides an engaging account of the facts underlying Pennoyer v. Neff (1877) and a careful analysis of both the lower court and Supreme Court opinions in the case. She places *Pennoyer* in the context of Justice Field's broader substantive due process jurisprudence. Geoffrey Hazard analyzes the Court's opinion in *Pennoyer* and places it in a broader historical context, examining jurisdictional limits in England in the eighteenth and nineteenth centuries. These works are:

Geoffrey C. Hazard, Jr., *A General Theory of State-Court Jurisdiction*, 1965 Sup. Ct. Rev. 241

Wendy Collins Perdue, *Sin, Scandal, and Substantive Due Process: Personal Jurisdiction and* Pennoyer *Reconsidered*, 62 Wash. L. Rev. 479 (1987)

## World-Wide Volkswagen Corp. v. Woodson (1980) in Context

Charles Adams describes the gruesome facts underlying *World-Wide Volkswagen* and recounts the protracted procedural history of the case. This work is:

Charles W. Adams, World-Wide Volkswagen v. Woodson—*The Rest of the Story*, 72 Neb. L. Rev. 1122 (1993)

## Minimum Contacts Test

A voluminous literature critiques the minimum contacts test, the purposeful availment requirement, and the Court's case-by-case, fact-specific jurisdictional analysis. Some scholars, including Bruce Posnak and Louise Weinberg, argue that the minimum contacts test is too unpredictable and breeds too much litigation. Posnak views jurisdiction as a matter of abatement, which demands "more formal, certain, simple and predictable rules." He criticizes the purposeful availment test as subjective, uncertain and unduly restrictive, precluding jurisdiction when it would be fair to exercise it. Posnak questions whether purposefulness is a good proxy for either fairness or the defendant's expectation of amenability to suit in the forum state. He nevertheless proposes a jurisdictional test that would eliminate consideration of the reasonableness factors (discussed below) and permit jurisdiction when the forum contacts are both purposeful and made for the defendant's benefit.

Louise Weinberg posits that the minimum contacts test does not serve any of the articulated purposes of jurisdictional limits: convenience, fairness, reasonableness or comity. She chastises the Court for "requiring minimum contacts for their own sakes." She recommends jettisoning the minimum contacts test and identifying the features of the rare case that would compel scrutiny of jurisdiction under the Due Process Clause. Peterson, too, complains that the purposeful availment doctrine has been "transformed into an independent test, as an end in itself . . . ." He would retain the minimum contacts test to protect defendants from unfair surprise.

Kevin Clermont proposes a tripartite conceptual structure that differentiates among what he calls pure territorial jurisdiction, venue and a constitutional requirement that the forum be a reasonable one. He argues that the Supreme Court should abolish the concept of pure jurisdiction and carefully differentiate between forum-reasonableness, a constitutional standard, and venue, a subconstitutional one.

Reexamining the purposeful availment test through the lens of mass tort litigation, Martin Redish and Eric Beste view it as an insurmountable obstacle to the effective resolution of mass tort claims in a single state court proceeding. They advocate in its place a pragmatic, individualized due process calculus. Under this approach, "interstate mass tort claims could be combined as long as no meaningful procedural inconvenience would result from the selection of the forum." Harold Korn, too, reexamines jurisdictional analysis with an eye to multistate mass torts. In an essay, he explores Judge Weinstein's path-breaking approach to jurisdiction in In re DES Cases (E.D.N.Y. 1992), which eschews reliance on the defendant's forum contacts and requires instead an " 'appreciable state interest' in the vindication of policies expressed in the forum's laws." In a later article, he derides the defendant-forum territorial nexus requirement that underlies the minimum contacts test.

Scholars have debated the role of interstate federalism in jurisdictional analysis. In separate articles, Daan Braveman, Stephen Gottlieb and Courtland Peterson doubt that jurisdictional limits are necessary to preserve interstate federalism. Martin Redish, too, maintains that the Due Process Clause protects private parties, not states, and concludes that federalism concerns are irrelevant in personal jurisdictional analysis. In place of the minimum contacts test, Redish proposes a new due process analysis that would consider the degree of inconvenience the defendant would suffer if compelled to litigate in the forum state; the degree of inconvenience the plaintiff would suffer if jurisdiction were denied; and the forum state's interest in applying its own law to the controversy.

Russell Weintraub, too, views the "federalism appendage to due process" as "misplaced." He recommends removal of "the federalism cloud from due process limitations on state court jurisdiction" and replacement of the minimum contacts test with a test that focuses on fairness to the defendant. He would consider the defendant's forum contacts only if the defendant has demonstrated that jurisdiction in the forum state "raises a serious likelihood of unfairness to him."

Harold Lewis traces the role of state sovereignty in personal jurisdictional analysis and welcomes sovereignty's "third death" in *Insurance Corp. of Ireland* (1982). He maintains that sovereignty concerns should play no role in jurisdictional analysis but should be addressed through the development of constitutional limits on choice of law under the Full Faith and Credit Clause.

In stark contrast, Allan Stein maintains that "jurisdiction, as exercises of power, ought to reflect the general limits on state sovereignty inherent in a federal system." He views jurisdictional doctrine as "inescapably political because it is tied to a power allocation between sovereigns." Stein criticizes the purposeful availment test in part because it "derive[s] from a vision of sovereign authority that is too limited and too dependent on consent."

These works are:

Daan Braveman, *Interstate Federalism and Personal Jurisdiction*, 33 Syracuse L. Rev. 533 (1982)

Kevin M. Clermont, *Restating Territorial Jurisdiction and Venue for State and Federal Courts*, 66 Cornell L. Rev. 411 (1981)

Stephen E. Gottlieb, *In Search of the Link Between Due Process and Jurisdiction*, 60 Wash. U. L.Q. 1291 (1983)

Harold L. Korn, *Rethinking Personal Jurisdiction and Choice of Law in Multistate Mass Torts*, 97 Colum. l. Rev. 2183 (1997)

Harold L. Korn, *The Development of Judicial Jurisdiction in the United States, Part I*, 65 Brook. L. Rev. 935 (1999)

Harold S. Lewis, Jr., *The Three Deaths of "State Sovereignty" and the Curse of Abstraction in the Jurisprudence of Personal Jurisdiction*, 58 Notre Dame L. Rev. 699 (1983)

Courtland H. Peterson, *Jurisdiction and Choice of Law Revisited*, 59 U. Colo. L. Rev. 37 (1988)

Bruce Posnak, *The Court Doesn't Know its* Asahi *from its* Wortman*: A Critical View of the Constitutional Constraints of Jurisdiction and Choice of Law*, 41 Syracuse L. Rev. 875 (1990)

Martin H. Redish, *Due Process, Federalism and Personal Jurisdiction: A Theoretical Evaluation*, 75 Nw. U.L. Rev. 1112 (1981)

Martin H. Redish & Eric J. Beste, *Personal Jurisdiction and the Global Resolution of Mass Tort Litigation: Defining the Constitutional Boundaries*, 28 U.C. Davis L. Rev. 917 (1995)

Allan R. Stein, *Styles of Argument and Interstate Federalism in the Law of Personal Jurisdiction*, 65 Tex. L. Rev. 689 (1987)

Louise Weinberg, *The Place of Trial and the Law Applied: Overhauling Constitutional Theory*, 59 Colo. L. Rev. 67 (1988)

Russell J. Weintraub, *Due Process Limitations on the Personal Jurisdiction of State Courts: Time for Change*, 63 Or. L. Rev. 485 (1984)

## Reasonableness Factors

World-Wide Volkswagen Corp. v. Woodson (1980) introduced the "reasonableness factors" into jurisdictional analysis. Bruce Posnak (cited above) argues that when coupled with the minimum contacts test, the reasonableness factors unduly complicate jurisdictional analysis and favor the defendant (because the plaintiff is required "to prove the same thing two different ways"). Posnak further argues that jurisdictional analysis should focus exclusively on the interests of the parties, and not on institutional interests (such as the forum state's interest and the shared interests of the several states in substantive social policy). Harold Lewis (cited above) agrees that "a state's interest in having its own law applied to a controversy or in providing a forum to resolve it" should not affect the personal jurisdictional calculus. While recommending a jurisdictional analysis under the Due Process Clause that focuses on the parties' interests, Martin Redish (cited above) would consider the state's interest in applying its own substantive law to the controversy.

## General v. Specific Jurisdiction

Arthur von Mehren and Donald Trautman coined the terms "specific jurisdiction" and "general jurisdiction." They view the defendant's mere presence within a state and the mere presence of the defendant's property within a state as problematic bases for general jurisdiction. They also question the appropriateness of assertions of general jurisdiction over corporations outside their state of incorporation or principal place of business.

Other scholars have addressed the general/specific jurisdiction divide, staking out competing positions on when a claim arises out of or relates to an in-state contact. Lea Brilmayer proposes a substantive relevance test, arguing that a contact is related to a claim only "if it is the geographical qualification of a fact relevant to the merits." She argues that alternative tests—based on the similarity between the forum contacts and the activity that gave rise to the claim, or on a historical connection between the contacts and claim–would support specific jurisdiction on very slim contacts.

Mary Twitchell, on the other hand, rejects the substantive relevance test, advocating a more expansive view of specific jurisdiction. Rather than dilute the requirements for general jurisdiction to reach cases involving tenuously related claims, she urges courts to expand the concept of specific jurisdiction "to include all decisions about exercises of jurisdiction over claims connected to the defendant's forum ties." Like von Mehren and Trautman, Twitchell suggests that general jurisdiction should be available only in the state in which the defendant maintains her "home base." Both Brilmayer and Twitchell have follow-up articles that respond to each other's work.

In separate articles, William Richman, Flavio Rose and Patrick Borchers return to the relatedness inquiry. Richman proposes a sliding scale of relatedness: "As the quantity and quality of the defendant's forum contacts increase, a weaker connection between the plaintiff's claim and those contacts is permissible; as the quantity and quality of the defendant's forum contacts decrease, a stronger connection between the plaintiff's claim and those contacts is required." Rose critiques the Ninth Circuit's "but for" test for specific jurisdiction and a number of alternative tests. He ultimately advocates a baseline rule of substantive relevance with two subject-specific exceptions. Borchers, too, grapples with relatedness and the standard for determining whether contacts are substantial enough to support general jurisdiction. He counsels against abolition of general jurisdiction and recommends legislation that articulates more definite bases for general jurisdiction, including defendant's domicile, habitual residence and situs of a branch facility.

In another article, co-authored with a group of students, Lea Brilmayer distinguishes between unique affiliations supporting general jurisdiction—domicile, state of incorporation and principal place of business—and nonunique affiliations—activities within the state that are unrelated to the dispute, such as presence, consent and ownership of in-state property. Unique affiliations are relationships that litigants have with only one state, making it fair to treat them as insiders. Brilmayer posits that while both unique and nonunique affiliations may support general jurisdiction, only the former justify the application of forum law.

In an article critiquing the leading decision on general jurisdiction, Helicopteros Nacionales de Colombia v. Hall (1984), Louise Weinberg chastises the Supreme Court for failing to consider the balance of conveniences and for relegating the widowed American plaintiffs to suit in a foreign country. She maintains that the minimum contacts analysis no longer serves the policy objectives of comity, convenience, reasonableness and fairness. Weinberg suggests that in suits against alien defendants, American courts should consider the national interest in providing a domestic forum and might even aggregate the defendant's contacts with the nation in assessing the defendant's amenability to jurisdiction.

These works are:

Patrick J. Borchers, *The Problem with General Jurisdiction*, 2001 U. Chi. Legal F. 119

Lea Brilmayer, *How Contacts Count: Due Process Limitations on State Court Jurisdiction*, 1980 Sup. Ct. Rev. 77

Lea Brilmayer, *Colloquy: Related Contacts and Personal Jurisdiction*, 101 Harv. L. Rev. 1444 (1988)

Lea Brilmayer et al., *A General Look at General Jurisdiction*, 66 Tex. L. Rev. 723 (1988)

William M. Richman, *A Sliding Scale to Supplement the Distinction Between General and Specific Jurisdiction*, 72 Cal. L. Rev. 1328 (1984) (book review)

Flavio Rose, *Related Contacts and Personal Jurisdiction: The "But For" Test*, 82 Cal. L. Rev. 1545 (1994)

Mary Twitchell, *The Myth of General Jurisdiction*, 101 Harv. L. Rev. 610 (1988)

Mary Twitchell, *Colloquy: A Rejoinder to Professor Brilmayer*, 101 Harv. L. Rev. 1465 (1988)

Arthur T. von Mehren & Donald T. Trautman, *Jurisdiction to Adjudicate: A Suggested Analysis*, 79 Harv. L. Rev. 1121 (1966)

Louise Weinberg, *The Helicopter Case and The Jurisprudence of Jurisdiction*, 58 S. Cal. L. Rev. 913 (1985)

## Jurisdiction in Cyberspace

Scholars debate whether existing jurisdictional doctrine can be adapted to address the issues that arise in cyberspace, or whether new jurisdictional principles need to be developed. Allan Stein maintains that "there is nothing about legal relations over computer networks that in any way challenges our conventional notions about how sovereign authority is allocated in the world." Because the Internet is not a political community that creates legal norms, he rejects the argument that cyberspace should be governed by a separate body of "cyberlaw." Stein maintains that courts are capable of applying existing principles to resolve the jurisdictional conflicts that arise in cyberspace.

Martin Redish disagrees to some extent, criticizing the current purposeful availment standard as incapable of effectively resolving jurisdictional issues involving the Internet. He rejects the purposeful availment test in the Internet context because the "technological impact of the Internet in many cases renders purposeful availment an all but meaningless concept from the perspective of out-of-state defendant activity, and imposes an unacceptably high barrier to the interests of both in-state plaintiffs and the states themselves." In its place, Redish offers an analysis that considers procedural burdens and fairness.

Henry Perritt anticipates the creation of new institutions dedicated to resolving disputes in cyberspace. He explores the use of international arbitration and a possible United States District Court of Cyberspace, which would have cyber-juries and electronic procedures for service, filings, hearings, orders, discovery and judgments.

Several scholars analyze the Anticybersquatting Consumer Protection Act ("ACPA"). Thomas Lee concludes that *in rem* jurisdiction under the ACPA is constitutional. He argues that property interests in Internet domain names registered through Network Solutions, Inc. ("NSI"), are located in the Eastern District of Virginia, where NSI is headquartered. He maintains that competing claims to domain names may be resolved in *in rem* proceedings in that district.

Suzanna Sherry, on the other hand, views the ACPA as a hasty, shortsighted and unnecessary legislative solution to a problem that would have been better addressed by the courts through common law lawmaking. She maintains that courts had little trouble asserting jurisdiction over cybersquatters even before the ACPA was adopted. She suggests that the *in rem* provisions cause confusion.

Finally, Jeremy Gilman surveys the courts' efforts to determine where Internet players are subject to jurisdiction. He analyzes the "sliding scale" test developed by a district court in Zippo Manufacturing Co. v. Zippo Dot Com, Inc. (W.D. Pa. 1997) and the effects test adopted by the Ninth Circuit in Panavision International, L.P. v. Toeppen (9th Cir. 1998). He maintains that even with the ongoing development of new technologies, courts are likely to resolve jurisdictional issues by applying traditional constitutional precepts.

These works are:

Jeremy Gilman, *Personal Jurisdiction and the Internet: Traditional Jurisprudence for a New Medium*, 56 Bus. Law. 395 (2000)

Thomas R. Lee, In Rem *Jurisdiction in Cyberspace*, 75 Wash. L. Rev. 97 (2000)

Henry H. Peritt, Jr., *Jurisdiction in Cyberspace*, 41 Vill. L. Rev. 1 (1996)

Martin H. Redish, *Of New Wine and Old Bottles: Personal Jurisdiction, The Internet, and the Nature of Constitutional Evolution*, 38 Jurimetrics J. 575 (1998)

Suzanna Sherry, *Haste Makes Waste: Congress and the Common Law in Cyberspace*, 55 Vand. L. Rev. 309 (2002)

Allan R. Stein, *The Unexceptional Problem of Jurisdiction in Cyberspace*, 32 Int'l Law. 1167 (1998)

## *Quasi-in-rem* Jurisdiction Today

Arthur von Mehren and Donald Trautman (cited above) were early critics of the distinction between *in personam* and *in rem* jurisdiction, arguing that all adjudications determine the rights and duties of persons. They recommend that courts decline to focus on power over persons and things, and focus instead on "the relationship of the parties and of the controversy to the forum, and . . . tak[e] other litigational and enforcement considerations into account."

Writing just a year after Shaffer v. Heitner (1977) was decided, Linda Silberman (cited above) reviews the history of *in rem* jurisdiction and carefully analyzes the various opinions issued in *Shaffer*. She notes that *Shaffer* did not explain whether the same type of contacts are required for both *in personam* and *quasi-in-rem* actions. She suggests that "there are at least three ways in which . . . an attachment [of property unrelated to the plaintiff's claim] can remain a valid source of state adjudicatory power": first, if the attachment of property, when coupled with otherwise insufficient contacts, satisfies the minimum contacts test; second, if the presence and attachment of more traditional types of property, like bank accounts, satisfies the minimum contacts test; and third, if no alternative forum is available to the plaintiff.

Holly Haskew agrees, arguing that *quasi-in-rem* jurisdiction should be allowed even if the defendant lacks minimum contacts sufficient to support *in personam* jurisdiction in the forum state. She maintains that "the presence of property alone establishes jurisdiction regardless of the defendant's contacts with the forum," and further argues that "a different and lesser level of minimum contacts satisfies the *International Shoe* test" in *quasi-in-rem* actions.

Michael Mushlin, on the other hand, sharply criticizes the post-*Shaffer* resurrection of *quasi-in-rem* jurisdiction in New York. He maintains that *quasi-in-rem* jurisdiction is likely to be unconstitutional because it deprives defendants of the use of their property before judgment. He further maintains that because *quasi-in-rem* judgments have limited preclusive effect, the use of this type of jurisdiction wastes judicial resources.

In a pair of articles, George Rutherglen describes the persistence of maritime arrest and attachment in the admiralty context after *Shaffer*. He notes that these pretrial remedies allow for assertions of jurisdiction in districts with which the defendant has no contacts other than the presence of the seized vessel. He advocates reforms to require that defendants in admiralty cases be subject to personal jurisdiction under standard rules except in exigent circumstances or when the plaintiff asserts a salvage claim or a seaman's claim for wages. Like Rutherglen, Angela Bohmann considers the extent to which *Shaffer* requires reconsideration of the unique jurisdictional rules that govern admiralty actions. She posits that most assertions of admiralty jurisdiction should be upheld even if minimum contacts are required.

These works are:

Angela M. Bohmann, *Applicability of* Shaffer *to Admiralty In Rem Jurisdiction*, 53 Tul. L. Rev. 135 (1978)

Holly S. Haskew, Shaffer, Burnham, *and New York's Continuing Use of QIR-2 Jurisdiction: A Resurrection of the Power Theory*, 45 Emory L.J. 239 (1996)

Michael B. Mushlin, *The New Quasi In Rem Jurisdiction: New York's Revival of a Doctrine Whose Time Has Passed*, 55 Brook. L. Rev. 1059 (1990)

George Rutherglen, *The Contemporary Justification for Maritime Arrest and Attachment*, 30 Wm. & Mary L. Rev. 541 (1989)

George Rutherglen, *The Federal Rules for Admiralty and Maritime Cases: A Verdict of Quiescent Years*, 27 J. Mar. L. & Com. 581 (1996)

Linda J. Silberman, Shaffer v. Heitner: *The End of an Era*, 53 N.Y.U. L. Rev. 33 (1978)

## Transient Jurisdiction

Albert Ehrenzweig was an early critic of transient jurisdiction, demonstrating that it lacked precedent in the English common law tradition and in early American history. It was only after *Pennoyer* required the plaintiff to "catch" and serve the defendant within the territory of the state that courts began to recognize transient presence as sufficient to establish jurisdiction. With the rejection of *Pennoyer*'s in-hand service requirement, Ehrenzweig predicted the demise of transient jurisdiction.

In the years following Shaffer v. Heitner (1977), many other scholars called for the rejection of transient jurisdiction. Donald Werner, for example, questions the viability of a number of presence-oriented bases for jurisdiction, including transient presence and doing business (as a proxy for corporate presence). He argues that "the 'catch as catch can' theory of *in personam* jurisdiction, based upon the unrelated physical presence of a defendant within the forum state is, and should be entombed along with the attachment basis of jurisdiction." Daniel Bernstine, too, argues that *International Shoe* and *Shaffer* presage the demise of jurisdiction over a defendant who is only transiently present in the state. Silberman (cited above) is somewhat more cautious, suggesting that the continued viability of transient jurisdiction depends upon whether or not *Shaffer* rejected the power theory of jurisdiction altogether.

These works are:

Daniel O. Bernstine, Shaffer v. Heitner: *A Death Warrant for the Transient Rule of In Personam Jurisdiction*, 25 Vill. L. Rev.3 8 (1979–80)

Albert A. Ehrenzweig, *The Transient Rule of Personal Jurisdiction: The "Power" Myth and Forum Conveniens*, 65 Yale L.J. 289 (1956)

Donald J. Werner, *Dropping the Other* Shoe: Shaffer v. Heitner *and the Demise of Presence-Oriented Jurisdiction*, 45 Brook. L. Rev. 565 (1979)

## Due Process Limitations on Assertions of Personal Jurisdiction by Federal Courts

Scholars have debated the territorial reach of federal court jurisdiction under the Fifth Amendment. Numerous scholars advocate a "national contacts" or "aggregated contacts" test, arguing that the Fifth Amendment permits federal courts to assert jurisdiction over defendants having minimum contacts with the nation as a whole. Thomas Green stakes out this position in a 1961 article on the jurisdictional reach of federal courts over corporate defendants. Marilyn Berger highlights the importance of federal courts hearing federal question cases and criticizes the patchwork statutory treatment of personal jurisdiction in federal courts. She advocates federal legislation that would "provide a uniform source of personal jurisdiction in federal question cases that would be coextensive with the grant of federal question subject matter." She posits that personal jurisdiction in federal question cases would be constitutional because "a relationship among the defendant, the litigation and the court would be established."

Robert Casad goes even further, arguing not only that the Fifth Amendment allows *federal* courts to exercise federal question jurisdiction based on national contacts, but also that Congress should adopt legislation to authorize *both state and federal courts* to exercise jurisdiction in federal question cases over any defendant possessing minimum contacts with the United States. In his view, "The same constitutional authority that gives Congress the power to create the federal cause of action, coupled with the Necessary and Proper Clause, should enable Congress to prescribe the conditions that will cause defendants to be amenable to jurisdiction for that cause of action."

Maryellen Fullerton, on the other hand, argues that "a nationwide personal jurisdiction statute providing that a defendant located in or having minimum contacts with the United States can be sued on a federal question in any federal court in the country would be unconstitutional." She posits that the Due Process Clause is concerned with fairness, not just sovereignty. In lieu of a national contacts approach, she proposes a three-factor test that would balance the inconvenience to the defendant, the defendant's reasonable anticipation of suit in the challenged location, and the government's interest in proceeding there.

Like Fullerton, Pamela Stephens and Robert Lusardi posit that the Fifth Amendment Due Process Clause requires consideration of fairness and reasonableness, in addition to territorial sovereignty. In Stephens's view, the standard for gauging the constitutionality of federal court personal jurisdiction should be the same in both federal question and diversity cases. She proposes a constitutional analysis that would consider the defendant's purposeful contacts with the United States, convenience and fairness concerns, and the other reasonableness factors outlined in *World-Wide Volkswagen*. Lusardi, too, recommends a multi-factor analysis, but he would examine the convenience concerns of both parties without favoring the defendant.

Commentators have discussed the 1993 amendment to Rule 4 of the Federal Rules of Civil Procedure, which added Rule 4(k)(2) and authorized jurisdiction over defendants sued on claims arising under federal law who are not amenable to the jurisdiction of any state. Dora Corby analyzes the Supreme Court's decision in Omni Capital International v. Rudolf Wolff & Co. (1987), the purpose behind Rule 4(k)(2) and district court interpretations of the Rule. In a pair of articles, Leslie Kelleher examines Rule 4(k)(2) in depth and argues that it violates the Rules Enabling Act. She posits that because the rule purports to govern amenability to jurisdiction, it impermissibly abridges a substantive right. She urges Congress to pass a nationwide long-arm statute rather than allow the Court to overstep its rule-making authority.

These works are:

Marilyn J. Berger, *Acquiring* In Personam *Jurisdiction in Federal Question Cases: Procedural Frustration Under Federal Rule of Civil Procedure 4*, 1982 Utah L. Rev. 285

Robert C. Casad, *Personal Jurisdiction in Federal Question Cases*, 70 Tex. L. Rev. 1589 (1992)

Dora A. Corby, *Putting Personal Jurisdiction Within Reach: Just What Has Rule 4(k)(2) Done for the Personal Jurisdiction of Federal Courts?*, 30 McGeorge L. Rev. 167 (1998)

Maryellen Fullerton, *Constitutional Limits on Nationwide Personal Jurisdiction in the Federal Courts*, 79 Nw. U. L. Rev. 1 (1984)

Thomas F. Green, Jr., *Federal Jurisdiction In Personam of Corporations and Due Process*, 14 Vand. L. Rev. 967 (1961)

Leslie M. Kelleher, *Amenability to Jurisdiction As a "Substantive Right": The Invalidity of Rule 4(k) Under the Rules Enabling Act*, 75 Ind. L.J. 1191 (2000)

Leslie M. Kelleher, *The December 1993 Amendments to the Federal Rules of Civil Procedure—A Critical Analysis*, 12 Touro L. Rev. 7 (1995)

Robert A. Lusardi, *Nationwide Service of Process: Due Process Limitations on the Power of the Sovereign*, 33 Vill. L. Rev. 1 (1988)

Pamela J. Stephens, *The Federal Court Across the Street: Constitutional Limits on Federal Court Assertions of Personal Jurisdiction*, 18 U. Rich. L. Rev. 697 (1984)

## CHAPTER 7: DUE PROCESS LIMITATIONS ON CHOICE OF LAW

### Constitutional Sources of the Limitations on State Choice of Law

Members of the academy have been less willing than the Supreme Court to conflate the limitations on state choice of law imposed by the Due Process and Full Faith and Credit Clauses. Some scholars highlight the distinctive role that the Full Faith and Credit Clause can and should play in restraining state overreaching in choice of law. Douglas Laycock, for example, argues that the Full Faith and Credit Clause requires "each state to give the law of every other state the same faith and credit it gives its own law—to treat the law of sister states as equal in authority to its own." (He also invokes the Privileges and Immunities Clause to bar states from favoring local litigants.) Lea Brilmayer, too, argues that the Full Faith and Credit Clause bars discrimination against other states, but in the choice of law context, she maintains that it only prevents a state from "refus[ing] to extend benefits of forum law without deferring to the laws of the other state." James Martin argues that the Full Faith and Credit Clause is the best candidate for limiting state choice of law because it "incorporates established concepts of mutual respect among sovereigns." He favors this approach in part because it focuses on the interests of states other than the forum state, while the Due Process Clause, with "its emphasis upon the relationship between the state and the individual," does not. Russell Weintraub argues that the Full Faith and Credit Clause imposes more stringent limits than due process where the need for national uniformity outweighs the interests of a state in applying its own law. (He recognizes that this standard rarely will require the choice of another state's law to govern a controversy not yet reduced to judgment.) Peter Hay, too, recognizes that both clauses play a role in limiting state choice of law, but he posits that federalism concerns, or the needs of the interstate system, factor into only the Full Faith and Credit Clause analysis. He maintains that federal law is needed to order intersystem relations.

Other scholars emphasize the role that the Due Process Clause plays in limiting state choice of law. Frederic Kirgis, for example, posits that "[d]ue process combines a check on power excesses by individual states with a regard for fundamental fairness to those who stand to lose by the exercise of the power to choose the rule supplied by a given legal system . . . ." According to Willis Reese, the Due Process Clause permits a state to apply its own law only if it "would be fair to the parties and also consistent with the needs of the federal (or international) system." In assessing fairness, he considers reliance upon a particular state's law and the expectation that a transaction will be upheld. In his view, the most important interstate system value "is that a state should not without good reason apply its law in disregard of the substantial interests of some other state or states." Like Reese, Russell Weintraub emphasizes the role that due process plays in protecting the parties' justifiable expectations and avoiding unfair surprise by barring the application of a law that the parties could not have anticipated at the time they engaged in their primary conduct. Robert Leflar, too, maintains that as a matter of logic and good sense, choice-of-law questions should be regulated by the Due Process Clause, with a "fair play and substantial justice" standard. In his view, the Full Faith and Credit Clause should be reserved to handle "denials of access to a local forum's courts and remedies for the enforcement of sister state claims and obligations whose substantive existence was independently assured."

Ralph Whitten maintains that the Full Faith and Credit Clause imposes no direct limitations on state choice of law, but it authorizes Congress to establish choice-of-law rules that would govern in state courts. He further concludes that the Due Process Clause regulates choice of law only to the extent that it bars states from enacting laws that retroactively deprive people of their rights.

These works are:

Lea Brilmayer, *Credit Due Judgments and Credit Due Laws: The Respective Roles of Due Process and Full Faith and Credit in the Interstate Context*, 70 Iowa L. Rev. 95 (1984)

Peter Hay, *Full Faith and Credit and Federalism in Choice of Law*, 34 Mercer L. Rev. 709 (1983)

Frederic L. Kirgis, Jr., *The Roles of Due Process and Full Faith and Credit in Choice of Law*, 62 Cornell L. Rev. 94 (1976)

Douglas Laycock, *Equal Citizens of Equal and Territorial States: The Constitutional Foundations of Choice of Law*, 92 Colum. L. Rev. 249 (1992)

Robert A. Leflar, *Constitutional Limits on Free Choice of Law*, 28 Law & Contemp. Probs. 706 (1963)

James A. Martin, *Constitutional Limitations on Choice of Law*, 61 Cornell L. Rev. 185 (1976)

James A. Martin, *A Reply to Professor Kirgis*, 62 Cornell L. Rev. 151 (1976)

Willis L.M. Reese, *Legislative Jurisdiction*, 78 Colum. L. Rev. 1587 (1978)

Russell J. Weintraub, *Due Process and Full Faith and Credit Limitations on a State's Choice of Law*, 44 Iowa L. Rev. 449 (1959)

Russell J. Weintraub, *Who's Afraid of Constitutional Limitations on Choice of Law?*, 10 Hofstra L. Rev. 17 (1981)

Ralph U. Whitten, *The Constitutional Limitations on State Choice of Law: Due Process*, 9 Hastings Const. L.Q. 851 (1982)

## Commentary on Allstate Insurance Co. v. Hague (1981)

The Supreme Court's decision in Allstate Insurance Co. v. Hague (1981) spawned an enormous body of scholarly literature. Russell Weintraub (cited above) untangles the state law insurance issues lurking in *Allstate*, concluding that the case was a false conflict: under both states' laws, stacking should have been permitted on the facts of the case. Arthur von Mehren and Donald Trautman, too, examine the underlying substantive issues. Focusing on state choice-of-law analysis rather than constitutional limits, Robert Leflar posits that "many American courts [today] would reach the same choice-of-law result that the Minnesota court reached" on the *Allstate* facts. Louise Weinberg compares the interests of Minnesota and Wisconsin, and she, too, concludes that "the scales are not as self-evidently tipped on Wisconsin's side" as others suggest.

Some scholars, including Andreas Lowenfeld, Friedrich Juenger and Louise Weinberg, defend the Supreme Court's decision in *Allstate*, arguing that the Court properly declined to scrutinize rigorously state choice-of-law decisions under the guise of constitutional law. Russell Weintraub agrees with the constitutional standard announced by the *Allstate* plurality and with the conclusion that the standard was met on the facts of the case. Robert Sedler advocates an approach of constitutional generalism, under which the broad, organic purposes and functions of the Due Process and Full Faith and Credit Clauses would be considered in assessing the constitutionality of state choice of law, rather than a specialized body of constitutional law designed to promote "conflicts justice." Under this approach, Sedler posits that the Constitution should impose only the most minimal limitations on choice of law.

Other scholars criticize the Court for wasting the opportunity to define and clarify constitutional limits on choice of law. John Kozyris chastises the Court for failing to offer "reasonably narrow limits of permissible variation" in state choice of law and for emphasizing *potential* contacts that do not materialize. Academics offer several possible approaches that the Court might have pursued. For example, in Bruce Posnak's view, a state can apply its law consistent with due process only if "a policy of its . . . law will be advanced by the application of that law to the instant facts." Willis Reese, too, maintains that a state has an interest in applying its law only if the policy underlying the law would be served by the law's application. In separate articles, Linda Silberman and Lea Brilmayer propose more restrictive approaches. Silberman advocates a non-unilateralism principle, "which would make activity by the defendant amounting to purposeful involvement in a state regime of law a prerequisite to the choice of that state's law." Brilmayer maintains that forum contacts create a legitimate interest in applying forum law "only if there is a regulatory connection between the rule and the contact. The rule must, in other words, be designed to prescribe the legal consequences of the in-state occurrence." She would require proof that the regulatory justifications offered for choice-of-law purposes also serve domestic functions. Martin modifies Brilmayer's approach by eliminating persons as contacts and by concluding that "[a] state may apply its own law to an issue in a case if at least one contact bears formal substantive relevance or informal policy relevance to the state's regulatory effort . . . ."

Courtland Peterson, too, considers the meaning of state interests and asks whether the interests required by *Allstate*'s constitutional analysis are the same as the "state interests derived from governmental interest analysis, for choice purposes," or whether "they have some other meaning in this constitutional setting." He questions whether traditional, territorial choice-of-law rules satisfy *Allstate*'s interest requirement. Aaron Twerski answers this question in the affirmative, positing that "[s]tate sovereignty implies a right of a state legal system to govern essentially local disputes." He maintains that the state in which actionable conduct occurs may apply its law even if the effects of the conduct are felt elsewhere. Jack Davies, a Minnesota legislator, also emphasizes the continued validity of territoriality.

Arthur von Mehren and Donald Trautman debate the extent to which the Supreme Court should attempt to exercise direct constitutional control over state choice of law. They conclude that the Court should adopt minimal standards of control but vigorously monitor lower courts to ensure that they apply these standards. They offer three steps to suppress "excessive parochialism," including elimination of a preference for forum law; a requirement that state courts offer persuasive reasons for any departure from choice-of-law norms; and a requirement that state courts interfere with or depart from a federal interest in national unity only in compelling circumstances.

Scholars have debated the relevance of a litigant's after-acquired domicile for purposes of due process analysis. Weintraub views consideration of after-acquired domicile as "sufficiently fair to squeeze past a due process standard." Weinberg and Martin agree. Silberman and Reese, on the other hand, view after-acquired domicile as irrelevant. Brilmayer expresses "reluctance" to consider it, and Peterson rejects a categorical approach to this issue, favoring a more "particularized inquiry."

These works are:

Lea Brilmayer, *Legitimate Interests in Multistate Problems: As Between State and Federal Law*, 79 Mich. L. Rev. 1315 (1981)

Jack Davies, *A Legislator's Look at* Hague *and Choice of Law*, 10 Hofstra L. Rev. 171 (1981)

Friedrich K. Juenger, *Supreme Court Intervention in Jurisdiction and Choice of Law: A Dismal Prospect*, 14 U.C. Davis L. Rev. 907 (1981)

P. John Kozyris, *Reflections on* Allstate—*The Lessening of Due Process in Choice of Law*, 14 U.C. Davis L. Rev. 889 (1981)

Robert A. Leflar, *Choice of Law: States' Rights*, 10 Hofstra L. Rev. 203 (1981)

Andreas F. Lowenfeld & Linda J. Silberman, *Choice of Law and the Supreme Court: A Dialogue Inspired by* Allstate Insurance Co. v. Hague, 14 U.C. Davis L. Rev. 841 (1981)

James A. Martin, *The Constitutional and Legislative Jurisdiction*, 10 Hofstra L. Rev. 133 (1981)

Courtland H. Peterson, *Particularism in the Conflict of Laws*, 10 Hofstra L. Rev. 973 (1982)

Courtland H. Peterson, *Proposals of Marriage Between Jurisdiction and Choice of Law*, 14 U.C. Davis L. Rev. 869 (1981)

Bruce Posnak, *The Court Doesn't Know its* Asahi *from its* Wortman*: A Critical View of the Constitutional Constraints of Jurisdiction and Choice of Law*, 41 Syracuse L. Rev. 875 (1990)

Willis L.M. Reese, *The* Hague *Case: An Opportunity Lost*, 10 Hofstra L. Rev. 195 (1981)

Robert A. Sedler, *Constitutional Limitations on Choice of Law: The Perspective of Constitutional Generalism*, 10 Hofstra L. Rev. 59 (1981)

Linda Silberman, *Can the State of Minnesota Bind the Nation?: Federal Choice of Law Constraints After* Allstate Insurance Co. v. Hague, 10 Hofstra L. Rev. 103 (1981)

Aaron D. Twerski, *On Territoriality and Sovereignty: System Shock and Constitutional Choice of Law*, 10 Hofstra L. Rev. 149 (1981)

Arthur T. von Mehren & Donald T. Trautman, *Constitutional Control of Choice of Law: Some Reflections on* Hague, 10 Hofstra L. Rev. 35 (1981)

Louise Weinberg, *Choice of Law and Minimal Scrutiny*, 49 U. Chi. L. Rev. 440 (1982)

Louise Weinberg, *Conflicts Cases and the Problem of Relevant Time: A Response to the* Hague *Symposium*, 10 Hofstra L. Rev. 1023 (1982)

## Commentary on Phillips Petroleum Co. v. Shutts (1985)

The Supreme Court in *Shutts* addressed constitutional limits on both jurisdiction and choice of law in the multistate class action setting. The academic literature addressing the jurisdictional issue is discussed above. Arthur Miller and David Crump recognize a relationship between the two issues: because the jurisdictional holding permits attorneys to file multistate class actions in whichever state they choose, limits on choice of law are necessary "to prevent forum shopping, unfairness to defendants, and interference with other states' sovereignty." In the absence of restrictions on choice of law, class counsel will file suit in a "magnet" state, or a state most likely to apply its law in favor of the class. Miller and Crump posit that while "the Court's guidelines limit the worst abuses, enough play in the joints remains to allow the magnet forum phenomenon to persist." They advocate a federal legislative solution.

Terry Kogan views *Shutts* as "offer[ing] little new doctrine to explain the constitutional limits on choice of law." He criticizes *Allstate* for fixating on state interests and paying only lip service to fairness concerns. He maintains that even though the *Shutts* Court purported to apply the *Allstate* test, it may have invalidated the choice of Kansas law out of concern for fairness to the litigants. Kogan advocates an analysis that "accord[s] priority to concerns of fairness over concerns of comity."

In a student comment, Ryan Phair "challenges the modern presumption that the choice-of-law problem precludes certification of a nationwide Rule 23(b)(3) class action." He argues that it may be constitutional to apply a single state's law to all claims in some multistate class actions, and in others, to use subclasses to overcome manageability concerns. He criticizes *Shutts* for limiting judicial creativity in the resolution of choice-of-law problems in multistate class actions.

Larry Kramer takes issue with the "single law" solution in mass tort cases. In his view, "choice of law . . . should not change simply because, as a matter of administrative convenience and efficiency, we have combined many claims in one proceeding; whatever choice-of-law rules we use to define substantive rights should be the same for ordinary and complex cases."

These works are:

Terry S. Kogan, *Toward a Jurisprudence of Choice of Law: The Priority of Fairness Over Comity*, 62 N.Y.U. L. Rev. 651 (1987)

Larry Kramer, *Class Actions and Jurisdictional Boundaries: Choice of Law in Complex Litigation*, 71 N.Y.U. L. Rev. 547 (1996)

Arthur R. Miller & David Crump, *Jurisdiction and Choice of Law in Multistate Class Actions After* Phillips Petroleum Co. v. Shutts, 96 Yale L.J. 1 (1986)

Ryan Patrick Phair, *Resolving the "Choice-of-Law Problem" in Rule 23(b)(3) Nationwide Class Actions*, 67 U. Chi. L. Rev. 835 (2000)

### Commentary on Sun Oil Co. v. Wortman (1988)

Louise Weinberg views *Wortman* as a disappointment because it immunized a traditional choice-of-law rule from constitutional scrutiny and because it "virtual[ly] abandon[ed] . . . reason." She criticizes Justice Scalia's due process analysis for identifying an interest that would support the choice of a forum state's shorter statute of limitations, but not its longer statute. She fears that *Wortman* stands for the proposition that "the 'traditional' choice always would be deemed to pass the rational basis test." She nevertheless concludes that *Wortman* correctly rejected the substantive model of choice of limitations law and may even have reached the right result.

Bruce Posnak (cited above), too, criticizes *Wortman* for failing to ascribe meaning to the state interest requirement and for creating an exception to the already minimal constitutional constraints on state choice of law for arguably procedural laws. He maintains that "current constitutional constraints on choice of law have become largely illusory and practically unimportant." He suggests that the forum should be free to apply its own law unless it clearly lacks a specific interest in applying its law and another state has such an interest, or the party opposing application of forum law can show detrimental reliance on the law of another state.

David Seidelson argues that the *Wortman* Court should have applied the *Allstate/Shutts* test to determine if Kansas had a significant interest in applying its own statute of limitations. He believes the Court should have examined the policies underlying the Kansas statute of limitations to determine if Kansas had such an interest. He analyzes the inconsistency between *Wortman*, which permitted Kansas to apply its own statute of limitations to claims governed by another state's substantive law, and a later Supreme Court decision, Ferens v. John Deere Co. (1990), which barred a federal transferee court from applying the statute of limitations of the state in which it sat.

George Brown begins with another apparent contradiction: the Supreme Court has condemned forum shopping between state and federal courts, but it has permitted, even encouraged, forum shopping between different state courts in decisions like *Wortman*. He explains away this contradiction by arguing that a bar on state/federal forum shopping serves federalism, while deference to state choice-of-law decisions in the interstate context likewise respects state primacy in private law (even if it encourages interstate forum shopping).

These works are:

George D. Brown, *The Ideologies of Forum Shopping—Why Doesn't a Conservative Court Protect Defendants?*, 71 N.C. L. Rev. 649 (1993)

David E. Seidelson, *1 (*Wortman*) + 1 (*Ferens*) = 6 (Years): That Can't be Right—Can It? Statutes of Limitations and Supreme Court Inconsistency*, 57 Brook. L. Rev. 787 (1991)

Louise Weinberg, *Choosing Law: The Limitations Debates*, 1991 U. Ill. L. Rev. 683

# Table of Cases

**A**

Abbott Labs. v. Gardner, 387 U.S. 136 (1967)
ABKCO Ind., Inc. v. Apple Films, Inc., 350 N.E.2d 899 (N.Y. 1976)
Adam v. Saenger, 303 U.S. 59 (1938)
Adames v. United States, 171 F.3d 728 (2d Cir. 1999)
Adams v. Robertson, 520 U.S. 83 (1997) (per curiam)
Addington v. Texas, 441 U.S. 418 (1979)
Adickes v. S.H. Kress & Co., 398 U.S. 144 (1970)
Advanced Mgmt. Tech., Inc. v. Fed. Aviation Admin., 211 F.3d 633 (D.C. Cir. 2000)
Aerojet-Gen. Corp. v. Askew, 511 F.2d 710 (5th Cir.), *appeal dismissed & cert. denied sub nom.* Metro. Dade County v. Aerojet-Gen. Corp., 423 U.S. 908 (1975)
Aetna Life Ins. Co. v. LaVoie, 475 U.S. 813 (1986)
Ake v. Oklahoma, 470 U.S. 68 (1985)
Akro Corp. v. Luker, 45 F.3d 1541 (Fed. Cir.), *cert. denied*, 515 U.S. 1122 (1995)
Al Odah v. United States, 321 F.3d 1134 (D.C. Cir. 2003), *reversed sub nom.* Rasul v. Bush, – U.S. –, 124 S. Ct. 2686 (2004)
Alabama v. Shelton, 535 U.S. 654 (2002)
Alaska Packers Ass'n v. Indus. Accident Comm'n, 294 U.S. 532 (1935)
Alaska Sport Fishing Ass'n v. Exxon Corp., 34 F.3d 769 (9th Cir. 1994)
Alford v. McGaw, 402 N.Y.S.2d 499 (N.Y. App. Div. 1978)
Alfred L. Snapp & Son, Inc. v. Puerto Rico *ex rel.* Barez, 458 U.S. 592 (1982)
Allen v. Illinois, 478 U.S. 364 (1986)
Allgeyer v. Louisiana, 165 U.S. 578 (1897)
Alli-Ballogun v. United States, 281 F.3d 362 (2d Cir. 2002)
Allied Corp. v. Acme Solvent Reclaiming, Inc., 771 F. Supp. 219 (N.D. Ill. 1990)
Allison v. Citgo Petroleum Corp., 151 F.3d 402 (5th Cir. 1998)
Allstate Ins. Co. v. Hague, 449 U.S. 302 (1981)
Alman v. Danin, 801 F.2d 1 (1st Cir. 1986)
ALS Scan, Inc. v. Digital Serv. Consultants, Inc., 293 F.3d 707 (4th Cir. 2002)
Amchem Prods., Inc. v. Windsor, 521 U.S. 591 (1997)
Am. Mfrs. Mut. Ins. Co. v. Sullivan, 526 U.S. 40 (1999)
Amoco Egypt Oil Co. v. Leonis Navigation Co., 1 F.3d 848 (9th Cir. 1993)

BE&K Constr. Co. v. United Bhd. of Carpenters, 688 So. 2d 246 (Ala.), *cert. denied*, 521 U.S. 1118 (1997)
Beard v. Beard, 21 Ind. 321 (1863)
Bearden v. Georgia, 461 U.S. 660 (1983)
Bearry v. Beech Aircraft Corp., 818 F.2d 370 (5th Cir. 1987)
Becherer v. Merrill Lynch, Pierce, Fenner & Smith, Inc., 193 F.3d 415 (6th Cir. 1999) (en banc)
Bedrejo v. Triple E Canada, Ltd., 984 P.2d 739 (Mont. 1999)
Beierle v. Zavares, No. 99-1383, 2000 U.S. App. LEXIS 13916 (10th Cir. June 12, 2000) (unpublished)
Bell v. Burson, 402 U.S. 535 (1971)
Bell v. Wolfish, 441 U.S. 520 (1979)
Bender v. City of Rochester, 765 F.2d 7 (2d Cir. 1985)
Benitez v. Wallis, – U.S. –, 124 S. Ct. 1143 (2004)
Benjamin v. Fraser, 264 F.3d 175 (2d Cir. 2001)
Benson & Ford, Inc. v. Wanda Petroleum Co., 833 F.2d 1172 (5th Cir. 1987)
Bensusan Rest. Corp. v. King, 937 F. Supp. 295 (S.D.N.Y. 1996), *aff'd*, 126 F.3d 25 (2d Cir. 1997)
Beverly Hills Fan Co. v. Royal Sovereign Corp., 21 F.3d 1558 (Fed. Cir. 1994)
Bi-Metallic Investment Co. v. State Bd., 239 U.S. 441 (1915)
Bijeol v. Benson, 513 F.2d 965 (7th Cir. 1975)
Bishop v. Wood, 426 U.S. 341 (1976)
Bittinger v. Tecumseh Prods. Co., 123 F.3d 877 (6th Cir. 1997)
Black v. Romano, 471 U.S. 606 (1985)
Blackmer v. United States, 284 U.S. 421 (1932)
Blair v. Equifax Check Servs., Inc., 181 F.3d 832 (7th Cir. 1999)
Blakely v. Washington, No. 02-1632, 2004 U.S. LEXIS 4573 (U.S. June 24, 2004)
Block v. Cmty. Nutrition Inst., 467 U.S. 340 (1984)
Blum v. Yaretsky, 457 U.S. 991 (1982)
Blumenthal v. Drudge, 992 F. Supp. 44 (D.D.C. 1998)
Bd. of Curators v. Horowitz, 435 U.S. 78 (1978)
Bd. of Educ. v. Shutz, 137 F. Supp. 2d 83 (N.D.N.Y. 2001), *aff'd on other grounds*, 290 F.3d 476 (2d Cir. 2002), *cert. denied*, 537 U.S. 1227 (2003)
Bd. of Natural Res. v. Brown, 992 F.2d 937 (9th Cir. 1993)
Bd. of Pardons v. Allen, 482 U.S. 369 (1987)
Bd. of Regents v. Roth, 408 U.S. 564 (1972)
Bd. of Trs. v. Ala. State Bd. of Educ., 479 U.S. 1085 (1987)
Bochan v. La Fontaine, 68 F. Supp. 2d 692 (E.D. Va. 1999)
Boddie v. Connecticut, 401 U.S. 371 (1971)
Boero v. Drug Enforcement Administration, 111 F.3d 301 (2d Cir. 1997)
Bogard v. Cook, 586 F.2d 399 (5th Cir. 1978), *cert. denied*, 444 U.S. 883 (1979)
Boit v. Gar-Tec Prods., Inc., 967 F.2d 671 (1st Cir. 1992)
Bolling v. Sharpe, 347 U.S. 497 (1954)
Bolton v. Gramlich, 540 F. Supp. 822 (S.D.N.Y. 1982)
Bonham's Case, 8 Co. Rep. 107a, 77 Eng. Rep. 638 (C.P. 1610)

**D**

Dow Chem. Co. v. Stephenson, 539 U.S. 111 (2003) (per curiam)
Dowling v. United States, 493 U.S. 342 (1990)
Draper v. Washington, 372 U.S. 487 (1963)
Dred Scott v. Sandford, 60 U.S. (19 How.) 393 (1856)
Drexel Burnham Lambert, Inc. v. D'Angelo, 453 F. Supp. 1294 (S.D.N.Y. 1978)
Drummond v. United States, 324 U.S. 316 (1945)
Dusenbery v. United States, 534 U.S. 161 (2002)

**E**

Edberg v. Neogen Corp., 17 F. Supp. 2d 104 (D. Conn. 1998)
EDIAS Software Int'l v. BASIS Int'l Ltd., 947 F. Supp. 413 (D. Ariz. 1996)
Edmonson v. Leesville Concrete Co., 500 U.S. 614 (1991)
Edwards v. Balisok, 520 U.S. 641 (1997)
Edwards v. City of Houston, 78 F.3d 983 (5th Cir. 1996)
Ehorn v. Sunken Vessel Known as the "Rosinco," 294 F.3d 856 (7th Cir. 2002)
Eisen v. Carlisle & Jacquelin, 391 F.2d 555 (2d Cir. 1968)
Eisen v. Carlisle & Jacquelin, 417 U.S. 156 (1974)
Elizondo v. Read, 588 N.E.2d 501 (Ind. 1992)
Elliott v. Weinberger, 1975 U.S. App. LEXIS 12532 (9th Cir. Oct. 1, 1975)
Elliott v. Weinberger, 564 F.2d 1219 (9th Cir. 1977), *aff'd in part, rev'd in part sub nom.* Califano v. Yamasaki, 442 U.S. 682 (1979)
Ellis v. District of Columbia, 84 F.3d 1413 (D.C. Cir. 1996)
Envtl. Def. Fund v. Higginson, 631 F.2d 738 (D.C. Cir. 1979)
Epstein v. MCA, Inc., 126 F.3d 1235 (9th Cir. 1997), *withdrawn and substituted by* 179 F.3d 641 (9th Cir.), *cert. denied*, 528 U.S. 1004 (1999)
Epstein v. MCA, Inc., 179 F.3d 641 (9th Cir.), *cert. denied*, 528 U.S. 1004 (1999)
ESAB Group, Inc. v. Centricut, Inc., 126 F.3d 617 (4th Cir. 1997)
Eskridge v. Wash. State Bd. of Prison Terms & Paroles, 357 U.S. 214 (1958) (per curiam)
Eubanks v. Billington, 110 F.3d 87 (D.C. Cir. 1997)
Evitts v. Lucey, 469 U.S. 387 (1985)
Ewing v. Mytinger & Casselberry, Inc., 339 U.S. 594 (1950)
Ex Parte Hull, 312 U.S. 546 (1941)
Ex Parte Newco Mfg. Co., 481 So. 2d 867 (Ala. 1985)
Ex Parte Quirin, 317 U.S. 1 (1942)
Excel Shipping Corp. v. Seatrain Int'l S.A., 584 F. Supp. 734 (E.D.N.Y. 1984)

**F**

Fahey v. Mallonee, 332 U.S. 245 (1947)
Fairchild Engine & Airplane Corp. v. Bellanca Corp., 137 A.2d 248 (Pa. 1958)
Far W. Capital, Inc. v. Towne, 46 F.3d 1071 (10th Cir. 1995)
Farbotko v. Clinton County, 168 F. Supp. 2d 31 (N.D.N.Y. 2001)
Farrar v. Hobby, 506 U.S. 103 (1992)
Feder v. Turkish Airlines, 441 F. Supp. 1273 (S.D.N.Y. 1977)
Fed. Deposit Ins. Corp. v. Mallen, 486 U.S. 230 (1988)
FTC v. Cement Inst., 333 U.S. 683 (1948)
FTC v. Jim Walter Corp., 651 F.2d 251 (5th Cir. 1981)

Grannis v. Ordean, 234 U.S. 385 (1914)
Great Am. Ins. Co. v. Louis Lesser Enters., Inc., 353 F.2d 997 (8th Cir. 1965)
Great Lakes Overseas, Inc. v. Wah Kwong Shipping Group, Ltd., 990 F.2d 990 (7th Cir. 1993)
Greene v. Lindsey, 456 U.S. 444 (1982)
Greene v. McElroy, 360 U.S. 474 (1959)
Greenholtz v. Inmates of the Neb. Penal & Corr. Complex, 442 U.S. 1 (1979)
Gregory v. Town of Pittsfield, 479 A.2d 1304, 479 A.2nd (Me. 1984), *cert. denied*, 470 U.S. 1018 (1985)
Gregory v. Town of Pittsfield, 470 U.S. 1018 (1985)
Griffin v. Illinois, 351 U.S. 12 (1956)
Griffis v. Luban, 646 N.W.2d 527 (Minn. 2002)
Grimes v. Vitalink Communications Corp., 17 F.3d 1553 (3d Cir.), *cert. denied*, 513 U.S. 986 (1994)
Grosjean v. Am. Press Co., 297 U.S. 233 (1936)
Grunin v. Int'l House of Pancakes, 513 F.2d 114 (8th Cir.), *cert. denied*, 423 U.S. 864 (1975)
Gutnick v. Dow Jones & Co., [2001] VSC 305 (S.Ct. of Victoria, Australia, Aug. 28, 2001), *appeal dismissed*, 194 A.L.R. 433 (Austl. 2002)

**H**

Haag v. Barnes, 175 N.E.2d 441 (N.Y. 1961)
Hagar v. Reclamation Dist., 111 U.S. 701 (1884)
Ham v. La Cienega Music Co., 4 F.3d 413 (5th Cir. 1993)
Hamdi v. Rumsfeld, 316 F.3d 450 (4th Cir.), *rehearing and rehearing en banc denied*, 337 F.3d 335 (4th Cir. 2003), *vacated*, No. 03-6696, 2004 WL 1431951 (U.S. June 28, 2004)
Hamdi v. Rumsfeld, 337 F.3d 335 (4th Cir. 2003), *vacated*, – U.S. –, 124 S. Ct. 2633 (2004)
Hamdi v. Rumsfeld, – U.S. –, 124 S. Ct. 2633 (2004)
Hammond Packing Co. v. Arkansas, 212 U.S. 322 (1909)
Hampton v. Mow Sun Wong, 426 U.S. 88 (1976)
Handschu v. Special Servs. Div., 787 F.2d 828 (2d Cir. 1986)
Hansberry v. Lee, 311 U.S. 32 (1940)
Hanson v. Denckla, 357 U.S. 235 (1958)
Harlow v. Fitzgerald, 457 U.S. 800 (1982)
Harold M. Pitman Co. v. Typecraft Software Ltd., 626 F. Supp. 305 (N.D. Ill. 1986)
Harris v. Balk, 198 U.S. 215 (1905)
Harris v. Hardeman, 55 U.S. (14 How.) 334 (1853)
Harris v. Rivera, 454 U.S. 339 (1981) (per curiam)
Harris v. United States, 536 U.S. 545 (2002)
Harris County v. Carmax Auto Superstores, Inc., 177 F.3d 306 (5th Cir. 1999)
Harrods Ltd. v. Sixty Internet Domain Names, 302 F.3d 214 (4th Cir. 2002)
Hartford Accident & Indem. Co. v. Delta & Pine Land Co., 292 U.S. 143 (1934)
Hasbro, Inc. v. Clue Computing, Inc., 994 F. Supp. 34 (D. Mass. 1997)
Hason v. Davis, 210 F.3d 354 (2d Cir. 2000)

Hatch v. District of Columbia, 184 F.3d 846 (D.C. Cir. 1999)
Hebert v. Louisiana, 272 U.S. 312 (1926)
Heck v. Humphrey, 512 U.S. 477 (1994)
Heckler v. Chaney, 470 U.S. 821 (1985)
Heckler v. Ringer, 466 U.S. 602 (1984)
Heckman v. United States, 224 U.S. 413 (1912)
Helicopteros Nacionales de Colombia v. Hall, 466 U.S. 408 (1984)
Heritage House Rest., Inc. v. Cont'l Funding Group, Inc., 906 F.2d 276 (7th Cir. 1990)
Heroes, Inc. v. Heroes Found., 958 F. Supp. 1 (D.D.C. 1996)
Hess v. Pawloski, 274 U.S. 352 (1927)
Hewitt v. Helms, 459 U.S. 460 (1983)
Hodel v. Va. Surface Mining & Reclamation Ass'n, 452 U.S. 264 (1981)
Hoffman v. State, 871 P.2d 27 (N.M. Ct. App. 1994)
Hoffmann-La Roche Inc. v. Sperling, 493 U.S. 165 (1989)
Hoke v. Henderson, 15 N.C. 1 (1833)
Hollingsworth v. Barbour, 29 U.S. (4 Pet.) 466 (1830)
Home Ins. Co. v. Dick, 281 U.S. 397 (1930)
Hooker v. Los Angeles, 188 U.S. 314 (1903)
Hoopeston Canning Co. v. Cullen, 318 U.S. 313 (1943)
Hornsby v. Allen, 326 F.2d 605 (5th Cir. 1964)
Hovey v. Elliott, 167 U.S. 409 (1897)
Hudson v. Palmer, 468 U.S. 517 (1984)
Hughes v. Rowe, 449 U.S. 5 (1980) (per curiam)
Huling v. Kaw Valley Ry. & Improvement Co., 130 U.S. 559 (1889)
Hunter v. City of Pittsburgh, 207 U.S. 161 (1907)
Hurtado v. California, 110 U.S. 516 (1884)

**I**

Iacaponi v. New Amsterdam Cas. Co., 379 F.2d 311 (3d Cir. 1967) (per curiam), *cert. denied*, 389 U.S. 1054 (1968)
Illinois v. Batchelder, 463 U.S. 1112 (1983)
Imbler v. Pachtman, 424 U.S. 409 (1976)
Imo Indus., Inc. v. Kiekert AG, 155 F.3d 254 (3d Cir. 1998)
In re Agent Orange Prod. Liab. Litig., 818 F.2d 145 (2d Cir. 1987), *cert. denied sub nom.* Adams v. United States, 484 U.S. 1004 (1988)
In re Agent Orange Prod. Liab. Litig., 996 F.2d 1425 (2d Cir. 1993), *cert. denied sub nom.* Ivy v. Diamond Shamrock Chems. Co., 510 U.S. 1140 (1994), *overruled in part*, Syngenta Crop Prot., Inc. v. Henson, 537 U.S. 28 (2002)
In re Application for Tax Deed, 675 N.E.2d 285 (Ill. App. Ct.), *appeal denied*, 679 N.E.2d 380 (Ill. 1997) (table)
In re Arizona Dairy Prods. Litig., No. Civ. 74-569A-PHX-CAM, 1975 U.S. Dist. LEXIS 15833 (D. Ariz. Oct. 7, 1975)
In re Asbestos Litig., 90 F.3d 963 (5th Cir. 1996), *vacated sub nom.* Flanagan v. Fibreboard Corp., 521 U.S. 1114 (1997)
In re Asbestos Sch. Litig., 620 F. Supp. 873 (E.D. Pa. 1985)
In re Brooks Fashion Stores, Inc., 124 B.R. 436 (Bankr. S.D.N.Y. 1991)

In re Cherry's Petition to Intervene, 164 F.R.D. 630 (E.D. Mich. 1996)
In re Chi., M., St. P. & Pac. R.R., 974 F.2d 775 (7th Cir. 1992)
In re Corrugated Container Antitrust Litig., 643 F.2d 195 (5th Cir. 1981), *cert. denied sub nom.* CFS Cont'l, Inc. v. Adams Extract Co., 456 U.S. 998 (1982)
In re DES Cases, 789 F. Supp. 552 (E.D.N.Y. 1992)
In re Diet Drugs Prods. Liab. Litig., No. 99-20593, 2000 U.S. Dist. LEXIS 12275 (E.D. Pa. Aug. 28, 2000)
In re Drexel Burnham Lambert Group, 960 F.2d 285 (2d Cir. 1992), *cert. denied sub nom.* Hart Holding Co. v. Drexel Burnham Lambert Group, 506 U.S. 1088 (1993)
In re Edwards, 962 F.2d 641 (7th Cir. 1992)
In re Engelhard & Sons Co., 231 U.S. 646 (1914)
In re Foreclosure of Tax Liens, 316 N.W.2d 362 (Wis. 1982)
In re Gault, 387 U.S. 1 (1967)
In re Gen. Elec. Capital Corp., MDL 1192, 2000 U.S. Dist. LEXIS 4808 (N.D. Ill. March 9, 2000)
In re Graham, 973 F.2d 1089 (3d Cir. 1992)
In re Integra Realty Res., Inc., 262 F.3d 1089 (10th Cir. 2001)
In re Int'l Telemedia Assocs., 245 B.R. 713 (Bankr. N.D. Ga. 2000)
In re ISCA Enters., 572 N.E.2d 610 (N.Y. 1991)
In re Maya Constr. Co., 78 F.3d 1395 (9th Cir.), *cert. denied*, 519 U.S. 862 (1996)
In re Murchison, 349 U.S. 133 (1955)
In re Nissan Motor Corp. Antitrust Litig., 552 F.2d 1088 (5th Cir. 1977)
In re N. Dist. of Cal., Dalkon Shield IUD Prods. Liab. Litig., 693 F.2d 847 (9th Cir. 1982), *cert. denied sub nom.* A.H. Robins v. Abed, 459 U.S. 1171 (1983)
In re Provident Hosp., Inc., No. 91-1025, 1991 U.S. App. LEXIS 21447 (4th Cir. Sept. 12, 1991) (per curiam)
In re Real Estate Title & Settlement Servs. Antitrust Litig., MDL No. 633, 1986 U.S. Dist. LEXIS 24435 (E.D. Pa. June 10, 1986), *aff'd without op.*, 815 F.2d 695 (3d Cir. 1987), *cert. denied sub nom.* Arizona v. Chi. Title Ins. Co., 485 U.S. 909 (1988)
In re Real Estate Title & Settlement Servs. Antitrust Litig., 869 F.2d 760 (3d Cir.), *cert. denied sub nom.* Chi. Title Ins. Co. v. Tucson Unified Sch. Dist., 493 U.S. 821 (1989)
In re Ruffalo, 390 U.S. 544 (1968)
In re Sawyer, 124 U.S. 200 (1888)
In re Silicone Gel Breast Implant Prods. Liab. Litig., No. CV 92-P-10000-S, 1994 WL 114580 (N.D. Ala. April 1, 1994)
In re Spring Valley Farms, Inc., 863 F.2d 832 (11th Cir. 1989)
In re Tax Foreclosure No. 35, 514 N.Y.S.2d 390 (N.Y. App. Div. 1987)
In re Temple, 851 F.2d 1269 (11th Cir. 1988)
In re Traffic Exec. Ass'n, 627 F.2d 631 (2d Cir. 1980)
In re Trans World Airlines Inc., 96 F.3d 687 (3d Cir. 1996)
In re U.S.H. Corp. of N.Y., 223 B.R. 654 (Bankr. S.D.N.Y. 1998)
In re Victor Techs. Secs. Litig., 792 F.2d 862 (9th Cir. 1986)
In re Virtual Vision, Inc., 124 F.3d 1140 (9th Cir. 1997)
In re Winship, 397 U.S. 358 (1970)

Indian Oasis-Baboquivari Unified Sch. Dist. No. 40 v. Kirk, 91 F.3d 1240 (9th Cir. 1996)
Ingraham v. Wright, 430 U.S. 651 (1977)
INS v. St. Cyr, 533 U.S. 289 (2001)
Inset Sys., Inc. v. Instruction Set, Inc., 937 F. Supp. 161 (D. Conn. 1996)
Ins. Corp. of Ir. v. Compagnie des Bauxites de Guinee, 456 U.S. 694 (1982)
Intercon, Inc. v. Bell Atlantic Internet Solutions, Inc., 205 F.3d 1244 (10th Cir. 2000)
Intermeat, Inc. v. Am. Poultry Inc., 575 F.2d 1017 (2d Cir. 1978)
Int'l Harvester Co. v. Kentucky, 234 U.S. 579 (1914)
Int'l Shoe Co. v. Washington, 326 U.S. 310 (1945)
Iowa Elec. Light & Power Co. v. Mobile Aerial Towers, Inc., 723 F.2d 50 (8th Cir. 1983).
Irving v. Owens-Corning Fiberglas Corp., 864 F.2d 383 (5th Cir.), *cert. denied*, 493 U.S. 823 (1989)
ISI Int'l, Inc. v. Borden Ladner Gervais LLP, 256 F.3d 548 (7th Cir. 2001)
Island Fin., Inc. v. Ballman, 607 A.2d 76 (Md. Ct. Spec. App. 1992)

**J**

Jackson v. Long, 102 F.3d 722 (4th Cir. 1996)
Jackson v. Metro. Edison Co., 419 U.S. 345 (1974)
Jackson v. Virginia, 443 U.S. 307 (1979)
Janmark, Inc. v. Reidy, 132 F.3d 1200 (7th Cir. 1997)
Jefferson v. Ingersoll Int'l Inc., 195 F.3d 894 (7th Cir. 1999)
Jenkins v. McKeithen, 395 U.S. 411 (1969)
J.M.S. & Assocs., Inc. v. Eastman Kodak Co., 156 F.3d 1230 (6th Cir. 1998) (table) (per curiam; unpublished opinion)
John Hancock Mut. Life Ins. Co. v. Yates, 299 U.S. 178 (1936)
John Walker & Sons, Ltd. v. DeMert & Dougherty, Inc., 821 F.2d 399 (7th Cir. 1987)
Johnson v. Avery, 393 U.S. 483 (1969)
Johnson v. Eisentrager, 339 U.S. 763 (1950)
Johnson v. Gen. Motors Corp., 598 F.2d 432 (5th Cir. 1979)
Johnson v. Robison, 415 U.S. 361 (1974)
Johnson v. Zerbst, 304 U.S. 458 (1938)
Joint Anti-Fascist Refugee Comm. v. McGrath, 341 U.S. 123 (1951)
Jones v. N. Am. Aerodynamics, Inc., 594 F. Supp. 657 (D. Me. 1984)
Jones v. United States, 463 U.S. 354 (1983)
Jones v. United States, 526 U.S. 227 (1999)
Jonnet v. Dollar Sav. Bank, 530 F.2d 1123 (3d Cir. 1976)
J.S. Serv. Ctr. Corp. v. Banco Cont'l, 425 N.Y.S.2d 945 (N.Y. Sup. Ct. 1980)
Juda v. Nerney, No. 99-2070, 2000 U.S. App. LEXIS 6914 (10th Cir. April 17, 2000)
Jurek v. Texas, 428 U.S. 262 (1976)

**K**

Kadonsky v. United States, 216 F.3d 499 (5th Cir. 2000), *cert. denied*, 531 U.S. 1176 (2001)
Kane v. New Jersey, 242 U.S. 160 (1916)
Kaplan v. First Options of Chi., Inc., 143 F.3d 807 (3d Cir. 1998)
Kaplan v. United States, 133 F.3d 469 (7th Cir. 1998)

Keenan v. Hall, 83 F.3d 1083 (9th Cir. 1996)
Keeton v. Hustler Magazine, Inc., 465 U.S. 770 (1984)
Keim v. United States, 177 U.S. 290 (1900)
Kelley *ex rel.* Mich. Dep't of Envtl. Quality v. Wagner, 930 F. Supp. 293 (E.D. Mich. 1996)
Kelly v. Borough of Sayreville, 107 F.3d 1073 (3d Cir. 1997)
Kelly v. Smith, 764 F.2d 1412 (11th Cir. 1985), *overruled on other grounds by* McKinney v. Pate, 20 F.3d 1550 (11th Cir. 1994)
Kelly v. Wyman, 294 F. Supp. 893 (S.D.N.Y. 1968), *aff'd sub nom.* Goldberg v. Kelly, 397 U.S. 254 (1970)
Kent v. United States, 383 U.S. 541 (1966)
Ky. Dep't of Corr. v. Thompson, 490 U.S. 454 (1989)
Kernan v. Kurz-Hastings, Inc., 175 F.3d 236 (2d Cir. 1999)
Kerrison v. Stewart, 93 U.S. 155 (1876)
Kerry Steel, Inc. v. Paragon Indus., Inc., 106 F.3d 147 (6th Cir. 1997)
Key v. McKinney, 176 F.3d 1083 (8th Cir. 1999)
King v. S. Cent. Bell Tel. & Tel. Co., 790 F.2d 524 (6th Cir. 1986)
Kirby v. Siegelman, 195 F.3d 1285 (11th Cir. 1999)
Kirkland v. Nat'l Mortgage Network, Inc., 884 F.2d 1367 (11th Cir. 1989)
Kitchen v. Upshaw, 286 F.3d 179 (4th Cir. 2002)
Klugh v. United States, 818 F.2d 294 (4th Cir. 1987)
Koch v. Lewis, 96 F. Supp. 2d 949 (D. Ariz. 2000)
Koch v. Lewis, 216 F. Supp. 2d 994 (D. Ariz. 2001), *appeal dismissed*, 335 F.3d 993 (9th Cir. 2003)
Konigsberg v. State Bar, 353 U.S. 252 (1957)
Kornblum v. St. Louis County, 72 F.3d 661 (8th Cir. 1995), *cert. denied*, 517 U.S. 1189 (1996)
Kowalski v. Tesmer, – U.S. –, 124 S. Ct. 1144 (2004)
Kreager v. Gen. Elec. Co., 497 F.2d 468 (2d Cir.), *cert. denied*, 419 U.S. 861 (1974)
Krecioch v. United States, 221 F.3d 976 (7th Cir. 2000)
Krell v. Prudential Ins. Co. of Am., 148 F.3d 283 (3d Cir. 1998), *cert. denied*, 525 U.S. 1114 (1999)
Krislov v. Aetna Plywood, Inc., 1999 U.S. Dist. LEXIS 19626 (N.D. Ill. Dec. 16, 1999), *aff'd sub nom.* Montgomery v. Aetna Plywood, Inc., 231 F.3d 399 (7th Cir. 2000), *cert. denied,* 532 U.S. 1038 (2001)
Kuenzle v. HTM Sport-Und Freizeitgerate AG, 102 F.3d 453 (10th Cir. 1996)
Kulko v. Superior Ct., 436 U.S. 84 (1978)
Kwong Hai Chew v. Colding, 344 U.S. 590 (1953)
Kyriaki v. W. Elec. Co., 647 F.2d 388 (3d Cir. 1981)

**L**

LaChance v. Erickson, 522 U.S. 262 (1998)
Lafayette Ins. Co. v. French, 59 U.S. (18 How.) 404 (1856)
Landon v. Plasencia, 459 U.S. 21 (1982)
Lane v. Brown, 372 U.S. 477 (1963)

Lanier v. Am. Bd. of Endodontics, 843 F.2d 901 (6th Cir.), *cert. denied*, 488 U.S. 926 (1988)
Larionoff v. United States, 533 F.2d 1167 (D.C. Cir. 1976), *aff'd*, 431 U.S. 864 (1977)
Lassiter v. Dep't of Soc. Servs., 452 U.S. 18 (1981)
Lauritzen v. Larsen, 345 U.S. 571 (1953)
Lawrence County v. Lead-Deadwood Sch. Dist. No. 40-1, 469 U.S. 256 (1985)
Lebowitz v. Forbes Leasing & Fin. Corp., 456 F.2d 979 (3d Cir.), *cert. denied*, 409 U.S. 843 (1972), *overruled by* Jonnet v. Dollar Sav. Bank, 530 F.2d 1123 (3d Cir. 1976)
Lebron v. Nat'l R.R. Passenger Corp., 513 U.S. 374 (1995)
Lee v. Hansberry, 24 N.E.2d 37 (Ill. 1939), *reversed*, 311 U.S. 32 (1940)
Lehr v. Robertson, 463 U.S. 248 (1983)
Leis v. Flynt, 439 U.S. 438 (1979)
Lepre v. Dep't of Labor, 275 F.3d 59 (D.C. Cir. 2001)
Lesnick v. Hollingsworth & Vose Co., 35 F.3d 939 (4th Cir. 1994)
Lewis v. Casey, 518 U.S. 343 (1996)
Lewis v. N.M. Dep't of Health, 94 F. Supp. 2d 1217 (D.N.M. 2000)
Little v. Streater, 452 U.S. 1 (1981)
Lochner v. New York, 198 U.S. 45 (1905)
Lockett v. Ohio, 438 U.S. 586 (1978)
Logan v. Zimmerman Brush Co., 455 U.S. 422 (1982)
Londoner v. City of Denver, 210 U.S. 373 (1908)
Long v. Dist. Ct., 385 U.S. 192 (1966)
Longyear v. Toolan, 209 U.S. 414 (1908)
L.A. Branch NAACP v. L.A. Unified Sch. Dist., 750 F.2d 731 (9th Cir. 1984) (en banc), *cert. denied*, 474 U.S. 919 (1985)
Louis K. Liggett Co. v. Lee, 288 U.S. 517 (1933)
Louring v. Kuwait Boulder Shipping Co., 455 F. Supp. 630 (D. Conn. 1977)
Ludecke v. Watkins, 335 U.S. 160 (1948)
Ludwig v. Bd. of Trs., 123 F.3d 404 (6th Cir. 1997)
Lugar v. Edmondson Oil Co., 457 U.S. 922 (1982)
Lujan v. G&G Fire Sprinklers, Inc., 532 U.S. 189 (2001)
Luken v. Scott, 71 F.3d 192 (5th Cir. 1995), *cert. denied sub nom.* Luken v. Johnson, 517 U.S. 1196 (1996)
Luna v. Black, 772 F.2d 448 (8th Cir. 1985)
Lyng v. Payne, 476 U.S. 926 (1986)

**M**

M.L.B. v. S.L.J., 519 U.S. 102 (1996)
Macarz v. Transworld Sys., Inc., Case No. 3:97CV2194 (JBA), 2001 U.S. Dist. LEXIS 18005 (D. Conn. May 11, 2001)
MacDougalls' Cape Cod Marine Serv., Inc. v. One Christina 40' Vessel, 900 F.2d 408 (1st Cir. 1990)
Mackey v. Montrym, 443 U.S. 1 (1979)
Madara v. Hall, 916 F.2d 1510 (11th Cir. 1990)
Madewell v. Downs, 68 F.3d 1030 (8th Cir. 1995)
Magee v. Amiss, 502 So.2d 568 (La. 1987)

Majique Fashions Ltd. v. Warwick & Co., 414 N.Y.S.2d 916 (N.Y. App. Div. 1979)
Malchi v. Thaler, 211 F.3d 953 (5th Cir. 2000)
Malinski v. New York, 324 U.S. 401 (1945)
Mallette v. Arlington County Employees' Supplemental Ret. Sys. II, 91 F.3d 630 (4th Cir. 1996)
Maritz, Inc. v. Cybergold, Inc., 947 F. Supp. 1328 (E.D. Mo. 1996)
Marrese v. Am. Acad. of Orthopaedic Surgeons, 470 U.S. 373 (1985)
Marshall v.Kleppe, 637 F.2d 1217 (9th Cir. 1980)
Marshall v. Jerrico, Inc., 446 U.S. 238 (1980)
Martin v. Mott, 25 U.S. (12 Wheat.) 19 (1827)
Martin v. Wilks, 490 U.S. 755 (1989)
Martinez v. California, 444 U.S. 277 (1980)
Mason v. Parker, 695 N.E.2d 70 (Ill. App. Ct.), *appeal denied*, 705 N.E.2d 439 (Ill. 1998)
Mathews v. Eldridge, 424 U.S. 319 (1976)
Matsushita Elec. Indus. Co. v. Epstein, 516 U.S. 367 (1996)
Mattel, Inc. v. Barbie-Club.com, 00 Civ. 8705 (DLC), 2001 U.S. Dist. LEXIS 5262 (S.D.N.Y. May 1, 2001)
May v. Baldwin, 109 F.3d 557 (9th Cir. 1997)
Mayer v. City of Chicago, 404 U.S. 189 (1971)
Maywalt v. Parker & Parsley Petroleum Co., 67 F.3d 1072 (2d Cir. 1995)
McAuliffe v. Mayor of New Bedford, 155 Mass. 216 (1892)
McDermott, Inc. v. AmClyde, 511 U.S. 202 (1994)
McDonald v. Mabee, 243 U.S. 90 (1917)
McGee v. Int'l Life Ins. Co., 355 U.S. 220 (1957)
McGuinness v. DuBois, 75 F.3d 794 (1st Cir. 1996)
McMillan v. Pennsylvania, 477 U.S. 79 (1986)
McNary v. Haitian Refugee Ctr., Inc., 498 U.S. 479 (1991)
McQuillion v. Duncan, 306 F.3d 895 (9th Cir. 2002)
Meachum v. Fano, 427 U.S. 215 (1976)
Medina v. California, 505 U.S. 437 (1992)
M'Elmoyle v. Cohen, 38 U.S. 312 (1839)
Memphis Cmty. Sch. Dist. v. Stachura, 477 U.S. 299 (1986)
Memphis Light, Gas & Water Div. v. Craft, 436 U.S. 1 (1978)
Mennonite Bd. of Missions v. Adams, 462 U.S. 791 (1983)
Metro. Life Ins. Co. v. Neaves, 912 F.2d 1062 (9th Cir. 1990)
Metro. Life Ins. Co. v. Robertson-Ceco Corp., 84 F.3d 560 (2d Cir. 1996)
Metro. Life Ins. Co. v. Ward, 470 U.S. 869 (1986)
Meyer v. Nebraska, 262 U.S. 390 (1923)
Michael H. v. Gerald D., 491 U.S. 110 (1989)
Mich. Nat'l Bank v. Quality Dinette, Inc., 888 F.2d 462 (6th Cir. 1989)
Middendorf v. Henry, 425 U.S. 25 (1976)
Mid-State Homes, Inc. v. Portis, 652 F. Supp. 640 (W.D. La. 1987)
Millennium Enters., Inc. v. Millennium Music, LP, 33 F. Supp. 2d 907 (D. Or. 1999)
Milliken v. Meyer, 311 U.S. 457 (1940)
Mills v. Duryee, 11 U.S. 481 (1813)
Mills v. Rogers, 457 U.S. 291 (1982)

Minichiello v. Rosenberg, 410 F.2d 106 (2d Cir. 1968), *cert. denied*, 396 U.S. 844 (1969)
Mink v. AAAA Dev. LLC, 190 F.3d 333 (5th Cir. 1999)
Missouri v. Lewis, 101 U.S. (11 Otto) 22 (1879)
Mitchell v. W.T. Grant Co., 416 U.S. 600 (1974)
Molski v. Gleich, 318 F.3d 937 (9th Cir. 2003)
Monfils v. Taylor, 165 F.3d 511 (7th Cir. 1998), *cert. denied*, 528 U.S. 810 (1999)
Montana v. United States, 440 U.S. 147 (1979)
Montanye v. Haymes, 427 U.S. 236 (1976)
Montelongo v. Meese, 803 F.2d 1341 (5th Cir. 1986), *cert. denied sub nom.* Martin v. Montelongo, 481 U.S. 1048 (1987)
Moody v. Daggett, 429 U.S. 78 (1976)
Moore v. Lindsay, 1989 U.S. Dist. LEXIS 18042 (W.D. Va. 1989)
Morris v. SSE, Inc., 843 F.2d 489 (11th Cir. 1988)
Morrissey v. Brewer, 408 U.S. 471 (1972)
Morton v. Beyer, 822 F.2d 364 (3d Cir. 1987)
Muhammad v. Close, – U.S. –, 124 S. Ct. 1303 (2004) (per curiam)
Mullane v. Cent. Hanover Bank & Trust Co., 339 U.S. 306 (1950)
Mun. Utils. Bd. v. Ala. Power Co., 934 F.2d 1493 (11th Cir. 1991), *cert. denied*, 513 U.S. 1148 (1995)
Murray v. Giarratano, 492 U.S. 1 (1989)
Murray's Lessee v. Hoboken Land & Improvement Co., 59 U.S. (18 How.) 272 (1856)

**N**

NAACP v. Hunt, 891 F.2d 1555 (11th Cir. 1990)
Nabisco, Inc. v. Amtech Int'l, Inc., 2000 U.S. Dist. LEXIS 305 (S.D.N.Y. Jan. 18, 2000)
Nat'l Collegiate Athletic Ass'n v. Tarkanian, 488 U.S. 179 (1988)
Nat'l Equip. Rental, Ltd. v. Szukhent, 375 U.S. 311 (1964)
NLRB v. Bildisco & Bildisco, 465 U.S. 513 (1984)
NLRB v. Donnelly Garment Co., 330 U.S. 219 (1947)
Nazarova v. INS, 171 F.3d 478 (7th Cir. 1999)
Neal v. District of Columbia, 131 F.3d 172 (D.C. Cir. 1997)
Nehemiah v. Athletics Congress, 765 F.2d 42 (3d Cir. 1985)
Neil v. Biggers, 409 U.S. 188 (1972)
Nelson v. Adams USA, Inc., 529 U.S. 460 (2000)
Nelson v. Forbes, 545 N.W.2d 576 (Iowa Ct. App. 1996)
Nevada v. Hall, 440 U.S. 410 (1979)
Nevada v. United States, 463 U.S. 110 (1983)
N.Y. Life Ins. Co. v. Dodge, 246 U.S. 357 (1918)
N.Y. Life Ins. Co. v. Dunlevy, 241 U.S. 518 (1916)
Ngiraingas v. Sanchez, 495 U.S. 182 (1990)
Niere v. St. Louis County, 305 F.2d 834 (8th Cir. 2002)
Nissan Motor Co. v. Nissan Computer Corp., 89 F. Supp. 2d 1154 (C.D. Cal. 2000)
North v. Russell, 427 U.S. 328 (1976)
N. Am. Cold Storage Co. v. City of Chicago, 211 U.S. 306 (1908)
N. Georgia Finishing, Inc. v. Di-Chem, Inc., 419 U.S. 601 (1975)

Nova Biomedical Corp. v. Moller, 629 F.2d 190 (1st Cir. 1980)
Nowak v. Tak How Invs., Ltd., 94 F.3d 708 (1st Cir. 1996)

**O**

O'Bannon v. Town Ct. Nursing Ctr., 447 U.S. 773 (1980)
O'Connor v. Lee-Hy Paving Corp., 579 F.2d 194 (2d Cir.), *cert. denied*, 439 U.S. 1034 (1978)
Ohio Adult Parole Auth. v. Woodard, 523 U.S. 272 (1998)
Ohio Bell Tel. Co. v. Pub. Utils. Comm'n, 301 U.S. 292 (1937)
Olim v. Wakinekona, 461 U.S. 238 (1983)
Olson v. Town of Fitzwilliam, 702 A.2d 318 (N.H. 1997)
Omeluk v. Langsten Slip & Batbyggeri A/S, 52 F.3d 267 (9th Cir. 1995)
Omni Capital Int'l, Ltd. v. Rudolf Wolff & Co., 484 U.S. 97 (1987)
Oppenheimer Fund, Inc. v. Sanders, 437 U.S. 340 (1978)
Ortiz v. Fibreboard Corp., 527 U.S. 815 (1999)
Ortwein v. Schwab, 410 U.S. 656 (1973) (per curiam)
Owen v. City of Independence, 445 U.S. 622 (1980)
Oxford First Corp. v. PNC Liquidating Corp., 372 F. Supp. 191 (E.D. Pa. 1974)

**P**

Pac. Employers Ins. Co. v. Indus. Accident Comm'n, 306 U.S. 493 (1939)
Palomar Pomerado Health Sys. v. Belshe, 180 F.3d 1104 (9th Cir. 1999), *cert. denied*, 528 U.S. 1074 (2000)
Panda Brandywine Corp. v. Potomac Elec. Power Co., 253 F.3d 865 (5th Cir. 2001)
Panozzo v. Rhoads, 905 F.2d 135 (7th Cir. 1990)
Parham v. J.R., 442 U.S. 584 (1979)
Parklane Hosiery Co. v. Shore, 439 U.S. 322 (1979)
Parsons v. United States, 167 U.S. 324 (1897)
Parratt v. Taylor, 451 U.S. 527 (1981)
Pasquier v. Tarr, 318 F. Supp. 1350 (E.D. La. 1970), *aff'd on other grounds*, 444 F.2d 116 (5th Cir. 1971) (per curiam)
Pate v. Robinson, 383 U.S. 375 (1966)
Patterson v. New York, 432 U.S. 197 (1977)
Paul v. Davis, 424 U.S. 693 (1976)
Paul v. Virginia, 75 U.S. (8 Wall.) 168 (1869)
Pearrow v. Nat'l Life & Accident Ins. Co., 703 F.2d 1067 (8th Cir. 1983)
Pembina Consol. Silver Mining & Milling Co. v. Pennsylvania, 125 U.S. 181 (1888)
Pennoyer v. Neff, 95 U.S. 714 (1877)
Pennsylvania v. Finley, 481 U.S. 551 (1987)
Pennsylvania v. New Jersey, 426 U.S. 660 (1976)
Pa. Fire Ins. Co. v. Gold Issue Mining & Milling Co., 243 U.S. 93 (1917)
Pennzoil Prods. Co. v. Colelli & Assocs., Inc., 149 F.3d 197 (3d Cir. 1998)
Penson v. Terminal Transp. Co., 634 F.2d 989 (5th Cir. 1981)
People *ex rel.* Devine v. $30,700.00 United States Currency, 766 N.E.2d 1084 (Ill. 2002)
Peralta v. Heights Med. Ctr., Inc., 485 U.S. 80 (1988)

Perkins v. Benguet Consol. Mining Co., 342 U.S. 437 (1952)
Perri v. Aytch, 724 F.2d 362 (3d Cir. 1983)
Perry v. Globe Auto Recycling, Inc., 227 F.3d 950 (7th Cir. 2000)
Perry v. Sindermann, 408 U.S. 593 (1972)
Peters v. Nat'l R.R. Passenger Corp., 966 F.2d 1483 (D.C. Cir. 1992)
Peterson v. Temple, 918 P.2d 413 (Or. 1996)
Petrovic v. Amoco Oil Co., 200 F.3d 1140 (8th Cir. 1999)
Phelps v. Hamilton, 122 F.3d 1309 (10th Cir. 1997)
Phil. & Reading Ry. Co. v. McKibbin, 243 U.S. 264 (1917)
Phillips v. Comm'r, 283 U.S. 589 (1931)
Phillips Petroleum Co. v. Shutts, 472 U.S. 797 (1985)
Picquet v. Swan, 19 F. Cas. 609 (C.C.D. Mass. 1828)
Pierce v. Society of Sisters, 268 U.S. 510 (1925)
Pifer v. Marshall, 1998 U.S. App. LEXIS 3189 (9th Cir. 1998)
Pizarro v. Hoteles Concorde Int'l, C.A., 907 F.2d 1256 (1st Cir. 1990)
Planned Parenthood v. Casey, 505 U.S. 833 (1992)
Plyler v. Doe, 457 U.S. 202 (1982)
Polk County v. Dodson, 454 U.S. 312 (1981)
Pollard v. Cockrell, 578 F.2d 1002 (5th Cir. 1978)
Ponte v. Real, 471 U.S. 491 (1985)
Porsche Cars N. Am., Inc. v. Porsche.net, 302 F.3d 248 (4th Cir. 2002)
Porter v. Nussle, 534 U.S. 516 (2002)
Porter v. Soice, 24 Fed. Appx. 384 (6th Cir. 2001) (unpublished)
Postal Tel. Cable Co. v. City of Newport, 247 U.S. 464 (1918)
Powell v. Alabama, 287 U.S. 45 (1932)
Preiser v. Rodriguez, 411 U.S. 475 (1973)
Prejean v. Sonatrach, Inc., 652 F.2d 1260 (5th Cir. 1981)
Procunier v. Martinez, 416 U.S. 396 (1974)
Provident Nat'l Bank v. California Fed. Sav. & Loan Ass'n, 819 F.2d 434 (3d Cir. 1987)

**R**

Rasul v. Bush, – U.S. –, 124 S. Ct. 2686 (2004)
Reed v. Int'l Union of United Auto. Workers, 945 F.2d 198 (7th Cir. 1991)
Regents of Univ. of Mich. v. Ewing, 474 U.S. 214 (1985)
Remick v. Manfredy, 238 F.3d 248 (3d Cir. 2001)
Renaud v. Wyo. Dep't of Family Servs., 203 F.3d 723 (10th Cir. 2000)
Rendell-Baker v. Kohn, 457 U.S. 830 (1982)
Reno v. Flores, 507 U.S. 292 (1993)
Republic of Panama v. BCCI Holdings (Luxembourg) S.A., 119 F.3d 935 (11th Cir. 1997)
Research Corp. v. Edward J. Funk & Sons Co., 15 Fed. R. Serv. 2d 580 (N.D. Ind. 1971)
Resnick v. Hayes, 213 F.3d 443 (9th Cir. 2000)
Revell v. Lidov, 2001 U.S. Dist. LEXIS 3133 (N.D. Tex. March 20, 2001), *aff'd*, 317 F.3d 467 (5th Cir. 2002)
Revell v. Lidov, 317 F.3d 467 (5th Cir. 2002)
Reyes v. Marine Mgmt. & Consulting, Ltd., 586 So. 2d 103 (La. 1991)
Reynolds v. Int'l Amateur Athletic Fed'n, 23 F.3d 1110 (6th Cir. 1994)

Reynolds v. Nat'l Football League, 584 F.2d 280 (8th Cir. 1978)
Rhoades v. Wright, 622 P.2d 343 (Utah 1980), *cert. denied*, 454 U.S. 897 (1981)
Richards v. Jefferson County, 517 U.S. 793 (1996)
Richardson v. Wright, 405 U.S. 208 (1972)
Riggins v. Bd. of Regents, 790 F.2d 707 (8th Cir. 1986)
Rio Props., Inc. v. Rio Int'l Interlink, 284 F.3d 1007 (9th Cir. 2002)
Rippey v. Smith, 16 Fed. Appx. 596 (9th Cir. 2001)
Rittenhouse v. Mabry, 832 F.2d 1380 (5th Cir. 1987)
Rivera v. Minnich, 483 U.S. 574 (1987)
Riverside & Dan River Cotton Mills v. Menefee, 237 U.S. 189 (1915)
Roberts v. LaVallee, 389 U.S. 40 (1967) (per curiam)
Robinson v. Hanrahan, 409 U.S. 38 (1972) (per curiam)
Robinson v. Metro-North Commuter R.R., 267 F.3d 147 (2d Cir. 2001), *cert. denied*, 535 U.S. 951 (2002)
Robinson v. Shewalter, No. 00-3211, 2000 U.S. App. LEXIS 31942 (6th Cir. Dec. 6, 2000)
Rochin v. California, 342 U.S. 165 (1952)
Rodgers v. Singletary, 142 F.3d 1252 (11th Cir. 1998)
Rodriguez v. Fullerton Tires Corp., 115 F.3d 81 (1st Cir. 1997)
Roe v. Wade, 410 U.S. 113 (1973)
Rogers v. Brockette, 588 F.2d 1057 (5th Cir.), *cert. denied*, 444 U.S. 827 (1979)
Rogers v. Peck, 199 U.S. 425 (1905)
Roller v. Holly, 176 U.S. 398 (1900)
Rosenberg Bros. & Co. v. Curtis Brown Co., 260 U.S. 516 (1923)
Ross v. Moffitt, 417 U.S. 600 (1974)
Rowan v. State, 30 Wis. 129 (1872)
Ruffin v. Commonwealth, 62 Va. 790 (1871)
Ruiz v. McKaskle, 724 F.2d 1149 (5th Cir. 1984)
Rumsfeld v. Padilla, – U.S. –, 124 S. Ct. 2711 (2004)
Rush v. Savchuk, 444 U.S. 320 (1980)
Rusk v. Cort, 369 U.S. 367 (1962)
Ruston Gas Turbines, Inc. v. Donaldson Co., 9 F.3d 415 (5th Cir. 1993)
Rutherford v. City of Cleveland, 137 F.3d 905 (6th Cir. 1998)
Rynsburger v. Dairymen's Fertilizer Coop., Inc., 72 Cal. Rptr. 102 (Cal. Ct. App. 1968)

**S**

St. Clair v. Cox, 106 U.S. (16 Otto) 350 (1882)
St. Joseph Lease Capital Corp. v. Comm'r, 235 F.3d 886 (4th Cir. 2000)
St. Joseph Stock Yards Co. v. United States, 298 U.S. 38 (1936)
Sallie v. Tax Sale Investors, Inc., 998 F. Supp. 612 (D. Md. 1998)
S.F. Arts & Athletics, Inc. v. United States Olympic Comm., 483 U.S. 522 (1987)
Sandin v. Conner, 515 U.S. 472 (1995)
Santosky v. Kramer, 455 U.S. 745 (1982)
Sarit v. United States Drug Enforcement Admin., 987 F.2d 10 (1st Cir. 1993)
Satsky v. Paramount Communications, Inc., 7 F.3d 1464 (10th Cir. 1993)
Savchuk v. Rush, 272 N.W.2d 888 (Minn. 1978) (en banc), *rev'd*, 444 U.S. 320 (1980)
Schall v. Martin, 467 U.S. 253 (1984)

Schluga v. City of Milwaukee, 101 F.3d 60 (7th Cir. 1996)
Schneiderman v. United States, 320 U.S. 118 (1943)
Scholz Research & Dev., Inc. v. Kurzke, 720 F. Supp. 710 (N.D. Ill. 1989)
Schrader v. Selective Serv. Sys., 470 F.2d 73 (7th Cir.), *cert .denied*, 409 U.S. 1085 (1972)
Schreiber v. Allis-Chalmers Corp., 448 F. Supp. 1079 (D. Kan. 1978), *rev'd on other grounds*, 611 F.2d 790 (10th Cir. 1979)
Schroeder v. City of New York, 371 U.S. 208 (1962)
Schware v. Bd. of Bar Examiners, 353 U.S. 232 (1957)
Schweiker v. McClure, 456 U.S. 188 (1982)
Scott v. Illinois, 440 U.S. 367 (1979)
Sea-Land Servs., Inc. v. Gaudet, 414 U.S. 573 (1974)
SEC v. Carrillo, 115 F.3d 1540 (11th Cir. 1997)
Sec'y of Pub. Welfare v. Institutionalized Juveniles, 442 U.S. 640 (1979)
Sedio, N.V. v. Bell, Kalnick, Klee & Green, No. 91-C-3691, 1992 U.S. Dist. LEXIS 874 (N.D. Ill. Jan. 28, 1992)
Segreti v. Gillen, 259 F. Supp. 2d 733 (N.D. Ill. 2003)
Seider v. Roth, 216 N.E.2d 312 (N.Y. 1966)
Sell v. United States, 539 U.S. 166 (2003)
Semtek Int'l Inc. v. Lockheed Martin Corp., 531 U.S. 497 (2001)
Shadwick v. City of Tampa, 407 U.S. 345 (1972)
Shafer v. South Carolina, 532 U.S. 36 (2001)
Shaffer v. Heitner, 433 U.S. 186 (1977)
Shapiro v. Thompson, 394 U.S. 618 (1969)
Shaughnessy v. United States ex rel. Mezei, 345 U.S. 206 (1953)
Shelley v. Kraemer, 334 U.S. 1 (1948)
Sheppard v. Maxwell, 384 U.S. 333 (1966)
Sherbert v. Verner, 374 U.S. 398 (1963)
Shriver Junior's Lessee v. Lynn, 43 U.S. (2 How.) 43 (1844)
Shute v. Carnival Cruise Lines, 897 F.2d 377 (9th Cir. 1990), *rev'd on other grounds*, 499 U.S. 585 (1991)
Sicari v. Comm'r, 136 F.3d 925 (2d Cir. 1998)
Siegert v. Gilley, 500 U.S. 226 (1991)
Silber v. Mabon, 18 F.3d 1449 (9th Cir. 1994)
Simmons v. South Carolina, 512 U.S. 154 (1994)
Simpson v. Loehmann, 234 N.E.2d 669 (N.Y. 1967)
Sims v. Artuz, 230 F.3d 14 (2d Cir. 2000)
Skipper v. South Carolina, 476 U.S. 1 (1986)
Slater v. Mex. Nat'l R.R. Co., 194 U.S. 120 (1904)
Slaughter-House Cases, 83 U.S. (16 Wall.) 36 (1873)
Slochower v. Bd. of Higher Educ., 350 U.S. 551 (1956)
Small v. United States, 136 F.3d 1334 (D.C. Cir. 1998)
Small Engine Shop, Inc. v. Cascio, 878 F.2d 883 (5th Cir. 1989)
Smith v. Bennett, 365 U.S. 708 (1961)
Smith v. Org. of Foster Families for Equal. & Reform, 431 U.S. 816 (1977)
Smith v. Robbins, 528 U.S. 259 (2000)

Smith v. Swormstedt, 57 U.S. (16 How.) 288 (1854)
Smith v. Texaco, Inc., 263 F.3d 394 (5th Cir. 2001), *withdrawn*, 281 F.3d 477 (5th Cir. 2002)
Smith v. Wade, 461 U.S. 30 (1983)
Sniadach v. Family Finance Corp., 395 U.S. 337 (1969)
Solesbee v. Balkcom, 339 U.S. 9 (1950)
Soma Med. Int'l v. Standard Chartered Bank, 196 F.3d 1292 (10th Cir. 1999)
Sondel v. N.W. Airlines, Inc., 56 F.3d 934 (8th Cir. 1995)
Songbyrd, Inc. v. Grossman, 206 F.3d 172 (2d Cir. 2000)
Sosna v. Iowa, 419 U.S. 393 (1975)
South Carolina v. Katzenbach, 383 U.S. 301 (1966)
S. Cent. Bell Tel. Co. v. Alabama, 526 U.S. 160 (1999)
S. Macomb Disposal Auth. v. Township of Washington, 790 F.2d 500 (6th Cir. 1986)
Southcenter Joint Venture v. Nat'l Democratic Policy Comm., 780 P.2d 1282 (Wash. 1989)
S.W. Airlines Co. v. Tex. Int'l Airlines, Inc., 546 F.2d 84 (5th Cir.), *cert. denied*, 434 U.S. 832 (1977)
Specht v. Patterson, 386 U.S. 605 (1967)
Speiser v. Randall, 357 U.S. 513 (1958)
Standing Stone Media, Inc. v. Indiancountrytoday.com, 193 F. Supp. 2d 528 (N.D.N.Y. 2002)
Stanley v. Illinois, 405 U.S. 645 (1972)
State *ex rel.* K.M. v. W. Va. Dep't of Health & Human Res., 575 S.E.2d 393 (W. Va. 2002)
State v. Homeside Lending, Inc., 826 A.2d 997 (Vt. 2003)
Stephenson v. Dow Chem. Co., 273 F.3d 249 (2d Cir. 2001), *aff'd in part by an equally divided Court*, 539 U.S. 111 (2003) (per curiam)
Stoll v. Gottlieb, 305 U.S. 165 (1938)
Stolz v. United Bhd. of Carpenters, 620 F. Supp. 396 (D. Nev. 1985)
Stomp, Inc. v. NeatO, LLC, 61 F. Supp. 2d 1074 (C.D. Cal. 1999)
Stoetzner v. United States Steel Corp., 897 F.2d 115 (3d Cir. 1990)
Sumpter v. White Plains Hous. Auth., 278 N.E.2d 892 (N.Y.), *cert. denied*, 406 U.S. 928 (1972)
Sun Oil Co. v. Wortman, 486 U.S. 717 (1988)
Sunburst Bank v. Patterson, 971 S.W.2d 1 (Tenn. Ct. App. 1997)
Superintendent v. Hill, 472 U.S. 445 (1985)
Swenson v. Thibaut, 250 S.E.2d 279 (N.C. Ct. App. 1978), *appeal dismissed*, 254 S.E.2d 181–83 (1979)

**T**

Tanner v. Illinois Tool Works, Inc., 1996 U.S. App. LEXIS 5378 (9th Cir. 1996) (mem.)
Tatro v. Manor Care, Inc., 625 N.E.2d 549 (Mass. 1994)
Taylor & Marshall v. Beckham, 178 U.S. 548 (1900)
Tellier v. Fields, 280 F.3d 69 (2d Cir. 2000)
Tenn. Valley Auth. v. Whitman, 336 F.3d 1236 (11th Cir. 2003)
Terrace v. Thompson, 263 U.S. 197 (1923)
Texaco, Inc. v. Short, 454 U.S. 516 (1982)

Texas v. Cobb, 532 U.S.162 (2001)
Tex. Trading & Milling Corp. v. Fed. Republic of Nigeria, 647 F.2d 300 (2d Cir. 1981), *cert. denied*, 454 U.S. 1148 (1982)
Textile Workers Union v. Lincoln Mills, 353 U.S. 448 (1957)
The Bremen v. Zapata Off-Shore Co., 407 U.S. 1 (1972)
The Japanese Immigrant Case, 189 U.S. 86 (1903)
Thomas v. Ramos, 130 F.3d 754 (7th Cir. 1997)
Thompson v. Whitman, 85 U.S. (18 Wall.) 457 (1873)
Ticketmaster-N.Y., Inc. v. Alioto, 26 F.3d 201 (1st Cir. 1994)
Ticor Title Ins. Co. v. Brown, 510 U.S. 810 (1993)
Ticor Title Ins. Co. v. Brown, 511 U.S. 117 (1994) (per curiam)
Tobin v. Astra Pharm. Prods., Inc., 993 F.2d 528 (6th Cir. 1993)
Torres v. Fauver, 292 F.3d 141 (3d Cir. 2002)
Torres v. $36,256.80 United States Currency, 25 F.3d 1154 (2d Cir. 1994)
Town of Phillipsburg v. Block 22, 528 A.2d 98 (N.J. Super. Ct. Ch. Div. 1987)
Township of River Vale v. Town of Orangetown, 403 F.2d 684 (2d Cir. 1968)
Toys "R" Us, Inc. v. Step Two, S.A., 318 F.3d 446 (3d Cir. 2003)
Troxel v. Granville, 530 U.S. 57 (2000)
Trs. of Dartmouth Coll. v. Woodward, 17 U.S. (4 Wheat.) 518 (1819)
Tulsa Prof'l Collection Servs., Inc. v. Pope, 485 U.S. 478 (1988)
Tumey v. Ohio, 273 U.S. 510 (1927)
Twigg v. Sears, Roebuck & Co., 153 F.3d 1222 (11th Cir. 1998)
Twining v. New Jersey, 211 U.S. 78 (1908)
Tyus v. Schoemehl, 93 F.3d 449 (8th Cir. 1996), *cert. denied*, 520 U.S. 1166 (1997)

**U**

United Elec. Workers v. 163 Pleasant St. Corp., 960 F.2d 1080 (1st Cir. 1992)
United Liberty Life Ins. Co. v. Ryan, 985 F.2d 1320 (6th Cir. 1993)
United Mine Workers v. Coronado Coal Co., 259 U.S. 344 (1922)
United States v. $8,850 in United States Currency, 461 U.S. 555 (1983)
United States v. Abilene & S. Ry. Co., 265 U.S. 274 (1924)
United States v. Alabama, 791 F.2d 1450 (11th Cir. 1986), *cert. denied sub nom.* Bd. of Trs. v. Ala. State Bd. of Educ., 479 U.S. 1085 (1987)
United States v. Balanovski, 236 F.2d 298 (2d Cir. 1956)
United States v. Cannons Eng'g Corp., 899 F.2d 79 (1st Cir. 1990)
United States v. Cardinal Mine Supply Inc., 916 F.2d 1087 (6th Cir. 1990)
United States v. Carrion, 488 F.2d 12 (1st Cir. 1973) (per curiam), *cert. denied*, 416 U.S. 907 (1974)
United States v. Clymore, 245 F.3d 1195 (10th Cir. 2001)
United States v. Combs, No. 95-50471, 1996 U.S. App. LEXIS 26739 (9th Cir. Oct. 9, 1996) (mem.)
United States v. Cotton, 535 U.S. 625 (2002)
United States v. Deninno, 103 F.3d 82 (10th Cir. 1996)
United States v. Donovan, 33 Fed. Appx. 823 (7th Cir. 2002) (unpublished)
United States v. Dusenbery, 201 F.3d 763 (6th Cir.), *cert. denied*, 531 U.S. 925 (2000)

United States v. First Nat'l City Bank, 379 U.S. 378 (1965)
United States v. Gagliardi, No. 98-1078, 1999 U.S. App. LEXIS 14780 (1st Cir. June 24, 1999)
United States v. James Daniel Good Real Prop., 510 U.S. 43 (1993)
United States v. Kras, 409 U.S. 434 (1973)
United States v. Leon-Leon, 35 F.3d 1428 (9th Cir. 1994)
United States v. Libretti, No. 99-8047, 2000 U.S. App. LEXIS 2499 (10th Cir. February 17, 2000)
United States v. Lindh, 212 F. Supp. 2d 541 (E.D. Va. 2002)
United States v. Marolf, 173 F.3d 1213 (9th Cir. 1999)
United States v. Martinez, 616 F.2d 185 (5th Cir. 1980), *cert. denied*, 450 U.S. 994 (1981)
United States v. McGlory, 202 F.3d 664 (3d Cir. 2000) (en banc)
United States v. Mendoza-Lopez, 481 U.S. 828 (1987)
United States v. Minor, 228 F.3d 352 (4th Cir. 2000)
United States v. Monroe Serv. Co., 901 F.2d 610 (7th Cir. 1990)
United States v. Morgan, 313 U.S. 409 (1941)
United States v. Morton Salt Co., 338 U.S. 632 (1950)
United States v. One Toshiba Color T.V., 213 F.3d 147 (3d Cir. 2000)
United States v. Orellana, No. 96-1795, 1996 U.S. App. LEXIS 29625 (1st Cir. 1996) (per curiam)
United States v. Perchitti, 955 F.2d 674 (11th Cir. 1992)
United States v. Poe, No. 99-5089, 2000 U.S. App. LEXIS 1905 (6th Cir. Feb. 7, 2000)
United States v. Raddatz, 447 U.S. 667 (1980)
United States v. Rodgers, 108 F.3d 1247 (10th Cir. 1997)
United States v. SCA Servs. of Ind., Inc., 827 F. Supp. 526 (N.D. Ind. 1993)
United States v. Sec. Indus. Bank, 459 U.S. 70 (1982)
United States v. Serafini, 781 F. Supp. 336 (M.D. Pa. 1992)
United States v. Texas, 158 F.3d 299 (5th Cir. 1998)
United States v. Verdugo-Urzuidez, 494 U.S. 259 (1990)
United States v. Warner, 32 Fed. Appx. 190 (8th Cir. 2002) (per curiam; unpublished)
United States *ex rel.* Knauff v. Shaughnessy, 338 U.S. 537 (1950)
United States *ex rel.* Negron v. State, 434 F.2d 386 (2d Cir. 1970)
United States *ex rel.* Vajtauer v. Comm'er of Immigr., 273 U.S. 103 (1927)
U.S. Indus., Inc. v. Gregg, 540 F.2d 142 (3d Cir. 1976)

**V**

Valmonte v. Bane, 18 F.3d 992 (2d Cir. 1994)
Vander Zee v. Reno, 73 F.3d 1365 (5th Cir. 1996)
Vencedor Mfg. Co. v. Gougler Indus., Inc., 557 F.2d 886 (1st Cir. 1977)
Verba v. Ohio Cas. Ins. Co., 851 F.2d 811 (6th Cir. 1988)
Vermeulen v. Renault, U.S.A., Inc., 985 F.2d 1534 (11th Cir. 1993)
Viam Corp. v. Iowa Export-Import Trading Co., 84 F.3d 424 (Fed. Cir. 1996)
Va. Hosp. Ass'n v. Baliles, 830 F.2d 1308 (4th Cir. 1987)
Vitek v. Jones, 445 U.S. 480 (1980)
Vlandis v. Kline, 412 U.S. 441 (1973)

**W**

W.H. Barber Co. v. Hughes, 63 N.E.2d 417 (Ind. 1945)
Waddell v. Forney, 108 F.3d 889 (8th Cir. 1997)
Wagner v. Hanks, 128 F.3d 1173 (7th Cir. 1997)
Waldron v. Raymark Indus., Inc., 124 F.R.D. 235 (N.D. Ga. 1989)
Walker v. City of Hutchinson, 352 U.S. 112 (1956)
Walker v. Sauvinet, 92 U.S. (2 Otto) 90 (1875)
Wallace v. Herron, 778 F.2d 391 (7th Cir. 1985)
Walsh v. Corcoran, 2000 U.S. App. LEXIS 5459 (4th Cir. March 29, 2000), *cert. denied*, 530 U.S. 1279 (2000)
Walters v. Nat'l Ass'n of Radiation Survivors, 473 U.S. 305 (1985)
Walters v. Reno, 145 F.3d 1032 (9th Cir. 1998), *cert. denied*, 526 U.S. 1003 (1999)
Walthall v. United States, 131 F.3d 1289 (9th Cir. 1997)
Ward v. Davis, 765 S.W.2d 5 (Ark. 1989)
Ward v. Village of Monroeville, 409 U.S. 57 (1972)
Warnell v. Ford Motor Co., 189 F.R.D. 383 (N.D. Ill. 1999)
Washington v. Glucksberg, 521 U.S. 702 (1997)
Washington v. Harper, 494 U.S. 210 (1990)
Washington v. Seattle Sch. Dist. No. 1, 458 U.S. 457 (1982)
Washington v. Wash. State Commercial Passenger Fishing Vessel Ass'n, 443 U.S. 658 (1979)
Watson v. Div. of Family Servs., 813 A.2d 1101 (Del. 2002)
Watson v. Employers Liab. Assurance Corp., 348 U.S. 66 (1954)
Webster v. Doe, 486 U.S. 592 (1988)
Webster v. Reid, 52 U.S. (11 How.) 437 (1851)
Weigner v. City of New York, 852 F.2d 646 (2d Cir. 1988), *cert. denied*, 488 U.S. 1005 (1989)
Weinberger v. Kendrick, 698 F.2d 61 (2d Cir. 1982), *cert. denied*, 464 U.S. 818 (1983)
Weinberger v. Salfi, 422 U.S. 749 (1975)
Weng v. United States, 137 F.3d 709 (2d Cir. 1998)
West v. Atkins, 487 U.S. 42 (1988)
W. Coast Hotel Co. v. Parrish, 300 U.S. 379 (1937)
W. Union Tel. Co. v. Pennsylvania, 368 U.S. 71 (1961)
Weston v. Cassata, 37 P.3d 469 (Colo. Ct. App. 2001), *cert. denied*, 536 U.S. 923 (2002)
Wetzel v. Liberty Mut. Ins. Co., 508 F.2d 239 (3d Cir.), *cert. denied*, 421 U.S. 1011 (1975)
White v. Nat'l Football League, 822 F. Supp. 1389 (D. Minn. 1993), *aff'd*, 41 F.3d 402 (8th Cir. 1994), *cert. denied*, 515 U.S. 1137 (1995)
Whiting v. United States, 231 F.3d 70 (1st Cir. 2000)
Wichita Fed. Sav. & Loan Ass'n v. Landmark Group, Inc., 674 F. Supp. 321 (D. Kan. 1987)
Wieman v. Updegraff, 344 U.S. 183 (1952)
Wien Air Alaska, Inc. v. Brandt, 195 F.3d 208 (5th Cir. 1999)
Wilkens v. Johnson, 238 F.3d 328 (5th Cir.), *cert. denied*, 533 U.S. 956 (2001)
Will v. Mich. Dep't of State Police, 491 U.S. 58 (1989)
Williams v. Burlington N., Inc., 832 F.2d 100 (7th Cir. 1987), *cert. denied*, 485 U.S. 991 (1988)

Williams v. New York, 337 U.S. 241 (1949)
Williams v. Oklahoma City, 395 U.S. 458 (1969) (per curiam)
Williams v. Pa. State Police, 108 F. Supp. 2d 460 (E.D. Pa. 2000)
Williams v. Rape, 990 S.W.2d 55 (Mo. App. 1999)
Williamson v. Bethlehem Steel Corp., 468 F.2d 1201 (2d Cir. 1972), *cert. denied*, 411 U.S. 931 (1973)
Willingway Hosp. v. Blue Cross & Blue Shield, 870 F. Supp. 1102 (S.D. Ga. 1994)
Willner v. Comm. on Character & Fitness, 373 U.S. 96 (1963)
Wilson v. City of New Orleans, Civ. Action No. 00-3115, 2002 U.S. Dist. LEXIS 1283 (E.D. La.), *aff'd without op.*, 51 Fed. Appx. 929 (5th Cir. 2002) (unpublished)
Winona & St. Peter Land Co. v. Minnesota, 159 U.S. 526 (1895)
Wisconsin v. Constantineau, 400 U.S. 433 (1971)
Wise v. City of Norfolk, No. 99-2135, 2000 U.S. App. LEXIS 11962 (4th Cir. May 30, 2000) (per curiam)
Witbeck v. Bill Cody's Ranch Inn, 411 N.W.2d 439 (Mich. 1987)
Withers v. Buckley, 61 U.S. (20 How.) 84 (1858)
Withrow v. Larkin, 421 U.S. 35 (1975)
Wiwa v. Royal Dutch Petroleum Co., 226 F.3d 88 (2d Cir. 2000)
WMX Techs., Inc. v. Miller, 197 F.3d 367 (9th Cir. 1999)
Wofford v. Eid, 671 So. 2d 859 (Fla. Dist. Ct. App. 1996)
Wolff v. McDonnell, 418 U.S. 539 (1974)
Wong Wing v. United States, 163 U.S. 228 (1896)
Wong Yang Sung v. McGrath, 339 U.S. 33 (1950)
Woodby v. INS, 385 U.S. 276 (1966)
Woodson v. North Carolina, 428 U.S. 280 (1976)
World-Wide Volkswagen Corp. v. Woodson, 444 U.S. 286 (1980)
Wozniak v. Conry, 236 F.3d 888 (7th Cir. 2001)
Wright v. Collins, 766 F.2d 841 (4th Cir. 1985)
Wuchter v. Pizzutti, 276 U.S. 13 (1928)
Wynehamer v. People, 13 N.Y. 378 (1856)

**Y**

Yakus v. United States, 321 U.S. 414 (1944)
Yick Wo v. Hopkins, 118 U.S. 356 (1886)
Young v. Harper, 520 U.S. 143 (1997)
Young v. United States *ex rel.* Vuitton et Fils S.A., 481 U.S. 787 (1987)
Younger v. Gilmore, 404 U.S. 15 (1971) (per curiam)

**Z**

Zachary v. Chase Manhattan Bank, 52 F.R.D. 532 (S.D.N.Y. 1971) (mem )
Zadvydas v. Davis, 533 U.S. 678 (2001)
Zeilstra v. Tarr, 466 F.2d 111 (6th Cir. 1972)
Zenith Radio Corp. v. Hazeltine Research, Inc., 395 U.S. 100 (1969)
Zimmer Paper Prods., Inc. v. Berger & Montague, P.C., 758 F.2d 86 (3d Cir.), *cert. denied*, 474 U.S. 902 (1985)

Zinermon v. Burch, 494 U.S. 113 (1990)
Zippo Mfg. Co. v. Zippo Dot Com, Inc., 952 F. Supp. 1119 (W.D. Pa. 1997)
Zobriscky v. Los Angeles County, 105 Cal. Rptr. 121 (Cal. Ct. App. 1972)

# Index

## ABOUT THE AUTHOR

RHONDA WASSERMAN is a Professor of Law at the University of Pittsburgh School of Law.

www.ingramcontent.com/pod-product-compliance
Lightning Source LLC
LaVergne TN
LVHW011906200926
848484LV00002B/542